SOCIAL SECURITY LAW

AUSTRALIA
The Law Book Company Ltd.
Sydney : Melbourne : Brisbane

CANADA AND U.S.A
The Carswell Company Ltd.
Agincourt, Ontario

INDIA
N. M. Tripathi Private Ltd.
Bombay
and
Eastern Law House (Private) Ltd.
Calcutta
M.P.P. House Law Booksellers
Bangalore

ISRAEL
Steimatzky's Agency Ltd.
Jerusalem : Tel Aviv : Haifa

MALAYSIA : SINGAPORE : BRUNEI
Malayan Law Journal (Pte.) Ltd.
Singapore

NEW ZEALAND
Sweet and Maxwell (N.Z.) Ltd.
Wellington

PAKISTAN
Pakistan Law House
Karachi

Social Security Law

by

Professor Harry Calvert

Professor of Law and Dean of the Faculty of Law,
University College Cardiff;
Chairman, Rhondda National Insurance Local Tribunal

assisted by

Susan V. Naylor

Tutorial Assistant, University College of Wales, Aberystwyth

SECOND EDITION

LONDON

SWEET & MAXWELL

1978

First Edition 1974
Second Edition 1978

Published in 1978 by
Sweet & Maxwell Limited of
11 New Fetter Lane, London,
and filmset in Great Britain
by Northumberland Press Ltd.,
Gateshead, Tyne and Wear
Printed by
Richard Clay (The Chaucer Press) Ltd.
Bungay, Suffolk
ISBN 0 421 22120 8

PREFACE TO THE SECOND EDITION

WHEN the first edition of this book was nearing completion in 1973, new social security legislation altered many features of the scene. An attempt was made to advert to the effects of this legislation, the Social Security Act 1973, with a view to more comprehensive treatment in a new edition once the new law had settled down. This new edition now appears, little more than three years after the first, and already the 1973 Act is history. The intervening years have seen changes more comprehensive than ever before in the legislative sources of social security law and the task of incorporating them into this new edition has been appalling. The Social Security Act 1975, the Social Security Pensions Act 1975, the Child Benefit Act 1975 and the Supplementary Benefits Act 1976 have left not a single stone of reference unturned and already they, and their attendant subordinate legislation which has been comprehensively consolidated and amended, are being eroded by new legislation. The aim has been to state the law comprehensively as of the start of 1977 and to incorporate reference to such subsequent developments as has been feasible. Thankfully, from an author's if not necessarily a social point of view, many basic principles and much central doctrine remains unchanged.

In addition to these alterations, the book has been changed in other respects. Some sections have been completely and many others largely rewritten; and new chapters have been added. In the first edition, treatment of industrial injuries was excluded. It was a marginal decision; such benefits were nominally a part of the social security scheme, but they savoured largely of compensation rather than income provision, had separate legislation and their own fund, and have received greater attention at the hands of other authors, particularly those working in the field of labour law, than the rest of social security benefits. Some reviewers thought the omission unfortunate and some at least of the justification for omission has disappeared in the intervening years with the merger of the legislation and funds. A chapter on Industrial Injury Benefits has therefore been included. A short chapter on Adjudication has also been added.

A very substantial contribution to the preparation of this edition has been made by Susan Naylor of the Law Department, University College of Wales, Aberystwyth. "Assistance" might seem to imply a rather menial role which is very far indeed from being the case. In addition to working on the book generally, Miss Naylor has become the prime begetter of the chapters on Retirement Pensions and Family Benefits and is responsible for much of the work in the chapters on Minor Benefits and Supplementary Benefits. Since the fist edition of this book appeared, there has been a tremendous surge of literature in the field of social security law and the book now has, again thanks to Miss Naylor, an appendix of further reading in the field.

The book still purports to be what it originally was, a students' book, but in a rather special sense. The category of students, for this purpose, embraces all, and not just candidates for this examination or that, who need to study social security law, whether for academic, research, advisory or adjudicative purposes. For none of these purposes is it, or can it be, a comprehensive source; but, equally, for all it should be a useful point of reference for the job in hand.

Blades, September 6, 1977   H.C.

CONTENTS

TABLE OF CASES

TABLE OF DECISIONS

*Note on Reported Decisions of the National Insurance
Commissioners in National Insurance and
Family Allowance cases*

Reported decisions of the Commissioners, cited frequently throughout this book, are the chief source of doctrine in United Kingdom social security law. They are published by HMSO individually, as reported and in bound volumes, every four or five years.

A standard method of citation has been used in all Great Britain cases since 1950. All reported decisions bear the prefix "R." There follows next, in brackets, the series symbol. Decisions are now reported in six series. The original four series are indicated thus:

(G) indicates the general series (Maternity benefit, Widow's benefit, Guardian's allowance, child's special allowance and death grant);

(P) indicates the retirement pension series;

(S) indicates the sickness benefit series; and

(U) indicates the unemployment benefit series.

(F) indicates the family allowance series (since 1960); and

(A) indicates the recently-added attendance allowance series.

Within each series, reports are cited by reference to number and year, thus; $R(U)$ 7/62 indicates reported unemployment benefit decision number 7 of 1962.

In Northern Ireland decisions, the same type of symbol is used in different order. Thus: R 7/62 (UB) indicates reported Northern Ireland unemployment benefit decision number 7 of 1962. The Northern Ireland series are:

D.G. Death Grant.

F.A. Family Allowances.

  M.B. Maternity benefits.
   P. Retirement pensions, Widow's benefit, Guardian's allowance and child's special allowance.
  S.B. Sickness Benefit.
  U.B. Unemployment benefit.

Prior to 1951, various methods of citation were used in Great Britain. The prefix "R" did not come into use until 1951. The earliest decisions do not even bear a series indication but are cited solely by reference to case number and year, with the suffix "K" or "K.L.," thus: *652/48 (KL)*. Most decisions before 1951, do, however, bear a series indication, prefixed by "C," thus: *C.U. 19/48*, sometimes with the suffix "K" or "K.L." They are, however, reported in order of case number within each year. The only exception is in the case of Scottish and Welsh decisions, indicated by the symbols "S" or "W" in the prefix, thus: *C.S.U. 14/48 (K)*. These Scottish and Welsh series are separately numbered and appear at the end of the annual list within each series. Thus, in the unemployment benefit series for 1948, *C.U. 109/48 (KL)* is followed by *C.S.U. 14/48 (K)* which is followed in turn by *C.W.U. 6/48 (KL)*.

There is a complete set of reported Great Britain decisions in the custody of the clerk of each National Insurance Local Tribunal who should allow consultation by or on behalf of bona fide appellants at reasonable times.

The decisions referred to in this book are set out in the following pages.

TABLE OF DECISIONS

Northern Ireland Decisions

TABLE OF STATUTES

976

1977

TABLE OF STATUTORY INSTRUMENTS

ABBREVIATIONS

Airmen's Regulations	1975 Social Security (Airmen's Benefits) Regulations (S.I. 1975 No. 494).
Attendance Allowance Regulations	1975 Social Security (Attendance Allowance) (No. 2) Regulations (S.I. 1975 No. 598).
B.J.I.R.	British Journal of Industrial Relations.
B.J.L.S.	British Journal of Law and Society.
B.T.R.	British Tax Review.
B.W.C.C.	Butterworth's Workmen's Compensation Cases.
Categorisation of Earners Regulations	1975 Social Security (Categorisation of Earners) Regulations (S.I. 1975 No. 528).
Child Benefit (Claims and Payments) Regulations	1976 Child Benefit (Claims and Payments) Regulations (S.I. 1976 No. 964).
Child Benefit (Determination of Claims and Questions) Regulations	1976 Child Benefit (Determination of Claims and Questions) Regulations (S.I. 1976 No. 962).
Child Benefit (General) Regulations	1976 Child Benefit (General) Regulations (S.I. 1976 No. 965).
Child Benefit (Miscellaneous Minor Amendment) Regulations	1976 Child Benefit (Miscellaneous Minor Amendment) Regulations (S.I. 1976 No. 1758).
Child Benefit (Residence and Persons Abroad) Regulations	1976 Child Benefit (Residence and Persons Abroad) Regulations (S.I. 1976 No. 963).
Child's Special Allowance Regulations	1975 Social Security (Child's Special Allowance) Regulations (S.I. 1975 No. 497).
Claims and Payments Regulations	1975 Social Security (Claims and Payments) Regulations (S.I. 1975 No. 560).
C.L.J.	Cambridge Law Journal.
C.L.P.	Current Legal Problems.
Computation of Earnings Regulations	1974 Social Security (Computation of Earnings) Regulations (S.I. 1974 No. 2008)
Contributions Regulations	1975 Social Security (Contributions) Regulations (S.I. 1975 No. 492).
C.P.A.G.	Child Poverty Action Group.
C.P.C.	Conservative Political Centre.
Credits Regulations	1975 Social Security (Credits) Regulations (S.I. 1975 No. 556).

Death Grant Regulations	1975 Social Security (Death Grant) Regulations (S.I. 1975 No. 565).
Determination of Claims and Questions Regulations	1975 Social Security (Determination of Claims and Questions) Regulations (S.I. 1975 No. 558).
D.I.G.	Disablement Income Group.
Earnings Factor Regulations	1975 Social Security (Earnings Factor) Regulations (S.I. 1975 No. 468).
E.A.T.	Employment Appeal Tribunal
Employed Earners (Employments for Industrial Injury Benefit Purposes) Regulations	1975 Social Security (Employed Earners Employment for Industrial Injuries Purposes) Regulations (S.I. 1975 No. 467).
F.I.S. (Claims and Payments) Regulations	1971 Family Incomes Supplements (Claims and Payments) Regulations (S.I. 1971 No. 227).
F.I.S. (General) Regulations	1971 Family Incomes Supplements (General) Regulations (S.I. 1971 No. 226).
General Benefit Regulations	1974 Social Security (General Benefit) Regulations (S.I. 1974 No. 2079).
Graduated Benefit Rights Regulations	1975 Social Security (Graduated Retirement Benefit) Regulations (S.I. 1975 No. 557).
Guardian's Allowances Regulations	1975 Social Security (Guardian's Allowances) Regulations (S.I. 1975 No. 515).
Hospital In-Patients Regulations	1975 Social Security (Hospital In-Patients) Regulations (S.I. 1975 No. 555).
I.L.J.	Industrial Law Journal.
Industrial Injuries (Airmen's Benefit) Regulations	1975 Social Security (Industrial Injuries) (Airmen's Benefit) Regulations (S.I. 1975 No. 469).
Industrial Injuries (Mariners' Benefits) Regulations	1975 Social Security (Industrial Injuries) (Mariners' Benefits) Regulations (S.I. 1975 No. 470).
Industrial Injuries Regulations	1975 Social Security (Industrial Injuries) Benefit Regulations (S.I. 1975 No. 559).
Irish J.	Irish Jurist.
J.D.P.	Justice, Discretion and Poverty.
J.P.	Justice of the Peace.
L.G.	London Gazette.
L.G.R.	Local Government Review.
Mariners' Benefits Regulations	1975 Social Security (Mariners' Benefits) Regulations (S.I. 1975 No. 529).
Married Women and Widows (Am. and Trans.) Regulations	1975 Social Security (Married Women and Widows) (Amendments and Transitional Provisions) Regulations (S.I. 1975 No. 562).
Married Women and Widows Special Provisions Regulations	1974 Social Security (Benefit) (Married Women and Widows Special Provisions) Regulations (S.I. 1974 No. 2010).

Maternity Allowance (Transitional) Regulations	1974 Social Security (Maternity Allowance) (Transitional) Regulations (S.I. 1974 No. 141).
Maternity Benefit Regulations	1975 Social Security (Maternity Benefit) Regulations (S.I. 1975 No. 553).
Medical Certification Regulations	1975 Social Security (Medical Certification) Regulations (S.I. 1975 No. 531).
Members of the Forces Regulations	1975 Social Security (Benefit) (Members of the Forces) Regulations (S.I. 1975 No. 493).
M.L.R.	Modern Law Review.
M.P.	Miscellaneous Provisions.
N.C.C.L.	National Council for Civil Liberties.
N.I.	National Insurance.
N.I.L.Q.	Northern Ireland Legal Quarterly.
N.I.L.T.	National Insurance Local Tribunal.
N.L.J.	New Law Journal.
O.E.C.D.	Organisation for Economic Co-Operation and Development.
Overlapping Benefits Regulations	1975 Social Security (Overlapping Benefits) Regulations (S.I. 1975 No. 554).
P.A.	Public Administration.
P.E.P.	Political and Economic Planning.
Persons Abroad Regulations	1975 Social Security Benefit (Persons Abroad) Regulations (S.I. 1975 No. 563).
P.L.	Public Law.
Polygamous Marriage Regulations	1975 Social Security and Family Allowances (Polygamous Marriages) Regulations (S.I. 1975 No. 561).
P.Q.	Political Quarterly.
Prescribed Diseases Regulations	1959 National Insurance (Industrial Injuries) (Prescribed Diseases) Regulations (S.I. 1959 No. 467).
SBAT	Supplementary Benefit Appeal Tribunal.
Short-Term Benefits (Transitional) Regulations	1974 Social Security (Short-Term Benefits) (Transitional) Regulations (S.I. 1974 No. 2192).
S.I.	Statutory Instrument.
S.J.	Solicitor's Journal.
S.S.	Social Security.
Supplementary Benefits (Claims and Payments) Regulations	1966 Supplementary Benefits (Claims and Payments) Regulations (S.I. 1966 No. 1067).
Supplementary Benefits (General) Regulations	1966 Supplementary Benefits (General) Regulations (S.I. 1966 No. 1065).
Unemployment, Sickness and Invalidity Benefit Regulations	1975 Social Security (Unemployment, Sickness and Invalidity Benefit) Regulations (S.I. 1975 No. 564).

Widow's Benefit and Retirement Pensions Regulations	1974 Social Security (Widow's Benefit and Retirement Pensions) Regulations (S.I. 1974 No. 2059).
1973 Act	Social Security Act 1973.
1975 Act	Social Security Act 1975.

INTRODUCTION

AN introduction ought to introduce a subject. I want, therefore, to define "social security law" for the purposes of this book and in order to do so I shall have to place it in a wider legal context. Then I want to outline the modern British social security system referring, where it is helpful to do so, to its historical and philosophical background. I hope that this will help to establish a framework for the rest of the book.

THE MEANING OF "SOCIAL SECURITY LAW"

By social security law I mean those legal mechanisms primarily concerned to ensure the provision for the individual of a cash income adequate, when taken along with the benefits in kind provided by other social services, to ensure for him a culturally acceptable minimum standard of living when the normal means of doing so fail. I am, of course, free to define it as I like for my own purposes; but if I expect it to have a wider appeal, I ought to justify my definition. I want to do so by placing "social security law" in a wider legal context.

The philosophy prevailing in a given society at any particular time profoundly influences its social objectives. These objectives are, in turn, a determinant of social policy. The law is one of the chief instruments whereby social policies are implemented. With modifications, this is a useful if simplistic model of social processes for the lawyer's purposes. The modifications are important.

First of all, the prevailing social philosophy is not necessarily either homogeneous or static. Secondly, different social policies may be advocated as means for attaining a single particular social objective. Thirdly, the law is an inefficient instrument of implementation in two ways. So far as some types of change are concerned, the wheels of the law grind exceeding slow and are not even very sure; and a rule, once introduced, tends to calcify the social policy which it implements for it does not fall into desuetude with the policy which gave it birth, but endures until positively thrust aside.

The modern social security system, like the legal system generally, manifests the characteristics of this model. The social philosophy which for so long dominated the scene, *laissez-faire*, caused individual freedom to be established as a primary social objective. This in turn favoured the policy of private enterprise free from intervention by the use of public powers. The consequential role of law tended, therefore, to be negative, directed chiefly towards the prevention of interference with private enterprise. Of course, the character of *laissez-faire* changed over the years. Absolute *laissez-faire* is anarchy, yet there was always a role for government. Its role was originally confined—national security, the keeping of the peace and the administration of justice loomed large. That role did, gradually, become more extended. Competing policies were articulated as to how individual freedom might best be attained, one voiced by the landowner, another by the *entrepreneur*, yet another by the worker. Some of these policies gradually found their way into the legal system; some did not. Many that did are still with us today; the policy is dead but the law still enshrines it.

For purposes of social security, the most significant fact is that although it still holds sway, the philosophy of *laissez-faire* no longer dominates the social scene. A rival, the philosophy of welfare, seeks to steal it. At times, it has occupied the greater part of the stage and thrust forward new social objectives amongst which collective social responsibility looms large.

Prevailing policies have tended to relegate private enterprise to a subordinate role and positively to favour intervention by the state. Legal mechanisms designed to regulate activity, redistribute wealth and, in particular, establish acceptable standards of life have resulted.

The scope of public law has, in consequence, become very much enlarged. Originally, it was essentially adjectival in character. It comprised constitutional law, concerned with the distribution of public power within the state and what eventually came to be known as administrative law, concerned with the legal techniques for regulating and controlling the exercise of this power. One area of substantive public law did emerge under the old philosophy and stands today as the obverse of administrative law, namely civil liberties. Until the nineteenth century, however, and consistently with the objectives established by the philosophy of *laissez-faire*, the concern of substantive public law was virtually confined to this area of freedom *from* interference. Entirely new areas of substantive public law have emerged as means to secure the implementation of the social policies aimed at attaining the objectives set by the philosophy of welfare. Of these new areas, the two chief ones are economic law and welfare law.

That economic law has such an important function is due to the fact that ours remains, fundamentally, a *laissez-faire* system. In the definition of social security law ventured above, I referred to the "normal means" of securing a culturally acceptable minimum standard of living. It is still the prevailing notion that individual initiative should be the primary source of provision, whether for the individual himself by the sale of the use of his labour or property, or for his dependants. The philosophy of welfare has, however, resulted in a host of legislative schemes designed to channel this economic activity for the collective welfare. It is exemplary of these developments that labour law, originally almost exclusively a part of private law, has now been largely consumed by public law and forms an important part of economic law.

The power of the state has not, however, been confined to regulating and controlling individual provision. It is inherent in the objectives set by the philosophy of welfare that adequate provision is a function not merely of individual initiative but also of social organisation and the notion of collective social responsibility necessarily involves that where individual initiative fails to ensure provision, in spite of the mechanisms of economic law, the state itself should intervene positively, not merely by regulating and controlling the activities of individuals, but by making actual provision itself. This is the scope of welfare law.

Within the field of welfare law there are many legal regimes concerned with making provision. In many cases, the state provides actual services itself, this for a number of reasons. In some cases, the scale of the service puts it beyond the economic power of the individual to secure it for himself. In other cases, supply is inelastic and the provision of cash would be an insufficiently sure way of ensuring that a necessary service was received. But ours remains, basically, a market economy. Alongside these instances of the provision of actual services, the concern of the law of public services, we therefore have schemes designed to provide the individual with the cash wherewithal to go out into the market and purchase his and his dependants' means. These schemes are the concern of social security law.

THE MODERN BRITISH SOCIAL SECURITY SYSTEM

Historians of social welfare have traced the social impulse that gives rise to the modern social services to a Christian influence to assist the underprivileged. For many centuries of English law, this impulse was satisfied, initially by private charity and philanthropy, later with state assistance: "The private social service which Christendom calls charity and the eighteenth century called benevolence has found ways ... of vesting itself with immortality. It has become a permanent endowment, a charitable foundation. It has asked the state for privilege and protection—the privilege of not dying and the protection that comes of legal recognition."[1] Positive state action, however, was impossible without machinery of administration. This really first emerged with parish organisation which became secular after the Reformation. Within a very limited sphere (the poor law) compulsory local rates replaced voluntary funding. The process was fortified with the establishment of county authorities and "the day on which the Tudor council first compelled a county bench to compel a parish to do the begging on behalf of its beggars was the day to which the social service (*i.e.* welfare) state can best trace back its origin."[2]

Voluntary charity still, today, discharges a not unimportant role, but a decreasing one. There has been a marked shift in its trajectory towards overseas aid and species other than the human. It became partially obsolescent with the first glimmerings of the idea of improvement—with the idea that man does not live by bread alone. In the Victorian era, under the influence of *laissez-faire*, the impulse was, and to an extent still is, directed towards self-improvement and the prevailing, paternalist, forces tended towards the provision of opportunities for self-help. The paternalist urge manifested itself in the provision of non-state schools and hospitals. Voluntary service was not only good for the bodies of its beneficiaries; it was also good for the souls of those who offered it.

The bubble burst. A fact which had throughout been obvious became, with the changing philosophy, worth stating. "In helping those only who help themselves, or who can get others to help them, we have left unhelped those who need help" said a Member of Parliament in 1870. The slump of the late nineteenth century destroyed the credibility of the myth that those left unhelped were in some way culpable and, ever since, the notion that the unemployed, sick and aged might be the victims as much of social malfunctioning as of their own ineptitude has been a more or less powerful motive in social service legislation. The First World War, with its massive increase in the scope and intensity of central government functions, built the engine to harness this power. The need to use it was made abundantly clear by the depression of the thirties and the necessary modifications were perfected as a result of the governmental apparatus created by the controls over production and distribution necessitated by the global War of 1939–45 and the election to office in 1945 of a government pledged to put that apparatus to reconstruction and welfare purposes. The social services had undergone a shift from being a casualty-rescue service to being a "centrepiece in the *tableau vivant* of the good society."[3]

When it comes to dating the origins of the modern system, a specific starting date is thus arbitrary. If, however, we restrict ourselves to modern social security systems, we can take the date 1883. Prior to that year, the function presently discharged by social security law was discharged by private arrangements made chiefly by the co-operative movement among workers.[4] In 1883, a scheme of compulsory state insurance was introduced by Bismarck in Germany, and extended in 1889 to cover cases of permanent incapacity. Austria followed suit in 1888 and Hungary in 1891 and the movement was established in Europe. By the beginning of the twentieth century, public opinion in the United Kingdom was coming to favour state organisation of schemes for the protection of the "deserving poor," especially those disabled for work by sickness. The return of a Liberal government in 1906 paved the way. Non-contributory old-age pensions at 70 subject to a means test were instituted in 1908.

Compulsory health insurance dates from 1912 (the Act of 1911) and became general in 1920. Contributory old-age, orphans' and widows' pensions were established by an Act of 1925 of that name. The dole came in with the Unemployment Act of 1934.

Parallel to these developments was the Poor Law which started in London in 1597 and was extended to the whole country in the charge of local boards (financed by local rates) by the nineteenth century. This survived with modifications until 1948.

By the start of the Second World War, the British social security set-up comprised a large number of separate and hetero-geneous schemes, each aimed at abating a given social evil, com-plex but uncomprehensive. The foundations of the modern system were laid by the Beveridge Committee. The first sod was cut in 1941 when the Committee was appointed "to undertake, with special reference to the inter-relation of the schemes, a survey of the existing national schemes of social insurance and allied services, including workmen's compensation, and to make recommendations." The Committee duly reported in 1942 and the Report was embraced by the Government in White Papers in 1944 and passed into law in the following four years. The Beveridge Report[5] and the White Papers[6] remain today the basic statements of policy of the social security system.

The modern scheme, then, derives from the Family Allowances Act 1945, the National Insurance Act 1946, the National In-surance (Industrial Injuries) Act 1946 and the National Assist-ance Act 1948. A mass of subordinate legislation accompanied these Acts. Acts and regulations have been frequently amended and consolidated down the years since, but still retain the basic form of the immediate post-War legislation. On the insurance side, there were important consolidations in 1965 and 1973, leading to the present consolidation, the Social Security Act 1975 (which combines the industrial injuries scheme with the general insurance scheme) the pensions provisions of which, however, will eventually be superseded by the Social Security (Pensions) Act 1975.[7] The former "national assistance" was re-vamped and re-named "supplementary benefits" by the Ministry of Social Security Act 1966 which, later amended and now codified as the Supplementary Benefits Act 1976, itself subsequently amended, now governs that area. Family allowances are in the process of being superseded by the child benefit scheme under the Child

Benefit Act 1975. A new scheme, designed to assist low-paid workers with families, was introduced by the Family Income Supplements Act 1970 and there have been very important developments in the fields of redundancy and unfair dismissals which many would regard as falling within a broader definition of "social security."

Regulations have experienced the same process of amendment and consolidation, most of the important ones being conveniently rationalised in 1975.

The ease and frequency with which the legislation can be amended does not ease the lawyer's task. Analysis and exposition are greatly hindered by the dynamic character of this body of law. Criticism is much complicated by the fact that the law currently contains the expression of competing social policies implemented at different times by different governments.

It is not only the lawyer's task which is thus complicated. The administrator's burden is rendered more onerous.

A number of different government departments are concerned with the administration of social security law in various respects —the Department of Employment and the Inland Revenue both have important roles to play. From the point of view of the claimant, however, the agency chiefly concerned is the Department of Health and Social Security, for it is the officials of that department in numerous local offices throughout the country who finally channel the benefits to those entitled to them. So far as supplementary benefits and family income supplements are concerned[8] a separate administrative agency is created, the Supplementary Benefits Commission. Appeals from the decisions of the Commission's officers lie to independent tribunals, the Supplementary Benefit Appeals Tribunals, which are supposed to be entirely free from the policies of the Commission. So far as family allowances and national insurance benefits are concerned, claims are determined in the first instance by insurance officers from whose decisions appeals lie to a much more complex tribunal structure than is the case with supplementary benefits. Insurance officers and tribunals are, however, the "statutory authorities" for purposes of determination of claims.

Certain questions which may arise in the course of determining claims fall to be decided by the Secretary of State from whose decision appeal lies to the High Court.[9] The claim itself is, however, determined by the statutory authorities. In national insurance claims, the insurance officer is not obliged to determine the claim; he may refer it to the first tier of tribunals, to a national insurance local tribunal.[10] If he decides the matter adversely to the claimant, the claimant may appeal to a local tribunal.[11] Appeal lies from the decision of a local tribunal to a National Insurance Commissioner at the instance of an insurance officer, the claimant, or the claimant's trade union etc., this latter and somewhat unusual provision allowing for appeal otherwise than at the instance of a claimant where the subject-matter of the dispute is of wider concern and an authoritative ruling by the Commissioner of more general interest.[12] In addition to appeals, provision is made for review of any decision, including decisions of a Commissioner, by an insurance officer or, on reference by him, a local tribunal. Review can only take place where there has been a relevant change of circumstances since the original decision or where the original decision was given in ignorance of or was based on a mistake as to some material fact. In the case of review of a Commissioner's decision, there must be fresh evidence to this effect.[13]

Local tribunals consist of a chairman (who is usually legally qualified) and two "panel" representatives, one panel being of employees and the other of employed persons and insured persons other than employees.[14] The Chief National Insurance Commissioner and other Commissioners must be chosen from amongst barristers or advocates of not less than 10 years' standing.[15] Commissioners normally sit alone but where a case involves a question of law of special difficulty, a tribunal of three Commissioners may be convened and they may decide by a majority.

Selected Commissioners' decisions are reported. Commissioners' decisions are binding upon local tribunals and decisions of a tribunal of Commissioners are of the highest authority of all. Commissioners also entertain appeals under the industrial injuries scheme. These appeals lie in the first instance to a local tribunal unless medical questions are involved. If such questions are involved, the insurance officer must refer to a medical board from whose decision appeal lies to a Medical Appeal Tribunal. That tribunal's decisions are conclusive on medical questions but appeal lies to the Commissioner on a point of law.

Subject only to review by the High Court by way of prerogative order, decisions of the Commissioners are final. Review by the High Court is limited and is accordingly rare. Commissioners' decisions thus form the chief source of doctrine on the matters with which this book is concerned and such decisions are accordingly frequently cited throughout.

TERMINOLOGY

In this book, the term "social security" is used to describe schemes designed to secure the provision of income. Other schemes having, for example, the provision of compensation for loss suffered (*e.g.* redundancy payments for loss of job security) may, of course, have the effect of yielding resources providing an income, but this is not their primary aim. Thus, redundancy payments and compensation for unfair dismissal are payable notwithstanding immediate re-employment with no consequential loss of income.

The industrial injuries scheme is a hybrid. Industrial injury benefit is payable only so long as earning is interrupted and thus savours of social security. The most important benefit, however, is disablement benefit with its attendant supplements; it is payable (though some supplements may not be) even though earning is not interrupted and is, in essence, a compensation scheme.

In other jurisdictions, "social security" is sometimes given an extended definition so as to embrace not only income provision schemes and some compensation schemes, but also some schemes, *e.g.* health services, providing services rather than cash. On the other hand, in popular usage in the United Kingdom today, "social security" is used much more restrictively, as synonymous with supplementary benefits.

Recent legislation has increased the confusion. Although the Act governing supplementary benefits was originally entitled the "Ministry of Social Security Act 1966" it was later re-entitled the "Supplementary Benefits Act 1966" and the 1975 "Social Security" Acts deal only with the former national insurance and industrial injuries schemes; indeed, the term "national insurance" survives for a few purposes (*e.g.* the title of the Commissioners) and for reasons of convenience the term is used throughout this book to refer to benefits formerly

administered under the National Insurance Acts but now
regulated by the equivalent part of the Social Security Acts.

A wide range of benefits is available under these various
schemes. A number of matters are, however, common to most of
these benefits. The first chapters are, accordingly, devoted to
these common matters, in particular to the question of contributions and benefits in general and general disqualifications.
Particular national insurance benefits are then dealt with one by
one. Family and supplementary benefits are then dealt with.
Since, however, the supplementary benefits scheme has been the
subject of much recent interest and therefore not a little
literature, that subject is not dealt with as comprehensively as are
the other benefits.

Chapter 1

FINANCE AND FUNDING

DIFFERENT sources of finance are resorted to for different parts of the social security system. Some parts, *i.e.* supplementary benefits, family allowances, family incomes supplement, are non-contributory, *i.e.* financed out of general taxation; others, *e.g.* unemployment, sickness and widows' benefits, are contributory, *i.e.* they are financed out of a fund the income of which consists in large part of cash contributions by prospective beneficiaries.

1. NON-CONTRIBUTORY SCHEMES

Non-contributory schemes are financed wholly out of general taxation. They are not separately funded. Non-contributory benefits accrue largely to the poor. Supplementary benefits and family incomes supplement are means-tested and although family allowances were not, and child benefit is not, "claw-back" (*i.e.* recoupment of a substantial part of the benefit in taxation in the case of standard-rate income tax payers) ensures that greater net benefit accrues to the poorer beneficiary. To the extent that general taxation is progressive, *i.e.* bears more harshly upon the wealthier sections of the community especially so far as direct taxation is concerned, non-contributory schemes can readily be seen to have a marked redistributive effect.

The cost to the Exchequer of non-contributory schemes is now in the order of £2,000m p.a. of which more than a half is accounted for by supplementary benefits and rather less than a half by other family benefits (much of that being recouped by claw-back). This is about a quarter of total social security expenditure, including contributory schemes.

2. CONTRIBUTORY SCHEMES

All national insurance and industrial injury benefits other than attendance allowance are contributory (though it should be noted that some benefits, *e.g.* guardian's allowance and attendance allowance have no contribution conditions, *i.e.* it is not necessary that the beneficiary or an associated person have contributed as a condition of entitlement to benefit). In this respect, national insurance is not unlike many types of private insurance seeking to make provision against similar contingencies, such as retirement, funeral expenses etc. Indeed, many of the benefits available under the national insurance schemes are the successors of formerly private schemes which were not compulsory and therefore not comprehensive.

Why finance such schemes out of contributions, *i.e.* specific sums paid into a separate fund for the purpose by persons covered by the schemes? It is certainly perfectly feasible to finance the whole of social security otherwise than by contributions and, indeed, modern thinking on the subject mainly concerns the move from financing by contributions towards negative income tax. Some foreign schemes, *e.g.* New Zealand, are non-contributory, being based on residence and employment record. Our scheme of contributions serves two purposes: (a) it yields funds for benefit: and (b) it established "deserts" by reason of having worked. One can have the latter without the former and still retain a point of distinction from supplementary benefits, if that be needed.

The persistence of contribution is mainly due to historical reasons. Individual contribution is, of course, inherent in private insurance schemes and, as is stated above, early social insurance schemes were modelled on private insurance. Beveridge might have heralded a departure from this philosophy but the Committee's terms of reference ("to survey ... existing ... schemes of social insurance and allied services...") did not encourage this. It is not surprising that it should appear as the third of Beveridge's basic principles[1] that "The State should offer security for service and contribution. The State in organising security should not stifle incentive, opportunity, responsibility...." Little attention is paid to alternative methods of financing. The only detailed consideration occurs in paragraphs 21–23 of the Report where the following justifications for retaining contribution are offered:

(a) "Contribution ... is what the people of Britain desire";

  (b) Contribution avoids the stigma of charity;
  (c) Contribution saves means-testing;
  (d) A departure from contribution would destroy incentive:

"Insured persons should not feel that income for idleness (*sic*), however caused, can come from a bottomless purse. The Government should not feel that by paying doles it can avoid the major responsibility of seeing that unemployment and disease are reduced to the minimum."

Much of this is dubious. Little evidence is offered for much of it, for example (a) and (d), and it consequently appears dogmatic. Contribution in its present form probably does avoid the stigma of charity[2] but whether this is a good thing may well be doubted. Would the "stigma of charity" still appear if all benefits, and not simply those confined to the desperately needy, were non-contributory? To the extent that one contributes to general taxation, *e.g.* when in work, is it in fact charity to receive support from general taxation when unemployed or retired? In any case, a substantial proportion of all national insurance benefits are "charitable" in the sense that contribution income is inadequate to meet the whole outgo and is supplemented by a contribution from general exchequer. How does contribution avoid a means-test? We do, in fact, have a means-test in the form of an earnings rule so far as some contributory benefits are concerned, but no means-test so far as some non-contributory benefits (*e.g.* child benefits) are concerned. One could have means-tests if the schemes all became non-contributory but there is nothing compelling about it. Finally, whether, in view of the competitive rates of supplementary benefits, there is anything in the incentive argument may well be doubted. Supplementary benefits are in fact met out of a "bottomless purse" and there seems to be a singular lack of any factual warrant for the assertion that contribution has anything whatever to do with governments becoming irresponsible.

As dogma, however, the Beveridge assumptions did, and perhaps still do, appeal to government. The White Paper[3] chants the response that "contribution has long been one of the essential features of British social legislation, and the Government believe that it reflects the desires and the characteristics of our people." It may still reflect the desires of a diminishing class—those who subscribe to the old nonconformist individualist virtues. But if it has a wider appeal, this can only be the result of ignorance. Contribution is a viciously regressive form of taxation, at all events in its flat-rate variant. Present-day minimum contributions represent about 8 per cent. of the income of low-paid workers and about 1 per cent. of those earning £100 per week.[4] Households with an income of £500 per annum contribute about 37 per cent. of income to public funds; those with £1,100 about 28 per cent.[5] The discrepancy is almost wholly attributable to contributions. In this, we are quite peculiar:

"... the main difference between us and our continental neighbours is in the role of social security contributions. We still have mainly a flat rate contribution system—a heavy weight of regressive taxation at the bottom of the tax structure and an inelastic source of revenue for social benefits. Such wage-related contributions as there are stop at a low income ceiling. The long awaited review of the whole social security system could be one of the keys to future progress in the Welfare State. But such a review is useless unless it is allowed to break through the whole of the public expenditure control system—to lay the Gladstonian ghost which still haunts the Treasury and the Bank of England."[6]

This is not the only matter for criticism. Contributions do not vary over time, once the age of 18 is reached. Yet capacity to pay varies considerably in the course of a normal life. As long ago as 1899, in his survey of poverty in York, Rowntree detected three marked periods of want—childhood, child-rearing and old age. One of our most serious social problems, that of family poverty, is simply the contemporary version of that middle period of want. It prompts the suggestion that it might be purposeful to vary contributions over time so that larger contributions were payable during the early, pre-family working years and particularly during the last, post-family working years when calls on income are at their lowest, allowing smaller contributions to be levied during the middle years. The case for some such approach is becoming more and more compelling in the case of certain less well paid middle-class occupations, such as teaching, where the early years can involve family poverty but the later years bring relative plenty. For the time being, however, the old system remains and, although there are some changes in detail, the new legislation marks no radical departure from it.

Sources of Funds for Contributory Schemes

Total social security outgo has now reached a level of about £10,000m per annum and of this approximately three-quarters is spent on national insurance and industrial injuries contributory benefits.[7] This expenditure is met from three main sources:

1. Contributions by employers and other contributors;
2. Exchequer contributions; and
3. Income from investments.

The third source is of trivial importance, accounting for approximately 1 per cent. of income. Viewed exclusively from the point of view of prospective beneficiaries, the investment policy[8] seems conservative, funds being devoted almost exclusively to public stocks. This may, however, be justifiable in terms of a broader national policy and in any case, even a very progressive investment policy would hardly add significantly to the income of the National Insurance Fund.

Exchequer contributions presently account for about 15 per cent. of the income of the National Insurance Fund. The size of the Exchequer contribution is now fixed at 18 per cent. of contribution income; it has been a permanent feature of the financing of the national insurance scheme and, to that extent, the insurance principle in a commercial sense has never been a feature of the scheme. Contributions of the various classes always have been and remain the chief source of Fund income. Again, however, actuarial principles have never governed the allocation of responsibility for contributing amongst various classes of contributor according to likely demands on the Fund. Very substantial employers' contributions have always been a feature of the scheme although the employers of most of the workforce, being corporations, are not prospective beneficiaries at all, and even such as are must contribute separately as regards their own entitlement. Under the present scheme, an inappropriate share of the burden is thrust on the self-employed.[9]

Viewed overall, however, the actuarial strategy, as revealed in annual House of Commons papers, is that contribution income as such from all sources, plus interest from investments, should be such as cover outgo in the short and long terms. Provision has to be made for ascertainable future demands greatly in excess of current demands, hence the enormous reserves yielding the income referred to above. Much the chief item here is provision for future retirement pensions which already account for over two-thirds of total national insurance[10] outgo and will eventually consume a greater share. Because of the extended contribution conditions and the refusal, in 1946, to include existing old-age pensioners, the annual cost of current retirement pensions was originally negligible. By the turn of the century, 50 years on, they will be a tremendous burden on the fund. Provision must be made now, hence the massive reserves. The position will eventually stabilise in the early years of the twenty-first century, inflation and constant changes in pension policy[11] permitting, when contributions, exchequer contribution and income from investments will neatly balance total outgoings in the form of benefits and cost of administration.

Contributions

Under the 1975 Act, contributions are of four classes[12]:

1. Earnings-related contributions in respect of employment;
2. Flat-rate contributions payable in respect of self-employment;
3. Voluntary contributions;
4. Contributions payable in respect of the profits or gains of a trade, profession or vocation.

Class 1

These consist of (a) primary Class 1 contributions from employed earners and (b) secondary Class 1 contributions from employers and other persons paying earnings. An "employed earner" is one "who is gainfully employed in Great Britain (or Northern Ireland as the case may be) either under a contract of service, or in an office (including elective office) with emoluments chargeable to income tax under Schedule E"[13] subject to extensive modifications in regulations.[14] Throughout the history of the scheme, this type of contribution has always been the most important in terms of its yield of funds. The criteria for liability for payment have, however, shifted to some extent. The

1965 Act spoke of "employed persons, that is to say, persons gainfully occupied in employment . . . being employment under a contract of service. . . ." The 1975 Act reiterates the 1973 Act's definition. Under all, "contract of service" means "any contract of service or apprenticeship whether written or oral and whether expressed or implied."[15] Thus, although the criteria are identical in some respects, it is not yet clear to what extent, if any, the substitution of the phrase "gainfully employed" for "gainfully occupied in employment" changes things. Some caution is therefore required in examining the older authorities.[16]

Employment under a contract of service remains the distinguishing characteristic of Class 1. The definition of a "contract of service" as opposed to a "contract for services" is a task undertaken by many authorities and much debated in the literature of tort and labour law. It is not intended here to enter into the general debate. Two matters, however, have a particular bearing on this debate as it relates to the social security scheme:

1. The vast majority of the authorities seem to assume that there is a single category of "contract of service" for all purposes, whether it be liability for national insurance contributions, or vicarious liability of a master for the torts of his servant. No doubt, when the term "contract of service" was incorporated into the legislation, the category established in tort law was in mind. Two points, one of policy, one of principle, should, however, be noted.

The first of these is that the questions being asked for purposes of contribution liability and vicarious liability are quite different in nature. So far as contribution is concerned, the chief question is whether or not an employee should be insured against unemployment, the chief difference between the "employed" and "self-employed" categories being that the former may enjoy unemployment benefit whilst the latter may not. If it be relevant that an employed person has little or no say over the question whether he should continue in employment, being subject to the employer's right to dismiss, then the latter's right to control him is central in importance. This is not the case with vicarious liability. Here, the question of policy is whether a third party, injured as a result of an activity carried on by the tortfeasor, should be able to call upon another person for compensation; and there may be a case to be made out for compensation if the activity was carried on on that latter person's behalf and perhaps for his benefit, even if he did not exercise stringent control over the activities of the tortfeasor.

The doctrinal difficulties which have beset the question of definition of a contract of service in recent years have centred around whether the "control" test or the "integration test" should govern. There is ample scope for the "integration test" in relation to questions of vicarious liability. It is submitted that the "control test," properly understood, is more apt for questions of contribution liability. I say "properly understood" because the "control test" has been subjected to much criticism which is inapt if one takes the "control test" as involving the question whether the parties have stipulated, expressly or by implication, that the "employer" shall have the residual *right to* control the activity carried on by the "employee." If it is the understanding between the parties (and these matters are often not spelled out before-hand) that in the final analysis the "employee" can be supervised and dismissed by the "employer," it is submitted that there is a contract of service. The world's most eminent surgeon can be subjected to a right to control in this sense by a health committee of corporation dustmen. It is, however, unlikely that that would be the understanding.

The question of principle is whether, in interpreting the phrase in a statutory context, courts must necessarily follow the developments and perhaps vagaries of judicial doctrine, especially where these developments have taken place in coping with an entirely different problem. In fact, courts have tended, when dealing with problems of contribution liability, not to embrace the integration test, and it might be a welcome development if they were to assert, in dealing with such questions, that a test different from that applicable to questions of vicarious liability should be resorted to.[17]

2. Some types of labour-relationship which might well be classified as "self-employment" according to the above tests are, by regulation, deemed to be contracts of service. These relationships (along with cases deemed to be self-employment and non-employment) are listed in Schedule 1 to the Categorisation of Earners Regulations. That Schedule provides, for example, for "employment as an interviewer for the purposes of obtaining information about the habits or opinions of members of the public

or any particular category or description of persons" to be treated as employment as an employed earner, thus creating liability for Class 1 contributions and seeking to settle, legislatively, a problem which had agitated both the courts[18] and the administration.[19]

Liability for contributions

The 1975 Act imposes upon the employee liability to pay his contribution and upon the employer liability to pay his.[20] Regulation provides,[21] however, that "earnings-related contributions shall be paid, accounted for and recovered in like manner as income tax deducted from emoluments of an office or employment" under P.A.Y.E. The primary factual liability is, therefore, the employer's who will deduct the primary Class 1 contribution from the employee's wages. For other purposes, however, it remains part of his emoluments.[22]

The opportunities for planning to restrict liability are severely limited. The Secretary of State may, "where he is satisfied as to the existence of any practice in respect of the payment of earnings whereby the incidence of earnings-related contributions is avoided or reduced by means of irregular or unequal payments, give directions for securing that such contributions are payable as if that practice were not followed."[23] Exercise of this power would impose a financial liability and it is presumably to be strictly construed. It assumes that but for the practice a liability would exist and cannot therefore be employed so as to create a liability which otherwise would not exist; and the means of avoidance must be "irregular or unequal payments," with the result that it is arguable that the power cannot be exercised where the means of avoidance is, or consists in part of, regular non-payment.

Class 1 contributions are levied by reference to gross earnings.[24] In assessing gross earnings, certain types of payment, such as certain holiday payments, payments in kind or by way of the provision of board or lodging or of other services or other facilities, and certain payments under discretionary trusts, may be disregarded.[25] There are clear opportunities for avoidance here, many of which would not fall under the head of "by means of irregular or unequal payments" for purposes of regulation 19

above. A note of caution, however, should be sounded. Failure
to pay contributions for which one is liable is an offence[26] and
in proceedings for an offence the decision of the Secretary of State
is conclusive for certain purposes.[27] These purposes include determining "a question whether the contribution conditions for any
benefit are satisfied, or *otherwise relating to a person's contributions* or
his earnings factor."[28] It is to be hoped that should the question
arise in the context of criminal proceedings the italicised phrase
would be construed, *eiusdem generis*, as referring only to contribution questions in relation to a particular benefit. The wider
construction means that the Secretary of State could create a
criminal liability and also decide the crucial question relating
to an accused person's guilt.

Class 2 and 4

"... every self-employed earner shall ... be liable to pay
Class 2 contributions" at a flat-rate, regardless of his income.[29]
Class 4 contributions are "payable in respect of all annual profits
or gains immediately derived from the carrying on or exercise of
one or more trades, professions or vocations, being profits or
gains chargeable to income tax under Case I or Case II of
Schedule D ..."[30] at a percentage rate on such profits or gains
between a lower and upper limit. A "self-employed earner" is
a person who is "gainfully employed ... otherwise than in an
employed earner's employment"[31] and "employment" includes
"any trade, business, profession, office or vocation."[32] Most self-
employed persons will therefore be liable for both Class 2 and
Class 4 contributions. The definition of the classes of contribution clearly opens the possibility of a single person being liable
for contributions of Classes 1, 2 and 4. Regulations in fact adjust
this liability in certain circumstances.[33]

Regulations again provide for a person who, prima facie, falls
within the class of self-employed earners to be treated as an
employed earner[34] and vice versa. The latter case embraces
ministers of religion and "Any employment ... as a self-employed
earner ... where the earner is not ordinarily employed in such
employment. ..."[35]

A person may be liable to pay contributions as a self-employed
earner or in respect of profits or gains in a trade or profession

notwithstanding that for lengthy periods no income accrues from his occupation. In the case of Class 4 contributions, contributions are levied on the basis of annual Schedule D returns, so that the liability accrues according to actual annual income. In the case of Class 2, however, contributions are payable weekly and remain payable even if no income accrues as long as the activity is carried on. Thus, a boarding house proprietor who spent the greater part of the year cleaning and decorating in preparation for the busy season was held to be self-employed throughout the year (*M36*). By contrast, a cricket umpire who kept fit in the winter by playing golf was held to be non-employed in winter (*M38*). A barrister would be self-employed and liable for contributions accordingly even during the early, lean years. To add insult to injury, he used to have to pay his share of contributions for the clerk who is an employed person (*M49*). In practise, this will no doubt remain so although legally the head of chambers is now liable.

Class 3

The purpose of Class 3 contributions is to allow a contributor to qualify for contributory benefits which would otherwise be denied him by paying contributions voluntarily in order to acquire the requisite earnings factor.[36] Such contributions may be paid at any time before the end of the second year following the year in respect of which they are paid.[37] In special cases, an even longer period is permitted. Thus, a break in the record of six months or more in the given year by reason of full-time education or apprenticeship, or imprisonment, entitles the contributor to six years in which to make good his record; whilst if the non-payment was due to ignorance or error without due care and diligence on his part, an even more extended period may be allowed.[38]

Inadequate provision for enabling a contribution record to be made good was an objectionable feature of previous schemes, and complaints to the Parliamentary Commissioner for Administration on this ground featured significantly in his case-load.[39] Problems will still arise over the exercise of the Secretary of State's discretion to extend the period for payment; and over the issue whether due care and diligence have been used.

Crediting contributions

Where there are two contribution conditions for a benefit (as is the case with the most substantial benefits), a contributor who loses the opportunity to pay contributions may, in certain circumstances, be entitled to be credited with them and thus qualify for the benefit.[40] The credits may be such as to make a year a reckonable year, where they are in respect of a year, and such as to equal the standard rate which would be payable on earnings at the lower earnings limit where the credit is in respect of a week.[41]

The commonest examples of crediting are starting credits, in respect of years before the age of 18, necessary in order to complete entitlement for, *e.g.* retirement pension (Class 3 credits) or unemployment benefit (Class 1 credits)[42] and credits receivable whilst unemployed or incapacitated.[43] A right to credited contributions may be retrospectively restricted under the Social Security (Miscellaneous Provisions) Act 1977.

Enforcement

The liability to pay contributions is enforceable by penal sanctions.[44] In such proceedings (which may only be instituted by the Secretary of State or his agent)[45] the presumption of innocence is largely eroded. The Secretary of State's certificate is conclusive for some purposes and "A certificate of a collector of taxes that any amount by way of contributions which a person is liable to pay to that collector for any period has not been paid ... shall until the contrary is proved be sufficient evidence ... that the sum mentioned ... is unpaid and due."[46]

A court before which a person is convicted of non-payment must order payment of unpaid contributions to the Secretary of State.[47] In cases where the employer has failed to pay and is a body corporate, contributions due may be recovered from any director who knew or could reasonably be expected to have known of the failure to pay.[48] This liability attaches notwithstanding the retirement in the meantime of a person who was a director at the relevant time.[49]

The time limit for instituting prosecutions is 12 months from the commission of the offence or three months from the receipt of sufficient evidence by the Secretary of State, whichever is the later.[50]

Two of the outstanding features of the law relating to contributions are its complexity and the extent to which the determination of questions of fact fall within the province of the Department which is, in some sense, usually a party to proceedings. In the determination of claims,[51] as well as in connection with prosecutions for non-payment of contributions, all may turn upon the Department's records. They are not invariably accurate.

Although it may be possible to appeal on questions of law[52] there is no formal appeal on a question of fact from some of the Department's determinations. But it is well worth noting that a complaint to the Parliamentary Commissioner for Administration may well result in a more thorough review by the Department than would otherwise have taken place. Complaints about errors in connection with contribution records are amongst the most common entertained by the Commissioner and any advisor will be familiar with the extent to which dissatisfaction on this score prevails. Resort to the Parliamentary Commissioner may open up opportunities for correction of errors and may also result in the granting of a discretionary remedy by the Department such as an *ex gratia* payment.

CHAPTER 2

BENEFIT

BEVERIDGE's aim was that the social security system should guarantee "the minimum income needed for subsistence."[1] The need which Beveridge had in mind was not merely biological or functional, for "what is required for *reasonable* human subsistence is to some extent a matter of judgment."[2] Estimates change with time, "and, generally, in a progressive community, change upwards." The Beveridge approach was to take the evidence of experts as to the standards currently prevailing, in fixing provisional levels, recognising that actual levels would need to have regard to the cost of living prevailing from time to time. Periodic reviews of the rates of both contribution and benefit have taken place and the latest legislation contemplates annual review, having regard to the general level of earnings or prices (in some cases, only the latter).[3]

This approach to the fixing of benefit levels is all right so far as it goes. In two respects, however, there is room for some disquiet:

1. As is stated above, Beveridge appreciated that "need," in reference to subsistence levels, is a cultural concept, and that notions of what is needed should have changed upwards, assuming ours to be a progressive society. The history of standard benefit rates over the 30 years since Beveridge does not suggest that this has happened.[4]

2. As appreciated by Beveridge[5] the cost of subsistence needs might vary considerably from person to person and particularly from one area to another. In the latter respect, the cost of rent looms large. Beveridge's view, however, was that "the principle that a flat rate of insurance contribution should lead to a flat-rate of benefit has a strong popular appeal" and that on balance, it was better not to attempt to adjust benefit rates in the light of regional costs etc. but to fix a single rate for all. The result is that standard benefit rates have never been adequate to meet the cost of rents inflated by housing shortages and the gap has been

bridged throughout by other sources, in particular national assistance (now supplementary benefits). There has, furthermore, never been any attempt to relate benefits to actual cost-of-living as it varies from one region to another, a matter of some significance when comparing the metropolitan area of London with other, less costly, parts of the country.

One other difficulty relating to benefit inheres in a discrepancy between the assumptions of the law and the facts of social life. For the legal system's purposes, the typical subject is the individual human being. It is in him that rights and duties inhere. So far as subsistence in social terms is concerned, the all-important entity is the dependency unit, usually a family of some sort. The subjects of the social security system live together and provide for themselves collectively in families in which individuals discharge different though complementary roles. Because, however, the concepts of the law do not readily accommodate the family as a legal entity, the social security system has to work through individuals as being on the one hand liable to maintain, and on the other hand, entitled to be maintained. The problem was seen in its starkest form in relation to family allowances, payable in respect of the children, belonging to the mother, drawn by the father and characterised as being for the benefit of the family as a whole.

The problem is complicated by the so-conceived social interest in legitimacy. The mores create a pressure towards households in which the "spouses" are married and the children legitimate; but the social facts are sometimes otherwise. In principle, a number of approaches are possible. At one extreme, the rules of the social security system could have regard only to legitimacy. This would leave illegitimate dependent adults and children without support. At the other extreme, it could have regard only to the fact of dependency; this would render marriage and being born within it equally irrelevant for purposes of maintenance under the social security system and would, in many cases, create a multiple dependency, one earner having several "families." The full range of benefits is available only for legitimate families; the illegitimate family will sometimes be taken care of, sometimes not.

Dependency is one reason for departure from the statutory flat-rate benefit prescribed. There are others. We shall therefore consider (1) reduction of benefit for various reasons; (2) increase of benefit for various reasons; and (3) extinguishment of title to benefit and repayment of benefit overpaid.

REDUCTION OF BENEFIT

Benefit may be reduced in the following circumstances:

1. Where there is an inadequate contribution record.
2. Where the beneficiary is in hospital.
3. Where there is overlapping entitlement to benefit.

INADEQUATE CONTRIBUTIONS

In order to establish title to any benefit, the contribution condition must normally be satisfied in full. This means that the contributions must have been paid or credited as required at the time required. Regulations may and do provide for full benefit to be paid in other circumstances, *e.g.* non-payment by the employer without the knowledge, connivance or consent of the insured person.[6] Otherwise, the claim to full benefit fails. Unless provision were made otherwise, title to any benefit would fail. Regulations, however, provide that in the case of partial satisfaction of the contribution conditions for certain benefits, a reduced rate of benefit may be paid.[7]

HOSPITAL IN-PATIENTS

The personal element in benefit, *i.e.* excluding any increase paid in respect of dependants, is designed to provide a basic standard of living for the beneficiary. If basic necessities are otherwise provided out of public funds, the case for full benefit continuing is weakened. Regulations therefore provide that the benefit of a beneficiary who receives or has received continuously for a prescribed period free in-patient treatment in a National Health Service hospital or other institution by arrangement may be reduced.[8] The extent of the reduction varies according to the duration of the spell in hospital and the existence of dependants of the patient.[9] Full benefit will not become payable again until discharge has been effected by and with the approval of an authorised person and it can be established that the beneficiary is neither receiving free in-patient treatment nor residing in any prescribed accommodation.[10]

For these purposes, the personal element in benefit includes any element in the benefit designed for the beneficiary personally such as increments to retirement pension by virtue of deferred retirement[11] and also, presumably, earnings-related benefits. The requirement that the receipt of treatment must be continuous is subject to a number of exceptions.[12] "Free" treatment is provided unless the patient, or someone on his behalf, pays charges designed to cover the whole cost of the accommodation or services.[13] It is accordingly not enough that some contribution towards the cost is made by the patient[14] or even, necessarily, that the patient has a right under his contract of employment by a hospital authority to free treatment.[15] Provided, however, that the whole cost of maintenance is borne by the patient or someone on his behalf (*e.g.* a charity) treatment will not become "free" merely because other patients similarly placed do receive some support from public funds.[16]

One may be a free in-patient and yet not receive treatment and therefore avoid the implications of the regulations[17] although "treatment" is, for this purpose, broadly defined.[18] Similarly, one may be receiving free treatment in a hospital but not as an in-patient, as where a nurse receives medical attention in her living quarters at a hospital[19] as opposed to receiving treatment in a "nurses sick-bay" in a hospital which has been held to be receiving free in-patient treatment.[20]

The period of in-patient treatment comes to an end with discharge by or with the approval of an authorised person. Discharge against the advice of the appropriate officer of the hospital will accordingly not suffice[21]; nor, *a fortiori*, will formal discharge in the case of a person who should have been detained but has escaped from hospital.[22] This may involve anomaly; an initial refusal might, but not necessarily would, have involved disqualification, depending upon whether the treatment refused was reasonable or involved major surgery.[23]

The defintion of "prescribed accommodation" has occasioned some difficulty.[24] There are special provisions relating to tuberculosis patients.[25]

OVERLAPPING BENEFITS

The conditions of entitlement to many benefits are such that a
claimant may qualify simultaneously for a number of benefits.
Since the social security scheme is aimed at abating need only
to the extent of providing a reasonably minimal standard of
living, it is manifestly contrary to the policy of the scheme that
a person should receive double or perhaps even triple benefit.
Regulations accordingly provide that excess benefits of this
character must be withheld.[26] Where there is overlapping entitlement, the basic principle is that the beneficiary shall receive
only one of the benefits, where they are of the same amount or,
"that one of them which would be ... payable ... at the higher
or highest rate.[27]

Non-periodic payments, such as death and maternity grant,
and certain other benefits, such as attendance allowance, are
excluded from this effect.[28] Benefit may also be withheld where
it is claimed in respect of another person who is a beneficiary
in his own right.[29] Thus, an increase for a dependent mother/
housekeeper with a personal retirement pension is not payable.[30]
The overlapping rules are not confined to national insurance
benefits. They extend, for example, to certain war pension
benefits payable under Royal Warrant[31] and to workmen's compensation[32] and industrial injury payments.[33] Not all payments
ultimately traceable to public funds, however, need be brought
into account.[34]

INCREASE OF BENEFIT

Benefit may be increased in the following circumstances:

1. In respect of dependency;
2. By way of earnings-related supplementation.

INCREASE OF BENEFIT FOR DEPENDANTS

In some circumstances the law imposes upon one person an
obligation to maintain another. A person may, however, in fact
maintain another without there being any legal obligation to do
so. The right to an increase of benefit in respect of a dependant
is not confined to those cases where there is a legal obligation

to maintain; nor, however, does it always exist where there is dependency in fact. An attempt is made to ensure that an increase in benefit is receivable in a number of commonly recurring cases of dependency in fact. It recognises four classes of such cases, namely children, spouses, certain relatives and some "housekeepers." In no other cases is an increase of benefit for a dependant payable. Thus, an increase may not be payable even though there is dependency in fact in the case of some relatives, some housekeepers, life-long friends, etc. In the case of children, guardian's allowance[35] or child's special allowance[36] may be payable and child benefit[37] may be receivable. Some adults may be entitled to benefit in their own right by virtue of their own contributions. Otherwise, dependency falls to be catered for by the supplementary benefits scheme.[38]

In the case of the four recognised classes (children, spouses, certain relatives and some "housekeepers") the exact circumstances in which a beneficiary may claim an increase vary from class to class. Even as regards a particular class, the conditions of entitlement to an increase vary according to the type of benefit. It is therefore useful to consider each class of dependant in turn, stating the general conditions which have to be satisfied for increase of any benefit and then dealing with those additional conditions of entitlement which are peculiar to a particular type of benefit. It will be seen that certain conditions of entitlement are common to two or more classes, *e.g.* the requirement of "residence with." These will be dealt with together at the end of this section.

1. CHILDREN

The law provides for an increase in certain specified benefits for any period for which the beneficiary is entitled to child benefit in respect of a child or children.[39] The specified benefits are unemployment benefit, sickness benefit, invalidity pension, maternity allowance, retirement pension and widow's allowance. Subject to exceptions, "child" bears the meaning attributed to it for the purposes of child benefits.[40] The most important of these exceptions allows a beneficiary to treat as a child of his family the child of a woman residing with him[41] if that child is either their illegitimate child or has been wholly or mainly maintained[42] by the beneficiary for six months prior to the day of claim.[43]

For the increase to be payable, the statutory condition must be satisfied. This requires either that the child be living with the beneficiary[44] or that the beneficiary be contributing to the cost of providing for the child in an amount equal at least to the amount of the increase[45] over and above any contribution required under the child benefit scheme[46] as a condition of entitlement to benefit for a child for the purposes of that scheme.[47] Where the beneficiary is a married woman residing with[48] her husband a further condition must be satisfied: the husband must be incapable of self-support.[49]

It will be seen that under the above rules, more than one person may qualify for an increase in respect of the same child. Section 43 imposes additional conditions to receipt of benefit in respect of children which will resolve some but not all of such contesting claims. Other cases, where a husband and wife are both entitled to an increase, are dealt with by regulations which provide that the increase shall be payable to the husband, if they are living together and otherwise (*e.g.* if permanently separated) to such of them as the Secretary of State may decide unless the parties agree otherwise.[50]

2. Spouses

The spouse in respect of whom the increase is claimed must be validly married to the beneficiary who must be either residing with[51] the dependant,[52] or contributing to his or her maintenance in an amount at least as great as the amount of the increase sought.[53] If the spouse in respect of whom the increase is claimed is a wife, there are conditions relating to her earnings outlined below. If the spouse in respect of whom the increase is claimed is a husband, he must be incapable of self-support.[54]

If the above conditions are satisfied, unemployment benefit, sickness benefit or maternity allowance may be increased provided that, where the increase is claimed in respect of a wife, she is not engaged in any employment from which her weekly earnings exceed the amount of the increase,[55] a condition which does not of course arise in the case of maternity allowance.[56]

Again, if the above conditions are satisfied, retirement pension or invalidity pension may be increased subject, in the case of a wife, to an earnings rule similar in operation to that applying to the retirement pension itself.[57]

Earnings

In calculating "earnings" for the above purposes, the Computation of Earnings Regulations apply.[58] All earnings, other than sums deductible under the regulations,[59] attributable to the wife[60] must be brought into account. Sick pay and holiday pay usually rank as earnings in respect of the week for which they are paid[61] notwithstanding that no work is done. It should be noted that the increase of benefit may be lost if the wife is engaged in employment notwithstanding that her actual earnings in a given week fall below the amount of the increase provided that the normal weekly earnings would exceed that amount.[62] Earnings need be neither earned in nor remitted to this country in order to be brought into account.[63]

Marriage

For many purposes, the existence of a valid marriage recognised by English law is an essential precondition to qualification for benefit or an increase of benefit. Where it is clear that there is no marriage, as for example where the person in respect of whom the claim is made is admitted merely to be a "housekeeper living with" the claimant[64] or where there has been a valid divorce[65] such a precondition is plainly not satisfied. Sometimes, however, the status of the parties may be highly dubious. This may be so either because it is not clear what in fact the relationship between the parties is, raising difficult questions of proof; or because although it is clear what the relationship is, the status of that relationship is not clear in law. The two chief questions which fall to be answered in such cases are, therefore, (a) the question of proof of marriage; and (b) the question of validity in law of an alleged marriage. In relation to both questions, the general principles of English and Scots law relating to marriage including the rules of conflict of laws apply.[66]

Proof

A marriage duly certified is prima facie valid.[67] In the absence
of a certificate, a ceremony followed by long cohabitation and
acceptance as man and wife may create a presumption of marriage[68] but it is essential that the parties shall intend to be
married.[69] The presumption may be rebutted by positive evidence of the invalidity of the marriage[70] and it will suffice to this
end to prove that no marriage was concluded in the manner
asserted by the person seeking to establish the presumption.[71]
So far as marriage under Scots law by habit and repute is concerned, the normal rules of Scots law apply.[72]

Validity

The formal validity ceremony falls to be determined according to the law of the place where it is celebrated. A Romany
ceremony is accordingly not valid in this country[73] nor is a
marriage without due publication of banns.[74] So far as essential
validity (*e.g.* capacity to marry) is concerned, the law of the
domicile (the subject of some doctrinal difficulty and statutory
amendment) governs. Thus, where the domicile is within
England and Wales, Scotland or Northern Ireland, marriage
within the prohibited degrees of consanguinity[75] or bigamously[76]
is void. A marriage which is merely voidable, as for non-
consummation,[77] is, however, valid for benefit purposes until
avoided.[78] The rules relating to domicile are complex[79] and
some of their difficulty is avoided by the Domicile and Matrimonial Proceedings Act 1973. In the context of social security
benefits, the problems that have been posed have usually surrounded marriages which, although valid by the law of the domicile, are polygamous or potentially polygamous in effect. Such
marriages were, for a long time, discounted for all purposes.
Since 1956,[80] however, some recognition has been accorded for
social security benefit purposes and the position which now
prevails is that for most benefit purposes a polygamous marriage
may be treated as a monogamous marriage for any period
during which it is in fact monogamous.[81] Generally, therefore,
the position is that an increase of benefit may be claimed for
such a period but only for such a period and not, even in

respect of the same marriage, for any period when it was in fact polygamous. The only exceptions arise in relation to retirement pensions for entitlement to which periods when the marriage is in fact polygamous may count to some extent.[82]

3. RELATIVES

Only prescribed relatives count. These are direct lineal ascendants and descendants and siblings, of the whole or half blood; and a widow or widower's parents-in-law.[83] Any such person who is a child is excluded but the class of prescribed relatives includes such as are related by adoption or would have been related if born legitimate.[84] It has been held that a person may be a relative by adoption even though no formal legal steps have been taken.[85] A similar charity was not bestowed on the claimant in *C.S. 2/48 (K)* who argued that if the illegitimate children of himself and his housekeeper had been born legitimate, his housekeeper would have been a "relative," *i.e.* his wife. He overlooked that an increase can only be claimed in respect of a "prescribed" relative and wives are not prescribed.

The legislation has always provided[86] for relatives by marriage to be prescribed but except to the extent above indicated, this has not been done.[87]

In addition to belonging to the prescribed classes, the relative must reside with[88] or be wholly or mainly maintained by[89] the beneficiary.[90] There can be no increase if the relative is detained in legal custody or, if a woman, supported by her husband or earning more than the amount of the increase.[91] If a man, he must be incapable of self-support.[92] Residence abroad disentitles except in certain sickness benefit cases.[93]

4. "HOUSEKEEPERS"

"Housekeeper" is a convenient if inaccurate[94] euphemism for the Act's cumbersome "female person (not a child) having the care of a child or children in respect of whom the beneficiary is entitled to child benefit".[95] Further conditions of entitlement are imposed by regulations.[96] She must reside with him, or be and have been employed[97] by him or be maintained by him, at a cost not less than that of the increase.[98] There can be no increase if she is detained in legal custody, or if she has another occupation in which her normal weekly earnings are more than the increase. This latter provision leads to anomaly in the case where the "housekeeper" takes care of lodgers. If she does so as the beneficiary's employee, he taking the profit, an increase may be payable. If, however, the beneficiary does not employ her for this purpose she may be held to be earning the profit from a gainful occupation of her own and, if the profit exceeds the amount of the increase, the increase will not be payable.[99]

"Having Care"

Whether the housekeeper "has care" of a child is a matter of degree. Whilst the child is away at boarding school, no care is involved[1] nor is it in the case of an older child who needs little more than general supervision.[2] "Care" does not, however, mean constant attendance, or exclusive or even main care. Provided that the housekeeper performs duties for the child to a substantial extent, the condition is satisfied.[3] A housekeeper may thus have the care of a child even though the beneficiary performs some duties and even if he has a wife living with him, if in fact the wife goes out to work and the housekeeper performs a substantial part of the duties of caring for the child.[4]

5. MATTERS RELEVANT TO MORE THAN ONE CLASS OF DEPENDANT

(a) *"Residing Together," "Residing With"*

A number of concepts used in the social security legislation, such as "residing with" and "residing together," have a common core.[5] "Residence" is a feature of other aspects of the social security scheme.[6] "Residence together" or "with" imports that the parties have a common abode under the same roof constituting their joint home.[7] It need not be an exclusive home[8] and it is not necessary that the arrangement be anything more than one of convenience.[9] If there is cohabitation of this character, the parties are "residing together." It does not, however, follow that they will cease to be so because they are living apart. So far as this is concerned, the 1975 Act[10] provides that two persons shall not be deemed to have ceased to reside together by reason of any temporary absence the one from the other. Where the two are married to each other, absence purely on the grounds of medical treatment at a hospital or similar institution is discounted altogether "whether such absence is temporary or not." Some authorities have sought to use a "one-year" rule as an indicator of temporariness[11] but it seems clearly to be understood that the presumption that an absence of over one year is not temporary is a rebuttable one. If there are special features, an absence may be temporary notwithstanding that it will be of some years' duration. Thus, common residence has been held to continue throughout a two-year prison sentence[12] and throughout the period of compulsory national service of two years.[13] The crucial feature in all these cases is that throughout the parties intend the absence to be temporary. Such an intention will preserve the character of the common residence unless the absence becomes prolonged.[14] If, however, the absence is not intended to be temporary, is prolonged, or if re-union is uncertain, residence together will have ceased.[15] One absence may thus be temporary although resumption of cohabitation is years away, whilst in another case common residence will be lacking even though the parties intend a resumption in a matter of days[16] for once residing together has ceased, a resumption of actual cohabitation (and not merely of intention) is necessary to restore it.[17] Nor will it avail that there have been occasional days of cohabitation in the meantime.[18]

Although a temporary absence in hospital can be ignored,[19] it used to be the case that a protracted stay frequently involved cessation of residence together.[20] It is now, however, provided that residence together shall be deemed not to have ceased merely because one party has in-patient status in hospital, even if the absence so caused is not temporary.[21]

(b) *"Incapable of Self-Support"*

A person is incapable of self-support "if (but only if) he is incapable of supporting himself by reason of physical or mental infirmity and is likely to remain so incapable for a prolonged period."[22] It follows that incapacity by reason of, for example, imprisonment or attendance at school is not covered.[23]

There is no statutory definition of "a prolonged period." The view was early taken that the incapacity must last at least for some months before it could be spoken of as prolonged in normal parlance, and five weeks was held inadequate.[24] Subsequently, the Commissioner came to apply a six-month rule in normal cases the implication being, however, that a lesser or greater period might be apt in special circumstances.[25] Strictly speaking, the words of the definition above-quoted seem to require a prognosis of a continuation of the incapacity. The question may, however, arise after the event, in which case, it may be proper to presume that medical opinion would have forecast the actual course of the incapacity. Regard may thus be had to actual duration in such a case.[26]

In an important respect, the above-quoted definition is ambiguous. The "prolonged period" may be taken as referring either to the total period of incapacity or the remainder of the period during which the person is "likely to remain" so incapable. If the harsher interpretation were adopted, it would follow that an increase of benefit would be lost once the person incapacitated was within six months of recovery. This interpretation has been rejected. It is enough that the likely total duration of the incapacity amounts to a prolonged period.[27]

(c) *"Contributing Towards the Cost of Providing For"*[28]

The underlying notion here is that a beneficiary ought not to receive more by way of increase of his benefit than he contributes towards the cost of providing for those in respect of whom the increase is paid. Normally, therefore, actual contribution is required. A mere unfulfilled obligation, even though imposed by an enforceable court order, will not suffice.[29] It also follows that actual payment of a contribution in excess of the statutory amount will not suffice if in fact the excess is paid wholly on account of arrears (*C.S. 74/55 (unrep.); R(U) 25/58*).

There are exceptions to the requirement of actual payment. One arises out of the "pump-priming" provision.[30] Regulation provides that notwithstanding that neither of the two conditions

of section 43 (1) are satisfied (*i.e.* child not living with; no contribution actually being made), a claimant may qualify for an
increase if (1) he undertakes in writing to contribute and (2) in
fact contributes upon receiving the increase. Payment of increase
under this regulation is, however, conditional. If the contribution undertaking is not honoured, entitlement may cease and
repayment may be required.[31] For the contribution undertaking to be honoured, the contribution must be made in the
week following that in respect of which the increase is received.[32]
A later payment will not suffice.[33] Anomalously, it thus seems
that a claimant denied the increase by the insurance officer, and
thus unable to make contribution in the following week, could
not qualify for payment in subsequent weeks even if he succeeded
on appeal.

There are also exceptions to the requirement that the amount
of contribution must not be less than the amount of increase for
which it qualified. One arises in connection with the "split
family" provision.[34] By way of illustration, consider a divorced
couple with three children, the two eldest living with the mother,
the youngest with the beneficiary. Without the "split family"
provision, the beneficiary would have to contribute to the extent
of an "eldest" plus an "other" child increase in order to qualify
for increase. The result would be that he would be left only with
the equivalent of an "other" child increase for the child living
with him who would be, in effect, a "sole" child in respect of
whom an "eldest" child increase would normally be payable.
To counter this, regulation 9 (2) requires him to contribute
only at the rate of two "other" child increases, thus leaving
him with the equivalent of an "eldest" child increase, a position which he could himself have brought about simply by
declining to contribute at all in respect of the other two
children.[35]

Regulation also allows the determining authority to reallocate
sums contributed towards providing for a wife or children so as
to maximise entitlement to benefit.[36] This, however, only allows
reallocation as between dependants for a week in respect of
which the payments are made; it does not allow reallocation
from one week to another contrary to the beneficiary's original
intention.[37]

(d) *"Maintaining"*

The concept of "maintenance" is not peculiar to the question of increase of benefit for dependants. It arises also, for example, in relation to the definition of "child" for purposes of child benefits.[38] To some extent, therefore, it may be fruitful to take note of authorities in these other areas. However, it cannot be assumed that the authorities are freely interchangeable. In some respects, as will be seen, the statutory authorities have given different answers to the same question arising in different contexts.

For purposes of increase of benefit for dependants, maintenance has a dual relevance. For some purposes, it is necessary that a beneficiary has "contributed to the maintenance" of the dependant. For other purposes, he must have "wholly or mainly maintained" the dependant. Where such a condition applies, the onus is upon the claimant to prove that it is fulfilled.[39]

"Maintaining" involves actually making available to the dependant funds attributable to the beneficiary. The existence of a legal obligation is not itself sufficient.[40] unlike the similar situation in relation to child benefits,[41] "maintaining" does not mean "actually making sure that the money is applied to the purposes of maintenance, but merely means taking all practicable steps to provide and hand over the money for those purposes." Accordingly, it suffices to hand over the money to be held by the clerk under a court order; it need not reach the dependant.[42]

It may be difficult to determine whether the funds made available are attributable to the beneficiary. No problem arises where the beneficiary directly makes available his own funds. The difficulty is encountered where funds have been handed over to the dependant by a third party, such as where the Air Ministry paid over to the wife of an airman a sum of £2 12s. 6d. consisting of an allotment of 17s. 6d. from her husband's pay plus 35s. marriage allowance. Here, the whole sum was attributed to the husband.[43] So also was an *ex gratia* payment of £2 per week paid directly to a wife by a husband's ex-employer, in *C.S. 58/49 (KL)*.[44] In *C.P. 96/50 (KL)* the question of attributability of a retirement pension payable to a wife on her husband's insurance arose. The pension was granted to the wife personally and not by way of an increase of the husband's retirement pension. It was payable to the wife and had to be separately claimed by her. Nevertheless, it was "derived from the beneficiary's own insurance contributions, *i.e.* as between the beneficiary and the claimant it is he who has made this provision for her maintenance" and payment was accordingly attributable to him; *a fortiori* if the payments had derived from a voluntary endowment policy. In a sense, a similar argument can be mounted in relation to supplementary benefits payable to a dependant, for the claimant, during his working life, will have contributed to general taxation and thus to the funding of supplementary benefits. It has, however, been decided that such payments fall the other side of the line.[45] The reason offered in this decision, that "an agency outside the family" had made the contribution, applies equally to all the cases considered above and cannot be regarded as a satisfactory basis for the distinction. It seems rather to be a question of whether or not the payment is ultimately attributable to some specific act or contribution of the beneficiary.[46]

The normal manner of paying maintenance is handing over cash. It often happens, however, that the dependant enjoys benefits other than cash, such as free accommodation. The value of such benefits may pose problems both of title and quantification.[47] If the property belonged originally to the beneficiary, its value or proceeds may be attributed to him.[48] By no means all the problems of determining when the value of property has become spent, or valuing a capital item in weekly income terms for benefit purposes, have yet been resolved.[49]

"Contributing to maintenance"

The contribution must be at not less than the rate of the increase. The legislation referred to above in relation to specific dependants requires that such contribution shall be made, first, during the period in question (*i.e.* the period of benefit) and, secondly, in normal times, *i.e.* when the beneficiary was in employment, or not incapable of work, or prior to his retirement.[50] The object here is to ensure that the national insurance fund is not called upon for the discharge of dependency obligations which the beneficiary did not himself honour previously.

"Dependency" here means actual, not legal dependency.[51] An exception is allowed where the dependency has only arisen subsequently. Here, the increase may be claimed notwithstanding that there was no maintenance in "normal times."

"Wholly or mainly maintaining"

A regulation lays down two conditions here. It should be noted, however, that whilst these conditions are necessary to entitlement, they will not necessarily be sufficient. The relevant regulation[52] only provides that the beneficiary shall not be deemed to be wholly or mainly maintaining another person unless two conditions are satisfied. It "does not provide that if those conditions are satisfied the beneficiary shall be deemed to be wholly or mainly maintaining that other person. The inference is that it was intended that the claimant in such a case should still be obliged to establish affirmatively that he can properly be regarded as wholly or mainly maintaining the other person ... during the period in question."[53] The two conditions are as follows:

(a) During the period of claim, the beneficiary must contribute to the maintenance of the dependant in an amount not less than the amount of the increase payable.

(b) Prior to the qualifying event (unemployment, sickness, etc.) the beneficiary must have been contributing to the maintenance of the dependant in an amount more than half the actual cost of the maintenance.

As to (a), the condition specified by the regulation would seem to be satisfied by the payment of the stipulated amount for one week; at all events, this would seem to suffice to prime the pump. As is above emphasised, however, these conditions are necessary but not sufficient. Over and above them, it has been held that at least two consecutive weeks' payments must be made[54] and that payments must be continuous.[55]

As to (b), because a contribution of half the actual total cost is required, it will be obvious that the beneficiary's right to an increase might be lost, even though he maintained his payments, if the dependant's other sources of income yielded more. This happened in R(S) 6/53 where a wife, receiving £1 per week from her husband, saw her national assistance allowance increased from 17s. 6d. per week to £1 2s. 6d. per week. The consequential loss to the husband might have been avoided had the increase been a temporary one. He might also have increased his contribution retrospectively and thus retained his qualification.[56]

Since these conditions are not necessarily sufficient, it follows that the right to an increase of benefit may be lost even though they are fulfilled. In particular, the right may be lost if the period of incapacity becomes so prolonged that actual wholly or mainly maintaining has ceased.[57] This will not readily be presumed. "Where the beneficiary has clearly repudiated his obligation to maintain the dependant or there is a definite agreement that a third party should assume liability for maintenance instead of the beneficiary it would be right to hold that the period has ceased to be one 'during which the beneficiary is wholly or mainly maintaining the dependant' even though only a few months, or even weeks, have elapsed since the beneficiary ceased in fact to maintain the dependant. Where there is no evidence of repudiation or transfer of the obligation to maintain but the beneficiary is in fact unable to maintain the dependant owing to his incapacity for work the answer to the question must depend upon how long the beneficiary has been prevented by his incapacity from wholly or mainly maintaining the dependant and whether it is probable that he will be able to resume maintenance within a reasonable time."[58]

The family fund

In calculating whether or not a maintainor is maintaining wholly or mainly, *i.e.* at half the actual cost of maintenance of a dependant or more, difficulty may arise in determining what the actual cost of maintenance of a particular dependant is. This will often be the case; the family's income may derive from a source or sources which are nominally appropriate to one dependant only, but actually used for the maintenance of all. This will frequently be the case where, for example, a deserted wife maintains the family by wages which are nominally her own, and maintenance paid by the husband, perhaps also nominally for the wife alone. In such a case, the actual cost of maintaining the children is obviously not nil, and the question arises of how to distribute the total family income amongst the various dependants in order to arrive at an "actual cost" figure. The device resorted to by Commissioners has been to add together all sums received by and used for the family's maintenance and to calculate the amount of maintenance for each by dividing the total by the number of persons in the family, non-earning children of school age counting as half.[59]

Multiple maintainors

Complications arise where a dependant is maintained by two or more maintainors (*e.g.* a widow maintained by two sons). Here, regulation[60] provides for their contributions to be aggregated for purposes of determining whether or not the dependant is wholly or mainly maintained, or maintained in the statutory amount. If this is so, and provided that both or all maintainors would otherwise qualify for benefit, then the increase may be paid to him who makes the largest contribution to the dependant's maintenance or, if all contributions are equal, to the elder or eldest contributor or, if a majority agree, to an agreed recipient designated in writing to the Secretary of State. All contributors must, however, be otherwise qualified for benefit, *e.g.* by virtue of unemployment.[61] This can work particularly harshly where, *e.g.* one son has made the major contribution towards the maintenance of a widowed mother and become unemployed, leaving a less well-paid son still in employment to bear the whole burden.

EARNINGS-RELATED BENEFITS

One of Beveridge's principles was that there should be a flat rate of benefit for a flat rate of contribution. It is a principle that has been eroded by successive measures, initially only so far as retirement pensions were concerned[62] but subsequently also for unemployment and sickness benefit,[63] maternity allowance[64] and widow's allowance.[65] The institution of universal earnings-related Class I contributions[66] adds an earnings-related dimension even to flat-rate benefit—the same benefit is more speedily and easily-earned, the higher the rate of contribution paid.

Pensions are now supplemented in a complex way—additional elements may accrue via the graduated pensions scheme existing prior to 1973; or via a recognised occupational pensions scheme. All pensions will eventually become earnings-related under the new scheme instituted by the Social Security (Pensions) Act 1975. So, too, will invalidity pensions, widowed mother's allowance and widow's pension.[67]

So far as unemployment and sickness benefit are concerned, the earnings-related supplement only becomes payable on the 13th day of a period of interruption of employment[68] and ceases to be payable after it has been payable for 156 days in the same period of interruption of employment. The same approach is adopted in the case of maternity allowance.[69] A widow's entitlement, however, starts immediately.[70]

In order to calculate entitlement to earnings-related supplement, it is necessary first to ascertain the relevant "reckonable weekly earnings." This is $\frac{1}{50}$th of the earnings factor for the relevant year[71] derived from Class I contributions actually paid. Subject to one important limitation, the amount of earnings-related supplement payable is:

1. One-third of the sum arrived at by deducting the current lower earnings limit (presently £13) from the reckonable weekly earnings in so far as they do not exceed £30; plus

2. 15 per cent. of the reckonable weekly earnings in so far as they exceed £30 but do not exceed the upper earnings limit (presently £95).

The limitation above referred to relates to the supplement in the case of unemployment, sickness and maternity payments. In no case is the total benefit receivable (personal benefit, increases for dependants and earnings-related supplement) to exceed 85 per cent. of the reckonable weekly earnings.[72]

Earnings-related supplement is not uncontroversial. On the one hand, it may be argued that higher contribution deserves higher benefit, and that at least in the short term, there is a case to be made for assisting with meeting the higher financial commitments that are likely to have accompanied higher earnings. On the other hand, there is substance in the argument that those who have enjoyed higher earnings are more likely to have a cushion for protection in hard times, whereas raw needs will make themselves more directly and viciously felt where a history of low earning has rendered it impossible for any provision to be made against the contingency.

EXTINGUISHMENT OF BENEFIT

Benefit is payable only so long as the conditions of entitlement are fulfilled. When any condition ceases to be fulfilled, entitlement automatically ceases and any further benefit paid is overpaid and may be recoverable.[73] Even, however, if the substantive conditions of entitlement are fulfilled and an order for payment obtained, benefit may be lost if it is not demanded in time. Generally, payment must be sought within 12 months of the accrual of the right to benefit. The right to benefit accrues on the date on which an instrument of payment accrues or on the date of receipt of a notice that a sum is available for collection, whichever means is used.[74] Even after the period of 12 months, payment may still be claimed by written notice to the Secretary of State provided that there existed, throughout until the notice is delivered, good cause for not giving earlier notice.

The above rule applies to "a person authorised or appointed to act on behalf of a beneficiary as it applies to a beneficiary." Commissioners used to distinguish between the case where a person was temporarily entrusted with the claimant's affairs and the case where a formal appointment of an agent was made under regulations. Benefit might not be lost in the former case but would be in the latter, for a person so appointed stands in the claimant's shoes for all purposes.[75] It is doubtful if this distinction can be maintained in the face of the present regulation.

The 12-month period for extinguishment of benefit must be distinguished from the periods of limitation for claiming as they relate to the various benefits. These periods of limitation are considered in relation to specific benefits *post*, but there is an absolute bar for all claims of 12 months.[76]

REPAYMENT OF BENEFIT OVERPAID

The legislation originally provided that any benefit overpaid (including benefit paid in pursuance of a decision of the statutory authorities subsequently reversed on appeal) should be repaid unless it had been claimed and received "in good faith." The Family Allowances and National Insurance Act 1961 substituted for this the requirement that the beneficiary and any

agent of his[77] should have "throughout used due care and diligence to avoid overpayment."[78] One respected authority tell us
that the new phrase "is intended to have substantially the same
effect as the phrase 'good faith'."[79] At least one Commissioner,
however, has entertained the notion that the interpretations
might differ.[80] The notion of "good faith" would seem to import
a subjective test, but Commissioners' Decisions repeatedly
allowed a more extended interpretation, such as, for example,
holding that there was no "good faith" where a claimant signed
a declaration as to earnings without reading it.[81] This result,
however, was arrived at by deduction from the onus of proof;
the claimant failed unless he positively proved his good faith.[82]
Accordingly, a claimant might succeed in avoiding repayment if
he could satisfy the statutory authorities of his good faith in the
matter, even though he might seem not to have used "due care
and diligence."[83] For this reason, it is doubtful if some of the
older decisions can stand in the light of the new formula. The
claimant in *R(G) 6/53*, who avoided repayment in respect of a
failure to declare earnings on grounds of her illiteracy, might not
be so lucky now. It is less clear whether reliance on the advice of
superiors will now excuse overpayment. Under the old formula,
it might do so provided there was genuine reliance[84] but not if
the object in seeking the advice was simply to seek a supporting
view for action which the claimant had in any case decided to
take.[85]

Repayment of benefit overpaid can be effected by way of
set-off as well as by order for the whole but the statutory
authorities have no power to direct repayment by instalments.[86]
The Department may, however, exercise a *de facto* discretion to
receive payment by instalments and has even been known to
abandon a demand for repayment of benefit overpaid, notwithstanding a lack of due diligence on the part of the claimant, if
such a course appears just.[87]

The notion that one need not reimburse what one had no
right to receive, provided that one exercised due care and
diligence, is not unquestionable. No doubt, in many cases repayment would result in hardship and hardship is to be avoided.
In some cases, however, repayment might involve no hardship
whatever. Resort to the supplementary benefits scheme[88] in case
of hardship might be a better way of resolving the difficulties.

OFFENCES IN CONNECTION WITH BENEFIT

Many offences arise in connection with the acts and regulations. It is an offence punishable by a £400 fine or three months' imprisonment or both (maximum) knowingly to make a false statement or representation or to produce or furnish any document or information known to be false for the purpose of obtaining any benefit or other payment under the Act.[89] It is as much an offence to make a false statement upon receipt of payment as it is in connection with the making of a claim for benefit. In *Tolfree* v. *Florence*[90] the accused obtained sickness benefit at a time when he was genuinely incapacitated on the strength of a "sick-note" predicting five days' incapacity. The claimant worked on two of these days but nevertheless asserted entitlement when he sought to cash the order for benefit afterwards. He was held to have committed the above offence.

An important part of the enforcement mechanism of the social security scheme is inspection. Inspectors appointed by the Secretary of State[91] have wide powers[92] including power to require information for the purpose of ascertaining "whether benefit is or was payable to or in respect of any person."[93] and it is an offence, *inter alia*, to refuse or neglect to answer any question or furnish any information when required so to do.[94] Thus, an employed person may be required to disclose the name and address of his employer[95] and be liable to a fine of £50 in the first instance, and £10 per day thereafter, in the event of a continuing refusal.[96] In the result, a person may be convicted and fined for failing to provide information which has nothing to do with his own liability to pay contributions etc., and which he might be unwilling to disclose for reasons not connected with national insurance, not least his own future employment prospects. For these reasons, the scope of such offences has been rightly criticised.[97] From this point of view, it is little consolation that proceedings for an offence cannot be instituted except by or with the consent of the Secretary of State or other officer authorised by him, or by an inspector.[98]

CHAPTER 3

GENERAL DISQUALIFICATIONS

MANY different types of benefit are receivable under the social
security schemes. Each benefit carries its own specific conditions
of entitlement and some are the subject of special grounds of
disqualification.[1] There are, however, certain general grounds
of disqualification applicable to all benefits. Some of these
grounds are procedural; others are substantive.

The procedural grounds relate to the making and determination of claims. Thus, claims must be made in the prescribed
manner and within the prescribed time limits[2] unless there is
good cause for the delay in claiming.[3] There is an absolute bar
against the making of a claim or the payment of a benefit
more than 12 months after the event in respect of which it is
payable.[4] The mere making of a claim does not establish
immediate title to benefit, even if in fact all the conditions of
entitlement are fulfilled—the benefit may be and frequently is
withheld pending proper determination of the claim.[5]

The substantive grounds are dealt with by section 82 (5) of
the 1975 Act. This provides that, subject to regulations, "a
person shall be disqualified for receiving any benefit, and an
increase of benefit shall not be payable in respect of any person
as the beneficiary's wife or husband, for any period during
which *the person*[6] (a) is absent from Great Britain; ("Northern
Ireland" in the Northern Ireland scheme) or (b) is undergoing imprisonment or detention in legal custody." It should be
noted that the disqualification attaches not only to the absence
or imprisonment of the claimant himself; the italicised phrase in
the above quotation applies equally to the beneficiary and the
dependant. An increase of benefit would thus not be payable for
a wife who was abroad even though the beneficiary was present.[7]

The word "period" in the above provision refers to a period
of calendar days. It was at first thought that entitlement
depended upon the state of things prevailing at the start of the
day in question and, thus, that the day on which a person

arrived in Great Britain would be a day of disqualification, he having been absent at its commencement.[8] It is, however, now settled that the word "during" means throughout. It follows that the period of disqualification does not include days during only a part of which the person was absent or imprisoned.[9]

ABSENCE

The provisions of the Act itself relating to absence are relatively simple. "Absence" is a matter of fact. One is "absent" whilst on holiday in the Isle of Man just as much as if one had emigrated to Chile.[10] The expressions "Great Britain" and "Northern Ireland" must be taken to have the meanings appropriated to them by the Union with Scotland Act 1706, art. 1, and the Government of Ireland Act 1920, s. 1 (2), respectively. Thus, "Great Britain" excludes the British Islands such as the Isle of Man[11] and "floating islands," *i.e.* British-owned and registered aircraft and ships outside the territory.[12]

These relatively simple provisions are, however, complicated in two important ways. First, regulations[13] establish the right to a broad range of benefits, notwithstanding absence abroad, on certain conditions. Secondly, international arrangements of various sorts exist whereby advantage may be taken of foreign schemes whilst abroad by virtue of participation in the United Kingdom schemes earlier.

1. Modification by Regulations

Many benefits are payable unconditionally during absence abroad notwithstanding the apparently categorical disqualification imposed by section 82(5)(a) of the 1975 Act. This is so with child's special allowance, guardian's allowance, retirement pensions,[14] disablement benefit[15] (but not supplements to it),[16] industrial death benefit[17] and death grant in respect of a death occurring in Great Britain.[18] In some circumstances, death grant may be payable in respect of a death occurring outside Great Britain.[19] Widows' benefits are also payable notwithstanding absence, except that *either* one spouse must have been present in Great Britain at the time of the death *or* the contribution conditions for mother's allowance or pension must be satisfied

in relation to the woman.[20] Attendance allowance is also stated
to be receivable notwithstanding absence abroad[21] but conditions elsewhere prescribed under section 35 (1) of the 1975 Act
require the claimant to be "ordinarily resident" and "present"
in Great Britain,[22] although "presence" is not interrupted by a
temporary absence.[23] But in the result, it is only a temporary
absence which can be ignored for attendance allowance purposes. This is also the case with constant attendance and special
hardship supplements to disablement benefit.[24]

Being "ordinarily resident" in Great Britain is also relevant so
far as avoidance of disqualification for age addition[25] and
entitlement to up-ratings[26] are concerned. Up-rating regulations
may and sometimes do entitle existing beneficiaries abroad to
up-rated benefits, but this may now be qualified by invoking
regulation 5 of the Persons Abroad Regulations confining the
right to, *inter alia*, persons "ordinarily resident" in Great Britain.
The notion of "residence" connotes association with a locality
"with some degree of continuity and apart from accidental or
temporary absence."[27] It used to be thought that residence was
only possible where there was a specific abode, but this view has
now been abandoned. It is possible, it seems, to have a number
of residences[28] though whether one could be "ordinarily resident" in more than one place for social security purposes is
doubtful.[29] However, notwithstanding absence and residence
elsewhere, residence in Great Britain may be retained so long as
there has not been an intention to abandon it.[30] If it is intended
not to return, residence is abandoned.[31] It is, furthermore, lost
immediately the intention is formed and cannot be regained
merely by changing the intention.[32] The residence must be re-
established.[33] Residence cannot be acquired simply by marriage[34] nor will it be re-established simply by resuming presence;
the resumption of presence must be accompanied by the intention to re-establish residence.[35] Provided that there is such an
intention, however, it does not matter that it is contemplated
that the presence will be of a limited duration.[36]

"Residence" also governs continuation of entitlement to an
increase of benefit for a spouse abroad. Provided that the spouse
in respect of whom the increase of benefit is payable continues
to reside with the beneficiary, title to the increase continues notwithstanding the absence abroad of that spouse,[37] mitigating the

harshness of the ruling, in *C.U. 28/49*, that an increase of benefit
is not payable in respect of a spouse absent abroad.

Maternity grant is normally lost through absence, title to it
in such circumstances being preserved only for wives abroad of
serving members of the forces abroad and even then only upon
different contribution conditions in the case of some post-
confinement claims.[38]

A range of benefits in respect of sickness and analogous
matters are subject to more complex conditions for the receipt
of benefit during a temporary absence abroad. So far as sickness
benefit, unemployability supplement and maternity allowance
are concerned, the conditions, in addition to the absence being
temporary[39] are:

(i) the Secretary of State must determine that it is reasonable
in all the circumstances that the disqualification should be
lifted; and, *either*

(ii) the absence is for the specific purpose of being treated for
an incapacity commencing before departure; *or*

(iii) the departure was preceded by at least six months'
incapacity which continues.[40]

Condition (i) above applies in the case of industrial injury
benefit, the other condition for receipt of which is that the
absence must be for the specific purpose of receiving treatment
appropriate to the relevant injury.[41]

Whether payment is reasonable is for the Secretary of State to
determine.[42] The function of the statutory authorities is thus confined to determining the maximum period within which the
other conditions of the regulation are satisfied.[43] If any of these
conditions is not satisfied, however, disqualification ensues;
there is no discretion to award benefit. The conditions are:

1. The absence must be temporary;
2. the claimant must be abroad for the specific purpose;
3. of being treated;
4. for incapacity which commenced before leaving Great
Britain.

(a) *The Absence Must be Temporary*

Where there is no prospect of the absence abroad coming to an
end and therefore no prospect of a return for an indefinite

period, the absence is not temporary.[44] Where the claimant is in hospital and the absence has lasted for more than a year it will be presumed that there is no prospect of a return for an indefinite period if discharge within six months cannot be foreseen.[45]

(b) *The Claimant must be Abroad for the Specific Purpose*

What is required is that the claimant *be* abroad for the purpose. "It is not essential for a claimant to prove that the specific purpose ... had been formed before he left."[46] Similarly, it is irrelevant that suitable treatment was available at home[47] and that the receipt of treatment was not the sole purpose of the absence.[48] The absence abroad must be referable to the purpose, however. It will not suffice if the absence is accountable by reference to some other purpose or that the treatment is a mere incident of an absence abroad explicable otherwise.[49] A good indication will be whether it is intended to return immediately after the treatment.[50]

(c) *The Purpose must be "Treatment"*

"Where a person goes abroad merely for the purposes of rest and freedom from worry in order to allow nature to continue the cure and recovery ... he is not going for the purpose of being treated."[51] Even if medicines are to be self-administered under a doctor's instructions, it is still not "treatment".[52] The test seems to be whether action of a medical character by some other person is involved.[53] Merely being "under a doctor's professional care" will not suffice if all that is prescribed is rest and recuperation,[54] but if convalescence under the care of nurses[55] or even psychological relief under the care of a doctor of divinity[56] is prescribed, this condition is fulfilled. Provided that such a purpose operates it is irrelevant that in the event the treatment is not received.[57]

(d) *Incapacity Commencing before Departure*

The incapacity must exist before the claimant goes abroad, even if the securing of treatment for it is not the purpose of his leaving. Benefit is thus not available to persons only becoming incapacitated after they have left the jurisdiction.[58] What is required is incapacity; mere undiagnosed ailments will not suffice.[59] Where pregnancy is the cause, entitlement to benefit depends upon whether it has reached an incapacitating state before the departure. If it has, benefit may be received[60] but if not, a subsequent incapacity attributable to the pregnancy will not help.[61] Commissioners have undergone a change of heart as to whether there may be an incapacity for this purpose even though a claim for sickness benefit would not have succeeded before departure. In both *C.S. 317/49 (KL)* and *R(S) 10/51* cognisable conditions had been diagnosed but the claimants had continued to work thus negativing "incapacity" in the technical sense for sickness benefit purposes. It was held that this was not fatal to avoiding disqualification under regulation 7. In *R(S) 1/75*, however, a claimant suffering from an undiagnosed abnormality associated with pregnancy and who had worked until her departure was treated as disqualified under regulation 7, there being no "incapacity for work" where in fact work was done.

Apart from regulation 7, special rules apply in the case of mariners left outside the jurisdiction on account of illness.[62]

Northern Ireland

In addition to the requirement that a claimant be not absent from the jurisdiction, the Northern Ireland scheme had a requirement peculiar to itself, namely, that a claimant shall have been resident in the United Kingdom for a period of five years immediately preceding the date on which benefit is claimed.[63] It has been held, consistently with developments in Great Britain[64] that a person may be resident for the purposes of this provision notwithstanding that he has no specific "place of abode" in the United Kingdom provided that "as part of his regular habit of life" he resides there from time to time.[65] This provision has, however, now been repealed.

2. INTERNATIONAL ARRANGEMENTS

(a) Reciprocal arrangements. Power for the Secretary of State to conclude arrangements with foreign countries on the basis of reciprocity has been included in the national insurance scheme throughout.[66] Frequent use is made of this power and such reciprocal arrangements now exist with most western and some eastern countries. These arrangements are bilateral and their terms differ in each case. Generally speaking, such an arrangement is only possible to the extent that parallel schemes exist, and, of course, each country's scheme tends to be peculiar to itself. Provided that there are similar schemes, however, *e.g.* in relation to benefits in respect of unemployment, and provided that the terms of the arrangement so provide, the result is that a claimant entitled to the relevant benefit under a United Kingdom scheme may become entitled to a parallel foreign benefit, when resident in the relevant jurisdiction, and vice versa.

(b) EEC arrangements. With the entry into Europe of the United Kingdom, reciprocal arrangements between the United Kingdom and states members of the EEC were superseded by arrangements governed by EEC Council Regulations, made under powers contained in the Treaty of Rome.[67] These arrangements by no means unify European social security schemes; they do not entitle a claimant to treat the whole of the EEC as a single jurisdiction, enabling title to a single benefit to be established by a single range of conditions of entitlement common throughout Europe. It is left to each member state to establish its range of benefits, (subject to treaties on the matter) and conditions of entitlement to them. The general effect of the EEC regulations is to harmonise reciprocity. Their general approach is that if a right to benefit is established in one country, it shall not be lost on transfer to another.[68]

In the result, the position of some claimants has become unfavourable by comparison with that which prevailed under the superseded bilateral reciprocal arrangements. For example, under the latter, contributions made by United Kingdom workers working in Germany could be taken into account immediately for unemployment benefit purposes upon return to the United Kingdom; that benefit might thus be payable immediately without more ado. Under the EEC Regulations, it is a necessary precondition to the receipt of that benefit on return to the United Kingdom, that the claimant shall have entered or re-entered insurance here, *i.e.* have got a job here and paid at least one week's contributions. This may well be desirable if it is conceived that there is a serious threat of the unemployed otherwise "shopping around" for the best benefits, but it certainly occasioned the defeat of the expectations of some United Kingdom migrant workers caught by the transition.[69]

(c) Although not an "international" arrangement, it should be noted that the Beveridge proposals were implemented separately in Great Britain and Northern Ireland and that the two schemes have remained theoretically separate ever since. For all practical purposes, however, they are virtually identical, the only significant difference being the former existence of residence requirements for unemployment and supplementary benefits in Northern Ireland because of the land frontier with the Republic of Ireland.[70] Without more, however, Northern Ireland workers would not qualify under the Great Britain schemes and vice versa. In fact, throughout there has been power to conclude comprehensive joint arrangements and section 142 of the 1975 Act continues this, constituting a joint authority to make arrangements for administering the two systems as one. This is done; the systems are separate in name only.

Whether in fact equality of treatment of beneficiaries as between Northern Ireland and Great Britain is secured by strict parity of contribution and benefit rates (involving transfers as between the funds) may well be doubted, as equally it may as between various regions of Great Britain, in view of economic and demographic differences.[71]

IMPRISONMENT OR DETENTION IN LEGAL CUSTODY

The concept of "imprisonment" has occasioned no difficulty. That of "detention in legal custody" has done so.

After some initial hesitation, it was settled in *R.* v. *National Insurance Commissioner, ex p. Timmis*[72] that it is not necessary that the detention have a punitive or corrective purpose. The disqualification may attach whenever a person is "detained by reason of a legal proceeding or as the result of a court proceeding." Although the *Timmis* case does not do so, Commissioner's decisions have made it clear that the proceedings thus referred to must either be criminal proceedings or be grounded on a criminal act.[73] It follows that it is not safe to characterise a detention simply by reference to the particular statutory authority under which it is ordered for the order might or might not be grounded on a criminal act. In both *R(S) 3/55* and *R(S) 5/55* the statutory authority for the making of the order was section 9 of the Mental Deficiency Act 1913. In the former case the detention did not result in disqualification since it did not arise out of criminal activities; but in the latter case disqualification did result since the detainee had been serving a prison sentence for a criminal offence and the order merely effected a transfer of custody. Conviction of a crime is not necessary. An accused person found unfit to plead and ordered to be detained in Broadmoor is "detained in legal custody" and disqualified from benefit.[74]

DETENTION

Where a person enjoys a measure of freedom from the detention, as under licence, does he remain disqualified or does the disqualification cease? A claimant allowed out from a mental hospital to work under daily licence was held to remain disqualified in *R(S) 23/54*. The claimant in *R(S) 10/56*, however, escaped the disqualification. He had been allowed out on licence first to reside at a hostel with his family and then, when he became ill, in a hospital where he was under the care of the staff. Although originally "detained in legal custody" he ceased to be so when he was released to reside with his family. Although while residing with his wife he might have been in her "legal custody," he was no longer "detained." He was under her "care and control" and she was obliged to give him "adequate care and supervision" but this fell short of detention. And his subsequent entry into hospital for treatment for a physical illness, although in pursuance of an order, did not alter the position.

This basic position is qualified in important respects by regulations in the case of certain of the benefits.[75] Disqualification is removed entirely in the case of guardian's allowance.[76] Where the detention in legal custody is "in connection with a charge brought or intended to be brought against a person in criminal proceedings" the disqualification only operates in the case of certain benefits if the proceedings conclude in the imposition of a penalty. The benefits here affected are sickness benefit, invalidity benefit, widow's benefit, child's special allowance, maternity allowance, retirement pension and age addition, and increases of benefit for dependants.[77] Persons on remand in custody or in prison for non-payment of a fine may thus preserve entitlement to these benefits though not, apparently, persons detained or interned as a result of the exercise of extraordinary executive powers for they are not in custody "in connection with a charge ... in criminal proceedings."

Many of the decisions discussed earlier have concerned cases where the claimant was detained in hospital in respect of a mental disorder. Although the principles on the basis of which they were decided still hold good, the actual facts of most of these cases would now be embraced by regulations.[78] In effect, it removes the disqualification in respect of all benefits if the claimant is detained in a hospital or similar institution as mentally disordered unless, before being so detained, he was already in "penal detention." The conditions of their preserving entitlement is that the proceedings do not conclude in a "penalty." It has been held that a suspended sentence of imprisonment is such a penalty and that the disqualification is accordingly not lifted in such a case.[79]

CHAPTER 4

UNEMPLOYMENT BENEFIT[1]

OUR social system puts primary reliance on earning from employment as a source of livelihood for the earner and his dependants. Manifestly, therefore, a failure of employment offers one of the primary occasions for the intervention of the social security system and is certainly one of the best-known.

In fact, a relatively small proportion of the entire social security budget is devoted to the relief of the unemployed. Even in times of high unemployment, unemployment benefit comes a bad third behind retirement pensions and sickness benefit in devouring funds. Furthermore, unemployment benefit is not even the sole means of relieving unemployment. Due to the fact that the contribution conditions are fairly stringent and that the benefit is relatively inadequate and short-term, many unemployed persons need to look to supplementary benefits either as a sole means of support during unemployment or at least as a way of supplementing inadequate unemployment benefits.

Although, in money terms, unemployment benefit is not of the first rank in importance, it is, however, the subject of a large number of claims. Even more is it the subject of a large number of contested claims. The vast majority of claims each year are for sickness benefit (about 10m. in recent years out of a total of about 16m.) but such claims are usually formal, turning almost invariably upon the presentation of a "sick-note." The 4½m. unemployment benefit claims which have become customary in recent years are by no means all so readily processed. It is not, therefore, surprising that the law relating to unemployment benefit should be the most complex part of the social security system.

STRUCTURE OF CHAPTERS ON UNEMPLOYMENT BENEFIT

The procedural law relating to unemployment benefit is briefly dealt with at the beginning of this chapter. This chapter is mainly concerned with the first part of the substantive law—the conditions of entitlement to unemployment benefit. In this connection, it should be noted that unemployment benefit and sickness benefit share a number of concepts and that some of the discussion of unemployment benefit relates also to sickness benefit.

Disqualification for unemployment benefit forms a large and controversial subject in itself and forms the subject of the next chapter.

PROCEDURAL LAW

CLAIMS

Claims generally are governed by the Claims and Payments Regulations which contain provisions specifically applicable to claims for unemployment benefit.[2] Normally, a claim for unemployment benefit should be made on the day in respect of which it is made.[3] In the case of spells of unemployment of more than a few days' duration, however, daily claim would provoke great inconvenience for claimants and administration alike. There is therefore power for the Secretary of State to give notice providing, in effect, that "signing on" on a particular day may rank as a claim in respect of a number of days.[4] If this is done, it is important that the claim be made on the day specified; failure to do so will result in disentitlement for all days before the date of claim and not merely for the day on which the claim should have been made, unless, of course, there was good cause for the delay.[5]

It is also a common administrative practice, obviously convenient for all concerned, to specify a particular time for "signing on," and it is not unknown for a claim made after the appointed time, but on the appointed day, to be treated as a late claim and benefit accordingly denied unless there is good cause for the delay. This is believed to be incorrect. Provided that the claim is made on the appointed day it would seem to be a proper claim and benefit ought not to be denied on this ground. The correct course would seem to be to proceed against the claimant for a breach of the regulations.

PROOF

On general principles and by implication from regulations,[6] it is up to a claimant to establish his entitlement to the benefit claimed.[7] The initial burden thus rests upon the unemployment benefit claimant to establish that the basic conditions of entitlement are fulfilled in his case, *i.e.* that he is unemployed, and capable of and available for work. He is not entitled to the benefit of any doubt, as is the accused in respect of a criminal charge. On the contrary, he must "substantiate his claim by proving his case, on the balance of probabilities, in the same way as a plaintiff would have to do in a civil action."[8] It is not, furthermore, enough simply to allege facts which, if true, would substantiate a claim. He must "furnish such certificates, documents, information and evidence for the purpose of determining the claim as may be required by the Secretary of State ..."[9] The claimant must therefore be prepared to subject his claim to the scrutiny of the insurance officer. If he does not answer frankly reasonable questions addressed to him by an insurance officer and give an account of his activities at the relevant time, if required, the insurance officer may fairly assume that the claim is not genuine. This is even more the case where the claimant's statement is established to be false in particular respects.[10]

This initial onus is of proof of unemployment, capability and availability. Once it is discharged, the onus shifts on to the insurance officer to establish reasons why the claim should be rejected. Whilst there is no hard-and-fast rule on the matter, the best evidence should be made available. Hearsay evidence may well justify a particular line of inquiry by an investigating officer but is highly unlikely to commend itself to a tribunal in rebuttal of a prima facie good claim. A *fortiori*, inconsistency in the second-hand evidence of a particular witness destroys its value.[11]

This secondary onus remains with the insurance officer not merely so far as contesting the facts alleged by the claimant is concerned, but also so far as establishing disentitlement for other reasons goes, such as the fact that the claimant has already worked to the full extent normal;[12] or that he is disqualified.[13]

THE SUBSTANTIVE LAW

Benefit is normally payable to a claimant satisfying the contribution conditions in respect of a reckonable day of unemployment forming part of a period of interruption of employment, provided that he is not disqualified for benefit. In the case of certain occupations there are additional conditions. Five separate matters thus fall for consideration. These are:

I. Contribution conditions, including period of entitlement to and requalification for benefit;

II. "Day of unemployment," described above as reckonable" because the first three such days in a period do not qualify;

III. "Period of interruption of employment" this being defined by the legislation in terms of days of unemployment or incapacity;

IV. Additional conditions; and

V. Disqualification.

1. CONTRIBUTION CONDITIONS

There are two contribution conditions for unemployment benefit. The first is that in any one tax year[14] prior to the date of claim, the claimant must have paid contributions yielding an earnings factor not less than 25 times that year's lower earnings limit. The second is that in the last complete tax year before the year of claim his contributions, whether actually paid or merely credited, yielded an earnings factor not less than 50 times that year's lower earnings limit.[15] Only primary Class I contributions at the full rate may be taken into account.[16]

A person of pensionable age who would have been entitled to a Category A retirement pension on the day of claim had he retired need not satisfy the above conditions.[17] Nor need a widow who would have been entitled to a Category B pension had she not opted to de-retire.[18]

Unemployment is classified as a short-term benefit.[19] Initial title to it is lost once the claimant "has been entitled" for 312 days (*i.e.* a year, the seventh day in the week being excluded[20]) in a single period of interruption of employment.[21] For this purpose, the claimant need not have claimed or drawn benefit; he will be treated as having been "entitled" on a day if in fact he satisfied the substantive conditions of entitlement notwithstanding that he did not claim.[22] If title is thus lost, there must be a further 13 weeks of full-time employment[23] in order for it to be re-established. It is not necessary to satisfy the contribution conditions *de novo*.

2. "Day of Unemployment"

The rates of benefit stipulated in respect of unemployment are presented as weekly sums.[24] As appropriate, benefit will be paid in the form of a weekly payment.[25] It is a common administrative practice for a claimant to be required to "sign on" once per week.[26] In spite of all this, unemployment benefit is a daily benefit, *i.e.* in order to succeed in a claim, the claimant must establish that each day in respect of which he claims is a day of unemployment.

That a claimant be unemployed on the day for which he claims is, of course, the most obvious condition of entitlement to unemployment benefit. However, "The concept of the day of unemployment is now complex and artificial; and the statutory authorities are compelled to make decisions which must seem to many to be complex and artificial. Some may be tempted to echo the words of the legendary Lord Mildew—'There is too much of this damned deeming.' "[27] Some complexity, be it by reason of "deeming" or not, seems inevitable, for the facts of industrial life are not simple. There are clear easy cases—one man paid for actual work under a contract of employment, another with no job, no pay and no contract. But all too often, there are variations on these three dimensions of work, pay and contract. A man may work and not be paid. Another may be paid but not work; and his pay may accrue under a contract or not. A third may be under contract but lack work and pay. Such instances could be multiplied. Because of them, it is not enough simply to understand what, in the normal case, consti-tutes a day of unemployment. It will be discovered that for a variety of reasons, benefit may be denied for a day on which one is in fact unemployed and yet allowed for a day on which one in fact works.

It is necessary, therefore, first of all to consider the "standard case", *i.e.* the criteria for prima facie characterisation of a day

as a day of unemployment, and then to consider two types of
exceptional case, (1) cases where a claimant may not rank a day
as a day of unemployment even though it is a day when he is
in fact unemployed, and (2) cases where a claimant may rank a
day as a day of unemployment even though he works on it.

The Standard Case

"Day"

Although "day" is not defined in the legislation, it is clearly
assumed that for general purposes it bears its ordinary meaning
of the period of 24 hours from midnight to midnight.[28]

Benefit is payable only for a complete "day" of unemployment. Laying-off for half a day (or even a long succession of half-
days) gives no basis for a claim even if it results in a drastic
reduction in earnings.[29] If any work at all is done (or payment
received in lieu thereof) the right to benefit falls. In *2/56 (UB)*
the power supply was cut off 20 minutes after the claimant had
arrived to start work. She was, nevertheless, to be treated as not
having been unemployed. The test adopted by Umpires under
the Unemployment Insurance Acts was adopted—". . . a
claimant must be deemed to be employed on any day on which
he has reached the point at which he is expected to work and
has actually commenced or had the opportunity for commencing
work."[30] Not even the opportunity for commencing work is
necessary if payment in respect of it is received. In *R(U) 35/51*, a
totalisator-operator who had attended the place of assembly and
received an attendance "allowance" of 10 shillings on the
occasion of a cancelled race-meeting was held to be not
unemployed. It might have been otherwise if the sum received
was no more than a reimbursement of expenses and subsequent
cases have emphasised that it is an essential condition of disentitlement to benefit that there should be an obligation to
undertake work if called upon to do so by an employer[31]
under a subsisting contract of service.[32]

"Unemployment"

The unemployment benefit scheme functions within a system
in which the primary source of subsistence incomes (for bread-

winner and dependants) is earnings from work, whether in an employed or self-employed capacity. For benefit purposes, one is employed during and only during such periods as one has an existing opportunity to secure earnings in this way. Otherwise one is unemployed.

This criterion is a purely factual one. It is irrelevant whether or not a contract of employment continues to subsist. "If an employer is entitled (under the contract) to stand a man off with neither work nor pay, . . . such person is unemployed for a period of suspension of service, notwithstanding that the contract has not been terminated."[33] This remains so even though the eventual removal of the suspension is accompanied by payment of the earnings withheld in the meantime. "It would be contrary to the manifest object of such a scheme that when this event has occurred and the insured person has suffered the loss of his means of livelihood he should be denied benefit because of the possibility that he might receive a payment at some unknown future date."[34] The same reasoning might be thought also to apply to the situation where wages, although earned, have in fact been unlawfully withheld from the earner. He, at all events, might be disposed to insist that he had lost his means of livelihood just as much as a man suspended without wages; but his claim for benefit would nevertheless fail.[35] The cases may be distinguished in that in the latter, the employee has an immediate enforceable right to payment throughout whilst in the former he has not, but in view of the cost and dilatoriness of litigation this distinction borders on the irrelevant.

It is crucial to determine whether an opportunity to secure earnings exists in respect of the day in question. If it does not, one is unemployed notwithstanding that, due to a rearrangement of the work pattern, total earnings for the week are not reduced. The three-day week resulted in many such rearrangements, entitlement to benefit turning on a number of variables. Workers covered by guarantee agreements[36] under which they were on call and paid for days on which they did not work were not entitled. Workers who were not on call and not paid were entitled.[37] A worker "on call" but not in fact called and *not* paid would presumably lack the opportunity to earn from work on the day in question and be unemployed. One not on call but paid anyway under his contract would presumably be regarded as earning from work and not "unemployed."

Provided that the opportunity to earn exists, it will not avail the claimant that he did not, in fact, seize it. This, presumably, is the reason why a deserter from the forces is not entitled to benefit when he loses his civilian employment but has not yet been discharged from the services.[38]

This latter point occasions difficulty in the case of persons, especially the self-employed[39] who can choose when to work, some occasions being much more profitable than others. In *R(U) 11/60* a salesman claimed benefit in respect of five days over the Christmas period, during which canvassing for sales would almost certainly have been a complete waste of time. His employers paid him no retaining fee; he looked to commission from sales for his entire income. He was, nevertheless, not unemployed. He could have worked. In this respect, he differs from a worker laid off by his employer because of a shortage of orders and from a person in self-employment whose business is temporarily closed down due to its seasonal nature and the impossibility of carrying on the business during the off-season.[40]

It will be apparent from the above that one need not actually work in order to be treated as employed, provided that one in fact earns in respect of one's employment. Payment, albeit much reduced, in respect of one's work for a particular day can thus destroy title to benefit for that day. The payment must, however, be "earnings" in respect of that day, and not a mere reimbursement of expenses.[41] Equally, a payment which is gratuitous[42] or which is an inducement to resume employment at a later date but carrying no obligation to work in the meantime even if called upon[43] does not import disentitlement. Considerable difficulty may be experienced in cases where the "work" done or "payment" received are of a nominal or peculiar kind. It is clear that payment in kind can rank as payment so as to involve disentitlement.[44] The difficulties arise from the question whether or not there has been such a payment. Where continuing employment is of a fluctuating nature, as in the holiday trade, it has been held that a person who, during the off-season, discharges nominal household duties and receives board and lodging at a reduced rate continues to be employed.[45] On the other hand, where a retired farm labourer continued to reside in the home of his former employer, paying a small sum for board and lodging, he was held to be unemployed.[46] This latter decision is, however, equally explicable by reference to the fact that the claimant was under no continuing obligation to work if called upon but was, on the contrary, entirely free to seek work elsewhere at any time.[47]

This general approach, that one cannot be considered to be unemployed for any day during which one has the opportunity to earn (or, *a fortiori*, for which one is in fact paid for work even if in fact one does none) is well-illustrated in its particular application in a couple of commonly-recurring and well-known industrial situations, namely days covered by guarnatee agreements and days of training.

Guarantee agreements

The basic unit of time for unemployment benefit purposes is the "day." Benefit is payable in respect of "days" of unemployment forming part of a period of interruption of employment, itself made up of "days" of unemployment or incapacity. In the realities of the employment situation, however, different units of time may be used. Where, in a particular employment, the basic unit is greater than a day, *e.g.* a week, the employee may be obliged to do, actually do, and receive pay for doing a stipulated amount of work as the week's work, and yet do no actual work on one or more of the "days" in the week. Where the usual amount of work is done in a given week, a claim for benefit is defeated, in the case of all except six day workers, by the "full extent normal" rule. That rule, however, does not bar a claim where, although a full week's pay is received, less work than usual is done for it. It being the policy of unemployment benefit law to insure against loss of income through unemployment, benefit manifestly should not be recoverable where no loss of income occurs. To some extent, the rule that days covered by guarantee agreements cannot rank as days of unemployment ensures that this is so.

Whether or not a guarantee covers the day in question calls for an examination of the contract of employment under which the claimant works. "It is always necessary to examine the particular agreement in question, in order to see what is its true meaning and effect."[48] In undertaking this task, the general principles of the law of contract apply. It has thus been held that amendments to a collective agreement purporting to alter the terms of a guarantee agreement could not take effect until communicated to and accepted by the individual parties concerned in a claim.[49] Similarly, a "paper" amendment by parties, designed solely to create the appearance of title to unemployment benefit but not intended to be accepted as binding by the parties, has been held to be ineffective.[50]

The rule that "where a guaranteed minimum wage is paid in respect of any week in which work is done ... the recipient of that wage is not unemployed during that week on the ground that the wage is a payment made in respect of each and all the days of the week ..." derives from doctrines developed by the Umpires under the pre-War legislation and dates at least from 1933.[51] Prior to the implementation of the post-War scheme, however, it had already become settled that in the case of a guarantee of employment for less than all the days in a week, days not covered by the guarantee could rank as days of unemployment.[52] The post-War scheme thus inherited a "distinction between a guarantee of so many hours' work in the week, and a guarantee of wages."[53] It proved to be a less than wholly satisfactory distinction in more than one respect. In the first place, a claimant guaranteed "thirty-four hours' employment a week" was allowed to include as days of unemployment two days off after he had worked more than 34 hours on the first four;[54] whereas one guaranteed 34 hours' wages was, in otherwise identical circumstances, not.[55] This was highly anomalous since the obvious intent of both agreements was the same. Secondly, the distinction was impossible to draw in cases guaranteeing both minimum wages and minimum hours necessitating an arbitrary classification.[56] Thirdly, evasion of disentitlement could easily be effected merely by making it clear in the agreement that the full guaranteed wage was not in respect of a full week, thus allowing days, *e.g.* after discharge, to be counted as days of unemployment.[57] The claimant in $R(U)$ 25/55, who worked under a guaranteed wage agreement providing for payment of the full amount in the event of employment being terminated on two hours' notice expiring at finishing time on Friday was discharged in this way, due to inclement weather, with a view to resuming work when the weather improved. He was allowed to rank the Saturday as a day of unemployment.

To some extent, these vices were due to a failure to focus upon the essential policy of the exception. For purposes of unemployment benefit, after all, the important feature of an employment relationship is not what the employer guarantees so much as what the employee's employment position is. This seems first to have been emphasised by a Commissioner in $R(U)$ *12/56* and is adopted by a tribunal of Commissioners in $R(U)$ *21/56*: "The ultimate question in these cases is not—what does the employer guarantee? but—what does the employee undertake in consideration of the employer's guarantee?" An employer may well guarantee wages, but what does he guarantee them *for*? In $R(U)$ *12/56*, he guaranteed them in consideration of the claimant making himself available for work on four days only—that was the limit of his obligation to work, therefore days off after the four could rank as days of unemployment. In $R(U)$ *21/56* this decision was contrasted with Umpire's Decision *958/41* in which the consideration for a guaranteed wage was the claimant's holding himself available for work on every day, he thereby being disabled from claiming benefit in respect of any day.[58]

This is not to say that the terms of the employer's guarantee are necessarily irrelevant. They may offer evidence as to the obligations which the employee has undertaken, as in $R(U)$ *15/61* where a guarantee of 34 hours' pay was taken to imply that the claimant was obliged to hold himself ready for work on at least four days (the minimum number in which the pay could have been earned). There is not, however, necessarily any correlation between the number of hours for which an employer guarantees payment and the number of hours which an employee is obliged to work (or be available therefor). A guarantee of 34 hours' pay minimum in respect of a week is not a contradiction in terms.[59] There remains the problem of determining the day on which a claimant is deemed to be employed where the agreement guarantees a certain number of days less than six but does not stipulate which they are. This was the situation in $R(U)$ *22/56* concerning a four-day agreement under which the claimant worked four days one week and three the next, in cycle. The tribunal indicated that in such a situation the fourth day should be assumed to be that of the four days sometimes worked which was not worked in the week in question. This does not, of course, solve all the problems.

Difficulties arise where the agreement provides that if the working week is cut short by certain events (*e.g.* power failures, shortage of materials etc.), the guarantee shall be reduced "in ratio" or "proportionately." Determination of the extent by which the period guaranteed should be reduced is a matter of construction of the contract. This has, however, resulted in drawing some distinctions which seem to lack difference. In *C.U. 56/57* (not reported), where the contract provided that the period be "reduced proportionately," the Commissioner held that the occurrence of a day's holiday during the week in question reduced the guarantee period from four to three days, thus enabling the fourth day to be ranked as a day of unemployment. In a number of other decisions, however, where contracts have made provision for reduction "in the same ratio," etc., the effect of a day's holiday has been to reduce a four day guarantee period to three and one-fifth days, the notional one-fifth of a day's work on the fourth day disentitling a claimant from ranking it as a day of unemployment.[60] This appears to be the most common type of case.

Termination of guarantee

Guarantee agreements contemplate that a worker may be released from the duty to render services on an ordinary working day. It has been said that "the worker may thereby be set free to seek employment elsewhere on that day, but the employer cannot, by waiving his rights, confer a title to unemployment benefit which would otherwise not exist."[61] This statement is true, but it is important to appreciate the sense and the context in which it is uttered. If an employer indicates to a worker that he does not intend to call upon him and in fact does not call upon him on a particular day, that worker is *in fact* free to take on other work on that day; but if, under the contract, he can still be legally called upon to work under the contract, no right to benefit arises. So much follows from the view of guarantee agreements adopted since *R(U) 21/56*. As a matter of principle, it would also seem to be the case that if an employer effectively waived his legal right to call in the course of the day of waiver itself,

no right to benefit would arise, for the worker would not have
been unemployed for the whole day.[62] In principle, however, it
would seem that a waiver of his legal rights by an employer
before the day in respect of which he waived would be effective
and, in that sense, he could create entitlement to benefit where
otherwise it would not have existed. This much has now been
recognised incidentally to deciding that such a waiver cannot
operate retrospectively.[63] This latter decision would seem to be
perfectly correct; the decision as to the right to benefit must
be made on the basis of the position as it actually stood on the
day in respect of which the claim is made. It remains the case,
however, that a legally effected waiver made one minute before
midnight can confer title to benefit in respect of the next day.[64]

The question is "what is a legally-effective waiver?" It has
been decided that the terms of a guarantee agreement cannot be
unilaterally abrogated. An employer who sought to do this after
negotiations for variation by agreement had failed and who instituted the regime, offering work on fewer days than normal,
in effect deprived his workers of benefit for the "off" days. The
agreement remained in force and presumably the workers were
entitled to enforce it by legal action.[65] On general principles of
contract, however, a wiser course would have been for them to
accept the employer's repudiation thus terminating the old contract of employment containing the guarantee and work for the
future under new contracts not containing such a guarantee.

The terms of the contract, including the guarantee, can be
varied by agreement; and such an agreement could be constituted by workers accepting in some positive manner a *fait accom-
pli* presented by an employer. Presumably, however, it would be
a question of construction of the agreement whether the contract
had been varied so as to exclude the guarantee. Certainly, a
mere re-arrangement of the hours or days worked would not
necessarily, by itself, imply waiver of the guarantee.[66]

The Employment Protection Act 1975

There is much to be said for relieving the national insurance
fund of the burden of financing short-term lay-offs and thrusting
it instead on the industries in question by way of guarantee
agreements. The first steps here have now been taken by the

Employment Protection Act 1975, which requires an employer himself to continue the wages of workers laid off for the first five days of lay-off in any quarter.[67]

Training

It is obviously desirable that persons who are unemployed should cease to be so as soon as possible and, if employment is not otherwise readily available, it is therefore desirable that training for employment should be undertaken. Such training may well involve "work" and an incident of it may well be the receipt of payment, *e.g.* as "living" or "expense" allowances. This may well create problems for unemployment benefit law, for whilst it may be wrong to award benefit to one who receives payment in respect of "work," it is equally to be avoided that an unemployed person should be deterred by denial of unemployment benefit from equipping himself for employment by training.

This problem was confronted by the umpires under the pre-War legislation. The umpire's solution[68] was to distinguish two different types of situation:

1. "Where a person is required to undergo a course of training with an employer as a condition of future employment for wages, and has accepted training with a definite understanding that he will be employed for wages by the person giving the training when he becomes proficient, he is to be regarded as employed during the period of the training."

2. "Where a person, whilst not employed for wages, occupies his time in learning a trade or in taking educational courses and is not doing so as a condition of future employment with the employer who is giving the teaching, he is not, merely by reason of his usefully occupying his time by fitting himself for future employment, to be regarded as employed and is entitled to benefit if he is available for work."

This approach was at first adopted by the Commissioner under the post-War scheme, expressly in *R(U) 4/59* which afforded an example of the first type of situation—a trainee bus-driver, being trained, paid a substantial allowance, and assured of employment if successful, by a bus company, even though not "employed" for contribution purposes.

Examples of the latter type of situation are to be found in *C.U. 162/50 (KL)* and *R(U) 30/51*, the latter a case where a claimant was assisted, without remuneration, by the firm of accountants with whom he hoped to work, in preparation for examinations, success in which would have qualified him for work. There was, however, no obligation, contingent or otherwise, to employ him.

In the latest decision, however, a Commissioner has declined to follow *R(U) 4/59* in adopting the pre-War solution, holding that the changed definition of "employed" under the post-War legislation calls for a new approach. Now, a person is "unemployed" unless he is gainfully employed in an employment. And he can only be gainfully employed if he is under a contract of service, or if he holds an office of profit, or carries on a trade or business, or exercises a profession or vocation.[69] This was not the case with the claimant in *R(U) 3/67* (nor, one infers, with the claimant in *R(U) 4/59*). He attended a selection and training course run by a firm and received a travelling and subsistence allowance. He had no unconditional right to appointment if successful; it was not clear whether he had a conditional right. The Commissioner did not regard this as relevant. The claimant was simply not gainfully occupied.

It does not follow that a person undergoing training will never be disentitled to rank the days in question as days of unemployment. In-service training during a contract of service might well be disentitling, provided it is for "gain," no matter that the remuneration is inadequate to live on. A person undergoing training in his normal occupation might well, if under a contract of service, be disentitled, it not being a permissible subsidiary occupation. In any training situation, a person might be disentitled to benefit simply by virtue of not being available for employment because of the training commitment.[70]

The legal position with regard to training takes no account of the important question—what remuneration is received in training. By definition, training is not immediately productive. Rates of pay, whatever form they take, may be inadequate to live on. On the other hand, an employer or prospective employer may well regard the payment of substantial remuneration during the training period as a necessary investment in order to secure the services of promising learners with scarce skills. Provided that the remuneration is more than a reimbursement of expenses actually incurred, there is no right to benefit if the training takes place under an existing contract of service, but benefit may be obtainable if it does not. And whether it does or not may depend entirely upon how the parties choose to arrange their affairs.

So much for the standard case. Prima facie, the above criteria determine whether a given day is a day of unemployment. It is necessary, however, to inquire whether the facts of any particular case involve any of the exceptions alluded to above, *i.e.* (1) cases where a claimant may not rank a day as a day of unemployment even though it is such a day by virtue of the above criteria, and (2) cases where a claimant may rank the day in question as a day of unemployment even though the above criteria are not satisfied.

(a) *Days of Employment by the Above Criteria which may not be so Ranked*

We are concerned here with the following matters:

    (a) Normal idle days;
    (b) Days after the full extent normal has been worked;
    (c) Compensated days;
    (d) Holidays;
    (e) Sundays;
    (f) Days of suspension;
    (g) Days of unavailability; and
    (h) Days of incapacity.

(i) Normal idle days

Umpires under the old Unemployment Insurance Acts developed a doctrine whereby benefit was not payable in respect of a day when a claimant would not normally work. Benefit was in respect of a failure of employment formerly held rather than a lack of employment. This policy was written into the 1946 Act and has remained to some extent in subsequent legislation. In its modern form, it is stated below. Section 3(1)(*a*) of the National Insurance Act 1966 proposed to displace it with the new, suspension, rule[71] but this latter rule has had but a limited sphere of operation and the normal idle day rule remains the rule so far as flat-rate benefit is concerned.[72] The rule provides:

"Where a person is an employed earner and his employment as such has not been terminated, then in any week a day on which in the normal course that person would not work[73] in that employment or in any other employed earner's employment shall not be treated as a day of unemployment unless each other day in that week ... on which in the normal course he would so work is a day of interruption of employment.[74]"[75]

A claimant can only get benefit for a day on which he is normally idle if he is off on all the days in a week when he would normally work. He can get benefit for a day in the week when he would normally work even though he is not off on all the normal working days. Thus, if X normally works Monday to Thursday and if, in a given week, he works Monday and Tuesday and is off from Wednesday, Wednesday and Thursday count as days of unemployment but Friday and Saturday do not.

The "normal idle day rule" is extensively modified by regulations.[76] These modifications elaborate upon the meaning of "termination of employment," and deny the application of the rule in certain specified circumstances. These modifications will be referred to in the discussion of the rule which follows.

Termination of employment

If the employment is terminated, all days of actual unemployment fall to be treated (apart from other exceptions) as days of unemployment. The normal idle day rule does not apply. For the purposes of the normal idle day rule, it used to be settled that "terminated" does not bear what might be considered to be its primary meaning—"brought to an end."[77] The meaning evolved by Umpires under the pre-War legislation[78] was: "finally discharged without any intention of resuming the relationship of employer and employee on the next available opportunity" and mere termination of the contract of employment might thus not suffice if, in fact, early resumption was intended. Notwithstanding the different statutory context, that interpretation was received into the post-war scheme.[79] The result was that the normal idle day rule applied to lay-offs even where the contract was terminated.

That this view of the meaning of "termination of employ-ment" is still authoritative is very doubtful indeed. In *R(U) 7/68*, a tribunal of Commissioners, dealing with the same phrase in the suspension rule[80] took the view that the employment should be regarded as terminated wherever the contract is terminated and further stated that this interpretation should be adopted not only in cases involving the suspension rule but also the com-pensation rule[81] and the holiday rule.[82] Admittedly, these dicta are *obiter* and no express inclusion of the normal idle day rule is made. One would expect, however, that the phrase "employ-ment ... has not been terminated" would be interpreted con-sistently throughout the legislation in the absence of any com-pelling reason otherwise; and it seems that if a claimant's employment has been treated as terminated for the purposes of earnings-related benefit, the new interpretation is to be adopted for purposes also of the normal idle day rule.[83] It is doubtful, therefore, whether the old view still holds good and what follows must, therefore, be read with this in mind.

Read literally, an offer of re-engagement 20 years on might be thought to be capable of being a "next available oppor-tunity." This, however, is not what is meant. A "next available opportunity" is opportunity presented before "the employee would normally be prepared to accept ... employment else-where."[84] It follows that once that point is reached, the employ-ment becomes "terminated" and the normal idle day rule ceases to operate. When that period is reached may well depend upon the industrial conditions prevailing in a particular region at the relevant time.[85] In three decisions, it has been decided that the mere fact that a claimant takes employment elsewhere during a "lay-off" period does not necessarily mean that his original employment is "terminated."[86] It seems, therefore, that a "next available opportunity" is one occurring before the claim-ant becomes prepared to seek permanent or regular employment elsewhere in place of his original employment.

Problems arise where a period of suspension is interrupted by a stoppage due to a trade dispute. If the "termination" is attri-buted to the latter event, disqualification for benefit ensues: if to the former, it does not.[87] Under the pre-War legislation, Umpires developed the rule that "an employee whose employ-ment has been indefinitely suspended less than 12 week-days

(exclusive of recognised or customary holidays) before the day
on which a stoppage of work begins at premises at which he
habitually seeks work must be deemed to have lost employment
by reason of the stoppage unless he can rebut this presumption
by definite evidence."[88] It appears that the evidence must be
such that it is clear that the stoppage is not a necessary condition of the claimant's actual unemployment. This "12-day" rule
is received into the post-War scheme.[89]

Notwithstanding that, by the above criteria, employment has
not been terminated, it may nevertheless be treated as having
been terminated (and the operation of the normal idle day rule
thus suspended) in a number of instances specified in regulations.
These include seven-day suspensions[90] and employments in
which there is neither a recognised or customary nor a regular
working week.[91] The exception which has most attracted the
interest of the statutory authorities is that relating to casual
employment.

Casual employment

Notwithstanding that employment has not been terminated,
it is nevertheless to be treated as having been terminated
and the operation of the normal idle day rule thus suspended
if it is casual employment, *i.e.* the standard case operates in the
case of casual workers.[92] The context in which the concept of
"casual employment" is found assumes that it can subsist consistently with an intention, by both parties, to resume employment at the next available opportunity, *i.e.* that the substantial
relation of employer and employee in fact subsists, even though
there may be no continuing contract of employment.[93] Whilst,
however, it *may* so subsist, it by no means follows that it *does*
so subsist, otherwise any suspended employment could be
argued to be casual employment and there would be no scope
for the normal idle day rule at all. Additional criteria therefore
have to be satisfied and it does not follow from the fact that
some fellow workers in similar circumstances are casual workers
that a particular claimant is. In order to escape the operation
of the normal idle day rule, a particular claimant must prove
that his particular employment is casual *in relation to him*.[94] In
the absence of any other evidence about the particular circum-

stances of his work, it may be that evidence as to the nature of the employment generally may warrant an inference in his particular case. But such evidence can easily be rebutted by reference to the particular circumstances of the individual claimant's employment record. In determining whether his employment is casual by reference to his employment record, the following matters must be considered:

(i) The frequency of recurrence of spells of work. Obviously, mere recurrence by itself is not fatal, for it is inherent in the concept of "casual" employment.[95] But if spells recur with a regular frequency (such as in *R 1/65 (UB)* where the claimant had found work in practically every week of the preceding year) this points to non-casual employment. Conversely, irregularity favours casualness.[96]

(ii) The duration of spells of work when they occur. "As spells of work diminish (in duration) so the probability of their being, in a true and practical sense, 'casual' increases."[97] Conversely, a series of long spells indicates non-casual work.[98]

(iii) The manner of recruitment and dismissal. If the method of recruitment is casual or if there is an absence of notice of dismissal, this will point in the direction of the employment being "casual."[99]

One final point should be emphasised. Work cannot be "casual" if there is an assurance of a resumption of work at the end of one spell, as opposed to a reasonable hope or expectation that it will probably be resumed at some time in the near future.

Normality

By definition, the normal idle day rule cannot apply unless there is a normal course of employment in relation to which a day is usually idle. Determination of the "normality" of the course of employment is necessary also for the application of the full extent normal rule and the criteria for this determination are discussed under that head.[1]

(ii) Full extent normal

"... a day shall not be treated as a day of unemployment if on that day a person does no work and is a person who does not ordinarily work on every day in a week (exclusive of Sunday ...) but who is, in the week in which the said day occurs, employed to the full extent normal in his case...."[2]

No account is to be taken, in determining either the number of days in a week on which he ordinarily works or the full extent of employment in a week which is normal in his case, of any period of short-time working due to adverse industrial conditions.[3] The rule does not apply unless there is a recognised or customary working week in connection with his employment or he regularly works for the same number of days in a week for the same employer or group of employers.[4]

This provision in effect requires one to discount all days of actual unemployment in a week during which the claimant has been no more unemployed than usual.[5] It is yet another example of doctrines evolved by the Umpires under the pre-War legislation finding statutory expression under the post-War legislation. In this case, however, there is a difference. Under the old law, benefit could only be claimed in respect of unemployment on a day which would normally have been worked.[6] Under the regulation, any day ranks (regardless of whether the claimant would normally have worked), provided the claimant has not worked for *all* the days he normally would. Thus a claimant with a normal four-day week, working three days in the week of claim, could claim three days of unemployment under the regulation but only one under the pre-War doctrine.

The concept of "normality" is common to both the "full extent normal" rule and the "normal idle day" rule and, in determining "normality," the authorities are, to that extent, interchangeable.[7]

The function of some parts of the rule is not immediately obvious. The rule as a whole is designed to disentitle a claimant to rank as a day of unemployment a day which ranks as such by the criteria of the standard case. One would think that the question would not arise in the first place if the claimant worked on the day in question—according to the standard case criteria, such a day could not be ranked anyway—yet the rule contains the condition "if on that day a person does no work." It is, of course, possible, that a claimant could rank, as a day of unemployment, a day on which he worked, for example under the "nightworker's regulation," but it is not easy to see why the operation of the rule should be suspended in such cases.

Similarly, the rule does not apply in the case of six-day workers, *i.e.* persons who do ordinarily work on every day in a week. This means that a worker who put in his normal number of hours on five days instead of six would be able to rank the sixth day as a day of unemployment whereas one who put in his normal number of hours in four days instead of five could rank neither of the two succeeding days. This distinction is not easy to understand.

In general, however, the function of the rule is clear. A claimant who has already earned his normal wages (though on fewer days than usual) does not suffer from the need which unemployment benefit is designed to abate, even though, technically, he may have a "day of unemployment." The full extent normal rule is designed to prevent him ranking such a day. In order for it to have this effect the following matters must be considered:

1. There must be a "normality" about the work. If there is not, the rule does not apply. In deciding this question, regulation 7 (2) must be borne in mind.[8]

2. The claimant must have worked to the full extent normal. This involves ascertaining what the "normal" extent of work is and deciding whether the extent actually worked at the given time is "full."

3. In deciding this, any period of "short-time" working due to "adverse industrial conditions" must be discounted.

Normality

In decisions such as $R(U)$ *32/51* and $R(U)$ *37/56*, Commissioners held that where there was no regular pattern of employment at all, there could not be said to be any "full extent normal" and there was, in consequence, no scope for operation of the rule at all. In the former case, a woman's occupation as a totalisator clerk was not limited to any particular days in a week whilst in the latter a once existing pattern of work had been departed from so often and so irregularly that it had become completely eroded. Provided, however, that a pattern of work continued to be discernible, notwithstanding frequent departures from it, the view of the Commissioners was that the rule could apply.[9] How compatible this attitude is with the terms of regulation 7 (2) is not yet clear. That provision conditions the operation of the rule upon there being "a recognised or customary working week" or "regularly" working "for the same number of days in a week for the same employer...." The latter alternative is fairly clear. It would seem to exclude any employment pattern based on a unit larger than a week. Not so the former. In relation to a given employment, a given week might be quite properly describable as "a recognised or customary working week" notwithstanding that it might differ from some other weeks provided that it occupied a regular place in a fortnightly, monthly or even seasonal rota-system of arranging work. Even without a rota, this might be argued to be so, provided there was a regular cycle.

Extent *"normal"* and *"full"*

In speaking of the "full extent normal *in his case*," the regulation clearly indicates that the crucial factor here is the character of the claimant's own employment. Commissioners have consistently disregarded, as irrelevant, attempts to refer to the characteristics of the work of fellow employees generally engaged in similar capacities.[10] Similarly, in numerous cases, Commissioners have made the point that it is the actual pattern of work which must be regarded.[11] The fact that a claimant's pattern of employment is against his wishes is neither here nor there.[12] Unfulfilled possibilities and speculations as to the future are irrelevant.[13] The paper rights and obligations of a claimant under his contract are equally irrelevant to the extent that they depart from the realities of the employment situation,[14] although it is submitted that in the absence of any other indication they would be acceptable as evidence of the actuality.[15] It has, indeed, been held that "... where a standard working week has been agreed between the claimant's employer and his trade union, that standard week is prima facie full-time working, and a working week which falls short of that standard is short-time working unless the deficiency amounts to less than an hour...."[16] It may be, however, that the standard working week generally agreed has been specifically modified.

"There may be cases where a claimant's working week is not regulated by an agreement applying to the industry generally or to the factory, or to the claimant's place of work. In those cases, the working week which is recognised as the standard working week under the claimant's contract of service must be taken as the measure of full-time working, and a working week which falls short of that standard is short-time working."[17]

In "full extent normal" cases, what the statutory authorities have to determine is whether the extent to which the claimant has worked during the week in which the day of claim falls is the "full normal" extent in his case. The central feature in this landscape is obviously what is *presently* normal, and it has been held that in the absence of evidence to the contrary, the fact that a claimant has already had a full week's work (notwithstanding that he did not work every day) will justify a finding that he is a person who does not ordinarily work on every day. Whilst, however, the statutory authorities are concerned with what is presently normal, the very idea of normality imports reference to other weeks, it may be both past and future. The extent worked in the present week can only be described as "normal" by comparison with other weeks. And "In the course of the long history of the decisions under the regulation a number of different types of case have emerged. There are those in which a clear and regular pattern of days worked and days not worked can be seen: it may be a regular weekly pattern, or the period may be longer...; it may even be a season.... On the other hand, there are cases ... where the weeks in which some days are not worked ... show no clear pattern."[18]

Where a clear pattern emerges from the past employment record, this will usually suffice by itself. Thus, where a married woman had done part-time work on only two days a week because there was no full-time work readily available to her, that had become her standard week by the date of her claim (three years later) and the rule applied.[19] This would remain her normal week even if the employment was terminated.[20] If, however, full-time employment has recently been lost and part-time employment undertaken involuntarily, *faut de mieux*, that reduced week will not become "normal" for some time, at all events so long as the claimant remains willing and able to resume the fuller week. In *C.W.U. 6/48* a period of some months was held to be insufficient for this purpose. In $R(U)$ *30/53* this was emphasised by the Commissioner in reversing the decision of a local tribunal which had held that a change in "normality" automatically accompanied a change in occupation:

"I think that might be true of a man who of his own free will adopted a part-time occupation with the intention of making that henceforth his normal occupation; it could truly be said of such a man that, as soon as he had made the change, part-time employment had become his normal occupation as soon as he undertook it. . . .[21]

"It is different, however, when a man, who regularly all his life has worked throughout the week, suddenly finds part-time work thrust upon him with no choice but to accept it or lose his employment altogether. I think it is wrong to say of such a man that he is 'a person who does not ordinarily work on every day in a week' as soon as he accepts part-time employment. . . . A man who has no practical alternative to accepting part-time employment . . . must, I think, be allowed a certain time in which to take stock of his position and to decide whether it is worth his while to continue as a part-time employee."

It is implicit in the above-considered decisions that an occupation which is, initially, abnormal, can come, by the passage of time and acceptance by the employee, normal in his case. It may be much easier to detect the point at which this transformation takes place in cases where there is a change, not in the occupation, but in the detailed work régime which accompanies it. Apart from the potential operation of regulation 7 (2) (considered above) an accepted and operative change in a rota-system of working may bring about an immediate change in normality. "When a person's working days are normally governed by a rota the days on which in the normal course he would not work have to be determined by reference to the rota and may vary from week to week."[22] In $R(U)$ *18/62*, a change in the rota-system, resulting in the claimant's working a five-day week in place of a former six-day week, was held to have brought about an immediate change in normality.[23] This is to be contrasted with $R(U)$ *9/62* where a new rota-system was introduced but never worked in the claimant's case because of short-time working. A Saturday on which, under the new rota, the claimant would have worked, could not be included as a day of unemployment in his case, this notwithstanding that the new rota was operated in the case of other employees.[24]

In all these "pattern" cases, a number of factors have to be permutated to yield a result. A mere change of job pattern may itself involve a change in normality immediately it is accepted and operated. A change in occupation, without more, will not. It depends upon whether it is voluntary or not. If voluntary, it may effect an immediate change in normality. If it is involuntary, it will not. In that case, it will depend upon whether the change is long or short term. If it is long term, it may involve a change in normality. If it is short term, it will not, unless it is accepted as a new arrangement of permanent or indefinite duration. Some of these possibilities are well illustrated in dicta from *C.U. 518/49* (*KL*), a test case:

"If, for example, when the claimant ceased to work full-time he changed his occupation (not merely temporarily) to one in which a normal full week's work is work for no more than part of the week, he might be said to be a 'person who does not ordinarily work on every day in a week' as soon as he makes the change. Thus, in Decision No. *C.U. 151/49* (reported) the employment had lasted only fifteen weeks, but there was apparently no suggestion that he had taken up this employment temporarily. Again, if a claimant, although he has been working only on some days of the week for a comparatively short time, has worked for a longer time at similar employments in the past, then despite an intervening period of full-time employment, he might properly be held to be 'a person who does not ordinarily work on every day in a week,' unless the period of full-time employment had lasted so long that his earlier period of employment on some days only of the week can reasonably be regarded as irrelevant. On the other hand, if a claimant took up, when unemployed, employment which did not involve working every day of the week as a stopgap, while looking for full-time employment, he could not properly be held to be 'a person who does not ordinarily work on every day in a week.'"

In the operation of these rules, it makes no difference whether a single employment or a number of employments concurrently is or are followed.[25] Thus, in *16/59* (*UB*), a claimant normally engaged in three separate concurrent employments was treated as "normally" employed on all days covered by these three employments notwithstanding that one of them had ceased; whilst in $R(U)$ *8/56* the "normality" of a claimant usually employed on only three days a week was not affected by his taking on temporary work in a different capacity on the other three days per week.[26] Where a pattern emerges, "normality" falls to be determined in the above manner. All that remains to be said is that in detecting an operative regular pattern, disruptions through holidays[27] temporary sickness[28] and possibly other events may be discounted. (A "holiday" may alter the "normality" for the week in which it occurs.)[29]

Where no clear pattern emerges from the claimant's employment record, it is obviously not possible to determine the "normal" by reference to such a pattern and some other approach is necessitated. Early in the history of the post-War scheme, the statutory authorities adopted the practice of referring to a claimant's employment record for the past year in order to decide upon the question of normality[30] though at first this seems to have been done as much for purposes of detecting a pattern as anything else. By the time of Decision $R(U)$ *14/59*, however, an adaption of this "year period test" specifically for the purpose of dealing with non-pattern cases appears. "If it is established that during the year ending with the day in question (or such other period as may provide a more suitable test in the particular case) a claimant has worked on less than 50 per cent. of the days of the week in question (excluding any day of incapacity for work or holiday and days on which he was unemployed because his employment had been terminated) that day should be held to be one on which in the normal course the claimant would not work. If the claimant has worked on as much as 50 per cent. of such days it should . . . be held that it has not been proved that in the normal course he would not have worked on the day in question."

The whole development of this doctrine is summarised and explained in $R(U)$ *14/60*.[31] A number of points should be noted. First, the normal period to be taken for this purpose is the year preceding the date of claim. If the circumstances of the case warrant it, however, either a longer or a shorter period may be more appropriate.[32] A change of employers or in the nature of the employment may justify taking a shorter period[33] though it will not, apparently, necessitate it.[34] Exceptional disruption (particularly of industrial circumstances) may warrant disregard of part of the year immediately preceding and a proportionate extension of the period.[35] Secondly, in ascertaining the number of weeks in the year on which a particular day was or was not worked, weeks affected by events such as sickness, holidays, etc. are again to be left out of account.[36]

Had regulation 7 (2) been in operation, many of the above cases would have fallen outside the purview of regulation 7(1)(e) altogether, for in many of them neither of the conditions laid down in regulation 7 (2) for the operation of regulation 7(1)(e) would have been fulfilled. These conditions are that there must be either a recognised or customary working week in connection with the claimant's employment or that he works regularly for the same number of days in a week for the same employer or group[37] of employers. These conditions do not, however, obviate the necessity for the "pattern" and "year period" tests for it remains possible for a claimant to have a customary or recognised working week, and yet work irregularly. If he works regularly, say one day less, the question of "pattern" becomes relevant. If he irregularly works fewer days, the "year period" test becomes operative.

"Adverse industrial conditions"

The regulation expressly requires "any period of short-time working due to adverse industrial conditions" to be left out of account in ascertaining what is "normal" or whether, in a particular week, the full extent normal has been worked. This exception was one provided for in *C.U. 518/49 (KL)* which launched the "year period" test and has been elaborated upon in subsequent decisions.[38]

The concept has, however, been differently described, the most favoured terminology being "exceptional industrial circumstances" and it may be that the statutory exception should be given wider scope than that formulated by the statutory authorities.

Two problems have occasioned particular difficulty. These are (1) the meaning of "short-time working" and (2) the scope of "adverse industrial conditions."

On the first of these matters, the "short-time working" referred to is not that forming part of the claimant's own personal experience but that prevailing in the factory or industry in which he works. *Ex hypothesi*, a claimant is engaged in short-time working. The relevance of "short-time working due to adverse industrial conditions" is "that it will show whether the claimant's loss of work is due to conditions which are not peculiar to himself but are of a general character." Only if this is so can the weeks in question be left out of account. Furthermore, the phrase implies "not merely a reduction of working hours from what has formerly prevailed, but a reduction of working hours below the level of the recognised or standard number of hours."[39] So cutting over-time regularly worked does not amount to "short-time working" and periods affected by such cuts need not be left out of account in working out the operation of the rules.[40]

On the scope of "adverse industrial conditions," the statutory authorities have taken a restrictive view. The meaning of "exceptional industrial circumstances" adopted in $R(U)$ *13/55* was "circumstances relating to ... work which were temporary and sporadic and brought about by conditions unlikely to continue" and this has been followed in subsequent decisions.[41] Thus, since "any estimate of the probable duration of a policy of restricted credit or of maintenance of a particular tariff, would seem highly conjectural," short-time working resulting from it should not be discounted.[42] The same view has been taken of a trade recession which provoked the practice of Saturday closing in the interests of fuel economy, the crucial factor being the lack of any evidence of the probable duration of the recession.[43] Where, however, the short-time working can be attributed to a particular event, the duration of which can be fixed with relative confidence, the weeks affected may properly be left out of account. This was the case in $R(U)$ *21/60*, where a change in demand from the employer's principal customer necessitated complete re-tooling which, although under way was occasioning short-time working in the meantime. In deciding whether short-time working is "unlikely to continue" it may be possible to use hindsight. In $R(U)$ *33/57*, the full working week had been restored before the Commissioner came to dispose of the claim. He held, however, that he could not have regard to that fact as evidence that the reduced working had been all along "likely to be temporary." It may be noted, in passing, that in an analogous situation in Redundancy Payments

Law, the House of Lords has taken the opposite view, endorsing a "hindsight" test for purposes of deciding whether or not a cessation of work was "temporary."[44]

Once the "normal extent" has been ascertained in this way, all that remains is to decide whether the extent to which the claimant has actually worked during the week in question is "full" by comparison with that "normal."

Whether "full" extent normal worked

Being "employed to the full extent normal" does not mean "employed for the number of days normal ... 'extent' is to be determined by reference to the total time worked.[45] If the total time (usually measured in hours) has been worked, the rule applies, notwithstanding that five days of work have been crowded into four.[46] Although Sunday is normally discounted in determining whether or not a claimant ordinarily works on every day in a week, any work done on a Sunday must be brought into account in calculating the extent actually worked.[47]

Because the measure of extent is the total time worked, a claimant may not have been employed to the full extent normal even though he has worked on the full number of days per week. This was the case in $R(U)$ *13/59* where reduced working (a half day) occurred on one of the normal days.[48] Whilst half a day is too much to ignore, however, the *de minimis* rule applies and a short-fall in the total time worked of less than one hour can be ignored.[49] Conversely, it was decided in $R(U)$ *2/58* that a claimant may be treated as employed to the full extent normal even if less than the full normal week is actually worked, provided that payment is received, and the claimant was on call, for the full normal week, as under a guarantee agreement. On this view, there is a large overlap between the full extent normal rule and that relating to guarantee agreements.

The regulation requires that the rule be applied to a claimant "who *is*, in the week in which the said day occurs, employed to the full extent normal in his case. ...." As previously drafted, the regulation used the phrase "has been" in place of the italicised word above and it had been held by the Northern Ireland Commissioner[50] that a claimant who, at the date of claim (say, a Monday) had not worked his full week, escaped the rule even though he subsequently completed his total time for the week. The new wording seems to involve denying benefit to any claimant who, on the day of claim, has worked to the extent normal at that stage in his week.

Criticism

It appears to be the policy of the "full extent normal" rule to ensure, so far as is administratively feasible, that compensation for loss of earnings due to unemployment is confined to those cases where there has been actual loss by comparison with what is usual in a claimant's case. If this is so, there are a number of respects in which the rule appears inefficient:

1. It functions according to loss of time, not loss of earnings. In many cases, the loss of the last day's work in a week will involve loss of overtime and, therefore, loss of a disproportionate amount of earnings. The rule takes no account of this. This is just one facet of the fact that scales of benefit are fixed by reference to minimum standards, not geared (except in the case of earnings-related supplements) to actual earnings.

2. The apparent function of the precondition that a claimant be not a person who ordinarily works every day in the week (*i.e.* six day a week workers) is to suspend the operation of the rule in their case, notwithstanding that a full week's work is done in less than six days. The result in such cases (subject to the other conditions of entitlement to benefit, such as that the day of unemployment must form part of a reckonable period of interruption of employment etc.) may be to make benefit payable in cases where a full week's earnings have already been gained. This is doubly anomalous when contrasted with workers on depressed earnings because of a normal short working week (to whom, therefore, the rule applies with full vigour).

3. The rule can work particularly harshly in the case of very short working weeks, *e.g.* a normal two-day week, where earnings are depressed accordingly. Here, no benefit may be payable for four days of unemployment. The temptation to avoid such employment is obvious.

4. The capricious nature of the rule is illustrated by the short full week. If one of two days' work is lost, this excludes the operation of the rule and opens the door to a claim in respect of

every other day's work in the week, thus rendering possible (subject to other exclusions) claim to five-sixths of a week's benefit. Or, in the case of a normal four-day week, the loss of a day's work (one-quarter earnings) may result in a claim for half a week's benefit.

The second of these anomalies could easily be removed by extending the operation of the rule to all cases where the full normal extent is worked, even cases where the claimant is ordinarily employed on every day in the week. The other anomalies, or at least equally anomalous alternatives, seem inherent in any scheme to confine entitlement to benefit to cases of loss of employment normally enjoyed which is not administratively top-heavy. Admittedly, abolition of the rule entirely might result in equal but different anomalies. It is not clear, however, that this would be the greater of the two evils. The chief result would be greatly to simplify procedure at the cost of a perhaps considerable increase in the number of cognisable days of unemployment. I am not aware of any published estimate of the cost which would be involved or of the savings which would be effected by such a step.

(iii) Compensated days

Regulation $7(1)(d)$ of the Unemployment, Sickness and Invalidity Benefit Regulations provides:

"a day shall not be treated as a day of unemployment if it is a day in respect of which a person receives a payment (whether or not a payment made in pursuance of a legally enforceable obligation) in lieu either of notice or of the remuneration which he would have received for that day had his employment not been terminated, so, however, that this sub-paragraph shall not apply to any day which does not fall within the period of one year from the date on which the employment of that person terminated."

This is the successor to other versions which have functioned in this sphere since the inception of the post-War scheme. One of the objectives of later versions has been to deal with the increasing number of contracts "terminated with what are often referred to as 'golden handshakes,'" that is, "to meet the increasing number of claims where persons have been dismissed with several thousands of pounds compensation and have sought to obtain unemployment benefit on the following day."[51] Progressive amendments have, however, also had the effect of simplifying the law in a number of respects. There used to be a somewhat complex method of determining whether or not accrued holiday pay should be treated as a form of disentitling compensation.[52] The latest versions, however, have omitted the words which seemed to embrace this situation and it now appears to be the case that accrued holiday pay does not fall within the rule, not constituting a payment in lieu of either notice or remuneration now covered by the rule. Similarly, old versions used to require, in the case of payments in lieu of notice, that receipt of them should be continuous.[53] Accordingly, it was arguable that if there was a gap during which payments were discontinued, disentitlement under the rule would cease. This appears now no longer to be the case.[54]

Types of payment covered

The present rule requires "a payment ... in lieu of notice or of remuneration which he would have received for that day had his employment not been terminated." It will be noted that where the payment is in lieu of "remuneration," "employment" is expressly required; not so where it is in lieu of "notice." Under the immediately preceding version of the rule the "notice" in lieu of which payment was made was notice "required to be given to him by his employer," thus expressly requiring employment. It was accordingly held that sums received by way of continuing income from former self-employment might be ignored.[55] It is not at all clear under the latest version that this conclusion follows. Suppose a continuing contract for services (self-employment) under which a claimant received a weekly retainer terminable by three months' notice on either side. If the contract was terminated and a sum equal to three months' retainer paid in lieu of notice, the conditions of the new rule would seem to be fulfilled and disentitlement would accordingly result.

It is perfectly possible for employment to be terminated without any right to notice accruing. This would be the case where serious misconduct justified summary dismissal without notice. It is presumably also the case, according to general principles of contract, that the contract can be varied by agreement so as to exclude any contractual right to notice. To some extent, it may be possible to avoid the compensated days rule by avoiding the right to notice in this way but a Commissioner has recently rejected the argument that where employment is terminated by agreement, and not by actual notice given by the employer, a sum paid in consideration is not "in lie of notice." It may not have been "in lieu of notice" actually required by reason of the employer terminating unilaterally, but it was nevertheless "in lieu of notice," *i.e.* in lieu of the notice which he would have had to give if he had terminated unilaterally as opposed to by agreement.[56] In that case, however, the employer had described the payment as being "in lieu of notice." If the parties genuinely intended to waive notice, or if, in a case of justified summary dismissal it was the employer's genuine intention not to pay in lieu of notice, a payment made on termination would not necessary invoke the rule,[57] for it is not all such payments but only those specified in the rule which bring about disentitlement. It was early decided, in *C.U. 639/48 (KL)*, that a sum paid by way of "compensation for loss of employment" (described in fact, as a "gratuity" though paid in discharge of a contractual obligation) could be ignored and subsequent decisions have sometimes drawn similar distinctions. Thus, redundancy payments under the Redundancy Payments Act 1965 have been held to be outside the rule being referable to past employment.[58]

Difficulty has arisen where a payment made on termination is greater than that required by the notice provision[59] and only the appropriate part of it is meant to be "in lieu of notice." It is not only payments "in lieu of notice" which bring about disentitlement; the rule also embraces "payments in lieu of . . . the remuneration" which the claimant would have received. The excess may be meant to be payment of "extra wages or salary"— does it disentitle as being "in lieu of . . . remuneration. . . ?" The case where the point calls for actual decision has not yet arisen, but the point has been considered by tribunals of Commissioners incidentally to deciding other cases, and they have disagreed as to what is the correct approach. Majorities have taken the view that the phrase "in lieu of . . . remuneration" applies only to fixed term contracts, a view which fully accords with the history of the provision and from which it follows that in any given case, the payment must be characterised as being *either* in lieu of notice *or* in lieu of remuneration, etc. It cannot be split. Thus, where three months' salary is paid, as to one month in lieu of notice and as to the other two months as "severance pay," only one month's disentitlement would ensue.[60] The minority view is that if such a payment was as to one month in lieu of notice and as to two months in lieu of remuneration three months' disentitlement would result.[61] It is a perfectly tenable view on the plain wording of the regulation and more fully accords with the policy of not paying benefit where the claimant is in fact paid in respect of his employment. The majority view is, of course, the more authoritative.

Difficulty has also arisen over determining the criteria according to which payments are to be characterised. If a payment is "wholly referable to past services" it will escape the rule.[62] If it is in lieu of notice, it will not. The parties may describe it as the former, meaning it to be the latter. How is it to be characterised? The approved criterion is that it is the actual substantial character of the payment which matters and not merely the description which the parties have attached to it.[63] What they say may, of course, be good evidence as to what its substantial character is, especially when the description is against interest (as where the dismissed employee describes it as "in lieu of notice," so that he loses benefit). Similarly, where the sum is fixed by reference to the amount of salary or wages which the employee would have earned but for termination,[64] the presumption is that it is compensation for that loss and therefore disentitling. The fact that the insurance card is not stamped is irrelevant.[65] It cannot be stamped after termination and the regulation only deals with the situation after termination. Where the payment is of a composite character, *e.g.* partly in lieu of notice and partly *ex gratia*, it is its overriding character that must govern.[66]

Where the payment etc. takes the form of damages for wrongful dismissal, or an agreed sum in lieu thereof, it nevertheless disentitles[67] since "compensation for the loss of the remuneration which the employee would have earned is the most familiar head of damage in an action for wrongful dismissal."[68] Compensation for unfair dismissal *or* a sum paid in compromise of such a suit is similarly treated.[69] It used to matter whether the sums received were similar in amount to the sums to which the claimant would have been contractually entitled, but under the new regulation, this requirement has disappeared. Accordingly, so long as the sums received contain an element in respect of the matters covered by the regulation, disentitlement results.[70] It has, indeed, recently been doubted whether the alleged distinction between "compensation" on the one hand and "damages" for other purposes on the other is "anything more than an argument about words." It may be true, as was suggested, that "damages, whether general or special, are a form of compensation" but that is not a sufficient reason for abandoning the distinction. The crucial question is not whether what is paid is "compensation" (or, to use the words of the rule, "payment in lieu") but what it is compensation *for*. It seems, therefore, still to be clearly arguable that if the payment received is genuinely and wholly in respect *not* of a period of notice or remuneration otherwise receivable, but of general loss of future employment security or some such other head, it will not disable a claimant from ranking the days following termination as days of employment.

Period covered

Subject to one exception (the limitation period of one year now contained in the proviso) the latest version continues the law formerly in force on the question of the period covered by disentitlement. It remains the stipulated period of notice or the unexpired contractual term regardless of the actual sum paid.[71] Where no actual period of notice is stipulated, disentitlement extends for a reasonable period.[72] The length of such period does not necessarily correspond with the period covered by the sum paid viewed as continuing wages. In *R(U) 10/58*, a six-month period was regarded as reasonable, though a sum equivalent to eight months' salary had been paid, and in *R(U) 37/53*, the court accepted the parties' agreement to treat one month as reasonable notwithstanding that three months' pay was involved.[73] Due to the inclusion in the latest version of the rule of the words "whether or not a payment made in pursuance of a legally enforceable obligation," decisions such as that in *R(U) 37/53* must be doubted[74] and the exceptional decision in *R(U) 5/60* will not be repeated. There, owing to the High Court's declaring the agreement under which the employee worked to be void, the contract was held to be frustrated by illegality with the result that no lawful period of notice applied, so that the payment "in lieu of notice" became wholly gratuitous and non-disentitling.

In the case of payments "in lieu of ... remuneration," no question of notice, reasonable or otherwise, arises. The period affected is the unexpired term covered, whether the remuneration is proportionate or not.[75]

The result, therefore, may well be that disentitlement may extend over a period considerably in excess of that apparently covered by a payment. In *R(U) 8/63*, a full 12 weeks' disentitlement (the contractual period of notice in respect of which the payment was made) resulted even though only seven weeks' pay was handed over.[76] On the other hand, a substantially larger sum than the strict legal entitlement will not import any greater disentitlement than for the period stipulated for.[77] Anything over and above this is gratuitous and is not to be taken into account.[78] This includes payments in respect of a period in excess of what is subsequently found to be "reasonable" and all payments such as in the case of *R(U) 5/60*.

Payments legally unenforceable

At one time, claimants not legally entitled to notice escaped the impact of the rule.[79] The regulation now, however, operates in case of any payment of the type stipulated "whether or not a payment made in pursuance of a legally enforceable obligation." So civil servants, dismissible without notice at Her Majesty's pleasure, are now caught by the rule if they receive a payment in fact in lieu of notice.[80]

The inclusion of the clause above has raised doubts about the position where a payment is made in lieu of notice but in excess of the amount legally obligatory to meet the legal requirement of notice. Where one month's notice is legally due and three months' salary is paid in lieu of notice, can the whole be regarded as in lieu of three months' notice, although in respect of the latter two months there is no "legally enforceable obligation?" If the parties have agreed to extend the legally-required period of notice, then such a payment would be in lieu of three months' notice and no problem would arise. If, however, it were not, the position is less clear. It has been suggested that it would have the effect of disentitling for the extra two months[81] but the better view would seem to be that it would be a question of fact whether that was the character of the payment, the new clause simply permitting evidence that it had that character.[82]

Criticism

The essential policy behind the "compensation" rule is, no doubt, sound. A Commissioner has, however, recently stated that the regulation "is drafted with such severity that it is likely to lead to hard cases"[83] and it does indeed seem now to be the case that a protracted period of disqualification could result from the receipt of a small sum of remuneration on termination. According to the decisions in *R(U) 2/68* and *R(U) 3/68*, acceptance of £100 as remuneration in respect of an unexpired term of five years would result in disentitlement for that period. Anomalously, a prospective claimant would, in such a case, be much better off to decline it, for the regulation attaches no penalty to voluntary non-compensation. This, too, seems anomalous.

The holiday position is not satisfactory, either. True, the rather cumbersome mechanisms for calculating whether or not accrued holiday pay should be taken into account have disappeared, but this is not necessarily wholly an improvement. A claimant who actually takes paid holiday may be disentitled.[84] One who, on termination, receives pay in lieu may avoid it, whether he takes the holiday or not.

There is, finally, apparent scope for abuse in the distinction which seems still to remain between the types of payment specified in the regulation and others, such as compensation for "loss of employment" as opposed to payment in lieu of notice or remuneration. It is not hard to dress up a payment as the former, especially if a short period of notice has been agreed beforehand with this prospect in mind. The parties might well agree to one week's notice, envisaging one year's salary equivalent as compensation for loss of prospects, with a view to avoiding disentitlement.

(iv) Holidays

The position with regard to holidays is complicated by two factors. First, whether a day is a day of holiday is one only of the variables relevant to the question whether it is a day of unemployment or not; others are whether or not it is a day in respect of which payment is received; whether or not the "employment" continues; whether or not the "holiday" is "recognised" or "customary." Secondly, the law relating to holidays has been confusingly affected by amendment of the unemployment legislation, sometimes with a view to altering the law relating to holidays, sometimes, unfortunately, affecting it incidentally and with consequences apparently unanticipated, so that it is now not easy to state the exact extent to which doctrine developed under earlier legislation still survives. For these reasons, the clearest method of approach seems to be to start by distinguishing cases in which payment is received in respect of a day of holiday from those in which it is not.

Cases in which payment is received

Where payment of wages in respect of a day is made, that day cannot rank as a day of unemployment, even if the claimant actually does no work. "When, in accordance with the terms of his employment, an employee is entitled to receive and does receive, from his employer part wages during periods when his actual services are not required, he continues during such periods to be in employment and is not unemployed."[85] This is the well-established principle which underlies guarantee agreements[86] and the standard case generally. It has been applied in numerous "holiday" cases. Doubt may arise whether a payment is a payment of wages attributable to an identifiable period. A lump sum at the start[87] or end[88] of holidays has been held to suffice. It is otherwise if the payment is a mere gratuity or retainer not paid in respect of an identifiable period, as in *R 3/63 (UB)* where none of the payment was receivable in respect of any part of the lay-off period but only when the claimant resumed work. It is equally irrelevant that a payment is received if it is clearly an advance of wages for the initial period of resumption.[89] In this connection, the intention of the parties is the governing con-

sideration, though in the absence of clear evidence of that intention, the size of the sum involved and its relation to the lay-off
period (*e.g.* "half wages") may be a relevant consideration.[90]
Provided these points are clear, however, the only question is
whether a payment admittedly made as an incident of the
employment can be attributed to a day alleged by a claimant
to be a day of unemployment.

On this question, the law as it stood before the amendment of
the old regulation 6(1)(*d*)[91] was fairly clear. That regulation
provided that where the employment had terminated but the
employee "continued to receive wages" a day in respect of which
he so continued could not rank as a day of unemployment. The
rule was of general application, covering not only the typical case
of a payment in lieu of a period of notice, but also holiday pay.
Since a "continuation" of receipt of wages was required, payments in respect of a period in the remote future clearly did not
qualify.[92] Where, however, the payment was not specifically
appropriate to a remote period difficulties arose,[93] and a series
of rules was evolved for determining when holiday pay could be
appropriable to a remote period difficulties arose,[93] and a series
constitute a "continuation" of wages. The amendment of regulation 6(1)(*d*) (now regulation 7(1)(*d*)) omitted the requirement
of continuity but also narrowed the class of payments which can
be brought into account, on the better view excluding holiday
pay as not being "remuneration ... in lieu of notice."[94]

The modern law therefore has to be sought outside the impact
of regulation 7(1)(*d*). In one situation, it seems fairly clear. The
old regulation 6(1)(*d*) never did apply where the employment
had not been terminated. Now, as then, no day in respect of
which payment is made may rank as a day of unemployment,
even though there is no continuity, provided it occurs during the
employment.[95] Even where the employment has come to an end,
however, regulation 7(1)(*d*) does not now operate.[96] The question to be settled here is whether a claimant who has been discharged with holiday pay can rank all days subsequent to the
discharge as days of unemployment, notwithstanding receipt of
the pay. It does not seem ever to have been argued before a
commissioner that no day in respect of which a claimant is paid
for work, whether done on that day or not, can rank as a day
of unemployment, merely as failing to fulfil the requirements of

the standard case. There have, however, been cases[97] where such an argument would, if successful, have resulted in a different eventual decision. It would seem that the better view is that once the employment has ended, a day may rank as a day of unemployment notwithstanding that payment is made in respect of it, if the payment in question is solely an accrued holiday payment.

Cases in which no payment is received

Where no payment is received and the claimant has either (i) been finally discharged, *i.e.* the contract of employment terminated,[98] or (ii) reached the seventh continuous day of a period of indefinite suspension, any day on which he does no work may be ranked as a day of unemployment even though it is, in some sense, a "holiday" and no matter the sense in which it is a "holiday." An extreme example of this occurs in *C.U. 427/50 (KL)* in which the Commissioner entertained an appeal on behalf of a claimant whose employment had clearly been terminated and who, having no work, went to spend a week's "holiday" in a nearby seaside resort. The employment having been terminated, no question of losing benefit under the "holiday" rules arose. The only question was whether he was still "available" for employment notwithstanding his absence.[99] "A person cannot be said to be on holiday within the meaning of Regulation [7(1)(j)] ... unless at the beginning of the period in question he had employment which had not been terminated...."[1]

If, however, there has been no termination or protracted period (seven or more continuous days) of indefinite suspension, the position falls to be resolved by regulation.[2] The relevant regulation is not confined in its express terms to cases where payment is not received and, indeed, technically applies whether or not it is. Cases where payment is received, however, will normally resolve themselves without need to resort to the regulation.

The regulation provides that "where ... employment has not been terminated, a day shall not be treated as a day of unemployment if it is a day of recognised or customary holiday in connection with that employment." It goes on to equate a suspension of seven days or more with termination and to deal with the problem which arises where a claimant changes from one occupation to another having already endured a greater number of days of recognised or customary holiday in the former occupation than confronts him in the latter.[3] Further provisions disable him from ranking as a day of recognised or customary holiday a day in respect of which he has received unemployment benefit, a Bank Holiday or other public holiday applying in his case.[4]

In deciding whether the regulation applies, it is obviously crucial to determine whether or not the employment has either been terminated or has been indefinitely suspended for seven days or more. In this context, "termination" bears the same, new, meaning attributed to it in $R(U)$ $7/68$ in relation to section $20(1)(b)$. So that: "It is important to keep in mind the distinction between the contract of service and employment under the contract, and to remember that in this legislation the words 'employed' and 'employment' seem to be used in more senses than one ... a person may be in employment in one sense but at the same time be unemployed in another sense." In the case from which this quotation is taken,[5] a Tribunal of Commissioners took the view that the claimant was employed under a "running" contract of service. In the relevant sense, therefore, the employment had not been terminated, although parts of the periods covered by it were periods (school vacations) when he was not actually employed. Today, therefore, the crucial question is: "Was there in existence on the day in question and throughout the relevant period a running contract of service, notwithstanding the fact that no work was required?"

The answer to this question requires ascertainment and construction of the agreement between the parties. Before the change of attitude evidenced in $R(U)$ $7/68$, construing the new regulations, it appears to have been considered that the existence of an intention to resume the employment after the break necessarily meant that the employment had not terminated, notwithstanding that the contract might have ended. It was so held in $R(U)$ $1/62$, which expressly rejected the approach now enshrined in the legislation and $R(U)$ $7/68$.[6]

On the other hand, a mere hope or prospect of resumption was not enough.[7] *A fortiori*, if the agreement to resume employment at a future date was only arrived at in the course of the break itself, the employment could not be considered to continue.[8] Many of these cases would be disposed of in an identical manner under the new legislation and interpretation. The difference is that whereas an intention to resume was formerly treated as conclusive of the matter (*i.e.* no termination) it is now merely evidentiary, albeit in some cases strongly so, that the contract is a running one and has not terminated. It remains clearly possible, if the parties make their intention abundantly clear, for the contract nowadays to terminate notwithstanding that he parties intend (albeit are not legally bound) to resume at the next opportunity. Actual termination of the contract is, however, a matter of substance and not merely of form. In $R(U)$ $2/51$, "the employers handed the claimant his insurance card at the beginning of the holiday, not with any real intention of discharging him or terminating his contract of service, but solely with a view to enabling him to obtain other employment, or possibly unemployment benefit, during the holiday." There being a real intention to resume, the days of holiday could not, under the old law, be ranked as days of unemployment. A similar conclusion might well be arrived at under the new law if the statutory authorities were satisfied that, notwithstanding the appearances, there was in fact a running contract.

If the contract has not terminated or the suspension continued for a sufficiently long period of time, the regulation applies. In such a case, however, not every day or period which, under the contract of employment, is a non-working day, is a "holiday" unable to be ranked as a day of unemployment.[9] The regulation is expressly confined in its operation to days of "recognised or customary holiday in connection with that employment." Even if there are, normally, such days, it is not entirely clear that they must be left out of account where the real reason for the lay-off is not holiday but shortage of work. In $R(U)$ $12/54$, the days in question were days of holiday notwithstanding shortage of work and a claim could not, therefore, be entertained. In *C.W.U.* $1/55$, however[10] it seems to have been held that a claim could be entertained in similar, though not identical, circumstances. The reasons for the decision in the latter case seem to be that there was no single holiday period for the whole staff, that they took holidays in relays, that employees were free to work their holidays if they chose, that the claimant sought to work the days of "holiday" in question but was disabled from doing so by shortage of work. The best reconciliation seems to be that if there would, in any case, be no work to do by reason of holiday, it is irrelevant if work would not be available for some other reason. But if the claimant has an option to work, but is disabled from exercising it not because he chooses to be on holiday but because of shortage of work, he may rank the day in question as a day of unemployment.

The core concept in the holiday regulation is "recognised or customary holiday in connection with that employment." Two problems emerge:

1. What is "in that employment"?

2. What are the criteria for determining whether a holiday is "customary" or "recognised"?

On the first of these matters, "unless there is definite evidence to the contrary a claimant who has taken employment in a particular establishment is subject to the holiday conditions prevailing there."[11] In *R(U) 31/56*, a claimant who had taken employment as a temporary postman over the Christmas period claimed in respect of New Year's Day which was observed as a customary holiday amongst regular workers in the postal branch where he was employed. Notwithstanding that he, unlike the rest, was a day-to-day worker, he was not entitled to benefit. "If a day-to-day worker normally seeks work in a particular market, the presumption is that he becomes bound by such agreements, express or implied, as govern employment in that market." However, "in a particular case, a claimant might be able to show that although a particular day was a holiday in the market in which he had been working, it was nevertheless not a holiday for him, because when that market was closed or on holiday he normally sought work elsewhere." An obvious case would be that of a seasonal worker being laid off during a slack period in his off-season work coincidentally with the customary holidays of his seasonal work.[12]

It does not follow, once a person has taken employment in a particular establishment, that the holiday customs applicable to one class of workers in that establishment necessarily apply to him. In *102/51 (UB)*, the Northern Ireland Commissioner considered the case of a third preference docker who had been laid off without pay for the duration of a holiday period applying only, under the relevant agreement, to first and second prefer-ence men. The case had been considered three years previously[13] when it had been held that *vis-à-vis* third preference men, the period in question was not "holiday." By the time of the 1951 decision, however, after five years' observance, it had become customary in the case of third preference men, and therefore applied to that class as well. A similar problem arises in the school cases, in the case of ancillary (*i.e.* non-teaching) staff. Here, it has repeatedly been held that "what is a holiday period for school teachers and their scholars is not necessarily to be re-garded as such for members of the non-teaching staff the nature of whose employment (if they were not attached to a school) would ordinarily give them only holidays of much briefer duration."[14] The criteria for definition of a "class" of employees for this purpose must, however, be relevant to the employment. In *R(U) 4/52*, a non-Jewish claimant was held to be on holiday and not, therefore, unemployed, when his firm closed, as it had for the past 10 years, on Jewish holidays.

The criteria for "customary" or "recognised" holidays were established under the pre-War legislation and effectively remain the same today. They are, said the Umpire in *U.D. 18284/32*, "those days which the employers and workers have agreed (whether expressly[15] or by implication based on acquiescence[16]) shall be non-working days. When those holidays have been defined and determined they become a normal incident of employment and an implied term of the contract of service which cannot be varied except by an express or implied agreement between the parties." It appears that the onus of proving that a day is a day of holiday in a particular establishment lies upon the insurance officer, but that that of proving that it does not apply to a particular class of worker lies upon the claimant.[17] The essence of the matter is the agreement, express or implied, between the worker and the employer. If a person agrees to take employment on terms which include a recognised holiday period, it is irrelevant that in the event he is laid off against his will, *e.g.* because he has not qualified for holiday pay.[18] It has been decided,[19] that "once the main body of employees has agreed to a period being treated as a holiday, it becomes a recognised holiday for all the employees (apart from the ex-cluded grades or classes) including the dissentients." It is sub-

mitted, however, that this would only be so if the employee
had either in the first place accepted employment on the basis
that he would be bound by such decisions as to the holiday period
or, if not, come to acquiesce in such arrangements. It is now
clearly arguable, in view of dicta in *Hill* v. *Parsons*,[20] that mere
tacit acquiescence would not suffice for this purpose.

Whilst tacit acquiescence might no longer suffice to characterise a day as a day of recognised holiday, it is clearly otherwise
with customary holidays. The regulation itself makes this clear
and it has always been the law that "if it has been the practice
for a number of years to close an establishment for the same
period of time each year, there arises the presumption that that
period has become *recognised* as a holiday for all employees."[21]
"Where during a substantial number of years a holiday has been
observed over a fixed period it must be inferred, unless there are
facts which negative the inference, that that holiday satisfied the
requirements of a recognised holiday, even though the period
of holiday does not synchronise with that generally recognised
as a holiday period in the district."[22] In *R(U) 16/55*, the practice
prevailed of taking December 24 and 27 as holidays when
Christmas Day and Boxing Day fell on Saturday and Sunday
respectively, and it was held that they could not be ranked as
days of unemployment.[23] Notwithstanding that an express works
agreement might provide otherwise, it may still be the case that
a particular day has become a day of customary holiday as in
R(U) 2/64, where, by long custom, the Saturday preceding the
annual fortnight's holiday had been taken off.[24] Finally, the fact
that the employers observe a practice of paying holiday pay to
certain employees in respect of a specified period affords some
evidence that that period is holiday *vis-à-vis* other employees,
even though no holiday payment is made.[25]

The holiday regulation does not apply, even though the
contract has not been terminated, if a period of indefinite
suspension has reached its seventh consecutive day. Whether or
not a period of "suspension" is "indefinite" seems to turn upon
the nature of the intention to resume. If both parties fully intend
to resume the contract of service when convenient, such as after
a specific period of holiday or other break in the employment,
it appears not to be "indefinite" but "definite."[26] Whilst the point
was not required, in the event, to be decided, the Commissioner

in $R(U)$ *16/54* seemed committed to the view that where the parties intended to resume at a definite date, the suspension was not indefinite. The inference is that where the parties intend to resume at some future, indefinite, date, the suspension is indefinite, and the regulation ceases to operate after the seventh successive day of such a period of suspension.

Criticism of the holiday rule

By and large, the holiday rule seems to achieve the objective in mind, that is, to ensure that unemployment benefit is not paid in respect of days for which the employee is, in effect, paid in the ordinary course of his employment. Some cases, however, give cause for concern. On the one hand, as we have seen, the result of the rule is that a worker on holiday may receive neither pay nor benefit (as where he takes employment so late in the works year that he fails to qualify for holiday pay at all). Also, a worker under a period of definite suspension may find himself in an inferior position when compared with a worker under a period of indefinite suspension who, however, in the event may resume long before the former. On the other hand, a worker whose employment has terminated may qualify for benefit (provided his "holidays" are neither recognised or customary) even though he negotiated successfully for wages in fact including an element in respect of "holidays."

Because of these anomalies there is great attraction in the suggestion that the scheme would be better served by the abolition of the holiday rule and by resolving the difficulties instead simply by reference to whether a claimant was paid for the day in question. If not paid, he should be treated as unemployed and entitled to benefit. If paid, he should not. The apparent simplicity of this suggestion is, however, deceptive. The hidden difficulty lies in the problem of determining whether or not the claimant was paid in respect of the day in question. There may, nominally, be no payment for the day in question, yet be a latent element in the normal weekly wages in respect of the "holiday." Or, by contrast, the pay for the day in question may be, in substance, a part of the earnings truly and wholly in respect of the working period but withheld for the "holiday." It is impossible to conceive of a satisfactory solution without imposing an extremely heavy burden of investigation and evaluation upon the statutory authorities.[27]

(v) Sundays

The amount payable by way of benefit for unemployment, sickness or invalidity for any day of unemployment or incapacity for work is one-sixth of the appropriate weekly rate.[28] The scheme, in other words, takes note, albeit crudely, of the fact that most earners earn a week's wages on six days, or less. One may, nevertheless, actually work on seven days a week; and, if one did, and became unemployed one might become entitled to benefit for the seventh day, *i.e.* for one and one-sixth the weekly rate of benefit per week, were provision not made otherwise.

The Act in fact provides that "Sunday or such other day in each week as may be prescribed shall not be treated as a day of unemployment or of incapacity for work and shall be disregarded in computing any period of consecutive days."[29] Regulations provide that persons working six days a week or less, including Sunday, may not rank as a day of unemployment the day off (in the case of six day workers) or the last day off in any week (in the case of persons normally working less than six days).[30] In many cases, the normal idle day rule[31] would suffice. It, however, only comes into operation when the employment has not been terminated and would not apply in cases where it was abnormal to have the Sunday or a substituted day off. The Sunday rule operates willy-nilly.

No doubt, in the case of most employment patterns, the Sunday rule achieves its objective, *i.e.* it ensures that a claimant who has lost a straight week's work receives no more than a straight week's benefit. In the case of exceptional work patterns, however, this may not be so. In some occupations, for example some having an annual seasonal character, the nature of the work regime may be such that the worker relies upon higher earnings for a long week during certain weeks of the year as a compensation for relatively lower, or no, earnings in other weeks. He will, nevertheless, receive only a week's benefit for the loss of what is really more than a week's work. There is no way in which he can receive more; yet there are many ways in which he might receive less than full benefit for the loss of work in an off-season week, *e.g.* the normal idle day rule, the full extent normal rule, and failure to satisfy the additional conditions for season workers.[32]

(vi) Suspensions

In strict legal terms and for many legal purposes, it makes sense to define unemployment in terms of whether or not there is a subsisting contract of service or apprenticeship. The facts of industrial life, however, do not fit this model sufficiently closely. Industrially-speaking, the important concepts are being sacked, or laid off, or put on short-time, or in work and to allow title to benefit to be determined simply in terms of the legalities would have obvious disadvantages. It would be little comfort to be regarded as in employment because one's contract subsisted if in fact neither work nor pay was available under it.

The unemployment benefit scheme has, in fact, always adopted a robust commonsense attitude as to what constitutes unemployment and accepted that if there is in fact neither work nor pay it matters little whether there is a contract.[33] However, the industrially-significant distinction between being sacked, *i.e.* finally dismissed, and laid off, *i.e.* suspended, received until recently insufficient attention. It may well be that it is now receiving the wrong kind of attention[34] but since 1966 express provision has been made in the legislation for taking note of suspensions.

In 1966[35] a new rule intended to displace the normal idle day rule was introduced. It has, however, been confined in that effect (*i.e.* displacing the normal idle day rule) to the earnings-related supplement to benefit and although provision for its eventual extension is made[36] such extension has, since 1969[37] needed an affirmative resolution of both Houses of Parliament.[38] Extension depends chiefly upon employers assuming a greater share of the cost of very short spells of unemployment due to lay-offs, a start on which has been made by the Employment Protection Act 1975.[39]

The new rule is couched in the following terms:

"... where a person is an employed earner and his employment as such has not been terminated but has been suspended by the employer, a day shall not be treated in relation to that person as a day of unemployment unless it is the 7th or a later day in a continuous period of days on which that suspension has lasted. . . ."[40]

Sundays and days of customary or recognised holiday do not count towards the six days.[41] Days of incapacity, however, which would be days of suspension but for the incapacity, are to be treated as days of suspension both for purposes of maintaining continuity of the period of suspension and calculating the six days.[42] Only days completely lost by suspension count.[43] Where the employment in question is in a subsidiary occupation which may be disregarded for ordinary benefit purposes[44] suspension in it is to be treated as termination and the suspension rule accordingly does not apply;[45] it seems likely that it was never meant to apply and that any application it might have had would be accidental and due simply to the fact that section $17(3)(a)$, dealing with the particular matter of earnings-related supplement would otherwise repeal *pro tanto* any prior and inconsistent general provision such as the power in section $17(2)$ under which the subsidiary occupations rule[46] was made.

It was in the course of interpreting the new suspension rule that Commissioners evolved the new meaning of "termination of employment."[47] Thus, when the rule requires of a claimant that "his employment . . . has not been terminated" it requires that his contract of employment has not been terminated. If his contract continues but he is laid off, (which, under the old view might have constituted termination) his employment has not been terminated and the suspension rule applies to him.

It is a further condition of the application of the rule that the claimant's employment shall have been suspended by the employer. In this respect, the rule seems to be aimed at only one or possibly two of the ways in which a lay-off can come about, namely exercise by the employer of a contractual right to suspend, or possibly of a *de facto* power to do so deriving from industrial practice regardless of the strict legal position. Prima facie, it seems as though a lay-off resulting from agreement between employee and employer, or compelled by external events, such as illegality, would not constitute suspension "by the employer" and thus would not involve the rule. Indeed, it might be argued and has been argued that the rule operates only in the case of disciplinary suspensions (the industrial meaning of "suspension") and not even to ordinary lay-offs effected by the employer even by contractual right.

This latter, most restricted, meaning was rejected by a tribunal of Commissioners in *R(U) 11/72*. In that case, they also decided that a claimant's employment was suspended by his employer where the suspension resulted from agreement between employer and employee, in much the same way that an employee could be said to have been employed by an employer upon agreeing to work for him. It was, however, expressly reserved for future decision whether a *de facto* unilateral suspension by an employer who had no legal right to suspend fell within the rule and one Commissioner emphasised, as must surely be the case, that the idea of "suspension" involves a contraction of the amount of work in relation to a previously established status quo and thus is not constituted by the mere fact of spells of work *per se*. So a worker whose regular established pattern was, say, three days on and three days off, would not *ipso facto* be suspended on the days off.

If this latter proposition is correct, then it may be most unwise for employees to accept an employer's proposal for short-time working. They will have been suspended. If they do refuse, and if the old contract is terminated, a new one for three-day working only being substituted, the rule may well be circumvented.

It has subsequently been decided that a *de facto* suspension by an employer brings the rule into operation even though he had no legal right to suspend.[48] The restriction of electricity supplies during the miners' strike of 1974 had caused the suspension. The chief reason offered for this interpretation was that effective administration of unemployment benefit would be rendered extremely onerous if an inquiry into the legal position had to be mounted every time there was a lay-off. Of course, there is a great deal to be said for effecting ease of administration but that means of effecting it could surely be frustrated quite simply by the worker, instead of merely accepting the lay-off, treating the contract as repudiated and therefore terminated by the employer's breach. The employment has thus been terminated, the rule is circumvented, and short-time working can proceed under a new arrangement. There can surely be no more certain way of easing administration of the rule than by by-passing its operation altogether.

This latter decision might or might not be viewed as a case where the contract of employment was discharged by frustration. It was certainly not treated as such by the Commissioner. It could, however, well be argued in an appropriate case (*e.g.* work on certain days being prohibited by law) that the "suspension" was effected by operation of law and not "by the employer" at all, *i.e.* neither legally, under the contract, nor in the exercise of a *de facto* power without contractual warrant; nor, it might be argued, had the suspension been effected by the employer by consent of the employee.

The effect of the rule is that lay-offs of six days or less do not count towards the 12 days of unemployment needed in a particular period of interruption of employment in order for title to earnings-related supplement to be established.

It is not only in relation to earnings-related supplement that special attention is paid to the position of the suspended worker. His legal position is extremely complex and at least one experienced Minister has expressed a desire for simplification.[49] That, however, seems over the horizon.

(vii) Availability

Unemployment benefit is designed primarily to meet the case of involuntary unemployment. It is assumed that a person should be able and willing to provide for himself by work if possible. It is therefore a condition of treating any day as a day of unemployment that he "is, or is deemed in accordance with regulations to be, available for employment in an employed contributor's employment."[55] The approach of the statutory authorities to this question is that "a claimant does not show that she is available for employment unless she is willing and able to accept suitable employment."[51]

The onus of proving availability rests upon the claimant. This onus is not discharged merely by proving that no offer of employment has been made.[52] "The fact that no ... situation has been offered ... does not preclude a finding that he was not available for employment on the date of his claim."[53] In order to establish "availability," the claimant must prove the following:

1. that there is a reasonable prospect of obtaining the work for which he holds himself available;

2. that he is willing and able to accept suitable work, if offered, at once; and

3. that this work is in an employed contributor's employment.

Reasonable prospect of obtaining work

It has frequently been held that if a claimant has no reasonable prospects of securing employment he cannot be regarded as "available" for work and thus cannot rank the relevant days as days of unemployment.[54] The most common application of this principle is in the situation where the claimant has placed restrictions upon the type of work he is willing to undertake. This is considered below under the heading "restricted availability." It may, however, apply for other reasons. In *120/52 (UB)* it was used to deny benefit in the case of an isolated day (which could otherwise have been linked with other days to make a period of interruption of employment) on the ground that alternative work of one day's duration only was not reasonably obtainable in that district. The same reasoning was applied to daily work generally in *R(U) 18/55*. In *R(U) 12/52*, a claimant was held unavailable on the grounds of his age and the fact that he was only available for the duration of school holidays, whilst in *R(U) 36/52* the claimant's obvious reluctance to accept employment with any but his existing, short-time employers, rendered him unavailable.

On the other hand, it is not necessary that work actually be available, provided that it is a reasonable inference that it might be forthcoming. In *C.U. 10/49 (KL)* a claimant was allowed benefit in respect of Wednesday and Saturday afternoons (her days off from college) since the possibility of part-time domestic work could not be ruled out.[55]

In principle, there seems to be no reason why the above principle should not apply in a case where a claimant is able and willing to take any work at all, whether part- or full-time. It has not, however, been applied in such a situation and it would undermine the scheme so to apply it. The point is unlikely to arise. Even in a depressed area in a time of recession, it cannot be said that there is no reasonable prospect of obtaining any work at all, albeit 700 miles away and in an unskilled capacity.

Willingness and ability to accept at once suitable work offered

The most common type of unavailability is the claimant's unwillingness or inability to accept an offer of work. This may arise for a number of reasons, such as a plain refusal to work, absence (*e.g.* on training or on holiday), illegality, being otherwise occupied and incapacity.

(i) Refusal to work—a claimant who refuses to work on a day is not available on that day.[56] *R(U) 4/53* affords a good example. There, a colliery worker on a five-day week was allowed to undertake voluntary Saturday work if he wished. His claim for unemployment benefit was rejected for he could not purport to be available for work consistently with having declined an opportunity which was open to him. Where a claimant is able and willing to take work which he has a reasonable prospect of securing, he may or may not be regarded as unavailable on a particular day according as to whether or not he is able and willing on that day. *R(U) 31/51* contrasts with *R 7/60 (UB)* in this respect. In the former case, the refusal of Saturday work (whether required or not) rendered the claimant unavailable on that day, but in the latter case, the claimant was entitled to benefit for a sixth day on the ground that the work she was willing to do was subject to a five-day week regime. She was available for the whole week since she was able and willing to work the full week in that occupation.

(ii) Absence for training.—It was held under the pre-War legislation[57] that a claimant who had left work in order to take an examination was not available for employment. The view has subsequently been taken, however,[58] that the mere fact of being engaged in training or examinations is not conclusive of the matter. If the claimant thereby renders himself unable to take work, or if the training takes place under an existing contract of employment, then unavailability may well be the result. But if he is in fact available, *i.e.* if he can readily be contacted and if at a moment's notice he can and will abandon the training or examination and take up a suitable offer, he may rank the day in question as a day of unemployment.

(iii) Absence on holiday—similar reasoning applies here. Under the pre-War legislation, the Umpires formulated certain conditions which became incorporated into a standard form[59] to be completed by claimants intending to be away from their normal residence on holiday. These conditions were:[60]

(a) The claimant must prove that he is ready and willing to curtail his holiday in order to accept at once any offer which might be notified to him.

(b) He must prove that he has taken reasonable steps to ensure that he could readily be notifed of any vacancy. "That his place of temporary residence was on the telephone service or had a postal and telegraph delivery which afforded a means of communicating with him" satisfied this condition.

(c) "He must prove that there was nothing connected with his absence from his locality or with the position of his place of temporary residence which would have prevented him from accepting at once any suitable employment which might be notified to him."

Though it is not clear that condition (c) ever had any function not covered by conditions (a) and (b), these conditions were nevertheless incorporated into the post-War scheme.[61]

It is clear that if a claimant absents himself from his normal residence with the result that he cannot be contacted in the event of an offer of employment, he has rendered himself unavailable.[62] It does not matter that he does not need to be contacted. The question is not whether work is available for him but whether he is available for work.[63] What is doubtful is the relevance of the conditions now contained in form U.I. 672H. The Commissioner pointed out, in *R(U) 4/66*, that these conditions were settled at a time of chronic wide-spread unemployment, during which "it was obviously unreasonable that a person should forfeit unemployment benefit merely because he left the vicinity of his Employment Exchange." In *R(U) 4/66*, he treated the information provided on the form as amounting to no more than slight evidence of availability and withheld benefit in the case of a dock worker in whose case the normal custom was to notify opportunities at a call stand each morning when work was available. By taking a week's holiday in London, the claimant had effectively rendered himself unavailable for employment notwithstanding that he could readily be contacted and was prepared to return immediately if called upon. In that case, he had "materially reduced his chances of obtaining suitable employment."[64] It would clearly have been otherwise if the claimant had been merely temporarily suspended and thus able to predict with probability that he would be called upon to resume his employment within a matter of days. In such a case[65] an absence during those days might well not materially reduce his chances.

(iv) Illegality—a person cannot be available for employment if he is legally prohibited from taking employment. In Northern Ireland, this is the position which appertains in the case of persons needing but lacking a permit to work under the Safeguarding of Employment Act (N.I.) 1947.[66] It would apply also to persons needing work permits under the Immigration Act 1971.[67] The former of these decisions leaves open the possibility that a person unable to work in Northern Ireland without a permit might nevertheless be entitled to benefit in Northern Ireland as being available for employment in Great Britain. Whether such employment would be "employed contributor's employment" for the purposes of the Northern Ireland legislation does not seem to have been considered. Arguably, it would not be.

(v) Being otherwise engaged—a person who is under a contractual obligation to work for an employer if called upon is not available for employment otherwise.[68] This is so even if the employer has made plain his intention not to call upon the employee.[69] The same principle applies to one undertaking public duties, albeit unpaid, *e.g.* as a Councillor.[70] If the obligation relates to a subsidiary occupation satisfying the conditions of regulation 7(1)(h), one of which is that the claimant must be available for employment in his full-time occupation, he will be *ex hypothesi* available.[71] Similarly, if the obligation to work is contingent upon reasonable notice of being required being given, a claimant may be treated as being available during periods when his services have not, in fact, been called upon, provided that the threat of such calls do not have the effect of depriving him of a reasonable prospect of obtaining suitable other employment.[72]

In considering whether or not a claimant is "willing and able" to accept an offer it is to be remembered that the offer must be suitable having regard to the nature of the claimant's skills, the duration of his employment in a particular occupation, the duration of his unemployment and the likelihood of alternative and more suitable offers being forthcoming.[73]

"Employed contributor's employment"

It is not enough that a claimant is able and willing to accept suitable employment which he has a reasonable prospect of securing. This was the case in $R(U)$ *14/51* where, however, the employment in question (as an "outworker") was only available on a self-employed basis, and benefit was consequently denied.

RESTRICTED AVAILABILITY

Most problems concerning availability arise from the imposition, by the claimant, of restrictions as to the days or hours on which, locality in which, or the nature or conditions of employment at which, he is prepared to work.[74] As stated above, a person cannot be treated as available for work which he has no reasonable prospect of obtaining. This situation almost invariably arises because of limits imposed by the claimant,[75] and it is a principle of general application that "a claimant's profession of ability or willingness to work must not be hedged about with restrictions which will render his chance of obtaining employment negligible."[76] In this connection, the following points should be noted:

1. In order to affect availability, the restrictions must relate to employment. In $R2/65(UB)$ the claimant had refused to undergo training which might materially have improved his prospects of employment. He was nevertheless entitled to benefit for he had not thereby restricted his availability for work. "'Employment' and 'training' mean different things. . . . Where the training offered was quite independent of any contract of service with any employer, its refusal cannot properly be held to constitute the placing of a restriction . . . on the conditions of employment which the claimant is prepared to accept."

2. The effect of restrictions must be considered in the light of the facts of each particular case. A restriction rendering a claimant unavailable in one locality might be not in the least unreasonable in another where work of the type wanted is more

readily available.[77] A restriction to "9 a.m.–5 p.m." will be unreasonable if unusual in the occupation in question.[78] Similarly, the longer a person remains unemployed, the more adaptable and accommodating he must become.[79]

3. A special problem arises in the case of women with domestic responsibilities. Here, the general rule is that "if claimants wish to be regarded as available for work they must make adjustments in their domestic arrangements to get, and retain, work.[80] "It is not enough for a married woman merely to say that the hours to be observed in a situation offered are not convenient to her; good and sufficient domestic or other circumstances must be shown and mere inconvenience to herself or her family is seldom sufficient reason for refusing employment."[81] Special circumstances may, however, be taken account of under regulation $7(1)(a)$ below.

REGULATION $7(1)(a)$

Notwithstanding that a person has imposed restrictions with the result that he has no reasonable prospect of securing employment, he may nevertheless be entitled to benefit if the restrictions can be justified on one of the three grounds stated by regulation[82] which provides:

"Where in respect of any day a person places restrictions on the nature, hours, rate of remuneration or locality or other conditions of employment which he is prepared to accept and as a consequence of those restrictions has no reasonable prospects of securing employment, that day shall not be treated as a day of unemployment unless—

(i) he is prevented from having reasonable prospects of securing employment consistent with those restrictions only as a result of adverse industrial conditions in the locality or localities concerned which may reasonably be regarded as temporary, and, having regard to all the circumstances, personal and other, the restrictions which he imposes are reasonable; or

(ii) the restrictions are nevertheless reasonable in view of his physical condition; or

(iii) the restrictions are nevertheless reasonable having regard both to the nature of his usual occupation and also to the time which has elapsed since he became unemployed."

It is to be noted that the regulation does not apply to all restrictions but only to those on the "nature, hours, rate of remuneration or locality or other conditions of employment." This certainly appears to be fairly comprehensive, but it excludes at least restrictions as to the number of days in a week upon which a person is prepared to work. The question which has to be considered is whether a given day is a day of unemployment and if, as a result of restrictions as to the number of days on which a claimant is prepared to work, he is not prepared to work on a given day, he is simply not available on that day, whether or not the reasons for the restriction would otherwise justify on the grounds of the regulation.[83]

Equally, the question of availability generally may still call for consideration, notwithstanding that one of the grounds of justification is established, if the alleged lack of availability is based as well on grounds other than reasonableness of restrictions relevant for regulation $7(1)(a)$ purposes.[84] If the only ground for alleged unavailability generally is one of the regulation grounds, however, that puts an end to the question of availability. Confusion arises because the regulation neither uses the term "available" nor refers to section $17(1)(c)(i)$ of the Act (stating that a day cannot be treated as a day of unemployment unless on that day the claimant is available for work). There thus appear, superficially, to be two grounds disentitling a claimant from ranking a given day as a day of unemployment, one, that he is not available, and two, that he has placed restrictions; and merely to justify the restrictions still leaves open the prospect of disentitlement by virtue of unavailability. This argument would, however, render the regulation otiose and was, for that reason, rejected in $R(U)$ $4/57$.

The first justifying ground in the regulation relates to "adverse industrial conditions."[85] The requirement here is that such conditions must be such as to be reasonably regarded to be temporary.[86] On this ground, the Commissioner has rejected a restriction confining availability to the off-season in the case of seasonal occupations, the slackness of the off-season trade not being exceptional and temporary but rather "the normal and annually recurrent industrial conditions ... regularly existing."[87]

The second justifying ground relates to the physical condition

of the claimant, and to "restrictions" in the plural. It may, therefore, be the case that one restriction may be "reasonable" by
reference to the claimant's physical condition, yet another or
others not so. In $R(U)$ *6/72* a claimant suffering from a heart
condition and hypertension could reasonably ask for work in his
home locality but could not reasonably expect exactly his usual
type of work at his usual remuneration.[88]

The main purpose of the third justifying ground "is to safeguard a claimant who restricts himself from accepting employment which is different from, or on less satisfactory conditions
than those in, his usual occupation. For a time, such a restriction
would be regarded as a reasonable one, but the longer he
remained unemployed the less reasonable that inflexible attitude
would become."[89] The restrictions must, however, relate to the
nature of the occupation, otherwise the door to the third ground
is not opened in the first place. In $R(U)$ *3/59*, the restrictions
were imposed for reasons personal to the claimant herself and not
because the nature of the occupation made their imposition
reasonable. The same point arose in $R(U)$ *1/69* where the claimant held himself available only on occasions (though rare) when
he was not required to work as an actor for the BBC. These
restrictions were not reasonable. "The fact that they arose by
reason of commitments entered into by the claimant with the
BBC and that as between the parties the commitments might well
be reasonable and that in any event they are part of a wider
agreement, which may well have been in the claimant's interest,
does not necessarily make them 'reasonable' for the purposes of
regulation $7(1)(b)(iii)$".[90] It is also clear that if the restrictions
are otherwise reasonable they do not cease to be reasonable
because they give rise to a lack of prospects of 'outside' employment.... This 'escape' provision requires, *inter alia*, that the
restrictions should be reasonable having regard to the nature of
the claimant's usual occupation. The restrictions in this case,
however, do not arise by reason of the claimant's occupation as
an actor but by reason of the particular commitments he had
chosen to enter into with the BBC and in my judgment were
not reasonable having regard to the nature of his usual
occupation."[91]

CRITICISM

It is undoubtedly in accord with the philosophy of the unemployment benefit scheme that a person who is unable to accept work if offered should be denied benefit. And it is but a small and perfectly warrantable extension of this principle to deny benefit in all cases where it is apparent from the start that work will not be taken if offered. Equally, the view is clearly taken that some circumstances (such as the desire to continue in one's own occupation; the need to take care of incapacitated members of one's family) may justify an unwillingness to take certain kinds of work. In two respects, however, the attempt to express these principles in rules of law seems unsatisfactory.

First of all, it is not easy to see why two independent provisions (section 17(1)(a)(i) and regulation 7(1)(a)) are necessary to express them. A simple expression of the requirement of availability followed by a list of justifying circumstances (including those at present operating under the section) would seem to be technically superior and would avoid some of the confusion which presently exists.

Secondly, there is a considerable overlap with the disqualification provisions relating to refusal of employment etc.[92] Such a refusal may have the effect of (1) disentitling a claimant to benefit for any day on which it persists (by rendering him not available) and (2) disqualifying him for a period of up to six weeks from the refusal (the practice not being to reimpose periods of disqualification in respect of a single continuing refusal). The position may thus result that one who recants his refusal may nevertheless continue to be disqualified, whilst one who does not may avoid any additional penalty. There seems to be a singular lack of discrimination here. The scheme might be much improved if the spheres of operation of disentitlement and disqualification were more rigorously distinguished, *i.e.* if the former were confined to cases of involuntary inability to take work and the latter to voluntary unemployment.

One further point may be mentioned. It seems anomalous that a claimant who, by reason of part-time work, perhaps on a small scale, is unavailable for work and therefore not entitled to benefit should be able to create entitlement simply by abandoning his part-time work. The subsidiary occupation rule only

applies if he *is* available. He is, presumably, not disqualified;
at all events, he is not so treated by the department.[93] This
would seem correct, certainly in the case where the part-time
work is in a self-employed capacity and probably also otherwise,
there being no "employed earner's employment" which he has
voluntarily left. It would make sense, at least in cases of chronic
unemployment and in times of acute unemployment, to permit
and perhaps even require part-time work, unavailability for full-
time work notwithstanding, subject to an appropriate abatement of benefit.

(viii) Days of incapacity

A day is not a day of unemployment unless on that day the
claimant is capable of work.[94] If he is, subject to the *de minimis*
rule, incapable of doing work which he may reasonably be
expected to do, the day will be a day of incapacity for sickness
benefit purposes,[95] provided the incapacity subsists for the whole
working day. If he is incapable of work for a part of the working
day, he is presumably, as to the rest of the working day, "capable
... on that day" and may rank it as a day of unemployment.

We have now considered the cases where, although the
claimant is actually unemployed, he is disabled by the law
from ranking the day in question as a day of unemployment.[96]
We come now to cases where the claimant may rank a day as a
day of unemployment notwithstanding that he earns from work
on it.

(b) *Days of Employment which may be Ranked as Days of Unemployment*

These are the cases of (i) nightworkers and (ii) subsidiary occupations.

(i) Nightworkers

The rule that if any work at all is done or payment received
in lieu thereof the right to benefit fails in respect of the day in
question (as exemplified in *R 2/56 (UB)* considered under "standard case" above)[97] may work very harshly where what is, in

substance, one day's work spreads over into a second day. "Day," for this purpose, means the period of 24 hours from midnight to midnight. Shift-work in many employments means that workers may start a shift on one day and end it on the next. If the "standard case" rule was applied to such a situation, neither day could rank as a day of unemployment. Thus, a claimant laid off for the whole of Monday, working Tuesday 6 p.m. to Wednesday 2 a.m. and laid off for the rest of Wednesday and Thursday until 6 p.m. would be entitled to rank only one day as a day of unemployment whilst one who did the whole eight-hour shift on a single day could rank two days (which would form a "period").

This obvious injustice is remedied by the "nightworkers' regulation"[98] which provides that "where a period of employment commencing on any day extends over midnight into the following day, the person employed shall, in respect of such period—

(*a*) be treated as having been employed on the first day only, if the employment before midnight is of longer duration than that after midnight, and, in that case, the first day shall not be treated as a day of interruption of employment; or

(*b*) be treated as having been employed on the second day only, if the employment after midnight is of longer duration than that before midnight, or if the employment before and after midnight is of equal duration, and, in either of these cases, the second day shall not be treated as a day of interruption of employment."

Where one day thus falls to be treated as a day of interruption of employment, the claimant will be treated as satisfying the requirements of availability or incapacity if he was available or incapacitated for that part of the day on which he was not actually working.[99]

The "nightworkers' regulation" used to apply only to unemployment benefit and used to contain a special provision attributing a Saturday/Sunday shift to the Saturday.[1] The new rule now extends to sickness benefit and is considerably simplified. In all cases, a shift spanning midnight is now attributed to the second day unless the greater part of it falls on the first day, in which case it is attributed to the first day. If the claimant's work pattern is settled and regular so that a particular day always falls to be regarded as a day of interruption of employment under the "nightworkers' regulation," it may become a normal idle day and thus unable to be ranked as a day of unemployment anyway.[2] Similarly, it may fall to be disregarded if, in that week, he works to the full extent normal in his case.[3]

It is not, however, every shift of nightwork which is the equivalent of a day's work. In some occupations (*e.g.* nightwatchmen) a substantial, and sometimes the entire, part of a week's work may occur in the single spell spanning midnight or perhaps even spreading into a third day. This was the situation which arose in *R(U) 18/56* where a trawler deckhand was on duty continuously from 6 p.m. on Monday to 2 a.m. on Wednesday, a total of 32 hours. He sought the benefit of the nightworkers' regulation in respect of the Monday. The problem which arises here is, of course, the opposite of that which occurs in the normal nightwork situation. Where, for example, a week's work is compressed into two spells spreading over four days, no injustice is involved in denying benefit for those four days, at least by comparison with an ordinary five or six day, daytime, worker. If, however, one takes as one's basis of comparison, say, a normally six-shift worker who compresses five eight-hour shifts into two entire 20-hour days, anomaly does result, for he may claim in respect of four days although he has lost only one day's work. In *R(U) 18/56*, the Commissioner denied the claimant the benefit of the nightworkers' regulation on the basis that it only applied where a shift began at some time within the 24 hours comprising one calendar day and ended at some time within the 24 hours comprising the following calendar day, conditions not satisfied where the work spread into a third day. This may well have been the ambit of the original rule (reference was made to Decision *6860/33* under the pre-War legislation) and certainly may, in some cases, fulfil the policy of the social security scheme. But this requirement, that the spell shall *end* on the following calendar day, is not, strictly, required by the regulation. What is required is that "a period of employment . . . extends over midnight into the following day," a condition which might properly be regarded as satisfied in the three-day spell situation.[4]

The interpretation adopted in *R(U) 18/56* does not, in fact, guarantee that the benefit of the nightworkers' regulation is not conferred upon workers who compress a substantial part of a week's work into a single lengthy spell. The spell in question in *R(U) 37/56* was 29½ hours and constituted about half a week's work. Because, however, it did not extend into a third day (it was from 11.30 a.m. Saturday to 5 p.m. Sunday), the claimant received the benefit of the regulation and was entitled to rank one day as a day of unemployment notwithstanding that he had, in effect, done three days' work.

(ii) Subsidiary occupations

A man who secures his livelihood mainly in one occupation may supplement it by engaging also in a subsidiary occupation. Unemployment benefit takes the place of income from a main occupation when the insured person ceases to be employed in it. The mere fact that he keeps on, or subsequently takes on, a subsidiary occupation should not and does not, by itself, cause him to be deprived of his right to benefit. If, however, his income from the subsidiary occupation is substantial; or if it prevents him seizing an opportunity to resume his main occupation, the case for receipt of unemployment benefit is considerably weakened.

Account has been taken of this throughout the whole duration of the national insurance scheme. The substantial content of the regulation dealing with it, however, has changed four times since 1948 (quite apart from consolidation), the last of these occasions being in 1960. Earlier authorities are not, therefore, necessarily reliable indicators as to how claims will be disposed of today.

The regulation which presently governs[5] provides as follows:

". . . a day shall not be treated as a day of unemployment if on that day a person is engaged in any employment unless the earnings derived from that employment, in respect of that day, do not exceed 75 pence, or, where the earnings are earned in respect of a longer period than a day, the earnings do not on the daily average exceed that amount, and unless he is available on that day to be employed full-time in some employed earner's employment and the employment in which he is engaged is consistent with that full-time employment,

and, if the employment in which he is engaged is employed
earner's employment, it is not in his usual main occupation."

This most recent regulation speaks of a person being "engaged in any employment." This represents a change in
phraseology from previous versions of the regulation which used
the phrase "following any occupation" around which a considerable doctrine had developed.[6] The extent to which this doctrine
survives is quite unclear.

Under both the former and present versions of the regulation
it was not and is not the apparent policy to exclude from benefit
all persons with an income from any source in excess of the
stipulated sum per day otherwise, presumably, a simple means
test would have been imposed. The old regulations drew the line
at income derived from "following an occupation," the new
regulations at income derived from being "engaged in employment." The question is whether the line has shifted. Little help
is derived from the legislation. "Occupation" was not defined
and in the current Act, "employment" is unhelpfully defined as
including "any trade, business, profession, office or vocation,"[7]
an employed earner being "a person who is gainfully employed
... either under a contract of service, or in an office ... with
emoluments chargeable to income tax under Schedule E."[8]
Regulations may, however, treat employments as being "employed earners'" notwithstanding the above criteria.[9]

Under the old regulation it was settled that an "occupation"
must involve some personal activity.[10] Devotional exercises and
domestic duties within a religious community would suffice[11] although persons so engaged might well not be *gainfully* employed.
It seems likely that the same distinction will be maintained in
relation to the definition of "employment" for this purpose. If
so, then the mere passive receipt of an income (as from mere
ownership as opposed to active management of property) would
not constitute an employment.[12] The mere ownership of property capable of being used for profit is not following an
occupation ... but when a person owns such property and holds
himself out as being prepared to use it for earning money whenever he can get customers he is following an occupation from
day to day and not merely on the days on which he finds
customers or makes a profit."[13]

The latter part of this quotation above raises the question of duration of an occupation and clearly suggests that it is not necessarily confined to periods of actual activity. The problem arises frequently in relation to occupations subject to seasonal fluctuation, the most common example of which is the boarding-house trade. Here, the view which has been taken is that a "person cannot be said to be engaged in an occupation during a period when there is no practical possibility of that occupation being followed merely because (the person) is prepared to follow it at any time,"[14] although "a person ... whose earnings are derived from rendering services can properly ... be regarded as following an occupation during a period when the rendering of services is temporarily suspended."[15] In practical terms, the distinction seems to turn upon whether the claimant is ready and willing to do work, given the chance. Thus, where a boarding-house is closed for the season, there is a break in the "occupation," whilst if customers are in fact sought, even though not obtained, the "occupation" continues even though no services are actually rendered.[16] This explains the ruling, in *211/49 (UB)*, that a claimant growing flax on rented land was not following an occupation on Sundays when it was customary not to work.[17]

A special difficulty arises in the case of a person who takes little or no active part in the business of a partnership of which he is a member. In principle, two views are open—(1) if he does no work, he is not "occupied"; (2) since he has rights and duties in relation to profits and management, he is actively involved. The first view is hinted at in *R(U) 11/57*, though the decision here relied upon[18] turns not upon the question whether the claimant was "occupied" but upon the fact that his inactivity did not warrant the appropriation to him of a sufficient share of the partnership income to disqualify him from pension by virtue of earnings, thus assuming without really considering the matter, that he was, in fact, "occupied." *R(U) 11/57* is, on this point, not easy to reconcile with *R(U) 15/56*, where, for a different (and not irrelevant) purpose, emphasis was placed upon the duties connected with the occupation rather than the actual behaviour in it, whilst in *R(U) 22/64* it was expressly held that the claimant was occupied, merely as a partner, even though he did little work in the business. This is believed to be the better view.

Once it is decided that the activity in question constitutes an employment, there remains the odd question whether it is being "engaged in." This question whether an "occupation" was being "followed" was first clearly raised in *R(U) 2/67* concerning attendance at a training centre for the mentally disordered in the course of which the claimant was engaged in the production of articles, for therapeutic purposes, receiving small incentive payments mainly as an encouragement towards rehabilitation and not as a reward for output. The Commissioner appreciated that "some meaning must be given to the word 'following'" but made no attempt to state what it was, otherwise than by illustration. Some of the activities illustrated are trivial (walking to the employment exchange to sign on and collect benefit; attempting to back a winner, filling up a football pool coupon) and in line with the criterion of substantiality of the activity hinted at in *R(U) 4/64*. This accords with principle, for if any bounds at all are to be drawn to the concept, a *de minimis* principle must be applied. But the other illustrations (cultivating a garden with a view to selling produce; knitting woollen garments in the hope of selling them) are not so easily explicable. Very hesitantly, one may venture the suggestion that, short of leading a vegetable-like existence, one must engage in some activity or another, and that if what is done is merely this, as opposed to clearly and markedly preferring a particular type of activity, there is no "engagement" in an "employment" in the sense of the regulation.

Earnings. Earnings in the subsidiary employment must not exceed 75p per day. Where the earnings are earned in respect of a longer period than a day, they must be averaged per day. In this connection, two types of problem arise. The first occurs in the case of allegedly joint employments and is that of appropriating a share of the allegedly joint income to one of the parties. (No problem arises where each partner is entitled to a separate share of profits.) In *R(P) 7/51* and *R(U) 11/57* (partnership cases) the approach adopted was to have regard to the actual contribution which the claimant made to the running of the business and, it being in both cases slight, no substantial appropriation of the joint income was warranted. In *R(U) 6/57*, however, the whole of the income was attributed to a claimant employed as a caretaker, notwithstanding that his wife offered him substantial assistance, on the ground that she was not contractually obliged to do so and that it was possible for the claimant to do all the work. The authorities can be reconciled on the basis that a share of "joint" income can only be attributed where legal entitlement and substantial activity actually coincide.

The second type of problem arises in connection with determining the days to which the income must be attributed. Where a substantial amount is earned (so that if averaged over all days, it would exceed the statutory rate) it is to a claimant's advantage to be able to attribute it all to as few days as possible. Where, however, the amount is so small that it might fall below the statutory rate if averaged over a large number of days, it is to his advantage to do this. The test, where the claimant is engaged under a contract of service seems to be to have regard to the contractual obligation in determining the days in respect of which the payment is received.[19] *R(U) 10/57* and *R(U) 23/57* both concern professional footballers who played on certain days only each week, and who could be called upon to train on any day, being paid a weekly wage, but who were in practice not called upon to train where it involved interference with the main occupation. They were held nevertheless to be obliged to attribute the whole of the earnings to the whole of the week. A similar view was taken of a director of a co-operative society in *R(U) 32/53* whose duties in that capacity continued throughout the whole year. In his case, unlike the footballers in the cases above, the effect of the averaging was to carry him below the statutory maximum. By contrast, in *R(U) 28/51* and *220/50 (UB)* claimants were obliged to attribute earnings to specific days, being employed on daily contracts.

Where there is no indication in the contract of employment on the basis of which it can be decided what earnings are to be appropriated to what day or days, the problem is more difficult. It is clear enough that the "earnings" must be attributed to all days during which the employment is engaged in;[20] and not to other days.[21] What creates difficulty is the case where the employment continues, but earnings fluctuate, with the result that they may fall above or below the limit, according to the selection of the period over which they are spread. This was the

difficulty in the not uncommon situation which arose in $R(U)$
1/67. The claimant and his wife had been running a boarding-
house business since June 1965. A profit and loss account for
the period down to October 31, 1965, showed a net profit of
£646. There was negligible income during November and
December and the claimant claimed unemployment benefit. A
number of possible approaches all yielded different results. One
might project forward the only information thus far available
(the profit from June to October); one might average over the
period thus far (June to December); one might take each day,
or week, or month in the November/December period; one
might take the financial year; or one might take the complete
trading cycle (which might or might not coincide with the
financial year). The legislation gives no guide as to this choice.
After a comprehensive consideration of the various possibilities,
the Commissioner, taking the view that "if the case is one for
averaging the statutory authorities must ... have an ultimate
discretion to decide, in the light of any evidence that may be
available, what period it would be fair and appropriate to take,"
decided to take a complete year from the start of the business,
"for that period gives a complete trading cycle." It would be
otherwise if there was a clear-cut suspension of trading activities
for a substantial period.[22]

The correct approach to these "spreading" problems has now
been greatly clarified. The regulation requires that attention
should first be directed to each day individually. If earnings for
that day exceed the statutory amount, that day cannot be
ranked. If they do not, the next thing is to inquire if payments
have been received in respect of a period longer than a day.
If not, that is the end of the matter. If so, the question is
whether the day under consideration forms part of the longer
period and, if so, what its share of the payment is.[23]

Where a claimant fails to produce a detailed statement of his
earnings, the statutory authorities have, in the past, gleaned the
information as best they can. In *220/50 (UB)*, information in the
case of a farmer was sought from the Ministry of Agriculture
as was the practice in national assistance cases. In national
insurance cases, it is submitted that by virtue of the rules relating
to onus of proof, it would be quite proper to dismiss a claim in
which proper evidence was not furnished and that the above

practice would only be necessary to rebut evidence adduced by a claimant.

Availability and consistency. A claimant must, on the day in question, be "available for full-time employment" notwithstanding his subsidiary occupation. Section $17(1)(a)(i)$ of the 1965 Act provides that "a day shall not be treated in relation to any person—(i) as a day of unemployment unless on that day he is capable of work and is, or is deemed in accordance with regulations to be, available for employment in an employed contributor's employment," a provision modified in regulations.[24] It would seem that the "availability" requirement is included in the subsidiary occupations regulation merely to rule out the argument that the "availability" condition need not be satisfied where there is a subsidiary occupation. It is identical in effect to the unavailable days rule.[25] The only difficulty is the reconciliation of the "availability" requirement with the "consistency" requirement. The distinction drawn in $R(U)$ $2/67$ seems to be that "availability" relates to the claimant in his peculiar subsidiary occupation and that "consistency" relates to that occupation quite apart from the peculiar terms of the claimant's employment in it. It is a distinction, however, which seems not always to be clearly drawn.[26] A number of decisions under the regulation turn upon the question whether the claimant could freely adjust the hours of *his* subsidiary occupation so as to enable him to take a full-time job were it offered.[27] In some of these cases,[28] the question has been treated as one of consistency (*e.g.* "as his part-time accountancy work was done in the evenings it was clearly 'consistent with' general clerical work"; he "could only follow the full-time employment ... by giving up the subsidiary occupation which was therefore clearly inconsistent with the full-time employment"). In $R(U)$ $24/58$, however, it is held that "the fact that a person ... does some work at a subsidiary occupation during normal hours does not prevent him from being available for full-time employment if it is plain that he will at once abandon his subsidiary occupation at any time at which it conflicts with normal full-time work." In $R(U)$ $12/55$, the same factor is regarded as both rendering the occupation inconsistent and the claimant unavailable. The distinction is clearly drawn in $R(U)$ $8/59$, where being

a professional footballer (in general) is held to be consistent with
being a warehouseman or packer, whilst the terms of the claimant's employment as a footballer are not such as to render *him*
unavailable, a distinction adverted to in $R(U)$ *4/64* and emphasised in $R(U)$ *2/67*:

"It cannot in my judgment be sufficient ... for the claimant
to show that on the day for which he claims benefit he could
have given up his occupation without notice and taken full-
time employment immediately in place of the occupation. That
may show that the *Claimant* was available for full-time employment, but not that the *occupation* was consistent with that full-
time employment."

Usual main occupation. If the subsidiary occupation is carried
on under a contract of service, but not otherwise, it must *not* be
the usual main occupation. If it is not carried on under a
contract of service, the condition does not apply. In deciding
whether or not it is carried on under a contract of service, the
usual approach is adopted. In *R 1/63 (UB)*, the claimant worked
as a process server. Those who engaged her (a variety of solicitors) were "not interested or concerned in the manner in which
she carrie(d) out her duties. She may use her discretion when
she will effect service ... and she may use whichever mode of
transport she wishes to carry out her work. There is ... a
complete absence of outside control and direction in the performance of her work" and she was, accordingly, not employed
under a contract of service, so that it did not matter whether it
was her usual main occupation. As to what is a "usual main
occupation" there is very little modern law. Until 1960, the
regulation contained in the requirement that the subsidiary occupation be "different in nature" from the full-time employment
for which she was available.[29] Under this regulation, the subsidiary occupation might have some features in common with the
full-time employment, provided that its nature differed in some
substantial respect. The new phraseology may be regarded as
having relaxed the stringency of this condition somewhat, suggesting that if the occupation is different at all, no disentitlement results. Whether or not "process-serving" was the claimant's
"usual main occupation" was considered, *obiter*, in *R 1/63 (UB)*,
but only in relation to the finding of the local tribunal that a

part-time occupation (such as that of process-server) can never be a person's main occupation. This was rejected by the Northern Ireland Commissioner. If an occupation is a person's only occupation, it must be his main occupation, notwithstanding that *vis-à-vis* another person it might be a subsidiary occupation and that it is only "part-time" work.

What at one time is a main occupation may, of course cease to be so, and vice versa. In *C.U. 30/49 (KL)*, a partner in a boarding-house left during the off-season to take other work. Upon his becoming unemployed in this other work, the question arose as to what was his "usual main occupation." In these circumstances, it was still "boarding-house keeper," but on another occasion, "if he should hereafter become unemployed again, and if he has in that time followed that other occupation long enough to enable one to say that it is his usual employment" benefit would be obtainable.

Critique. It is doubtful if anything more than an earnings rule, if that, is needed in order to achieve the broad objectives of this part of the national insurance scheme. Regulation $7(1)(h)$ does contain a built-in earnings rule—if the earnings exceed 75p per day, benefit cannot be claimed. A claimant must in any case, under section $17(1)(a)$ be available for full-time employment. If he secures the opportunity of it and cannot take it because of his subsidiary occupation, he will normally be disqualified under section $20(1)(b)$ or (c),[30] which rather leaves the "consistency" requirement without any useful function. A person earning under a contract of service would simply not be "unemployed," whether in his usual main occupation or not, and if his earnings are very depressed (as the present earnings rule requires) it seems excessively harsh to deprive him of support because he is doing his usual work. To some extent, his position is ameliorated by family incomes supplement, but this is so whether it is his usual occupation or not, and if it is not, he qualifies for unemployment benefit as well.

If benefit were not payable to any person earning in excess of 75p per day but were payable to any person earning less than that amount, a deal of mainly purposeless complexity would be avoided and a greater approximation to social justice achieved.

It has been suggested that rather than cutting off benefit

entirely at what is still a low level of earnings, it would be more equitable to pay reduced benefit on a sliding scale. The Department has considered this suggestion but rejected it for two reasons. First, it is a fundamental condition for the payment of unemployment benefit to a person who has a part-time job that he be available for full-time work. This principle would be eroded by a sliding scale allowing benefit to people with relatively substantial earnings. Secondly, any form of sliding scale is bound to be administratively complicated and would probably lead to a delay in payments.

The first reason is not compelling. It does not answer the case of the claimant with more than the statutory level earnings who nevertheless *is* available for employment and, in any case, it is not beyond question that the requirement of availability must be maintained at all costs, especially when it is clear that no work is or will be available for the claimant. The second reason is doubtful. The attendant complications are not, apparently, overwhelming where an earnings rule is applied to a benefit, as in retirement pensions, and a delayed payment, even if necessarily so, may be preferable to none at all. As to whether it would be necessary to delay payments, it is an existing practice in some cases to make an interim payment and balance up later.

Days of disqualification

Certain grounds of disqualification are dealt with in the next chapter. Regulation $7(1)(b)$ of the Unemployment, Sickness and Invalidity Benefit regulations prevents a day of disqualification being treated as a day of unemployment.

Low paid employment

Certain employments of a casual or subsidiary nature, or in which a person is employed only to an inconsiderable extent used to be treated as non-employment for contribution purposes. Employments so characterised were non-employment for all purposes and under prior schemes it was held that a day on which a person followed an occupation which was "non-employment" must be treated as a day of unemployment even though he worked for pay on it.[31]

This reasoning is no longer available—there are "non-employed" persons' contributions no longer and the power to disregard certain occupations exists only for the purpose of exempting from liability to pay contributions otherwise payable, or of creating liability to pay which otherwise would not exist.[32]

3. Period of Interruption of Employment

Unemployment benefit is payable in respect of unemployment forming part of a period of interruption of employment.[33] Sickness benefit is payable in respect of a day of incapacity for work forming part of such a period.[34] There is, however, a "three-day rule"[35] under which no benefit is payable for the first three days of any period of interruption of employment. These are commonly called the "waiting days." The reason for the "waiting days" rule is that it relieves the statutory authorities of the administration of a vast number of very small claims. Many schemes, however, seem to find such a burden tolerable.

The "waiting" period was originally one week. It used to be the rule that benefit for the waiting days could eventually be claimed if, during the period of 13 weeks commencing with the first day of a period there were a further nine days of unemployment forming part of the same period but this proviso has now disappeared, not without political controversy.

Any two days of interruption of employment (*i.e.* days either of unemployment or incapacity for work), whether consecutive or not, within a period of six consecutive days, are to be treated as a period of interruption of employment and any two such periods not separated by a period of more than 13 weeks are to be treated as a single period of interruption of employment.

It is to be noted that in deciding whether two periods of interruption of employment must be linked together to form a single period, the 13-week period runs from the end of the first period of interruption of employment.

In deciding whether two days of interruption of employment occur within "six consecutive days," Sundays may be ignored. Other days, however, may not, even though they could not be

ranked as days of unemployment anyway. In *R(U) 33/59*, the
claimant was unemployed on Monday in one week and Tuesday the next. He sought to ignore not only the Sunday but also
the Monday of the second week on the ground that he was disentitled to treat it as a day of unemployment under the normal
idle day rule. It was held that the days did not occur within the
period of six consecutive days.

In *R(U) 12/58*, however, the question was whether Sunday
could be ignored in deciding whether more than 13 weeks had
elapsed between the end of one period of interruption and the
commencement of the next. In this case, the Act contains no
express exception of Sunday and it was accordingly decided that
13 weeks and one day had elapsed between the Saturday in the
first week and the Monday of the 15th.

The statutory authorities require a genuine "interruption of
employment." If therefore it is clearly established that an employer has planned lay-offs mainly with a view to maximising
the benefit rights of his employees, entitlement may be lost. It
must, however, be established that maximising the workers'
entitlement was the predominant if not the sole motive in
making the arrangements.[36]

Effect of Failure to Claim

Regulations[37] provide that a person who fails to make a timeous
claim for benefit shall be disqualified therefor, and that a day of
disqualification cannot be a day of unemployment.[38] Prima
facie, therefore, it looks as though it is within the power of a
claimant to determine whether an old period of interruption of
employment continues or a new one starts, simply by claiming
or not. Regulations, however, also provide that if, but for not
claiming, he would have been entitled to benefit for a day, that
day shall be treated as a day of entitlement for purposes of determining the duration of a period of interruption of employment.
He can escape this consequence only by proving that he did not
intend to cause a new period to commence by declining to
claim.[39]

It remains possible to escape this consequence by ensuring
that conditions of entitlement other than claiming are not fulfilled, such as by making oneself unavailable for work.[40]

4. ADDITIONAL CONDITIONS

In the case of certain peculiar types of occupation, regulations lay down special conditions, and sometimes a relaxation of other conditions, of entitlement to unemployment and other benefits.[41] Title to benefit in the case of share-fishermen has occupied a great deal of the attention of the statutory authorities. Whatever the occupation, however, additional conditions attach if the claimant's employment in it is seasonal in character and the case of seasonal workers therefore requires closer attention.

Seasonal Workers

"The main purpose of insurance against unemployment is to insure against a risk rather than a certainty of unemployment. If a person accepts an occupation where the work and the pay are intermittent and the holiday period is long, he or she must be taken as accepting the employment with those incidents of it."[42]

Work-patterns vary. A person's employment normally continues throughout the year; earnings rates will reflect this fact. A person engaged in this normal employment risks unemployment; its consequence is loss of earnings. Unemployment benefit is designed to fill this gap.

In much the same way that a day's pay can be earned in an eight-hour shift; or a week's pay earned in five days, so also a year's pay can, in some occupations, be earned in six or nine months. It is a settled feature of such work patterns that there will be no work for a substantial part of the calendar year. It may therefore be that unemployment during this part ought not to create need. The fact is that, in many seasonal jobs, need does exist during the off-season. The work with all its defects is taken in default of any better alternative.

The social security scheme nevertheless proceeds on the basis that it is no function of unemployment benefit to provide a means of livelihood during times when the possibility of work is totally lacking. Seasonal workers must fulfil conditions over and above those generally applicable before they can qualify for benefit. This matter is dealt with by the Seasonal Workers Regulation.[43] This regulation defines what is meant by a "seasonal worker" and his "off-season" and then proceeds to set out the additional conditions which he must satisfy.

(i) "Seasonal worker"

A "seasonal worker" is a person whose normal employment is for a part or parts only of a year in an occupation or occupations of which the availability or extent varies at approximately the same time or times in successive years; or any other person who normally restricts his employment to the same, or substantially the same, part or parts only of the year.[44]

By "employment," the regulation means "gainfully occupied under a contract of service." A person so occupied during what would otherwise be an off-season is not a seasonal worker notwithstanding that this occupation is a low-paid subsidiary one which can be ignored for unemployment benefit purposes. He may thus be "unemployed" for unemployment benefit purposes and yet employed throughout the year for purposes of determining whether he is a seasonal worker.[45] It will not, however, suffice that he received a small sum by way of a gratuity during the off-season from his seasonal employer. Such a person is the beneficiary of an act of grace, not an employee.[46]

Characterising an employment as "normal" has proved problematical. It is clear that the fact that a claimant does not desire it is irrelevant[47] as is the fact that he is compelled by circumstances under his control to take it or is anxious to change it.[48] It is, equally, settled that "the primary question raised by the definition is not whether a claimant follows an occupation which is of a seasonal nature, but whether he ... is a seasonal worker."[49] The definition "relates not to the industry generally, but to the circumstances of the individual claimant. It is therefore possible for two claimants working alongside in the same industry to have a different status according to the individual employment record."[50] "What has to be considered is whether the particular occupation which is followed is of a seasonal nature and it is none the less so because other people follow it permanently and not seasonally."[51] Furthermore, the definition speaks of "normal" employment and not an "only" employment.[52] If, however, the claimant is in fact "normally employed" for a certain part of the year, it does not matter that

that employment is in different occupations in different years. He is, nonetheless, a seasonal worker.[53]

What "normal employment" means is, therefore, fairly clear. The difficulty attends determining, in any given case, what the claimant's "normal employment" is. The difficulties have been considerably eased by the adoption by the Commissioner of a "three-year rule":

The three-year rule

"In a case where he has followed such employment for three years or more without substantial employment in the off-season in any of those years there is a strong presumption that his normal employment is of a seasonal nature and that he has become a seasonal worker within the meaning of the regulations even though it is his age or infirmity or other circumstances beyond his control which have prevented him from obtaining employment all the year round. This presumption could only be rebutted by showing that the last three years do not afford a proper basis for estimating the person's prospect of employment, for example because his failure to obtain substantial employment in the off-season was due to abnormal conditions in industry or other exceptional circumstances."[54]

The rule speaks of a period of "three years or more." In the absence of any good reason for going back more than three years, the three-year period should be adhered to.[55] One year, it seems, means nothing; two could be coincidence; normality is, prima facie, created by three years' consistency. The function of the rule is, however, purely evidentiary and if, for some good reason, that evidentiary function would not be discharged by adhering to the three-year period, it may be departed from. Cognisably abnormal years can be omitted and the period lengthened accordingly.[56] Or it may be that normality can be clearly established in less than three years, as might be the case where a claimant had clearly taken a different employment with established characteristics on a permanent basis, or even contracted to work in his existing employment for the future only on a seasonal basis.[57] Clearly, a person cannot frustrate the three-year rule merely by declining the seasonal work during the third year.[58]

There have been some changes of mind by Commissioners as
to when the three-year period begins and ends. At first, the rule
was that the three years involved were those dating back from
the date of claim.[59] Subsequently, a Tribunal of Commissioners
refused to accept a shortening of the period by having reference
to the past three on-seasons only.[60] Later still, another tribunal
in effect accepted a lengthening of the period by taking as the
date from which one counted back the three years, the date not
of claim but of the end of the latest spell of work in the seasonal
employment thus excluding from the calculation any part of the
alleged current off-season.[61] The latest decision[62] accepts the
argument, rejected in previous cases, (though left open in *R(U)*
6/64) that the delimitation of the three-year period should have
regard to the definition of "year" in the regulation. That definition is "the period of 12 months commencing with the first day
in the calendar year on which the person concerned begins a
period of normal employment."[63]

Operation of the "three-year rule"

"If, after examining a claimant's employment history and
applying those tests, it was found that the claimant had had for
three consecutive years ... no 'substantial amount of employment' in his off-season, he was normally to be held to be a
seasonal worker, but, if he was found to have had a 'substantial
amount of employment' (*i.e.* normally one-fourth)[64] in his off-
season in one or more of those years he was not to be held to be
a seasonal worker." In making this determination, "regard shall
be had to factors inherent in the nature or conditions of the
occupation or occupations in which that person is engaged and
not to factors abnormal to that occupation or occupations notwithstanding that those factors persist for a prolonged period."[65]
In *R(U)* *14/61* the majority of a tribunal of commissioners
attached importance to "a factor inherent in the occupation of
fishing, that the presence of fish in any given area at any
time may be uncertain and unpredictable" whilst the minority
decision turned upon the fact that "the adverse weather conditions which resulted in the absence of winter fishing were ...
a factor abnormal to the occupation and not inherent in it."[66]

Rebuttal of the presumption

The three-year rule creates a presumption. It is rebuttable. The mere fact that the claimant has had an occasional and in-considerable spell of off-season work will not suffice to rebut the presumption that he is a seasonal worker if that is the pre-dominant feature of his three-year record.[67]

Change of normality

One who has been a seasonal worker may have ceased to be so. This might be the case because the seasonal employment had ceased to exist[68] or because the worker has, with justifi-cation, genuinely abandoned all hope of ever again securing employment in his seasonal work.[69] Even where he remains in the same job, the character of his work may change. What was seasonal work may become non-seasonal work. Once the status of a seasonal worker has been acquired, however, it will nor-mally be retained in the absence of any clear evidence as to its loss, until the three-year rule has again operated, this time in the claimant's favour. This means that he must be able to point to a three-year period in which he has had substantial work in what would formerly have been his off-season.[70]

The burden of proof rests on the claimant to prove that he has ceased to be a seasonal worker and he will not normally be able to do this until a change has taken effect.[71]

The "on" season

Seasonal work may be involuntary (*i.e.* attributable to the fact that the work itself is of a limited availability or extent) or voluntary (*i.e.* attributable to the fact that the claimant has re-stricted his employment in it). Where it is involuntary, the availability or extent of the work must be for part or parts only of a year which vary at approximately the same time or times in successive years.[72] Here, "approximately" is the key word. The dates of the "on season" need not coincide exactly each year. Nor can a fixed margin of variation be determined for what would be tolerable for would vary with the length of the "on season." "The length of the spells of employment concerned

may have a bearing on the matter.... If a person did a week's
work in the first week of January, and in the following year a
week's work in the first week of March, I certainly would not
regard these, with a variation of nine and a half weeks, as being
at approximately the same times in successive years" said the
Northern Ireland Commissioner in a case where the spells
averaged 12 weeks with a variation of eight and a half weeks.
This he regarded as a borderline case, coming down on balance
against the claimant being a seasonal worker;[73] whilst in $R(U)$
8/62, where the average spell was of seven months' duration, the
Commissioner decided that the claimant was a seasonal worker
notwithstanding that the variation was nine to ten weeks.[74]

Where the seasonal character of the work is due to the
claimant's restricting his employment, the requirement is that
the work must be restricted to "the same, or substantially the
same, part or parts only of the year."[75] The meaning attributed
to this phrase by the regulation indicates that spells on work can
be aggregated and that if the total spells off work do not exceed
seven weeks the status of seasonal worker and its accompanying
disabilities are not acquired. In calculating this period of seven
weeks, however, public holidays must be included even though
they could not constitute days of unemployment.[76]

In a sense, of course, anyone who chooses to work in an occupation where there is a likelihood of periodic unemployment
may be said to be restricting his employment opportunities.
This, however, will not suffice. For him to "restrict" his employment, it seems that the opportunity of more extended employment must have been open to him.[77]

(ii) The "off" season

The statutory definition of this term is that it connotes the
spells off work in aggregate, ignoring, for this purpose, spells of
seven days or less. By inference from the regulation considered
above, an off-season cannot consist of less than seven weeks.[78]

Where there is just one single spell in work in a season and
one spell off, the on- and off-seasons are readily distinguishable.
Both, however, may consist of an aggregate of spells on or off
work. It will readily be seen that according as to what spells are
aggregated, the on-season may be longer or shorter. The more

spells that are aggregated and the longer the on-season consequently is, the greater will be the amount of work required to
constitute "a substantial amount of work in the off-season" and
the fewer will be the spells available to count towards it. In some
such instances, no problem will arise for such spells as do not
meet the basic criteria for seasonal work (*i.e.* the extent varying
at approximately the same time or times in successive years)
cannot be included in the on-season. Logically, such as do meet
these criteria should be included in the on-season, but Commissioners have been more generous in their interpretation. The
on-season should consist of the period of more or less continuous
employment in the year. "Where a claimant has only short
periods of employment at irregular intervals and of irregular
duration during a period of the year during which he is for the
most part normally unemployed, it is appropriate to treat the
whole of this period as prima facie the off-season, and the
occasional irregular work as work obtained by the claimant in
the off-season" rather than aggregate it as part of the on-
season.[79]

Determination of the "on" and "off" seasons

Unless it is inappropriate, for example because the spells are
abnormal,[80] the commencement and termination of the "on"
and "off" seasons are determined by reference to the "three-year
rule," *i.e.* the average dates of commencement and termination
in the three full years are taken as being the limits of the normal
season.[81] By the same token, the average lengths of these seasons
are taken to be the normal lengths of seasons.[82]

(iii) Additional conditions to be satisfied by seasonal workers

The additional conditions for receipt of benefit (which apply
only to claims in respect of unemployment during the off-season)
are as follows:

1. Registration for employment through the two years preceding the date of claim (or since the claimant became a seasonal
worker if he did so within the two-year period) except for:

(a)   periods when incapable of work;
(b)   inconsiderable periods; and

(c) temporary periods of non-availability by reason of
     domestic necessity, compulsion of law or "any other cir-
     cumstances ... of an exceptional character;" *and*

2. Having done or having prospects of doing a "substantial
amount" of work during the off-season.[83]

So far as the first condition is concerned, the obligation to
register for work is removed only in the cases expressly stipulated.
It is no excuse that the claimant was self-employed.[84] As to what
amounts to an "inconsiderable period" of non-registration, a
period of nine days has been held to be "inconsiderable"[85] whilst
periods of 12[86], 19[87] and more[88] days have been held to be
considerable. The mere fact that the claimant lives at a distance
from the local employment exchange will not constitute "circumstances ... of an exceptional character."[89] Engaging in six
weeks of study during an off-season in order to improve one's
qualifications has been held to do so.[90]

In examining whether the second condition is fulfilled, the
statutory authorities have first to determine what work is done
or in prospect during the off-season, and then to determine
whether it is sufficient to meet the condition. In discharging the
first of these tasks, little difficulty is occasioned in determining
what work *has been* done. It is clearly proper to take into account
the number of days by which the actual "on" season in a
particular year obtrudes into what is normally the "off" season.[91]
Both in respect of work done and work in prospect, work in
another district should be taken into account.[92] The chief difficulty is encountered in making an estimate of the work in
prospect during a particular off-season. It frequently happens
that what was "in prospect" at the time when the claim was
made has become "in retrospect" by the time an appeal comes
to be heard. This fact yields a convenient device for disposing
of appeals (not available to the insurance officer processing the
original claim) for "what in fact has happened is prima facie
evidence of what could reasonably have been expected to happen"[93] although "on investigation this evidence may turn out to
be of no weight because it may be shown that what happened
was so exceptional that no reasonable person could have expected
it at the material time."[94] The presumption thus created may
be rebutted[95] if, for example, the unanticipated work was
fortuitous[96] or exceptional[97] or had no reasonable bearing on

what was expected to happen.[98] The appeal in such cases savours of a review; indeed, the question may arise by way of a review and falls to be disposed of in the same way.[99]

The "three-year rule" may be used to determine the amount of work reasonably in prospect. Again, however, it is to be remembered that the rule is evidentiary only and if there is clear reason to suppose that the off-season employment available in the past is unlikely to be available in the current season, it will not help the claimant.[1]

Once it has been settled what work has been done or is in prospect, it remains to be decided whether it satisfies the requirements of the regulation. The regulation in fact offers a definition of what is a "substantial amount of employment" during the off-season. It must be "equal in duration to not less than one-fourth (or such other fractional part as the determining authority may, in the circumstances of any particular case, consider reasonable) of the current off-season." The determining authority has thus first to determine what fraction is reasonable. Taken literally, the regulation would allow the fixing of a part greater than one-fourth. However, "it would never be reasonable to take this course; the authorities must fix one-fourth of the current off-season or some lesser fraction. The regulation leaves them an unfettered discretion in fixing this lesser fraction but the discretion must be exercised judicially and certain considerations should be borne in mind," such as that since it is permitted not to register in certain circumstances (*e.g.* domestic necessity, compulsion of law) it seems reasonable to disregard such periods in deciding the dimensions of the off-season one-fourth of which should be worked.[2] Subject to this, the appropriate fraction is one fourth unless there are exceptional reasons for departing from it[3] and even a fraction of a day less than one-quarter of the off-season will result in disentitlement.[4]

Once the appropriate fraction has been determined, it is a matter of deciding the length of the off-season, usually by reference to the three-year rule, taking the appropriate fraction of it and measuring it against the sum of the days actually worked and in prospect.[5]

One question remains unanswered. It is a not infrequent occurrence for a person to be incapacitated for work during his off-season. This clearly relieves him from the first condition (registration for employment) and there is authority for the proposition that such a period should be disregarded in deciding the dimensions of the off-season.[6] There is also authority for the proposition that such a period should be disregarded in deciding of work in order to constitute a "substantial amount" of employment[7] and that it should be ignored altogether.[8] It will be obvious that disentitlement might or might not result according to the manner in which the incapacity is taken account of. The authorities can be reconciled. If the illness is chronic so as to be an enduring influence in the claimant's work pattern, it should be ignored.[9] If it is exceptional, it should be excluded from the off-season[10] unless it clearly constitutes an interruption of the off-season work and therefore consists of days on which the claimant would otherwise have worked, in which case the days of incapacity can be counted as days of work.[11]

Conclusion

Once the assumptions on which the seasonal workers rules stand are made, a complex and somewhat arbitrary set of rules becomes inevitable. Those assumptions are questionable.

First of all, it is not at all certain that, in the case of a worker during his off-season, we are dealing with a case where unemployment is a certainty. In a sense, it is a "certainty" in many occupations that unemployment will occur in the course of the working life but we do not deny benefit when the event falls in. It is not so much a matter of certainty or not, as of degrees of risk. And once it is recognised as being a matter of degree, the whole principle of excluding from benefit becomes questionable.

Secondly, we do not know whether the assumptions we make about seasonal work are at all warranted. We know nothing about the characteristics of the workers involved or of their earning patterns.

The rules are, at the time of writing under review.

SUMMARY

One thing at least should be obvious from the foregoing. Legislators and the statutory authorities have taken great pains to try and adjust the unemployment scheme to the realities of the industrial situation. It is, however, a difficult task even to approach near perfection and in at least two respects the scheme should be questioned.

First of all, it might be thought that an efficient system of social security would offer protection against all forms of failure of earnings from work but as we have seen, the United Kingdom schemes depart from this apparently simple model at a number of points. The most obvious of these is the fact that unemployment benefit is a short-term benefit—chronic unemployment is outside its purview. Another concerns the contributory nature of the scheme—the persistence of the Beveridge insurance principle in spite of the fact that substantial Exchequer contributions have throughout been needed in order to give the system even the appearance of a vague actuarial soundness. In relation to unemployment benefit in particular, we have seen that benefit may be payable on various grounds although work is available as an alternative whilst on the other hand and on other grounds it may be denied although it is perfectly clear that no work is obtainable.

Secondly, if one looks at many of the complexities of the unemployment benefit scheme one observes that they are directed towards the problem of temporary very short-term unemployment. It is, of course, perfectly true that from the individual worker's standpoint, he is left in need of the means of subsistence whether he has been finally dismissed or merely temporarily laid off. The national insurance fund is, however, not the only source of relief to which he might look. The fact that the fund picks up the burden means that the employer is enabled to off-load some of the costs of his business, *i.e.* wage costs in slack periods, whilst in the analogous case of other costs he must continue to bear the burden and spread it over good times and bad times alike. There is no public fund which will take over the lease of his factory during a shut-down; his bank does not suspend interest on his overdraft when production stops. Yet the rest of the country's work force and other contributors are required to take over the costs of his workers when he does not require them. The unemployment benefit scheme does not merely facilitate this by acknowledging that a man who is still under contract to an employer is unemployed for benefit purposes. It encourages it by giving him a right to hold out for a considerable time for re-employment in his old job.

Ogus has summarised the arguments admirably.[12] First, it is undesirable from an economic and social viewpoint that other contributors should subsidise those industries which regularly lay off workers temporarily. This represents a transfer of resources from enterprises offering steady employment to those where it is capricious. On the margin, an enterprise which, unemployment benefit apart, is economically unviable may survive whilst a sound one may fail. Secondly, (a fact recognised to some extent in the somewhat arbitrary and unjust "waiting days rule") the administrative costs of paying benefit for short spells is unduly high. Thirdly, employment agencies which are closely involved in the administration of unemployment benefit are not geared to providing temporary work as an alternative to benefit.

Present levels and methods of payment of wages are such that it is not feasible to expect the employee to bear the cost of temporary unemployment (although in the case of a seasonal worker and the self-employed, he may be required to). Ogus argues, and there is much to be said for his view, that the employer could bear the burden more cheaply and distribute the cost through the price of goods and services to the consumer. To some extent, the Contracts of Employment legislation has tended in this direction but it would require near-universal guarantee agreements to warrant the appropriate change in the benefit system, *e.g.* by making unemployment benefit unpayable for the first week. A start has been made with the Employment Protection Act 1975 but there is still some way to go.

CHAPTER 5

DISQUALIFICATION FOR UNEMPLOYMENT BENEFIT

CERTAIN grounds of disqualification apply to all benefits under the scheme. Examples are being absent from Great Britain (or Northern Ireland as the case may be)[1]; undergoing imprisonment or detention in legal custody[2]; and failure, without good cause for the delay, to claim within the stipulated time.[3] Apart from these general grounds, however, certain other grounds are peculiar to specific benefits. This is the case with unemployment benefit.

"The basic purpose of unemployment insurance is to provide against the misfortune of unemployment happening against a person's will $(R(U)$ $20/64$, para. 8). But the ... Acts do not go so far as to exclude, from insurance cover, all self-induced unemployment...." The legislation "imposes a disqualification ... not in every conceivable case of self-induced unemployment, but only in certain specific instances."[4] Thus, whilst the general principle underlying the various grounds of disqualification is that benefit should not be paid to a claimant who has brought about his own misfortune, he actually loses his right to benefit only in the specific circumstances stated in the legislation; and the onus is upon the insurance officer to establish that this is so.

Two main heads of disqualification are considered below. One of them contains a number of sub-heads each stating a separate ground of disqualification. In claims before the statutory authorities there are no rigid pleadings and it is possible for a claimant, initially disqualified on one ground, to find the first ground abandoned on appeal and the refusal of benefit argued to be justified on an alternative ground. It is in fact open to a tribunal to consider whether or not a claimant is disqualified on grounds other than those relied upon in the decision appealed from[5] but in such a case, special precautions should be taken in order to ensure that the claimant is not prejudiced by the surprise. The tribunal should ensure that the new ground is explained to the claimant so that he may be enabled to speak to it, the record should show in terms that this has been done[6] and it might well be that an adjournment would be the proper course for the tribunal to take where a claimant would not otherwise be able adequately to defend himself from the new charge.

The two main heads of disqualification concern: 1. loss of employment by reason of a stoppage of work due to a trade dispute; and 2. self-induced unemployment. They differ *inter alia* in that in the case of the trade dispute disqualification the disqualification lasts so long as the stoppage continues, whilst in the case of self-induced unemployment it lasts for a period of up to six weeks. It can happen, however, that where one ground of disqualification is followed, during or at the end of the period of disqualification, by another (such as unreasonably refusing an offer of suitable employment), a second term of disqualification may follow upon the first. It is perfectly possible, by continuing to induce one's own unemployment, to remain disqualified indefinitely.[7]

1. The Trade Dispute Disqualification

Disqualification for unemployment benefit because of a trade dispute has been a feature of the national insurance scheme since its inception in 1911 and its history is pithily summarised in the Report of the Royal Commission on Trade Unions and Employers' Associations 1965–1968 under the Chairmanship of Lord Donovan.[8] "At the outset the problem presented itself as to what was to happen when persons became unemployed, not through the ordinary fluctuations of trade or business, but because of industrial dispute. The purpose of the insurance scheme was to protect those who lost their employment because of such fluctuations, and not because of strikes or lockouts" (*ibid.* para 956). The difficulty is that strike or lock-out, in addition to having the direct result of rendering participants unemployed, may have further repercussions eventually becoming indistinguishable from the ordinary fluctuations of trade or business. Workers may be laid off because of an unavailability of parts due to a strike elsewhere. A lockout may increase the supply of labour in a particular locality and cause others totally unconnected with the dispute to lose work. Benefit may properly be regarded as payable in such cases, provided there is no other closer connection with the original dispute. The problem is where to draw the line before such remote effects, for if disqualification were confined to actual strikers it would be possible, by a withdrawal of labour by a few key workers, to provoke lay-offs of many workers who could thus be sustained by social security benefits even though very much involved in the original dispute. The law which we shall be examining is the result of efforts to solve this problem.

It is sometimes stated that the approach of government to this problem should be and is one of neutrality. "The merits of the dispute are not relevant. It simply does not matter how unreasonable one or other of the parties to the dispute have been. Moreover, while it is necessary that the claimant should have lost employment by reason of a stoppage of work which was due to the trade dispute, it doesn't matter whether he ceased employment following a strike or lock-out."[9] In this respect, however, a number of points are worth noting:

1. If "neutrality" means that unemployment benefit should ignore the strike or lockout and its consequences, then it fails to do so, for it does award benefit in some situations (such as those instanced above).

2. If, on the other hand, "neutrality" means that it should treat employer and employee alike in the administration of benefits, then no matter how adequately formal neutrality is achieved (both sides are equally denied benefit) substantially it is not, for only one side would be entitled anyway.

3. If "neutrality" consists in withholding benefit from a party at fault, again it fails. For quite apart from the problem of attributing "fault" in the case of a strike (*cf.* a capricious reduction of wages and a "blackmail" demand for double wages), it treats strikes (where workers take the initiative) and lockouts (where employers take the initiative) alike.

In some circumstances, indeed, disqualification seems to operate as a sanction in breach of neutrality. In *R(U) 41/56*, colliery repairers laid off as a result of a strike who would otherwise have been entitled to benefit became disqualified by refusing to work as "brushers" in which capacity they would not have been asked to work (although they were contractually required to work) but for the strike. Disqualification is here being thrust upon persons not involved in the dispute, but made to become participants in it by virtue of the act of one party, the employers, requiring them to "blackleg." The same reasoning would apparently apply even if there were no contractual obligation to do the work.[10]

The basic trouble is that some strikes and lockouts are reasonable and others are not. Some lockouts are the equivalent of unfair dismissal (in which case benefit would almost certainly otherwise be payable) whilst some strikes may amount to an unjustifiable refusal such as would otherwise disentitle or disqualify. In $R(U)$ *19/53*, in order to enforce new (and, as the employees conceived it, less favourable) terms upon employees, the employer gave them notice of termination of existing contracts and offered fresh contracts on the new terms. The stoppage which in fact was constituted by the refusal to accept the fresh contracts was treated as being due to a trade dispute and disqualification ensued. This reasoning would apply equally if the proposal was to cut wages by 99 per cent. In such a case, there can be little doubt that such an offer would not be "suitable" or "reasonable" for purposes of disqualification under the heading of self-induced unemployment but this, as the Commissioner in $R(U)$ *19/53* asserts, is irrelevant. Equally, it would seem to apply if the dismissals were wrongful, for there is authority for the proposition that the right to benefit may be lost even in a case of wrongful dismissal, if it is in pursuance of a trade dispute.[11] In none of these circumstances is it any justification of the existing law that the statutory authorities would be involved in difficult problems of evaluation of the merits of a dispute. They are presently involved in just such problems in deciding upon the "suitableness" of an offer or the "reasonableness" of a refusal for purposes of disqualification under the other heading.

One is left with the fact that industrial disputes often have important political overtones and that the law's blank refusal to evaluate their merits is referable as much to desire to avoid involving the statutory authorities in political controversy as to spare them administrative unease. To the extent that the law is regarded as unsatisfactory, it may well be solely because it seeks to abandon the quest for justice in order to avoid controversy. By doing so, however, the risk that the statutory authorities would forfeit the confidence of workers, which they presently enjoy, is avoided.

The Act provides that "A person who has lost employment as an employed earner by reason of a stoppage of work which was due to a trade dispute at his place of employment shall be disqualified for receiving unemployment benefit so long as the stoppage continues. . . ."[12] Notwithstanding that he is thus prima facie disqualified, a claimant may still escape if he can establish either of two things:

1. That, "during the stoppage, he has become bona fide employed elsewhere in the occupation which he usually follows or has become regularly engaged in some other occupation" or

2. "That he is not participating in *or financing* or directly interested in the trade dispute which caused the stoppage of work; *and that he does not belong to a grade or class of workers of which, immediately before the commencement of the stoppage, there were members employed at his place of employment any of whom are participating in or financing or directly interested in the dispute.*"[13]

The repeal of the italicised words above is proposed in the Employment Protection Act 1975[14] which, however, at the time of writing, has not yet been brought into force in this respect.

The trade dispute disqualification is a complex provision. It applies to supplementary benefit claims as well as to unemployment benefit claims (appeals in both respects going to national insurance tribunals). It is of considerable social and economic importance. Each phrase has its own meaning and function and the law is best appreciated by considering each phrase separately.

(a) *Losing Employment by Reason of a Stoppage of Work*

At least three types of problem may arise in connection with determining whether there has been a "stoppage of work":

(i) whether a "stoppage" consists in the cessation of workmen's labour or in the halting of the process of production at his place of employment;

(ii) whether, and if so in what circumstances, a partial cessation may amount to a "stoppage";

(iii) where A takes industrial action with the result that B's employment is affected, whether the disqualification provision is concerned with A's or B's employment or both, in determining whether there has been a "stoppage."

The first of these questions arose in argument in *R 4/63 (UB)* where nine members of a workforce of 12 engaged in drilling operations in connection with a geological survey went on strike. The three non-strikers were, however, able to keep the drilling operations going. The case was actually disposed of on the ground that notwithstanding that drilling continued there was, nevertheless "a sufficient interference with the labouring activities on the site to mean that work which could have been done but for the dispute was prevented from being done." *Obiter*, however, the Commissioner did express a tentative view that "'stoppage of work' refers to the cessation of the workmen's labour rather than the stoppage of the work of the factory."[15]

The answers evolved by the statutory authorities to the second question above fit neatly with that evolved to the first. It has been decided that a work to rule does not amount to a "stoppage of work" notwithstanding that it causes considerable unemployment to others and regardless, presumably, of the fact that it necessarily interferes with the process of production at the place of work.[16] At the same time, an actual cessation need not be total provided it involved an appreciable number of employees.[17] In *215/49 (UB)* 190 workers out of a total workforce of 1,400 were held to suffice. Where a "go-slow" provokes dismissals of those involved in it (*i.e.* a lockout), those dismissals constitute a "stoppage."[18]

The third question poses a problem one solution to which is implicit in *19/59 (UB)*. There, notwithstanding that the industrial action brought about a cessation of the work of many other workers, there was no "stoppage." Those who lost work did so "because the volume of work at the firm diminished as a result of a trade dispute, but not because of a stoppage since there was no stoppage." The reasoning here is not compelling but the actual decision fully accords with the policy underlying this head of disqualification. The same cannot be said of *R(U) 3/69* in which workers laid off as a result of the action of pickets were held to have "stopped" notwithstanding that they were not parties to the original dispute. And little consolation is to be derived from the rationalisation there adopted, that the two groups of workers were involved in a separate "trade dispute" resulting in the "stoppage."[19] Suppose that picketing by workers in dispute who are not stopped interrupts the flow of materials so that other workers are stopped. It is surely more in accordance with the policy of the disqualification provision to allow benefit than to disallow it (on the reasoning in $R(U)$ $3/69$) on the ground that they have lost employment by reason of a stoppage due to a trade dispute.

(b) *Whether the Unemployment is "By Reason of" a Stoppage "Due to" a Dispute*

The question frequently recurs whether a person unemployed for an allegedly extraneous cause is in fact disqualified under this head. Obviously questions of causation are involved here. The terminology of the section poses two questions of causation: (1) whether the unemployment is "by reason of" the stoppage; (2) whether the stoppage is "due to" the dispute. In many situations, these two questions are not clearly distinguished in the authorities. Due in part to the fact that under the above-mentioned interpretation of "stoppage" the loss of the employment and stoppage of work are often the same thing, the question which most frequently emerges is the simple one of whether the unemployment in respect of which benefit is claimed is attributable to the trade dispute or not.

On the one hand, there are cases where the occurrence of a stoppage subsequent to the claimant's becoming unemployed is totally unconnected with his loss of work. Here,[20] *e.g.* where the claimant has been finally discharged for other reasons regardless of the dispute, no disqualification results. Discharge before a stoppage is not, however, necessarily unconnected with it. Thus, where the claimant has voluntarily left his employment in anticipation of a strike[21] a sufficient connection is established and disqualification results. In the two earlier of these cases, it seems to be suggested that notice (*e.g.* by means of strike notice) of the impending stoppage must have been issued, but in the latter case, this requirement is dispensed with. "The claimant must have known that ... the stoppage of work would occur" notwithstanding that actual strike notice had not been given. The same principle applies where the claimant is disabled by the stoppage from resuming work after a lay-off[22]; and where he has been finally discharged in anticipation of the stoppage.[23]

In all these decisions, the causal connection must be positively established, though it may be inferred from the surrounding circumstances.[24] In the case of certain types of employment, however, this may be extremely difficult to prove. Umpires under the pre-War legislation thus evolved the "12-day rule" to cover such cases, and it has been received into the post-War scheme: "In the case of a worker whose employment is irregular or intermittent it may be difficult to decide when a stoppage of work due to a trade dispute occurs during one of his workless spells, whether his lack of employment is due to the trade dispute or to normal unemployment. The Umpire therefore ruled that if an employee whose employment was irregular has been out of work for more than twelve days before the stoppage due to the trade dispute begins, his lack of work (after the stoppage has begun) will be presumed to be due to normal unemployment and benefit will be payable. If however, a stoppage due to a trade dispute occurs at premises, where he normally works, twelve days or less after his last employment his lack of work (after the stoppage has begun) will be presumed to be due to the stoppage and he will thus be disqualified for receiving unemployment benefit. In any case, either presumption can be rebutted by satisfactory evidence."[25] Sundays are included in the 12-day period.[26] The burden of proof that the unemployment is not due to the stoppage rests upon the claimant where he loses work within the 12-day period[27]; otherwise, it rests upon the insurance officer.

The presumptions created by the 12-day rule can be rebutted. All the cases, however, concern rebuttal of the disqualifying presumption by the claimant. Whilst it remains doctrinally possible for a claimant discharged more than 12 days before the stoppage to be disqualified as a result of rebuttal by the insurance officer of the presumption operating in the claimant's favour in such a case, there is no reported decision where that has happened. The claimant may rebut by proving that he would have continued to be unemployed notwithstanding the stoppage, *e.g.* because of redundancies in the labour force[28] which may be inferred from the fact that others laid off when the claimant was laid off have been reinstated.[29] On the other hand, it will not do merely to establish that the particular work on which the claimant was engaged has come to an end, for there might, but for the stoppage, have been other work for him to do.[30]

Whilst the 12-day rule has been expressly received into the post-War doctrine[31] its modern relevance has recently been doubted, at least in relation to the type of work to which it has been most commonly applied, *i.e.* dock work. "There is an obvious element of arbitrariness in this so-called rule; and it may well be that, having regard to the general decasualisation of dock labour, the inference or presumption which it embodies is less readily justifiable nowadays in relation to dockers." However, "I simply reserve my opinion as to the validity and applicability of the rule in present-day circumstances."[32] Mature reflection might justify the survival of the rule at all events in relation to other types of irregular or casual employment.

In none of the above cases is a distinction drawn between the two causal requirements above referred to. In the rather peculiar situations contemplated by some decisions, however, such a distinction seems to have a place. These are cases where there are two independent potential causes for the unemployment, either of which would, by itself, be sufficient. Here, the approach differs according as to whether the disqualifying event occurs first in time. If it occurs first, it causes disqualification throughout the period of the stoppage notwithstanding that some other event, which would also have caused the unemployment, supervenes.[33] If, however, the unemployment is originally caused by a non-disqualifying event, no disqualification results so long as that first cause continues to operate,[34] though once it ceases to operate, disqualification may ensue.[35] The contrast is neatly pointed by $R(U)$ *11/52* and $R(U)$ *12/61*. In the former case, the claimant was given notice before the stoppage took place, effective after it had started. He was held to be disqualified throughout the stoppage, notwithstanding that he would in any case have been unemployed once his notice took effect.[36] In the latter case, the claimant was suspended three days before the stoppage and would normally have resumed work four days after its commencement. Here, the disqualification only operated after the first four days. These decisions are more easily understood if they are related to the first causal requirement, *i.e.* that the loss of employment must be "by reason off" a stoppage, always remembering however that once a loss so caused is identified, disqualification continues "so long as the stoppage of work continues."

In one other situation, attention is focused exclusively upon one only of the causal elements outlined above, this time whether the stoppage of work is "due to" a trade dispute. In $R(U)$ *17/52* there was undoubtedly a trade dispute at the place of work, and the claimant had undoubtedly lost employment, along with a number of others, by reason of a stoppage. But it was found as a fact that the stoppage (occasioned by dismissal of the men concerned) was referable not to the trade dispute but to the employer's determination, at an opportune time when materials were short, to get rid of men whom he regarded as troublemakers.[37]

(c) *Trade Dispute*

"Trade dispute" is partially defined as "any dispute between employers and employees, or between employees and employees, which is connected with the employment or non-employment or the terms of employment or the conditions of employment of any persons, whether employees in the employment of the employer with whom the dispute arises, or not."[38] This is described as a partial definition because it is confined to declaring the parties between whom a trade dispute may subsist and what its subject matter may be. On the question of the essential nature of a "dispute" it is silent. Other authorities are not and a considerable doctrine has developed.

It is clearly possible for there to be a difference or issue without there actually being a "dispute." "A question between employer and employee (or, presumably, between employees and employees) must reach a certain stage of contention before it may properly be termed a dispute."[39] However, "to say that there is no 'dispute' until hostile action has been taken seems to me to confuse the 'dispute' with the 'stoppage.'"[40] The mere fact that a difference may be classified as an "issue" for the purposes of other legislation, does not mean that it cannot be a "dispute" for unemployment benefit purposes.[41] The "dispute" need not involve the claimant as a party. It is enough that he suffer loss of employment by reason of a stoppage due to a dispute between other parties[42] provided, of course, that the other requirements of the trade dispute disqualification are satisfied.

"Dispute" is, it seems, confined in its operation to the area of legitimate difference. Whilst the law purports to adopt a neutral stance, this is only so where the parties are legally free to differ. Where the difference arises because the employer refuses to do something which he is required by law to do, there is no "dispute" and no disqualification results if unemployment occurs in consequence.[43] Similar reasoning might be thought to apply where one or other of the parties is in breach of contract or even a non-binding collective agreement. This, indeed was once the law but is authoritatively considered to be so no longer.[44] This reasoning would, however, apply equally in the case where employees were in breach of the law, and locked out by an employer. It would be highly anomalous if, in such a case, the penalty of disqualification could be avoided and there is obvious scope for the maxim *ex turpi causa non oritur actio*. It is, however, clear that mere failure to comply with the non-binding recommendations of some body, albeit under authority of statute, does not fall under his heading. In such a case, there may well be a "dispute" and disqualification would ensue.[45]

The "trade" element in a "trade dispute" is present if there is an appropriate dispute "between employers and employees or between employees and employees. . . ." Disqualification may thus extend to one losing employment as a result of picketing in consequence of another dispute between the picketing faction and their employers, for here there arises a second and distinct dispute between the claimant's faction and the pickets.[46] It is, however, submitted that the decisions in the above cases may be doubted in the light of the fact that unlawful picketing seems to have been used. In such a case (*i.e.* where the difference arises as a result of the illegal conduct of one of the parties under the above-mentioned doctrine) there would seem to be no cognisable "dispute." It is certainly to be doubted whether the policy of disqualification embraces such a case.

The statutory definition of "trade dispute" seems to be broader than at first glance it might seem. Where A employs B and C a trade dispute can clearly subsist between A and B and B and C. However, where X is employed by another, a dispute can also subsist as between A and X and, apparently, between B and X.[47] In other words, there can be a dispute between an employer and one who is an employee albeit of a different employer; and between employees of different employers.

It is possible for one who is not, according to general principles of contract law, an "employee" nevertheless to be treated as such for purposes of disqualification. This is certainly so in the case of persons who, though in fact self-employed, are treated as "employed" for contribution purposes.[48] $R(U)$ *32/57* poses a different question. Here, several employees including the claimant were dismissed and the rest stopped work in sympathy. The dismissal resulted from a disagreement about work targets which had been a matter of controversy for some time. The claimant was held to be disqualified, *i.e.* to be an "employee" for the purposes of the disqualification provision, notwithstanding that his dismissal had terminated the employment, on the basis that his dismissal was an incident in a continuing "dispute" even though that the actual stoppage resulted from the dismissals. The implication is, however, that he could not have been disqualified, not being an employee, had the "dispute" been born of his dismissal.[49] $R(U)$ *32/57* may be explained on the ground that the dismissal was "furtherance" not "severance."[50]

The dispute must be "connected with the employment or non-employment or the terms of employment or the conditions of employment of any persons. . . ." The definition thus seems to embrace any dispute as to what should or should not be made the subject of a contractual term between the parties though not where action is motivated by personal as opposed to trade considerations.[51] It used to include a dispute as to whether or not compulsory membership or non-membership of a trade union should be a term of the contract of employment[52]; after some considerable doubt due to proscription of the closed shop by the now-repealed Industrial Relations Act 1971 this view probably now represents the law again.

It seems, according to $R(U)$ *26/59*, that a dispute, not as to whether a particular stipulation *should be* a term or condition of the contract but as to whether it *is* such, is not a trade dispute. In that case, employees walked out when a foreman withheld money which they alleged was due to one of them as an income tax rebate. The Commissioner held that there was no trade dispute, relying upon relevant pre-War decisions[53] on disputes as to alleged underpayment. There, the Umpire stated: "There was no trouble in these cases about the terms of payment under the contracts of employment or as to what should be the terms of future employment, but whether the claimants had been underpaid or overpaid for work actually done. . . ." Whilst there undoubtedly is a logical distinction between what is and what ought to be included in the contract, there are a number of reasons for doubting the relevance of it in the present context. In the first place, except where one party is involved in illegality (thus carrying the disagreement outside the scope of "dispute" anyway,[54]) the policy of neutrality bears equally on both situations. In the second place, difficulties are posed by the "it is and if it isn't it should be" type of argument which is common in industrial disputes. Thirdly, it is a distinction which seems to be coolly ignored in *R(U) 3/71* where the Commissioner, without adverting to *R(U) 26/59*, or to the point there made and here under consideration, treated a dispute as to whether or not a machine was safe as a trade dispute. This is thought correct.

Termination of dispute

A dispute may come to an end by compromise, albeit uneasy, or by one party or the other capitulating; or it may be that the differences prove irreconcilable and one or both parties may reach the stage of deciding to sever relations finally. If this comes about, the dispute is just as much at an end as if they had agreed and there is no longer any basis for disqualification.[55] Similar reasoning apparently applies once differences have been resolved, where one party continues the stoppage for disciplinary reasons. Here again there is no dispute and therefore no disqualification.[56]

Difficulties here arise from the fact that disqualification attaches to loss of employment due to a stoppage whether that stoppage arises by strike or by lockout,[57] and both these concepts, particularly the lockout, are ambiguous. Where an employer issues notices of dismissal in consequence of a dispute with workers, his action may constitute a furtherance of the dispute (in which case disqualification attaches,[58]) or a final severance of relations (in which case there is no disqualification though

there may be misconduct or some other ground resulting in disqualification under section 20 (apparently the ground in $R(U)$
33/51). Into which category it falls seems to depend upon the
intention of the employer in issuing notice. The mere issue by
itself does not evidence a dispute.[59] Where, however, it is seen
to be not the wish of the employer to terminate the relationship
permanently, the dispute is furthered and disqualification
attaches[60]; and it continues to attach so long as any matter in
dispute is unsettled or until hope of settlement is abandoned. It
is belived that $R(U)$ *27/56* is wrong in suggesting that if notices
would not have been issued but for the dispute disqualification
necessarily attaches. Where the dispute causes one party to have
no desire for further dealings with the other, the matter is at an
end and there can be no disqualification.

(d) *Place of Employment*

In relation to any person, "place of employment" "means the
factory, workshop, farm or other premises or place at which he
was employed, so however that, where separate branches of work
which are commonly carried on as separate businesses in separate
premises or at separate places are in any case carried on in
separate departments on the same premises or at the same place,
each of those departments shall for the purposes of this paragraph
be deemed to be a separate factory or workshop or farm or
separate premises or a separate place, as the case may be."[61]
This definition falls into two parts, the first of which elaborates
upon the meaning of "place of employment." It is for the
insurance officer to establish that this part of the definition is
satisfied.[62] The second part of the definition states circumstances
in which separate places of employment may be deemed to exist.
It is for the claimant to allege and prove matters under this
second part.[63]

The prima facie meaning of "place of employment"

The first part of this definition defines "place of employment"
very widely. "The presence of, and necessity for, the exception
in the second part does not suggest that the first part should
be narrowly construed. It has always been widely construed by

the Commissioner."[64] Thus, the whole of the Ford Plant at Dagenham, covering a vast area and intersected by public roads and railways, and consisting of a number of separate divisions in which different activities are carried on, has been held to be, prima facie, a single "place of employment."[65] In similar vein, Commissioners have consistently held that the place of employment of dock workers and shipwrights etc., is the whole of the docks within which they may be called upon to work on vessels, and not merely the particular vessel on which they happen to be working at a particular time.[66]

It is not enough, for the purposes of the definition merely to establish that there is *a* place of employment with which the claimant is associated. It must be *his* place of employment. Difficulties may, therefore, arise where one part of a claimant's work is done in the place in question, and another part outside it. In *250/49 (UB)*, the Northern Ireland Commissioner held that the fact that up to 50 per cent. of the claimant's time was spent inside factory premises was enough to render those premises his place of employment. This test of "substantiality" was not, however, resorted to in *R(U) 6/51*. The question there was whether taxi drivers, who spent most of their time on the streets, and taxi-cab washers, responsible for cleaning and maintaining the cabs wholly on garage premises, shared the same "place of employment." The Commissioner held that they did, the place of employment of the drivers being "the premises of the owners of the cabs where the hiring takes place." At first blush, this reasoning is not easy to reconcile with that in *R(U) 26/57* where it was held that the place of employment of a chipper and scraper was the docks on which he worked, the fact that his employers did not own them being immaterial. The definition, however, appears to require that there be a specific "factory, workshop, farm or other premises or place" and it may be thought to follow that any claimant's "place of employment" is the specific place with which his work is most substantially connected. "The streets" in *R(U) 6/51* would not qualify on this basis whilst the docks in *R(U) 26/57* would. It would therefore seem proper to select the employer's premises as the "place" in the former case but be unnecessary to do so in the latter.

The exception

Notwithstanding that persons involved in the stoppage have the same actual place of employment as the claimant, he may still avoid disqualification if his particular "department" can be deemed separate under the second part of the definition. These requirements were not satisfied in $R(U)$ $6/51$ above (the taxi-cab case) because "the maintenance and cleaning of the cabs are integral and inseparable parts of the business of cab hiring" and "the work of cleaning and maintaining taxi-cabs is (not) commonly carried on as a separate business." This latter point was fatal in the Ford case[67] also. The question there was whether the work of the "Trim Shop" in which the strike occurred could be said to be "commonly carried on as a separate business." The only evidence on this point was that the company, in seeking to obtain trim from an alternative source, had been able to locate only one supplier. It therefore followed that trim manufacture was "certainly not commonly carried on as a separate business."[68] It has, however, been held that the transport section of a firm of ship repairers did constitute a separate place of employment, for its work was commonly carried on as a separate business in separate premises etc.[69] The second part of the definition is actually dealing with cases where different activities are carried on in the same premises or at the same place. A physical or topographical separation of activities is not, therefore, necessary to the operation of the exception. The concept of a "department" used in that section embraces administrative or organisational division as well.[70]

It will be remarked that determination of the question whether or not there is a common or separate place of employment calls for the answering of questions of degree at many points and it is perhaps not surprising that it should have attracted criticism. In evidence before the Donovan Commission[71] the Confederation of British Industries argued for a more extended definition, whilst the Trades Union Congress wished to see the definition further narrowed. The former body attached great importance to the tendency in recent years "to break down the production processes between a number of establishments with a high degree of inter-dependence" so that an employee at one existing place of employment might well be directly interested in the outcome of a dispute at another place of employment forming part of the same industrial concern. The latter body argued that the modern tendency to integrate different processes of production in the same place involved in disqualification workers who were formerly free from that risk. The Donovan Commission rejected both these suggestions. That of the CBI was turned down mainly on the ground that it would be administratively very difficult to determine, in some cases, whether there really was a sufficient community of interests to warrant disqualification. That of the TUC was declined on the ground that it would enable trade unions, by selective strikes, to bring work to a standstill at the cost of the disqualification for benefit only of the members in a particular department, the rest being entitled to draw benefit. On this latter point, three members of the Commission dissented on the ground that the risk of selectivity was slight and should be run in order to avoid "the greater injustice of penalising men who are not concerned in a trade dispute simply because it is the common practice of an industry to locate people doing their work in a particular way."

(e) *Duration of Stoppage*

If the loss of employment is not by reason of a stoppage of work due to a trade dispute, but merely coincides with such a dispute, no disqualification results.[72] Equally, if the industrial action taken constitutes a final severance of relations and is not merely "a move in a contest between an employer and his employees, the object of which is that employment shall be resumed on certain conditions," *i.e.* a furtherance of the dispute,[73] no disqualification results. Given, however, that the original loss of employment is by reason of a stoppage due to a trade dispute, then disqualification ensues and remains so long as the stoppage continues, notwithstanding that relations between the particular claimant and his employer are later finally severed. In *R(U) 1/65*, a number of strikers were finally discharged on the day after the strike commenced but were held to be disqualified until the end of the stoppage several weeks later, for the general stoppage *vis-à-vis* other employees continued during that period.[74] This rule applies even where the stoppage has ended *vis-à-vis* the particular class or grade of workers to which the claimant belongs, other members of his class or grade having resumed work. He remains disqualified so long as the stoppage con- tinues as regards other workers.[75] Only when there is no longer a stoppage due to the dispute at all, either because of a general settlement or a final discharge of all workers involved, does the disqualification end.[76] Even where the place of work was closed down and machines moved to another plant the stoppage was held to continue, it not being established that the employer had no intention of ever again resuming production at the original place of work.[77]

It would be logically open to the statutory authorities to hold that provided the stoppage *was* originally due to a dispute, dis- qualification might continue even after the dispute had ended *vis-à-vis* all workers, so long as the stoppage continued (as it well might, after a settlement, due to the time lag in re-establishing production in some industries). There is, indeed, authority for the proposition that "a stoppage of work continues (and, with it, disqualification) after the settlement of a dispute for such time as is necessary to remedy disrepair naturally resulting from the stoppage of work."[78] $R(U)$ $25/57$ holds, consistently with this, that "where the dispute is settled ... the stoppage of work which was due to the trade dispute comes to an end when there is a general resumption of work following such a settlement, though ... not necessarily immediately after the settlement." In some cases, however, the resumption will be gradual, different groups of employees returning to work at different times. In such cir- cumstances, it has been held that the stoppage ended when the first group of workers returned to work under the settlement.[79] In principle, the position would seem to be different where workers drift back, as the strike is progressively abandoned, without any specific settlement being reached. Here, the dispute continues as regards those who have not returned and there is, for them, a continuing stoppage due to the dispute. In such a situation, there is authority that "the stoppage of work comes to an end when the employers have got all the workers they require, that is, when work is no longer being stopped or hindered by the refusal of workers to work on the employer's terms or the refusal of employers to employ the workers on the workers' terms."[80]

(f) *Bona Fide Employment Elsewhere etc.*

Disqualification ceases, in the words of section 19, "where ... (the claimant) has become bona fide employed elsewhere in the occupation which he usually follows or has become regularly engaged in some other occupation." The rationale here seems to be that a *second* loss of employment in respect of which the claim is made is not "by reason of a stoppage of work due to a trade dispute" which provoked the *first* loss of employment and is not therefore tainted by the disqualifying factor. In order to escape by this route, the claimant used to have to satisfy the statutory authorities that he had finally severed relations with the first employer and "genuinely taken fresh employment elsewhere in such a way as to be altogether unaffected by the continuance of the stoppage."[81] It followed that if the new employment was "a temporary expedient to tide (the claimant) over the period of the stoppage and no permanent severance of relations with his original employer was intended" the disqualification resumed upon the second loss of employment.[82]

In one, commonly accepted, sense of the term "bona fide," a person may become employed elsewhere, or in a different occupation, bona fide, and yet intend to resume his former occupation at the end of the stoppage. All that is required is that he be honestly and genuinely employed in the second occupation. In the latest decision[83] this latter view is adopted. It may still be relevant to consider whether relations with the old employer have been finally severed and whether the new employment is permanent or not but only for the purpose of testing the genuineness of the new employment, *i.e.* they are now merely evidence, it may be thought slight, as to the seriousness of the purpose of the second employment. In effect, unless the second employment is a mere sham and the claimant not genuinely employed at all, the disqualification will not attach.

Provided that he is bona fide employed elsewhere, there being no intention to prefer the original employer when the opportunity arises, the disqualification ceases, even if the new employment is only for a day, and destined to cease before the end of the original stoppage.[84] It also seems, from these two decisions, that a worker may become employed "elsewhere" notwithstanding that the new work is at the same "place of employment." The point is not actually canvassed, but in both cases, the new employment was as a docker on a different vessel at a different berth (and for a different employer) but at the same docks as his original work. It may well be that in the light of other decisions that the place of employment of a docker is the entire docks[85] these decisions would not be followed were the point specifically argued.

Avoidance of disqualification dates only from the obtaining of the new employment, each day's claim having to be considered on its merits according to the position as at the time it is made.[86]

(g) *Participating in or Financing or being Directly Interested in the Dispute*

Disqualification can be avoided by proving that the claimant is not participating in or financing or directly interested in the dispute *and* that he does not belong to a grade or class of workers of which there were members at his place of employment who are so participating in, financing or directly interested.[87] The Act places the onus of proof squarely on the claimant.[88] It is, however, not impossible to discharge. Whilst a claimant must fail in the absence of any evidence on the point[89] the onus upon him is that of proving a negative, and such an onus must be viewed realistically.[90] Relatively slight evidence may therefore amount to prima facie discharge of the onus which then shifts to the insurance officer to produce rebutting evidence.[91] It is not fatal to a claimant's case merely that the area of dispute has been extended so as to involve him.[92]

Whilst a person may be "directly interested in" a dispute without knowing of his interest,[93] "participating in or financing" involve active support by claimants.[94] A number of pre-War decisions, mainly concerning unlawful picketing, settle that a person does not become a participant in a trade dispute merely by being prevented from working by violence or intimidation.[95] However, "a different situation arises when persons refrain from working or presenting themselves for work, not because they are prevented by violence or intimidation from so doing, but because they acquiesce in a request not to do so."[96] Picketing may, furthermore, lead to a second dispute, between pickets and the workers picketed, in which case the latter are actual parties.[97]

"Participating"

A person participates actively in a dispute if he knowingly does something or refrains from doing something which contributes to the continuance of the dispute. $R(U)$ *41/56*, where the claimant was contractually bound to make himself available for two kinds of work, affords a good illustration. He usually worked as a repairer, but could be required to work as a brusher. On the occasion of a strike by brushers, he declined to take on their work and by this refusal was held to have participated in the dispute. A similar decision was reached in $R(U)$ *19/55* where the claimant, employed as a ripper but laid off by a strike of fillers, declined to offer himself at his place of employment for alternative work which was available for him. In this case, there is no finding that he was contractually bound to take the alternative work.

Questions of participation may also arise in relation to activities within a union pursuing the dispute and occasioning a strike. The claimant in $R(U)$ *5/66* belonged to a class of workers most of whom had declined to attend the union meeting at which the stoppage was voted for. The local tribunal took the view that their failure to take what steps they could to prevent the stoppage involved them in the dispute as participants. The view of the Commissioner, however, was that whilst there might have been circumstances justifying such a finding, there was no evidence of them on which a tribunal could act. Mere abstention by itself did not amount to participation. A similar question arises in R *3/68* *(UB)* where the matter received rather more attention. There, a claimant attended a union meeting, at which it was proposed to authorise an extension of the stoppage, in order to protest that the meeting had not been properly called, with a view to ensuring that the stoppage was not extended. In fact, it was a closed meeting, he had no right to attend, he was asked to leave and retired to the back of the hall where he continued to protest. He was not disqualified as participating in the dispute. In the course of his decision, the Commissioner makes it plain that "anyone who attended the meeting and voted in a manner calculated to prolong the stoppage of work participated in the dispute." Further than this, "It might be argued ... that anyone who attends a meeting of this type and votes in favour of a resumption of work also participates, although from the opposite point of view." But "what the claimant in the present case was seeking to do was to dissociate himself from the dispute and at the same time advocate a return to work." It would seem that the second of these dicta (participating by voting in favour of a resumption of work) could only be justified on the basis that a person so voting also showed himself willing to accept the decision of the meeting, identifying himself with other participating factions if his view did not prevail. It is hard to see how anything short of this will suffice. What is required is participating in the dispute, not participation in a meeting concerning the dispute.

There was general acceptance of the present position so far as participating is concerned, in evidence before the Donovan Commission, and no change in the law was recommended.[98]

"Financing"

"The theory upon which the disqualification is based is that the act of the union in paying strike benefit and thus financing the trade dispute is the act of each and every one of its members. As members of an unincorporated association of individuals bound by a common contract providing, *inter alia*, for financial support for fellow-members on strike, all must be regarded as involved in the act individually as well as collectively. Expressed in another way, the union acts as agent for its members."[99]

As the above quotation indicates, almost all the decisions concerning the question whether a person is "financing" a dispute have been cases where a trade union to which they belonged has made payments to workers on strike or locked out.[1] The same principles would apply, however, to an individual worker making payments to another involved in the dispute. In principle this could apply within the family context where one member of the family out of work lent financial support to another on strike. Payments to strikers by a union are attributed to its members on the basis that those members have a proprietary interest in the funds of the union, including its investments. The actual wording of the decision in *R(U) 4/58* suggests that disqualification might be avoided by showing that no subscriptions by the member concerned had been expended on the investments from the interest on which strike payments were made, *i.e.* that the payments must be traceable to the subscriptions. This, however, is misleading. Disqualification would result in any case where funds in which a person had a proprietary interest were disbursed on strike payments,[2] though union rules might condition the acquisition of full membership (and, with it, proprietorship) upon payment of subscriptions.

Because a proprietory interest in the union's funds is the touchstone, it matters not that the member's subscriptions are in arrears[3] (though it might be otherwise if falling into arrears automatically terminated membership and proprietorship); or that they are paid to a different branch from that involved in the dispute.[4] The *de minimis* principle is equally irrelevant.[5] Since "financing" is based on the existence of a proprietory interest, disqualification might be avoided by resort to the device of the discretionary trust, though the statutory authorities have in other areas manifested a healthy disposition to have regard to the realities.

Two particular problems have occasioned some difficulty:

(i) Can a member "finance" where payments are *ultra vires?*

(ii) To what extent may payments made *ex post facto* effect disqualification?

On the first of these questions there is some conflict of authority. A pre-War decision[6] tentatively approved in $R(U)$ *2/70*, proceeded on the commonsense basis that if a union in fact makes payments, its members are "financing" the dispute, even though its rules prohibit such payments. The snag here is that if the appropriate legal proceedings were subsequently taken against the officials making the *ultra vires* payments, the funds might be completely restored with the result that none of the members' property would have been used to support the workers stopped. This, no doubt, is the thinking behind the suggestion in $R(U)$ *12/71*, where it is implied that *ultra vires* payments could be ignored. It was not, however, so decided, the payments being held, in the event, to be *intra vires*. Since it is perhaps unlikely that legal proceedings would be taken or, if taken, would result in a complete restoration of funds, the former view is perhaps more realistic though it bears harshly upon members who would have every reason to expect that the terms of their membership would not involve them in "financing" in such circumstances.

The second question is more complex. Since unemployment benefit is a daily benefit, it is payable or not in respect of a given day according as to whether the conditions for entitlement are fulfilled on that day or not. It is clear that if strike payments have actually been properly made in respect of a day there is "financing" on that day. It is equally well settled that once the union has undertaken to pay, disqualification attaches to all future days covered by the undertaking though some doubt arises if the undertaking is subsequently dishonoured.[7] The difficulty arises where payment is undertaken or made *ex post facto*, *i.e.* in respect of earlier days in the stoppage. Here, the strikers will receive belated support from the union's funds but, as of the day of claim, there will be neither actual payment nor even an undertaking to make it. *C.U. 274/50 (KL)* has been taken as authority for the proposition that a decision to pay *ex post facto* may disqualify in respect of earlier days, at all events where the likelihood of eventual payment existed from the start. That reasoning has now been rejected—it would introduce elements of uncertainty into the question of title to benefit and make the insurance officer's task impossible.[8] It is believed, in fact, that as far as it goes, *C.U. 274/50 (KL)* is correct. It decides merely that where there is a union decision to pay but no date of decision is given, a claimant has failed to discharge the onus of proving that he is not financing the dispute—the decision might have preceded the day of claim.

The position thus seems to be that a member will be treated as financing on any day on, and in respect of, which there exists an obligation (at all events if honoured) to pay strike pay. If the union's rules provide for automatic payments in the event of a stoppage, then members are financing from the start without more ado. If there is no such certainty, a subsequent payment may be related back to the date of the decision authorising payment but no earlier.[9]

It will be noted that the explanation of the basis of disqualification by reason of "financing" offered at the head of this section turns upon the union being an unincorporated association whose property therefore is that of its members. Dicta in the House of Lords in *Bonsor* v. *Musicians' Union*[10] suggested that in some sense, a trade union might be viewed as a separate legal entity, and in *R(U)* *12/71* it was argued that it followed from this that members no longer "owned" the union's property and could not, therefore, be said to be financing when the union, a distinct legal person, paid strike pay out of its property. The Commissioner rightly rejected this argument—the actual decision in *Bonsor*'s case does not confer juristic personality on trade unions but turns, rather, on the limited authority of the union's agents. The validity of the argument as to what the position would be *if* the union had been a separate legal entity is not, however, assailed and acquired a temporary new relevance by virtue of section 74 of the Industrial Relations Act 1971 which provided that upon registration a trade union became a body corporate, all property and funds, of whatever nature, vesting in the new body corporate. Members would thus lose any proprietory interest in the property or funds of the union and proprietorship, as a rationale of "financing," would no longer operate.

The rules relating to financing were stringently criticised by the Donovan Commission. "... [T]he logic squares very uneasily at times with reality. It must be obvious beforehand in most cases that a strike in one department at a place of employment is likely to throw out of work employees in another department who may have no interest in the dispute whatever. If one of the employees in this other department is a member of the union supporting the strike, it is again a little unreal to treat him automatically as a party to the union's action if he knows full well in advance that the result will be to bring considerable financial hardship upon himself, and also perhaps upon his family. Of course, such a man may be willing to accept such hardship in the interests of union solidarity; on the other hand he may regard the strike as quite unjustified and unworthy of support. At the present time he is penalised whatever view he takes.... It is open to a claimant for unemployment benefit to evade the disqualification ... simply by resigning from his trade union at any time during the trade dispute. He is entitled to benefit if he can show that he 'is not' financing the dispute. This use of the present tense involves that the question must be decided, if need be, each time the claimant applies for benefit, which he will usually do each week. On the basis that membership of the union paying strike pay is a 'financing' of the trade dispute, the claimant can cease to finance by ceasing to be a member. This of course may involve him in difficulties with the union if he is entitled to benefits dependent upon continuous membership; but no union, we think, would have any great legal difficulty in devising a rule to meet such a case, providing that the member rejoined after the trade dispute was over.

A situation can arise in which claimants may be refused benefit if a strike by their fellow union members is official and therefore financed by their union, but may be granted benefit if the strike is unofficial and there is therefore no financing by the union. In such circumstances an advantage is given to unofficial action which might not always be marginal and which should if possible be removed.

The theory that a member must be regarded as automatically involved in union decisions will be much more difficult, if not impossible, to sustain if and when trade unions are given corporate status."

For all these reasons, the Donovan Commission (with one dissentient) took the view that a claimant should no longer be regarded as financing a trade dispute merely on the ground that he is a member of a trade union paying strike pay to those on strike.[11]

"Directly interested"

Where a non-striker or members of his grade or class who are not stopped are laid off as a result of the stoppage it may nevertheless be regarded as proper to disqualify if they stand to benefit as a result of the outcome of the dispute. The dispute may, for example, be about a bonus scheme affecting all classes, though the action may be taken by only one class.[12] No objection to this position was lodged in evidence before the Donovan Commission. The actual law relating to interest, however, goes beyond this simple proposition.

It is obvious that everyone laid off as a result of a stoppage has, in one sense, an interest in its outcome—he wants to get back to work. Disqualification, however, turns not upon interest in the outcome of the stoppage as such, but upon interest in the dispute and accordingly, the mere fact that a claimant will benefit by resuming employment when the stoppage ends does not, of itself, disqualify him.[13] Of course, he may himself become involved in a new dispute if his eventual return to work is delayed because of a dispute with his employer about the terms on which he should resume.[14]

Equally, it is clear that a person may be "interested" for reasons other than financial ones. No doubt, a pecuniary interest will be the most common type, but an interest is equally constituted by, for example, standing to be affected by the outcome of a dispute as to conditions relating to heating or ventilation in the place of work.[15]

A person is interested in a dispute if his own conditions of employment stand to be affected by decisions upon the point at issue.[16] If he does not stand to gain or to lose anything in his conditions of work, in his terms of employment or in amenity, he is not interested.[17] The effect must be substantial. ". . . [A]n interest in the mere formal maintenance of an industrial agreement divorced from any probability of material change" does not constitute a sufficient interest for the purposes of the disqualification provision.[18] On the other hand, a sufficient interest is shown if settlement of the dispute will have practical effects, such as on the amount of work likely to be available to the claimant, notwithstanding that no formal change in his position results.[19] It has been held to be a sufficient interest that, as a result of a recognition dispute, a claimant might be "compelled to work side by side with persons, other than tradesmen, who are not members of his Trade Union and also that the position of the Union, in subsequent negotiations with the employers, will be seriously affected."[20]

Obviously, in deciding whether a person is interested in a dispute, the statutory authorities are involved in predicting what the consequences of its outcome will be, so far as the claimant's conditions of work are concerned. In so forecasting a future course of events, there can be no certainty one way or the other, only a greater or lesser probability. The approach which Commissioners have adopted is to ask whether an effect is "probable."[21] This appears to call for a decision to be made on the balance of probabilities. It must be emphasised, however, that the probability which must be sought is that of interest or involvement, not change. It was rightly held, in *R(U) 25/56*, that a claimant was directly interested where the outcome of the dispute would result in either alteration or *affirmation* of his conditions of service. It was sufficient that as a result of the dispute, those conditions would probably be in issue.

The interest must be "direct."[22] This calls for a judgment as to whether the causal connection between the dispute and a probable effect on the relevant conditions of employment is sufficiently close.[23] It was on this point that the existing rules came in for criticism before the Donovan Commission. The TUC complained about the way in which the term "directly interested in the dispute" had at times been interpreted and applied by the adjudicating authorities, and cases were cited to the Commission "in which the decisions on the point seem[ed] to conflict or [were] at any rate very difficult to reconcile" and it was suggested that there were "periodical trends during which a clear distinction [was] drawn between direct and indirect interests, while at other times the distinction [became] blurred."[24] However, "the problem of distinguishing between direct and indirect interests is notoriously difficult, and the line between major and minor interests could also not be drawn with precision. These are all matters of interpretation and therefore matters for the courts alone, unless Parliament wishes to attempt the task of clarification itself which so far it seems studiously to have avoided." The Commission was not itself able to suggest any definition which would put all doubts at rest.[25] The latest, post-Donovan, decisions do, however, seem to make the question easier to answer. Both concern a common industrial phenomenon, the desire to maintain differentials between different classes. This phenomenon is not, by itself, sufficient to establish a direct interest. "... [A] claimant should not be regarded as having a direct interest ... unless there is a close association between the two occupations concerned, and the outcome of the dispute is likely to affect the claimant, not at a number of removes, but virtually automatically, without further intervening contingencies."[26] Such an effect would be automatic, and the interest therefore direct, if there were in force an express agreement for the maintenance of differentials.[27]

In one other respect it is not at all clear that the law embraces any sensible policy. A person may be "directly interested" even if the only effect likely to be produced *vis-à-vis* him is an adverse one; and even though he is utterly helpless to do anything about it. It makes sense to insist that a man pick up the burdens of a stoppage where he stands to benefit by its outcome or at least where it is in his power to do something about it (in which case, he will probably be "participating"). It is, however, hard to see what principle justifies the infliction upon him of the additional burden of disqualification for unemployment benefit where he is thrown out of work by the action of others which threatens only to prejudice his employment position.

Grade or class

A claimant may not avoid disqualification under the proviso to section 19 (1) if he belongs to "a grade or class of workers" members of which were employed at his place of employment, any of whom are participating in or financing or directly interested in the dispute. His liability to disqualification is not lost merely because he has temporarily ceased to function as a member of that grade or class[28]; even more is this the case where he has, as a member of the grade or class, two capacities and is, for the time being, acting in only one of them, the dispute concerning members of his class acting in the other.[29] In this case, a toolsetter/overseer was held disqualified in connection with a dispute about the conduct of overseers, even though he was, at the relevant time, functioning only as a toolsetter. It is sufficient to disqualify that a single one of the class was participating, etc.[30] If it is not known whether even one of the claimant's grade or class is participating, etc., he may still fail, for the onus is on him to prove that there are none,[31] though no doubt matters must be viewed realistically. It is to be emphasised that by virtue of this part of the proviso, a person may be unable to avoid disqualification even though his grade or class is not a party to the dispute, and even though he himself is personally and actively opposed to the stoppage and does all he can to avoid or terminate it. It is enough that fellow class- or grade-members participate, etc. in an irrelevant dispute between two other factions.[32]

The major point of difficulty which has arisen in administering this provision is the settling of the criteria for appropriating a particular worker to a particular class or grade. The safest and most readily workable guide is that offered by the Umpire in pre-War *Decision 8344*. Here, he points out that a worker may fall within more than one class and/or grade according to the principle of classification involved and takes the view that, in any given case, the relevant principle should be determined by reference to the subject-matter of the dispute. This approach seems to have been approved by a Tribunal of Commissioners in *R(U) 25/53* and offers the best guarantee of avoiding anomaly.[33] The Donovan Commission (see below) seems to assume that the class or grade is settled, without reference to the dispute, for all purposes, and, indeed, in a number of cases, Commissioners have done exactly this, ignoring the relevance of the subject-matter of the dispute. The clearest example here is *R(U) 17/51*. There, compositors went on strike. The claimant was one of 33 readers thrown out of work by the strike. Three of the 33 were "dual ticket holders," *i.e.* compositors also. The claimant was held to be disqualified because he was a member of a grade or class (readers) three of whom (*qua* compositors) were financing the dispute as members of the compositors' union. If the subject-matter of the dispute is taken into account in settling the relevant class, then the fact that some compositors are readers is no more reason for disqualifying readers than is the fact that some compositors are workers of 10 years standing a reason for disqualifying all such workers.[34] Were the earlier cases to be followed in determining the criterion of relevance by reference to the subject-matter of the dispute, this criticism of the Donovan Commission would fall.

In evidence before the Donovan Commission, the then Ministry of Social Security sought to justify the "grade or class" provision, not on the basis that members will necessarily have any interest in the dispute, but on the principle that "members of a grade or class have a mutual 'interest' as members of that grade or class which justifies treating them alike for unemployment benefit purposes in trade disputes."[35] The arguments of the Ministry did not, however, commend themselves to the Commission:

"In our view the reasoning ... is fallacious. In order to ascertain whether a class of persons has a common interest simply because it is a class one needs to know what common attribute it is which marks such persons off as a class. This the law makes no attempt to do." (In fact, this is not correct; the law has attempted to do just this, see above.) "It simply assumes, apparently, that if a group of workers in the same place of employment can by some means be identified as a 'class' or 'grade' then automatically they possess a common interest as such: and no investigation is required to disqualify them from receiving ... benefit beyond discovering whether there is at least one of the class participating in the dispute.... Moreover, the grade or class provision will operate if only one member of the grade or class is 'financing' the trade dispute ... if A were a storeman in a works comprising different departments and a dispute occurred in the foundry shop which led to a stoppage of work, during which the union concerned paid strike benefit, A would be disqualified for receiving unemployment benefit if he happened to belong to the same union. So would all the other storemen, although they might belong to a different union or unions."

For these and other reasons, the Donovan Commission favoured the total abolition of the "grade or class" provision.[36] That might, indeed, be a wise step, but until it is taken (as it will be under the Employment Protection Act 1975) some problems remain. There has been some controversy about whether, in any given case, regard is to be had to "class" or "grade" or both. In *Decision 8344*, the Umpire stated that "what the section means is that if the dispute relates only to men of a particular grade, one must see whether the applicant belongs to that grade; if the dispute relates to a class of workers one must see whether the applicant belongs to that class." Provided that it is properly understood, this dictum is believed to be correct. The difficulty is that a particular dispute may relate to (1) a class as such or (2) a grade as such or (3) both. And, a grade as such or a class as such may or may not be a sub-category of a class as such or a grade as such respectively. Thus, a dispute involving the terms and conditions of foremen welders might involve all welders as a class, or merely foremen welders as a grade. And foremen welders as a grade might or might not be a sub-category of welders as a class, according as to whether the dispute related to them as foremen or as welders.[37] If, in a given case, the subject-matter of the dispute makes "class" relevant and grade irrelevant, then a claimant will be disqualified if he belongs to the relevant class notwithstanding that his grade is not involved as such.[38] Of course, if his grade was involved either by itself, or together with his class, whether as a sub-category of it or otherwise, there is no problem.

The Commissioner has attempted to evolve a criterion for membership of a "grade" or "class" by reference to "points of similarity and difference."[39] Such an approach is bound to lend substance to the criticisms voiced by the Donovan Commission (above) unless regard is had to the relevance of such points to the dispute in question. If this is done, then classification for all purposes becomes unattainable. If it is not done, a positive or negative answer can be yielded simply by the selection of points.

Critique

The provisions relating to disqualification by reason of a trade dispute are complex. They are a primary source of aggravation of the administration of unemployment benefit. In addition, they are in some respects obscure as appears from the difficulties that have arisen on appeals. They are, finally, in some respects inapt or unjust, at least in the view of such an esteemed body as the Donovan Commission. If they were necessary, none of this would matter.

It is salutary at this point to recall the function of this head of disqualification. It is not to ensure that benefit is withheld from claimants who are responsible for their own need. This is, or could easily be, taken care of by section 20 which imposes disqualification where a claimant becomes unemployed as a result of his own misconduct or voluntary leaving etc. If the trade dispute disqualification were removed from the statute book, the result would be that in the trade dispute situation, the statutory authorities would have to determine whether a claimant locked out had been guilty of "misconduct" and whether one on strike had "voluntarily left without just cause" for purposes of deciding whether to impose a disqualification of up to six weeks, in the first instance. Thereafter, each refusal of a suitable opportunity would warrant further periods of disqualification.

In this light, it is the plain and only function of the trade dispute disqualification to spare the statutory authorities the perhaps unwelcome task of passing judgment on the "merits" of an industrial dispute and prejudicing the confidence reposed in them by workers. Indeed, it is even less than this, for the strict sphere of the function of the statutory authorities would be to decide upon the merits not of the dispute itself, but the action (the strike or lockout) taken in consequence of it. It would, for example, involve no judgment on the merits of the dispute itself for the statutory authorities to say that a lockout was too hasty and extreme a response to it.

The anomaly may be brought into focus by considering the case where an employer proposes deleteriously to alter the terms and conditions of employment or employees. If an individual employee refuses to accept the change and quits his employment, the statutory authorities have to decide whether he had "just cause" for voluntarily leaving, under section 20. The same applies if several or all employees quit spontaneously. It is if, and only if, there is a concerted stoppage with a view to coercing the employer to change his mind that the trade dispute disqualification comes into operation. It is at that point that the employees (and perhaps others) become disqualified, "just cause" notwithstanding, in order that the law can seem to adopt a pose of neutrality.

"Neutrality" is not a supreme end of law in itself. If it were, the law would seek to be neutral as between murderers and persons killing in self-defence, or between debtors and creditors. It is plainly arguable that too high a price has been put upon it in the context of unemployment benefit.

Certainly some of the complexity and some also of the injustice will be removed from the trade dispute disqualification when section 111 of the Employment Protection Act 1975 is brought into force. It will not, however, remove all cause for disquiet.

2. SELF-INDUCED UNEMPLOYMENT

"The object of the provision for disqualification in the subsection is not to punish the insured person but to protect the unemployment insurance fund from claims in respect of unemployment which the insured person has brought upon himself...."[40] Provision is made, however, for repentance. A period of unemployment having its origins in a voluntary act may continue against the will of the person unemployed. It would, however, be very difficult, as well as administratively very burdensome, to seek to decide in each case whether the initial voluntary act had spent itself. The Act therefore fixes a maximum period of disqualification of six weeks, and it is assumed that unemployment in excess of that ordered is involuntary.

The 1975 Act provides that

"A person shall be disqualified for receiving unemployment benefit for such period not exceeding 6 weeks as may be determined ... if—

(*a*) he has lost his employment as an employed earner through his misconduct, or has voluntarily left such employment without just cause;

(*b*) after a situation in any suitable employment has been properly notified to him as vacant or about to become vacant, he has without good cause refused or failed to apply for that situation or refused to accept that situation when offered to him;

(*c*) he has neglected to avail himself of a reasonable opportunity of suitable employment;

(*d*) he has without good cause refused or failed to carry out any official recommendations given to him with a view to assisting him to find suitable employment, being recommendations which were reasonable having regard to his circumstances and to the means of obtaining that employment usually adopted in the district in which he resides; or

(*e*) he has without good cause refused or failed to avail himself of a reasonable opportunity of receiving training approved by the Secretary of State in his case for the purpose of becoming or keeping fit for entry into, or return to, regular employment."[41]

Each of the clauses of this provision specifies circumstances in which a person who is unemployed becomes disqualified for benefit. None of them, however, simply requires the finding of facts—all call for evaluations, in one guise or another, as to whether disqualification is deserved. In some clauses (*e.g.* (*b*), (*d*) and (*c*)) this is explicit, disqualification being conditioned upon an absence of "good cause." But even though "good cause" (or "just cause," the formulation appearing in part of clause (*a*)) may not be expressly required in some of the other clauses, something resembling it is nevertheless hidden in the words chosen to express the reasons for disqualification. In clause (*a*), "misconduct" is required and the authorities indicate[42] that this means a sufficiently reprehensible degree of objectionable conduct. In clause (*c*), the unemployed person must have neglected to avail himself of a "reasonable" opportunity of "suitable" employment, no disqualification attaching if either the opportunity is unreasonable or the employment unsuitable.[43]

This formulation has implications for the burden of proof. Once the claimant has proved that he is unemployed, the onus shifts onto the insurance officer to establish the facts warranting disqualification,[44] and they must be clearly proved, particularly where the charge is one of misconduct in which case direct evidence should be adduced.[45] If insufficient evidence is adduced, the claimant is entitled to benefit without more.[46] On general principles, however, once the ground of disqualification is established, disqualification must follow unless the claimant can, in cases where it is relevant, establish good or just cause. Here, the onus would seem to be on him.

We now turn to the individual clauses:

(a) *Misconduct and Voluntary Leaving*

Benefit is forfeited if the claimant "has lost his employment in an employed contributor's employment through his misconduct, or has voluntarily left such employment without just cause."[47] From the wording of the clause, it appears that one who loses employment as a self-employed person because of misconduct, or who voluntarily ceases to be self-employed, is not disqualified from receiving benefit (though, of course, his right to it, *e.g.* in respect of contributions, would have to be established positively). It has, however, been held that disqualification is not avoided merely because one is subjected to disciplinary suspension rather than discharged finally. He has, it appears, "lost his employment" for the period of the suspension even though he remains under his contract of employment and will definitely resume work under it at the end of the period of suspension.[48] This interpretation is fully consistent with that adopted elsewhere in unemployment benefit law.

At first blush, the spheres of operation of the two branches
of clause (*a*) look clear and mutually exclusive. If one is dismissed by the employer, one seems to be disqualified if the
reason is "misconduct." If one quits of one's own accord, one
seems to be disqualified unless one had "just cause." One cannot it would seem, "leave voluntarily" if one is sacked. The
simple view of clause (*a*) thus presented is, however, not in
accord with the behaviour of the statutory authorities in dealing
with cases under clause (*a*) where the misbehaviour of the
claimant has provoked his dismissal by the employer. On a
number of such occasions, the Commissioner has held that a
claimant has left voluntarily. In *105/50* (*UB*), a claimant who
had failed to comply with a rule of her employers that she should
forward medical certificates when off sick was held to be disqualified for leaving voluntarily and one is left in some puzzle-
ment to understand why failure to comply with a reasonable
instruction could not be classified as misconduct. Even more
perplexing is *R(U)* *16/52*. Here, the claimant had refused to
undergo an X-ray examination in connection with her employment. She was held to have left voluntarily (having been given
notice by her employer) and the Commissioner expressly finds
that there was no misconduct on her part. Two tentative explanations may be offered. First of all, it has been stated that "in
some cases a claimant's actions may fall short of 'misconduct'
and yet justify a finding that he voluntarily left his employment
without just cause."[49] It may be speculated that in *R(U)* *16/52*,
the claimant's conduct was not sufficiently reprehensible to
amount to "misconduct," yet nevertheless posed an insuperable
bar to her continued employment. Secondly, it is arguable in
principle (though unsupported by authority) that misconduct
relates only to the manner of doing the job and not to behaviour
concerning one's qualifications for holding it.

The latest decision in this area holds out a hope of rationalisation. The claimant in *R(U)* *5/71* refused on principle to register
with the General Teaching Council for Scotland, registration
having become a necessary precondition to continued employment. He was given notice of dismissal but persisted in his
refusal. Even after his dismissal had taken effect, he could have
secured reinstatement by registering. The Commissioner recognised that whilst "prima facie a person who has been dismissed

has not left voluntarily," nevertheless, "it is proper to examine the reality of the transaction and not merely its outward form. A person who has been (in form) dismissed, may nevertheless in certain circumstances be held truly to have left voluntarily: but it is not always so, even when the dismissal was the predictable result of the employee's failure or refusal to do something which it was within his power to do." However, the Commissioner did not find himself "compelled by any supposed rule of law to treat" the claimant as having in fact left his job voluntarily. To describe him as having done so would have been "a simple misuse of language" and the most appropriate ground on which to disqualify was that the claimant had neglected to avail himself of a reasonable opportunity of suitable employment. Why the refusal to register did not constitute "misconduct" is not considered. The decision, however, does enable us to hope that the scope of "voluntary leaving" may be confined to areas where the claimant either leaves of his own accord or voluntarily does something which must result in the termination of his employment.

The loss of employment must be causally connected to the misconduct. There is obviously no problem of this type where a man is sacked for misconduct. The position is equally clear where he is sacked solely for some other reason (*e.g.* laid off as redundant) whether or not he happens also to have been guilty of misconduct. The problems arise where two causes figure in a dismissal, one of them being misconduct. There have been two cases where the misconduct contributed along with other causes to a dismissal, but might not have been sufficient, by itself, to bring it about. In the first of these cases[50] it was held to warrant disqualification merely that the misconduct was a necessary element in provoking the dismissal. In *R 8/60 (UB)*, however, disqualification was not imposed notwithstanding that the misconduct was a necessary element (a "contributing cause"), in the dismissal, because it would not, by itself, have provoked it (*i.e.* been sufficient). It is submitted that whilst both of these approaches can be verbally reconciled with the text of section 20, the former is the correct one. Any consequence (in this case, loss of employment) is always, logically, the product not of a single but of a number of necessary conditions. The "sufficient" cause (*i.e.* one which, by itself, would have produced the given result) exists only in the realm of fancy. If the loss of employment would not have happened but for the misconduct, then it "occurs through" that misconduct, and it is irrelevant that in different circumstances that misconduct might not have provoked that loss. It is to be remembered that this problem only arises once "misconduct" is established. In many cases, it may well be that no real problem exists because there is no conduct sufficiently reprehensible to be classified as "misconduct." One suspects that in *R 8/60 (UB)*, where the employers frankly stated that if it had not been for a shortage of work they would have given the claimant another chance, it might have avoided confusion to have found that there was no "misconduct" at all, but rather that in a short-time situation the employer chose to dispense with the services of an employee whose conduct was less satisfactory than that of others.

Whilst the misconduct must thus be causally connected with the loss of employment, it need not be directly connected with the employment itself, *i.e.* it can relate to conduct outside work.[51] Thus, lorry-drivers have been held to have been dismissed through misconduct where they became legally disabled from driving by virtue of disqualification notwithstanding that the offence in respect of which the penalty was incurred involved the claimant driving his own vehicle in his own time.[52] Again, "an offence of dishonesty which induced an employer to dismiss a man from a position of trust would amount to misconduct, even though the offence had nothing to do with the man's employment."[53] In *R(U) 10/53*, an employee not in a position of trust was held to have committed misconduct when he stole cigarettes from a fellow employee's pocket at a welfare club dance whilst in *R(U) 1/71* the misconduct consisted in the commission of a sexual offence with only the most remote and tenuous connection with the employment. None of these four instances concern conduct in the course of the employment. Each has an indirect connection with it in some sense, but the nature of that connection differs in each of the four cases. The connection is obvious in the cases where the misconduct results in the loss of a legal qualification essential to the job in question, such as a driving licence. In the fraud cases, the misconduct may be argued to evidence the lack of a quality, trustworthiness, the possession of which is reasonably regarded as being essential.

Where an employee's behaviour towards fellow employees[54] or clients[55] is such as to impair good industrial or business relations, it may be said to bear upon the man's suitability for the job, notwithstanding that it takes place outside working hours. The connection in $R(U)$ *1/71* is not immediately obvious. The claimant was a gardener employed by a local authority but not, according to his uncontradicted evidence, required to work in public parks. A tenuous connection with the work was, however, established by the fact that he might, nevertheless, "have opportunities of embarrassing the public by some form of indecency."

The general principle seems to be that "if a person is guilty of such misconduct as would induce or compel a reasonable employer to dispense with his service, on the ground that he was *not a fit person to hold his particular employment* having regard to that misconduct, he incurs disqualification ... even though the misconduct is unconnected with his employment."[56] Two points should be noted as regards the italicised words. First, they involve the proposition that conduct which would amount to misconduct in relation to one job may not do so in relation to another not requiring such a high standard of behaviour. This is well exemplified by the case of a policeman convicted of traffic offences which would be irrelevant or excusable in many other cases.[57] Secondly, they seem to import some relation between the conduct and the employment. If the conduct complained of has nothing whatever to do with the employment, it cannot it seems amount to "industrial misconduct" involving disqualification. A sufficient nexus was established in $R(U)$ *1/71* in the concern of the local authority for its public image. It would be hard to link a conviction for common assault upon a non-fellow-worker outside hours to many occupations, though even here the connection might be sufficient where the work involved personal contact with members of the public.[58]

One type of case instanced above poses a particular problem. Where a job involves trust, a reasonable employer might well dismiss a man convicted of fraud as untrustworthy. It is tempting to justify this on the basis that the fraud evidences a defect of character relevant to the job. Yet a fraud committed before entering employment, but unknown to the employer, might equally well evidence such a defect of character. It has, however, been held[59] that the misconduct must occur during the

currency of the employment lost. It is submitted that this
approach is not the most apt in the circumstances. The crucial
question in principle is that of the evidentiary value of the conduct complained of. A fraud committed years before, whether in
the course of the employment lost or not, might be thought to
have slight evidentiary value as regards present untrustworthi-
ness for there has been ample opportunity for reformation. A
fraud committed immediately before entering the employment
lost might, however, be good evidence of current untrustworthi-
ness.

Types of misconduct

There is no exhaustive list of types of misconduct. Any behaviour impairing the carrying on of the employer's business
may suffice. The most obvious and common type of case is
simply doing the job badly, illustrated by the case of the
manager of an inn charged by the police for supplying liquor to
guests outside permitted hours, thus putting the licence at risk.[60]
It is equally misconduct to use obscene language and make improper suggestive remarks to fellow-employees[61] with the result
that harmonious relations between fellow-workers are impaired. Stealing from the place of work,[62] failing to
observe agreed industrial relations procedures[63] etc. may also
amount to misconduct. Not all disruptive behaviour or bad
work, however, necessarily amounts to misconduct. It is not constituted merely by a lower than average volume of production[64];
nor will the disruption of good relations with fellow-employees,
as by unsuccessfully bringing criminal charges, necessarily suffice, provided that the charges were brought in good faith.[65]

Unexplained absence from work is another common ground.[66]
Even if the reason is sickness, there is an obligation to inform the
employer so as to enable him to make necessary arrangements.[67]
It would, presumably, be otherwise if the sickness disabled the
employee from informing the employer. The misconduct consists not in being sick but in failing to take reasonable steps to
prevent the resulting disruption and inconvenience.

Insubordination may or may not amount to misconduct. An
unjustifiable refusal to carry out a reasonable order will.[68] A
good example is a refusal to work overtime contractually stipu-

lated for.[69] It is not, however, a "reasonable" order (though it may be reasonable as a request) to require an employee to undertake overtime not contractually required;[70] nor is a refusal unjustifiable if the order involves undue hazard or danger.[71] Even if the order is reasonable, a failure to comply with it may be excused, *e.g.* if it is reasonably misunderstood.[72] Provided that there is justification, it is irrelevant that a refusal has some ulterior motivation, such as dissatisfaction with wages.[73]

Misconduct "may be constituted by mere carelessness; but it is too much to expect that all people will at all times be entirely careful; and in considering whether a person has been guilty of misconduct it is necessary to discriminate between that type and degree of carelessness which may have to be put up with in human affairs, and a more deliberate or more serious type of carelessness which justifies withholding a benefit."[74]

Behaviour alleged to amount to misconduct often forms the subject-matter of proceedings in a court of law or other tribunal, giving rise to the status of the findings of such a body in connection with claims for benefit. "It is well-settled that a conviction by the competent court should be accepted as proof of the commission of the acts alleged," especially if the accused pleaded guilty,[75] but even if he did not.[76] Misconduct, even of a criminal nature, may, however, be constituted even though no criminal charges are brought[77] and, indeed, even an acquittal does not necessarily negative a finding of misconduct for it may be constituted by behaviour which does not import criminal liability. In *R(U) 8/57*, an employee acquitted of embezzlement was held to have been rightly disqualified for misconduct for even if the criminal charge was not established, he was at least guilty of serious negligence in the handling of the employer's funds. It is submitted, however, that where the alleged misconduct and the subject-matter of the criminal charge are one and the same, an acquittal would negative liability to disqualification.[78]

In recent years this problem has been raised in an acute form by the creation of new remedies in the event of loss of employment in certain circumstances. It is theoretically possible for a dismissal by reason of redundancy for the purposes of the Redundancy Payments Act 1965 to involve disqualification for unemployment benefit by reason of misconduct or voluntary leaving, although at first blush one might have thought the two mutually exclusive. Similarly, on first impression it might well be thought that a dismissal which is "unfair" for the purposes of Trade Union and Labour Relations Act 1974 could hardly be justified by reason of misconduct for the purposes of unemployment benefit.

There is much to be said for rationalising these procedures so that incongruity is avoided, although there are serious administrative obstacles to be overcome in order to do so.[79] At present, however, they are not rationalised and apparent anomalies will continue. They occur for a number of reasons. First of all, there are differences in the nature of proceedings before national insurance tribunals and industrial tribunals. Secondly, the manner in which the onus of proof shifts is not identical in the two types of proceeding. Thirdly, as long as there are separate proceedings, employer or claimant may seek to "improve" his evidence in the light of the first experience. Fourthly, a dismissal may be held to be unfair for procedural reasons whilst in relation to unemployment benefit the substance governs. Fifthly, it is not necessarily to be assumed that the same standard prevails in the different types of proceedings. If proper procedures are observed, it may be proper, from the point of view of unfair dismissal proceedings, to dismiss a worker who has demonstrated chronic minor inefficiency which is, however, insufficient to be considered misconduct or to provoke dismissal for voluntary leaving purposes. The national insurance authorities have accordingly taken the view that the findings of an industrial tribunal are not conclusive for disqualification purposes although they are, of course, evidence to be taken into consideration.[80]

Voluntary leaving without just cause

One who voluntarily leaves his employment without just cause is disqualified for receiving benefit. The onus of proving that he left voluntarily lies upon the insurance officer; that of establishing just cause rests upon the claimant.[81]

Voluntary leaving is usually constituted by the employee handing in his notice. If he does so, he will normally be regarded as having left voluntarily and it makes no difference that the employer chooses to dispense with his services summarily and pay wages in lieu of notice.[82] Exceptionally, however, an employee may be held not to have left voluntarily even though he has handed in his notice. This was the position in *R(U) 1/58* where, because of his conviction of a criminal offence, the claimant's action was merely an anticipation of a decision by his employers to dismiss him, and not voluntary leaving.

By contrast, a claimant may be held to have left voluntarily even though he was dismissed by his employer. If he has "invited dismissal," *i.e.* "in accordance with his own desires brought about the termination of his employment,"[83] he has, in substance, left voluntarily. It all depends upon whether he can fairly be said to be responsible for the severance of the relationship of employer and employee; whether the dismissal is the "natural consequence" of his action.[84] Normally, the employee must have acted or threatened to act in a manner involving a deliberate repudiation of his contract of employment.[85] As is pointed out above, this view of "leaving voluntarily" involves overlap with the ground covered by dismissal for "misconduct."

There seems to be an overlap also with paragraph (*c*) of section 20 (1), concerning failure to take a reasonable opportunity of suitable employment. In *R(U) 15/53*, the claimant had been summarily dismissed when he refused to accept a summary change in the terms of his employment in breach of contract resulting in a substantial drop in wages. He was held to have left voluntarily (though he had just cause), a view which is tenable if, as is often the case in unemployment benefit law, one has regard to the realities, rather than the legalities of the employment situation. In a similar situation in *R(U) 5/71*,[86] however, the Commissioner took the view that the claimant's action constituted failure under paragraph (*c*), though in this case the claimant was free to resume his employment whenever he chose to accept the new conditions.

Even though it is established that he left voluntarily, a claimant may still avoid disqualification if he can establish just cause. "So long as he does not break his contract with his employer, the individual is free to leave his employment without due regard to the interests of the rest of the community."[87] However, he "does not show just cause merely by demonstrating that he was acting reasonably in relation to his own interests.

The interests of others (the Fund and other contributors), have to be taken into account. The notion of 'just cause' involves a compromise between the rights of the individual and the interests of the rest of the community."[88] "It is not practicable to lay down any hard and fast rules to guide the statutory authorities as to the precise circumstances in which just cause or no just cause for leaving is shown. Each case must depend upon its own particular circumstances."[89] It is, however, possible to give some indication of the operation of this "defence" by reference to certain commonly occurring situations.

In broad terms, instances of alleged "just cause," in relation to voluntary leaving, are of three types:

1. Those where some feature of the existing employment is put forward as justifying the leaving.

2. Those where circumstances in the claimant's personal or domestic life are alleged to warrant the leaving.

3. Those where the claimant leaves in order to better himself.[90]

As to 1, it is clearly the case that leaving may be justified by objectionable features of the employment left, such as, for instance, the terms and conditions of employment being such as not to permit the employee to earn a proper livelihood.[91] Not any grievance will do. Normally, it must be substantial and personal to the claimant.[92] Even, however, if it is substantial and personal to the claimant, it will not necessarily (though it may) justify immediate leaving. The question here is whether immediate leaving is a proportionate response to the grievance complained of. If the employer offers no choice, leaving may be justified. *R(U) 18/57* affords a good illustration. Here, the employer ordered an apprentice to undertake work, which was admittedly outside the proper scope of the apprenticeship, failing which he must quit. Here, there was no doubt about the impropriety of the order, "there was no truly controversial issue between the parties" and there was no room, in view of the employer's ultimatum, for negotiation. Hence, the leaving was justified. But, "where an employed person has a legitimate grievance about his employment, he is not necessarily entitled, in the absence of immediate rectification of his grievance, to make himself a burden upon the insurance fund by throwing up his employment.... It is generally the duty of persons in such a situation to endeavour to have their grievances remedied through the proper channels, as for example by negotiation through their trade union."[93] It is emphasised that this is so even though the employer is clearly in the wrong in an important respect[94] so that ultimately, if all else fails, leaving may be justified. Nevertheless, all else must first be done. There is even authority for the proposition that even then leaving may not be immediately justified. If he has time and opportunity to do so, a claimant should first seek other employment before quitting the job that he has,[95] though no doubt this would not be insisted upon where continuation was intolerable.[96]

Under this heading, reference should be made to a number of cases concerning dismissal for refusal to join or continue membership of a trade union. The attitude of Commissioners has been that leaving might be justified if the claimant was being coerced to join against his will[97] or was in genuine dispute with his union,[98] but not if his refusal was for no substantial reason.[99] In any case there is still room for the requirements that grievance procedures should be exhausted and other employment sought.

As to 2, above, even though there are no objectionable features to the employment, good and sufficient personal or domestic reasons may justify leaving.[1] A wife may have to quit in order to join her husband who has taken employment elsewhere[2]; an employee may have to quit in order to visit or care for a dying father.[3] In an extreme and pressing case, the fact that the only decent accommodation for a man's family is so far away as to disable him from travelling to his work may justify leaving.[4] In all these cases, however, every effort should be made to secure alternative employment before the first job is left, and the timing of the leaving adjusted accordingly.[5] In the case of married women leaving in order to join husbands, it is arguable this practice is wrong. A wife who discharges her common law duty to live with her husband may be argued not to leave voluntarily. The practice is, however, a reasonable one and there is a case for amending the legislation so as to warrant it.

As to 3, above, this is really no more than a special instance of 2, above. Whilst it may be perfectly understandable for a man to quit employment in order to obtain a gratuity payable on

termination[6] or because there is no further financial gain to be
derived from a deferment of retirement[7] this fact does not
establish just cause, though it may warrant a reduction in the
period of disqualification.[8] Similarly, whether or not a man is
justified in leaving in order to get a better job turns upon the
reality of his prospects of doing so and the nature of the employment left.[9] Disqualification may be avoided if the claimant has
a better job to go to, even if it falls through.[10] But it may be
fatal if the claimant has not made exhaustive inquiries in order
to make certain that the new job is more or less immediately
available.[11] It may, however, be just cause for an employee
who genuinely believes work to be beyond his capacity and
unfair to his employer to quit in order to try and find employment more suitable in his case[12] even if no opportunity is
immediately available.[13]

Paragraphs (b), (c), (d) and (e). Each of those last four
paragraphs of section 20 (1) sets out a separate ground of
disqualification. Several concepts are, however, common to two
or more of them. It is proposed, therefore, to refer briefly to
each of the paragraphs separately, dealing with matters peculiar
to each, after which certain common matters, *i.e.* whether a
claimant has received an opportunity or offer, whether employment is "suitable," whether he has been guilty of a
"refusal," and whether he had "good cause," will be considered
separately.

(b) *Failure to Apply for a Notified Situation Vacant*

A person incurs disqualification if, without good cause, he
refuses or fails to apply for a situation in any suitable employment properly notified to him, *i.e.* "notified by the Employment
Service Agency, a local education authority or some other recognised agency, or by or on behalf of an employer."[14] Although
the most common channel of notification would be the Employment Service Agency and although paragraph (b) speaks of
"properly notified," it is plain from this definition that there
need be nothing formal or official about the method of notification. Merely being informed by or on behalf of an employer
seems to suffice.

(c) *Neglect to Avail of a Reasonable Opportunity of Suitable Employment*

There is a certain vagueness about this ground of disqualification, a feature of many parts of section 20. In the first place, overlap with paragraph (*b*) at least will clearly be involved in some cases. Facts constituting a failure to apply or refusal to accept for purposes of paragraph (*b*) may also constitute "neglect to avail" for purposes of paragraph (*c*) with this difference, that "good cause" will justify under the former, but not under the latter.[15] In practice, this will be unimportant because of the second respect in which paragraph (*c*) is vague. It contains a number of terms ("neglect," reasonable," "suitable") all of which may permit the same type of excusing evaluation attending a finding of "good cause." Thus, "In an appropriate case, a person's attitude towards some feature of a proposed employment may properly be regarded as making that employment not 'suitable' in his case: or as making the opportunity of such employment not a 'reasonable' opportunity: or, possibly, as making it inappropriate to describe his attitude as 'neglect' of anything."[16] The best example is a conscientious objection to a particular employment as opposed to a merely "intellectual" objection (the distinguishing feature alleged to be that the former must operate in the sphere of religion or morals).[17]

In *R(U)* 5/71, the requirement that Scottish teachers should register did not make an opportunity "unreasonable" *vis-à-vis* a claimant who refused to register; nor did it make the employment "unsuitable." And it did constitute "neglect to avail." This latter term seems to include doing anything likely to impair one's prospects of appointment. It covers not only an express refusal to take the job, or to fulfil a precondition of appointment to it such as registration in *R(U)* 5/71 but also presenting oneself in a dirty or unkempt condition for interview with a prospective employer.[18]

(d) *Failure to Carry Out Recommendations*

A person who fails without good cause to carry out "official recommendations" reasonable in his circumstances and in the light of job-hunting practices in his locality in order to help

him find work incurs disqualification. "Official recommendations" are recommendations in writing made by an officer of
the Employment Service Agency, a local education authority or
the Secretary of State.[19]

(e) *Refusal of Approved Training*

A person who, without good cause, fails to undergo approved
training in order to become or remain fit for regular work
incurs disqualification. The course of training must have been
approved by the government before the opportunity is offered.
"The proposed trainee should be told that it has been approved
in his or her case" so that "it would then be known that a
refusal would be a refusal ... involving a risk of disqualification."[20] Hence it is not sufficient that the training should have
been approved before it is refused, if it was not approved at
the time it was offered.[21]

Approval by the Secretary of State carries the question of
suitability of the training outside the purview of the statutory
authorities but nevertheless leaves them with a wide area of
jurisdiction in other respects, particularly:

(1) whether the claimant has without good cause turned it
down;

(2) whether his behaviour constitutes a refusal or failure to
avail; and

(3) whether a given opportunity was "reasonable."[22]

We may now turn to the matters listed above as being common
to two or more paragraphs:

(i) Whether an "oportunity" or "offer" has been received

An offer, or information about an opportunity must be
effectively communicated to the claimant and should enable
him to consider the terms of employment etc., under consideration.[23] The quality of his response (*e.g.* whether he has
"good cause" for his refusal) "must be determined in relation
to the terms of employment as represented to the claimant ... it
is immaterial that they are less favourable than the actual conditions of employment."[24] This statement was, however, made
in a case where even the less favourable terms communicated

did not justify the refusal. The position is therefore technically open where refusal seems justifiable on the basis of inaccurate information conveyed. Even more is it unsettled what the position would be if the actual job might properly have been refused, but the information conveyed makes refusal seem unjustifiable. It is believed that disqualification should not attach in either of these two latter cases. In the first case the claimant's failure to take reasonable employment etc. is hardly voluntary since he did not know of its existence. In the latter case, he ought to accept the "offer" but would be justified in leaving the "employment" immediately.

The statutory authorities will not countenance an offer of the same employment as that of which a previous refusal remains the subject of appeal. As long as a matter is *sub judice*, an offer of the same employment should not be made.[25]

(ii) Whether employment is "suitable"

The questions whether employment is suitable and whether a person has good cause for refusing it are rarely distinguished in the cases. It has indeed been stated that the two questions are "in effect one. They are inextricably interwoven, because the good cause (if any) for the refusal is the unsuitability of the employment for the claimant."[26] It is not uncommon for a Commissioner to hold that a claimant had good cause for refusal *because* the employment was unsuitable.[27] Whilst this approach may have a certain brusque realism about it, there is no denying that it flies in the face of the accepted canons of statutory interpretation, for it clearly renders one concept or the other otiose. From this point of view, decisions such as *R 6/60 (UB)* (where the decision is stated in the alternative) and, even better, *R 22/60 (UB)* (where the Commissioner decided that since the claimant in any case had good cause, the question of suitability need not be considered) are preferable. Even these decisions, however, suffer from the vice of obscurity as to the exact scope of the two concepts, whilst in the case of other decisions, one can see no reason at all why "good cause" should have been preferred to "unsuitability" as a ground of decision[28] and vice versa.[29]

The onus of proving unsuitability rests in the first instance upon the claimant.[30] "The very notion of a 'disqualification' implies an allegation that the case is an exception from the normal, and on ordinary principles of evidence one would expect the burden of proving the exception to lie in the first instance on the party alleging it." However, "if the insurance officer makes out a prima facie case that the situation was suitable for the claimant the onus is then upon the claimant to show that the situation was not in fact suitable employment in his case."[31] If the employment is not in fact suitable, disqualification is avoided, and it is irrelevant that the claimant's motivation for the refusal related to some other feature of the employment.[32]

Some statutory guidance as to the meaning of "suitable" is offered by subsection (4) of section 20. This provides that in three instances, employment shall not be deemed "suitable" and that in one it shall not be deemed "unsuitable." The three instances of deemed non-suitability are:

1. vacancies due to a strike etc.;
2. work in the home district at the usual job on less favourable terms;
3. work away from home at the usual job on unfavourable terms.

The instance of deemed suitability is that of work in a different job on terms not less favourable than those offered by good employers, after the lapse of a reasonable time looking for the usual work.

Subsection (4) does not, however, state a comprehensive definition of "suitable." The three instances of deemed non-suitability state circumstances in which, if the conditions stated are satisfied, the statutory authorities are forbidden to decide that employment is suitable. The converse is not true. If the conditions of the three grounds are not satisfied, it does not follow that the employment is "suitable." The statutory authorities have a discretion and it is still open to them to decide that disqualification should not be imposed, *i.e.* that the employment is unsuitable for some other reason. The same applies to the instance of deemed suitability. "If the only reason for saying that the employment is unsuitable is that it is employment of a kind other than employment in the claimant's usual occupation, the statutory authorities, if the conditions in the concluding words are satisfied, are forbidden to say that it is unsuitable. [I think that the operation of these concluding words must be extremely limited in view of the presence of the all-important word 'only.'] Here again however the converse is not true. If the concluding words do not compel the statutory authorities to decide that the employment is suitable, that does not mean that they must necessarily decide that it is unsuitable."[33]

The slightly obscure purport of subsection (4) is at least in part due to its legislative history. In view of this, and because of the fact that the matters dealt with by it are by no means comprehensive, the concept of "suitability" is better approached from a different direction. As a general proposition (and bearing in mind that the onus of proof is on the insurance officer) the position is as follows. Prima facie, employment is not suitable unless it is in the claimant's usual job, in his home area, on conditions not less favourable than usual and is otherwise satisfactory. If any of these four elements is lacking, and particularly if there is deemed non-suitability under subsection (4), the employment is not suitable. The insurance officer may, however, except where there is deemed non-suitability, persuade the statutory authorities that the employment is nevertheless suitable. In particular, if he can establish the conditions of the one instance of deemed suitability he is entitled to succeed. The four elements above referred to will now be considered separately.

Work in the claimant's usual job

"Prima facie, employment in an occupation other than the claimant's usual occupation is not suitable...."[34] However, "under the concluding words of the subsection it may be deemed not to be unsuitable after 'the lapse of such an interval from the date on which he becomes unemployed as in the circumstances of the case is reasonable.'" Although the concluding words of subsection (4) refer to "the date on which he becomes unemployed" it has been held that the relevant date is that on which the claimant registers for work, notwithstanding that he has in fact been unemployed for a considerable time before then. In $R(U)$ $3/63$, the claimant became unemployed eight months before he registered and refused work three weeks thereafter. The interval was therefore three weeks only and this was too early a date to require him to change jobs. What is a reasonable period in any given case depends very much upon individual circumstances. If it is clear that the claimant has been and will continue for some time to be unfit for his regular work, it may well be reasonable to expect him to change.[35] If the claim for unemployment benefit results from short-time working and it is likely that full-time working will be resumed in the future, it may be reasonable for a claimant to refuse alternative work for a lengthy period.[36] During this reasonable period, a claimant will not, by taking temporary work of a different kind, prejudice his right to resume his usual work.[37] He will not, however, be allowed to escape disqualification merely by asserting that the work is of a different kind; he must make reasonable inquiries or he will incur disqualification.[38] Beyond this, it is impossible to be specific. Whether a reasonable time has elapsed depends upon the view taken by the statutory authorities.[39]

Work in the claimant's home area

Prima facie, a man is entitled to work in his home area. If, however, he has been unemployed for a long time; if he has no personal or domestic ties or if they can be reconciled with his moving; if there is little or no prospect of his obtaining work at home; and if he is not too old to move, it may be reasonable to require him to do so,[40] especially if the work offered is of a permanent character. If he is offered work in his usual occupation, it will not be suitable if it is "at a rate of remuneration lower, or on conditions less favourable, than those generally observed in that district by agreement between associations of employers and employees, or, failing any such agreement, than those generally recognised in that district by good employers."[41] In *R 5/61 (UB)*, work was considered unsuitable because the prospective employer, unlike many others, did not provide transport.

Conditions not less favourable

Prima facie, work is unsuitable if the terms are less favourable than usual. The standard of comparability, if he changes his area, is set out above. In the home area, the matter is dealt with by subsection (4): the work must not be "at a rate of remuneration lower, or on conditions less favourable, than those which he might reasonably have expected to obtain having regard to those which he habitually obtained in his usual occupation in that district, or would have obtained had he continued to be so employed." It will be noted that the criterion here is personal—comparison is to be made with the claimant's own employment history, rather than with general standards prevailing in another district[42] or another job.[43] A cut in salary[44] or a loss of security or responsibility[45] may suffice. Even though the standard is personal, however, comparison with the claimant's actual previous job is not required. Reference must be made to his "usual occupation" in that district, and it might be that different terms and conditions applied within the same occupation, as between different employers. In *R(U) 9/64* it was held that employment in the same place in the same occupation was not unsuitable merely because the previous employer paid for tea-breaks whilst the one under consideration did not. There were really two sets of standard terms in the same occupation and it was sufficient that the employment offered measured up to the lower of the two. *R 16/60 (UB)* suggests that in such a situation, the standard to be met is that of the "good employer." If this means that one may ignore a notoriously underpaid sector of the same occupation, this is consistent.

Otherwise satisfactory

It is often stated that the employment must be "suitable in the claimant's case." There have been many cases where employment has been argued, often successfully, to be unsuitable for personal or domestic reasons. This is very much the case so far as women with family responsibilities are concerned.[46] A physical incapacity exposing the claimant to an abnormal degree of risk might suffice[47] as might the absence of reasonable means of transport for getting to the work.[48] Particularly difficulty is encountered in the case of young persons whose parents forbid them to take certain kinds of work. Parental objection does not by itself justify a refusal to take work but has to be considered on its merits. If the employment is otherwise suitable and the parental objections unreasonable, disqualification may attach to refusal.[49] Normally, however, a parental objection sincerely raised on religious grounds will be considered reasonable.[50]

(iii) **Refusal**

An outright refusal of an offer creates no problems. It is just as much a refusal for a claimant to make an unacceptable counter-offer, *i.e.* to attach to an "acceptance" qualifying conditions which any reasonable employer would reject.[51] It is not settled what the position is if the counter-offer is a reasonable one nevertheless rejected by the employer.

Difficulty is occasioned where the claimant accepts the offer but causes the employer not to employ him by disclosing some fact which puts the employer off. If the disclosure is of the truth, it seems that no refusal is constituted, at all events if it is relevant. Thus, in *110/49 (UB)*, the claimant had informed the employer of his intention to resume work with his former employer at the earliest opportunity.[52] In *126/50 (UB)*, however, the claimant was disqualified. He had represented that he would be likely to take other work in the near future whereas in fact he had no such prospect at an early date.

"Good Cause"

As stated at the head of this section, "good cause" for his action figures as an avenue of escape for a claimant under several of the clauses of section 20. In addition, "just cause" enables him to avoid disqualification for voluntary leaving under clause (*a*). Much of the doctrine relating to "just cause"[53] also applies to the other clauses. In one respect, however, it would seem that "just cause" in clause (*a*) operates differently by virtue of the claimant's having been in employment immediately prior to the occurrence of the disqualifying event—his leaving. As we have seen, certain causes of leaving (grievances, personal reasons leading to the seeking of employment elsewhere, etc.) may be held to be just or not according to whether the claimant's response to them is reasonable or not. He must exhaust grievance procedures; he must seek as far as possible to assure that work awaits him elsewhere before he leaves. Whilst there is no decision squarely on the point, it is extremely doubtful if "good cause" would be held to function similarly in relation to the other clauses, *e.g.* if a claimant would be held not to have good cause for refusing to avail himself of a suitable opportunity because he declined to take work and put grievance procedures into operation immediately in order to remedy some vice in the employment (which might or might not be otherwise unsuitable).

The determination of questions of "good" and "just" cause is very much a matter of equitable jurisdiction. There are no statutory limits to the type of factor which may be held by the statutory authorities to constitute good or just cause. Past decisions (dealt with below) are therefore little more than illustrative of the type of factor likely to be viewed sympathetically in a subsequent case. Before considering these instances, one obvious point should be stated. The establishment of good cause is not a solid gold guarantee of the right to benefit. The husband who, in *R(U) 6/59*, left his work to look after the children while the wife worked had just cause for doing so. But he was clearly unavailable for work and was therefore disentitled to benefit.

Good cause may be constituted by matters such as a refusal, on grounds of conscience, to work on Sundays, but not, apparently, on grounds other than conscience.[54] It has been held that a claimant who refused employment as a deck-chair attendant on the ground that he feared he might become a seasonal worker did not have good cause, even though he was disabled and had recently had two deaths in the family.[55] The latter distressing events were presumably irrelevant to the work.

Certain types of factor occur more frequently. The following will be considered individually: personal and domestic circumstances; trade union policies etc.; change of work; and health.

Personal and domestic circumstances

Although this is a common type of factor,[56] no general principles emerge beyond that the personal or domestic circumstances must be relevant to the work, and that their impact is largely a matter of evaluation—of how much sympathy they exact. The special provision made in the case of married women should be noted:[57] the question whether a married woman is disqualified has to be determined on the same basis as that applicable to a single woman, giving, however, such consideration to "the responsibilities arising from her marriage as is reasonable in the circumstances of the case."[58]

Trade union policies etc.

It frequently happens that a claimant has refused work, etc., because acceptance of it would have conflicted with his trade union's policies or instructions to him.[59] The consistent view of the statutory authorities has been that observance of trade union policies or instructions does not constitute good cause etc., by itself. The question must be decided by reference to the factor in the employment which provokes the applicability of the policy or the instructions. This may or may not constitute good cause. Where trade union interests are put forward as "just cause" for voluntary leaving, disqualification may be constituted under the trade dispute disqualification.[60]

Change of work

Whether good cause is constituted by virtue of the fact that the work offered differs from that normally done depends upon a number of factors. Generally speaking, a claimant initially has a right to secure work in his normal occupation. This right, however, wanes with time. What period is reasonable in this context depends upon the circumstances. One relevant circumstance is the character of the alternative work offered. If it is work which could be left at any time in order to return to the normal work, it will not readily be conceded by the statutory authorities that there is good cause for its refusal.[61] Similar considerations apply where it is work of a short duration, *e.g.* seasonal work, and thus unlikely to interfere substantially with the resumption of the normal occupation.[62] Where, however, the alternative work offered involves jettisoning the claimant's considerable training and experience and seriously prejudicing his prospects of resuming his former employment, that there is good cause will be much more readily conceded.[63]

Health

Incapacity for work may found entitlement to sickness benefit. Short of this, however, it may have a dual impact on entitlement to unemployment benefit. First, reduced capacity may oblige a claimant to take alternative work (by virtue of severely limiting his prospects of resuming his former occupation) in circumstances which would otherwise have offered him good cause for refusal. In the second place, ill-health resulting in reduced capacity may justify refusing work which should otherwise have been accepted.[64] The crucial factor here is the state of health as the claimant reasonably believed it to be at the time of the refusal etc. It is irrelevant that it subsequently turns out that the medical advice on which he acted was wrong.[65]

PERIOD OF DISQUALIFICATION

Section 20 provides for disqualification "for such period not exceeding six weeks as may be determined." The section seems clearly to call for the exercise of discretion by the statutory authorities in fixing an appropriate period. The view formerly adopted, it seemed erroneously, by the Commissioner was that it was the duty of the statutory authorities to disqualify for the whole six weeks unless the claimant showed circumstances justifying a reduction.[66] In a recent decision, however, this error is corrected. Section 20 vests a discretion in the statutory authorities, unlimited save only that it should be exercised in a judicial manner. The correct approach is therefore for the statutory authorities to consider, in each case, what period of disqualification is appropriate and not to impose the maximum unless mitigating circumstances are proved.[67]

In considering what term to impose, one starts from the policy behind disqualification. Its purpose is not to punish the insured person but to protect the fund from claims in respect of a need which the insured person has brought upon himself.[68] "It follows that the fact that the insured person has been fined or imprisoned for his offence is not in itself a reason for reducing the period of disqualification."[69] Equally, however, where there are other reasons for imposing a reduced period, the period should be reduced—disqualification should not be used to penalise a claimant.[70] Where it is clear that the impact of the claimant's voluntary unemployment is spent in less than six weeks, it may be proper to terminate the period of disqualification then (see below).

Grounds for Reduction of Period

Frequently, the discretion to reduce the period of disqualification is exercised on grounds of sympathy with the claimant's plight.[71] This seems quite proper if it is confined to cases where the claimant's conduct posed no conscious threat to the national insurance fund. But it seems dubious, in the light of the above stated policy, if the motive is that greater "punishment" is not deserved. Decisions reducing the period on grounds of the claimant's subsequent recantation[72] seem to savour of the latter, though this objection disappears where the repentance has led to re-engagement[73] for here, the call on the fund is abated.

Peculiar rules apply in the case of misconduct. All the circumstances have to be taken into account, including whether the claimant realised or ought to have realised that what he was doing involved a risk of dismissal and a consequential demand on the fund.[74] Via this roundabout route, "mitigating circumstances" may be taken into account.[75] As the misconduct becomes less and less closely related to the employment there is more and more justification for reducing the period of disqualification.[76] "Misconduct may consist of many different degrees of culpability and may depend on a variety of circumstances which the particular claimant might or might not anticipate would lead to loss of employment."[77] Reduction of the period may not be used as a means of taking account of a conflict of evidence.[78]

Commencement and Termination of the Period of Disqualification

Commencement

"The general rule is that disqualification should run (normally) from the day following the end of the employment in question" (or, presumably, the refusal, etc.).[79] In cases of unnotified sickness, the appropriate date is not the last date on which work was done, but the date on which the claimant is discharged.[80] There were, however, well-established exceptions to the above "rule." Thus, where wages were received in lieu of notice, the period of disqualification only commenced at the expiry of the week covered by the wages.[81] Holiday pay, if attributable to the period after the employment ceased, was formerly treated in a similar manner[82] but under the "new view" of holiday payments[83] now falls out of account altogether.[84] A claimant who received benefit in ignorance of the disqualification was not entitled to evade the full period which accordingly commenced on the first day of the benefit week following the date of the decision. This is in accord with the other exceptions. It was also acknowledged, however, that if a claimant refrained from claiming benefit and thus failed, officially, to be "disqualified" he should not be prejudiced, but should be subjected to disqualification from the date on which he would have been disqualified had he claimed.[85]

In fact, this "rule" and "exceptions" can all be stated much more simply. A claimant liable to disqualification is disqualified from the date on which he would otherwise have been entitled to get unemployment benefit had he claimed, unless he has actually received it.

Termination

Once commenced, the period normally runs for an unbroken period for its duration (six weeks or the lesser period imposed) notwithstanding that benefit has actually been paid on a day during that period.[86] Some difficulty is encountered where the employment would have come to an end before the end of the period of disqualification. In *R(U)* *5/54*, a claimant had left voluntarily at a time when his job only had three weeks to run. Here, a period of three weeks only was imposed. If, however, it is merely speculative that the employment would have ended, that alone is no ground for a reduced period.[87] It seems, however, that once the period is settled, the disqualification continues, notwithstanding that the actual unemployment comes to an end by the claimant's taking work which he subsequently loses. This happened in *R(U)* *13/64*. The law here loses touch with its purpose. It is harsh to disqualify a man on the grounds that his unemployment is voluntary when he has in fact voluntarily taken other work which he has involuntarily lost.

Chapter 6

BENEFITS RELATING TO SICKNESS

Where primary reliance is placed upon earning capacity as a source of a minimum income, loss of that capacity due to inability to work by reason of sickness is an obvious target of an efficient social security system. English law has long recognised this. For centuries, equity recognised the care of the sick as a charitable activity.

Modern statutory provision was first made by the Workmen's Compensation Acts from 1897 onwards. These, however, only applied in cases where the disability stemmed from injury arising out of and in the course of work, and even then in by no means all such cases. Industrial injuries benefits have now succeeded workmen's compensation and preserved an anomaly; injury in a vehicle accident inside the factory gates leads to one type of benefit—the same accident in all other respects occurring outside the factory gates may well lead to sickness benefit instead. Industrial injury benefits are differently structured and give title to higher basic rates.[1] It is not easy to see why injury at the hands of a blameless employer should confer greater benefits than injury at the hand of a blameless outsider.

The first provision for sickness benefit as such (i.e. without regard to the source of the sickness unless, perhaps, self-imposed) was made by Part I of the National Insurance Act 1911, Part II dealing with the health service. Existing schemes were rationalised as a result of Beveridge, amongst whose "five giants" disease figured. The main attack on disease is, of course, mounted by the National Health Service. In so far, however, as disease leads to want by virtue of incapacity for work, that want falls to be catered for by the social security system. It remains a corollary of regarding the more or less free National Health Service as the chief weapon in the assault on disease that needs may be partially catered for by that service and therefore not need to be satisfied wholly by the social security system.[2] Most cases of reduction of benefit due to in-patient status in

N.H.S. hospitals are, as one would expect, sickness benefit cases.

The Beveridge scheme as incorporated in the post-War legislation included only one type of sickness benefit. This benefit continues in respect of cases of relatively short-term sickness. Since then, however, it has been recognised that needs arising from sickness are not simple, and other types of benefit suited to special needs have been instituted. The first of these were "invalidity benefit," taking account of long-term needs resulting from prolonged or chronic illness or disability, and "attendance allowances," providing benefit where an invalid's need for constant care and attention either disables a close relative from working or requires the employment of another in order to ensure that the care is given. Provision is also made in the latest legislation for non-contributory invalidity pensions[3] and invalid care allowance,[4] whilst mobility allowance[5] also goes some way towards alleviating hardship for the disabled.

SICKNESS BENEFIT

CLAIMS

Claims are made in the normal manner. The period of limitation within which a claim must be made varies. In the case of "original claims" the period is 21 days from the earliest day in respect of which the claim is made. Otherwise, claim must be made within six days; or, if it is a claim in respect of a continuing spell of sickness already the subject of a claim, within 10 days of the day in respect of which the claim is made.[6] There was at first some doubt about the validity of prospective claims[7] but prospective medical certification and, with it, claim, is now permitted within the limits prescribed by regulations.[8] Any disallowance by an insurance officer, including prospective disallowance, must be limited to the period covered by the claim.[9]

THE PRESENT LAW

To some extent, the conditions of entitlement to unemployment, sickness and invalidity benefit are integrated. Thus, for example, in order to be a day in respect of which benefit is payable (a day of unemployment or incapacity as the case may be) it must form part of a period of interruption of employment[10] and such a period may consist of days of both kinds.

The statutory provisions relating to unemployment and sickness benefits are presently consolidated in sections 14–17 of the 1975 Act. In so far as these provisions relate to sickness benefit, entitlement to benefit is established by fulfilment of conditions relating to contributions, capacity, and the avoidance of disqualification.

CONTRIBUTIONS

There is only one important difference between the contribution conditions for unemployment benefit and sickness benefit, at least so far as full benefit is concerned.[11] Whereas the "appropriate class" of contribution for unemployment benefit is Class I (employed earners and employers),[12] in the case of sickness benefit, it is Classes I *and* II (self-employed persons.)[13] For sickness benefit, the requisite condition may be satisfied by aggregating contributions from each class. If the principle behind this distinction is that a self-employed person is the master of his own fate so far as having to work is concerned, or even if it lies merely in the practical difficulty of proving unemployment in the case of self-employed persons, it is not entirely apt. It is, no doubt, true in many cases that the self-employed businessman may, by his own efforts, determine the amount of work he has to do. Equally, in the case of, say, a barrister, whether he is unemployed at any given time may be extremely hard to determine. The fact that a distinction can clearly be drawn in some cases, however, proves merely that some distinction, not necessarily the above one, might be drawn. Practices which have developed since 1946, particularly that of labour sub-contracting,[14] make out a case for rethinking the distinction.

EXHAUSTION OF RIGHT TO BENEFIT

Once, in respect of any single period of interruption of employment, a person *has been entitled*[15] to sickness benefit for 168 days, he ceases to be entitled to it and normally becomes entitled instead to invalidity benefits,[16] payable at a higher rate. The words "has been entitled" have occasioned some unresolved difficulty.[17] In *R(S) 27/52* a Commissioner decided that where benefit had not been "receivable" in respect of some of the days because of failure to make a timeous claim, the claimant was not "entitled" in respect of those days.

In *R(S) 1/56*, however, a case where a sickness benefit claimant had been receiving industrial injuries benefit, the reasoning which prevailed was that the "incapacity for work" which was an essential condition for receipt of the latter benefit, constituted "entitlement" for sickness benefit. The reasoning in the two decisions appears to be inconsistent. According to the former, a claimant is not entitled so long as any of the essential pre-conditions for receipt (including procedural ones) remains un-fulfilled. According to the latter, entitlement is established once the substantial conditions ("incapacity for work") are fulfilled, notwithstanding that for procedural reasons benefit may not be receivable. (It might have been possible to arrive at the same decision in the 1956 case, by reference to the overlapping bene-fits legislation, by reasoning compatible with that in the 1952 case, but this was not done.)

The conflict is not easy to resolve. Policy-wise, the 1952 decision seems satisfactory, because failure to claim social security benefits is unlikely to delay an illness on its course to becoming chronic. At the same time, the phrase used is "been entitled," not "received," suggesting that there must be some limit to the conditions non-fulfilment of which may result in non-receipt of benefit, such as failure to cash orders. It is sug-gested, however, that the 1952 decision hints at the proper distinction—"entitlement," involving the notion of "title," is a legal concept and would seem to arise when all the necessary legal conditions are fulfilled. Actual receipt may necessitate the fulfilment of further, non-legal conditions, but they are irrele-vant. Procedural conditions are, however, legal conditions and a failure to fulfil them would seem to result in failure of "title."[18]

Capacity

Day of Incapacity

Sickness benefit is payable in respect of any day of incapacity for work which forms part of a period of interruption of employment.[19] This latter term bears the same meaning for both sickness and unemployment benefit.[20] It follows that where the normal week consists of some days of work and others involving a different activity, as in *R(S) 8/61*, where the occupation involved three days per week attending classes at a polytechnic, no benefit is payable for those other days.

Because "incapable" is given a fairly broad meaning, it is possible to be "incapable" (*i.e.* unfit to do work which one might reasonably be expected to do) and yet work. Actual work is, however, fatal to a claim unless it is *de minimis* (below) or permissible under regulation 7(1)(g) of the Unemployment, Sickness and Invalidity Benefit Regulations, *i.e.* the earnings from it are normally less than £9 per week and either:

(i) it is done under medical supervision whilst a patient in hospital or a similar institution, or, if not,

(ii) the claimant has good cause for doing it.

It is perhaps anomalous to have an earnings limit for this particular purpose. It seems to function as a crude evaluator of the substantiality of the work done rather than as a means-test for, provided that one does no work, one may draw unlimited wages as well as benefit.

"Subject to the *de minimis* rule, a day is not a 'day of incapacity for work' unless the claimant is incapable of work[21] throughout the 24 hours of that day, counting from midnight to midnight, or is deemed in accordance with regulations to be so incapable of work."[22] It has been held that the *de minimis* rule does not warrant the ignoring of periods of five, two or even one hour.[23] Fifteen minutes has been ignored.[24] The "nightworkers' regulation"[25] was not originally applicable in sickness benefit cases[26] but subsequent amendment has removed the anomaly and the smaller part of a shift of work spanning midnight can now be ignored so as to allow the day on which it occurs to be treated as a day of incapacity. One situation remains uncertain in its effect. If a night shift which would, if completed, have been attributed to the second day under the "nightworkers' regulations" is prematurely terminated by sickness so that the greater part of the period actually worked falls on the first day, can the second day be treated as a day of incapacity? The legislation is ambiguous—"period of employment" (the night shift) can be interpreted so as to mean either the period of work originally contemplated or the period actually worked. The obvious solution is to ensure that a day qualifies for benefit where a day's earnings are substantially lost, but amendment of the legislation would be necessary in order to achieve this result—no single interpretation of "period of employment" would permit distinguishing between those situations where no further work was done on the second day, and where a new shift, attributable under the "nightworkers' regulations," was begun. In those probably rare situations where the effect of premature termination of a night shift by reason of illness is loss of the whole shift's pay, the case for allowing a day of incapacity is unanswerable but not, under the present legislation (which uses hours actually worked as the criterion, whether paid for or not) necessarily admissible.

It is provided by regulations[27] that "a person who at the commencement of any day is, or thereafter on that day becomes incapable of work . . . and does no work as an employed earner or self-employed earner on that day shall be deemed to be so incapable of work throughout that day." So one does not lose benefit merely because one is fit during non-working hours. The regulation is, however, couched in terms so wide as to allow payment of benefit to a claimant fit to work during working hours provided only that he was incapable at some other time and did not in fact work.

A day of departure from Great Britain (normally resulting in disqualification for sickness benefit) was held, in *R(S) 3/59*, to be excluded from a period of disqualification and thus capable of being treated as a day of incapacity, the same view having been taken with regard to unemployment benefit in *C.U. 54/48 (KL)*.

Specific Disease or Bodily or Mental Disablement

A day shall not be treated as a day of incapacity for work unless on that day the claimant is, or is deemed to be, incapacitated "by reason of some specific disease or bodily or mental disablement."[28] Obviously, therefore, if personal circumstances other than disease or disablement enter into a determination of incapacity, such as, in *R(S) 13/54*, a claimant's need to look after her invalid mother, title to sickness benefit is not established.

The dividing line between a cognisable psychological state
and chronic malingering is a fine one. The former will clearly
suffice[29] even though the effect of the medical evidence is merely
to suggest that it would be "inadvisable" for the claimant to
work. Otherwise, the decision seems to turn upon whether or not
a claimant really believes that there is something wrong with
him. The claimant in *R(S) 6/59* was suffering from "Mun-
chausen's Syndrome" and regularly visited hospitals complain-
ing of symptoms consistent with disease of the kidney or ureter.
The Commissioner took the view that "If I felt satisfied ... that
the claimant's condition was a psychosis, so that, despite the
absence of organic disease, it was reasonable to infer that the
symptoms of which he complained were real to him with the
result that he attended hospital in the genuine belief that benefit might be derived from doing so and for the genuine purpose
of having their cause ascertained, I should hold that there was
no evidence to rebut the prima facie evidence of incapacity....
But on the facts ... I am not satisfied. The balance of probabilities appears to me to support the view that the claimant's
condition was due to a defect of character and not to disease or
mental disablement."

Alcoholism seems to be classifiable as a "disease or disablement"[30] though its causes may be such as to result in disqualification for benefit.[31] Pregnancy has occasioned some difficulty.
A woman entitled to a maternity grant in respect of a confinement used to be disentitled to sickness (and unemployment)
benefit for the four weeks following the confinement[32] but is so
no longer. Apart from this, decisions have made it clear that
disease associated with pregnancy qualifies just as does any other
disease or disablement.[33] Considerable doubt, however, surrounds disablement by pregnancy quite apart from any associated disease. Dicta in *C.S. 221/49 (KL)*, in which disease is defined as "a departure from health capable of identification by its
signs and symptoms, an abnormality of some sort," state that
pregnancy is not a bodily disablement, nor a disease. At the
same time, it is said, in *R(G) 3/54*, that at the time of the
confinement, a woman "would clearly be incapable of work by
reason of bodily disablement" and this is thought to be the
better view. This is, in any case, a satisfactory reconciliation.
Pregnancy does not, *ipso facto*, involve disablement. Whether or

not it does (even apart from any associated disease) is a question of fact calling for a consideration of the impact of the stage of pregnancy reached in relation to the actual job done. If, in fact, the woman is disabled by the pregnancy from doing her work (as, presumably, she would be at least during the process of childbirth) then she is surely suffering from a "bodily disablement."

Incapacity for Work

Unless the sickness incapacitates for work,[34] no question of benefit arises.[35] Difficulty arises, however, where the sickness has the indirect effect of disabling a claimant from undertaking his work. In *R(S)* *8/53*, the Commissioner took the view that a disabled claimant with an artificial leg, unable to attend work because of inclement weather, was not thereby entitled to sickness benefit. The reasoning is not compelling—"The claimant was not incapable of work, but was prevented by circumstances beyond his control from reaching his place of employment." The better reasoning, hinted at in the decision, is the "outwork" *rationale*,[36] that is he was not incapable of work because he could have done suitable work had it been brought to him. This avenue is not, however, open in *R 2/58 (S.B.)*, a Northern Ireland decision purporting to follow *R(S)* *8/53*, in which the claimant's assertion that he would have been incapable of reaching *any* work available went unchallenged. This rule is not a happy one—it is abundantly plain that a person deprived of the power to earn by virtue of a disease or disability which precludes access to all work available is a victim of the precise species of need for the abatement of which sickness benefit is designed. Carried to its logical conclusion, it would follow that a person whose work at his place of work consisted exclusively of mental activity would be disentitled to sickness benefit if he were bed-ridden by a physical disablement rendering his place of work inaccessible. He would be "capable" of the work, if he could get there.

This anomaly is highlighted by the fact that certain other cases of indirect incapacitating clearly qualify. Some of these are established by regulations and are dealt with under the heading "deemed incapacity" below.[37] One other common case

arises where a person capable of light work, sickness notwithstanding, cannot actually attend his place of work by virtue of
attending for treatment. Here, if, when the claimant attends for
treatment he is precluded from attending work on the day in
question, he is "on that day as much 'incapable of work by
reason of some bodily disablement' as if [he] had gone to hospital
for a week. The fact that the disablement would not by itself
have prevented [him] from doing light work (or even [his]
ordinary work) is immaterial."[38] Whether a claimant is actually
so precluded is a question of fact, more readily established in the
case of employed than in the case of self-employed persons, the
latter being more readily able to adjust the hours of work so as
to accommodate attendance for treatment.[39]

Reduced Capacity for Work

The most common type of sickness benefit case is that where
the disease or disablement has the effect of partially disabling the
claimant from work. In deciding upon the question of incapacity
"functions which can only be performed with substantial pain
should be included in the estimate of a claimant's degree of
capacity."[40] On the other hand, "work includes part-time work"
and if a capacity for the latter remains, benefit is not payable.[41]
Nor is it payable if the disablement is in respect of a particular
kind of work only, the claimant remaining fit for alternative
work. On this ground, in *C.S. 561/50 (KL)*, a merchant seaman
certified as disabled from going to sea by virtue of needing a
course of dental treatment, was refused benefit (see also, *1144/49
(SB)*). There is, however, a qualification of this rule. "In a case
of temporary illness of short duration, a claimant's incapacity for
work should be judged by reference to his normal field of employment because he could not in such circumstances reasonably be
expected to embark on a new career, but, when a claimant's
disabilities last for a long period, the field of employment to be
taken into account must be enlarged."[42] If, in fact, the illness
is long term, capacity for alternative work disentitles for benefit,
even though the claimant's past experience and means cause him
to decline to consider the alternative.[43] Furthermore, the alternative types of work need not actually be available.[44] Benefit has
been refused even in the case of acute agoraphobia on the

ground that outwork in the claimant's own home remained notionally available.[45] There must, however, be a limit to this rule if benefit is ever to be payable. If the allegedly alternative work could not be available, benefit ought not to be refused. It has been decided that the mere fact that a claimant might be trained so as to become capable of alternative work does not justify withholding benefit,[46] nor does capacity for the sort of work classifiable as "non-employment" for contribution purposes.[47]

Diminution of Capacity to Perform Existing Work

"Whether a given disability renders a person incapable of work depends not only on the nature of the disability ... but also on the personal capacities of the individual, and on the nature of the work."[48] A negligible amount of work can be ignored.[49] What is negligible is a question of fact. Instances which have been regarded as negligible include the signing of cheques for a business,[50] collecting the proceeds of two boys' newspapers rounds and paying the bills,[51] and feeding and tending 100 hens on a smallholding.[52] A considerable amount of work was treated as "negligible" in *C.S. 449/50 (KL)*; a similar decision again would seem unlikely in view of regulation $7(1)(g)$.[53] Three and a half to four and a half hours' work a day was held to be too much in *C.S. 9/48 (KL)*.

Whether or not the work is negligible calls for the same approach whether employment or self-employment is under consideration.[54] In many types of self-employment, however, a claimant may be rendered unable to pursue the more active roles of his normal occupation and yet remain able to contribute to the functioning of the business in a supervisory capacity. A professional man suffering from a broken wrist but able to dictate letters, supervise staff and answer the telephone has been held not to be incapable of work.[55] A manual labourer with such a disability would certainly be incapacitated.[56] The question is one of fact in each particular case.[57] Something resembling a rule emerges in the case of working housewives: "If a woman is capable of doing the domestic work of a normal household, that would be evidence to support the view that she was capable of remunerative work because by doing for an employer what she does for her family she could reasonably be expected to obtain remuneration. At the other extreme, a woman living alone in a small house or flat might be able to cook her own food and make her own bed and yet that would not be sufficient reason for inferring that she was capable of remunerative work, because for so limited a performance of work no employer would normally be expected to engage and remunerate her."[58]

Deemed Incapacity

Regulation 3 of the Unemployment, Sickness and Invalidity Regulations provides: "(1) A person who is not incapable of work may be deemed to be incapable of work by reason of some specific disease or bodily or mental disablement for any day on which either—

(a)   (i) he is under medical care in respect of a disease or disablement as aforesaid,

      (ii) it is certified by a registered medical practitioner that by reason of such disease or disablement he should abstain from work, and

      (iii) he does not work; or

(b)   he is excluded from work on the certificate of a Medical Officer for Environmental Health and is under medical observation by reason of his being a carrier, or having been in contact with a case, of infectious disease."

Obviously, all the stipulated conditions must be satisfied; the claimant in *R(S) 8/61* failed because, although excluded from work on the certificate of a Medical Officer of Health due to contact with measles, she was not under medical observation by reason thereof. In *R(S) 8/53*, benefit was denied because the doctor, considering the claimant incapable of work, did not advise him to abstain!

The power to deem is discretionary; satisfaction of all the conditions will not necessarily be enough. Even under previous regulations[59] (which provided that a claimant "shall, if an insurance officer, a local tribunal, or the Commissioner, as the case may be, so determines, be deemed to be incapable") the Northern Ireland Commissioner decided[60] that an appellant who satisfied the conditions in (a) above could nevertheless be denied benefit if in fact he was clearly capable of work. *A fortiori*, this is the correct approach now that the regulation is expressly and unambiguously discretionary.

PROOF OF INCAPACITY

The vast majority of claims for sickness benefit are processed and benefit awarded without the aid of a tribunal being invoked or questions of strict proof arising at all. The prospective claimant visits his doctor and obtains his "sick-note" on the strength of which claims will normally be admitted.[61] Not that this procedure meets with the approval of all involved. The medical profession in particular does not take kindly to functioning as a certifying authority and some bodies have advocated the abandonment of "sick-notes," substituting therefor formal declarations by claimants, sanctioned by perjury or some allied statutory offence.

It was certainly the case, during the doctor's strike of 1970, that the number of claims for sickness benefit (for the duration of the strike made on the basis of a questionnaire, not a sick-note) fell strikingly. This, by itself, is however, equivocal. Some decline could surely be attributed to the change in procedures itself causing some confusion and disabling some claims from being made. The latest regulations,[62] however, have relaxed the obligations thrust upon doctors and as a corollary, vested a more substantial power in the statutory authorities to determine whether an incapacity exists.[63]

Medical ethics have resulted in a practice, now expressly permitted by regulations,[64] of not disclosing to a claimant or his representative medical evidence, knowledge of which would be harmful to the patient. There is obviously a case for doing this in some circumstances, yet, as a complaint to the Parliamentary Commissioner for Administration indicates,[65] it can lead to misunderstanding and can result in injustice. The Department of Health and Social Security has now modified its procedures to the extent of inquiring what the claimant and his family already know, so that information is not purposelessly withheld. What they do not know, however, may still be withheld in the interests of the patient, so that misunderstanding and injustice may still occur.

Even where the claim reaches a tribunal, the doctor's evidence will commonly be accepted without question. A local national insurance officer may, however, seek a second opinion from the regional medical officer of the Ministry of Health if he has reason to doubt the claimant's doctor's evidence. If this happens, the regional medical officer will ask the claimant's doctor for information likely to be of assistance. A regional medical officer normally sends a copy report to the claimant's own doctor immediately, thus providing that doctor with an immediate opportunity of checking the medical officer's findings.[66] This is in line with the policy of the tribunals, in all cases where medical facts are in question, of securing as much relevant evidence as possible and of ensuring that harmful evidence is made available to the party, whether claimant or insurance officer, against whose contentions it bears[67] although exceptional circumstances might warrant non-disclosure according to the practice described above.[68]

Where medical facts are in issue the best evidence will, obviously, normally be that of medical experts. In the absence of any good reason for not calling it, a claim will normally be rejected[69] (as it was in *R(S) 13/51*) where the claimant had not considered himself ill enough to consult his doctor. Whilst, however, a doctor's evidence will normally be necessary, it does not follow that it will be sufficient to ground a claim. Where, although "incapable" (*i.e.* not reasonably capable) a claimant nevertheless works, he loses his right to benefit, medical certification notwithstanding.[70] *A fortiori*, mere medical inspection will not, by itself, necessarily suffice.[71] Actual hospitalisation will normally warrant the inference that the patient is "incapable" but even this appears to be rebuttable. It will not, however, do merely to establish that there was no actual disease or physical disablement, for "even though he has been admitted (to hospital) only for investigation ... a man cannot be expected to work if there are reasonable grounds for belief that he is suffering from a disease, while the matter is under investigation."[72]

The Department's own record of the claimant's claims history may function as a useful indicator of the likelihood of his claim being good. It can cut both ways. A claimant who had previously on several occasions avoided examination by a Ministry doctor predictably had his claim disallowed on repetition of this practice.[73] Similarly, a claim calls for careful scrutiny when, for the third year in succession, it is for a short period covering Christmas, especially if the "sick-note" has been issued without attendance.[74] In general, however, the claims history will be, by itself, equivocal. A long series of short claims relating to a particular illness may evidence constant recurrence of the complaint, or malingering. The details of the history, the circumstances in which the claims were made and the manner in which they were disposed of on previous occasions are all relevant.[75]

The primary instrument whereby general practitioners are enjoined to take the task of certification seriously is examination by a Ministry doctor. No doubt, many claims are rejected on the strength of such second opinions. In cases appealed to a Commissioner, however, it is far from the case that the evidence of the Ministry's own doctor is invariably accepted—quite the contrary. In seven reported cases, the evidence of the Ministry doctor was rejected in five cases where it was unfavourable to the claimant and accepted in one case where it was favourable. In only one case was it accepted where unfavourable.[76] In many cases, of course, there will have been an exchange of views and further evidence will be adduced as a result.[77]

Once a claimant proves incapacity, he gets the benefit of a presumption of continuance in so far as consistent with the nature of the original medical evidence contained in the certificate.[78] If, however, the claimant returns to work or otherwise breaks the continuance, the presumption is rebutted and the claimant is put to further proof, not only of incapacity thereafter, but even of each day prior to the act of discontinuance.[79] Mere receipt of another benefit or pension conditioned upon incapacity will not be treated by itself as establishing title to sickness benefit.[80]

Expert medical evidence would seem to be the best way of seeking to establish the medical facts relating to incapacity, though it is to be remembered that there are other aspects, such as the nature of a particular industrial process, that are no more within the knowledge of a doctor than of a priest. If there is doubt about the efficaciousness of the present procedures, it is on the ground that the medical profession may be a reluctant and, in some cases, a less than diligent participant in them. It must, however, be said that in addition to formal sanctions being available in case of gross abuse, the medical profession itself takes a serious view of carelessness in this sphere of administration and there would seem to be little that could be done to improve methods of proof. To depart from medical certification might well make the doctor's lot a happier one. It is unlikely to result in more reliable methods of proof.

DISQUALIFICATION[81]

Disqualification in cases of sickness and invalidity benefit is dealt with by regulations[82] which authorise disqualification of a claimant for a period of up to six weeks on the grounds stipulated below:

1. That ". . . he has become incapable of work through his own misconduct, except that this disqualification shall not apply where the incapacity is due to venereal disease or, in the case of a woman who is not a wife, or being a wife, is separated from her husband, to pregnancy. . . ."

"Drinking to such an extent as to endanger health is prima facie misconduct, and if it is a direct cause of a person's incapacity for work that person has become incapable of work through his own misconduct." This presumption can be rebutted by proof that the alcoholism was "really involuntary," *i.e.* the result of an "impairment of will power" due to circumstances beyond the claimant's control.[83] The same reasoning applies to a number of other sources of incapacity, such as venereal disease and pregnancy (specifically excluded by the regulation itself) and, in the present stage of medical knowledge, presumably smoking and over-eating. If a distinction is to be drawn, it can only be the dubious one that incapacity from excess alcohol is a more probable consequence than disablement from tobacco or over-eating. A literal interpretation of the regulation leads to the conclusion that it may be misconduct for a wife living with her husband to become pregnant. This would seem absurd in the case of such a wife becoming pregnant by her husband, but not so where the pregnancy results from adultery. It would nevertheless be anomalous not to except such a pregnancy.

2. That ". . . he fails without good cause to comply with a notice in writing given by or on behalf of the Secretary of State requiring him to attend for and to submit himself to medical or

other examination on a date not earlier than the third day after the day on which the notice was sent and at a time and place specified in that notice...."

Time begins to run only when the claimant receives the notice, the first of the "three clear days" being the day after that on which he receives it.[84]

3. That "... he fails without good cause to attend for, or to submit himself to, medical or other treatment; provided that this disqualification shall not apply to any failure to attend for or to submit to vaccination or innoculation of any kind or to a surgical operation, unless the failure is a failure to attend for or to submit to a surgical operation of a minor character, and is unreasonable...."

In one respect, this particular ground of disqualification falls short of its objective, *i.e.* seeking to ensure that benefit is confined to cases of involuntary incapacity. In *R 2/60 (SB)* a Ministry medical officer had, after examination, suggested that a claimant suffering from rheumatoid arthritis was suitable for a course rehabilitating him for alternative employment, and the claimant's own doctor had certified him as fit to attend it. Attendance at the course, we may presume, would have increased his chances of obtaining work, his existing incapacity notwithstanding. Nevertheless, he could not be disqualified for non-attendance. "I cannot see how a course of gardening, even under medical supervision, can possibly be construed in its widest sense, as treatment for rheumatoid arthritis."[85] Clearly, either the regulation or the interpretation here put upon it, is defective. It might be considered that it would not be too artificial to interpret the words "other treatment" as embracing therapy aimed at removing the social disabilities resulting from the physical incapacity.

The criticism might also be made of *R(S) 3/57* relating to the first of three following "rules of behaviour":

4. That "... he fails without good cause to observe any of the following rules of behaviour, namely:

(1) to refrain from behaviour calculated to retard his recovery, and to answer any reasonable inquiries (not being inquiries relating to medical examination, treatment or advice) by the Secretary of State or his officers directed to ascertaining whether he is doing so;

(2) not to be absent from his place of residence without leaving word where he may be found;

(3) to do no work for which remuneration is, or would ordinarily be, payable unless it is work" which is described in regulation $7(1)(g)$.[86]

The view taken in *R(S) 3/57* was that "recover" above meant "recover from the disease or disablement causing incapacity" and that accordingly training, which would not have removed the disability but which would have enabled him to take other work, could be refused with impunity.

The provision which has occasioned most difficulty is rule (3) above. Work for which payment would normally be made disqualifies even if no payment is in fact made unless *all* the conditions stipulated are satisfied.[87] Thus, it avails nothing that the work was undertaken under medical treatment if the claimant was not, in fact, a patient in or of a hospital.[88] *A fortiori*, medical advice merely to "get some fresh air" cannot be used as an umbrella for earning as a taxi driver.[89] In genuine cases, however, the tribunals have not shown themselves to be unduly rigorous in ensuring that the conditions are fulfilled. In *R(S) 3/52*, work in a factory for rehabilitation purposes done under the general supervision of a tuberculosis officer was held to be "undertaken under medical supervision" and as "part of his treatment," whilst the requirement that the claimant had to be a patient "in or off" a hospital was satisfied by his out-patient status, in which capacity he attended for examination every two months.

"Good Cause"

It will be noted that in the case of grounds 2., 3. and 4., above, provision is made for ignoring the existence of grounds for disqualification given "good cause." The onus of proving "good cause" is on the claimant and should be clearly discharged.[90] Whilst what constitutes "good cause" in any particular case calls for an evaluation, it is possible to detect in the decisions of Commissioners a disposition to view more sceptically claims of "good cause" for undertaking remunerative work than for other reasons,[91] though even here, medical encouragement or authorisation of the work may confer upon it the character of "good cause."[92] Where remunerative work is not involved, Commissioners seem to have been quite lenient in some cases. Thus, a Christian Scientist's genuine conscientious beliefs were held to be a sufficient excuse for refusing treatment and it was irrelevant whether they were reasonable or not.[93] This is in marked contrast with the position of the claimant in $R(S)$ *21/52* who was disqualified for aggravating influenzal bronchitis by undertaking a 60-mile drive in March. In this latter case, the claimant was ignorant of the rule. Had he known of its content, who can say what action would have been compelled by his conscience?

Period of Disqualification

Disqualification is meant to be effective and should strike at the period when it will be most effective. Normally it should take effect from the day after that for which benefit has last been paid, where the ground of disqualification supervenes. Otherwise, it should date immediately from the day on which entitlement for benefit would otherwise have been established.[94] The length of the disqualification depends entirely upon the circumstances of the case but is limited by regulation 11 to six weeks. Where, however, the ground of disqualification is of little practical effect, a short period would be appropriate.[95]

CRITICISM

The sickness benefit rules assume that loss of work through illness necessarily involves loss of income from work. There is no "earnings rule" and it is not a condition of benefit that income from work cease. In the case of most occupations, this assumption may well be warranted. It is clear, however, that in some it is not and that salary or wages continue to be paid in whole or in part, absence through illness notwithstanding. In these cases, sickness benefit may simply be an additional bonus payable for the duration of the spell off work. Illness may well involve a person in extra expenditure but not, surely, to the extent per week of sickness benefit. No doubt, extra income functions to some extent as a solatium for the discomfort attending the illness, but this is hardly a function of the social security system.

One by-product of the institution of sickness benefit has been that in many occupations which previously carried a continuation of full pay during illness, employers have now adopted the practice of paying on a scale equal to full pay less the amount of sickness benefit recoverable. Even in such a case, the employee is still better off, since the benefit is not taxable. Even more so, however, is the employer better off—in such a case, sickness benefit is not so much guaranteeing a continuation of a minimum income to the claimant as relieving the employer of a substantial part of his wages burden. It is quite certain that sickness benefit was never intended to do this.

If the only alternative to this generosity were means-testing, on the supplementary benefits model, one would have to tolerate it, for the insurance principle is incompatible with such means-testing. In many other parts of the social security schemes, however, an earnings rule is imposed *e.g.* in relation to retirement pensions.[96] There is abundant scope for an earnings rule in the case of sickness benefit. Such benefit is, after all, the object of one of the largest items of national insurance fund outgoings and the potential savings are considerable.

INVALIDITY BENEFIT

Invalidity benefit was introduced by the National Insurance Act 1971, s. 3, in order to make better provision for the chronically sick. It consists, in substance, of a device for allowing sickness benefits to be paid at a higher rate in some cases of prolonged illness.[97]

The benefit becomes payable when a claimant who satisfies the contribution condition for sickness benefit in full passes the 168th day in any single period of interruption of employment. It consists of an invalidity pension, payable in all cases, and an invalidity allowance payable to persons five years below pensionable age and varying in amount according to age. The highest rate of allowance, is payable to beneficiaries under the age of 35 at the date of qualification. A middle rate is payable for persons between 35 and 45 and a lower rate for persons over 45.[98]

Grounds of disqualification are the same as for sickness benefit.[99]

Invalidity benefit is now governed by sections 15–16 of the 1975 Act.

ATTENDANCE ALLOWANCE

Beveridge's detection of sources of need has now been seen not to have been comprehensive. In the same way that the need for child's special allowance was not foreseen,[1] so also the scope of the need occasioned by chronic sickness and incapacity was not accurately forecast.

Chronic illness may do more than merely disable the patient from earning a living. It may have the effect of disabling others also. The need for constant care and attention, due to, for instance, incontinence, may mean that a member of the family who might otherwise have worked and provided support cannot be spared so as to do so. Not only this, but the constancy of the need for care may impose demands which it is unreasonable to expect any person single-handed to satisfy. For these reasons, a new benefit, attendance allowance, was instituted by the National Insurance (Old Persons' and Widows' Pensions and Attendance Allowance) Act 1970 (hereafter, "the 1970 Act"). It is now governed by section 35 of the 1975 Act. In this latest form, account is taken of the fact that needs for attention may vary. Formerly payable at a flat-rate, the allowance is now payable at two levels—a higher level where the demand for attention is very heavy; and a lower level where it is less so.

CONDITIONS OF ENTITLEMENT

Attendance allowance was one of the first of an increasing number of benefits under the national insurance scheme which are non-contributory and in respect of which it was never required that any person be insured under the scheme. Allowances today remain payable out of general exchequer and not out of the national insurance fund.[2] There are, accordingly, no contribution conditions. The chief conditions of entitlement therefore relate to the disability of the claimant (the medical conditions). Other conditions relate to presence or residence in Great Britain (or Northern Ireland as the case may be),[3] to procedures in connection with claims, and as to special circumstances warranting modification of the general conditions of entitlement in special cases.

The Medical Conditions

There are two conditions: a day-time condition and a night-time condition. Both require that a "person"[4] be "so severely disabled physically or mentally that . . . he requires from another person either (i) . . . attention throughout the day in connection with his bodily functions or (ii) continual supervision . . . in order to avoid substantial danger to himself or others." In the case of the day-time condition, the attention must be "frequent" and "throughout the day" whilst in the case of the night-time condition it must be "prolonged or repeated . . . during the night." If "continual supervision" grounds the claim, it must be throughout the day or night as the case may be.

Whilst the general thrust of these conditions is obvious, delimiting their precise scope is difficult, yet it is necessary if, for example, bandaging a cut finger is not to qualify. A number of problems of interpretation thus arise and not all have yet been happily resolved.

The definition of "day" and "night" has been particularly controversial.[5] Claimants have pressed for 6 a.m. and 6 p.m. as the borderlines[6] and a Commissioner has held that the words must be given their ordinary meaning and the change recognised as occurring at sunrise and sunset.[7] The view that the terms need to be interpreted differently in relation to different ages of disabled persons and different household routines[8] was early expressed in a Northern Ireland decision and a similar view expressed later in Great Britain.[9] The matter has now been considered by the Divisional Court in *R. v. National Insurance Commissioner, Ex parte Secretary of State for Social Services*,[10] and it has been held that the distinction between "night" and "day" should be drawn according to the domestic routine of the household in question. The purpose of the distinction is to recognise the greater onerousness of night-time attendance and "night" should be regarded as commencing when those added burdens need to be assumed in the particular household in question. This seems eminently sensible as far as it goes. What is left unclear is whether the criterion relates to the "night" of the attendant or that of his charge, for they may, of course, differ and added burdens may accompany each. At one point, in the Divisional Court's judgment delivered by Lord Widgery C.J., he fixes upon the position of the attendant having to get out of bed in order to minister to his charge, but later approves the proposition that "night" would begin when a child (presumably not the attendant) was put to bed. It would seem purposeful to regard "night" as commencing whenever added burdens needed to be assumed, regardless of which event they accompanied.

Less satisfactorily tied in to the policy underlying allowance is the decision, in $R(A)$ $1/75$, that the conditions are met by the mere fact of attendance being required, regardless of whether or not it is provided. That decision seems compelled by the wording of the legislation; yet it seems to involve viewing the allowance as a solatium for incapacity rather than as a means of ensuring attention.

"Attention" denotes some personal service of an active nature[11] and involves actually ministering to the claimant's needs. Although perhaps closely linked to it, it is to be distinguished from supervision which involves merely being in attendance in order that attention can be given if required.[12] Beyond this, there is still a lack of clarity about the meaning of "supervision." It surrounds the taking of the initiative of "attending" to the charge's needs. On the one hand, it has been suggested that the supervisory role can be passive, so that, for example, one could supervise even whilst asleep, provided one were prepared to respond to a call to provide attention if required.[13] On the other hand, two commissioners have expressed the view that a claimant who was able to summon assistance if required might well not require the kind of supervision required by the Act.[14] If attendance allowance recognises the fact that requiring attention may involve the hiring of help, or at least depriving another person of the opportunity of earning, then the former view is perhaps to be preferred, merely being on hand to respond to calls being equally demanding in such terms.

The supervision must be "continuous," a different notion from "continual." The question is one of frequency or regularity, albeit discontinuous, not of continuity.[15] The requirement of continuity should, therefore, be considered over a period and not in relation to each day or night forming part of the period of claim, nor according to a rigid arithmetical formula (*e.g.* 51 per cent. of the days or nights in question). What period is appropriate presumably depends upon the features of each particular case, though it would seem helpful to consider each "cycle" of treatment where it assumes a cyclical character. It has been held that the requirement of "continuousness" was satisfied in the case of a claimant suffering from a kidney complaint whose treatment necessitated spending three nights each week on a dialysis machine, at which times supervision was required, although not continuously.[16]

As to what may constitute "substantial danger" there can be no hard-and-fast criterion. The matter is essentially one of degree; indications are that it must be more than a nearly minimal risk. Paraphrases of "substantial" such as "considerable" and "big" have been approved.[17] The claimant is obviously expected to run some risk himself. What are not yet clearly distinguished are the substantiality of the risk that harm will occur and the substantiality of the harm that would occur should the risk fall in. The legislation gives no clear pointer here.

Claims

Although claims are made to an insurance officer in the first instance in the normal way[18] the question whether the claimant satisfies the medical conditions must be referred by the insurance officer to the Attendance Allowance Board,[19] a new body specially constituted for the purpose when attendance allowance was introduced. The Board consists of from four to nine members of whom all may be, and all but two of whom must be, medical practitioners. The board may delegate individual cases to one or two medical practitioners and this is in fact the normal channel of administration.[20]

Whether it was necessary to create a new body rather than vest a new jurisdiction in the existing Medical Board (which has, throughout, answered the disablement questions arising in connection with disablement benefit under the industrial injuries scheme) may be doubted. At the time, the Council on Tribunals expressed concern[21] and although some reassurance was forthcoming it remains hard to see why, contrary to the Franks Committee's principle of non-proliferation of new tribunals, the duplication is fully justified. This is especially so in view of the Board's practice of delegating above referred to.

As a law-determining agency, the Attendance Allowance

Board was certainly unsatisfactory initially. It is not required that a lawyer be a member; nor has a practice of using the two "free" places so as to provide legal expertise developed. Yet the need for it was made abundantly clear by the way in which the Board processed its first cases[22] and although problems of interpretation diminish as a result of appeals, not all the difficulties have yet been resolved.

Allowance is not payable before the date of claim.[23] It is, furthermore, only payable in respect of a period commencing after six months during which the relevant conditions have been satisfied[24] although the claim itself may be made prospectively and allowed on the basis of the Board's certificate that the claimant is likely to satisfy the relevant condition for the 6-month period and thereafter.[25] It appears that a prospective claim such as this can succeed on the basis of a certified likely need for attention, even if, in the event, it is not actually needed. Admittedly, if due care and diligence are not used to avoid overpayment, the allowance will be repayable[26]; and the Secretary of State might in such a case seek a review[27] resulting in loss of entitlement. But neither of these events will necessarily follow and it remains advisable, certainly in marginal cases, to make a prospective claim.

Appeals

Appeal lies at the instance of the claimant or the Secretary of State to a National Insurance Commissioner within three months of the making of the decision appealed against, unless, for special reasons, the Commissioner extends the time.[28] The right of appeal is, however, qualified in three important respects:

(a) the leave of a Commissioner is required;

(b) Appeal lies only against a Board's review decision, not an original decision; a claimant's first recourse must therefore be to seek review from the Board;

(c) appeal lies on a point of law only, although this does extend further than might at first seem obvious. It covers not only resort to erroneous propositions of law, but also the following matters:

(i) Decisions and findings unsupported by or contrary to the evidence;

(ii) Breach of the rules of natural justice; and
(iii) Failure adequately to state reasons for the decision, as required by regulations.[29] In this connection, it is not enough merely to state the conclusion and the bare findings of fact necessary to support it. A claimant (and, presumably, the Secretary of State) is entitled to know why his evidence has failed to satisfy the Board.[30]

Modifications of Entitlement

Regulations modify entitlement in the case of persons in hospital or certain other accommodation[31] and children[32] taking account of the fact that the cost of attention may in some cases be already borne by public funds and not be a charge on the claimant or his family; and of the fact that a measure of attention is in any event normally required by a child according to its age and development, and that therefore a greater degree of attention than normal should be required for the allowance.

So far as the first modification is concerned, the statutory requirement is that the claimant be "living in accommodation provided for him in pursuance of, or provided for him in circumstances in which the cost of the accommodation is or may be borne wholly or partly out of public or local funds in pursuance of" certain enactments listed in the Schedule to the Regulations.[33] Some difficulty has attended determination of the scope of this provision. It has been decided, as clearly seems to be the case, that it is not necessary for the accommodation to be provided, equipped or maintained by a public authority. It is sufficient that they make and bear the cost or some of the cost of an arrangement whereby accommodation is provided by a private individual, as in fostering arrangements under section 12 of the Health Services and Public Health Act 1968.[34] It has also, however, been decided that it is not sufficient merely that public or local funds finance an arrangement whereby care is provided for a claimant.[35] A distinction seems to be drawn between arrangements for the provision only of maintenance for the claimant and arrangements for the provision of accommodation for him, with or without maintenance. The former would not result in modification of entitlement.

Conclusion

There can be no doubt that the institution of attendance allowance is a welcome addition to the range of weapons in the social security armoury and that it goes a long way towards alleviating the hardship of a group regarded by most people as particularly deserving of help. The only criticism to be ventured derives from the absence from the social security scheme of a general disability benefit as such. As a former Chief National Insurance Commissioner has pointed out:

"... the benefit which the Legislature was introducing ... was not an invalidity benefit nor a disablement benefit but an attendance allowance. If the claimant's present condition had been due to a road accident for which a third party was to blame he would undoubtedly have been awarded very heavy damages. If it had resulted from an industrial accident for which he was insured, he would doubtless be entitled to disablement benefit at a substantial weekly rate based on an assessment of the degree of disablement probably at 100 per cent. Yet he has been awarded an attendance allowance only at the lower rate. An even more striking contrast is afforded by the case, which has received much publicity recently, of a boy who has only one useful limb out of the four, but has been held not to be entitled to an attendance allowance at all. The question, however, whether the whole basis of the benefit ought to be altered is one for the Legislature."[36]

It is surely odd that a disabled person should be subjected to a supplementary benefit means-test so far as his basic subsistence income is concerned, yet be entitled as of right to his non-contributory attendance allowance, no more (albeit no less) a provision for his basic needs.

The new benefits (described in Appendix I) have extended the range of cover in respect of sickness and disablement.

CHAPTER 7

WIDOW'S BENEFITS

IN our social system, in which a family usually looks to an individual breadwinner as a primary source of maintenance, the loss of that breadwinner again constitutes an obvious source of need. Where the loss occurs otherwise than by death, the continuance of maintenance may be secured by a number of devices. Where the cause is separation or divorce, continuation of maintenance may be enjoined by the court; where it is detention in legal custody, reliance is presently placed on the supplementary benefits system, if needed. Beveridge's view was that this type of event (which might be occasioned by the fault of the wife anyway) was not really insurable and should not, therefore, be embraced by the national insurance scheme.[1]

Widowhood may, it is true, occur through the fault of or with the consent of the wife; and suicide of the husband may be considered to be doubtfully an insurable event. Nevertheless, in the vast majority of cases, widowhood will be occasioned by unforeseeable, uncontrolled and blameless events. Its consequences may be complex and may vary from one case to another. In almost all cases, one need will arise—that of readjusting to the new circumstances brought about by the death of the husband during a period when adequacy to cope, both emotional and physical, may well be at a very low ebb. At the same time, taking a longer view, Beveridge thought "there is no reason why a childless widow should get a pension for life; if she is able to work, she should work."[2] Ideally, therefore, the scheme in this respect should be such as to alleviate the immediate hardship by cushioning and the prospective longer-term problem by encouraging self-support. This is the function of widow's allowance, the most generous of the national insurance benefits.

The immediate personal crisis of the widow is not, however, the only possible consequence of widowhood. In addition to being the economic unit of maintenance in our society, the family is also the basic educational unit. And the mother's function of caring and providing for the children of the family, a function not readily reconcilable with earning by work outside the home, continues notwithstanding the death of the father. Beveridge therefore recommended and the scheme now contains provision for the payment of widowed mother's allowance to cater for this need.

A system which consisted exclusively of short-term widows' benefits would assume that once the initial shock had passed widows should provide for themselves (old-age can be treated as a separate source of need and be separately provided for).[3] In the case of women widowed late in life this assumption will often be totally unwarranted; there may be no marketable skill and it may be too late to acquire one. Beveridge contemplated this but concluded that "the principle that any person physically fit for work should be entitled to retire from work upon pension before reaching the minimum pension age ... cannot without grave danger be admitted in any scheme of social insurance."[4] Notwithstanding this dire warning, the government announced in the White Paper,[5] and incorporated into the scheme, provision for widow's pension in response to this need and no cognisable harm has resulted.

Although there have been subsequent modifications, these three types of benefit—allowance, mother's allowance, and pension—are still the basic instruments for dealing with need created by widowhood. We shall deal with those elements which are relevant to all three types of benefit—marriage, widowing and disqualification—and then deal with the peculiarities of each type.

MARRIAGE[6]

Marriage has a dual relevance to widows' benefits. It is, of course, an essential precursor to a widowing—no benefit is payable even to a faithful, life-long sole cohabitant; and a remarriage disqualifies for receipt of benefit.[7] What is required, in both cases is "a marriage in the sense of the law of Great Britain (or, presumably, Northern Ireland respectively): *i.e.* the voluntary union for life of one man and one woman to the exclusion of all others."[8] All polygamous marriages were thus originally excluded, though *de facto* monogamous ones now qualify for such

period as they are in fact monogamous.[9] Void marriages will
not do.[10] This rigorous insistence upon marriages valid according
to United Kingdom law means, of course, that the dependants
of insured persons who have lived with, cared for and been
supported by them for many years and who may even be married,
polygamously, according to their personal mores, are excluded
from benefit, on the one hand, and on the other may continue
to receive it in respect of an earlier, valid, marriage in circumstances in which a subsequent, valid, marriage would disqualify.
This latter situation will rarely occur. The justification is no-
where made explicit in the preparatory documents of the scheme.
It is apparently to be assumed that the social interest in con-
ducing parties to marry monogamously outweighs all other considerations, though it is hard to understand how this can justify
a complete disregarding of the interests of an innocent party to
a bigamous union.

The position with regard to voidable marriages is more
complicated. Prior to 1971, the position had to be considered
in relation to each week of claim. The marriage was regarded
as subsisting during each week prior to annulment but, as
from annulment, it was treated as never having existed.
Accordingly, the widow's status as a widow was suspended prior
to annulment but revived on annulment[11] (and by parity of
reasoning, a woman so "married" would be entitled to widow's
benefits if her "husband" died prior to annulment but not if he
died after).[12] Legislation in 1971, however, provided that "a
decree of nullity granted ... on the ground that a marriage
is voidable shall operate to annul the marriage only as respects
any time after the decree has been made absolute, and the
marriage shall, notwithstanding the decree, be treated as if it
had existed up to that time."[13] The result is that a voidable
marriage is valid prior to annulment and, as respects the period
prior to annulment remains a valid marriage for the purposes
of any legal incidents attaching, after annulment. Prior to the
1971 Act, title to widow's benefits was restored on annulment.
After it, the remarriage remains a remarriage and they are
lost.[14]

Divorce presents a clearer case. The marriage is over for benefit
purposes and no title accrues by reason of the death of the
former husband. Subsisting benefit is, however, clearly lost by

the subsequent marriage and its termination by divorce does not affect the position.[15]

WIDOWING

Obviously, the husband must die. The only problems that arise here relate to proof. It is not unknown for a husband to disappear with no clear evidence one way or the other. In such a case, the onus is upon the claimant.[16] It will not necessarily be regarded as discharged by satisfaction of the requirements of a statutory presumption of death for this may have a limited application only.[17]

DISQUALIFICATION

Benefit "shall not be payable for any period after the widow's death or remarriage or for any period during which she is co-habiting with a man as his wife. Whereas death or remarriage terminates the right to benefit absolutely, so that accrued pension rights in respect of the first marriage may be lost yet not restored in respect of the second marriage,[18] cohabitation merely suspends such rights in the meantime.[19]

These provisions seem less than satisfactory in two respects. First, it is to be noted that remarriage terminates not only the part of a widowed mother's allowance payable in respect of the widow, but also the part payable in respect of the children, *i.e.* the scheme makes no provision for a man to insure in respect of his children in the event of his death regardless as to whether the widow remarries or not.[20] A widow's prospects of remarriage are certainly not enhanced by this fact. A second husband might not feel the same moral scruple to provide for the welfare of another man's children; and in any case, there might be the children of two families to care for.

Secondly, there is room for another look at disqualification on account of cohabitation in the case of widow's allowance. This benefit is payable only for the 26 weeks following upon the death. As a result of investigation, some 200 cases of co-habitation annually come to light, effecting a saving of the order of £2,000 per week (and it will rarely be for the whole 26 weeks) less the cost of investigation. Measured by the standards of social security funding, these sums are not large, though if there were no countervailing reason they would, of course, be worth saving. In the case of widow's allowance, there are strong countervailing reasons. No matter how sympathetically and discreetly the investigations are carried out, the suggestion of cohabitation must and does cause great pain and distress to innocent victims of an allegation at a time in their lives when they are emotionally extremely vulnerable. This debit cannot be quantified in cash terms but many will think it clearly capable of outweighing the credit attributable to the net saving.[21]

WIDOW'S ALLOWANCE

No specific period of time is an accurate measure of the duration of the immediate stress and hardship of widowhood in all cases, and verification of the actual period in each case would be difficult and, administratively, extremely cumbersome. A somewhat arbitrary period has therefore been selected. It was originally 13 and is now 26 weeks.[22] The personal element in the allowance is the most generous of the social security benefits and increases for children are at the higher level. Allowance is, of course, payable from the day of death.[23]

WIDOWED MOTHER'S ALLOWANCE

If, at the end of the 26-week period during which widow's allowance is receivable, the widow is left with the charge of any of their children, she becomes entitled to widowed mother's allowance for so long as this situation prevails.[24] The allowance per child remains the same as in the case of widow's allowance. Her personal allowance is reduced to the ordinary long-term rate.

The provisions for determining whether or not there is a qualifying child or children are complex and incorporate reference to the child benefit legislation.[25] A number of alternative conditions are prescribed. The material time for satisfying them is the date of the death of the husband. Thus, where at the death, the child of the husband's brother, though living with the husband and wife, was maintained by the brother whose issue he was, albeit at a minimal rate, no title to the allowance was established, notwithstanding that the wife subsequently adopted the child.[26] Provided that the conditions are satisfied then, however, allowance remains payable so long as they remain satisfied

—a temporary cessation of qualification does not necessitate a fresh claim upon requalification, though a failure to apply for reinstatement of the allowance in due time might result in loss of the allowance through delay without just cause.[27]

One of the alternative qualifying conditions is that the child resides with the widow. The usual rules relating to residence apply.[28]

WIDOW'S PENSION

Pension is payable to widows in respect of whom are satisfied (a) the relevant contribution conditions[29] and (b) one other from amongst three further conditions. These are:

1. That at the time of the husband's death, the wife was more than 40 years old[30]: or

2. That the widow has ceased to be entitled to widowed mother's allowance at a time when she was over 40.[31] Actual title to mother's allowance must be established[32]: or

3. That upon ceasing to be entitled to another widow's benefit prior to 1957 she was and has remained since incapable of self-support by reason of infirmity.[33]

The full rate of pension is the standard long-term rate but a lower rate may be payable according to the age at which pension was first receivable.

The statutory age for pension was originally 50. Between the ages of 40 and 50, a pension is now receivable, but the rate at which it is paid follows a sliding scale. For each year by which the widow was less than 50 on the death of her husband, the pension is reducible by 7 per cent. of the maximum each part year counting as a whole. Thus in the case of a woman aged 40 the pension would be reduced by 70 per cent.[34]

Incapacity for self-support may justify the award of a pension under head three above. Such an award, however, requires that the authorities be satisfied on two points:

1. That there is an infirmity. If there is no infirmity, obviously there can be no incapacity due to it.[35] Whether or not there is an infirmity is a medical question falling for determination by a medical board whose certificate is conclusive of the matter.[36]

2. That there is a resulting incapacity. This is a matter for determination not by a medical board, but by the statutory

authorities on all the evidence[37] though obviously medical
evidence as to the likely effect of an infirmity will be weighty.
The regulation requires that the claimant should continue to
be incapable of self-support by reason of the stipulated infirmity.
Title to pension is thus lost, notwithstanding that incapacity continues, if one infirmity is removed only to be replaced by
another[38] though *sequelae* of an operation will be treated as the
same infirmity.[39] Variations in the degree of infirmity will not,
however, break the continuity provided that periods of resulting
capacity are short and infrequent.[40] Normally, evidence that
the claimant is leading an active and industrious life (*e.g.* keeping
house and looking after children)[41] suggests that there is no
incapacity. Such a presumption is not, however, irrebutable[42];
indeed an unsuccessful attempt to work is strong evidence of
incapacity.[43]

An incapacity to work is not all that is required. There must
be an incapacity to earn "a reasonable standard of living"[44] by
which is meant a standard related to but higher than National
Assistance Board (now Supplementary Benefits Commission)
scales. The actual level regarded as satisfactory has varied with
increases in such scales and in the cost of living.[45]

Whilst it clearly furthers the policy of widow's benefit to make
payment of pension conditional upon incapability of self-support,
it is not at all clear why it should be necessary to attribute such
incapability to infirmity. The policy requires that it should be
attributable to the loss of the husband. Provided that it is,
whether for social, emotional or medical reasons, the case is made
out.

Finally, why not widower's pensions? Whilst the assumption
that death of a wife creates a need for support is clearly not
warrantable in all cases, it may well be in some. It is, no doubt,
rare for the wife to be the sole breadwinner, but where it is
established that she is, why not a pension for the surviving husband? And it is much less uncommon for husband and wife both
to make substantial contributions to the family fund and for the
loss of the wife to impose exactly the sort of stress against which
the present benefit is directed. It should be a sufficient test for
identifying families in which this is the position that the wife is
classified as employed or self-employed, though on insurance principles, additional contribution conditions should be imposed.[46]

Chapter 8

MINOR BENEFITS

MATERNITY BENEFIT

CONFINEMENT may operate as a source of need in different ways. First of all, the process of child-bearing and initial costs of rearing can be expensive and thus subject the family fund to exceptional demands. Secondly, in the case of working wives, it deprives the family of a breadwinner for what may be, and some would say should be, a protracted period. The first cash benefits in respect of maternity were provided in the National Insurance Act 1911. The system was drastically revised in the 1946 Act and ever since then has undergone a great deal of change in respect of the structure, value and qualifying conditions of the various benefits.[1] In 1974–75 some 47 million pounds[2] was paid out in the form of maternity benefits, in respect of 659,000 claims.[3]

The basic law is now to be found in sections 21–23 of the 1975 Social Security Act[4] and in regulations, especially the Social Security (Maternity Benefit) Regulations 1975. A separate benefit is provided in answer to each of the sources of need outlined above. The added expense of confinement is catered for by the provision of a maternity grant, once-for-all of £25. The loss of earning capacity is, in appropriate cases compensated for by a maternity allowance at the standard short-term benefit rate.

MATERNITY GRANT

Grant is payable to a woman who has been confined[5] or is pregnant and within 11 weeks of the expected week of her confinement.[6] A woman may qualify on her own or on her husband's contributions.[7] One of them must have paid contributions of Class 1, 2 or 3[8] in respect of any one tax year before the date of confinement,[9] or, where her husband has died or attained pensionable age before that date, then before the date of those events.[10] Where a claim has been made in expectation of confinement, the contributions must have been paid before the beginning of the expected week of confinement.[12] The earnings factor derived from such contributions must not be less than the year's lower earnings limit multiplied by 25.[13] The second condition is that either of them must have paid or been credited with contributions, the earnings factor derived from which being not less than the year's lower earnings limit, multiplied by 25, in respect of the last complete tax year before the beginning of the relevant benefit year.[14] If a woman qualifies for a maternity allowance, whether at the full or at a reduced rate, she is eligible for a maternity grant.[15]

If contributions are not paid by the woman herself, they are required to be paid by her husband. Concubinage will not suffice because "a husband means a man to whom a woman is married." Special regulations deal with polygamous marriage[16] and special provision is also made with regard to voidable marriages.[17]

The qualifications must exist at the relevant time. "When a statutory benefit is payable on the occurrence of a certain event subject to certain conditions being satisfied, there can be said to be a presumption to the effect that benefit is only payable if the conditions are satisfied on the date on which the event happens."[18] It will not suffice, therefore, that, in the case of post-confinement claims, the contribution conditions are satisfied by one who only became a husband after the confinement, or who ceased, by virtue of a divorce, to be one before it.[19] Since the Act[20] expressly provides for title to grant on the husband's insurance record to survive the death of the husband before the relevant date (although only in respect of a child who is his) this seems highly anomalous. The anomaly is not much abated in the pre-confinement cases. Here, the rule is that the qualification conditions are satisfied if they are satisfied at any time during the period of 11 weeks, ending with the contribution week of the expected confinement.[21] This means that termination of a marriage by divorce before the confinement but during this 11-week period does not negative title to grant. It remains capricious that the right to grant should depend upon whether the date of the decree absolute happens to fall inside or outside this period.

In the case of both pre-confinement and post-confinement divorce, there is a case for allowing the grant on the insurance of a man who fathers the child, especially if he becomes a husband shortly after the confinement, or ceases to be shortly before. This, of course, would not be necessary if the contribution conditions for maternity grant were themselves abolished.

MATERNITY ALLOWANCE

Maternity allowance is payable to a woman who has been confined[22] or to one who is pregnant and within 14 weeks of the expected week of confinement. A woman entitled to maternity allowance in expectation of confinement ceases to be so entitled if her pregnancy is terminated otherwise than by confinement before the 11th week before expected week of confinement.[23] The allowance is payable only on her own insurance record and not that of her husband, since the purpose of the allowance is to compensate for loss of her earning power. The contribution conditions are laid down in Schedule 3, Pt. I, para. 3 to the Social Security Act 1975.[24] The claimant must have paid contributions of Class 1 or 2,[25] and the earnings factor derived from them must be not less than the lower earnings limit multiplied by 25. These must be paid in respect of any one tax year, before the beginning of the maternity allowance period. Furthermore, contributions of an earning factor of not less than the year's lower earnings limit multiplied by 50 must have been paid or credited, in respect of the last complete tax year before the relevant benefit year. Regulations provide that maternity allowance is payable at reduced rate where contribution conditions are not satisfied in full.[26]

Maternity allowance, under the 1975 Act attracts an earnings-related supplement, and increases for child and adult dependants. The earnings-related supplement is payable in respect of every day in the maternity allowance period which falls after the 12th day of a period of interruption of employment. Entitlement to the supplement is exhausted after 156 days in the same period of interruption of employment[27] and days for which earnings-related supplement to unemployment or sickness benefit has been received during this period go to make up the 156 days.[28]

The allowance is payable weekly, the period depending on the circumstances. Where a woman has already been confined, without previously making a claim in expectation of her confinement, the period is seven weeks, from the date of confinement.[29] Where a woman fails to make a claim in expectation of confinement but is confined more than 11 weeks before the expected week of confinement, then the maternity allowance paid is 18 weeks, beginning with the week of actual confinement.[30] If she is confined not more than 11 weeks before the expected week of confinement, maternity allowance is payable from the first day of the week of confinement until the last day of the sixth week after the expected week of confinement.[31] Regulations[32] provide for an extended period of allowance where the woman "had good cause for her failure to make a claim in respect of expectation of her confinement."

In respect of a claim in expectation of confinement, maternity allowance is normally payable over an 18-week period, beginning with the 11th week before the expected week of confinement.[33] Since the expectation is by no means always fulfilled the actual period of allowance may fall to be adjusted in the light of events.[34] Also a claim which would have succeeded in expectation may fail if made after the event notwithstanding that earning capacity may have been affected. In $R(G)$ *14/52*, a woman claimed a maternity grant after confinement. Since she had had a miscarriage she was unable to obtain a certificate of confinement as required but produced a certificate of expected confinement, given after the miscarriage had occurred. The Commissioner held that since she had made a claim after the confinement, only a certificate of confinement would suffice. It is, however, the expected date which matters so far as claims before the event are concerned, not the actual date. Thus whilst a decision may be reviewed in the light of fresh evidence as to what a reasonable expectation would have been[35] what actually evenes is not directly relevant.[36]

Regulations provide for pre-confinement claims in which the expected week of confinement fails to coincide with the actual week of confinement. Where the confinement occurs more than 11 weeks before the expected week of confinement, the maternity allowance period is 18 weeks, beginning with the week in which the confinement takes place.[37] Where the confinement has not occurred before the end of the expected week of confinement, the maternity allowance period is extended for another six weeks, and failing confinement, further extended to six weeks, until confinement occurs whereupon it is extended until the end of the sixth week after confinement. Proof that the confinement is still expected must be rendered.[38]

Provision is made for disqualification for allowance on grounds of working, failing to take reasonable health precautions or failing to submit to examination,[39] in accordance with regulation 4 (3). In all these cases, the statutory authorities may disqualify the claimant "for such part of the said period as may be reasonable in the circumstances." Under regulation 9(1)(a), however, they have no discretion to disqualify a person for less than the number of days on which he worked, although, of course, they may do so for more. There are additional safeguards where disqualification results from a failure to submit to a medical examination under regulation 9(1)(c). There, disqualification may not be retrospective, and may not extend beyond the date of confinement.

The concepts of "pregnancy" and confinement are common to both grant and allowance and will now be dealt with.

PREGNANCY

So far as pregnancy is concerned the question whether benefit was payable in respect of a condition where the foetus had early ceased to develop has fallen for decision.[40] The view taken is that "The popular meaning of pregnancy certainly appears to draw no distinction between a living and a dead embryo or foetus.... It would be very unfair ... to hold that the claimant ceased to be pregnant at the end of three months simply because the embryo or foetus ceased then to be a living organism." In so far as the function of the allowance is to compensate for the disablement associated with the process of child-bearing, this must surely be correct.

CONFINEMENT

"Confinement" is partially defined in the Act,[41] and means "labour resulting in the issue of a living child or labour after

28 weeks of pregnancy resulting in the issue of a child whether alive or dead." The Act does not make it clear whether "confinement" embraces merely the actual parturition, or also the period of labour preceding and recovery following upon it. One Commissioner has opted in favour of the former, more restrictive view, although this was in connection with the now abolished home confinement grant.[42] It is clear, however, that the section requires "a child" and in view of this it is not surprising that the Commissioner should have held that delivery of a "hydatidiform mole" is not a confinement.[43] The availability of sickness benefit in such cases renders this anomaly insignificant.

A day for which there is entitlement to maternity allowance is deemed to be a day of incapacity for work.[44] A claim for maternity allowance may be treated as a claim in the alternative for sickness benefit or invalidity benefit.[45] If accompanied by a certificate of expected confinement, or other evidence complying with the requirements of regulation 2 of the Medical Evidence Regulations 1976, a claim for sickness benefit, or maternity allowance may, unless otherwise directed, be treated as a claim for sickness benefit or invalidity benefit for a period beginning with the 11th week before the expected week of confinement, and ending at the end of the sixth week after the confinement or after the week in which it was to be expected that the confinement would occur, whichever is the later.[46] Where it is certified that the woman has been confined, the claim for maternity allowance may be treated as one for sickness or invalidity benefit for a period, beginning with the week of actual confinement and ending six weeks after the week of confinement or week of expected confinement whichever is the later. However, this provision "neither confers title to Sickness Benefit nor restricts right to it. It is solely concerned with pregnant women who have claimed a maternity allowance but who, for some reason, are not entitled to it. It does no more than define the period for which, having made an abortive claim to maternity allowance, they may be treated as having claimed Sickness Benefit."[47]

A claimant must furnish evidence of pregnancy and the stage which it has reached, or of confinement, as the case may be. A claim[48] for benefit must be accompanied by a certificate given either by a doctor or a certified midwife on the form provided by the Secretary of State,[49] or by such other means as may be sufficient in the circumstances of any particular case.[50]

After its various fluctuations, maternity benefit has probably settled down to its most satisfactory form, the two species of benefit directly responding to the two main sources of need. Such scope for criticism as does exist is directly attributable to the application of the insurance principle. The Committee on one-parent families commented in respect of maternity grant[51]: "Among the mothers who do not qualify for maternity grant are likely to be very young mothers . . . others not qualifying include wives of students, wives of polygamous marriages, common law wives, and wives of long-stay prisoners and women who have recently arrived from abroad. . . . If[52] the aim is to help groups, like young unmarried mothers, who may have no contribution record there is no half-way house between the present contribution conditions and no contribution conditions at all. The real issue is whether maternity grant ought to be provided on a universal basis like family allowances which do not depend on satisfaction of any contribution conditions."

Any such suggestion is, however, likely to bring out the doom-watchers in force, prognosticating the beginning of the end for the contributory principle in the national insurance scheme, and improvement could be made without departing from the insurance principle. It has been suggested that maternity grant should be given for illegitimate children on the putative father's record, particularly where he accepts paternity before or after the child's birth, or where an affiliation order has been issued against him after the child's birth.[53] Such improvements are, however, only half-measures, and must be recognised as such.

The Finer Committee considered that since the benefit represented only a minor part of the scheme, and since the cost of extending it would not be prohibitive[54] and would not weaken the insurance principle, it should be made non-contributory. The government, however, has declined to implement the proposal.[55]

The fact of the matter is that the insurance principle is founded on the virtue of providence—the insured person making adequate provision for events which might befall—and pays too little, indeed no regard to the interests and welfare of the unborn or newly born child. If one could be assured that the parents of all such children would unhesitatingly apply for supplementary benefit in case of need, this would not matter. One can not.

DEATH GRANT

Death grant "is designed to insure that a modest sum shall be available to meet the whole or part of expenses which are usually visited upon an insured person's family or friends in connection with his death or funeral.[56] It is a once for all payment (presently a maximum of £30) not designed to provide a continuing income for dependants. It was instituted as a "challenge to the orgy of industrial assurance in which the British people have hitherto indulged in order to enable them to meet the cost of a funeral and thus avoid the hated pauper's burial."[57] In 1938, there were approximately 100 million such policies current, attracting an annual premium income of an average of £7·20 per contributing family at a time when earnings were much depressed.[58] It is a peculiar benefit in that it is aimed at the abatement of a self-inflicted need and has thus been described as "the boldest feature" of the social security scheme.[59] It is, however, clearly not a major part of the scheme, accounting for less than half a per cent. of outgo on the contributory scheme, and as incomes rise and attitudes towards disposal of the dead change, it must come to rank as one of the foremost contenders for restriction and eventual abolition. As it is, it is riddled with anomalies.

Death grant is payable "in respect of the death of any person"[60] in respect of whom the contribution conditions are satisfied.[61] The contributor must have paid or been credited with at least 25 contributions of any class prior to April 6, 1975 (or the date he attained pensionable age, if earlier) or must have paid contributions of any class yielding an earnings factor of at least 25 times the relevant year's lower earnings limit in the last complete tax year before that in which the death occurred, unless the contributor is himself dead. In this latter case, the year concerned is the last complete tax year before the year in which he attained pensionable age or in which he died if under pensionable age.[62]

Both in Great Britain[63] and Northern Ireland[64] it has been held that the grant is not payable in respect of a stillbirth, it being "impossible to speak of the death of a person unless that person lived," the criterion of living being breathing. This result is not compelling as a matter of interpretation—"death" can be a state as well as a process—and, this aside, clearly reveals a lacuna in the legislative scheme designed to implement the policy behind death grant. The purpose of the grant is to give some relief in cases where the family resources are suddenly burdened with the cost of a funeral and attendant expenses. This emergency may well be considered to exist as much in the case of a stillborn child as in the case of a child dying immediately after birth. Stillbirth is not such a common phenomenon that the award of the grant in that circumstance would impose an intolerable burden upon the Fund.

Proof of death is a matter for all the evidence, medical certificates not, apparently, being conclusive. In $R(G)$ $3/51$, it was held that a midwife's certificate, whilst conclusive in respect of a claim for maternity grant,[65] was not conclusive so far as a death grant claim was concerned. It was, in fact, discounted as a result of a post-mortem examination. Claims for death grant should be accompanied by a death certificate and, in the case of a child, a birth certificate and such other information as is necessary to verify that the contribution conditions have been satisfied in respect of it. If the Secretary of State requires it, an estimate or account of an undertaker must be supplied.[66]

The death must occur within the relevant jurisdiction[67] unless it can be brought within one of the exceptional categories set out in the regulations[68] most of which categories embrace cases of being qualified for other social security benefits immediately before death notwithstanding absence from the country. In $R(G)$ $6/57$ a widow failed to found her claim to death grant on her title to widow's benefit, the regulation not being satisfied by a title to benefit established *eo instante* with the death as opposed to before it. A person's right to death grant is suspended during a period of imprisonment or detention in legal custody. He is not absolutely disqualified.[69]

Death grant used to be regarded as an aid to those burdened with the cost of disposing of a deceased person. That, after all, was its designed objective. Under later regulations, however, it has come to be regarded as payable, prima facie, to the deceased's estate. In order to qualify as a claimant, therefore, a person must fall within the category of person's comprising "persons over the age of 16 claiming as personal representatives, legatees, next of kin, or creditors of the deceased (or, where the deceased was illegitimate, to or amongst other persons over the age of 16)."[70] "Creditors" include any person who gives a written undertaking to pay the whole or part of the deceased's funeral expenses.[71] The discrepancy is well illustrated by *R(G)* *3/63* where payment of grant to a hospital almoner for transfer to the secretary of a charity nominated by the deceased was refused. The Commissioner took the view that "personal representative" was to be construed strictly, so as to embrace only executors and administrators. The Minister would not come to the charity's aid, taking the dubious view that the appointing discretion was not available because of the subsequent express listing of persons entitled to claim under the regulation above. The Commissioner was, however, clearly of the opinion that the Crown could have claimed as being entitled on an intestacy.

Under the previous law, which required that a claimant should "incur or intend to incur expenses," it was held[72] that a claimant whose intent was to pay a deceased's funeral expenses if death grant could be paid to him did not qualify. It seems to be supposed that the new regulation obviates this difficulty. There is still, however, doubt with regard to a conditional undertaking to pay expenses. A person undertaking in writing to pay the whole or part of the funeral expenses of the deceased may rank as a "creditor" within the meaning of the regulation (see reg. 27 (4). The deceased's estate, however, is regarded as relieved, *pro tanto*, from any obligation to reimburse him.[73]

It was at one time an anomaly of death grant that one could establish title to a grant of several pounds merely by establishing expenditure of one pound.[74] This anomaly is not entirely removed, for there is still no general limitation of grant to the amount of expense actually incurred,[75] and whilst the Minister appears to have a discretion whether or not to award grant,[76] he has no power to vary its size otherwise than in accordance with rules which bear no relation to the amount of expenditure. It was once the justification for this anomaly that one should avoid "subjecting bereaved person to inquiries into the details of their expenditure or the reasonableness of the amount, provided that the amount was not nominal and would represent some degree of financial sacrifice to the average weekly wage earner.[77] Now that death grant is treated as a debt to the estate, this justification will have no application in very many cases. It is, furthermore, incongruous that no such solicitude is shown to a widow suspected of co-habitation.[78]

In another respect, the new rules have merely altered the nature of the unsatisfactory character of the previous law. Under the latter, since several persons might qualify for grant by virtue of "incurring expenses of an appreciable amount," the Minister had power to select from amongst qualified potential claimants. This might easily produce a situation in which one was over- and another under-compensated. The present position is that the Secretary of State has a discretion to distribute (including, apparently, to apportion) the grant[79] but cannot be readily controlled in the exercise of this discretion. The only apparent controls of a legal character are the usual ones that the power must be exercised in good faith for the purposes for which it was conferred.

"FUNERAL"

It has been settled,[80] after some vacillation, that the term "funeral" embraces both the actual burial and also the ceremonies associated therewith. The cost of a wreath of flowers may now be included as an expense. Even loss of earnings necessitated by attendance at and travelling to and from the funeral may, it seems, be included.[81]

SIZE OF GRANT

The normal grant is £30. Reduced grants are payable as follows: under the age of three, £9; aged three to six, £15; aged six to 18, £22·50; aged 55 (man) or 50 (woman) on July 5, 1948, £15.[82] This attempt to combine insurance principles with the cost of funerals is not a happy one.

CONCLUSION

With the infusion of the notion of compensation to the estate, the basis of death grant changed. It is no longer directly geared to relief from hardship due to bereavement, though it will no doubt, coincidentally have this effect in many cases. Whether the founding fathers of the present national insurance scheme would have approved such a policy is doubtful. What is clear is that the insurance principle as applied to this benefit is actuarially somewhat wild. The net result is that death grant really amounts to nothing more than a near universal subsidy of the estates of deceased persons and thus an acceptance of the notion that the cost of disposal of the dead should be a charge on the public purse. The implementation of such a notion would be better effected entirely separately from the social security scheme and the insurance principle.

GUARDIAN'S ALLOWANCE

The death of his parents deprives the orphan of the usual and legally obligatory source of maintenance during childhood, whilst he is still disabled from providing for himself. Guardian's allowance is the response of the government in the post-Beveridge White Paper[83] to the obvious source of need thus uncovered. The apparent policy is to provide financial support for guardians, *i.e.* those assuming responsibility for the upkeep and upbringing of orphans, on a scale more fully compensatory than child benefit, the level of which takes account of an existing parental obligation to maintain. The current rate is £7·45. The allowance is paid to about 5,000 recipients, a cash expenditure of comparatively small proportions which, most would agree, is money well-spent.

The 1975 Act provides[84] for the payment of the allowance to a person "in respect of a child where he is entitled to child benefit in respect of that child,"[85] if the conditions contained in section 38 (2) and (3) are satisfied. The former requires either the death of both parents or the death of one parent and the disappearance or imprisonment of the other. These conditions are, however, subject to modification by regulations[86] which may require the satisfaction of certain conditions relating to "nationality, residence, place of birth and other matters."[87]

There are no contribution conditions and entitlement no longer depends upon the parent being an insured person.[88] It had long been accepted that guardian's allowance did not really belong in an insurance system at all, and this was reflected by a liberal interpretation put upon the insurance condition, making entitlement something of a lottery.[89] Insurability is replaced by conditions relating to locality and "other matters." It is doubtful if the power to prescribe "other matters," as yet unexercised, authorises the imposition of conditions relating to contributions; "other matters" has the distinct appearance of being *ejusdem generis* and thus of being confined to "other matters" of the same kind as nationality, residence, and place of birth (although the use of the phrase "other *such* matters" would have removed all doubt on this point).

Regulations[90] provide that at least one of the child's parents (natural, or, if adopted, adoptive[91]) must have been born in the United Kingdom or present in Great Britain for a minimum of fifty-two weeks in any two-year period after reaching the age of sixteen, at the date of the death of the parent whose death gives rise to the claim. Absences on account of prescribed activities are ignored. These conditions are deemed to have been satisfied in respect of a pre-1975 death if the parent was an insured person under the 1965 Act.[92] It is questionable whether even such lax conditions as to residence are really necessary— the position of the parent may be thought not to be particularly relevant; the welfare of the child and the need thus thrust upon the guardian would seem to be the paramount considerations. The imposition of residential qualifications upon the guardian would seem to offer a sufficient safeguard. Rates of allowance are not so high as to make the importation of dependants a viable commercial practice.

Entitlement to child benefit is determined in accordance with the provisions of the Child Benefit Act 1975[93] and it is accordingly possible for those having responsibility for an orphan to fail to qualify for the allowance even though no one else is entitled.[94] This was the position under the Family Allowances Acts, but the mode of its happening is changed under the Child Benefit Act. Formerly, allowance was payable to a person "in respect of a child of his family." It was therefore possible for a person to qualify for guardian's allowance even though there was no entitlement to family allowance because other conditions of entitlement to family allowance were not fulfilled. Now, all conditions of entitlement to child benefit must be fulfilled; it is not sufficient merely that the child be in the "family."

"Parent" is not defined in the legislation and has been liberally interpreted. The policy seems to be that so long as anyone who can fairly be described as a "parent" and thus under some sort of obligation to maintain, is alive, the burden of such maintenance should not be thrust upon public funds. The decisions have mainly had regard to this. It is established that a "natural father" may be a parent for these purposes.[95] This is fortified by regulations[96] although the interpretation of "parent" as including "natural father" is inconsistent with the common law as exemplified in _Re M. (an infant)_.[97] What is less clear is whether a step-parent is a "parent." Under the 1946 Act it was expressly stated that he was but there is no such provision in the 1965 and 1975 Acts. Furthermore, the 1975 Act requires that "both" parents be dead whilst previous Acts required simply that the parents be dead. The implication seems to be that only two persons can now rank as "parents" for guardian's allowance purposes whereas previously three or more might have so ranked, _e.g._ as a result of the remarriage of one of the original parents. At all events, step-parents seem to be excluded administratively; it is understood that the Department makes provision for the payment of guardian's allowance to step-parents who are maintaining an orphan notwithstanding the prohibition of payment to parents imposed by section 38 (6).

The Act[98] allows a claimant to dispense with establishing the death of a second parent, provided that at the date of the death of the first, the claimant was unaware of and has failed after all reasonable efforts to discover the whereabouts of the second parent.

The formula used in the 1946 Act was that the parent "cannot be traced." The earlier (pre-1957) authorities ($R(G)$ _8/51_, $R(G)$ _10/52_, $R(G)$ _11/52_, $R(G)$ _10/55_, $R(G)$ _13/56_) are therefore no longer necessarily apposite. On the amended version the Northern Ireland Umpire, in _R 2/61 (P)_,[99] sets out the considerations which it becomes the duty of the statutory authorities to examine in such cases: "(i) The person claiming the allowance must show that he was at the date of the death of the deceased parent unaware of the whereabouts of the surviving parent. (ii) There must be 'efforts to discover' those whereabouts which are, or would have been, reasonable in the opinion of the statutory authorities, *i.e.* there must, in the circumstances of the particular case, be avenues of inquiry open to the particular claimant which it would have been reasonable to expect him or her to have pursued with the knowledge and facilities available to him, the test under the amended regulation clearly being a subjective one.... (iii) The onus lies upon the person claiming the allowance to show that he has made such efforts to the best of his particular ability." It is to be noted that section 38(2)(*b*) does not expressly state at what time a "failure" after all "reasonable efforts to discover the whereabouts of the other parent" may properly be registered. Since the conditions must be satisfied at the date of claim, the failure must clearly have taken place by then. What creates problems is the prospect of a discovery of the other parent's whereabouts, or of information justifying further efforts to discover them, after the date of claim. The normal rule is that entitlement to benefit only continues so long as conditions for it remain fulfilled. The trouble here is that a "failure" connotes a state of affairs at a particular point of time and does not have the appearance of being able to function as a continuing condition. Notwithstanding this, the Commissioner has held, in *R*(*G*) *3/68*, that the relevant statutory authority must dispose of a claim in the light of the facts as known at the time the decision on the claim falls to be made.

The Act[1] allows allowance to be paid as if both parents were dead where one is dead and the survivor is in prison and serving a sentence of imprisonment for life or for a minimum of 5 years, or "is in legal custody as a person sentenced or ordered to be kept in custody during Her Majesty's pleasure or until the directions of Her Majesty are known."[2] Under the former regulations[3] the allowance was not payable where there was a right of appeal until the time limit for making the appeal had expired, or until the appeal had been adjudicated upon, whichever was the later. There is no such provision in the latest regulations so presumably allowance is payable notwithstanding the possibility of an appeal unless conviction is subsequently quashed or sentence reduced to below five years. It has been held, in *R*(*G*) *4/65*, that an accused person found unfit to plead and ordered, under section 63 of the Mental Health (Scotland) Act 1960, to be detained in hospital does not satisfy the requirements of this regulation

and guardian's allowance is consequently not payable in such
a case.

Regulations modifying the provisions of the Act have in the
past given rise to great difficulties.[4] Fortunately, much of the
confusion is dispelled by the 1975 legislation. The new regulations state a number of closely circumscribed, though not wholly
mutually exclusive, grounds upon which the strict requirements
of the Act can be relaxed. Regulation 2 provides that where
a child is adopted his adoptors, or, if only one, his adoptor, are
to be treated as his parents for the purposes of section 38 (2).
In the case of an illegitimate child, other than one who has been
adopted, proof of the death of the mother alone will suffice
provided that any person found by a court of competent jurisdiction to be the father, or admitted or established to be such
in the opinion of the determining authorities, is also dead.[5] Where
paternity is not established or admitted, the death of the mother
will suffice,[6] but not, it would seem, if she merely disappears
or is imprisoned. The same applies with a single adoptor. The
lacuna is somewhat surprising and may well be inadvertent,
particularly since regulation 4 expressly provides that the provisions relating to imprisonment or disappearance are inapplic-
able in that case whereas regulations 2 and 3 make no such
provision. (Regulation 4 deals with the children of parents (or
adoptors) whose marriages have been terminated by divorce and
provides that the allowance is payable on the death of one parent
provided that the child was not in the custody of nor maintained by the other.)

It is an overriding provision of the Act that "no person shall
be entitled to a guardian's allowance in respect of a child of
which he or she is the parent."[7]

Where both husband and wife are prima facie entitled to the
allowance in respect of the same child and are living together,
only the latter is entitled to the allowance but it may be paid
to either unless the wife objects.[8] Only natural persons qualify
for entitlement to the allowance; power is, however, given in
the Child Benefit Act 1975 for child benefit to be conferred on
voluntary associations and if this creates entitlement to the
benefit, entitlement to guardian's allowance may follow.[9] The
power thus to confer benefit does not, however, extend to state
institutions.

CHILD'S SPECIAL ALLOWANCE

In terms of the source from which the means of livelihood is derived, dependants (married women, children, etc.) form one of the largest groups in our society. In their case, severe need will commonly arise as a result of the death of the person, usually a husband and father, liable to maintain them. That this was so was, of course, appreciated by Beveridge and in consequence the need is usually met by the payment of widow's and associated benefits. Neither the Beveridge proposals nor the post-War legislation, however, catered for one particular type of need thus arising. Where a mother was divorced from a father she would not qualify for widow's benefits on his death, not being, technically, "widowed." There could, therefore, be no increase of benefit for dependent children notwithstanding that the father may, during his lifetime, have been liable to maintain them and was in fact maintaining them.

There may well be circumstances when this withdrawal of maintenance and lack of benefit works grave injustice on the mother. There is no provision, however, under the national insurance scheme, for benefit for her. It is, no doubt, the case that benefit as of right would be gratuitous in many cases where the mother has successfully established a new, self-supporting, pattern of life on her own; and supplementary benefits may therefore be regarded as an appropriate mechanism in the case of the mother (though it may be mentioned in passing that the difficulties of conditioning benefit as of right in such a case are no more insuperable than in the case of widow's benefit). In the case of young children, however, the possibility of self-help can be entirely ruled out and the case for provision of benefit as of right is unanswerable. The National Insurance Act 1957, therefore instituted such a benefit, child's special allowance, which is now dealt with by section 31 of the 1975 Act and regulations.

Section 31 provides:

". . . a woman whose marriage has been terminated by divorce shall be entitled to a child's special allowance . . . if—

(a) the husband of that marriage is dead and satisfied the contribution condition for a child's special allowance as specified . . .; and (*b*) she is entitled to child benefit in respect of a child and either—

(i) she was so entitled immediately before that husband's death, or

(ii) in such circumstances as may be prescribed he was then so entitled, and

(*c*) either—

(i) that husband had before death been contributing at not less than the prescribed weekly rate to the cost of providing for that child, or

(ii) at the date of that husband's death she was entitled, under an order of court, trust or agreement which she has taken reasonable steps to enforce, to receive (whether from that husband or from another person) payments in respect of that child at not less than that rate provided or procured by that husband:

Provided that the allowance shall not be payable for any period after the woman's remarriage or for any period during which she is cohabiting with a man as his wife."[10]

This provision is expressly subject to section 43 of the 1975 Act[11] which requires that in order to be entitled to the allowance, either the beneficiary must be treated for the purposes of the Child Benefit Act 1975 as having the child living with him or the requisite contributions to the cost of providing for the child are being made.

A voidable marriage which has been annulled is treated as if it had been a valid marriage which was terminated by divorce at the date of the annulment.[12] A bigamous marriage is, however, not voidable but void *ab initio* and the allowance accordingly cannot be claimed even by an innocent party.[13] There seems to be no reason in principle why such an innocent party should be treated unfavourably by comparison with a party (not necessarily "innocent") to a voidable marriage.

The contribution condition for child's special allowance has been greatly relaxed in the latest legislation. The contributor must in any one tax year have paid contributions yielding an earnings factor not less than 50 times that year's lower earnings limit.[14]

The part of section 31 which has occasioned most difficulty is that requiring that the husband has been contributing towards the child's maintenance at the prescribed weekly rate.[15] The difficulty arises where there is an interruption or cessation of contributions by the father prior to his death or where such contributions are variable and irregular. The statutory authorities have consistently taken the view that the expression "had before his death been contributing" must mean "had immediately before his death been contributing" (subject to an important qualification) otherwise the words would be mere surplusage—he can hardly contribute *after* his death.[16] This interpretation has been fortified by reference to the alleged policy of the section, which is "clearly to compensate a divorced woman, who has been deprived of financial assistance for the maintenance of a child by the death of her former husband." The assumption which is drawn from this is that the fact that the husband had ceased to contribute to the cost of providing for the child (subject to the qualification mentioned above and dealt with below) before his death would necessarily mean that no loss to the claimant would result by reason of his death.[17] It is a highly questionable assumption in some circumstances. The wife and mother may have been obliged to go progressively deeper into debt over a prolonged period and to rely upon the eventual discharge of the liability to pay by the husband and father. That reliance may well be misplaced in many cases but it is somewhat unedifying for the state to make its obligation to pay vary according to the disability, indolence or neglect of the father to discharge his.

We are spared some of this spectacle by the important qualification above referred to, which is that temporary and involuntary failures to contribute may be ignored; and by the further qualification that "at his death" has been taken, in effect, to mean "at the onset of a disabling terminal illness." Thus, in *R(G)* *15/59*, the former husband became unemployed over four months before he died; remained unemployed for some seven weeks; resumed employment for four weeks and then entered hospital where he died six weeks later. Throughout the whole of this period, he made no contribution to the child's maintenance. The Commissioner took the view that, for purposes of determining whether allowance was payable, the six weeks of terminal illness could be ignored entirely. The remaining question was whether the non-payment of contributions during the 11 weeks preceding the admission to hospital could be regarded as temporary and involuntary. It could be regarded as "involuntary" in that it was provoked by unemployment (and it appears that the duration of the resumed employment was so short as to be ignored). And it could be regarded as temporary because he had, during that 11-week period, manifested his continued affection and concern for the children implying, it seems, a lack of intention finally to cast them off.

It would have been otherwise had it been clear at the start that he was unlikely ever to resume work. In *R(G) 3/60*, allowance was refused where the former husband had become incapable of work for some 21 months before his death. Although involuntary, the cessation of contributions could not be said to be temporary for it was clear at the outset that he was unlikely ever to be able to resume them. It was, furthermore, not possible to treat the whole of this period of incapacity as a terminal illness. That concept is, it seems, limited to the terminal phase of an illness, *i.e.* the phase during which it is clear that the patient must die. Where it is not clear from the circumstances (*e.g.* a chronic illness) that a cessation is to be permanent, there is no hard and fast rule for determining whether it is temporary or not. The longer it continues, the less likely it is to be temporary.[18] Furthermore, a cessation which appears at first to be temporary may have to be viewed differently in the context of the husband's entire contribution record.[19]

Problems also arise in connection with averaging. The former husband's contribution may have exceeded the prescribed rate in some weeks and fallen short of it in others. No problem presents itself in the simplest case—where there has been no long terminal illness, no involuntary and temporary cessation of contribution and a short period only between divorce and death. Here, it is simply a matter of dividing the total amount of the contribution by the number of weeks. It is settled that in a more complex case, periods of terminal illness and of involuntary and temporary cessation of contribution can be ignored entirely (*i.e.* the weeks so covered left out of account altogether). It seems also to be the case that payments may be attributed to a week if the former husband has done everything in his power to ensure that they were made then. In *R(G) 17/59*, the husband had died immediately after the divorce, having entered into undertakings to make payments but neither been able to make them nor sign covenants to do so. It was held that sums paid by his personal representatives to the former wife could be brought into account.

What is not settled is the total period over which it is proper to average. A former husband may have been guilty, during the early years of a divorce, of persistent neglect to contribute to the child's maintenance and yet, for perhaps a year before his death, have done so regularly. Averaging over a year might establish entitlement to the allowance, yet over a longer period might not. In the light of the avowed policy of the allowance, the relevant consideration would seem to be whether the former wife has come to depend upon the contributions and it is not necessary for this purpose that they should have been paid consistently throughout the period of the divorce. Though this approach does not yield an automatic test it does suggest a potentially more just one—whether the former wife has received the prescribed rate of contribution for a sufficient period to cause her to rely upon it. Precedents in other areas of national insurance law suggest that there is room for a "year-period" test here.

The allowance was at first limited in amount by reference to the amount actually contributed by the former husband but this limitation has now disappeared. It is now payable at the rate of £6·45 for the first or only and £4·45 for each other child.

In the past 10 years the number of children in respect of whom an allowance is payable has more than doubled and in 1975 stood at 997. The number of families benefitted had similarly increased from 311 (1966) to 621 (1975). This is, no doubt, a direct reflection of the increase in the number of marriages ending in divorce. It may be that child's special allowance, presently, at £200,000 per annum, the least expensive benefit of all, will come to consume a larger share of the social security budget.[20]

CHAPTER 9

RETIREMENT PENSIONS

INTRODUCTION

THE most predictable source of need is the inability to provide for oneself due to old age. One may, with luck, live and yet avoid unemployment or widowhood—not senility. Within the public sector, provision for old age looms very large as a consumer of the available resources. In 1975, 8,243,000 pensioners received a retirement pension or old age person's pension, and 22·7 per cent. of these received supplementary benefits in addition.[1] The annual cost of social security benefits in 1975, at rates applying at the end of that year, was about £9,712 million. Retirement pensions accounted for £5,200 million with supplementary benefits and old person's pensions accounting for a further £420 million and £32 million respectively. Furthermore, the proportion of public funds spent on retirement pensions is increasing. The proportion of the total population over pensionable age has nearly trebled since public provision was first made in 1908, now stands at 17 per cent.[2] and is likely to increase still further before it settles back. Furthermore, not all the old yet participate in the present national insurance scheme. The need to fulfil onerous contribution conditions has meant in the past that not all entitled so far as age is concerned have been entitled to a retirement pension and all are still not adequately provided for. Indeed, it will not be until pensioners falling out of the scheme come to balance those entering at the start of their careers that the plateau will be reached, by which time retirement pensions are likely to account for about three-quarters of national insurance outgo.

The scale and predictability of the financial problems raised by old age has coloured attitudes towards the part that the state should play. No social security scheme has sought to satisfy all the demands of the aged claimant. To an extent all assume that the provision of benefits above a certain level should be left private initiative, and few would disagree with Beveridge that "the State ... in establishing a national minimum ... should leave room for voluntary action by each individual to provide more than the minimum for himself and his family...." Provision for old age, therefore, occupies an important place in the private sector as well as in the public sector, and the growth of occupational pension schemes in recent years has been phenomenal. It is estimated that there were recently some 11 million members of occupational pension schemes in employment with a further three million beyond retirement in receipt of occupational pensions. The value of occupational pension rights in Great Britain in mid-1975 was £42,000 million including about £12,000 million in respect of pensions then in payment. The *total* value of accrued rights for the whole population over the age of 16 was, at April 1, 1976, £178,000 million. Public intervention in the private sector (tax relief for approved occupational pension schemes) exceeds in value the total contribution paid by the Exchequer into the National Insurance Fund[3] and is as much a part of state social security as the public sector scheme itself.

The assumption that the state should work in partnership with private pension schemes gives rise to complex policy considerations. The question of the applicability of the insurance principle assumes a different aspect when the subject in question is senior citizens subjected to an inescapable disability after a lifetime of productive activity and contribution to national prosperity. It is further complicated because of the very predictability of the event. Should those who make private provision for themselves be compelled to participate in a state scheme or should they be allowed to opt out and, *pro tanto*, undermine the state scheme? If the insurance principle is applied, what is the place of an earnings rule or a retirement condition? If the scheme is to be compulsory, to what extent? Should contributions and benefits be flat-rate or earnings-related? Should actuarial principles be applied? What provision should be made for the probability of continuing inflation?

The complexity of these problems might not be as confusing if coherent and consistent solutions to them were pursued in the relevant legislation. Unfortunately, this is not the case. The scheme as we find it, is in some respects identical to that launched by Beveridge, and in others, totally different. We have retained some of the features of that scheme, whilst abandoning to a marked extent the fundamental principles upon which they were based. Furthermore, whilst it usually happens that a change of the party in power results in the infusion into the law of the policy solutions which it, the party now in power, favours, it rarely happens that all traces of the former party's now offensive policy solutions are removed. The latest pension scheme to be advanced is the third pension plan to be put forward by a government in less than six years.

Beveridge was totally committed to the insurance principle, believing that "Benefit in return for contributions rather than free allowance is what the people of Britain desires." The payment of retirement pensions today is still tied to the insurance principle but, for the most part, the link between the two is little more than fictitious (a fiction which, it might be added, assumes all too real proportions to those who fail to qualify by virtue of it). Successive government measures have underlined the increasing irrelevance of the insurance principle. The raising of supplementary benefit levels effectively above those of national insurance benefits has brought about a situation in which the contributor gets precisely nothing for his troubles, the avoidance of which was one of Beveridge's justifications for contribution. At present, the basic rate of Category "A" retirement pension (at rates applying in November 1976) for a single person is £15·30, and for a couple £24·50.[4] A single pensioner on supplementary benefits—regarded for most purposes as the *minimum* level of subsistence—can expect to receive £15·70, a couple £24·85 (plus payment of rent and rates). Thus a pensioner with no source of income other than his retirement pension is automatically eligible for supplementary benefit. It is hardly surprising then that pensioners form the largest group of persons on supplementary benefit, accounting for 60 per cent. of all claimants. Ninety-four per cent. of these also have a retirement pension of some kind.[5] The aim of the new pension scheme, implemented by the Social Security (Pensions) Act 1975, is to provide an adequate income during retirement and it may well be that, for future generations of pensioners, the scheme, when it matures will "fulfil the Government's pledge to bring to an end the massive dependence on means-tested supplementary benefits." For the time being, however, the Government has undertaken only to maintain the relationship of current pension rates to the general level of earnings or prices, and it looks very much as though, for the present generation of pensioners, at least, supplementary benefits will remain "the sad hall-mark of old-age."[6]

Although the insurance principle has been retained, all pretence of the application of actuarial principles has now been abandoned. Earnings-related contributions go to finance flat-rate benefits, and contributions have come to rank as a some-what regressive and not very rational form of taxation. Furthermore, the system is financed on a pay-as-you-go basis, and contributions are collected through P.A.Y.E. Another corollary is that the Exchequer element in the pension is paid as of right to persons who neither need it nor actuarially deserve it.

Moreover the scheme has been extended by what amounts to little more than a fiction, to cover those persons who, it is acknowledged, would not normally qualify if required to satisfy the stringent contribution conditions on the basis of their own records. Thus, widows, divorcees, and under the new scheme, widowers, are deemed to satisfy conditions which, manifestly *they* have not satisfied. The insurance principle is thus preserved but evaded in certain cases in which its strict application would cause particular hardship. There are a number of things to say about this. First, it is thoroughly artificial. There is a certain resemblance between the use of fictions in the early common law and the apparent maintenance of the insurance principle whilst covertly departing from it in response to changing social pressures. The system is initially gradually modified, and in the end changed completely. Second, it is hard to see the logic of extending entitlement only to a particular point. Why this far? Why not further? It is now accepted that one set of contributions can support two pensions in some circumstances; why not in others? Why is a re-divorced woman confined to using her last husband's contribution record? Why does a life-long cohabitant have no such right in any circumstances? It seems odd to justify the practice on the ground that the woman is usually younger than her husband though it is hard to see how the insurance principle can otherwise be made to fit. Yet she may be much older. Is it the expectation that a woman, well on in years, should enter or re-enter employment in order to qualify on her own contributions? Apparently not—the requirement of registration for work under the supplementary benefits scheme is waived. There is, of course, a difference—the retirement pension scheme is contributory, the supplementary benefit scheme is not, which is where we came in.

The Government concede that the contribution principle "is not and never has been an insurance principle in the commercial sense," but, nonetheless, attach great importance to its retention, primarily it seems, as a "reaffirmation of public faith in the security of benefit rights."[7] It may be a harsh, but it is not an inaccurate, paraphrase to say of the insurance principle thus understood that it is a piece of psychological sleight-of-hand, designed to persuade the pensioner that he has earned a pension which in fact he owes very largely to employers and tax-payers generally. That particular piece of deception, however, offers no prospect of a departure from the insurance principle at all events in the near future.

It is very difficult to offer a rational critique of the law in the light of so contradictory and indeterminate a policy regime. It is proposed to state the broad aims of the scheme propounded by Beveridge, after a brief account of events prior to that time, and examine briefly the main respects in which the current scheme and that presented by the new Pensions Act [8] differ from that expressing the Beveridge philosophy.

The necessity for public provision for old age was recognised for centuries in the Poor Law. The Old Age Pensions Act 1908 was the first national scheme and provided non-contributory pensions to persons over 70 subject to a means test. The benefit levels, were not, however, even minimally adequate as a sole source of income and required supplementation, either under the Poor Law or by private provision. A contributory scheme was introduced by the Widows, Orphans and Contributory Old Age Pensions Act 1925 which reduced the qualifying age to 65. All the pre-1948 schemes, however, were seriously defective in one respect. They lacked the condition that the income must have ceased and they thus failed very substantially to relate aid to the specific source of need *i.e.* cessation of income due to cessation of employment by reason of age. In this respect the post-Beveridge scheme differs, being conditioned on retirement; in others it is the successor in title to the 1908 and 1925 schemes. The scheme proposed by Beveridge had the following characteristics:

(i) Taking into account the Exchequer contribution, the scheme was to be actuarially justifiable.[9]

(ii) It was to be funded by flat-rate contributions.

(iii) It was to be conditioned for the first five years after attaining pensionable age on retirement.

(iv) Benefits were to be flat-rate and payable as of right *i.e.* not means-tested.

(v) Benefits were to be at a level favourable by comparison with the subsistence level of the proposed national assistance (now supplementary benefits).

Except for rejecting a Beveridge proposal for the gradual build-up to the proposed level of benefit, and lowering the level, the Government accepted the Beveridge proposals.[10]

The resulting legislation remained substantially unaltered until 1959, when earnings-related pensions were introduced.[11] The same Act also introduced a further element into pensions policy by permitting contracting out of the new graduated scheme. The Act was primarily aimed at removing an increasing flat-rate benefit funding deficit due to inflation and politically irremediable by such an unpopular procedure as a substantial increase in flat-rate contributions. Thus graduated contributions purportedly introduced to finance graduated pensions were being used to an increasing extent to finance flat-rate benefits. It cannot, therefore, be convincingly argued that earnings-related benefits stood on their own merits as a primary aim of the revised scheme.

The scheme was placed on a more rational basis in 1973, when the hybrid system of flat-rate and graduated contributions was replaced by fully earnings-related contributions, for basically flat-rate benefits. This came into effect in 1975. The provision of earnings-related benefits was regarded primarily as the responsibility of the private sector, but the 1973 legislation established a state reserve scheme to cover those employees without adequate occupational cover. These latter proposals were scrapped with the change of government. Further legislative proposals were

published in the White Paper *Better Pensions* and implemented
by the latest Pensions Act due to come into effect in 1978.
Briefly the new scheme places more emphasis on state pensions
than did its predecessor. Pensions are to be fully earnings-
related and divided into two parts; the basic element and an
additional component, based on the contributor's 20 best years
of earnings. Contracting out of part of the state cover is permitted, subject to fairly rigorous conditions. The scheme will
reach maturity after 20 years.

A factor of overriding significance in recent years has been
the effect of inflation.[12] If eradication of poverty is the aim of
the social security scheme, the need to protect the value of
pensions in an inflationary period is obvious. Less obvious,
perhaps, are the means by which this might best be done. The
fact that three pension schemes have been advanced in the past
six years is a reflection of the failure of successive governments
to reach agreement on the measures needed to safeguard
pensions.

The 1973 scheme (now contained in the 1975 consolidating
legislation) imposes a statutory duty on the Secretary of State
to maintain the relationship of flat-rate benefits to the general
level of earnings or prices. The new pensions scheme will extend
this protection to both the additional component and its equivalent in contracted-out schemes.

It is proposed first of all to consider the standard case of a
person retiring at pensionable age on a flat-rate pension and
then proceed to consider Category B pensions, deferred retirement and deretirement, the earnings rule, earnings-related
pensions and non-contributory pensions. The chief source of the
law is now sections 27–30 of the 1975 Act and numerous
regulations made thereunder. A successful claim must be made
in proper form and the fulfilment of conditions in relation to
age, contributions, retirement and notice thereof is necessary.

1. CLAIMS

Claims for a retirement pension must be made not more than
four months before or three months after the date on which the
claimant becomes entitled, apart from satisfying the condition
of making a claim, thereto.[13] One who fails to claim within this

period forfeits benefit in respect of any period more than three months before the date of the claim, although where good cause for delay is shown the limit may be extended up to 12 months.[14] Even if good cause for delay is not shown it may be possible to persuade the Department to make an *ex gratia* payment where a claimant has been prejudiced as a result of a failure adequately to brief him as to his position.[15]

A person may submit further particulars on an approved form to the Secretary of State with a view to securing a determination, in advance of claim, of any question (other than a question about retirement) provided that he does so not more than four months before attaining pensionable age. This is so even though he has no intention of retiring on that date.[16]

2. AGE

A beneficiary must be over pensionable age.[17] This means 65 in the case of a man and 60 in the case of a woman.[18] The difference was originally introduced in 1940, to enable wives to draw pensions at the same time as their husbands, who were usually older than they, at a time when the state did not provide increased pensions for dependent wives under pensionable age. In 1946, for the first time, such provision was made, and the original justification disappeared. Other explanations have been advanced. It has been attributed to the common pattern of life prevailing in the early years of this century when social principles were crystallising. The woman's lot was to bear children, as many as possible, therefore the youngest would be born late and their rearing would not end until the mother was well past the age at which self-support by work was a reasonable prospect. Therefore the pension should enter her life-cycle at approximately this point. This reason has ceased to operate with the change in the standard pattern of family life—indeed it is questionable whether it ever was a sensible basis for policy. The Report of the Committee on Equal Status for Men and Women[19] lists a further four justifying grounds: (a) the average age disparity between men and women; (b) the fact that women, in effect have two jobs—running a home and going out to work; (c) the reduced working efficiency of women in their 60s and; (d) a woman's greater proneness to illness. It has been estimated that the capital value of a flat-rate pension paid to a woman at 60, taking into account the difference in expectation of life[20] is twice as much as the same pension paid to a man of 65. It is believed that none of the reasons given above offer adequate grounds to justify this difference in treatment.

There is insufficient evidence to support the arguments advanced in (c) and (d). Indeed, as was pointed out in the Report, "In one sense, the only reliable measure of overall morbidity consists of mortality rates. These indicate that women enjoy *better* health." As for (b) whilst it is certainly true that many women do have a dual responsibility, it must be remembered that this responsibility is by no means confined to women. An increasing number of men have sole responsibility for their children and the sharing of responsibility is common.[21] Indeed, it is worth mentioning that up to 1974 single-parent fathers were *expected* to go out to work, irrespective of their family responsibilities and that their right to supplementary benefits was made conditional on their registration for work. There was no such requirement in the case of one-parent mothers. It is also noteworthy that this requirement may be waived in the case of women widowed in late middle age with no experience in the employment field and where there is some evidence of ill-health, but that no such dispensation is granted to widowers in similar circumstances. The ages of 60 and 65 are quite arbitrary, being "medically-speaking pulled out of a hat"[22] and it makes no more sense to have as the statutory age difference, that of the average couple on retirement, than it is to build a car with room for 4·2 people because that is the size of the average family. In fact, a set degree of disability because of age in the average case varies both over time and with occupation. The average 75-year-old is healthier than he was 50 years ago (although not more than he was five years ago). Septuagarians of Social Class 1 are healthier than their fellows in Class 5 (67 per cent. fit as against 20 per cent. fit). The disparity in age may have had some justification as a balancing measure so long as unequal pay for equal work was the norm. It should not, however be allowed to co-exist with other more efficient mechanisms for achieving the same end. "Equal Status must mean equal pension ages. Any other arrangement can only be based on the assumed requirements of each sex, an approach which we consider to

be incompatible with equal status."[23] Nonetheless, notwithstanding the advances made in this field, unequal treatment is
still advanced as a justifying ground for the retention of the
age difference. In 1975 Mrs. Castle, then Minister of Health
and Social Services stated that "the lower retirement age for
women is some compensation for them for the lower wages they
have been drawing all these years, when everyone will agree,
many women have been exploited and have been paid merely
sweated wages. No one can pretend that they will get real
equality in pay and job opportunities for some time ahead."[24]
It is as well to remember that the social security system was
designed to meet current needs, not to compensate for failure
to meet past ones. The Government have repeatedly stated that
they have no plans to alter the situation. In 1976 Mr. O'Malley
told the House of Commons that "a reduction in men's pensionable age is ruled out for the forseeable future on grounds
of cost . . . on the other hand the government believe that raising
the pensionable age for women would be unfair to women who
have contributed over the years in the expectation of a pension
at 60."[25]

The former reason may well be sound. It was recently estimated that the cost of lowering the age of retirement to 60 would
be in the region of £1,560 million.[26] The latter justification,
however, applies only in the case of those women who are already
participating in the scheme. It does not, and cannot apply to
those women who are not yet participating or who have been
participating only for a short time. If provision can be made,
in a new pension scheme, for the gradual phasing out of lower
contributions having due regard for the interests of those already
participating who might be adversely affected thereby, then
surely it can be made for the gradual raising of the pension age.
The age at which people are allowed to retire clearly influences
the age at which they actually do retire. The unjustified inequality of treatment in the public sector stultifies the proper
development of occupational pension schemes in the private
sector. There is little doubt that the statutory age difference is
a significant factor in the determination of retirement age in
the private sector, and that, because of the difficulties involved,
"change cannot be imposed on occupational pension schemes
before equal pension ages are achieved in the state scheme."[27]

If abatement of need is the aim there are weighty arguments for raising the pension ages considerably for women but also for men. Beveridge did, after all, intend social insurance to be integrated with the health service in the fight for social progress; sickness benefit is available to those who are not capable of work. When it comes to easing the cost of social insurance and redistributing the national insurance fund more equitably, nothing is so ripe as the immense amount spent on pensions to the able-bodied and prematurely retired. The solution that seems to meet with most approval is the introduction of a flexible pensionable age. This has, however, been ruled out for the time being on the grounds of cost.

The required age must, of course, be proved in connection with a claim. A person is deemed to attain a given age at the commencement of the relevant anniversary of the date of his birth.[28] A birth certificate is the normal manner of proof. If none is available, the best other evidence should be tendered.[29] It should furthermore be sought in good time. "Cases where claimants are unaware of their true age fall into two categories. On the one hand there is the type of case in which the claimant, not knowing his age, assumes, without being able to show any good ground for the assumption, that he is younger than he is, in fact, and neglects to make enquiries ... indifference in the matter of establishing ... rights and responsibilities in claiming retirement pension could not be accepted as good cause for ... delay on giving notice of retirement. On the other hand, there is the case in which the claimant's erroneous belief is based on reasonable grounds. ..."[30] The fact that a claimant had consistently been given the wrong date of birth by his parents has been held to be reasonable cause for delay, but the safe course to pursue is always to check.

Prior to 1973 it was clear that title to retirement pension was not instituted merely by the attainment of pensionable age. Then, as now, pension was payable only from the next pension day. Since being of pensionable age and retired disqualifies for other benefits, there may be a hiatus of some days between the cessation of one and the commencement of the other. Formerly it was clear, and in the case of Category B retirement pension, still is clear, that this hiatus is not merely one of payment (for pension is payable in advance)[31] but of entitlement. The reasoning behind this seems to be that, although the legislation provides for pension for life from the date of retirement, this is expressly made subject to the provision of the Act, including regulations made thereunder.[32] The current legislation, however, contains no such qualification in relation to a Category A retirement pension and therefore the strict legality of the restriction in the regulation must be open to question on grounds of *vires*. *R1/62 (P)* assumes that one is entitled as from the date of attainment of pensionable age, but is believed to have been wrongly decided.

3. CONTRIBUTION CONDITIONS

Entitlement to a retirement pension is dependent upon the satisfaction of a number of conditions. To qualify for a full pension, a person must first of all have paid at least 50 contributions, of any class before April 6, 1975[33] or he must have paid Class 1, 2 or 3 contributions[34] producing an earnings factor of at least 50 times the year's lower earnings limit, in any tax year after April 6, 1975.[34] In both cases the contributions must have been paid before the contributor attained pensionable age. Secondly, one, and in the case of married women, two, further conditions must be satisfied. The contributor must have paid or been credited with Class 1, 2 or 3 contributions, producing an earnings factor 50 times the year's lower earnings limit, in respect of every year of the requisite number of years of his working life.[35] Working life is defined as "the period between (inclusive) the tax year in which he attained the age of 16, and (exclusive) the tax year in which he attained pensionable age or died under that age"[36] and contributions must normally have been paid or credited for nine-tenths of that time.[37]

A woman who has married before attaining the age of 55, and who is still married to the same man on reaching the age of 60 is precluded from getting a Category A retirement pension unless, in addition, she has the required earnings factor for at least half the years between marriage and pensionable age. This so-called "half-test" is abolished as from April 6, 1979.[38]

A woman whose marriage is terminated otherwise than by death, prior to attaining pensionable age is not, of course, entitled to either widow's benefit or a Category B retirement pension—she is entitled only to a Category A retirement pension, which as we have seen is subject to stringent contribution conditions. To avoid hardship in the event of non-fulfilment of such conditions, special provision is made to enable women, whose marriages have been terminated otherwise than by death to satisfy these conditions by using the contribution records of their former husbands to supplement their own, so that, in effect, full pension can be claimed on the basis of their combined records.[39] Regulations provide for the modification of the above conditions in respect of certain persons insured under the former Act.[40] Contributions paid under that Act are re-expressed in terms of "reckonable" years by means of a formula provided in the Regulations.[41]

The legislation makes similar provision for widows, so as to confer on them some of the benefits of the deceased husband's contribution record.[42] The right to use the contribution record of a former or late spouse ceases on remarriage.[43] There have been numerous complaints to the Parliamentary Commissioner concerning misunderstandings or alleged wrongful advice about the effect on the rights of married women or widows of remarriage before the age of 60.

Benefit at a reduced rate may be payable in the event of partial satisfaction of contribution conditions.[44] *Pro rata* benefit is awarded depending on the proportion of full contributions between 25 per cent. and 98 per cent. Prior to April 6, 1975 claimants with a deficient contribution record were paid pension according to a system of banding.[45] The system is still applied to the records of some 400,000 pensioners and can result in injustice. A pensioner who has paid an average of 21 contributions, for instance, has paid 41 per cent of the contributions needed for a full pension, but under the banding system, will receive only 35 per cent. of a full pension. The Department of Health and Social Security have reviewed this rule, after the matter was referred to the Parliamentary Commissioner for Administration[46] but have concluded that it would not be worth the excessive work involved in instituting a new *pro rata* system for the 400,000 pensioners who are affected. Some very easy and untroublesome progress towards justice might, however, be made by merely raising the part-pension rates.

The Commissioner has held that a pension payable to a wife on her husband's insurance record is a contribution by him to her maintenance for family fund purposes on the basis that the contribution requirement makes retirement pension analogous to an endowment policy.[47] In some cases the analogy will be dubious (*e.g.* where there is an excessive number of credited contributions). It is necessary in the above case to distinguish an earlier case,[48] on the ground that in that earlier case the pension was payable on the wife's own insurance, and there may well be other situations in which the first case will prove unsound.

4. RETIREMENT

A beneficiary must have retired from regular employment.[49] All that is required is that he has become "over pensionable age" and has retired. It does not say has "retired in consequence of attaining that age."[50] Retirement may consequently take place at any age; pension will nevertheless be payable at pensionable age, provided, of course, all the other conditions are satisfied. On a strict interpretation, it at first appears that to qualify for pension one must, at some time, have been in regular employment, since one must have "retired" from it. This is not so.[51] If it has not taken place before, retirement is deemed to take place when the age of 70 (man), or 65 (woman) is reached.[52]

Decisions whether or not to award pension are made on the basis of the claimant's answer to a questionnaire. This questionnaire assumes that in order to have retired a claimant must have ceased, or must intend on the due date to cease finally to be gainfully *occupied*. (It is not clear why the Department retains the old terminology. Perhaps it is assumed, somewhat prematurely, that no significant alteration in meaning is made by the change of wording.) Whether, strictly speaking such a stringent requirement is *intra vires* is questionable. The Commissioner has, however, been confronted with the question on many occasions and no objection has been taken to this understanding of "retired." It was indeed expressly authorised in *141/49(P)* and must now be taken to be the authoritative interpretation notwithstanding that nothing in the legislation requires a positive intention not to work again (as opposed to the absence of a positive intention to work).[53] What is required then is an unconditional cessation of, or an intention finally to cease regular employment. Section 27 (3) seems to assume that to be in "regular employment" one must be "an earner." The latter term was substituted under the 1975 legislation for that of "engaged in gainful occupation" which was felt to be too ambiguous. The relationship between the two is unclear.[54] There are no grounds for regarding them as identical in meaning but as yet, no attempt has been made on the part of the Commissioner to distinguish them. However, old decisions, concerning the law which incorporated the phrase "in a gainful occupation" must obviously be read with this caution. The term "earner" clearly includes both employed and self-employed persons in gainful employment, although subs. 3 is worded in such a way as to leave open the possibility that an earner might also be someone deriving remuneration otherwise than from gainful employment and therefore neither of these. Decisions have made it clear that "regular employment" is not limited to employment under a contract of service, but includes employment under a contract for services.[55] This would seem implicit in the statutory definition of "employment" as including "any trade business, profession, office or vocation."[56]

A gainful occupation certainly included "An occupation in which a person is engaged with the desire, hope and intention of obtaining for himself directly and personally remuneration or profits in return for his services and efforts."[56] Thus it has been held that a convent sister confined to activities such as writing letters and arranging flowers in consideration of board and lodging was, nevertheless, engaged in gainful occupation,[57] though in her case pension was payable by reason of the inconsiderable extent of the activities.

By contrast, a property owner deriving a substantial income from letting has been held not to be gainfully occupied though the decision would have been otherwise if he had performed "any appreciable amount of work" in connection with the ownership.[58] A shareholder in a registered company would be in an analogous position. The mere holding of shares would not constitute a "gainful occupation" but active participation in the management or running of the business would. In the case of partnership the mere status of partner involves this. "A partner in a business partnership[59] has an ostensible authority to deal on behalf of the partnership and he carries a corresponding responsibility for the acts of the partnership. Within the partnership itself, he is entitled to an active voice in the management of affairs. Neither in relation to the outside world nor in relation to his co-partner or co-partners is he in the position of a mere investor of capital drawing interest or dividend."[60]

It may be commented in passing that at this point the questionable nature of one of the assumptions of the social security scheme becomes apparent. The assumption that a cessation of earnings from employment produces need is clearly unwarranted in all cases of substantial unearned income. Why, in view of this fact "retirement" should have been selected as a condition for pension is unclear.

The above definition of "gainful employment" is not exhaustive. "It may well be that there are cases when it is important to consider what was the hope, intention or desire of the person alleged to have been employed or self-employed during the relevant period.... When, however, the person in question is receiving money during the course of his employment, it is not, I think, very important to consider what his hopes, intentions or desires were at the time he entered upon his employment or during its course. I do not consider that if a man is in fact paid money for services during the course of his employment the fact that when he entered into his employment he had no hope, intention or desire of obtaining gain is of the slightest relevance."[61]

"Gainful employment" is relevant to the question of liability to contribution[62] and increase of benefit for dependants and is discussed more exhaustively under that head.[63] Two decisions should, however, be noted here. They concern the same claimant. In 1965 he "retired" from employment as an accountant in a firm of chartered accountants, but in 1966 he was paid £1,000 for advisory services rendered to his former firm during his retirement. The insurance officer contended that these were earnings from gainful employment and extinguished his entitlement to pension. However, the services which the claimant had rendered were inconsiderable and "he was not contractually obliged to render such services nor had he any contractual right to be paid for them and the services were not rendered in the hope or expectation that they would be paid for." In these circumstances the sum received was not "earnings from a gain-

ful employment."[64] Similar payments were made in subsequent
years and the insurance officer again tried to treat the pension
as extinguished. This time, largely on the basis of the claimant's
own admission for revenue purposes that the sums were "fees
for advisory services" and that he was entitled to earned income
relief, the sums were held to be earnings from gainful employment. It should be noted that throughout its period the claimant
was receiving an annuity from the firm and no question of
treating that annuity as "earnings" arose.[65]

The suggestion in these decisions seems to be that the sum
accruing must accrue in consideration of the services rendered
if they are to be treated as "earnings from a gainful employment." No doubt, the most important matter is the understanding, usually the contractual arrangement, between the
claimant and the payor; if it were clearly the case that the
payment would be made whether or not services were rendered
it might not amount to "earnings." However if, in substance,
it was clearly understood that services would have to be rendered
when called upon, liability to reduction, or extinguishment of
pension would not be avoided merely by disguising the payments
as a gratuity or accrued annuity.

If either employment or gain ceases, one is no longer "gainfully employed." It matters not that income *e.g.* holiday pay
continues to accrue provided it is payment for pre-retirement
services.[66] In *C.P. 106/49* the money was in fact paid in respect
of post-retirement services and the Commissioner regarded it
as significant that he was "not ... dealing ... with a case of
earnings derived after the date of retirement from an occupation
followed before that date. They may stand on a different footing,"
and the best explanation of *141/49 (P)* may well be that the
farmer in that case had in fact ceased to be "occupied" even
though the arrangement under which he transferred his land
and business was void with the result that he remained, in law,
responsible for its management.

Equally, even if the occupation continues, there may be a
retirement if such gain as accrues does so irrespective of the
occupation[67] as where an invalid brother who performed tasks
such as feeding fowl and collecting eggs on his brother's farm
was held to be retired, maintenance by the brother being an
act of brotherly consideration rather than in respect of the work.

If, however, the payment is made in respect of the occupation, that renders it a gainful occupation. It was decided in *R(P) 1/65* that provided this is so an occupation does not cease to be gainful merely by virtue of the fact that engagement in it is voluntary or uninfluenced by the prospect of gain.

The retirement consists of "the giving up of a business, profession calling or means of livelihood. It therefore means much more than a temporary suspension from employment and implies a retirement which is final and permanent."[68] The intention of the claimant with regard to his future is obviously therefore a relevant consideration. "In deciding whether a claimant can be treated as retired, it is necessary to take into account not only what he is actually doing but also his intentions for the future. If he states that he intends to engage in any gainful occupation, his title to retirement pension would have to be determined in the same way as if he were actually engaged in that occupation. If on this basis, he cannot be treated as having retired, the position is not affected by the fact that he has not recently had any work and has no immediate prospects of any."[69]

It is of course, what the claimant's actual intention is, not what he or anyone says it is that matters; and ascertainment of that intention is a matter, notoriously difficult, of evidence.[70] Difficulty has been encountered in cases where the intention has been ambivalent. In one case, the claimant gave notice of retirement even though he intended to engage in employment several months later if he was successful in obtaining it.[71] In another, a miner who was completely disabled by injury entertained the illusory hope of returning to work.[72] Another claimant intended to take all the work he could get but anticipated reasonably that it would be very little.[73] In the first and third cases, pension was refused. In the second, it was granted. The matter must be viewed as at the time of making the claim.[74] It cannot be judged in the light of events as they work out. It seems that if, at the time the claim is made, there is no reasonable expectation of work, no matter how strong the desire for it, a claimant may be treated as having retired.[75] If there is a reasonable expectation of work, however, there can be no retirement even if, in the event, no work is obtained.[76]

What is most common is for the intention to be, not to give

up all activity, but to engage in the same one to a lesser degree,[77] or a different and less onerous one. It is quite clear that such a course will not necessarily amount to retirement.[78] Whether or not it does depends upon whether the case can be subsumed under one of the four conditions of section 27(3)(*b*) of the 1975 Act on fulfilment of which a claimant *may* be "treated as having retired from regular employment ... notwithstanding that he is or intends to be an earner. ..." These conditions are alternatives; it suffices to satisfy any single one. They are:

(i) that the claimant is or intends to be an earner only occasionally;

(ii) that the claimant is or intends to be an earner to an inconsiderable extent;

(iii) that the claimant is or intends to be an earner otherwise in circumstances not inconsistent with retirement;

(iv) that his earnings can be expected not to exceed or only occasionally to exceed the earnings limit (£35) beyond which progressive reduction of pension is encountered. In this connection it should be noted that pension may be reduced or lost entirely according as to whether the earning is accompanied by deemed retirement or not.

The learning on these four conditions is somewhat confused and tribunals have not always clearly distinguished between them. It is accordingly not always clear on what basis a claim has been decided.[79] The conditions would appear to be mutually exclusive. A claimant could therefore succeed under condition (iii) notwithstanding that the considerableness of extent and the frequency of occasion were such as to preclude success under heads (i) and (ii) provided the work was "otherwise" consistent with retirement. On this point, the opinion of the tribunal in *R(P) 8/54* has confused the position and impaired clear doctrinal development. The actual decision (that employment for $12\frac{1}{2}$ hours per week in the school meals service was not "otherwise inconsistent with retirement") is unobjectionable. So, also, is the injunction in that decision that "attention should be directed to the nature of the occupation itself."[80] It is the tribunal's statement of the interrelation of the different conditions which causes confusion:

"It is clear from the use of the word 'otherwise' in (iii) that the legislature contemplated that the circumstances in which a person was engaged in an occupation might justify his being treated as having retired from regular employment, even though he was not engaged, or did not intend to engage in his occupation only occasionally or only to an inconsiderable extent.

In order to decide whether a claim falls within (iii) it is therefore necessary to have regard to the circumstances of the occupation looked at as a whole. The number of hours worked though material is not conclusive (unless the hours are short enough to justify a finding that the occupation is engaged in only to an inconsiderable extent). . . ."

Thus, in the tribunals' view, the extent (and presumably also the frequency) of the work has a dual relevance. If inconsiderable the occupation may be ignored under the first condition. A corollary, one would have thought, was that if the extent was not inconsiderable, the occupation could not be ignored in point only of extent. But the tribunal now tells us that quite part from the first condition, extent is material (though not conclusive) so far as the third condition is concerned. The words of the statute require that the employment be "otherwise" consistent and it is tempting to suggest, as a straightforward matter of interpretation, that this must mean "otherwise" than in respect of frequency of occasion (condition (i)) and considerableness of extent (condition (ii)).[81] The opinion expressed in *R(P) 8/54* is, strictly speaking, *obiter* and there is something to be said for adopting as the rule in relation to condition (iii) that one must look to all the circumstances of the occupation otherwise than circumstances relating to frequency and extent.

This approach obviates some of the confusion which surrounds the later decisions. It is somewhat perplexing to find a person whose average number of hours is well inside the limit prescribed under condition (ii) saved under condition (iii), as happens in *R(P) 4/55*. And it is even more disconcerting (since at least the right end-result is arrived at in *R(P) 4/55*) to find a claimant denied pension because of the confusion. In *R(P) 12/55*, the Commissioner expressly finds that the occupation in question (keeping a small sweet shop in a room in the claimant's own house) "is a characteristic occupation for a woman who has retired from a more strenuous occupation," enough, one would have thought, for condition (iii). Unfortunately, the shop was open for a number of hours per week vastly in excess of that regarded as necessary to qualify under condition (ii). The conditions are alternates. But if the question of extent can be raised under condition (iii), as it was in this case, the single factor of extent prevents fulfilment of either condition. The claimant failed. Unease also attends decisions such as *R(P) 8/55* (condition (iii) not satisfied because of number of hours worked) and *R(P) 18/56*, which contains extensive discussion of the number of hours per week which might be consistent with satisfying condition (iii). In *R(P) 6/55* the claimant was denied pension, the Commissioner remarking that "regular work week by week in the service of an employer for as much as 20 hours a week where the work involved is substantially continuous during the hours of work [has] features which would render it unreasonable to speak of a person engaged in it ... as having retired from regular employment." The claimant was denied pension under condition (iii) on grounds of both regularity and extent.

There is, however, a better reconcilation of these cases with section 27(3)(b). The legislation requires that the employment be otherwise consistent with retirement. The alternative view is that regard may be had under condition (iii) to both extent and regularity but that neither of these may be the sole factor in preventing the fulfilment of the condition. *All* the circumstances must be taken into account. On the other hand, conditions (i) and (ii) clearly exclude consideration of any circumstances other than those specified therein. This latter approach is entirely consistent with the approach adopted in *R(P) 8/54* and subsequent cases.

At the end of the day, however, it must be asked if any useful purpose is served by having a number of alternative conditions, whichever interpretation is adopted. The conditions are selected on a somewhat arbitrary basis. One might just as well include, for good measure, that the employment be lacking in responsibility, or that it is free from the normal restraints of business; there seems to be no reason for attaching special sanctity to extent and regularity. Indeed, it seems odd that, whereas in respect of regular work exceeding 12 hours a week the nature of the work is a material factor in determining the question of retirement, prima facie no such regard need be paid to the nature of the work of, for example, a blast furnace stoker, provided that he confines his activities to under 12 hours per week. The sensible solution would seem to be the enactment of a single general requirement, directing the statutory authorities to have regard to all the circumstances subject to an overriding minimum earnings rule below which retirement must be presumed (if, that is, a retirement condition is to be retained at all).

(a) *Occasional Employment as an Earner*

The decisions are virtually unanimous in regarding this condition as involving the regularity of attendance at work. A claimant is not engaged "only occasionally" when he "works regularly at fixed recurring weekly periods and not merely now and then as occasion requires."[82] If regular daily hours are worked, the first condition is not met.[83] The key-note here is regularity. Regular work cannot be only occasional[84] even if it is part-time. Thus a steady three days work per week is not merely "occasional."[85] Availability during ordinary business hours is fatal.[86]

(b) *Engagement to an Inconsiderable Extent*

"The word 'inconsiderable' in the expression 'to an inconsiderable extent' is a relative term, that is to say, it has relation to, or is proportioned to, something definite in extent."[87] In order to secure uniformity in the administration of a similar provision under earlier legislation, the Umpire laid down a general rule[88] which was subsequently incorporated for national insurance purposes by the Commissioner.[89] It was:

"A claimant is engaged or intends to engage in his gainful occupation 'to an inconsiderable extent' if he proves that he engages in it or intends to engage in it for not more than twelve hours a week; or, alternatively, for not more than one-fourth of the normal hours of a full working week in that occupation, whichever of these alternatives is more favourable to the claimant."

The "twelve-hour rule" remains the primary criterion of "inconsiderableness." The general rule has been followed on innumerable occasions.[90] In an unreported decision[91] it is suggested that "where a person is engaged in regular part-time employment, the extreme limit of what can reasonably be regarded as consistent with retirement is round about eighteen hours a week, and then only if the work is light and such as would normally fall within the compass of a retired person." This statement seems, however, to refer to satisfaction of condition (iii).

The decisions are all agreed that the criterion is one of quantity measurable in hours. Where the extent of work cannot be measured in hours, the question of retirement must fall for decision under some other head. If it is clear that a trivial amount of work is involved, no difficulty is presented.[92] At the other extreme, if it is "clearly implicit in his duties ... that he ... should be present throughout the day,"[93] or if he is "in charge" all the time[94] or available to serve customers on demand[95] he is not engaged to an inconsiderable extent, even though the actual work be not onerous, or even though there be, apparently, no actual active work at all. This is not to say that a person whose work consisted merely of "standing by" for a considerable period of time would not be entitled to pension. The relevant question in such a case would be whether the work fell under the third condition. Nor is it to say that one whose earnings were, in consequence, slight, could not be regarded as retired. It has been decided, in *R(P) 1/52*, that low earnings are no indicator of "inconsiderable extent" and such a question would now fall for decision under the fourth condition.

(c) *Engaged in Circumstances Otherwise Not Inconsistent with Retirement*

It must be obvious that a continuation of an employment "steadily and regularly pursued for ... years as a means of livelihood" is extremely unlikely to be regarded as consistent with retirement.[96] It used, indeed, to be thought that a claimant must "show some specific circumstance causing a change of occupation or an alteration in the terms of an occupation" but this view has now been authoritatively rejected[97] and it is plain that a reduced scale of activity will not necessarily be regarded as inconsistent with retirement.[98] It is easier, however, to state, negatively, what will not necessarily fail to satisfy the third condition than to say, positively, what will satisfy it. The question has occupied the attention of the Commissioner on very many occasions, but no clear statement as to what should be the governing criterion emerges. Many of the decisions focus upon the nature of the work as giving the clue. In *R(P) 6/54*, the decision turns upon the fact that "the character of ... work had ... changed." More specifically, the condition is regarded as satisfied in *R(P) 7/56* because the claimant "would not be expected to work so hard" and as unfulfilled in *R(P) 12/53* because the work would not be free from the restraints of normal business. Similarly, in *R(P) 18/56*, pension was refused substantially because the work to be done evidenced no peculiar characteristics rendering it consistent with retirement. The claimant would have been fully occupied during the hours on duty and no special privileges would have been accorded to her. In *R(P) 19/56*, the fact that a partner retained his legal right to profits (though he ploughed them back) and his liabilities and powers (though he chose not to exercise them) was treated as rendering the work "inconsistent with retirement."

From these decisions focusing attention on the nature and characteristics of the work proposed to be undertaken has emerged the criterion that the work must be "of a kind which a retired person might reasonably be expected to do"—superficially singularly unhelpful, but rendered less so by the explanation offered by *R(P) 16/56*. What is meant is "work of a kind which a person who has reached an age when he is unable or unwilling to face the exertions of full-time employment would be likely to undertake. Work as a caretaker is work of that kind...." In that case, however, the amount to be done and the responsibilities attached to it rendered it inconsistent.[99]

Other decisions, however, seem to approach the question from a different angle. The reasons for which, and the attitude with which, the post-retirement work is approached seem predominant. In *R(P) 3/52*, the claimant was awarded pension in spite of the substantial nature of the occupation, because she had "left employment in which she was earning a wage sufficient to support her in reasonable comfort, not ... because she desired to change her employment or could expect to benefit by the change, but because she was driven to sacrifice her own interests by a sense of duty and the claim of blood relationship." It was "essentially not 'a business relationship.'" In *R(P)* *10/52* the predominant factor seems to be the attitude of the claimant towards his work. He is "free to abandon it whenever he likes"; it is "a self-imposed occupation."

In principle, a number of different permutations of the relevance of "nature of work" and "motivation" might function as guides to the role of condition (iii). Inevitably, there are decisions where the two criteria seem to be treated as equally relevant. Thus, in *R(P)* *7/52*, the decision was treated as turning on the "amount of time and labour spent on the gainful occupation, and the degree of diligence and earnestness with which it is pursued, and whether the primary purpose of the occupation is for profit or for recreation." In those decisions where special consideration seems to have been given to the question, however, whilst the two criteria emerge as relevant, they do so on the basis that one functions as strongly evidentiary of the other. *R(P)* *2/53* suggests that the relevance of examining the character of the work is to ascertain whether it amounted to work or merely to a post-retirement occupation. The clearest explicit statement of this view occurs in *R(P)* *11/55*[1] elaborating upon the general approach adumbrated in *R(P)* *8/54*, and stating that the test to be applied is to see whether there is any feature in the occupation and way it is done, which is characteristic of the way elderly people who have given up their regular occupations follow a post-retirement employment. Of course, if this view is correct, it should be doctrinally possible for an occupation the nature of which is entirely equivocal to be treated as consistent with retirement if accompanied by the right motivation, but inconsistent if accompanied by the wrong motivation. Something very like this is to be found in *R(P)* *8/56* where the occupation in question was crofting the nature of which, said the Commissioner, was "inconclusive." Whether or not it qualifies turns upon whether it is regarded as a "full-time occupation and employment" or whether the croft is "little more than a home and garden."

The position towards which decisions have tended is that an occupation may be disregarded, notwithstanding that it is gainful, if it is undertaken primarily as a post-retirement hobby, or amusement—a method of keeping the retired person occupied. If it is too onerous, if no special conditions attach to it, if it does not differ from any other business occupation, it fails to qualify. It should be stated clearly, however, that this is not the explicit approach of the Commissioner but an attempt to rationalise the various decisions. Furthermore, in the light of the avowed policy of the retirement pensions scheme, it is not the best approach. The function of the retirement condition is to seek to confine the award of pensions to those presumably in a state of increased need (by comparison with pre-retirement earnings). The question whether there has been a retirement should be answered in the light of this function, *i.e.* is the activity in question such as to bring about increased need? Prior to 1961, this interpretation of condition (iii) would have been perfectly admissible. In 1960, however, retirement condition (iv) (earnings) was added, and such an interpretation of condition (iii) as is above suggested became incompatible. It would have been better had the conditions been rationalised in the light of the addition of the low-earnings condition but they were not. It would, of course, be best if they were now to be rationalised by legislative action but the opportunity has been declined in the 1975 Acts. Until then, it may perhaps be noted that conditions (i) (irregularity), (ii) (extent), and (iv) (low earnings) have been interpreted consistently with the above-stated function of the concept of "retirement," and urged that in so far as is possible, a similar approach should be adopted to condition (iii). In other words the attitude should be that work not inconsistent with retirement in that it is such as not to obviate increased need should be ignored.[2]

(d) *Low Earnings*

Prior to 1960, the law relating to earnings was that, provided you were retired or entitled to be treated as retired, you could earn up to a certain amount without impairing the size of your pension, and that thereafter the pension would be progressively reduced according to the amount of earnings. It remained, however, essential that you be *retired*. Many claimants failed to understand this requirement and assumed that title to pension was established on the attainment of pensionable age merely by reduction in the amount of earnings below the statutory level.

Whilst this was, by reference to the legislation, a misunderstanding, it was, anomalously, fully in accordance with the
original policy. It was, as it were, the legislation which was out
of line, for it had never been intended that one should be disentitled to receive pension at a time when one's need for it had
greatly increased by virtue of reduced activity at pensionable
age. The legislation was brought into line in 1960 (National
Insurance Act 1960, s. 3) by the addition of a new alternative
retirement condition, namely, "if his earnings can be expected
not to exceed, or only occasionally to exceed, the amount any
excess over which would ... involve a reduction of the weekly
rate of retirement pension awarded to him" under the earnings
rule (below). The sum currently fixed under the earnings rule
is £35 per week.[3] Since the new condition was added, the other
conditions, with which there is considerable overlap, have
diminished in importance.

It will be noted that an expectation of reduced earnings satisfies this condition. Thus, in *R(P) 1/62*, no objection was taken
to a claim by a boarding-house proprietress who stated that she
intended to reduce the scale of her activities which, previously,
had been considerably in excess of the limit. It seems, furthermore, that the statutory authorities will have regard to the
factual family situation in appropriating earnings, rather than
the strict legal position. In *R(P) 1/76* a wife assisting her husband
in running a small business yielding £20 per week (in excess
of the then limit) was treated as earning a half-share of the
profits, even though she did not actually receive it, with the
result that the share attributable to the husband was below the
earnings limit. One unexpected paradox has appeared but seems
to have been satisfactorily resolved. The earnings of the claimant
in *R 1/63 (P)* were such that if national insurance contribution
was deducted, they fell below the limit and thus entitled the
claimant to be retired. The trouble was, that if she could be
treated as retired, there was no longer any obligation to pay
contributions. The Commissioner avoided this impasse by pointing out that the essence of condition (iv) was the impact of
earnings upon a pension if one was awarded. One had, therefore, to start with the assumption that a pension was awarded,
from which it followed that no contribution would be deducted
from the earnings, which, thus, would disentitle to a pension.

When it is intended to continue work after attaining pensionable age it is advisable to seek the Department's opinion beforehand as to whether the work pattern contemplated will be regarded as consistent with retirement. This will enable any necessary adjustment to be negotiated with the employer beforehand. If the advice turns out to be erroneous there is a prospect of redress via the Parliamentary Commissioner.[4]

5. Notice of Retirement

It is a condition for receipt of a retirement pension that a claimant shall have complied with the prescribed requirements as to notice of the date of his retirement.[5] He may not be treated as having retired earlier than three months before the giving of notice unless he can establish good cause for delay, in which case the period is 12 months.[6]

It used to be the case that no award could be made before the date of the notice and the related authorities[7] are presumably still good in so far as they hold that there is no discretion to pay pension in respect of a date earlier than that authorised by the legislation, in the absence of "good cause." Provided, however, that notice has been given in a proper manner, title is established and cannot be defeated by an erroneous denial of pension, even for two years.[8]

Regulations[9] allow claims at any time during the four months preceding entitlement. The notice should be in writing and must specify a date which may not precede the date of attainment of pensionable age nor be later than four months from the date of giving of notice. It must, of course, be a notice of "retirement" and will consequently be ineffective if what is notified is not "retirement."[10] In such a case, if pension is awarded, it will be recoverable unless good faith can be shown.[11] There is, however, a discretion for the Department to accept informal notice and notice of appeal to the local tribunal has been accepted as notice.[12]

The notice should be given to the Secretary of State which, in effect, means to the local office.[13] Where, however, a reciprocal arrangement exists with another country notice to the relevant authorities in that country may be accepted, such authorities being treated as agents of the Secretary of State for this purpose.[14] Presumably the same would apply under the European Community arrangements.

6. CATEGORY B PENSION

A woman may be entitled to a Category B pension in her own right by virtue of her husband's contributions.[15] Whilst the husband is alive and receiving pension the position will not be practically different from that of a wife in respect of whom an increase is payable for the amount receivable is the same in both cases.[16] The chief practical difference arises where the husband is dead. Here a woman receives a Category B retirement pension at the higher rate, the same as for a Category A pension.[17]

Subject to one exception, it is a condition of a woman's becoming entitled to a Category B pension that her husband has satisfied the appropriate contribution conditions.[18] Even the one exception is more apparent than real for it substitutes, for the condition that the husband has satisfied the contribution conditions, a condition that the woman was a widow and entitled to a widow's pension, and entitlement to a widow's pension is itself conditioned on the husband's having, before his death, satisfied contribution conditions identical to those for retirement pension.[19]

It is a second condition of entitlement to pension by virtue of a husband's insurance that a woman shall have reached pensionable age.[20]

The third condition of entitlement to a Category B retirement pension is that the woman shall have retired from regular employment.[21] There is one exception to this which arises when the husband is dead.[22] Here, pension is, in effect, discharging the function which widow's pension would have discharged had the widow been under pensionable age. If the husband is alive then he too must have reached pensionable age and have retired from regular employment.[23]

The woman loses her entitlement to pension if the marriage is dissolved prior to her attaining pensionable age. There used, further, to be a condition of contemporaneity, entitlement to pension being established only when all the conditions were contemporaneously satisfied. The position now is somewhat confused. Regulation[24] provides that a woman, whose marriage is terminated otherwise than by death after she attains pensionable age is entitled to a Category B pension "as if her husband by that marriage had died on the date of that termination." If this means that her case falls under the fourth head of entitlement the result in *R(P)* *14/56* is avoided. The fourth head, however, clearly requires that the husband be dead, not that he be treated as being dead. On the other hand if it is brought under the first head it must satisfy the contemporaneity condition, contained therein, since the regulation is clearly stated to be "subject to the provisions of the Act" *i.e.* including those relating to contemporaneity. In that case the result in *R(P)* *14/56* would remain unchanged and Regulation 4 (2) would be quite otiose.

It will be obvious from the foregoing that a woman may achieve dual qualification. The Act[25] provides that no person shall be entitled to more than one pension for the same period, but in such a case she may opt in writing for the pension of her choice, failing which she will be credited with the choice of pension offering the highest rate.[26] A rather more paternalistic approach was adopted in the 1973 legislation, under which no such option was permitted, and the reversion to the pre-1973 position appears to be a somewhat regressive step.

Certain provisions due to come into effect in 1979 enable women and surviving spouses to take advantage of both pensions, to the extent provided in the Act.[27] Under the same legislation, for the first time in the state scheme, a widower will be entitled to a Category B pension on the basis of his wife's contributions provided (i) he was married to her when she died, (ii) they were both over pensionable age and (iii) she was entitled (or would have been had she retired) to a Category A pension.[28]

7. DERETIREMENT

A retired person may elect to terminate his retirement and resume employment at any time during the five years following upon his attainment of pensionable age.[29] A married woman entitled to a Category B pension may not make such an election.[30] Where, however, the husband and wife have both become entitled on his contributions the consent of the wife to the election is required.[31] The consent must not be unreasonably withheld.[32]

It is up to the husband to persuade the tribunal that the consent is unreasonably withheld.[33] Where financial detriment to the wife is involved a withholding of consent may be proper. Pique or obstructive or improper motive might well, however, be unreasonable. The criteria are those applicable in the analogous situation in relation to leases.[34]

Notice in writing of the deretirement must be given to the Secretary of State.[35] The notice may or may not specify the date of retirement.[36] In the former case, the date specified must be within a period of 28 days following upon the date of the giving of notice.[37] Where the notice is posted, this is deemed to be the date of postage, not the date of arrival.[38] A notice may not be antedated.[39] Furthermore, where the consent of the wife is required, the date of the deretirement may not take effect prior to the date of consent if that be in writing, unless the consent is unreasonably withheld whereupon it takes effect as above provided the determining authorities make no order to the contrary. There is, however, no requirement that the consent be in writing. Where no date is specified, deretirement takes effect on the date on which the notice is given. Obviously, deretirement terminates all rights to a pension.[40] Only one election is permitted.[41] Other provisions apply in special cases.[42]

Notice may not be given by a person who does not ordinarily reside in this country.[43]

8. DEFERRED RETIREMENT

The statutory pensionable age is minimum retirement age. There is of course no requirement that retirement must take place at that age. There are a number of factors to be taken into consideration in determining the date of actual retirement.

Contributions are payable by a person over pensionable age who has not retired, unless he has not satisfied the contribution conditions for a retirement pension, prior to the attaining of that age.[44] Flat-rate unemployment and sickness benefit will be available to him at the same rate as the pension, subject to certain disregards, but he is not entitled to any earnings-related supplement. If he is entitled to earnings-related graduated pension, he may therefore be better off if he retires. On the other hand, unlike retirement pension, neither unemployment nor sickness benefit are taxable, and it might therefore be to his advantage not to retire for so long as he is incapacitated.

Pension advantages accrue as a result of deferred retirement. Where a person does not retire at the statutory age or where he ceases to be retired after that date, he may be entitled to an increased pension when he actually does retire. Under the former Act increments, expressed as a fixed sum of money, were calculated by the number of contributions paid after the statutory pensionable age.[45] This is still the case in respect of increments earned before April 5, 1975.[46] The weekly rate of pension is increased by 6p for every nine contributions paid since the attainment of pensionable age. After 1975, such increments are to be increased by the same percentage as the basic pension is increased.[47] Contributions paid before 1975 must be paid during the contribution year in which they are payable or within a year from then. Contributions paid after the time limit may count for increments only if the Secretary of State is satisfied that the failure to pay them was due to ignorance or error on the part of the insured which was not due to any failure on his part to exercise due care and diligence.[48] In a case referred to the Parliamentary Commissioner[49] the view was taken that although the Department had not sent out its usual reminders that there was a default of payment in the contributions, nonetheless there was no maladministration in the Department refusing to find that a claimant had exercised "due care and diligence" mainly on the basis that there was no legal obligation to remind. It is arguable, however, that where a practice of reminding is in fact adopted, a situation is created where contributors rely on being reminded and that normally all the care and diligence that is due from them in the circumstances is to respond to the reminders when received. The position is entirely different under the new scheme in respect of increments earned after April 1975 since pension entitlement no longer depends on the payment of contributions in the same way.

Under the 1975 legislation increments are calculated by reference to the number of days between pensionable age and retirement, and are expressed as a percentage of the basic pension.[50] In calculating the basic rate, no increase of benefit may be included other than that of invalidity allowance payable within 13 weeks and one day immediately prior to the date of attaining pensionable age. After 48 days, the basic pension is increased by $\frac{1}{8}$ per cent. for every six days, excluding Sunday, from the date on which the person reached pensionable age to the day before the date of retirement. The requirement of a 48-day period is omitted in the case of a person who is entitled or has a prospective right to an increase in pension under the former Act. Contributions paid before 1975 but not already accounted for are counted as six days of increments under the new scheme. Only those days in which a person would have been entitled to a pension had he been retired, are reckonable days of increment. Thus, days on which a person is imprisoned or detained in legal custody do not count. Neither does any day in respect of which certain stipulated benefits are paid. These include both unemployment and sickness benefit.[51]

A wife or widow entitled to a Category B retirement pension is entitled to receive some benefit by virtue of her husband's deferred retirement.[52] She would of course be entitled to an increased pension if entitled on her own insurance. A woman who opts to recover on her husband's contributions cannot supplement her pension by her own deferred retirement prior to his death[53] but a woman who elects to return to work after her husband's death may supplement her Category B pension in respect of days worked after his death.[54]

A widow entitled to a Category B pension continues to be entitled to any increase to it by virtue of her husband's deferred retirement entitlement even though she remarries provided she does so after pensionable age.[55]

9. The Earnings Rule

For the first five years of pensionable age, a number of devices seek to operate so as to ensure that payment of pension is confined to cases of loss of earning power. The necessity for retirement is one such device. Even more obviously so is the rule that pension may be abated or even lost if, in fact, substantial earnings accrue. The "earnings rule" has, as we saw in relation to condition (iv) of deemed retirement, a subsidiary function. Its main function, however, is stated by section 30 of the 1975 Act. This provides that a pensioner within five years of pensionable age shall lose 5p of the pension for each complete 10p earned between

£35 and £39 and 5p for each complete 5p earned over £39 "for the week ending last before any week for which he is entitled to pension."

The rule operates separately in respect of the husband's and wife's element in an increased pension. The single man's pension of £15·30 thus disappears at an earnings level exceeding £52·30 per week, no difference in total income resulting from earnings between £39 and £52·30 per week. It is to be remembered, of course, that the effect of earnings more than £35 may be to evidence non-retirement, resulting in disqualification for the entire pension.

Under the previous legislation, pension would be reduced if earnings exceeded the specified rate "for the calendar week ending last before any week for which he is entitled to a retirement pension." There were conflicting decisions as to the meaning of "calendar week" and the former word is omitted from the 1975 provision. There is provision for the definition of "week" in this context to be prescribed by regulations but the power has not yet been exercised. The difficulties of defining "week" therefore remain.

Regulations did at one time define "week" for the purposes of the earnings rule in terms of "the period of seven days preceding pension day" and it therefore followed that a deduction could be made from pension six times in respect of five weeks' work (the working week ending on Saturday and the pension week on Wednesday).[56] In a different context, "week" has been held by a tribunal of Commissioners to have its "ordinary meaning," namely the calendar week commencing at midnight on Saturday/Sunday,[57] and this meaning was later adopted for the expression "calendar week" even though qualified by reference to "ending last before any week for which he (the claimant) is entitled to the pension" as in the present legislation.[58] The expression "week for which he is entitled to pension" means the period of seven days following the pension day of payment, which is normally Thursday,[59] and it is clearly arguable that in such a context "week ending last before" means simply the period of seven days preceding the week of entitlement notwithstanding the absence of any express definition. There is nothing compelling about this interpretation but it is available and no decision has yet canvassed the various possibilities with sufficient thoroughness. When this is done, it will be relevant to bear in mind that the commonest "payment" week for employment purposes begins on Monday and ends before Sunday. Ease of administration would attach to an interpretation which took account of this fact.

For the purpose of the "earnings rule," the crucial question is, of course, that as to the meaning of "earnings." Reduction of pension is only required in case of "earnings." It is not required in case of other sources of income. The legislation[60] in a not altogether unprecedentedly unhelpful manner, merely tells us that it "includes any remuneration or profit derived from an employment." Commissioners' decisions over the years evolved a complex gloss on earlier regulations, a congeries of rules for determining net earnings. Anomalies developed. The whole structure has now been considerably rationalised, though not all problems solved, by more comprehensive regulations.[61] In one respect, indeed, they have added to the difficulties. Under the old law, as exemplified in decisions such as *R(G) 1/64*, and others[62] derivation from an occupation (presumably, there-fore, gainful) was an integral part of the definition of earnings.[63] As the law now stands, however, this is no longer clearly so, this by reason of the use of "includes" in the definition section, implying the logical possibility, at least, of earnings derived otherwise than from a gainful occupation. The current regula-tions deal only with the computation of earnings derived from gainful employment. The point has not yet troubled the Com-missioner and, indeed, the imagination boggles at concocting examples. Yet stranger things have happened and under the old law it was held that the fees of a director who performed no duties were earnings, it being "not possible to say that a director has no occupation."[64]

It is clear that "earnings" is a wider category than "wages." In *R(P) 9/56*, the claimant drew the sum of £2 per week from a business as wages and also received a share of profits averaging more than £5 per week. His contention that only the wages were "earnings" was rejected. We have seen that director's fees may be included, even if no duties attach.[65] It is not even necessary that cash should be earned. "Remuneration includes whatever the person receives for his services. It includes not only cash, but money's-worth such as the value of uniform or of board and accommodation, or of a rent free cottage or meals supplied."[66] The principle holds good though actual examples are in some respects superseded by new regulations.[67] "Earnings" does not, however, embrace all income, however derived. A claimant who was entitled to a half-share in the capital and income from her late husband's estate, irrespective of whether or not she lived and worked at a farm forming part of that estate, was held not to be in receipt of earnings, even though she was occupied in running the business.[68] It does not follow from this decision that receipts must be made in discharge of an obligation in consideration of services etc. rendered in order to be "earnings." *Ex gratia* payments qualify, provided they are in fact made for services rendered.[69] At first blush, it does not seem easy to reconcile with $R(G)$ $9/55$ the decision in $R(G)$ $1/60$. In the latter case, a shareholder and managing director of a company was also a consultant on terms that she would be paid a sum by which her dividends fell short of £350 per annum. It could thus be said that she would receive £350 per annum "irrespective or not of whether" she functioned as consultant. As long, however, as dividends fell short, she was in fact paid in consideration of her services and was thus liable to reduction of pension.

It is, of course, highly anomalous in this latter case, that the claimant's liability to reduction should have turned upon the source from which her income was derived, rather than upon the question whether she continued to receive it or not. This, however, is an anomaly due to the somewhat irrelevant confinement of reduction to cases of "earning." Thus dividends payable to a shareholder in a company cannot be taken into account, it being "impossible to regard the income produced by the securities as a remuneration or profit derived from an occupation."[70] If a person, on reaching pensionable age and being retired, suffers no diminution of income because his income, being unearned, continues before as after attaining pensionable age, there is no more reason for exempting him from reduction than for exempting an earner. The obvious policy objectives are secured rather by an "income" rule than an "earnings" rule.

There is no requirement that earnings be earned in or remitted to this country before they need be brought into account.

In $R(P)$ *1/70* the profits from a business in Italy counted as
"earnings" even though, by reason of currency regulations, they
could not be remitted to the claimant in England. The earnings had, however, been received and it is possible, notwithstanding $R(P)$ *5/53* below, that "earnings' unlikely ever to be
received might be left out of account.

Regulation requires that in cases of gainful employment, the
earnings shall be "derived" therefrom.[71] Earnings, it appears,
are "derived" when the obligation to pay them accrues, even if
actual payment is deferred,[72] at all events provided that payment is eventually received. If no obligation accrues, as in the
case of *ex gratia* payments, the actual week of payment is
obviously the crucial one.[73]

Difficulty is posed by those sources of earnings where income
is "not immediately ascertainable" for a particular period for
purposes of reduction or where a person's earnings do not
consist of "salary, wages, fees or other payments related to a
fixed period." This situation is dealt with by regulation[74] which
provides for the determining authorities to "calculate or estimate the amount of those earnings, for any day or week on or
in which that person is following the employment from which
they are derived, as best they may, having regard to the
information (if any) available to them and to what appears to
them to be the probabilities of the case." First, earnings are not
"immediately ascertainable" if anything remains to be done to
determine the amount due, such as the employer confirming
commission earned.[75] Secondly, the averaging can only be done
in relation to periods when the occupation is being followed,
which may be a matter of degree. In $R(P)$ *4/56* a widow's
boarding-house profits could be averaged over a year, and not
merely the busy weeks, because she had made efforts to get
boarders all year round, even though with no marked success.
One cannot be confident that slight efforts with no prospects of
success would necessarily have sufficed. A year has also been
held to be a reasonable period in the hotel trade, presumably
on the ground that that is the duration of the seasonal cycle.[76]
Where the payment is in respect of a specific period such as an
annual bonus[77] such a period is obviously a reasonable one for
the purposes of the calculation. There appears, indeed, to be a
rule that "a period of one year is an appropriate period to take

as a matter of general practice"[78] departure from which may be justified by exceptional circumstances.[79] Re-estimation whenever circumstances change is obviously desirable.[80]

Payments to be disregarded

Regulation[81] allows disregard of non-transferable meal vouchers to the value of 15p per day; meals provided at the place of work; accommodation to be occupied as a condition of employment; and "food or produce provided by the employer to the person for his personal needs and those of his household." Christmas bonuses, in the form of sums of money up to £10, may be disregarded, provided they are paid in December. There appears to be no limit to the value of remuneration in kind paid by way of Christmas bonus. A sum may not be treated as a bonus if it is one of a series of sums payable at intervals of less than a year or is payable for work done and accrues as overtime or an incentive payment or is "otherwise directly related to his hours of work or to the amount of work performed by him."[82] "Incentive payment" appears to be confined to those cases where the payment is directly related to the quantity of work. Bonus paid merely to induce employees to remain with the employer clearly is not an "incentive payment ... for work done"!

There is an obvious scope for planning both in relation to these exemptions and in relation to the guidelines indicated in regulation 2 (3) considered above.

Deductions

Regulation[83] provides an exhaustive list[84] of permissible deductions. It includes matters such as the cost of travel, tools, protective clothing, national insurance and industrial injuries contributions etc., cost of meals during work etc. Two items have received considerable attention from the Commissioner:

1. Expenses reasonably incurred "in respect of ... the making of reasonable provision for the care of another member of his family because of his own necessary absence from home to carry out his duties in connection with that employment." The taking of the employment must be a necessary condition of the incurring

of the cost. If it would have been incurred anyway, it cannot be deducted.[85] The cost of food for children is an obvious example.[86] An expense is thus incurred "in connection with" an employment if the employment could not be taken without incurring it.[87] More than this, however, seems to be required. The expense must be an incident of the employment and not something disconnected with though consequent upon it. There is some difficulty in reconciling the authorities here. One early authority[88] asserts that "in connection with" means "in consequence of" whilst two later ones[89] state that it does not. The earlier decision is not considered in the later ones. The phase "in consequence of" is, however, ambiguous and it seems to be given a different meaning in the earlier case than in the later ones. It is believed that the distinction above drawn offers the best reconciliation of this apparent conflict.

These rules can lead to anomaly. They mean that if a claimant goes out to work in order to send her child to a boarding school, the cost cannot be deducted.[90] But if the child is sent to the school in order to enable her to work, it can.[91] It seems that the original policy of the earnings rule has been lost sight of in making these decisions. It should not matter if the motive for taking work is sending the child to school, provided that the work cannot be taken without the child being sent to school. It can hardly be a significant factor whether a working wife likes housework or not.

The provision made must be "reasonable." Previously, it was required to be "necessary" and the change of words could warrant a less generous approach on the part of the statutory authorities.[92] An expense incurred merely for convenience or comfort will not suffice—the cost of having a meal cooked for the child of a low-wage earner has been treated as a matter of convenience.[93] In judging what is reasonable regard must be had to the claimant's earnings. An expense is regarded as unreasonable "in so far as it exceeds the expense which a reasonable person whose income was limited to her earnings would incur for that purpose." It is, however, permissible to allow deduction of such part of an expense as is reasonable. The policy thus enshrined is not beyond question. It means that the identical expense may be deductible in whole in the case of one earner but only in part in the case of another. There is something to be said for adopting a common standard for all rather than one which reflects the economic circumstances of the particular claimant.

2 "Any other expenses (not being sums the deduction of which from wages or salary is authorised by statute) reasonably incurred ... in connection with and for the purposes of ... employment." The exclusion from this category of "sums ... authorised by or under any enactment" confirms that tax cannot be deducted. There had been some confusion on this point, one view being that tax was deductible,[94] the other that it was not, being a part of the "net remuneration or profit."[95] Commission payable to an employment agency on securing employment[96] and rent of business premises[97] have been held to be reasonable. On the other hand, the cost of sub-employment unknown to an employer has been excluded merely on the ground of the employer's ignorance and consequent non-acquiescence, reasons the relevance of which is not clear.[98] The statutory criteria do not seem to involve such a consideration at all. The decision in *C.P. 2/48 (KL)*, amounting really to the proposition that a husband cannot charge his wife board and lodging, is a happier one.

The "expenses" referred to in this provision must be "related to the person, that is to the particular individual concerned and not to an abstract ordinary reasonable person, and the expenses incurred by the person concerned must be in connection with the employment; they must also be reasonable expenses. The words must be read together so that the expenses must be reasonable not only in relation to the subject-matter of the expenditure and the amount spent on it but also in connection with the employment... The remaining question is one of fact and of degree, namely whether expenses claimed in certain circumstances fall within or outside the words of the regulation.[99]" In that case, the claimant was allowed to deduct a reasonable (but not the whole) sum in respect of travelling home at lunchtimes, a proper diet being necessitated by his suffering from a duodenal ulcer, that expense being reasonably connected with his employment. Under the new regulations referred to above, he might be allowed to deduct travelling expenses under another head.

Method of Calculation of Earnings

Regulations[1] provide for the use of returns or statements for tax purposes, to facilitate calculation of earnings which are not immediately ascertainable. Special provision is made for the payment of certain benefit.[2] Regulations also govern the calculation of earnings derived from taking in lodgers.[3] In the absence of any other basis, the insurance officer may use a previous year's figures, making an appropriate adjustment as necessary.[4] In other cases, in the absence of reasonably proper and satisfactory details being supplied by a claimant, the insurance officer may reasonably use supplementary benefit assessment methods in order to make his determination and assist the tribunal.[5]

The Social Security Pensions Act 1975 removes the earnings rule from the additional component in the new pension, and from any preserved graduated pension payable under former schemes. Its abolition is justified on the ground that to retain the full rule would be to discriminate unfairly between members of state and occupational schemes but it affords least benefit to those with the smallest pensions, a result which would not universally be described as equitable.

The Social Security (Miscellaneous Provisions) Act 1977 imposes a statutory duty on the Secretary of State to uprate the earnings limit in line with earnings. The earnings rule has never been popular and both major parties have undertaken to abolish it. For the time being, however, this is ruled out on grounds of cost. Objections to the rule rest primarily on the ground that it is a disincentive to work involving abnormally high marginal rates of taxation. The extent to which it does so act is the subject of a departmental inquiry established under the above Act to review the operation of the rule and the cost of its abolition. This latter move may well be a logical development and may be argued to reflect the prevailing (although actuarially inaccurate) view of pensions as deferred pay. Nonetheless, it can certainly be argued that there are more pressing claims on limited funds than the provision of benefits for those who still enjoy a perfectly adequate income from wages. If pensions are to become a solatium for senescence the decision should be made advisedly.

ADDITIONS TO FLAT-RATE PENSION

The Present Scheme

"Flat rate of subsistence benefit; flat rate of contribution"[6]—
these were two of the six fundamental principles upon which
Beveridge stationed his proposals. Both have been abandoned.
The first departure came in the National Insurance Act 1959,
introducing graduated contribution and benefit mainly as a
politically palatable method of coping with a flat-rate funding
deficit. The financial proposals frankly contemplated the
diversion of part of the graduated contribution income to the
funding of flat-rate benefits which had come to be in deficit
through inflation. Graduated benefits were, in consequence,
actuarially a poor return on the additional contributions.
Although contracting out was allowed (and, thus, rejection of
the graduated element in benefit) higher contributions were
nevertheless required from persons contracted out.

The 1959 Act (later the 1965 Act as amended by the 1969 Act)
provided for an addition to the flat-rate contribution of a sum
equal to weekly earnings between £9 and £18, from both
employer and employee. Class 2 and 3 contributors were thus
excluded.

In its 1966 Act, the Labour Government introduced supplementary graduation, contributions to equal half a per cent.
of weekly earnings between £9 and £30. Consistently with
Labour philosophy there was to be no contracting out of this
supplementary scheme which extended not only to pensions but
also to other benefits. The 1973 Act (now the 1975 Act) replaced
the hybrid system of flat-rate and graduated contributions by a
system of fully earnings-related contributions for employed
earners—Class 2 and 3 contributions remain flat-rate. There is
both an upper and a lower limit on earnings on which contributions are payable.

So far as benefit is concerned, section 36 of the 1965 Act provides for a weekly addition to the pension of two and a half
pence for each contribution unit or part exceeding half thereof.
A contribution unit consists of amounts of graduated contribution. These amounts are £7·50 units in the case of men and
£9 in the case of women[7] the difference being due to actuarial

reasons. If employer's contributions of an equivalent amount are taken into account, the total amounts of these units are £15 in the case of a man and £18 in the case of a woman. A widow is entitled to take the benefit of half her former husband's entitlement to graduated pension, as well as her own. Under the Social Security Pensions Act 1975, this may be extended to cover widowers.[8]

No new graduated payments will be made after April 6, 1975 but accrued rights to it are preserved by regulations.[9] Under the 1973 Act (now the 1975 Act) graduated benefits were not made subject to the annual review proposed for benefits on the grounds that to do so would be unfair to members of recognised occupational pension schemes, for whom no such cover was provided. The Social Security Pensions Act 1975, coming into effect on April 6, 1978 provides statutory authorisation for the making of regulations allowing graduated pensions to be increased with the line of prices.[10]

Under the 1973 Act benefits were to be basically flat-rate; the provision of earnings-related benefits to supplement the basic pension was regarded primarily as the responsibility of the private sector, state earnings-related pensions being offered merely in default of a satisfactory private occupational scheme. Additional state pension was to accrue under the reserve pension scheme, established by the Act, but contracting out of the scheme was permissible subject to certain conditions. The scheme embodied in the 1973 Act, however, was unacceptable to a subsequent Labour Government and for the most part has been shelved. The Labour Government, in turn, has published its own proposals, which are given legislative effect in the Social Security Pensions Act 1975, due to come into force on April 6, 1979. In many respects they differ radically from the previous scheme. The Act replaces the existing pension with one divided into two components, the basic component and the additional component.[11] The former is a flat-rate sum, representing a 100 per cent. return of average weekly earnings up to the basic level. At present the basic component stands at £15·30. When the scheme is fully mature, the additional component will represent a quarter of average weekly earnings between the basic level and a ceiling of seven times that level, based on the contributor's best 20 years of earnings. The scheme, which reaches maturity after 20 years, provides for an accrual rate of $1\frac{1}{4}$ per cent. of average earnings between the lower and upper ceilings. Those who have contributed for 20 years will be entitled to the full 25 per cent.[12] Although calculation of the pension is based on his 20 best years, nonetheless entitlement to pension continues to be conditioned on the payment of contributions throughout working life. Contributions are no longer obligatory from persons over pensionable age, although liability for secondary Class 1 contributions remains. Furthermore, the right of women to pay contributions at a lower rate is withdrawn as from April 6, 1977 except in respect of those women who have exercised their option prior to that date.

Contribution conditions have been significantly relaxed in certain cases to cater for particular needs, going some way to meet the view expressed earlier, that it is high time the insurance myth was decently interred. Some of the resulting provisions have been referred to in previous paragraphs. Married women are no longer required to satisfy the half-test and special provision is made for persons precluded from regular employment by responsibilities at home.[13]

A surviving spouse or married woman, entitled but for section 27 (6) to both a Category A and a Category B pension, is able to maximise benefit from the two entitlements. Furthermore, the right of a woman whose marriage has been terminated to aggregate her contributions with those of her husband (former or late) is extended to cover the spouse of either sex, and for the first time provision will be made for the payment of a Category B retirement pension to a widower on the basis of his late wife's contribution record.

The familiar arguments against earnings-related benefits, because of their "inherently inegalitarian" nature, apply with most force to post-retirement benefits. It may be unreasonable to require a man substantially to reduce his standard of living whilst he is temporarily incapacitated from earning his usual wage. Indeed, it may not be open to him immediately to do so; certain financial commitments will remain outstanding for a while—hire-purchase payments, mortgage payments etc. But these arguments are far less convincing when applied to a retired person over pensionable age. It is not the function of the State to perpetuate the inequalities produced by the labour market. That

it should do this at all is bad enough; that it should do this
after working life is over is even less excusable.[14]

Contracting Out

Since 1959 insured persons entitled to a pension under a
private pension scheme have been able to be contracted out if
the terms offered are at least as favourable as the most favourable benefits under the state scheme. Other conditions must
also be complied with. The scheme enacted in the National
Insurance Act 1965 is to be replaced by a new scheme coming into
effect in 1978. The 1965 Act itself has been largely repealed but for
the purposes of facilitating the winding up of the old scheme
provision has been made for the continuance in force of certain
sections of that Act. In particular, sections 58 and 59 (which
provide that an employer must make a payment in lieu of
contributions to the national insurance fund if, at the end of a
person's service is a non-participating employment, he is not
assured of equivalent pension benefits) have both been amended
by regulations[15] so as to cover schemes which have ceased to be
non-participating schemes by virtue of the repeal of the Act.
Such a payment must now be made, in similar circumstances,
in respect of the "settlement period" which for most purposes,
ends on April 5, 1980.[16]

The Social Security Pensions Act 1975

This Act, coming into effect for the most part in 1978–79 marks
a shift in emphasis in the respective roles of state and private
pension schemes. About half the working population is covered
by occupational pension schemes. Full contributions are payable by all employed employees up to the basic level, and in
return, they will be covered for the basic component of the
state pension. Contracting out of the additional component is
permitted subject to rigorous conditions in return for a reduced
contribution liability of 7 per cent. The Treasury supplement
to the Fund will be calculated on the contributions which
would have been paid had the employment not been contracted
out.[17]

The conditions for contracting out are more rigorous than

anything hitherto devised. For a scheme to be contracted out it must fulfill certain minimum requirements as follows:

(i) It must provide for the minimum benefits specified in the Act.

(ii) It must be specified in a contracting-out certificate issued by the Occupational Pensions Board. The Board have a wide discretion for these purposes, and can withhold or cancel a certificate, even though the scheme otherwise satisfies the contracting-out conditions if, in the opinion of the Board "there are circumstances relating to the scheme or its management which make it inexpedient that the scheme should be contracted out.[18]"

(iii) Its rules must comply with the requirements of any regulations prescribing their form and content and with any requirement as to form and content imposed by the Board as a condition of contracting-out.[19]

The requirement of minimum benefits includes the satisfaction of a minimum level of both personal and death benefits. That level may be met by compliance with the standard laid down in the Act or in other not inferior ways.

First, the scheme must provide its members with a pension which is as much as the additional component they would have received under the state scheme. This is known as the "guaranteed minimum." A new development in the state intervention in private pension schemes is that the government have assumed responsibility for inflation-proofing this sum.[20]

Secondly, the scheme must provide for an annual accrual rate of at least $1\frac{1}{4}$ per cent. of the average or final salary revalued in line with the general level of earnings. Accrual may cease when half-salary is reached.[21] The Board have a discretion to accept a lower percentage if they are satisfied that the benefits as a whole are not less favourable.

Thirdly, in the event of the member's death provision must be made for the payment of a widow's benefit to his wife during any period for which a Category B retirement pension or a widowed mother's allowance or pension is payable.[22] The scheme must provide for an annual accrual rate of five-eighths of her late husband's average or final salary revalued in line with the general level of earnings[23] and it must provide her with at least half of his guaranteed minimum pension. If death occurs before he attains pensionable age the pension may be commuted to a lump sum but the guaranteed minimum pension must always be in the form of a pension.[24]

Fourthly, the scheme must be soundly funded[25] the supervision of the financial arrangements being within the jurisdiction of the Board.

Prior to 1975, one of the chief vices of many occupational pension schemes was that benefit under them ended or was drastically reduced upon termination of employment whether in the form of premature retirement, transfer to another employment or dismissal. Occupational schemes must now conform to the "preservation requirements" in such circumstances. These are contained in the 1973 Act[26]; the statutory standard is five years' pensionable service under the scheme in question by a contributor aged at least 26 years on the termination of that service. A scheme conforms to the preservation requirements if it entitles members to short-service benefit or if it provides for the transfer of accrued rights to another scheme with the employee's consent.[27]

In the event of prior termination, the Social Security Pensions Act 1975 permits an employer to pay a state scheme premium equivalent to the amount which would have been payable in respect of the employee had he not been contracted out. The payment of this sum extinguishes the member's (or, if dead, his wife's) accrued rights to a guaranteed minimum pension under the scheme.[28] If the employee is not brought back into the state scheme his guaranteed minimum pension must be preserved or, if he consents, transferred to another scheme. A similar premium is payable in the event of termination of contracted-out employment.[29] Significantly, provision has been made for the protection of accrued pension rights of early-leavers against the effects of inflation.[30] Under section 35 (7), liability to revalue the preserved pension may be limited to 5 per cent. plus the payment of a limited revaluation premium into the National Insurance Fund.[31] Alternatively, the scheme may provide for a rate of interest of at least $8\frac{1}{2}$ per cent. compound for each relevant year after his service terminated, even though the increase in earnings factor is less than that for that year. An election to pay a state scheme premium must be notified in writing not more than one month before or six months after the date of termination of contracted-out employment.[32] Where the scheme itself ceases to be contracted out, the time is six months from the date of certification that the earner's rights are not subject to approved arrangements. The time limit may be extended.[33] The state scheme premium must be paid within the six months after the termination of contracted-out employment or one month after the receipt of notice certifying the amount payable whichever is the later, although the time limit may be extended.

The Act forbids discrimination "between different earners on any grounds other than the nature of their employment," where the employer elects to contract employees out.[34] Discrimination is also forbidden "between different earners on any grounds other than their respective lengths of relevant service"[35] by an employer when electing to pay a contributions equivalent premium under section 42 (2) or (3). This does not apply in respect of women employees paying reduced contributions; nor where the earner's accrued rights are transferred; nor where he has elected under the rules of the scheme that his pension shall be preserved,[36] but in these circumstances, an employer may not discriminate between different earners falling within the same class of case.

All occupational pension schemes financed as prescribed under section 41 (1) must comply with the "equal access" requirements. Subject to certain exceptions, these are that "membership of the scheme is open to both men and women on terms which are the same as to age and length of service needed for becoming a member and as to whether membership is voluntary or obligatory."[37] These requirements have been modified where pension schemes provide for different pension ages.[38] Rules creating a discretion which may result in discriminatory treatment do not contravene the equal access requirement provided the rules themselves are capable of applying to either sex.[39] The duty of ensuring that the rules of a scheme conform to the "equal access" requirements rests upon the trustees and administrators of the scheme. The Occupational Pensions Board is the determining body on whether the schemes rules comply with the requirements and, if they do not, the Board may direct the administrators to modify the rules accordingly and may even, if necessary, modify the rules themselves. The recent

sex discrimination legislation incorporates the "equal access"
requirements into the equality clause and provides a means of
redress for the individual employee.[40] Complaints will be heard
by an industrial tribunal with an appeal on a point of law to the
Employment Appeal Tribunal. The appropriate remedy in such
cases is a declaratory order. Damages may not be awarded by
the industrial tribunal although they may require the employer
to make a contribution to the resources of the scheme to provide adequate benefits to which the employee would otherwise
earlier have been entitled to. The Board has similar powers
where the rules of a scheme are modified retrospectively under
section 56 (4); and under the Equal Pay Act 1975, the Central
Arbitration Committee may also have jurisdiction in respect of
discriminatory rules where access to a scheme is governed by a
collective agreement or wages order.

Responsibility for the supervision of contracted-out employments rests with the Occupational Pensions Board, established
under the 1973 Act. The Board has jurisdiction to determine
any question as to whether employment is contracted out and
there is a right of appeal on a point of law from its decisions
to the High Court.[41]

11. Non-Contributory Pensions

The contribution conditions for the species of retirement pension
discussed above prevented retirement pensions as of right from
becoming universal. For a number of reasons (*e.g.* being over
pensionable age at the inception of the scheme) an old person
might fail to satisfy the contribution conditions and thus be left
to his private resources or, more often, supplementary benefits.

The first halting steps to deal with this phenomenon were
only taken in 1970 by the National Insurance (Old Persons'
and Widows' Pensions and Attendance Allowance) Act of that
year, section 1 of which instituted a separate retirement pension
for the rapidly declining group who were over pensionable age
on July 5, 1948. Under the 1975 Act, this pension is described
as a Category C retirement pension.[42] The claimant must have
been resident in Great Britain for at least 10 years between
July 5, 1948 and November 1, 1970 and must have been ordi-

narily resident in Great Britain on the latter date or on the date of his claim for the pension.[43] His wife may also be eligible for a Category C pension if she is over pensionable age and has retired from regular employment. Special provision is made for women whose marriages have been terminated whether by death or otherwise, who were married and over pensionable age on July 5, 1948.[44]

The National Insurance Act 1971 took these developments a step further in establishing a pension as of right for all persons over 80 who were not otherwise adequately provided for under the scheme.[45] Under the 1975 Act, this is described as a Category D retirement pension.[46] Entitlement is conditional on the claimant being resident in Great Britain for at least 10 years of the 20 ending on the day he reaches the age of 80 years. He must also have been resident in Great Britain either on the date of attainment of the age of 80 years or on the date of the claim if later.

In both cases, pension is payable at a higher and lower rate, the latter being confined to the case where the beneficiary has been a married woman since entitlement was established.[47] The current higher and lower rates are £9·20 and £5·60 per week. There is a statutory obligation placed on the Secretary of State to maintain the value of each pension in relation to the general level of prices or earnings.[48]

Age Addition

The 1971 Act[49] establishes the right of all the above pensioners to an extra payment at the age of 80 and above of 25p per week to make extra provision for the extra and long-term needs of the aged.[50] Age addition is paid weekly in advance usually on the same day as the pension.[51]

OVERSEAS PENSIONS

An accrued right to retirement pension may be attained notwithstanding that the pensioner ceases to be resident in Great Britain or Northern Ireland. Residences abroad, however, disqualifies for increases in pension until such time as residence at home is resumed unless regulations or an up-rating order specifies otherwise.[52]

Chapter 10

INDUSTRIAL INJURIES BENEFITS

A. INTRODUCTION

ALTHOUGH not peculiar to it, the incidence of injury, disablement, death and disease arising out of work burgeoned as a result of the industrial revolution. Where earnings from work form a chief source of income for a family, such events are particularly apt to cause need. A worker so affected was not necessarily without redress at common law. Generally, however, redress at law was totally inadequate. Usually fault would need to be proved and would in any case be insufficient if countered by the defences of common employment, *volenti non fit injuria* or contributory negligence. Perhaps more important, the cost and delays of litigation would normally deter the injured worker from even contemplating legal redress.

The usual result would therefore be that the injured worker would be left to bear the whole cost of industrial injury. The employer could contract for other labour; the injured worker could not, *ex hypothesi*, contract for other work. This was manifestly unsatisfactory and its unjustice might to some extent be recognised by the employer *ex gratia*. That this was clearly inadequate is evidenced on the one hand by schemes for self-help arranged through the medium of growing trade unions and friendly societies; and on the other hand by a movement for legislation which would improve the injured worker's lot.

At a time when the former development was accelerating, the latter culminated in the Workmen's Compensation Bill 1896, and it is interesting to note that the only significant opposition to the Bill came, not from an employers' lobby, but from Members of Parliament voicing trade union and friendly society interests. The Bill nevertheless became law as the Workmen's Compensation Act 1897, the grandfather of the modern industrial injuries scheme.

The 1897 Act was directed against a number of evils. It was

clearly inequitable that the worker should be left to bear the whole of the burden of injury; therefore the cost should be shared between worker and employer. It was not fair to confine the employer's liability to cases where he and he alone was at fault; injury could result without fault and the employer should shoulder a share of the burden regardless of his fault for it. Finally, the worker should not be put to litigation before the courts to enforce his rights. The abolition of the fault principle and resort to arbitration would obviate this. The worker's entitlement would derive simply from the fact of his having suffered personal injury caused by accident arising out of and in the course of employment.[1]

The ensuing half-century evidenced increasingly the in-adequacies of this scheme, inadequacies which persisted through amending and consolidating Acts the chief of which were the extension of 1906 and the consolidations of 1925 and 1934. To some extent, the problem of the impecunious employer was met by compulsory insurance in the mining industry. It was also recognised that the "equity" of sharing costs between worker and employer was apparent only. Whatever proportion he had to pay, the employer would simply treat it as one of the costs of his business and pass it on to his customers. Whatever propor-tion the average worker had to bear he would bear personally. The whole cost was therefore shifted progressively on to the employer.

Other vices persisted. The Act, said Lord Wright,[2] "was in-tended to be administered with as little technicality as possible: yet thousands of reported cases have accumulated round it, and fresh ones are likely to go on accumulating so long as the act remains in its present form." The reasons were, in retrospect, obvious. Abolishing the requirement of "fault" removed only one of the questions which courts could entertain. Others—what was "personal injury"? "accident"?; when did an accident arise "out of and in the course of employment"?[3]—remained and lawyers extracted stupendous mileage out of them. Arbitration did not stem the flow—an appeal might establish him to have been wrong in law, and even if the prospects seemed unlikely the inequality of arms between employer and worker nevertheless made the threat of litigation a powerful bargaining counter for the former.

Not unnaturally, many employers insured against the contingency and insurance companies played a large part in spoiling the scheme. Claims contended by insurance companies often exacerbated relations between employers and workers. The latter might steer clear of light or part-time employment for fear of prejudicing his claim by mitigating his loss. There were demarcation struggles where two or more potential payors were involved and arguments about causation in some cases such as those concerning pneumoconiosis and silicosis. It might be prudent to discharge a worker or refuse to employ him if a claim was anticipated, and there was no profit in and no attempt at rehabilitation desirable though it might be from an individual and social viewpoint.

Most of these vices blossomed under the care of insurance companies spending 7–45 per cent. (on average 20 per cent.) of premium income on administration and litigation. Others were inherent. Only partial compensation, often by a lump-sum, was aimed at and the scheme could therefore never be more than merely palliative. The class of dependants was badly defined and hard cases proliferated. Incapacity alone triggered the scheme; non-incapacitating disablement did not. Most vicious of all, the injured worker could still end up with nothing —he had to opt between his common law rights and compensation under the scheme and the former might turn out to be non-existent.[4]

Beveridge

It is not surprising that Beveridge found the workmen's compensation scheme inadequate. It is more surprising that the Committee arrived at the conclusion that in the proposed post-War scheme special provision should be made for the industrially incapacitated. The social scene had changed considerably over the decades since the 1897 Act and the Committee was proposing more striking changes still. In 1897, industrial injury might well mean poverty, destitution and even starvation. Today, as a result of Beveridge, between the industrially injured and his dependants and such a sorry end there stand not only the social security benefits described in the foregoing chapters but also devices such as the national health and social work services and industrial training and rehabilitation schemes. In some respects this range of benefits is inferior to the generally higher flat-rate industrial injury benefits (though sickness benefit with earnings-related supplement can overtake injury benefit). The question then is, is a separate scheme for the industrially-injured justified by the need to make available a higher range of benefits? Children have to go to school; workers have to use the roads to get to work; the housewife has to cook and clean—all flirt with sources of serious injury and disablement. Why single out industry for special treatment?

Beveridge confronted the anomaly and indeed recognised that "what is needed is not a special arrangement for the industrially-disabled but rather a comprehensive scheme covering all casualties, however caused."[5] However, "such a proposal ... could not arise out of the scheme of workmen's compensation as it stands today."[6] It could, however, have arisen out of the proposed social insurance scheme as a whole, and why rationalisation in this context was not considered remains a mystery.

It seemed to the Committee that special provision should continue to be made for the industrially-incapacitated for three reasons:

1. "... many industries vital to the community are also specially dangerous. It is essential that men should enter them and desirable, therefore, that they should be able to do so with the assurance of special provision against their risks."

2. "A man disabled during the course of his employment has been disabled while working under orders. This is not true of other accidents or of sickness."

3. "... only if special provision is made for the results of industrial accident and disease, irrespective of negligence, would it appear possible—as on grounds of equity and for the avoidance of controversy it is desirable—to limit the employer's liability at common law to the results of actions for which he is responsible morally...."

It is not easy to see how these reasons can support the Beveridge proposals. The first of them might have justified special provision for highly hazardous occupations if the economic model implicit in it bore any relation to reality. However, it takes the Committee only two paragraphs to conclude that provision should not be so-confined and if identical cover is to attach to all occupations one is left wondering what it is that will attract the work-force to the hazardous jobs. That is, of course, to use Beveridge's model, men shopping around, weighing the pros and cons, and choosing a job accordingly, whereas the facts of industrial life are that most are conduced to take whatever work is available.[7]

The second reason is, if anything, even less adequate. Workmen's compensation was, and industrial injury benefit is, payable not only when the victim was working under orders but also where he was doing a range of incidental things; whereas many groups injured by more or less coerced activities (travelling to work; attending school; working in the home) are excluded.

The third reason again departs from reality. Employer's liability was not, prior to workmen's compensation, co-extensive with his moral culpability and has been extended rather than contracted coincidentally with social insurance.

Whether the abandonment of any special treatment for the industrially-injured would have been tolerable 30 years ago, as now, is speculative. It is now an industrial reality, a privilege as dear, perhaps, to those in whom it inheres as any other. That, when the general provision for the disabled which Beveridge conceived to be needed is made and when better provision is made for the dependants of deceased persons, the last shreds of a rational case for separate treatment will have disappeared can hardly be controverted. The efficiency of its administration will not justify its retention. The apparent costs of administration (8 per cent. of outgo) are the highest in the social security system and are, in fact, much higher than appears. The mere fact of incapacity will, in the vast majority of cases, justify sickness or invalidity benefit. In industrial injury cases, the administrative cost is incurred largely in determining whether the added margin of benefits is payable. In some cases, pounds are spent on deciding upon title to pence.[8]

THE WHITE PAPER[9]

The Beveridge proposals did not survive the White Paper unscathed. Beveridge had recommended special risk premiums for specially dangerous occupations—the White Paper preferred contributions to be flat-rate throughout. It rejected the proposed earnings-related pensions and lump-sum payments generally for dependants. The latent logic had prompted Beveridge to propose that all cases of incapacity, whether derived industrially or otherwise, should be treated undifferentially for the first 13-week period and that special provision for industrial cases should start only then. The White Paper restored complete irrationality by instituting differential treatment from the start.

In all other respects the scheme deriving from the White Paper and enshrined in the National Insurance (Industrial Injuries) Act 1946 expressed the Beveridge scheme. Changes that have taken place since have not radically altered the substance of the scheme. The most significant of them have concerned the administrative structure. Initially the scheme was contained in its own separate legislation, was financed by its own contributions (though commonly collected with national insurancé contributions) and had its own fund. The top-tier adjudication in claims was the Industrial Injuries Commissioner, although usually the National Insurance Commissioner simply changed hats.

In the latest legislation[10] the legislative schemes are merged. There are no longer separate contributions but a single, consolidated one. The funds have been merged, benefits under both heads now being payable out of a single National Insurance Fund. And Commissioners now wear a single hat. In all other respects, continuity is preserved. There still exists an obviously dwindling number of cases of title to benefit under the pre-1948 Workmen's Compensation Acts.[11] Such cases may fall for consideration under the Old Cases Acts [12] under which it is possible for some incidents of the new scheme (*e.g.* certain supplements to disablement benefit[13]) to attach to pre-1948 benefits.

B. THE MODERN SCHEME

The modern scheme makes available a range of benefits in case of an employed earner suffering "personal injury caused ... by accident arising out of and in the course of his employment"[14] or in respect of any prescribed disease or other personal injury due to the nature of his employment.[15] The benefits are:

(i) injury benefit payable in respect of up to six months' incapacity for work;

(ii) disablement benefit payable as compensation for loss of physical or mental faculty regardless of incapacity for work;

(iii) death benefit payable to dependants on the death of the earner.[16]

These benefits may be augmented by increases for dependants and supplements in certain cases.[17] Rates of benefits, increases and supplements are as set out in Part V of Schedule 4 to the 1975 Act as amended by up-rating legislation. Injury benefit is paid at rates more generous than the non-industrial long-term benefits such as invalidity and Category A retirement pension. A 100 per cent. disablement pension is the most generous benefit of all, higher even than widow's allowance, and may also attract supplements. Death benefits (*e.g.* widow's pension) may be eventually more generous than their non-industrial equivalents, though the initial widow's rate is identical.

The cost of these benefits is a relatively small part of total social security outgo representing, at about £250 million per annum, about 2½ per cent.[18] Although the vast majority of claims are for injury benefit, disablement benefit and death benefit (particularly the former) may be payable for life and are the big spenders.

<h2 style="text-align:center">CLAIMS</h2>

The periods of limitation for injury benefit claims are the same as those for sickness benefit claims. An original claim must be made within 21 days, the first claim in respect of a subsequent injury within six days and continuation claims within 10 days.[19] In all cases, a late claim involves loss of benefit in respect of days earlier than those periods unless there is good cause for delay.[20] Claims for disablement and death benefits must be made within three months subject to similar penalties, except that where the disablement benefit is payable as a gratuity[21] it remains payable in full the late claim notwithstanding.[22] Supplements to disablement benefit are subject to the same rules as disablement pension.[23]

One peculiar feature attends industrial injury benefits. The event which ultimately founds entitlement to benefit may take some time to do so. There may be no resulting incapacity and hence no title to injury benefit whilst disablement may take some time to develop. By that time, it may not be easy to prove the cause to the satisfaction of the statutory authorities. Provision is therefore made for one who suffers personal injury through an accident at work to ask for a declaration of accident. He may do this in connection with a claim for injury benefit which is otherwise disallowed[24]; or he may seek a declaration simpliciter notwithstanding that no claim is made.[25] The statutory authorities are not compelled to issue a declaration if they think it unlikely that the question will even arise.[26] If a declaration is made it is conclusive of the fact that the accident arose out of and in the course of employed earner's employment within the jurisdiction.[27]

ADJUDICATION

All claims fall to be determined by the statutory authorities, *i.e.* an insurance officer, local tribunal or Commissioner as the case may be. The exclusive authority to decide upon certain questions arising in connection with claims is, however, vested in persons other than the statutory authorities who are bound, in determining claims, by decisions upon such questions. Thus, a decision upon the question whether a person is employed in employed earner's employment for industrial injury benefit purposes falls to the Secretary of State[28] from whose decision the only appeal is to the High Court on a question of law.[29] The Secretary of State has similar powers in respect of constant care[30] and exceptionally severe disablement[31] supplements to disablement pensions[32] and also in relation to some questions relating to death benefit.[33]

In practical terms, the most important of these questions determinable otherwise than by the statutory authorities are the disablement questions.[34] These are the questions "whether the relevant accident has resulted in a loss of faculty" and "at what degree the extent of disablement resulting from a loss of faculty is to be assessed, and what period is to be taken into account by the assessment."[35]

These are usually the crucial questions in claims for disablement benefit and must be referred to and determined by a medical board or a medical appeal tribunal.[36] A claimant who is dissatisfied with the final assessment of a medical board may

appeal to a medical appeal tribunal. There is no right of appeal
in the case of a provisional assessment until after two years from
the first reference to a board.[37] The Secretary of State may,
however, require an insurance officer to refer such a case to a
medical appeal tribunal[38] and this is frequently done at the
instance of a claimant.[39]

C. BENEFITS IN RESPECT OF INJURY CAUSED BY ACCIDENT ARISING OUT OF AND IN THE COURSE OF EMPLOYMENT

The most confused and controversial questions in industrial
injuries law concern the formula originally enshrined in the
Workmen's Compensation Act 1897 and now contained in
section 50 of the 1975 Act. As a description of the general aim
of the legislation it is perhaps inadequate. As a technical legal
delimitation of the circumstances in which, and in which alone,
benefit is to be payable it is a disaster. As will be seen, it results,
after 80 years of dissection and parsing, in benefit being denied
where health is indubitably severely impaired as a result of work;
and granted where the causal connection is remote and obscure.
That it should have survived is a tribute to legal conservatism.

In its latest version, the formula requires that an "employed
earner" have suffered "personal injury ... by accident arising
out of and in the course of his ... employed earner's employment." Each element must be considered separately.

"EMPLOYED EARNER"

The concepts of "employed earner" and "employed earner's
employment" are, of course, used throughout the scheme and
are relevant to liability to contribute and entitlement to other
benefits.[40] Somewhat confusingly, they bear a meaning different
in some respects for purposes of industrial injury benefits. The
Act allows employments not within the class to be treated as
being within it and vice versa[41] and regulations have been made
to that effect.[42] Some important differences result. Thus, the
"lump" is treated as employed earner's employment for general
purposes[43] but not for purposes of industrial inquiries.

Provision special to industrial injury benefits is also made in the case of illegal employments. Where the contract if void or the employment otherwise illegal, there is presumably no "employed earner's employment" and therefore no basis for benefit. The Secretary of State may, however, direct that such "employment" be treated as employed earner's employment and benefit may thus become obtainable.[44]

"Personal Injury"

"Personal injury ... means injury to the living body of a human being."[45] In contradistinction to phrases such as "physical injury" it appears to include mental as well as physical injury,[46] but excludes damage to an artificial leg etc., notwithstanding that actual incapacity for work is occasioned thereby.[47]

There is no doubt that mental impairment can rank as personal injury.[48] The problem which usually arises here is not as to whether such "injury" can rank at all but as whether, or to what extent, it was caused by accident.

"Injury Caused by Accident"

Throughout the whole history of the law it has never been entirely clear what limits are to be drawn to the range of harms insured against under the schemes. The phrase "injury caused by accident" is perfectly apt to describe a large core of clear cases. An event readily-describable as an "accident" (a roof-fall; a machine-failure) culminates in a consequence readily-describable as an injury (a broken back; a mangled arm). This, no doubt, is the sort of thing in mind as the evil against which the original Act was directed. Within seven years of its passing, however, a Lord of Appeal in Ordinary, in the leading case, was commenting that in this respect, "the Act did not seem to have had the benefit of careful revision,"[49] and the need remains, all these decades on.

The difficulties arise from inherent inadequacies in the formula and from a failure to remedy them on the part of courts which have grappled with them. The inherent inadequacies stem mainly from the fact that the formula chosen seems in some respects inapt to describe certain types of work-caused harm which one would expect a scheme to cover. What of tuberculosis contracted by a T.B. nurse in the course of her work or silicosis in a quarry-worker? Where is the "injury caused by accident"? As will be seen, in some such cases, courts have contrived to detect "accidents" and consequential "injuries" whilst in others they have striven and failed. A further source of complication is the fact that "accident" as commonly used may quite intelligibly be used of both the causal event and its consequence as well as of the two combined, a fact which is not aided by the form of the legislation where "out of and in the course of employment" is quite capable, grammatically, of qualifying "personal injury," "accident" and "personal injury caused by accident." Similarly, does the Act require identification of a specific causal factor (the "accident") and a separate cognisable consequence flowing from it (the "injury")? A man experiences strain through raising a heavy weight which is normal in his occupation, or cuts his hand on a jagged piece of metal. Is there injury and, if so, what prior "accident" "caused" it? Or will it do simply to say of the entire incident that he suffered an accidental injury?

Early attempts to answer these questions resulted in different approaches in Scottish[50] and English courts.[51] The English courts inclined towards dissecting the formula into its component parts and adopting a literal approach to this interpretation. Accordingly, a man suffering a strain in the normal course of his work could not recover for what he did was done deliberately and it was not therefore fortuitous and accidental. It mattered not that the *injury* was unforeseen and unintended. The Scottish courts had approached the matter more robustly. If, at the end of the day there resulted what in common parlance could fairly be described as an "accidental injury" that was enough.

Arbitration fell to the House of Lords in *Fenton* v. *Thorley and Co.*[52] and the award went in favour of the Scottish approach. The expression "injury by accident" seemed to Lord Macnaghten to be a "compound expression." "Injury" and "accident" are used interchangeably in the legislation and ought not to be construed as separate elements. It is in this context that his famous dictum, that "accident" means "an unlooked-for mishap or an untoward event which is not expected or designed,"[53] should be read. It would not necessarily be required that the claimant should establish the specific causal event. If personal injury was caused to a worker by *something* arising out of or in the course of his employment he was prima facie entitled to compensation. The apparent inference that the "something" was an accident might be displaced by proof that the injury was attributable to his own misconduct or some extraneous cause but the function of "accident" was simply to exclude non-work sources.[54]

Fenton's case has frequently been followed, by the House of Lords itself, most famously in *Brintons Ltd.* v. *Turvey*,[55] the anthrax case. In that case, the majority concluded that a textile worker who contracted and died from anthrax had suffered "personal injury caused by accident" but found it necessary to identify a specific causal factor (the entry via the eye of the guilty anthrax bacillus) of which the physiological damage was a consequence. Lord Robertson dissented, not liking what he conceived to be the logic, that the contraction of any disease must involve "accident" in its broadest sense and Lord Lindley qualified his assent by stating that the mere fact of a disease resulted from work would not suffice; it must be established that the disease resulted from "accident."

Immediately thereafter, the Court of Appeal baulked at the logic. In *Steel* v. *Cammell, Laird*[56] they declined to accept, as "injury caused by accident," lead-poisoning the onset of which was gradual. For Collins M.R., it was crucial that the appellant could not point to a particular accident on a particular day. The same result followed the next day in *Marshall* v. *East Holywell Coal Co.*, and *Gorley* v. *Backworth Collieries*.[57] Ostensibly following *Fenton* v. *Thorley and Co.*, Collins M.R. expressed the reasoning of the Court of Appeal in the following terms:

> "The injury was the gradual result of the process of friction of the pick and pressure of kneeling. . . . To be an accident, it must be something which is capable of being described as having occurred on a particular date and it must be an accident in the popular meaning of the word."

Thus was the distinction between "accident" and "process" born,[58] and it has bedevilled industrial injuries law ever since; not that the Court of Appeal's original distinction survived for long. It did not. There is an unreal ring to the assumption of the House of Lords, in *Grant* v. *Kynoch*,[59] that blood-poisoning as a result of infection by streptococci and staphylococci must have occurred as a result of contact at a particular time and by the time of *Burrell (Charles) & Sons Ltd.* v. *Selvage*,[60] two years later, a changed rationale has appeared. The "injury" need no longer result from a particular event at a particular time; it will suffice if it results from a series of such events. By *Pyrah* v. *Doncaster Corporation*[61] in 1949 we have such a series constituted by individual "assaults" by particular bacilli culminating in tuberculosis. "Process," however, survives, no longer in contradistinction to a single specific event, but in contrast to any discontinuous series of events, no matter how numerous and protracted and no matter how insignificant each one considered in isolation.

"Process" in this variant is finally apotheosised, however unconvincingly, in *Roberts* v. *Dorothea Slate Quarries Co. Ltd. (No.* 1*)*.[62] The alleged "injury" in that case was silicosis and the alleged cause was the series of "accidents" constituted by the innumerable instances of bombardment by individual particles of silica dust. Lord Parker draws a distinction between "a series of specific and ascertainable[63] incidents" and "a continuous process going on substantially from day to day." Appealing to the same source of inspiration as the House in *Fenton's* case ("the meaning of the words in ordinary popular language") he arrives at the opposite conclusion.[64]

There is force in the argument that in common parlance a "disease" is something different from an "injury" and the wry observation of Lord du Parcq, in the *Dorothea* case, that to wander from one dictum to another "may take one on an interesting and attractive journey, but is all too likely to lead to a destination far removed from any end contemplated by the legislature," is not without point. But it is fair to say, also, that it is no remedy simply to run off at random to another end equally uncontemplated by the legislature, for that is what has resulted. Did the legislature intend, by "injury caused by accident" to embrace a locomotive-driver who progressively aggravated a hernia by pulling a heavy lever[65] but not a pugfeeder who strained his chest muscles raising heavy weights (process)?[66] Was it meant to include a "ganglion of the hand" resulting from exposure to intense heat and powerful ultra-violet radiation over a period of "some days"[67] but to exclude osteoarthritis of the fingers caused by three days of hand leather-stretching?[68]

A part, at least, of the uncertainty which flows from the distinction between "accident" and "process" is due to a failure adequately to define what is meant by "process." Does it differ from a series of "accidents" because it is continuous whereas they are discontinuous[69]; or is it because of its duration, a "process" taking a greater length of time to develop than an accident which must have the quality of "suddenness" and occupy a lesser period of time?[70] Other difficulty is occasioned by the failure to state clearly what phenomenon it is that we should be examining in seeking a "process." Is it the causal factor, which must operate long or discontinuously[71]; or must the consequential condition develop discontinuously or over a lengthy period[72]; will either do—must we look at the composite happening? These distinctions are often not made and frequently confused. Until they are distinguished and the position clarified, entitlement to benefit will remain a lottery in such cases.

Even, however, were these vices removed, the fundamental one would remain. The requirement of "accident" will necessarily result in excluding from consideration some diseases about whose attributability to work there is little doubt yet whose criteria for prescription as industrial diseases[73] are inadequate or dubious. "Accident" has too fine a mesh to ensure that only non-work originated harm is sieved out. This has been obvious from the earliest days and it is simply scandalous that it should have been allowed to remain so all these years.[74]

The problem for the legislature is not at all an insuperable one. What is needed is some phrase, such as "impairment of health caused by work factors . . . ," which would catch all work-derived harms and exclude others, and leave the rest to the burden of proof,[75] with prescription of diseases allowing it to be dispensed with in appropriate cases. There is often a strong case for leaving untouched a formula which has served its purpose well, albeit now archaic. That cannot be said of "injury caused by accident."

"Arising Out of And in the Course of Employment"

The phrase "personal injury caused by accident" attempts to describe the harm insured against. The phrase "arising out of and in the course of employment" seeks to link it to the work.

Again, no difficulty will be encountered in the vast majority of "core" cases; by any criterion the harm will clearly qualify or equally clearly fail to do so. Again also, however, the fringe cases cause great difficulty.

Adjudicating authorities have adopted two distinct approaches to the interpretation of the phrase. There is some authority for viewing the phrase as a whole: "Ultimately, the decision must depend on the interpretation, and application to the facts of the particular case, of the 'composite expression' 'accident arising out of and in the course of' the employment."[76] A greater weight of authority, however, approaches the problem by treating the phrase as consisting of two distinct and separable elements each with its own function. Lord Wright, in *Weaver* v. *Tredegar Iron Co.*[77] identified these elements succinctly as "the causal element" ("out of") and "the time element" ("in the course of") and this is the commonest approach.[78] It is, furthermore, the approach implicit in the legislation, some provisions of which require the distinction to be drawn.[79] Some confusion may be avoided if they are kept separate.[80] Whether, however, policy dictates this or, indeed, whether it requires two elements at all, is not clear. It is true that an accident could occur whilst the claimant was within his working hours[81] but have nothing whatever to do with his work[82] such as his being struck by lightning. It is not, however, easy to imagine examples of accidents arising "out of" the employment but not "in the course of" it; and such examples as can be imagined prompt one to ask if denial of benefit accords with the policy. It might, for example, be argued that a man who suffered injury as a result of contact with a noxious substance, derived from work, on his work-clothes when he removed them on arriving home, has suffered as a result of an accident arising "out of" though not "in the course of" his employment. Such an argument would likely fail, as it should, on some such ground as that the "accident" did arise "in the course of employment" in that although the injury was occasioned later, the accident began to work when the substance got onto his clothes. But this is, in effect, to say that any accident which arises "out of" the employment can be causally-linked to a point in time which falls within the "course of employment" and thus to render the latter requirement otiose. Perhaps that is right. Perhaps the question should simply be whether the claimant suffered harm as a result of his work. For the present, however, it is not. The accident must arise "in the course of" and "out of" the employment.

"In The Course Of"

To say of an accident that it arose "in the course of" employment is to say "that the accident occurred at *a time when* the man was actually doing something he was employed to do."[83] It would seem to be a simple matter to decide this point yet it has occasioned more difficulty than any other single question in industrial injuries law. The difficulties have attended determination of the start and end of the course of employment and breaks during it.

So far as determining the start and end of the course of employment are concerned, the difficulties have surrounded journeys to and from work. After some vacillation, it was settled by the House of Lords, in *St. Helen's Colliery Co. Ltd.* v. *Hewitson*[84] that the key was contractual obligation. The employer had arranged travel facilities which, under their contracts of employment, workers were entitled but not obliged to use and it was held that an accident occurring whilst the worker was on his way home on the transport provided did not arise in the course of his employment. In cases concerning the start and end of the course of employment his criterion has been applied consistently since.[85]

Once he is "at work" and before he leaves it, he is "in the course of" and the only problem concerns deciding employment when he arrives at it. The view which has prevailed here is that once he arrives on the employer's premises, he is at his place of work and the course of employment has begun.[86] This extends to cover means of access to and egress from the employer's premises provided that the public do not make use of them.[87] Marginal situations cause discomfort but that is inevitable. A worker is crushed and injured whilst pressing to board a train at a halt for the purpose on the employer's premises. Once on the train, which he is not obliged to use, he is no longer in the course of his employment, but until then, he is.[88] The public are allowed to use a path across the premises; a worker using it slips and falls. She is "in the course of employment" because she has reached the premises and the public's use of the path is not relevant.[89]

It may, of course, be that the worker is obliged to travel in the course of his work. A commercial traveller whose duties require him to travel from one customer to another may well be as much "in the course of" his employment when between customers as when dealing with them.[90] There must, however, be something more than the general obligation to get to work. It has been held that the journey from home to the place of work may count as "in the course of employment" where the worker is required to make a special journey in haste in an emergency[91] or, more doubtfully, where by special arrangement he is *allowed* to take a particular train but required, if he does so, to proceed from the station to work by the most direct route and as quickly as possible.[92]

The rule that whilst at the place of work a worker is "in the course of" his employment is subject to one important qualification—that whilst there he is doing what he is employed to do or something reasonably incidental to it.[93] The corollary is that if there has been a break in the course of employment, an accident does not arise in the course of it. There has been considerable confusion on this point over the years. Some cases seemed to require that the worker be under a duty to engage in the activity from which the harm resulted whilst others upheld awards even though there was clearly no duty to perform the act in question.[94] Some at least of this confusion can be dispelled if certain distinctions are borne in mind. The first is the distinction between acts performed by the worker and risks to which he is subjected. The former certainly relates to the question whether the workman has interrupted the course of his employment. The latter relates rather to the question of causation and to the question whether an accident arose "out of" his employment.[95] The second is the distinction between discretion as to the manner in which a particular work objective, which is obligatory, is to be attained, and discretion to perform acts which are unconnected with the work objective. In the former case, the course of employment will not be broken and the act in question will be, *ex hypothesi*, "reasonably incidental" even though not obligatory.[96] In the latter case, the acts in question are equally not obligatory and may, but also may not, be reasonably incidental.[97] It is sometimes suggested that whether an act is "reasonably incidental" is a matter of degree in this latter type of case.[98] So far as determining the course of employment is concerned, this must be so only to the extent that the worker has ceased entirely to do "his work" and is doing something else instead. Many of the cases seem to be cases where the worker is, in effect, doing two things at once—*e.g.* tending a machine and talking to a fellow employer about non-work matters. Here, on principle, there can have been no break in the course of employment and attention should be concentrated on the question of causation. If the accident arose "out of" his work activity (as by reason of his machine being defective), he may be entitled to his award. If it arose "out of" the second, non-work activity, he may lose notwithstanding that the accident arose in the course of his employment, because it did not arise "out of" that employment.

The most recent High Court decisions on these matters illustrate the difficulties admirably. In *R.* v. *National Insurance Commissioner, ex p. East*[99] certiorari was sought to quash the decision of the Commissioner in a case where the claimant had arrived at her place of work half an hour early, changed into uniform supplied by the employer, gone to the canteen for a cup of coffee, and slipped and fallen suffering injury. According to the Commissioner, no question arose as to whether there had been a break in the course of employment[1]; it had simply not begun at all because her visit to the canteen was for her own convenience and purposes and had no sufficient connection with what she was employed to do.[2] According to the Divisional Court, however, he was clearly wrong in law[3] in so holding. As a matter of law he should have held that when the claimant arrived at the factory and went to put on her uniform she entered upon the course of her employment and did not subsequently break it.

R. v. *National Insurance Commissioner, ex p. Michael*[4] concerned a policeman injured whilst playing football for his constabulary during off-duty hours. Participation was encouraged, *inter alia* by a contractual arrangement under which on-duty time could be spent playing football if the policeman played during off-duty hours when asked. The Commissioner held that the activity was not reasonably incidental to the employment[5] and the Divisional Court refused to disturb the decision although Lord Widgery L.C.J. was "by no means sure" that he would have reached the same conclusion had he been sitting as Commissioner himself.[6]

The approach of the court in the later case is preferable in that "whether or not something is or was reasonably incidental to a person's employment is more often than not purely a question of fact and degree."[7] What it is that must be "reasonably incidental" would seem, however, to be a matter of law, and on this question the Divisional Court does not entirely prevent confusion, seeming to be indifferent as to whether it is the activity engaged in or the risk which attends it which must be "reasonably incidental."

"Out of" the Employment

"'Arising out of' no doubt imports some kind of causal relation with the employment."[8] "What kind?" is the problem. It does not necessitate "direct or physical causation."[9] "It is enough that the exigencies of employment brought the workman within the range of the particular danger and exposed him to its impact, whereas but for his employment he would not have been exposed."[10] The source of the accident thus need not be a "work risk" in the narrowest sense; but there must, it seems, be at least a "superficial nexus"[11] and the point is commonly made that an accident does not arise "out of" employment if it results from the falling in of a risk to which the claimant is exposed simply as a member of the public and not in any sense by reason of his work.[12] Section 55[13] clearly assumes that an accident caused, *e.g.* by lightning, would not otherwise qualify notwithstanding that it happened "in the course of" employment. It is, at the same time, frequently difficult to understand how, as a matter of fact, some risks can be viewed as impending solely by reason of the work as, for example, in the case of road accidents.[14] And there is the highest judicial authority for the proposition that it is "an irrelevant circumstance that the risk in question was a danger to which all persons in the same area were also subjected."[15] The rationale most commonly adopted is that a sufficient nexus is established if the exigencies of the work caused the claimant to be at the spot where the risk fell in[16]; and "work" in this context includes activities reasonably incidental to the work, even, if appropriate, rest periods.[17] This does not, however, solve the problems; it renders the requirement that the accident arise "out of" the employment otiose for it implies that entitlement ensues so long as the claimant is "in the course of" his employment.

The only possible reconciliation of these different criteria lies in regarding the nexus as being sufficient where the claimant is exposed, by the exigencies of his work, to a greater risk than he would otherwise be subjected to, notwithstanding that others in the same locality are subjected to the same risk. Even here, it is impossible to glean from the authorities any indication as to what the standard of comparison (the claimant not at work; or at his base; or in the United Kingdom?) is to be. The truth of the matter is that we are again being invited to draw distinctions by the application of criteria which, although ostensibly mutually exclusive, in fact overlap. Workers are frequently, by the exigencies of their employment, exposed to risks (which suggests entitlement) to which the public are equally exposed (which suggests non-entitlement).

Complications arise where causes apart from the work also operate. In some cases, a prior cause will have brought about a pre-existing injury or disease. In others, a subsequent cause will have operated so as to produce the eventual injury.

Pre-existing injuries

Injuries wholly attributable to prior causes do not rank notwithstanding that an accident arising out of the employment has occurred. Because of the pre-existing injury, pain and discomfort which would not otherwise be experienced may be caused by the accident but this by itself makes no difference.[18] Even if the injury itself is aggravated, entitlement may still not be established; the aggravation of injury "must be material, *i.e.* of some substance."[19]

If, however, the work accident contributes in substantial degree to the eventual totality of injury, then the injury is caused by accident.[20] The contrast is neatly pointed by $R(1)$ *73/51* and $R(1)$ *12/52*. Both cases concern accidents at work to claimants suffering from pathological conditions rendering the bones liable

to spontaneous fracture. In the first case the evidence suggested
that the leg had fractured spontaneously and prompted the
accident which, accordingly, did not arise "out of" the employment.[21] In the second case, however, the fall provoked the
fracture, although such an injury would not have resulted but
for the pre-existing condition, and the statutory requirement was
satisfied.

These cases also illustrate the approach to another and separate
problem. The victim must be taken as he is found. Provided
that a physiological[22] injury is sustained as a result of the work
accident "the claim would not be defeated merely because some
disease or some congenital weakness contributed to the injury
or incapacity."[23]

Intervening new causes[24]

It sometimes happens that the accident occurs as a result
of the work *and* later events. The work is a *necessary* condition
of the accident—it would not have happened *but for* the work;
the work is a *"causa sine qua non."*[25] But, equally, it would not
have happened had the intervening new cause not occurred; so
although the work is a *necessary* condition, it is not a *sufficient*
condition by itself.

Such trying questions of causation are by no means peculiar
to industrial injuries law. Similar problems arise in connection
with fixing liability for the purposes of tort, crime and many
other branches of law. They are rarely happily resolved. Industrial injuries law is no exception. The authorities are consistent, however, in holding that it will not suffice merely that
the work risk is an essential condition.[26] What is not easy to
understand is what more is needed. It is suggested that there
must be a "complete chain of causation unbroken by the intervention of some new cause," that the cause must have been
"directly," a *causa causans.*[27] We are told that it must be the
"effective cause" and not merely a condition.[28]

It is easy to distinguish between two groups of cases, at each
extreme, simply by reference to the fact that one of the two causes
is, by itself, "sufficient" and the other is, in consequence, not
"necessary."[29] Sometimes, the confusion results from a lack of
clarity as to whether this is so or not. In *R(1) 54/52* a miner

suffering from pneumoconiosis contracted carcinoma an operation for which might or might not have prolonged his life, but was not undertaken because of the pneumoconiosis. The problem is at first viewed as being whether death would have ensued from the carcinoma alone (in which case the pneumoconiosis would not be an essential condition at all). But later, something more is required, it being insufficient to establish that "but for the pneumoconiosis (he) would not have died when he did." It would be "something more" if it were established that the pneumoconiosis prevented an operation which would have prolonged life. In the event, it was decided that it did not.

In cases where there are two necessary causes it is impossible to distinguish logically in terms of differences in their causative qualities. Every event is the outcome of a congeries of condition each of which is logically as necessary as the rest. It is perfectly possible but not purposeful to distinguish chronologically—on this basis, a worker critically injured at work but dying because of a failure of a life-support system would fall outside the scheme. It appears that in these cases, a choice is made whether to regard the first, work, cause as significant and operative according to an evaluation as to its substantiality.[30]

In cases of "intervening new causes," therefore, it seems that a solution lies via two questions:

(i) Is the first, work, cause a necessary or sufficient cause of the accident? If it is neither, it does not arise out of the employment and that is an end to the matter. If it is a sufficient cause by itself, the accident does so arise and that is equally an end to the matter. If it is a necessary but not sufficient cause, a further question must be asked;

(ii) How substantial a role does it play in bringing about the event? If the role is as in the example of the critically-injured worker above-cited, almost any adjudicator would regard its role as very substantial and regard the accident as within the scheme. If, as in *R(1) 38/51* a relatively slight injury at work is merely a minor one of a number of factors provoking a depression resulting in suicide, its role would be generally considered to be insubstantial. The degree of substantiality is not an observable fact; it calls for an evaluation as to significance. This being so, the decision is necessarily in some part subjective and unpredictability in many cases is inevitable.

In spite of the doubts surrounding its application in some circumstances, the requirement that the accident has arisen out of and in the course of employment serves adequately to identify the type of harm which, generally, it is the aim of the scheme to cover. There are, however, a number of statutory relaxations of this requirement. The first of these is designed to circumvent a deficiency which arises from the problem of proof. The others, however, are deliberate attempts to extend the range of cover to a number of sources of harm which are not, in common parlance, inherent in the work. These are in part codification and in part amendment of doctrines developed under the pre-War scheme.

(i) *The presumption that an accident arising in the course of employment arises out of it*

The primary onus of establishing the facts on which title to benefit depends lies on the claimant. Prima facie, therefore, he must prove, *inter alia*, that the accident arose in the course of employment *and* that it arose out of it; and failure to do so means withholding of benefit. Hardship might well result, and indeed under the Workmen's Compensation Scheme did result[31] in cases where the specific cause of the accident was obscure. This was particularly the case where the worker had been killed in circumstances unknown to dependants claiming death benefit.[32] The situation could also arise, however, where whether the accident was connected with the claimant's work, albeit tenuously, was a fact peculiarly within the knowledge of a third party via whose agency the accident had been caused.[33] The resulting injustice was merely fortified by the fact that the required connection with the work was so tenuous; was, indeed, as has been suggested above, virtually fictitious in some cases. A claimant might fail merely through inability to explain how the accident happened even though it was extremely likely that, if he could explain, it would be regarded as having arisen out of the employment.

Under the workmen's compensation scheme, adjudicators were often willing to infer from the known fact that the accident arose in the course of the employment the unknown fact that it arose out of it.[34] This was formalised in the immediate post-War legislation[35] and is now contained in section 50 (3) of the 1975 Act in the following terms:

> "... an accident arising in the course of ... employment shall be deemed, *in the absence of evidence to the contrary*, also to have arisen out of that employment."[36]

Such controversy as there has been has surrounded the effect of the italicised phrase. The Commissioner early on took the view that the presumption only operated where there was "nothing in the known circumstances from which it could reasonably be inferred that the accident did not arise out of the employment." Where there were known facts which would justify such an inference, the presumption disappeared entirely and the claimant was put to proof.[37]

Cases continued to be disposed of on this basis[38] until 1958 when the Divisional Court was asked to correct the decision of a Commissioner who had directed himself in these terms.[39] The Court was invited to hold that a claimant was entitled to the benefit of the presumption unless it was proved positively by the insurance officer (presumably on the balance of probabilities) that the accident did not arise out of the employment. It declined. Any evidence at all to the contrary[40] brought the presumption down; the claimant was not entitled to the benefit of it until the contrary was proved.

In the *Richardson* case above, a bus-conductor on duty had been assaulted by a gang of youths and the view which was taken was that the accident could only be said to have arisen out of the employment if he had been singled out for attack because of his employment.[41] The "evidence to the contrary" offered was that the youths had been attacking other people. This by no means proved that the youths had not attacked the conductor because he was a bus conductor—two passengers, indeed, were not assaulted and there was evidence that conductors were becoming increasingly the targets for such assaults. But there was *some* evidence[42] that the attack was indiscriminate and it did not need to' be sufficient evidence.

The interpretation here adopted is perfectly tenable but it should be noted that its effect is to erode the potential of section 50 (3) to ensure that benefit is payable for work injuries despite the problem of proof. Although benefit is now payable in the

Richardson situation[43] it will not be payable in other situations,
even though the accident occurs in the course of employment,
simply because of ignorance as to how or why it occurred. It
is some consolation in this regard that at least some hard evidence
must be tendered to produce this result; a mere "speculative
inference," *i.e.* a supposition, will not suffice.[44]

(ii) *Acts in contravention of orders, etc.*

   Where responsibility for injury to an employee is being exacted
from an employer, it is just to allow him to disclaim on the
grounds that he had prohibited and perhaps even that he had
not authorised the act resulting in the injury. There is a similar
appeal about the argument that liability for benefit should be
excluded where the injury resulted from acts of the claimant
which were contrary to law or the employer's orders. In the
common law situation, the view likely to prevail in these circumstances is that the accident did not arise out of and in the
course of employment.[45] So far as industrial injuries benefits are
concerned this, it appears, is to confine too narrowly the coverage
of the scheme and the act accordingly expressly provides for such
acts to be included in certain circumstances. An act is to be
deemed to arise out of and in the course of employment notwithstanding that the employee was acting in contravention of
any statutory or other regulations applicable to his employment,
or of any orders given by or on behalf of his employer, or that
he was acting without instructions from his employers, if two
conditions are satisfied. These are:
   (i) that the accident would have been deemed to have arisen
out of and in the course of employment but for the prohibition,
etc.; and
   (ii) that the act was done for the purposes of and in connection
with the employer's trade or business.[46]
   The first point to note about this provision is that it is not
necessary to resort to it in every case of breach of a prohibition
etc. The rules, etc., in question must be "applicable to his
employment." If they are not (as, for example where a claimant
travelling on his employer's business was injured alighting from
a moving bus contrary to regulations[47]) the conditions predicated
by the section are not present and the only question is as to

whether the accident actually arose out of and in the course of employment. Or it may be that an apparent breach of rules etc. is not really such because the alleged "rules" are only nominally and not really such, never having been applied, or having been waived, by the employer.[48] The only qualification here is that it must be within the employer's (or other relevant person's) authority to waive the rules and the authority to do so must have been exercised. So it has been held that the effect of statutory rules cannot be affected by tolerance or, presumably, the express endorsement by the employer of a practice involving this breach.[49]

The second and most important point to note about section 52 is that in many cases it will not save a claimant because he was not doing his own job anyway and would not, therefore, be within the scope of his employment, even apart from the prohibition, as required by condition (i) above. It is sometimes the case that what is done is prohibited in effect because it is not his job, so that stepping outside the course of employment and breaking the rules are constituted by a single act, as where a repairer fires a shot contrary to a regulation providing that "no person other than a shot-firer shall couple any shot firing cable to any detonator...."[50] Most frequently, however, the prohibition is a general one and the question whether the accident would otherwise be within the course of employment fails to be decided according to the usual criteria and is not concluded by the prohibition itself.[51] This is yet again one of those areas where apparently mutually exclusive criteria are invoked to effect a distinction which in fact, to the extent of overlap, they are incapable of drawing. In *Bresnahan's* case[52] and in $R(I)$ $I/70$, in which it was distinguished, the claimant's injuries arose from driving a vehicle without authority but in order to facilitate the doing of the authorised work. The precedents had sought to distinguish between acts wholly different in kind from what the claimant was employed to do, and acts within the scope of employment but done in a prohibited manner. These criteria will, however, yield either desired result according as to whether attention is focused upon the end in mind in performing the act or the intermediate means selected to do it. The true criterion is whether the use of the means selected was in fact authorised or permitted by the employer. Adopting this approach, the

Commissioner in *R(1) 1/70* felt able to distinguish the case before
him on the ground that, whereas in the *Bresnahan's* case it
appeared that had the employer or his agent known of the act
he would immediately have prohibited it, in the case before him
it was not clear that the act would not have been tolerated.

The second condition required to be satisfied in order to save
a claim under section 52 is that the act must have been done
"for the purposes of and in connection with the employer's trade
or business." Again, in many cases the same single feature of
a case will foreclose all answers. Conduct which is in breach
of a prohibition or outside the course of employment (enough
by itself—both conditions must be satisfied) will, for the same,
obvious, reason, not be done for the purposes of and in connection
with the employer's trade or business.[53] The question is in what
circumstances is there scope for each of the two conditions to
operate separately?[54] One possibility is that the first condition
is concerned with "the accident" whilst the second is concerned
with "the act" but no attempt has been made to mine this
particular vein.

A second possibility is that each condition embraces circumstances excluded by the other.[55] The origins of condition (i) seem
to assume that an act can be done for the employer's purposes
but not in the course of the claimant's employment and this
would clearly seem to be the case as where one worker engages
in work totally different from his own but nevertheless for the
employer.[56] There is also some authority for the converse
proposition that not all acts which are "in the course of employment" are necessarily done "for the purposes of and in connection
with the employer's trade or business,"[57] *i.e.* acts which are reasonably incidental to the work which the claimant is employed to
do but which are not part of the doing of the work itself.

This would seem to be the most satisfactory view of section 52
as a whole—that an infringement of a prohibition etc. can be
ignored provided the claimant was actually doing work he was
employed to do and not something different or merely incidental
to it. It is, however, a view which is not easy to reconcile with
a number of decisions where the section has been successfully
invoked in respect of acts which seem clearly to be merely
incidental.[58] These decisions seem simply to ignore that condition (ii) needs to be satisfied in a meaningful way.

(iii) *Travelling*

As has been indicated above[59] an employee travelling in the discharge of the duties of his employment is acting in the course of his employment whilst one undertaking the journey to and from work in the usual manner is prima facie not in the course of his employment and accordingly does not fall within the scheme. He may, however, nevertheless do so if the requirements of section 53 are satisfied. Section 53 extends to cover employees travelling as a passenger to and from work even though there is no obligation to use the vehicle in question, provided he has the express or implied permission of the employer.[60] The circumstances must be such that had the journey been obligatory the accident would have been regarded as arising out of and in the course of employment[61]; and the vehicle (which includes a ship, vessel, hovercraft or aircraft)[62] must be being:

(i) operated by or on behalf of the employer or some other person by whom it is provided in pursuance of arrangements made with the employer; and

(ii) not operated in the ordinary course of a public transport service.[63]

Provided all these conditions are satisfied, the accident may be deemed to arise out of and in the course of the employment.

Section 53 has been given a somewhat restrictive and rather technical interpretation. The claimant must have been "travelling"—it will not suffice that the accident occurs whilst he is between buses on a journey involving a change.[64] He must be travelling "as a passenger," not as a driver, even if he is a driver only for the purpose of getting to work.[65] The requirement that he must have the employer's express or implied permission will usually be met easily, but a fellow-worker driven home without authority by the van-man after a pub-crawl should not presume too much.[66] "To or from" has not been fully exploited; cover does not wax and wane with the bends in the road—it is enough to be *en route* even if a change of buses is involved (as long as one is "travelling")[67]; and the bus need not go the whole way.[68]

The real thrust of the section is to extend cover to transport facilities laid on by the employer even though the employee is not required to use them and it is to that extent irrational—the employee for whom no special arrangements are made remains uncovered completely. The central feature of the section is that the transport must be operated by or on behalf of[69] the employer or some other person by whom it is provided in pursuance of arrangements made with the employer.[70] The making of "arrangements" requires more than merely that the employer request a transport undertaking that a service be laid on.[71] At the same time, it is clear that a binding contractual arrangement is not required.[72] There must, it seems, be a bilateral element to the "arrangement" though it will be enough that, for example, the employer's contribution consist of an adjustment of work schedules so as to facilitate the provision of an economic service.[73] Where, indeed, the service is laid on, not by a transport undertaking but by one of a number of associated employers for the employees of all, *e.g.* the main contractor for, *inter alia*, employees of sub-contractors, it may be possible to infer that the "arrangement" exists as a part of the longer congeries of bilateral relations.[74]

Even though all these criteria are met this will not be enough if the result is that the vehicles laid on are operated in the ordinary course of a public transport service, as may well be the case; the best response to an approach by an employer to a transport undertaking may well be for the latter to lay on a public service. If the service is confined to the particular employees and the public excluded, it is clearly not a "public transport service."[75] It may be, however, that the public are allowed to use the service to a limited extent and here it may be difficult to characterise the service as one thing or the other. Where the service is "open" for one part of the route but "closed" for the rest, it qualifies for the "closed" section at least.[76] It is an open question whether it qualifies otherwise. It is possible that it will, if its main function is as a service for particular employees and if, for example, it is not scheduled, does not use all normal stops, uses private roads and has a special fare-structure.[77]

(iv) *Emergencies*

In the same way that travelling can be within the course of employment (so that saving by section 53 is not necessary) so also it may be within the scope of employment to cope with an emergency[78] as in the case of police and fire service employment. It will commonly happen, however, that an emergency will arise and that ordinary workers will, in the urgency of the moment, seek to cope with it, notwithstanding that they are actually employed to do something entirely different. So, of course, might ordinary members of the public who happened to be at the scene. There is no way in which an ordinary passer-by can invoke the aid of the industrial injuries scheme should he be injured thereby. An employee might, however, be able to do so. Whether he would do so would depend on whether he could satisfy the terms of section 54. For him to do so, the accident must happen to him "in or about any premises[79] at which he is for the time being employed for the purposes of his employer's trade or business"[80] and he must be "taking steps, on an actual or supposed emergency at those premises, to rescue, succour or protect persons who are, or are thought to be or possibly to be, injured or imperilled, or to avert or minimise serious damage to property."[81] If so, the accident is deemed to arise out of and in the course of his employment.

(v) *Skylarking etc.*

In considering the question whether the accident arose "out of" the employment, it was seen that the accident must have at least some tenuous causal connection with the employment. It is possible, therefore, for an accident to escape the scheme if in fact it is clearly caused by factors which have nothing whatever to do with the employment.[82] If this is the case, it is hard to see why any consequential injury should be considered to be an "industrial" injury. It may, nevertheless, qualify if section 55 applies.

Section 55 requires an accident which would not otherwise be so treated to be treated as arising out of employment if certain conditions are satisfied. It was first introduced into the scheme as a result of the *Richardson* decision[83] but is not particularly apt as a response to the defects revealed by that case. It will be recalled that Richardson failed because the presumption in section 50 (3) was defeated by "evidence to the contrary" notwithstanding that that evidence did not prove the contrary. Section 55 gives a claimant the benefit of a conclusive presumption as to the cause of the accident if the accident arises in the course of employment and if certain conditions are satisfied. The first condition requires that the accident either be caused by "another person's[84] misconduct, skylarking or negligence, or by steps taken in consequence of any such misconduct, skylarking or negligence, or by the behaviour or presence of an animal (including a bird, fish or insect), or is caused by or consists in the employed earner being struck by any object or by lightning. . . ."[85]

The second condition is that "the employee did not directly or indirectly induce or contribute to the happening of the accident by his conduct outside the employment or by any act not incidental to the employment."[86]

Up to a point, these exceptions to the requirements that the accident arise out of and in the course of the employment do serve the purpose of ensuring that benefit is payable in respect of an industrial accident which might otherwise fail to qualify. They do, however, go beyond this and result in benefit being paid where the work is quite immaterial to the injury suffered. In many such cases, the claimant might well be thought to be deserving but so, also, might others who have suffered injury in the same circumstances; yet they will not qualify because, quite irrelevantly, they were not at work at the time.

D. THE BENEFITS

1. INDUSTRIAL INJURY BENEFIT

An employee is entitled to injury benefit in respect of any day during the injury benefit period on which, as the result of the relevant injury, he is incapable of work.[87] The "injury benefit period" is the period of 156 days (excluding Sundays) beginning with the day of the accident subject to the proviso that injury benefit is not payable to a claimant who has become entitled to disablement benefit in respect of the same incident.[88] A claimant is "incapable of work" if he is incapable of doing work which he can reasonably be expected to do.[89] In order to rank for benefit, the day must form part of a period of interruption of employment; none is payable for the "waiting days."[90]

The average weekly intake of new claims has declined very markedly in recent years—by one-third over a decade. It is payable at a higher rate than sickness benefit[91] (for which a person "incapable of work" will usually be qualified whether as a result of industrial injury or not) but the latter attracts earnings-related supplement whereas injury benefit does not. It accordingly follows that a worker earning as little as £9 or £10 more than the lower earnings limit will be better off on sickness benefit with earnings-related supplement, once he qualifies for the latter, than an injury benefit.[92] In substance, therefore, injury benefit is a very short-term benefit only for all workers and a true, *i.e.* six-month, short-term benefit only for low-paid workers. When assessing the costs of administration of injury benefit, it is worthwhile remembering that they are substantially incurred in deciding upon entitlement only in the margin between sickness benefit and injury benefit and that in some cases the margin is a few pence only.

Although there are many more claims for injury benefit than for both disablement and death benefit, injury benefit accounts for only about 35 per cent. of total industrial injuries outgo compared with about 50 per cent. on disablement and 6–7 per cent. on death benefits which, in addition to being large, may be very long-term.[93]

2. Disablement Benefit

Most social security benefits are aimed at abatement of need by provision of income when other sources are inadequate. Disablement benefit, the chief of the industrial injuries benefits, is not. It stands not upon the principle of income-provision (though it may, as may common law damages, incidentally discharge this function) but upon that of compensation—making amends for a loss. Disablement benefit is payable regardless of income. It is receivable as well as earnings from work and regardless of whether or not the disablement has diminished earning capacity (though such considerations may affect entitlement to certain supplements). If abatement of need is the aim of social security, disablement benefit should be located elsewhere. Industrial injury, however, commonly has as its consequences the creation of need requiring abatement *and* loss deserving compensation. In the United Kingdom and in most continental countries the two have historically been treated together and schemes dealing with both consequences are usually regarded as part of the social security system. In the United Kingdom, the latest legislation fortifies the link. Hitherto, industrial injuries had their own legislation and fund. In 1973 each was merged with its national insurance twin and the 1975 Act states a unified and integrated scheme of regulation and finance.

Disablement benefit is payable in respect of the loss of faculty, mental or physical, resulting from an accident arising out of and in the course of employment.[94] "Loss of faculty," includes disfigurement.[95] Disablement normally starts with incapacity and disablement benefit is usually not payable in respect of any of the 156 days following the accident if injury benefit is paid. If, however, incapacity does not accompany the disablement, disablement benefit may be payable immediately after the three "waiting days."[96]

The amount of disablement payable depends upon two factors:

  (i) the degree of disablement; and
(ii) entitlement to certain supplements which may accompany disablement.

The degree of disablement may vary from 1 to 100 per cent. If the degree assessed is less than 20 per cent., the benefit is payable as a "gratuity" which is normally a lump sum but which may be paid in instalments.[97] If it is 20 per cent. or over, the benefit is payable as a weekly pension.[98] The maximum gratuity is payable in respect of a 19 per cent. assessment for life or seven years or more. The maximum gratuity must be reduced proportionally for a degree of disablement of less than 19 per cent. and for a duration in years of less than seven.[99]

The crucial questions so far as disablement benefit is concerned are, therefore, whether there has been a loss of faculty resulting from the relevant accident and, if so, what degree of disablement should be assessed. These, known as the "disablement questions" are the peculiar province of medical boards (and, on appeal, medical appeal tribunals)[1]—the medical authorities.

Assessment of Degree of Disablement

The most straightforward type of assessment which the medical authorities can be called upon to make is in the case where a claimant who, prior to the accident, was perfectly sound in health, is, as of result of it and only it, disabled. After considering this straightforward type of case it will be necessary to consider complications which arise where there was a pre-existing condition, or where the accident was not the sole source of the disability.

What the medical authorities have to assess is the degree of disablement resulting from the loss of faculty deriving from the injury brought about by the accident.[2] They must take account of "all such disablement" to which the claimant may be expected, having regard to his physical and mental condition at the date of assessment, to be subject during the period taken into account by the assessment "as compared with a person of the same age and sex whose physical and mental condition is normal."[3] Other characteristics are to be ignored.[4] The assessment may be final or provisional. A final assessment is an assessment in respect of the period "during which the claimant has suffered and may be expected to continue to suffer from the relevant loss of faculty."[5] If the condition of the claimant does not permit a final assessment because of the possibility of changes, a provisional assessment or, if necessary, a series of provisional assessments must be made, each for whatever period is reasonable in the light of his condition.[6]

The degree of disablement is stated as a percentage, total disablement as indicated below being rated at 100 per cent.[7] and degrees of less than 1 per cent. being ignored.[8] For gratuity purposes (1–19 per cent.) the actual degree is used for calculating the benefit.[9] For pension purposes, banding is used so that a degree of 20–24 per cent. would be treated as 20 per cent. and one of 25–34 per cent. as 30 per cent. etc.[10]

Disablement can take many forms, some more common than others. A guide to the appropriate percentage is offered in the form of a tariff which ranges from 100 per cent. for, *e.g.* "loss of both hands" and "loss of sight to such an extent as to render the claimant unable to perform any work for which eyesight is essential," to 2 per cent. for a "guillotine amputation of a fingertip without loss of bone."[11] Where the *sole* injury suffered appears on this tariff, the degree must be assessed according to the tariff unless it would not be a reasonable assessment, in which case the degree should be increased or reduced as reasonable, except that it need not be reduced in the case of a 100 per cent. disablement on grounds of off-set[12] if the medical authorities are satisfied that 100 per cent. is in any case reasonable.[13]

Multiple Causes

Special provisions apply in the case of "disabilities which, though resulting from the relevant loss of faculty, also result, or without the relevant accident might have been expected to result, from a cause other than the relevant accident...."[14] The three cases dealt with are:

    1. Congenital defects and pre-existing injuries or diseases;

    2. injuries or diseases received or contracted after and not directly attributable to the relevant accident;

    3. multiple accidents, diseases, etc.

Congenital defects and pre-existing injuries, etc.

In these cases, the extent to which the claimant would in any case have been disabled had the accident not occurred is to be left out of account, *i.e.* "offset." It is *not* a question of apportioning the eventual degree of disability as between its different causes according as to their conceived significance. In effect, separate assessments must be made, one of the actual ultimate total degree of disability and another of the hypothetical degree which would have attached had the accident not occurred, and the latter figure subtracted from the former. As a result of a pre-existing disposition to hysteria, a claimant might become 100 per cent. disabled by an injury which would have left a normal person only 20 per cent. disabled. 100 per cent. might nevertheless be the proper assessment if, but for the accident, the hysteria would not have manifested itself at all.[15]

Post-accident injuries, etc.

Here, the assessment must initially be made on the hypothesis that the second cause had not operated, *i.e.* an assessment must be made on the basis of the degree of disability which would have resulted if the second cause had not occurred. Where, approaching it in this way, an assessment of 10 per cent. or less results, it must stand. Where, however, an assessment of 11 per cent. or more results, the medical authorities must hypothesise further. They must first make a second assessment as to the degree of disablement which would have resulted had only the second, non-accident, factor operated. And, secondly, they must make an assessment of the total degree of disability from which the claimant actually suffers as a result of both causes. If the difference between the total degree and the hypothetical degree attributable to the accident is greater than the hypothetical degree attributable to the non-accident cause, the claimant is entitled to the benefit of that excess. Take, for example, a claimant who loses a foot in an industrial accident (30 per cent.) and a hand in a subsequent non-industrial accident. The notional initial assessment would be 30 per cent.; but, since it exceeded 10 per cent., the authorities must assess the loss of hand alone (60 per cent.) and the actual total eventual disability (100 per cent.), and credit the claimant with an additional 10 per cent., *i.e.* 40 per cent. in all.[16]

Multiple accidents, etc.

Where a succession of accidents or diseases have contributed to a claimant's eventual disablement, the assessment is to be made in relation to the latest event in the series.[17] He may, of course, have succeeded in respect of earlier claims in which case special provisions considered below may apply to the question of adjusting his benefit in respect of successive accidents. Even if he has not claimed in respect of the earlier accident, it may affect his eventual assessment as a pre-existing injury or disease.[18]

A person already in receipt of a disablement pension in respect of an earlier accident may, if he would otherwise become entitled to a gratuity in respect of a later accident, elect instead to have consolidated pensions reflecting the degree of disablement resulting at the end of the day.[19] He must, however, so elect before his claim is determined and even then he may not elect if his existing pension is 100 per cent. or in so far as the total amount receivable as pension would exceed 100 per cent.[20]

Increases of Disablement Pension

Disablement benefit is aimed primarily at compensating for a
loss of faculty due to industrial injury and basic benefit is
accordingly payable even though there is no loss of earning
power. A loss of earning power in some degree will, however,
frequently accompany disablement. The scheme accordingly
makes available a range of supplements to disablement pension
in these circumstances. The supplements are unemployability
supplement (which may itself be increased in some circumstances); special hardship allowance; constant attendance allowance; hospital treatment increase; and increase for exceptionally
severe disablement.

(i) Unemployability supplement

This is payable where the beneficiary is incapable of work
and likely to remain so permanently.[21] He may be treated as
"incapable of work" even though he is in fact capable of a
limited amount of work. The test is whether the disablement
is likely to prevent his earnings in a year exceeding a prescribed
amount not less than £104.[22] The unemployed wife of a beneficiary in receipt of unemployability supplement may be entitled
to unemployment benefit at the higher rate.[23] Unemployability
supplement is payable at the same rate as invalidity and
Category A retirement pension.[24] It is a comparatively rare
supplement, approximately 500 beneficiaries being in receipt at
the end of 1974.[25]

A claimant who is more than five years short of pensionable
age is entitled to an increase of unemployability supplement.[26]
This is payable at different rates according to age exactly as
in the case of invalidity supplement.[27]

(ii) Special hardship allowance

Special hardship allowance is designed to compensate for loss
of earning power as a result of the disablement. It is the most
important of the supplements to disablement pension, about
140,000 allowances being currently payable,[28] many of these in
respect of pneumoconiosis sufferers. A person entitled to un-

employability supplement would normally qualify for a special hardship allowance. He may not receive both.[29]

The key to entitlement to the allowance is that the claimant be, or have been, since he came off injury benefit, incapable (and likely to remain so if it is a prospective claim) of following his regular occupation and any alternative employment of equivalent standard suitable in his case.[30] If this is so, the amount of increase is to be determined by reference to his probable standard of remuneration in employments which he is capable of following with his disability and which are suitable in his case, as compared with earnings in his regular, pre-disablement, occupation, subject to a statutory maximum.[31] When measuring standards of remuneration and also in determining incapacity, account is to be taken of promotion which might reasonably have come his way, or which a person in his occupation would normally have come to enjoy, respectively.

Calculation of entitlement turns upon comparing pre-disablement and post-disablement earning capacity. Claimants, however, must take the employment scene as they find it. In *R.* v. *National Insurance Commissioner, ex p. Mellors*[32] the question arose as to entitlement where the claimant, having previously earned £28 for a week of 36½ hours, found himself working a 65-hour week for £27 in his post-disablement work. On a common-time basis, his earnings were much reduced. The proper basis of comparison, however, is "the remuneration which the beneficiary is likely to receive in his new employment working the hours which are normal for persons working in that class of employment" with "the remuneration which he was receiving working . . . normal hours in his earlier employment."[33] "Normal hours" includes overtime normally worked but excess overtime is to be discounted.[34] Like, however, must be compared with like. A claimant who moves from a relatively low-paid locality to seek post-disablement work in a higher-paid locality should not suffer from the comparison of relatively higher pay in the new locality with relatively lower-paid work in his former occupation. He is entitled to an assessment of the value of his pre-disablement work in the locality in which he later finds himself.[35]

Since basic disablement pension is not aimed at compensation for loss of earnings, and special hardship allowance is payable simply on the basis of the difference between pre- and post-earning capacity, it is possible for a claimant to receive in total more by way of post-disablement benefit (including increases for dependants) than he earned previously.[36]

(iii) Constant attendance increase

A 100 per cent. pensioner in need of constant attendance is entitled to an increase[37] so long as he is not receiving free in-patient treatment in a hospital.[38] The amount of increase varies with the circumstances. If the beneficiary is to be a substantial extent dependent upon the attendance for the necessities of life and likely to remain so for a prolonged period, he is entitled to the basic increase, presently £8·70 per week, unless part-time attendance suffices in which case whatever increase is reasonable in the circumstances may be ordered. If greater attendance is needed by reason of exceptionally severe disablement, a greater increase not exceeding £13·05 is obtainable, unless it is such that he is entirely, or almost entirely, dependent on the attendance for the necessities of life, in which case the limit is £17·40 per week.[39]

In assessing the need for attendance, account may be taken, not only of disabilities compensatable under the Industrial Injuries Acts, but also certain others, such as those compensatable under the Workmen's Compensation and War Injury Schemes.[40] At the end of 1974, 2,600 allowances were in payment.

(iv) Hospital treatment increase

Notwithstanding that his disablement has been assessed at less than 100 per cent., a beneficiary is entitled to receive pension at the rate of 100 per cent. for any period during which he is receiving, as an in-patient in a hospital or similar institution, medical treatment for the relevant injury or loss of faculty.[41] Where the disablement is assessed at less than 20 per cent., the basic benefit remains payable as a gratuity, the hospital treatment increase taking the form of a weekly payment in an amount equal to a 100 per cent., pension minus a weekly equivalent of the gratuity in an amount fixed by regulations.[42]

Entitlement to the increase continues throughout breaks in hospital treatment of not more than one week.[43]

Hospital treatment allowance is the least common of the supplements, approximately 100 only being in payment at the end of 1974.[44]

(v) **Exceptionally severe disablement increase**

One qualified (or who, but for hospital treatment etc. would be qualified) for constant attendance allowance (above) may qualify for a further increase if his need for attendance is likely to be permanent.[45] The current rate is £8·70 per week. About 900 such increases are in payment.[46]

(vi) **Increases for children**

Where death results from an industrial accident, the deceased's dependants may be the direct beneficiaries in respect of death benefit.[47] In cases of injury and some cases of disablement benefit, an increase of benefit may be payable in respect of certain dependants.[48] In the case of disablement benefit, increases only attach in the case of a pensioner entitled to an unemployability supplement.[49]

Increases may be payable in respect of children in respect of whom child benefit would be payable,[50] spouses,[51] prescribed relatives[52] and "housekeepers"[53] in much the same way as they are payable in respect of other social security benefits discussed earlier.[54]

3. DEATH BENEFIT

If the earner dies as a result of personal injury caused by accident arising out of and in the course of employment[55] or as a result of a prescribed disease[56] a fairly extensive class of persons may become entitled in principle to death benefits.[57] Not all may benefit; where two or more qualify, it may be necessary to prefer.[58] The following are the potential beneficiaries:

(i) Widows[59]—the widow must have been residing with the deceased at his death, or receiving or entitled to receive maintenance in a sufficient amount. If so, she is entitled to a pension

for life or until remarriage. Upon remarriage, she becomes entitled to a terminal gratuity equal to a year's pension. Cohabitation causes the right to pension to be suspended.

For the first 26 weeks, the pension is payable at a high rate. Thereafter, it continues at a middle rate if conditions similar to those for entitlement to a widowed mother's allowance or widow's pension[60] are satisfied[61]; otherwise it is payable at a low rate equivalent to 30 per cent. of the widow's pension rate.

The vast majority of recipients of pensions in respect of industrial death are widows.

(ii) Widowers[62]—a man who is permanently incapable of self-support and who was, until the accident, wholly or mainly maintained by his wife is entitled to pension for life equivalent to the middle rate industrial death pension, payable to a widow, described above.[63] There is no provision for termination on remarriage or suspension on cohabitation.

(iii) Children[64]—an allowance is payable to the person, if any, who becomes entitled to claim child benefit for them after his death, in respect of any children for whom the deceased was entitled to child benefit during his life. Where that person is the deceased's widow, the allowances are payable at a higher rate equivalent to the increases which a widow entitled to a widow's allowance or widowed mother's allowance receives.[65] Otherwise the increases are payable at a lower rate equivalent to the increases which attach to unemployment and sickness benefit.

(iv) Parents[66]—a parent substantially maintained by the deceased at his death may be entitled to benefit. If he was wholly or mainly maintained, he may be entitled to pension, otherwise a gratuity. A mother is liable to lose the right to pension on marriage or to its suspension on cohabitation unless the object of her marriage or cohabitation was already on the scene when the deceased died.

(v) Relatives[67]—a prescribed relative wholly or mainly maintained, or substantially maintained and permanently incapable of self-support (or the wife of such a person), may be entitled to benefit. It may be a pension or a gratuity; it may be affected by marriage or cohabitation; it may cease on restoration of the capacity for self-support.

(vi) "Housekeepers"[68] having care of the deceased's children may benefit.

E. PRESCRIBED DISEASES

Incapacity, disablement and death can, and frequently do, all result from work otherwise by reason of an injury caused by accident. It has long been recognised that certain diseases are a peculiar hazard of certain occupations. The justice and propriety of extending the benefits of the industrial injuries scheme in such cases can hardly be questioned.

In the case of some diseases it is possible to do this via the injury/accident route. Other industrial diseases, however, fall victim to the accident/process distinction and accordingly cannot lead to benefit in this way. Even were this not so, to put the claimant to proof that the contraction of the disease "arose out of and in the course of his employment" in the case of many well-known industrial diseases would often result in farce or scandal. It would be farcical if it involved going through the motions of proving a fact which could never be less than highly probable in the circumstances; this being so, it would be scandalous if benefit were denied.

For these reasons, it has long been recognised that an alternative route to benefit should be opened up and this was done, originally via the workmen's compensation scheme. At the same time, it is necessary, so long as the policy of special treatment for industrial risks continues to be espoused, that the route shall not be so open as to allow passage to those suffering as a result of non-industrial diseases. Account therefore has to be taken not only of the fact that a particular disease might be considered to be an occupational hazard but also of the incidence of its contraction quite apart from occupation. Some attempt must be made to sieve out the case of the claimant contracting a disease which he might well have contracted because of his work but which is in fact contracted outside. This attempt is, as we shall see, made. In the result, two routes to benefit are opened up but a third remains closed. A workman who contracts a disease at work, because of his work, may nevertheless fail because it is neither an "accidental injury" (being a "process") nor the product of a risk sufficiently peculiar to his occupation to have warranted recognition as such. He, or his dependants, ought to be allowed to prove, if he or they can, that he contracted a disease by reason of his work and is thereby incapacitated, disabled or dead. The opportunity is denied.

We have no measurement of the numbers of workers who are denied benefit for this reason. All we know is that such cases continue to occur. There is a measure of the numbers using the prescribed diseases route. So far as injury benefit is concerned, prescribed diseases account for only 2 per cent. of all spells of certified incapacity[69] and are on the decline in this respect.[70] They account for 2·3 per cent. of days in respect of which injury benefit is paid.[71] So far as injury benefit is concerned, non-infective dermatitis accounts for two-thirds of the spells on benefit and traumatic inflammation of the tendons of the hand or forearm for three-quarters of the rest.[72]

So far as disablement benefit is concerned, prescribed diseases cases are again a minority source, although now a more substantial one, accounting for 21 per cent. of all pensions.[73] Of these, the vast majority derive from pneumoconiosis (18 per cent. of the total). Approximately 40,000 persons are presently in receipt of pensions in respect of diseases, two-thirds for a degree of disablement of 20 or 30 per cent.[74]

Any disease or injury may be prescribed in relation to any earners if the Secretary of State is satisfied that:

"(a) it ought to be treated, having regard to its causes and incidence and any other relevant considerations, as a risk of their occupations and not as a risk common to all persons; and

(b) it is such that, in the absence of special circumstances, the attribution of particular cases to the nature of the employment can be established or presumed with reasonable certainty."[75]

The Secretary of State merely requires to be "satisfied" that this is the case. His discretion would appear to be practically uncontrollable. In exercising it, he may provide for the causal presumption to be rebuttable and he may require service at a particular time or for a stipulated length of time in the prescribed occupation as a condition of entitlement to benefit.[76] Both devices are used.

The process of prescription can be lengthy. The establishment of sufficiently clear and sufficiently exclusive causal link may involve protracted medical research from the time when the link is first hypothesised. The Secretary of State usually consults the Industrial Injuries Advisory Council[77] and its reports are the usual basis for prescription. Some 50 diseases are currently prescribed, along with their *sequelee*.[78] The most common type is poisoning in the case of persons in occupations exposing them to that particular risk. Another example is anthrax in relation to occupations involving "the handling of wool, hair, bristles, hides, skins or other animal products or residues, or contact with animals infected with anthrax."[79] Perhaps surprisingly "primary carcinoma of a bronchus or of a lung" is prescribed in relation to certain occupations even though it is commonly attributable to other causes[80]; the presumption is, however, rebuttable.[81]

A similar point can be made in respect of tuberculosis which is prescribed in relation to occupations involving close contact with a source of infection for example as a nurse, research worker or pathologist.[82] There might be something to be said for generalising such a provision so as to embrace all infectious and contagious diseases to the risk of contraction of which medical workers are peculiarly exposed by reason of their work. Again, the presumption can be rebuttable, although in the case of tuberculosis it is conclusive.[83]

Pneumoconiosis receives special treatment. Prescription may and does extend not only to the normal *sequelae* of the disease but also to accompanying tuberculosis and, in certain circumstances, to accompanying emphysema or chronic bronchitis.[83] In the latter case, account may only be taken of the accompanying diseases if the degree of disablement apart from them (*i.e.* in respect of the pneumoconiosis and tuberculosis) would by itself exceed 50 per cent.[84] Special medical panels are constituted for pneumoconiosis purposes.[85]

F. DISQUALIFICATION AND REPAYMENT OF BENEFIT OVERPAID[86]

Subject to important qualifications, the general grounds of disqualification[87] apply. There are the customary exceptions to the absence disqualification in the cases of airmen[88] and mariners.[89] Disqualification on grounds of imprisonment or detention in legal custody does not apply at all to disablement pension for a year; or, where he is prosecuted for a crime, during such time as he is detained in custody pending trial[90]; or in certain other circumstances. Disqualification may be imposed for retarding recovery.[91]

Repayment of benefit overpaid may be ordered where the claimant has not throughout used due care and diligence to avoid overpayment. Where, however, he would have been entitled to a lesser benefit (*e.g.* sickness benefit) instead of injury benefit the order for repayment must be confined to the difference.[92] Benefit overpaid and ordered to be repaid may be recovered by deduction from subsequent benefits to which the person ordered to repay (or, on his death, his dependants) may become entitled.[93]

G. SUPPLEMENTARY SCHEMES

Provision is made for the Secretary of State, by order, to institute a supplementary scheme, providing for additional payments in the cases of the statutory benefits or for payments otherwise, on the submission of "a body of persons claiming to represent, or to be entitled to be treated as representing, employed earners of any class and their employers."[94] The Secretary of State has a discretion in the matter and must consult unrepresented earners before making an order.[95]

The only supplementary scheme so far implemented is the Colliery Workers' Supplementary Scheme.[96] Under it, the National Coal Board pays a periodic sum in order to finance higher rates of benefit in the case of disablement or death resulting from colliery accidents as defined. In the case of disablement benefit, the rate is usually increased by one-third, provided that the total income receivable by way of benefit shall not exceed the rate of pre-accident earnings.

H. CONCLUSION

If asked simply whether a social security system should make provision for persons whose health is impaired as a result of their work, the vast majority of people nowadays would answer in the affirmative. That speculation, however, falls far short of justifying the industrial injuries scheme as we know it today. On the one hand the scheme embraces many injuries and disablements which are not, in any generally acceptable sense, work-caused, but are irrationally associated with work because of some irrelevant association with it. On the other hand, benefit is totally denied in cases where there is negligible doubt that a disease was contracted as a result of the work, because it is neither prescribed not an accidental injury. Add to this the fact that we are still fundamentally confused on some basic doctrinal questions and the disposition to self-congratulation is likely to wane. If we are to have an industrial injuries scheme at all, it is time we had a radical look at what we are doing.

But should there be special treatment for industrial injuries at all, in contrast to the injuries sustained by other persons in relation to activities which can hardly be distinguished from industrial activities in terms of involuntariness and importance, such as accidents in the home or on the roads or at school?

There is no rational case for the retention of injury benefit alongside earnings-related sickness benefit, and even if there were, account should be taken of the extraordinarily high real costs of administration of injury benefit. There is a case for disablement benefit, though only because there is a case, not yet met, for providing disablement benefit generally, whether its source be work, or the home or a congenital condition, and it is better to have adequate provision for some than for none. A general disablement benefit scheme would, it is true, be expensive. It may be remarked, in passing, that in some cases, industrial disablement benefits can be generous and that a generalised scheme could justifiably be pitched at a lower level.

The radical new look at the industrial injuries scheme, therefore, should not merely seek to remove anomalies and uncertainties in the existing scheme. It should ask, as Beveridge effectively did not, whether we should have it at all. The answer to that question might be yes, but only because the scheme is an established part of the industrial scheme conferring privileges upon workers at work and otherwise denied to all. Politically, that is a powerful consideration; there are no votes in abolition; the industrial injuries scheme may well remain as the incubus of social security.

CHAPTER 11

FAMILY PROVISION

NOTE is taken of the size of family and therefore the scope of need by virtue of dependency in a number of ways. Under both the national insurance scheme and the supplementary benefit scheme (as, of course, the industrial injuries scheme) an increase of benefit is payable in respect of most dependants. This aspect of family provision is dealt with in connection with the appropriate schemes.[1] Certain other aspects of family provision secured by public law, such as free education, free school meals and milk, etc., are available but are outside the scope of this work. The legal device which at present involves the largest sums of money is not, in fact, concerned with the positive provision of cash payments or equivalents in kind, the traditional form of social security benefit, but with allowances for dependants under the income tax scheme. Child relief is available to a taxpayer, provided he is the child's parent or has the custody of and maintains him at his own expense, in respect of a child living with him.[2] It is not proposed to deal in any detail with the child allowance scheme; nonetheless, the close relationship between tax and social security systems is of very great significance. As Kincaid shows,[3] "There is no good reason why social security should be defined solely as a system of schemes whereby people in danger of poverty are given cash to meet essential needs. A very large part of social security is in fact managed through the tax system by the mechanism of giving people tax relief. There is no essential difference between a family allowance obtained in cash from the Post Office and a children's allowance by which a person is allowed tax exemption which he otherwise would have to pay. In either case, the effect is the same. The Government makes special financial concessions to people with children."

The need to rationalise the various forms of state support for families has become more and more pressing. The schemes are administratively cumbersome and, in so far as they duplicate each other, extremely wasteful. The current system of giving tax concessions to families is unsatisfactory for a number of reasons. Its benefits are confined solely to taxpayers, thus excluding persons whose earnings are too low to bring them into the tax bracket. Furthermore, the value of such allowances is directly proportionate to the income earned; the higher one's income, the more valuable the relief resulting from avoidance of payment of higher rates. There is no provision to ensure that those who have the chief responsibility for the upbringing of the family (usually the mother who is thus precluded from working at all events whilst the children are young) receive the benefit of any allowances the effects of which are presented in the husband's wage-packet. Moreover, lack of co-ordination between the two systems, combined with a range of other benefits all independently means-tested, results in the "poverty-trap" whereby an increase of gross income on the part of certain low income earners in receipt of means-tested benefits results at best in an extremely high marginal tax rate and often in an actual loss, through a combination of direct taxation, loss of benefits and imposition of graduated national insurance contributions.

The new child benefit scheme proposes the replacement in part of child allowances by the payment of cash sums. In the following pages, it is proposed to examine the provisions of the new child benefit scheme, and then to deal with other facets of the social security system directed specifically towards family provision, namely the family incomes supplement scheme, educational maintenance allowances and the special position of one-parent families.

A. CHILD BENEFIT

1. INTRODUCTION

Our society looks mainly to income from employment as a means of meeting needs. In most cases, it is an adequate means and most social security benefits are designed to cope with the situation where, for one reason or another (retirement, sickness, unemployment etc.) income from employment stops.

In some cases, however, income from employment is not adequate. "A national minimum (income) for families of every size cannot in practice be secured by a wage system, which must be based on the product of a man's labour and not on the size of his family."[4] More accurately, the size of a man's wage is determined not by the extent of his and his dependant's needs, but by the demand for his services on the labour market. The basic factor here is the personal skills which he, as a worker, has to offer; the size of his family is irrelevant. In practice, some slight account is taken of family needs in the employment market. Private family allowances may occasionally be paid; ideas of "need" in the average family function as a subsidiary factor in collective bargaining, *i.e.* in fixing demands, but they do so undifferentially—the wage demanded may have reference to the need to maintain a family, but different rates for one- and 10-children family are not demanded.

Without the aid of social security therefore, widespread and severe family poverty would prevail. The need has been long recognised. As early in 1796, Pitt introduced a Bill to provide for not less than one shilling per week out of the rates for the third and subsequent children (second and subsequent in the case of widows) but it lacked adequate support. It was left to the twentieth century and the work of Eleanor Rathbone to emphasise the dire need and provoke action in abatement of it.

The springboard was Beveridge whose main justification for action was the reason stated above. There was, however, a subsidiary justification: "With its present rate of reproduction, the British race cannot continue."[5] This assumes two things: (i) that there was a need to encourage population growth; (ii) that payment of family allowances would have this effect. Today, neither of these propositions is unquestionable. The first is perhaps understandable (though not necessarily correct) when one bears in mind that it was formulated in the midst of a World War at a time when the future of "the British race" was to some extent a matter of doubt and when "cannon-fodder" was a scarce good. It is much less so today when the question of population growth might be more responsibly viewed in global terms. The second proposition (and, particularly, the corollary that refusal of allowances will prevent large families) is singularly lacking in detailed evidence. It is important to appreciate exactly what conclusion is warranted by the imposition of the economist's market model upon this situation. If all children were the product of a decision and if the decision to have children turned solely upon the accompanying added income, no one would ever have children, since family allowances are not paid for the first child, and for the rest, do not and were never meant to relieve parents of anything but a small proportion of the cost of rearing children. The existence of family benefits is therefore but one factor (if it figures at all) in decisions about having children. It is almost certainly an unimportant factor and would affect decision only on the margin. This is to say that in a very small proportion of cases, the removal of family benefits might provoke parents who would otherwise have had more children not to have them. More important, however, such removal would, in the vast majority of cases, not affect the decision at all and widespread family poverty would again result. The chief victims would again be the children who had not participated in the decision and who were unable to help themselves.

It is, of course, in principle possible to limit allowances *as of right* to, say, the first three or four children, and to condition payment thereafter on need and in theory this could be done either as a part of the child benefits scheme or of the sup-plementary benefits scheme or of the family supplement scheme. The problem here, as with all other means-tested benefits, is that of take-up, *i.e.* ensuring that benefits are received by those qualifying for them. It is a problem so far unsolved.

One attempt has been made to limit the amount of allowance in respect of the later children in large families. In 1956, the Northern Ireland government, which has its own scheme, pro-posed to do just that. A higher proportion of Roman Catholic families than of Protestant families in Northern Ireland were, however, "large" and widespread criticism of these proposals ensued. The Unionist members of Parliament at Westminster reported to the Prime Minister of Northern Ireland that there was likely to be substantial opposition in Great Britain to this departure from parity with the Great Britain scheme and the proposals were, therefore, abandoned.

This fact, that the chief beneficiaries of a family benefits scheme are the children themselves, tends at times to be lost sight of. Beveridge debated whether to make the family allow-ances scheme contributory or not and eventually decided against contribution only because contributions would have to be too high and actuarial problems would arise by virtue of some child-assistance being envisaged as being in kind in the form of free school meals and milk. The allowances obviously have to be paid to someone to administer in favour of the child, and the parent is the obvious payee. But to consider that payment should be conditioned on contributions by the parent is to put the needs of his children in the same category as unforeseen redundancy or sickness as a threat to the parent's livelihood, against which he should prudently provide. Many will consider that children, by virtue of their own humanity and helplessness, should be adequately provided for in their own right, regardless of the degree of thrift, providence and foresight manifested by parents.

Albeit for the wrong reasons, the Beveridge recommendations for a scheme of non-contributory allowances was therefore right. The idea was for free school meals and milk and for an allowance of eight shillings per week per child up to the age of 15 or, if in full-time education thereafter, 16. Payment was to be made "to those responsible for the care of those children"[6] seeming to emphasise that the important factor was the obligation to maintain. Beveridge considered but rejected certain variations on the theme. There were inadequate reasons for the progressive reduction of the allowance in respect of each successive child, and for varying rates according to the age of the child and the value of benefits received in kind. Nonetheless, he conceded that "in practice, the allowance should not be uniform but graded by age since the needs of the children increase rapidly with age."

The White Paper accepted the substance of the Beveridge proposals. It emphasised "First, that nothing should be done to remove from parents the responsibility of maintaining their children, and second that it is in the national interest for the state to help parents to discharge that responsibility properly."[7] The aim was therefore not to make provision for full maintenance but rather to go some way towards assisting parents to do the job. The government settled for an allowance of five shillings per week, payable to the father and cashable by the mother in the normal case, but for the second and subsequent children only. The normal age limit was to be 15, but this could be extended to July 31 after attaining the age of 16 in respect of a child at school or apprenticed. Aid beyond these limits should be means-tested.

The family was to be defined by blood, not household. In most cases, of course, the natural father and/or mother will be the maintainers of their children and the government contemplated that "if the presumption that the parent is the maintainer is upset, arrangements will have to be made to reckon the child a member of the family of the person actually doing the maintaining."

This identification of the "issue" parent as being primarily entitled may have reflected then existing notions of family responsibility but complicated the resulting legislative scheme and may have caused injustice at times. It disappears under the new scheme.

The Beveridge proposals, as modified by the White Paper, passed into law as the Family Allowances Act 1945 and governed the position until 1977. The last consolidation was the Family Allowances Act 1965. Allowances were taxable and, after 1968, also subject to claw-back, *i.e.* coincidental reduction in children's allowances for income tax purposes.

A movement to rationalise the various schemes of family provision had been gathering momentum for some time, culminating in the publication of a government Green Paper, *Proposals for a Tax Credit Scheme*, in 1972. This proposed a partial merger of the personal taxation and social security schemes with two principal objectives in mind: first, to simplify the tax system and, secondly, to improve income support for the poor. Under the proposed scheme, tax credits were to replace personal allowances, family allowances and family income supplement. The national insurance and supplementary benefit systems were to be retained. Tax credits have not been designed with the intention of guaranteeing in every case that a family with no further help from the state would have enough to live on. The self-employed, recipients of supplementary benefit ineligible for national insurance benefits, and earners below the minimum qualifying level, were to be excluded from the scheme but the payment of tax-free child credits, in the form of cash payments made to the mother, was to be universal.[8] As Tony Atkinson shows, the proposed scheme would have had a limited redistributive effect and, moreover, would have been very costly to implement.[9] Consequently, only the child credit proposals survived the change of government; the rest of the proposed scheme was abandoned.

The Labour Party manifesto of 1974 committed the Labour government to "a new system of child care allowances for every child, including the first, payable to the mother." This was given legislative effect in the Child Benefit Act 1975 which repeals the Family Allowances scheme. The Act contemplates the replacement of the hybrid system of child allowances and family allowances by a "single, universal, non-means-tested, tax-free, child endowment," payable to the mother for every child for which she is responsible. The scheme, originally intended to come into force in 1976, was postponed for a year for all families other than for single-parent families, on economic grounds. For the latter, a modified form of family allowances, extending to the first child, was introduced for the interim period.

The scheme has three principle advantages. Its benefits are not confined to persons above the tax-threshold; it reduces dependence on means-tested benefits thus avoiding the problems of take-up which seem insuperable in that form of benefit; and it extends to the first child.

The subsequent history of the scheme has been tortuous. In May 1976, the Government announced its intention of implementing a part only of the original scheme the following year, due to its effects on the government's pay policy and public spending programme. The proposed merger of the tax and family allowance schemes, an integral feature of the original proposals, was to be postponed indefinitely, because of the reduction in take-home pay which its full implementation would inevitably entail. Instead, family allowances, posing in the guise of child benefit, were to be extended to the first child of every family and were to remain taxed and subject to claw-back. The benefit was to be paid at the same rate as had been family allowances, *i.e.* £1·50 for every second and subsequent child and £1 for every first child. A premium of 50p was to be payable to one-parent families. This was substantially lower than the rates originally put forward (around £2·50). The new scheme as modified was estimated to cost some £95 million.

The following month, details of a cabinet meeting in which

plans for the total abandonment of the scheme were discussed were "leaked" to the Press.[10] The resulting outcry forced the Government to reconsider the position and in September a further change of policy was announced, following the recommendation of a special Labour Party/TUC joint committee set up specifically to deal with the question.

The Present Scheme

The scheme taking effect on April 4, 1977 contemplates the gradual phasing out of tax allowances for children. Tax relief for children under 11 will be phased out over a three-year period but residual allowances for children over this age will remain. From 1977, child benefit is to be untaxed and exempt from claw-back, and is to be payable at the rate of £1 for the first and £1·50 for each subsequent child, except in the case of one-parent families where £1·50 is payable in respect of every child including the first. Tax allowances are reducible by the amount which would have been consumed in tax, or clawed-back (*i.e.* £104 for the first and £130 for each subsequent child) under the Government's earlier proposals. Further reductions are to be made in 1978 and 1979. Special provision is made for a widow whose allowances were not subject to claw-back under the former scheme. The allowance for the first child in the case of other one-parent families will also be reduced by £104 notwithstanding that benefit is paid at a higher rate, but this is intended to be a temporary measure only.

Like family allowances, child benefit is not age-related, although power to make regulations permitting differential rates is contained in the Act. The power is unlikely to be exercised within the immediate future.[11] The benefit is to be financed out of general taxation[12] and no question of deprivation of benefit on grounds of an inadequate contribution record arises. The Act requires the Secretary of State to review the rates in force (which he is not allowed to reduce)[13] but it imposes no obligation on him to uprate the benefit in line with the cost of living on the principle that, unlike other benefits, it is not the sole source of income for most recipients,[14] a proposition which is untrue in the case of many benefits so reviewable and, in any case, dubious.

Under the new arrangements, the majority of families will be in much the same position as before (the usual net gain being about 30p). Persons below the tax-threshold will get most benefit from the introduction of a first child benefit; persons on a marginal rate of tax of more than 55 per cent. will suffer a loss.

It seems clear that the scheme, with its varying rates of tax and benefit, will be administratively much more complex than was originally contemplated. Nonetheless, it is worth stressing an obvious point—the paramount objective of the social security system is not the production of administrative simplicity (though, equally obviously, considerations of cost/benefit impose limits); abatement of need is.

It is now proposed to deal with the details of the child benefit scheme. Many of these have not yet been settled, hence a complete account is impossible. It must be further added that, of necessity, reliance will be placed on Commissioner's decisions under the former scheme where it seems that the doctrine developed by them has a place. There is, however, room for doubt about the relevance of some of them.

2. The Right to Child Benefit

Section 1 of the Child Benefit Act provides that "a person who is responsible for one or more children in any week ... shall be entitled to a benefit (to be known as child benefit) for that week in respect of the child or each of the children for whom he is responsible," if certain other conditions, *e.g.* relating to residence, in the Act are satisfied.

"Week"

The conditions contained in section 1 must be satisfied at the beginning of the week, *i.e.* Monday,[15] although regulations may and do provide otherwise.[16]

"Child"

The meaning of "child" is dealt with by section 2:

"A person shall be treated as a child for any week in which—
    (a) he is under the age of sixteen; or

(b) he is under the age of nineteen and receiving full-time education by attendance at a recognised educational establishment."

No difficulty arises under (a). On the other hand, (b) clearly presents problems of interpretation. Interpretation may be simplified, though justifiable conclusions not guaranteed, by the definition of "a recognised educational establishment" as "an establishment recognised by the Secretary of State as being, or as comparable to, a university, college or school."[17] Presumably, "school" will be given the same meaning as under the Education Acts 1944–76, section 114 of which defines it as "an institution for providing primary or secondary education being a school maintained by a local education authority or an independent school or a school in respect of which grants are made by the Minister to the proprietor of the school." If it was the intention of the legislature to include persons receiving education otherwise than at school under special arrangements made under the Education Act 1944, section 56, or section 14 of the Education (Scotland) Act 1962, it is doubtful if they have achieved it. On a strict interpretation, the power to "recognize" does not necessarily extend to such a scheme of education —there will not necessarily be an "establishment" "comparable to ... a school" especially, for example, in the case of home tuition—it is the "establishment" and not the standard of education which must be comparable. Regulation 5 of the Child Benefit (General) Regulations provides for persons being so educated to be treated as receiving full-time education. It does not, in express terms, "recognise" anything. It is therefore clearly arguable that it creates no right to benefit either because the requirement of "attendance at a recognised educational establishment" is not dealt with by the regulation or, if it is, because the regulation is *ultra vires*. Under the old scheme, the Parliamentary Commissioner took the view that "full-time instruction in a school" did not include the education at home, even by a retired professor of classics.[18] The Secretary of State had considered whether to broaden the definition of "child" so as to embrace such cases but decided against it on the ground that any such change would lead to uncertainty and complications, especially in the case where there was a gap between leaving school, *stricto sensu*, and starting work. "Full-time" is potentially ambiguous. *R(F) 4/62* concerned a child over school-leaving age whose only recorded activity was to attend a course of instruction at a secretarial college involving her in $13\frac{3}{4}$ hours' instruction per week. She was taking the "full" course and devoting the whole of her activity to it. The course of instruction in question nevertheless occupied only half the day and was not, therefore, a full-time course of instruction.

In the normal course of a child's educational career, breaks in full-time education or instruction do, of course, occur, *e.g.* in the case of sickness or holidays; or in the case of transition from school to some other form of training. Were provision not made otherwise, it would be arguable that title to allowance would be temporarily lost during such break although the need would continue unabated. Provision otherwise is made by regulation 6 of the Child Benefit (General) Regulations which provides that a period of interruption of full-time education of up to six months may be ignored "to the extent to which it is accepted that the interruption is attributable to a cause which is reasonable in the particular circumstances of the case." The time limit may be extended only where the interruption is attributable to the child's physical or mental ill-health. In calculating the 6-month period, regard must be had to any part of the period falling before the child attains 16. This seems inequitable in view of the fact that persons under 16 qualify irrespective of whether they are in full-time education.

The regulation introduces a wide measure of flexibility into the law. Under the previous scheme, it was settled that full-time instruction in a school could be deemed to continue during school holidays only where the child was intended to resume schooling at the end of the holidays.[19] The position probably remains the same albeit for different reasons—regulation 6 is concerned only with the "interruption" of full-time education. On one interpretation, this would exist provided that there was an intention to resume education at some future date. The intention is not always clearcut. Very often, the child's future course may turn upon future events. It may be the intention that the child shall take up a particular occupation if the opportunity offers, but failing this return to school. In this type of situation, it is the "predominant wish of the persons concerned" which is to govern.[20] In that case, it was the predominant wish of the parents and the school authority that the child should pass his examinations and leave school, but they intended that he should return to school if he failed, which was not unlikely. Title to allowance was thus lost. In the event, he passed the examinations. The results did not become known and he could not commence work until six weeks later—even so, he could no longer be considered a "child" and the same result would have ensued, for the period of the vacation, even had he failed and returned to school when, of course, title would have been re-established.[21] One can envisage cases where the idea of the "predominant wish" might seem to lean to anomaly. The fond parent might have the predominant wish that the child should become a professional footballer but at the same time entertain the realistic expectation that the opportunity would not be offered and that a continuation of schooling would follow. "Predominant wish" is perhaps best understood as indicating predominant realistic expectation.

What the position would have been had the child in $R(F)$ 7/64 failed his examinations (which he did not do) is unclear under the present regulations. Under the old regulations, it appears that title to allowance would have been lost until he actually returned to full-time education when it would be re-established.[22] Whilst there is no initial intention to resume schooling, education is nonetheless resumed. It is therefore suggested that in these circumstances regulation 6 will apply. This interpretation would be consistent with later developments under the old law, contained in $R(S)$ 3/70, in which it was suggested that determination of the claim should await the outcome of events and that payment in full should be made if school were resumed. There are no logical reasons why the statutory authorities should not be allowed to continue this practice.[23]

Provision is further made for treating a person who has ceased to receive full-time education as continuing to receive it for a maximum period of 13 weeks. This is subject to the overriding qualification that no person may take the benefit of the regulation for any period in which he is over 19.[24]

Apprentices under the former scheme may, transitionally, continue to be treated as children until they cease to be apprentices or reach 19[25]; otherwise, employed trainees are excluded from the scheme, as are students on advanced courses,[26] though where no net payment is received for a period of over six months, benefit may be payable.

Age

Age is to be proved in the same manner as under the social security legislation,[28] *i.e.* by furnishing certificates of the registrar of births, deaths and marriages. A person is deemed to attain a particular age on the commencement of the relevant anniversary of his birthday.[29]

Person Responsible for a Child

A person is to be treated as responsible for a child in any week if:

(a) he has the child living with him; or

(b) he is contributing to the cost of providing for the child at a weekly rate which is not less than the weekly rate of child benefit.[30]

In conferring priority on a person with whom the child is living rather than on the child's parent, the Act marks a major shift of policy which is consistent with the aims both of equity and administrative simplicity.[31]

Almost invariably, a child who is physically cohabiting with a parent will be "living with" that parent and there is a strong presumption to that effect. Exceptional circumstances may, however, rebut that presumption. In this respect *R(F) 3/63* and *R(F) 1/71* may be contrasted. The facts in the two cases are not readily distinguishable. In both, a claimant grandmother, her daughter (the mother) and an illegitimate child born of the mother were living in the same household. In both cases, the mother went out to work and the grandmother had charge of the upbringing of the child. If there is a difference it is that in the 1971 decision, the mother "had delegated all her maternal parental duties for an indefinite period and for twenty-four hours a day" whilst in the 1963 decision, the mother saw to the child during the night and was regarded by the child as "mother." It was held in the 1963 decision that the presumption that the child was living with its mother (therefore an issue family to be preferred to the maintenance family of the grandmother) had not been rebutted; but in the 1971 decision that it had, *i.e.* the mother was no longer "living with" the child for family allowance purposes. She was a sort of lodger in the same household. "The fact that (she) could at any time have resumed her parental role did not affect the situation existing at that time ... the normal relationship of parent and child did not in fact exist."[32] The child is, of course, capable of "living with" both, in which case the mother would have priority.[33]

A person who has the child living with him continues to be eligible for benefit in any week notwithstanding temporary absences.[34] Any time spent away at a recognised educational establishment may be ignored. Up to 84 consecutive days (and any two days separated by an interval of not more than 28 days may be treated as "consecutive") spent as an in-patient in a hosptial or like establishment receiving treatment may be discounted, and further absence may be ignored if the person "regularly incurs expenditure in respect of the child."[35] The circumstances in which a person is to be treated as regularly incurring expenditure have yet to be prescribed. Whether it is sufficient to spend any money at all on the child (*e.g.* buying a stamp for a weekly letter) to fall within the regulation remains to be seen. There are similar provisions covering a child who is living in residential accommodation under section 12 of the Health Services and Public Health Act 1968 or section 27 (10) of the National Health Service (Scotland) Act 1947.[36] Apart from this, absences for any reason not exceeding 56 days in the 16 weeks immediately prior to the relevant week may be ignored.[37]

By section 3(3)(*a*) one may be "living with" a person notwithstanding absence at school. In *Hill* v. *Minister of Pensions and National Insurance*[38] a local authority took two children into care under section 1 (1) of the Children Act 1948 and put them into residential schools. The mother claimed family allowance in respect of them as "issue" children "living with" her relying on section 17 (7) of the Family Allowances Act 1965 (the predecessor of section 3(3)(*a*)). She was held, however, not to be entitled. That they were not actually living with her was due, in the opinion of Lord Goddard L.C.J., not to the fact that they were at school, but to the fact that they were in care.

Presumably, had they been taken into care but not sent to school, there would have been nothing onto which the section could fix. If the issue arose again, the child would be excluded by virtue of Schedule 2 of the Act and regulation 16(5)(a) of the Child Benefit (General) Regulations.[39]

"Providing for"

A person is treated as responsible for a child if he contributes to the cost of providing for him at an amount which is equivalent to, or in excess of, the weekly rate of child benefit.[40] The significance of this alternative means of entitlement is considerably reduced, now that priority is conferred on the person (including a voluntary organisation[41]) with whom the child is living rather than on a providing parent. It will be only in a very small number of cases that contribution *per se* will lead to entitlement to child benefit.

Regulations prescribing the circumstances in which a person is to be treated as so contributing have not, as yet, been published. The Child Benefit (General) Regulations as amended by the Child Benefit (Miscellaneous Minor Amendments) Regulations make provision for joint contributors, *i.e.* where the contributions of more than one person are aggregated so as to produce the required amount. In such a case, only one contributor, elected by his fellow-contributors or, failing election, selected by the Secretary of State, is entitled to the child benefit. This applies equally to husband and wife. Regulation 2 (2) provides that after such an election or selection has been made, the person entitled must subsequently show that he is himself contributing to the cost of providing for the child at the required rate. This appears to suggest that the value of child benefit may be treated as a contribution to the cost of the child, endorsing the view expressed in *R(G) 3/61*. This would, of course, be subject to any subsequent defining provision.

One requirement under the old scheme seems equally relevant to the new. *The contribution must be from the contributor to the beneficiary.* This means in the first place that *the contribution must be sufficiently referable to the contributor*, a matter in some doubt in *R(F) 2/62*. There, a local authority had taken a claimant's four children into care under section 1 of the Children Act

1948 and obtained orders under section 26 of that Act against the putative father. Under these orders, the authority received 17s. 6d. per week for each child (the minimum was then eight shillings as compared with today's £1·50). The claimant claimed family allowances as contributing towards the cost of providing for the children her argument being that the same result could have been arrived at by her obtaining affiliation orders and making payments for the children. The crucial point was that she had not done so. Her title was, however, lost for largely procedural reasons. If she "had obtained an order ... or had even made an agreement with (the father) to pay sums for the children's maintenance, and on her instructions the money had been paid for convenience direct to the local authority then I think that those payments could have been regarded as being contributed by the claimant to the cost of providing for the children. It would have been *her* money."[42]

The statement at the head of this section means in the second place that the *contribution must reach its destination*. In *R(F) 9/61*, the children were living with their grandmother, who largely maintained them. Under a court order, the father paid weekly sums into court for the maintainance of the separated mother and children. On the wife's authority, payments were occasionally remitted in lump sums to the grandmother, but this ceased when the wife disappeared. The question was whether the father "contributed" merely by making the weekly payments. It was held that he did not.

The children could be included in the father's family only for those weeks during which the grandmother received payments. "The cost of providing for a child is contributed to for the purpose of section 3 (2) [now s. 3(1)(b)] ... only when the contribution reaches the person maintaining the child ... if the right of a person maintaining a child to include that child in her (or his) family is to be defeated by contributions made by a parent it is for the parent to take such steps as will ensure that the contribution reaches that person promptly."[43]

Spreading

Problems arise where spasmodic payments are made in a few weeks of amounts which, if spread, would qualify for more weeks.

This problem arose incidentally in *Re P. (Infants)*,[44] concerning the question whether there had been a "persistent failure to discharge the obligations of a parent" for purposes of section 5 (2) of the Adoption Act 1958. Here, maintenance contributions totalling £29 had been made spasmodically over an otherwise barren period of two years, by a parent who had drawn family allowances during this period. Pennycuick J. seems to spread this amount over the whole two years in order to establish that there had been disentitlement to allowance for the whole period, *i.e.* persistent failure. This, however, was not necessary. Had the payments not been thus spread (and Pennycuick J.'s judgment does not expressly do it) there would still have been disentitlement for most of the time and, presumably therefore, still a failure to discharge etc., by depriving them of the benefit of the allowance.

This simple method may be manifestly unsatisfactory in some cases, *e.g.* where generous payments have been made for a shorter period, followed by none over a much longer period. Here, it might be unjust to deny any right to allowance. The approach of Commissioners has been more sophisticated and more satisfactory. Take *R(F) 8/61*: here, the children were admitted to an orphanage managed by a charity. The father continued to obtain allowance and agreed to pay the charity 30 shillings per week. He made five payments at irregular intervals, four of them being of multiples of 30 shillings. He did not specify any particular period for these payments. It was held: (1) prima facie children could only be included in the father's family in the week of contribution at the statutory rate. (2) In the instant case (where there were arrears), payments in any week over 30 shillings should be attributed to arrears, and there could be no retrospective qualification for allowances (title falling to be determined according to the position as at the time in question). "The question to what period payments relate is a question of fact. They must be attributed in our view to the period to which they were intended to be attributed, the intention expressed by the payer being a vital factor. Here an important distinction must be drawn between payments wholly or in part intended to cover a specific future period and payments in arrear and payments of arrears. Whilst we cannot accept the view that a lump sum payment without more can be regarded as a contribution at the minimum or any other rate for whatever future period it would cover, we do not doubt that a payment understood to be made to cover a specific future period may count as a contribution throughout a period, for a payment in advance can in a practical sense help to support a child. Arrears appear to us to be in a completely different position. We express no opinion on the question whether, where the person maintaining the child has agreed to payment in arrear, or has obtained an order for it, payments in arrear may constitute contributions for the period covered by the payments. Payments of arrears in our judgment cannot assist the parent under s. 3 (2)."[45]

This decision signposts the direction of solution of many of the problems but falls short of solving them all. The basic statutory requirement must here be borne in mind. It is that the claimant must contribute to the cost of providing for the child at a rate equivalent to the rate of benefit for that week. All other questions are questions of fact, as to whether this statutory requirement is fulfilled.[46] The statement in *R(F) 8/61* above, that "payment *of* arrears in our judgment cannot assist the parent under section 3 (2)" seems to suggest that if the payment is in respect of a prior week, or weeks, it cannot be attributed to the week of claim (the current week). Strictly speaking, the same reasoning would seem to apply to payment *in* arrears (*i.e.* payment in due time but in respect of an earlier week). It may however, be possible to distinguish between payment *of* arrears and payment *in* arrears. In the latter case there has, but in the former case there has not, been due discharge of the obligation to provide created by the maintenance agreement or order. Even this, however, does not avoid anomaly. Take the case of a father who agrees to pay £10, in respect of every five weeks, in arrears. If his claim in respect of each of those five weeks is to be regarded as proper by virtue of the fact that his payment is not yet overdue, what is the position if he does not pay until the sixth or seventh week? By that time, his payment is overdue; it becomes a payment *of* arrears. The same reasoning would presumably apply to the sixth to tenth weeks—a claim here would be justified by reference to the payment due in the tenth week. It too might be late, and therefore become a payment *of* arrears. It would certainly be anomalous were he to be treated

more favourably than one who had not benefited from an agreement or order for payment in arrears in the first place.

It is manifestly unjust to deny benefit to a man who pays
regularly and generously in arrears. It is manifestly anomalous
to treat one man differently from another where both are paying
off arrears. The Commissioner had not yet been provided with
the opportunity to resolve this dilemma, nor the analogous one
which arises in relation to future payments. The solution probably lies in the fact that where benefit has been paid on the
assumption that the conditions of entitlement would be met
by a due payment in due course, and that assumption turns
out, in the event, to have been unwarranted, then benefit has
been wrongly paid and would be recoverable.

In *R(F)* *1/73*, the question arose whether payments in kind
could similarly be spread forward. It was held that although
there were "no hard and fast rules" the question being one
of fact, nevertheless, as a general rule, contributions in kind
should be attributed to the week in which they are made and
not spread forward; in particular, only in the most exceptional
circumstances[47] should they be spread over the estimated period
of their life. The Commissioner stated that "the approach to
the matter which I adopt has the advantage of keeping payments
in money and in kind so far as possible in line. If a parent
thinks that her child living with a foster mother needs a winter
coat and gives the foster mother some money to buy one, I
have never heard it suggested that such a contribution should
not be treated as a contribution during that week in the same
manner as normally happens with money contributions." The
reasoning of the Commissioner is not very clear and no authorities other than those dealing with payments in kind are cited
in the decision. It may be that where money is given to purchase
a specific item it will not be spread forward, but it seems
established that money contributions in general may be so
spread, contrary to what seems to be suggested. The Commissioner appears to reject any distinction between payments in
kind and cash payments but, in so doing, creates a precedent
for differential treatment: payments in kind will usually be
treated as contributions for the week in which they are made
save in exceptional circumstances. Similarly with money payments (although it is unclear whether, in actual practice, spread-

ing forward is limited to exceptional circumstances). But cash payments for a specific article may not be spread.[48]

One-parent Families

Child benefit is payable at the rate of £1·50 for all children including the first, provided they are living with the parent. Providing for them, under section 3(1)(b), is insufficient to qualify for the premium of 50p for the first child.

The premium is payable if the parent:

(a) has no spouse or is not residing with his spouse, and
(b) is not living with any other person as his spouse.[49]

"Parent" includes a natural parent in the case of an illegitimate child and a step-parent. Since section 24(3)(c) of the Child Benefit Act was repealed by the Children Act 1975, no reference is made to the position of adoptive parents. The validity and hence consequences of an adoption presumably fall to be determined according to the provisions of the Adoption Act 1976. The general principles of conflicts of laws remain unaffected.

In *R(F) 1/65* a successful claimant had been domiciled in the Republic of Ireland and had adopted a child also domiciled there according to Republic of Ireland law. On coming to Great Britain, the claim for family allowance in respect of the child as an "issue" child succeeded without more. "If both (*i.e.* adopters and child) had the same domicile at the time of the adoption, it must next be determined what the effect of the adoption is under the law of the place of domicile. If, by that law, the child has the status of a legitimate natural child of the adopter ... that child will retain that status for the purposes of the Family Allowances Act."[50] This was followed in *R(F) 3/73* in which allowance was refused on the grounds that Moslem law did not recognise adoption as a mode of affiliation. In *R(F) 1/65*[51] the domicile of the child as well as that of the adopter appeared to be relevant, although the Commissioner declined to decide what the position would be if the domiciles of adopter and child were different.[52]

Effect is given to polygamous marriages by regulation 12 of the Child Benefit (General) Regulations. Provided that the law under which the marriage was celebrated permits polygamy,

a polygamous marriage has the same consequences as a monogamous marriage for any period during which neither spouse
has an additional spouse.

Regulation 11 (1) of the Child Benefit (General) Regulations
provides that spouses "shall not be treated as having ceased
to reside together by reason of any absence the one from the
other which is not likely to be permanent" and as long as they
are neither separated under a court order or by deed, nor apart
for more than 90 days, an absence is to be treated as not likely
to be permanent. The regulation does not require spouses to
be treated as no longer residing together if they are separated
under a court order etc., or apart for more than 90 days, and
it remains a question for the statutory authorities in any case
whether there has been a cessation of residing together. If the
sole reason for them being apart is hospital treatment they may
not, even then, be treated as having ceased to reside together.
The same applies to spouses who have been treated as living
together for purposes of family allowances or child interim
benefit immediately prior to their supersession by child benefit.[53]

Different terminology is used in the case of parents who are
not married to each other. Here, "temporary absences" are
ignored for the purposes of determining whether the parties
are residing together.[54] The statutory authorities are given no
further guidance.

As with supplementary benefits[55] and widow's benefits,[56]
cohabitation is here again operating as a ground for disentitlement, this time to a child's premium of 50p per week. If the
cohabitation rule with its attendant embarrassment is to be
seriously administered in this situation, it can hardly be a profitable undertaking. It would, however, be costly to pay the
premium to all, as opposed to only single-parent families, and
it would be discriminatory against married couples to pay it
not to them but to unmarried couples.

The withholding of the premium from *de facto* single "parents"
such as grandmothers seems clearly to lack justification. Such
cases cannot be numerous and the arguments for a premium for
single, *de jure*, parent families apply with equal force in such cases.

The premium is not payable where either a child's allowance,
a guardian's allowance or certain dependant's allowances are
payable.

Voluntary Organisations

In general, child benefit is not payable to a body corporate but special provision has been made for voluntary organisations.[57] These are defined by section 24 (1) of the Child Benefit Act as bodies "other than a public or local authority, the activities of which are carried on otherwise than for profit." For these purposes, the child must live on premises provided or managed by an organisation or must be boarded out under certain enactments.[58] It is not sufficient that the organisation is contributing to the child's upkeep. Throughout the relevant period, the child must in fact be living on the premises, subject only to absences of not more than 56 days (84 days in the case of hospital treatment).[59] Benefit is limited to the lower rate of £1 per child.[60]

Although it is easy to sympathise with the policy of paying benefit to such organisations, it deserves to be noted that they may already receive a number of actual or notional subsidies from public funds, especially if, as is likely, they enjoy charitable status. The policy underlying family allowances and child benefit turns upon wages being fixed by the labour market rather than by considerations of size of family; and that underlying the special treatment of single-parent families turns up the difficulties attending a single-parent securing wages from work at all. It is hard to see how the first of these policies can have any application at all to a voluntary organisation and the second is far from apt. There is something to be said for rationalising, consciously and outside the social security system, aid to voluntary organisations providing for the care of children.

Priorities as Between Competing "Parents"

Several persons may, according to the above criteria, be prima facie entitled to benefit in respect of the same child. In this event only one is entitled and his priority is determined in accordance with Schedule 2 to the Child Benefit Act. Overall priority is granted to any person to whom an award of benefit has already been made, in preference to a subsequent claimant, provided that the week in question is within three weeks of that claim.[61] Subject to this, priority is conferred on a person

having the child living with him. Where a husband and wife
reside together, the latter is entitled, and in a one-parent family,
the parent is entitled, as is the mother of an illegitimate child.
In other cases, the parties concerned may choose as between
themselves.[62] In default of agreement, the Secretary of State
may decide. Where the contributions of a number of people
are aggregated, the parties must again choose from amongst
themselves and, failing this, the Secretary of State may decide.[63]

It is clear that Schedule 2 is not intended to be resorted
to only in the event of a dispute between the heads of two
families but operates automatically to disentitle anyone who
has a lesser priority.[64] It is possible to disclaim priority under
regulation 14 of the Child Benefit (General) Regulations, but
such a disclaimer is effective only until a further claim is made.

Under EEC Regulations[65] the order of priority in respect
of persons from other Member States working in Britain is altered
to enable the worker here to claim benefit in respect of his
family living in another Member State.

Exclusions

The Act contains a general power to provide for exclusions.
Certain of these are contained in the First Schedule to the Act,
including the exclusion, common to all benefits, of children
"undergoing imprisonment or detention in legal custody."[66] A
child will not be treated as being thus excluded unless he has
been sentenced in respect of a crime to imprisonment or borstal
training or detention under certain Acts,[67] or has received a
comparable sentence elsewhere than in Great Britain. Detention
by reason of mental disorder does not cause him to be excluded
unless he has been serving or was liable to serve a sentence
of detention.[68] In this case, exclusion ceases when the sentence
could, according to the certificate of the appropriate Secretary
of State, soonest have ended.[69]

Certain children in care are also excluded.[70]

In all cases, the exclusion only operates from the ninth consecutive week and even then not if the child actually lived with
or would ordinarily have lived with the claimant during that
week.[71]

Exclusion may also operate in certain other cases, such as

those of persons exempt from income tax under certain legislation; married children in some cases; disabled children entitled
to non-contributory invalidity pension; and, from October 1977,
students on advanced courses in whose case scales of parental
contribution in connection with grants will be adjusted accordingly.[72]

Employed trainees

In marked contrast to the family allowances scheme, apprentices (or, now, employed trainees) are deliberately excluded
from the child benefit scheme, probably on the ground that
the general level of wages paid to trainees has risen sufficiently
to render less justifiable further family subsidy in respect of them.
It is thus no longer possible to train for the job whilst in it[73]
and remain eligible for a child benefit. In most cases trainees
will fail to qualify for benefit on account of not being "in full-
time education by attendance at a recognised educational
establishment." Those who escape this net will nevertheless be
excluded by virtue of paragraph 1 (2) of the First Schedule
"if the education in question is received by the child by virtue
of his employment or of any office held by him." The wording
of the exempting clause is very wide and no help is given as
to its meaning. He must be "employed" or hold "office" by
virtue of which he receives the education. Day release education
for the purposes of acquiring a skill plainly falls within the schedule. A person sponsored through college by another for whom he
intends later to work might or might not be embraced by the
clause. It would seem to depend upon whether he is under
a contractual obligation with the "employer" or not. An analogy
can be drawn with the situation so far as training is concerned
in connection with claims for unemployment benefit.[74]

There is a minimum earnings rule satisfaction of the requirements of which can result in entitlement to benefit for a limited
period. His net earnings (after certain deductions including
matters such as tuition fees, books, etc.[75]) must be nil for a period
of not less than six months. It should be remembered that
even if all these conditions are satisfied, the other, general, ones
remain, *i.e.* he must be receiving full-time education in a recognised educational establishment.

A deduction of the cost of returning home for a mid-day meal (though not of the meal itself) was allowed as a deductible expense in *R(F) 4/63*. In *R1/64 (FA)*, however, the Northern Ireland Commissioner declined to follow suit taking the preferable view that such an expense is not necessary but merely a matter of personal convenience. Under the new scheme, there appears to be no requirement that the expenditure, to be allowable, should be reasonable, nor that it should necessarily be incurred in connection with the receipt of the education.[76] The regulations contemplate reimbursement by the employer of expenses incurred by him for the specified purposes and it seems to be assumed that an employer would not reimburse expenses for non-work purposes.[77]

There are transitional provisions affecting families entitled to family allowances under the old scheme in respect of apprentices. Their entitlement to the same rate of benefit under the new scheme continues for up to three years continuously. Title to benefit is lost if the apprenticeship is broken; it cannot be revived.[78] An apprentice who was an eldest child never did qualify for family allowances therefore no entitlement is carried over. Child benefit would be payable at the higher rate of £1·50 for the second child in such a case. Entitlement also ceases within the 3-year period when the apprentice reaches the age of 19 years.

The Family Allowances Act definition of an "apprentice" was "a person undergoing full-time training for any trade, business or profession, office employment or vocation" and not in receipt of net earning exceeding £2 per week. This definition means that status as an apprentice for benefit purposes may be lost even though the child continues to be an "apprentice" in common parlance,[79] as, for example, by an increase in net earnings which might result simply from a decrease in deductible expenses without any increase in gross earnings.[80]

Persons to whom Benefits are Payable

Benefits belong to the wife in a two-parent family and the sole parent in a one-parent family.[81] The husband has no right as such to receive payment of benefit.[82] However, arrangements may be made whereby payment may be made to the husband.[83] There are three circumstances in which payment may be made to a third party other than on death.[84] These are (1) where such payment is requested by the person entitled; (2) where it is necessary for the protection of that person or a child; and (3) where a person who would otherwise have been entitled to receive the benefit is absent from Great Britain.[85] In any case where a person entitled is unable to act, the Secretary of State may nominate a person over 18 years of age to receive payment on that person's behalf.

Benefit is inalienable.[86] Attempts to assign are void, although the effectiveness of voidance as a sanction may be doubted. Amongst small-time moneylenders, the allowance book is a common and very good security. Certainly, section 12 allows a borrower to cock a legal snook at the lender, but all this means is that if the borrower sued for the return of the book, the moneylender would have no defence, and the idea of litigation in this situation is laughable.[87] And if the borrower simply refuses to repay the debt, the moneylender just cashes the allowance. It might make a difference if a fine were payable by anyone lending on the security of an allowance book. It might soon become undesirable as a security.

Section 12 (1) also provides that on the bankruptcy of a person by whom benefit is receivable, no rights in benefit shall pass to any trustee etc. Unlike the position under the Family Allowances and Social Security Acts, there is no provision to the effect that benefit is not to be included in the bankrupt's means for the purposes of section 5 of the Debtors Act 1952. In *Re P. F. and M. L. E., Bankrupts*[88] a husband and wife were adjudicated bankrupt. The wife had to her credit in a bank money consisting, *inter alia*, of sums received by way of family allowances. It was ordered that such money should be held in trust for the children free from any claims arising out of the wife's adjudication. "... section 1 of the former Act provides for the payment of an allowance which is declared to be 'for the benefit of the family as a whole.' That phrase points the very purpose of the Act.... To put it another way, the administration of the allowance is committed to the household, but it is so committed for the benefit of the family as a whole."[89] Child benefit on the other hand is not expressed to be "for the family as a whole" and the same reasoning would not be available in the case of the child benefit.

A corollary of this, so far as divorce is concerned, is seen in *Powell* v. *Powell* ([1951] P. 257). The allowances can apparently be treated as part of the wife's income for purposes of calculating what would be an appropriate sum for maintenance in divorce, but should not be treated as part of the husband's contribution to household income (for purposes of assigning a proportion, usually one-third, of the total income to the wife). Jenkins L.J. was in favour of either treating it as part of the wife's income or leaving it out of account altogether and treating it merely as a matter to be borne in mind in considering what provision should be made for children. Lord Evershed M.R. preferred not to take it into account at all.

Claims and Payments

The period of entitlement under the Child Benefit Act is a week, *i.e.* a period of seven days beginning with a Monday. In this, it differs from the family allowances scheme under which allowances were payable for a continuing period until a lapse of entitlement. Obviously, this does not mean that a fresh claim must be submitted every week, but a person in receipt of benefit for any period is under an obligation to inform the Secretary of State of any circumstances which he might "reasonably be expected to know might affect the right to benefit" and a failure to do so is a summary offence, punishable by three months' imprisonment and/or a fine of up to £50 (the maximum permitted under the enabling legislation).[90] The requirement of "reasonableness" is a new development.[91]

Proper claim is a condition of entitlement and claims made more than 52 weeks after the week in respect of which they are made are out of time.[92] Prospective claims are allowed if the determining authorities are satisfied that the conditions of entitlement will be met within 56 days. If benefit has actually been paid (as opposed to merely awarded) to another person, no subsequent claim in respect of the same period can be entertained unless it is required to be repaid by that person without appeal, or in fact voluntarily repaid by him.

The right to payment of benefit is extinguished if payment is not sought within 12 months although the time limit can be extended where there was good cause for delay.[93] Benefit wrongly paid is to be treated in the same way as other social security benefits wrongly paid[94] and overpaid benefit may be recovered by deduction from other social security benefits.[95] Repayment of benefit is not required where due care and diligence to avoid overpayment has been exercised[96] but where arrangements have been made to pay benefit to a person other than the one entitled, the exercise of due diligence etc. by the one will not exonerate the other.

Section 11 of the Child Benefit Act makes it an offence punishable by three months' imprisonment and/or a £50 fine knowingly to make any false statement or false representation or to produce or furnish or cause to be produced or furnished any information which is known to be false in a material particular. That this control functions with less than perfect efficiency is well illustrated by *R.* v. *Curr*[97] where a moneylender who received allowance books as security and sent women friends to cash the orders was charged with soliciting women to commit the above offence. He was acquitted. He could only be guilty of soliciting if the women knew the allowances to be not properly receivable by them and this had not been established. Nor was it conspiracy for the women again required knowledge that the allowances were not properly receivable by them. The decision is perhaps unfortunate in its findings of fact since instructions on the books clearly indicate who is and who is not entitled to receive allowances and one shares Fenton Atkinson J.'s expressed regret at the conclusion he felt compelled to arrive at.

The case is also interesting as regards the significance of "false representation" since one of the charges concerned obtaining property by falsely pretending that payment was received for the benefit of the person named in the order book. This conviction was quashed on the ground that it was not established that the allowances were not in fact received by the accused for the benefit of the beneficiary. This depended upon the relationship between the accused and the beneficiaries—on whether there was an attempted assignment or merely an authority to collect the allowances.

Proceedings under the Act must be instituted within 12 months of the commission of the crime[98] although this bar can be avoided simply by charging the offender with common law conspiracy. As under the social security legislation, a husband

and wife are competent to give evidence against each other
but cannot be compelled to do so, nor to disclose any com-
munication passing between them during marriage.[99]

Nationality, Presence, Residence

There is no longer any requirement of a nationality link as
there was under the family allowances scheme.[1] Such requirements as there are relate solely to presence and residence. The
general rule is that a person may not receive child benefit in
respect of a child unless that child is present during the week
in question and either he or one of his parents has been present
in Great Britain for a total of six months during the previous year.[2] Absences of less than 26 weeks may be ignored
if intended at the outset to be temporary and remaining
throughout temporary. If the absence is not intended to be
temporary at the outset, the right to benefit is lost immediately
upon its commencement.[3] This was the position in *R(F) 3/64*,
where the claimant and her husband lived in Great Britain
with their four children until November 2, 1962, when the
parents and two children left for Uganda in order that the father
could take up work. Two children were left at school in
England and the father's work would involve him in returning
to Great Britain from time to time (including a six months'
stay in barrister's chambers). Whilst in Great Britain, he intended to visit the children left at school. It was thus argued
that there was dual residence and that the qualification for allowances would be retained provided that six months' absence was
avoided. Had the question been one of "residence" the claim
might well have succeeded.[4] However, ". . . the question is not
whether the claimant's husband resides in Uganda or Great
Britain or both, nor even whether he has a residence in Great
Britain, nor indeed, whether his absence is temporary. The question is *whether the absence was 'for a purpose other than temporary
purpose'* . . . his purpose in this case was . . . to live and earn
his living in Uganda, his home country, in some branch of the
law . . . it is quite impossible to say that his purpose was a
temporary purpose."

The requirement of presence is similarly waived in the case
of the child where his absence was intended to be temporary

from the outset and is either limited to 26 weeks or is due to his receiving full-time education by attendance at a recognised educational establishment and is limited to 156 weeks. It is also waived where the absence is for the "specific purpose of being treated for illness or disability of mind or body" in which case the period of absence permissible is in the discretion of the Secretary of State.[5] A child born to the mother abroad will not ordinarily become resident when first present unless at birth the mother's absence was temporary.[6]

Where the requirements relating to the child are satisfied, the second condition relating to the person entitled is also waived, so that nothing more is required of him than his actual presence in Great Britain. There are three further circumstances where this will suffice. First, when his spouse, with whom he resides, satisfies section 13(3)(b) of the Child Benefit Act; secondly, where he is an employed or self-employed earner paying Class I or II contributions during the six months prior to the relevant week and likely to be in Great Britain for six months thereafter; thirdly where he is actually present in Great Britain and likely to be so for six months and either was entitled or had a spouse who was entitled to child benefit for at least one week during the preceding year. Temporary absences of up to 28 days may be ignored in the first and third cases.[7]

The second qualification relating to children and their parents has also been considerably modified and is regarded as having been satisfied:

(i) where the child is in fact in Great Britain and one of his parents satisfies section 13(3)(b) of the Child Benefit Act;

(ii) where title to guardian's allowance is capable of vesting in a person were he entitled to benefit and the child is in Great Britain; and

(iii) where the child is in fact in Great Britain but is not residing with his parents, but living with someone else who satisfies the conditions and is likely to be doing so permanently.

There are additional provisions dealing with special categories of persons.

Reciprocal Arrangements

The Child Benefit Act does not extend to Northern Ireland but similar measures have been introduced into Northern

Ireland by the Child Benefit (Northern Ireland) Order 1975.[8]
Provision is made for reciprocal arrengements.[9]

For Great Britain, reciprocal arrangements with other states
are authorised under section 5 of the Child Benefit Act and
by the Child Benefit (Residence and Persons Abroad) Regulations which continue arrangements made under the family
allowances scheme to child benefit. The reciprocal arrangements
thus continued applied to 11 countries and were scheduled to
the regulations.[10]

Europe

Under Council Regulation 1408/71, a person from another
Community Member State, working in Great Britain, is entitled
to family benefits in respect of his family residing elsewhere.
Prior employment in another Member State is treated as
equivalent to presence in Great Britain for the purpose of any
residential qualifications.[11] To prevent overlapping of benefit
his spouse is disentitled to any allowance to which she might
have been entitled in her own state. This is subject to one
exception—the right of the worker and not that of his spouse
is suspended if his spouse "exercises a professional or trade
activity," *i.e.* is gainfully employed.[12]

The effect of the regulation on the order of priority under
the Child Benefit Act is unclear. By virtue of Schedule 2, priority
is conferred on the wife in a two-parent family and not on
the husband (although payment may be made to him).[13] The
Commissioner in *R(F)* *1/76* assumes that the regulation reverses
the order of priority so as to enable the husband to claim allowance "for himself or on behalf of his wife" although, in the event,
such a finding was unnecessary to the decision. It is, however,
difficult to see how, in a subsequent case, a different result might
be arrived at. In *R(F)* *1/76* a husband and wife, citizens of
the Republic of Ireland, drew allowance for their three children
whilst residing in this country. In 1967 the wife, together with
the children, returned to Ireland where her fourth child was
born. Before leaving, she handed in her allowance book but
subsequently her husband, prompted by the Department of
Health and Social Security, drew allowances for his children
and continued to do so until 1973 when it was discovered

through the Irish authorities that the children had been absent for six years. The Secretary of State sought repayment of the allowances dating back to the date on which the absence had ceased to be temporary.[14] It was argued *inter alia* that even though the husband was not entitled to family allowances under the Family Allowances Act, he was so entitled under the European legislation. The claim was rejected on the grounds that his wife was exercising "a professional or trade activity" in 1973 within the meaning of Article 10 (1) and that therefore his title to benefit under the Regulation had been suspended.

European legislation is at present aimed at co-ordinating the various systems of the Member States. In the preamble to Council regulation 1408/71, it is stated that "it would be preferable to lay down rules common to all the member states and efforts should continue to this end," *i.e.* harmonisation. There is a long way to go before that goal is reached.

B. FAMILY INCOMES SUPPLEMENT[15]

It is clear that, at its present level, the child benefit scheme has a limited effect as a weapon against family poverty and that in some cases further state provision is needed. In theory, it is desirable to direct assistance to areas of most need. This is the principal goal of the supplementary benefit and family incomes supplement schemes, both of which are confined in their operation to low-income groups. The first is available where the head of the family is not in full-time work and is a general, not a family, benefit scheme, being payable to individuals in need. The second is available to a head of a family in work. In practice, means-tested support falls short of its objective. Many people apparently entitled to such support simply fail to claim for a variety of complex reasons. These are too deep-rooted to be eradicated merely by instituting a large-scale publicity campaign.[16] In the initial stages of the family incomes supplement scheme, a take-up level of at least 85 per cent. was anticipated.[17] Yet despite intensive advertising, the level has never exceeded 75 per cent.[18] Furthermore, in many cases, the progressive withdrawal of means-tested benefits by reason of increased earnings effectively wipes out any advantage to be gained from such a rise, thus preventing many low-income families from ever improving their position. It is against this background that we must examine the family incomes supplement scheme.

Family incomes supplement is specifically designed to supplement the earnings of low-income families. "It is to help a family that is not entitled to supplementary benefits to improve its income where its income at the moment is below supplementary benefit level."[19] It is therefore confined to families where the head of the family is in remunerative full-time work.[20] The Act of 1970 provides for the payment of a weekly income supplement of one-half of the difference between the resources of the family and the prescribed amounts where the former falls short of the latter.[21]

There are a number of conditions which must be satisfied before the supplement is payable. First, as already stated, the head of the family must be engaged and normally engaged in remunerative full-time work. A family consists of a man or a single woman at work plus, if a man, his wife or cohabitant and any children maintained by them both.[22] In the case of a two-parent family (*i.e.* a family with two adults) it must be the man who works. It is not sufficient if it is merely the woman, although in the latter case supplementary benefits may be available provided her earnings fall within the permitted levels.

It should be noted that the Act imposes two distinct requirements. The head of the family must be actually engaged in remunerative full-time work at the time he submits his claim *and* he must normally be so engaged. Under the regulations[23] work is treated as being "full-time" if it is over 30 hours per week. No attempt is made to define "remunerative" and it is assumed that it has a similar meaning to that of "gainful" in "gainful employment" covering both employed and self-employed persons.[24] This is less flexible than the supplementary benefit scheme were no definition of "full-time" is given, the intention being to leave people free to adjust their hours so as to bring themselves within whichever scheme they prefer. It should be remembered, however, that supplementary benefit is not payable to a person who is "voluntarily unemployed."[25]

Family incomes supplement is available only where there are children "whose requirements are provided for in whole or in part" by either member of the family.[26] For this purpose, a person is treated as a child if he is under 16 years of age, or is receiving full-time instruction at a school.[27] It was originally the intention of the Government to confine the payment of the supplement to parents. Having regard to the purpose of the scheme, *i.e.* to assist earners having responsibility for a child, it is clearly wrong so to confine it and it is now payable to any person caring for a child.[28] This is subject to one exception in the case of children boarded out.[29]

Regulations provide for the situation where a child falls into more than one family. In this event, the parties may choose among themselves which of them shall receive the supplement and, if agreement cannot be reached, the decision will be made by the Secretary of State.[30]

The resources of the family may not exceed the prescribed limit stipulated in the Act and regulations. This currently stands at £41·50 per week for a one-child family and is raised by £3·50 for each additional child.[31] Resources comprise the aggregate of normal gross income of all the family, although regulations may exempt a child's income in certain circumstances.[32] There is no capital limit. Regulations also fix the method of calculating "gross income."[33] Earnings are averaged over a five-week period (or, if payment is monthly, over a two-month period) immediately prior to the date of claim and entitlement calculated accordingly. Where this period would not yield a fair assessment because, for example, of abnormally long or short hours having been worked during it, or because of abnormal fluctuations in earnings, the determining authorities may select another, more appropriate, period.[34] Salary, wages or fees paid for a limited fixed period must also be taken into account as must the net profits of a business or any other income. In this case, the method of assessing a normal weekly income is left to the determining authorities.[35] Certain disregards are permitted.[36]

The maximum supplement paid under the scheme is £8·50 for a one-child family plus an additional 50p for the second and subsequent children. Thus a one-child family with a reckonable income of up to £24·50 per week would qualify for a maximum entitlement (£27·00 for a two-child, £34·00 for a four-child family, etc.). Since no account is taken of rent, it is possible for a family to be in receipt of the supplement and yet remain below the poverty line as determined by supplementary benefits criteria.

A family is required to be "ordinarily resident" in the United Kingdom with at least one adult member resident in Great Britain.[37] These qualifications will not be regarded as satisfied, however, if any member of the family falls within the Northern Ireland scheme.[38]

The Supplementary Benefits Commission[39] is charged with the administration of the scheme.[40] There is a right of appeal to a Supplementary Benefit Appeal Tribunal[41] but very few appeals are successful.[42] Provision is also made for the Commission to review its original determination and the review decision is similarly subject to appeal. Benefit may be suspended pending review.[43]

Initial claims must be made jointly, other than in the case of families headed by a single woman, unless the Secretary of State is satisfied that such a requirement is unreasonable.[44] Generally, there is no right to benefit for any period prior to the date of claim, but a claim may be back-dated for three months if the delay is not the fault of the claimant. A renewed claim, on the other hand, may be made within four weeks before or after the relevant date.

Benefit commences on the Tuesday following the making of a successful claim[45] and once entitlement is established it will usually continue uninterrupted for 52 weeks notwithstanding a change in circumstances (including the death of or a change in the family of the recipient).[46] The period of entitlement may be reduced from a year to not less than four weeks where the determining authorities are clear that supplement at least at some level should be paid but are uncertain as to at what rate above that level it should be paid.[47] Entitlement to benefit is extinguished after 12 months unless a written request for payment is submitted and if it is submitted after the end of that period there must be good cause for the delay.[48]

There is one particular case where a change of circumstances is relevant. This is designed to prevent duplication of benefit. Where one party has to resort to supplementary benefits because of the refusal or neglect of the other party to maintain his family, the supplement ceases to be payable to the latter.[49] Subject to this, the Act contains no provision for disqualification, *e.g.* on grounds of unreasonable refusal to take suitable higher-paid employment, such as are to be found in other areas of social security law.

Sums wrongly paid can be recovered if the recipient cannot satisfy the determining authorities that he has disclosed all material facts. There appears to be no time limit within which such action must be taken and it must cause some disquiet that the burden of proving his "innocence" is thrust upon the recipient.[50] Criminal proceedings may be taken against a person who knowingly makes a false statement or representation or produces information which he knows to be false in a material particular. There is a maximum penalty of three months' imprisonment and/or a £100 fine.

The family incomes supplement scheme accounts for a small proportion of total social security outgo accounting for some £13 million in 1975–76.[51] In its first full year (1971) the supplement reached more than 80,000 families but, after touching a peak of more than 180,000 families in 1972 declined rapidly, benefiting less than 60,000 by 1975,[52] probably due to the fact that rates of supplement fell far behind wage inflation. The effect of child benefit on the numbers involved has yet to be assessed. A recipient of the supplement is automatically eligible for a number of other benefits, *e.g.* remission of dental and optical charges, free prescriptions, free milk and vitamins for children under 16 and expectant mothers, free school meals, refund of fares for hospital treatment and, under section 1 (6) of the Legal Aid Act 1974, free legal advice provided disposable capital is not in excess of £250.

C. EDUCATION MAINTENANCE ALLOWANCES

Under the Education Act 1944[53] local education authorities are empowered to pay any fees, allowances and other expenses with a view to "enabling pupils to take advantage without hardship to themselves or to their parents of any educational facilities available to them."

Education maintenance allowances are confined to persons over minimum school leaving age. The original policy was merely to enable children of low-income families to continue at school.

The allowances were "not intended to compensate parents for loss of earnings by their children."[54]

Since the Local Government Act 1958, the allowances have been administered exclusively by local education authorities; the Department of Education and Science accepts no responsibility for them. The grants are discretionary and vary considerably from area to area, both as to the amount and the numbers of allowances paid. This lack of uniformity and the obvious discrepancy between the allowances and student grants[55] has been the subject of much recent criticism, though it is by no means entirely unprecedented.[56] In 1974 it was recommended that the scheme be put on a mandatory basis with a standard rate of allowance but this has been rejected by the Government in the belief that the question "... can be studied effectively only in the wider context of family support through the social services.... The starting point would be that maintenance (as opposed to any special educational expenses) of children under 19 in full-time education and living with their families is part of the maintenance of the family as a whole for which public support, if it is needed, is given through the social security system."[57]

Information available on the operation of the scheme is minimal. In 1975/76 it was estimated that £1,475,000 was spent by local authorities, the average annual payment being £125. The most recent estimate of the numbers in payment is 6,880.[58]

D. THE SPECIAL POSITION OF ONE-PARENT FAMILIES

Until the introduction in 1976 of child interim benefit, no special provision was made within the social security system, for one-parent families other than those of widows. Of these alone could it be said that they bore no "blame" for the termination of the marriage (not, one might point out, entirely self-evident) and therefore posed no threat to that institution. The needs of other lone parents were subordinated to the overriding requirement that the integrity of marriage be preserved.[59]

Beveridge had proposed the institution of a "separation benefit" to the "innocent" wife, but this was rejected in the subsequent White Paper and general, means-tested, benefits remained, as before, the only form of state-support available in such cases. Some 20 years later, "the old tariff of blame which pitied widows but attached varying degrees of moral delinquency to divorced or separated women or to unmarried mothers is becoming irrelevant in the face of the imperative recognition that what chiefly matters in such circumstances is to assist and protect dependent children, all of whom ought to be treated alike irrespective of their mother's circumstance."[60]

The publication of the report of the Finer Committee "on the problems of one-parent families"[61] in 1974 focused attention on the plight of such families. An analysis of the 1971 Census figures by the Statistics and Research Division of the Department of Health and Social Security indicated that one in every 10 families with dependent children were one-parent families. Most of these were women of whom about half were dependent upon supplementary benefit. The Committee concluded that the evidence "overwhelmingly confirmed the general impression of financial hardship amongst one-parent families."[62] The principal reasons for this hardship were: the inability of recipients of supplementary benefits to improve their position by supplementing their entitlement by part-time work without a corresponding reduction in benefit (where earnings exceeded a low level of disregard)[63]; low earnings due to the disparity in wage levels between men and women, and reduced availability on account of family commitments; the inadequacy of maintenance payments as a regular source of income. To meet these difficulties, the Finer Committee recommended the creation of a non-contributory social security benefit for one-parent families with the "aim of guaranteeing to lone parents a sufficient level of maintenance to offer them a real choice between working and staying at home to look after the children without inequity to low-income two-parent families."[64] This was to be known as a guaranteed maintenance allowance. It was to be paid at a higher rate than supplementary benefits and was to be taxed for the purpose of gaining entry into the tax-credit scheme which was then proposed but which is presently defunct. The allowance was to be available only to those who qualified on the grounds of income and status. It was to be divided into two distinct portions, an adult portion and a child portion. The latter was to remain unaffected by any change in income. The former, on the other hand, was to be means-related but it was not to be entirely extinguished until gross earnings reached average male earnings. Therefore it was to be reduced by half the difference between earnings (less certain disregards including expenses incurred in child care) and the prescribed limit (this being fixed as the same level as the earnings disregard under the supplementary benefit scheme). The allowance was to be payable only to a lone parent. Like widow's benefit, it was to cease on remarriage or cohabitation. A minimum qualifying period of three months was to be imposed where no formal evidence of separation, *e.g.* a court order, was available. Benefit was to be payable for a similar period notwithstanding any change in circumstances save that of remarriage. The scheme was to be administered independently of the Supplementary Benefits Commission, by post.

The recommendations of the Finer Committee have been rejected by the government primarily because they substitute one means-tested benefit for another at excessive administrative cost.[65] Instead, family allowances for the first child in the form of child interim benefit was introduced a year in advance of the full child benefit scheme and an additional 50p premium is payable under the latter.[66] The creation of an entirely new benefit designed to meet the needs of one-parent families has been ruled out, at least for the immediate future, and for many such families, supplementary benefits will remain the primary source of income.[67]

CHAPTER 12

SUPPLEMENTARY BENEFITS

1. INTRODUCTION

"CONDITIONS may arise where this outer wall (social insurance) breaks down or has gaps and the government, on its different levels, intervenes to restore needy persons to the minimum standard considered as decent. The legislative programs by which this public aid is accomplished are usually designated by the generic term *Public Assistance*."[1]

Public assistance (in the United Kingdom called national assistance from 1948 to 1965 and supplementary benefits since this latter date) remains a fundamental part of the social security system. It is fundamental in the sense that it is the haven of last resort for the needy; in that more persons benefit from it than from any other social security benefit; and it is also, historically, the first scheme to appear on the scene, indeed the only scheme for virtually three centuries from the end of the sixteenth, though increased national wealth and the growth of social work as a profession are both necessary conditions of its present scope and effectiveness.

The Poor Law

The poor law is the historical precursor of the modern scheme. In its inception, it was a mixture of employment and social security law, being aimed at both finding and making work for those who could work and providing relief for those who could not. The process starts with legislation applying to the City of London in 1547 (extended in 1598 and 1601) to urban corporations in 1575 and to rural parishes in 1598 (being made permanent in 1601).[2]

Right from the start, two defects were built into the poor law system. One plagued it throughout its life until it was replaced by modern national assistance; the other is still present. The

first was making the cost of relief a charge upon the parish
with the result that in badly depressed areas it was never
possible to finance the scheme at an adequate level.[3] This vice
appeared in its most extreme form in the Irish famine in 1847.
The ensuing century witnessed a series of attempts to distribute
the burden more evenly, an aim only finally achieved in 1948.

The second defect was confusion between the lack of willingness and the lack of opportunity to work. The early legislation
did distinguish—it contemplated workhouses for those willing
to work and houses of correction for those presumed not to be
willing. The two institutions, however, became confused with the
result that all beneficiaries of the poor law, even if willing to
or disabled from working, became stigmatised as idle, work-shy
social parasites. "Oliver Twist had to suffer from the fundamental confusion that dogged the whole history of the English
poor-law. The discipline suited to the able-bodied pauper was
extended to the young and old."[4] Deterrence from a presumed
laziness became a cardinal objective of social policy, colouring
poor law administration and causing the confession of need to
be equated to the profession of vice.

Although successive attempts have been made to cure this
defect, notably that of 1966, clearly the most successful so far,
there still remain on the one hand, a diffuse public demand for
the pursuit of a deterrent policy in administration, and on the
other hand, a reluctance on the part of some persons to claim
benefits to which they are clearly entitled.

Beveridge

Beveridge entered upon the scene at a time when the poor law
and public assistance were highly unpopular in some quarters.
The standard of living which they offered was extremely low.
As a matter of policy, they were administered in a humiliating
manner in order to discourage anyone from enjoying benefits
unless he was utterly desperate to do so. Nevertheless, Beveridge
advocated the substantial continuation of public assistance,
though it was to be rationalised, centralised and improved in
some respects, in the form of "national assistance" and the
National Assistance Act 1948 resulted.

Beveridge did not advocate a continuation of the policy of

deterrence, but he clearly contemplated that the scheme would be unattractive. It was—all the old objections to public assistance were carried over. The result was that amongst those deterred from availing themselves of benefits were those above-mentioned, people, especially old people, genuinely in desperate need, but repelled by the idea of being characterised as "paupers" and receiving state "charity." The Ministry of Social Security Act 1966 (now codified as the Supplementary Benefits Act 1976) sought to remedy this evil.

Supplementary benefits, as provided for by the 1976 Act, do *not* mark a radical departure from the substance of the 1948 scheme. The 1966 scheme marked rather "a change as much in attitude as in purely legal entitlement."[5] The 1966 scheme's main objective was, in fact, not to change the law so much as to remove the psychological barriers to prospective beneficiaries by verbal and administrative devices. The scheme was no longer to be administered by a separate government department from the rest of social security—all would be handled by a single department, coming into line with Beveridge after 23 years. One's prospect of receiving benefit is now in some cases called a "right," a fact emphasised by the accompanying publicity, though the same conditions have to be satisfied as had to be under the 1948 scheme in order to persuade the old National Assistance Board to exercise its "discretion." The aim is now to administer all aspects of the social security system on the same premises, so that a prospective beneficiary is more assured of receiving the help he needs and is at the same time spared the public demonstration of his need. Prior to 1966, the number of beneficiaries *per annum* averaged less than two million. Immediately after, it rose to over two and a half million and now stands at about $4\frac{1}{2}$ million, 8 per cent. of the total population, accounting for 2·3 per cent. of public expenditure.

Events since Beveridge have, however, brought about some confusion of policy. Under Beveridge, both insurance and assistance were aimed at providing "subsistence," the only distinguishing feature of the latter being that assistance should be "given always subject to proof of needs and examination of means" for "it must be felt to be something less desirable than insurance benefit; otherwise the insured person gets nothing for his contributions."[6] One wonders how substantial the distinc-

tion was even in 1942—whether it was worth the "premiums"
just to secure a different method of administration.

The Scheme Today

The present position really is rather ludicrous. In cases of need,
the insured person does now get nothing at all for his contributions in very many cases, for supplementary benefit levels,
including a rent allowance, will normally be substantially higher
than national insurance benefit levels and most distinctions in
administration were eroded by the 1966 Act. Only the means-
test remains as an important distinguishing feature of the supplementary benefits scheme and even this is administered as pain-
lessly as possible in most cases. Even in this respect, anomaly
is further heightened by the fact that most national insurance
benefit levels are not justifiable on strict actuarial principles
by reference to the contributions which insured persons pay. A
substantial part of national insurance fund income is derived
from contributions by employers and by the Exchequer. Yet
there is no means-test for entitlement to that element in benefits
which is referable to either of these sources.

What Beveridge originally contemplated was that the numbers
of persons drawing national assistance would diminish over the
post-War years, settling down eventually to being a very minor
part of the social security set up, functioning as a safety net
for the odd few who failed, for some reason or another, to secure
protection from national insurance.[7] The opposite has happened.
There has been a retreat from social insurance. National
insurance contributions are now less a premium against specific
risks and more a regressive form of taxation. Supplementary
benefits are coming more and more to be a chief mechanism
for ensuring that adequate standards are reached, albeit in most
cases by topping up income from other sources, including national
insurance benefits. The supplementary benefits scheme can fairly
be viewed as being the basic social security scheme (as it was
in the days of the poor law though with the objectionable
features of that institution) rather than, as Beveridge contemplated, an ancillary and unimportant feature. The overwhelming
majority of people are, as Beveridge contemplated, covered by
insurance against the major risks (unemployment, sickness, old

age, etc.); yet few people reach subsistence level without resort to some other source of income, and in a vast number of cases this alternative source is supplementary benefits in one form or another. Thus, in 1975 more than half of the $4\frac{1}{2}$ million supplementary beneficiaries were pensioners, the overwhelming majority of whom were also in receipt of retirement pensions. Just under half of all registered unemployed persons received supplementary allowances; for most of these, this formed the exclusive source of assistance. 40 per cent. of all one-parent families relied on supplementary benefits, a third of these exclusively, and of the 242,000 sick and disabled supplementary beneficiaries, only 32 per cent. received other social security benefits.[8]

It must be emphasised that it is totally erroneous to assume that persons in receipt of national insurance but not supplementary benefit payments are provided with a subsistence income by national insurance. In the overwhelming majority of these cases, national insurance payments by themselves would be inadequate for this purpose. It is only by virtue of other, private, sources of income, such as savings and sick-pay, that subsistence is reached, if at all. It is therefore true to say that the supplementary benefits scheme is the only one which ensures a subsistence level of income and that the national insurance scheme functions only to contribute to this end.

2. Sources of Supplementary Benefits Law

As with the child benefit and national insurance schemes, the basic sources are to be found in public documents—Acts of Parliament and regulations made under them. The chief source is the Supplementary Benefit Act 1976, a consolidating statute (hereinafter referred to as "the 1976 Act") which provides a flexible legislative framework for the operation of the scheme.

One's "right" to supplementary benefits, or one's prospect of benefiting from an exercise of discretion to award benefits, depends in large part on the application of rules. Not all these rules are, however, legislation in a formal sense—some are merely internal departmental rules more analogous to instructions issued by an employer to his employee than to general law. Although the difference between the two types of rule may be significant when, as very rarely happens, supplementary benefit decisions reach the courts of law, in the vast majority of cases they discharge the same substantial function—they constitute the body of rules which is applied indiscriminately to the facts of the given case by the "front-line" administrator making the initial decision. The chief distinction between the two types of rule is one of form. Rules given formal legislative effect are published; internal rules are, for the most part, not published. For this reason, a large part of the body of rules which, in practice, actually determines how supplementary benefits are distributed, is inaccessible. An award of benefit may well depend upon the determination of one of the Commission's officers that there exists a "need" (which may require to be "exceptional" or "urgent") and he may make that determination according to internal rules structuring the manner in which the Commission's "discretion" is to be exercised.

Discretion is not, of course, peculiar to supplementary benefits law. In other areas, settled practices grow up as to how such discretions are to be exercised in a "normal" case and the expectation is created, and usually fulfilled, that the discretion will be exercised in a fair, judicial manner.[9] Information about such practices has a three-fold relevance for prospective beneficiaries. In the first place, it may enable purposeful and reliable advice to be given as to the advisability of pressing a claim or appealing against a rejected one. Secondly, it offers a check as to the extent to which the scheme is achieving justice in the sense of treating like cases alike. Thirdly, the practices may be improper and it is in the public interest that it should be possible to curb improper practices.

That "rules" of administration of this type do exist and are applied in the area of supplementary benefits is admitted. From the little that we know of them, most of them seem to originate in practice directives from the Commission to inferior officials, some of them in consequence of decisions of the appeal tribunals. The most important of these directives constitute the "A Code" which, however, is available only to the staff of the Commission and not to the public. The *Handbook* itself is a publication of those parts of the "A Code" which the Commission thinks it desirable to make available to the public. It is not, and does not purport to be, a comprehensive statement of the law.

No adequate reasons have ever been offered for the refusal to publish the "A Code" and other internal rules. They are said to be "largely unintelligible to the lay reader"[10] and both detailed and subject to frequent modification,[11] criticisms equally apt in the case of most modern legislation. Yet the Commission's rules are withheld from professional advisers. They are said to concern internal procedure which, however, is crucially ambiguous. If "internal procedure" referred only to processes which had no bearing on claimants the point would be a valid one, but there is every reason to suppose that it refers to the processes whereby claims are determined and notified. It is claimed that "no bureaucracy can be expected to publish everything it needs to tell its staff." Yet arguments in favour of the publication of the "A Code" do not go this far and admit the case for withholding publication of some rules, *e.g.* those relating to the prevention and control of fraud, publication of which would be self-defeating. What is not admitted is that everything withheld falls into these two narrow categories. It is clearly the case that rules governing the determination of claims and having nothing to do with fraud are withheld. It seems all too likely that the Commission wishes to avoid some of the consequences of fuller publication. These might well include criticism of the Commission's procedures and an increasing practice of challenging the Commission's decisions by reference to its own internal rules, at present *ex hypothesi* impossible.

The Commission argues that simplification and not publication is what is required. If, by this, it is meant that the existing rules are unnecessarily complex and that publication of them would not improve the quality of decision-making then, obviously, simplification is needed. But, even if it were true that publication would not help, one is still at a loss to understand why the rules should be classified and why the threat of prosecution under the Official Secrets Acts should be held over the head of a claimant who wishes to consult the rules—it is not a crime, surely, to waste one's time.

One is forced to conclude that the interest chiefly served by the insistence on keeping the rules secret is administrative convenience. This is certainly a legitimate interest, but it ought not to be preferred to the primary objective of the scheme, which is abatement of need. It is the fear that non-publication effects exactly this preference which motivates the demand for publication. It is hard to see how else that fear can be abated.

This would not be so bad if these administrative rules broke the surface, as in most other areas they do, as a result of judicial or quasi-judicial consideration of them. Supplementary Benefit Appeal Tribunals are not, however, open to the public; nor are reports of their proceedings systematically or officially published. Tribunals may withhold the identity of their members and prohibit the use of tape-recorders, powers which the Council on Tribunals thinks it desirable they should retain; though no objection is taken to the compiling of notes of a hearing; and it is even accepted that an appellant may use such notes in order to obtain publicity for a claim.[12] The ostensible reason for this secrecy is to protect claimants from the fear of revelation of their personal circumstances which, if it happened, might deter potential beneficiaries from claiming or appealing. In other areas of social security law, however, this same objective is achieved consistently with publication of reports of tribunal decisions simply by withholding the identity of claimants in the reports. In the area of supplementary benefits, this is not done. There is not even provision for the publication of reports with the consent of the claimant, though recent regulations have allowed individuals to attend for bona fide research purposes with the claimant's and the chairman's consent.

Again, it is not clear what interest is served by the rigorous insistence on privacy of tribunal proceedings. One writer[13] has it that "the official who is afraid of the Press is usually either mistaken or inefficient, or has something to hide" and echoes the House of Lords[14] in urging publicity for tribunal proceedings. The Franks Committee did endorse the practice of privacy, but stated no case for excluding publicity which would not be satisfactorily answered by anonymity. There seems, in short, to be no good published reason why, as a general rule, some reporting of proceedings should not be permitted, as is done elsewhere. After all, decisions are occasionally appealed to higher courts and reports of proceedings published in full, even to identification of parties in some cases. Furthermore, not all supplementary benefits litigation goes to the tribunals. Some matters[15] are heard by magistrates and appealed to higher courts with full publicity.

By contrast, it has been alleged and seems credible, that evil does result from non-publication of reports. Lynes[16] states that in a number of instances tribunals have deliberately failed to follow decisions and cites the case of payment of travelling expenses for wives on benefit wishing to visit husbands in prison. Titmus has argued that the imposition of a rigorous system of precedent would destroy the flexibility of the scheme and turn it into a playground for lawyers; but, with respect, this is an argument against rigour, not against precedent. The argument for precedent is simply that prevailing notions of justice require that as long as the policy remains the same, like cases should be treated alike. The argument against rigour is that it inhibits desirable developments in policy. All that a flexible system of precedent requires is that in a like case treated in an unlike manner, the reasons should be published. What secrecy permits is the treatment of like cases in an unlike manner for no known reasons, and anyone who has been involved with the affairs of claimants knows how frequently this suspicion is found and how hard it is to lay. What has to be explained is why, if a claimant wishes the public to be admitted to the hearing or a report to be published, this should be denied ostensibly in order to protect his interests. One is again tempted to conclude that administrative convenience is being accorded higher priority than it merits.

At present, therefore, the sources of supplementary benefits law available to the public are quite inadequate. The Commission's *Handbook* is invaluable but admittedly far from comprehensive. Decisions may occasionally reach the High Court and be reported. Some spasmodic and necessarily low quality reporting occurs in publications such as *Poverty*. The legislation itself, published in a comprehensive and convenient form by HMSO, prescribes basic conditions of entitlement to benefits and sets the bounds within which the commission and tribunals must operate but tell us nothing of the topography of the territory surrounded by those bounds. There is now a mine of useful information as to how discretions are generally exercised in Lynes's *Penguin Guide to Supplementary Benefits* and there is little purpose to be served in merely repeating the contents of this work and the *Handbook*. For the rest, there is nothing. We know a little about a lot of the law, and a lot about a little of it. This chapter concentrates on the little we know well. The reader who wishes to acquire a comprehensive knowledge of the administrative practices of the Commission, particularly with regard to the exercise of discretions, should familiarise himself with the works mentioned above.

3. The Administrative Structure

Overall charge of administration now falls to the Commission which took over from the National Assistance Board under the 1966 Act.[17] Their overriding obligation is "to exercise the functions conferred on them ... in such manner as shall best promote the welfare of persons affected by the exercise of those functions."[18] The Commission consists of a chairman, deputy chairman and at most six other persons including at least two women. It may decide upon its own procedures from time to time.[19] The day to day work, including decision making, is in fact done by officers. The Act allows it to be delegated to employees of any government department or local authority as convenient.[20]

Members of the Commission are disqualified from sitting in the House of Commons and the now-defunct Northern Ireland Assembly.[21]

Claims[22]

Procedure is very simple. Claims can be made in the first place merely by filling in the appropriate form which may be obtained not only from the local office but also from the Post Office. The only exception here is the unemployed claimant who uses form BI obtainable at the employment exchange. Once claim is made, the Commission takes the initiative, usually seeking to interview the claimant at home.

A supplementary pensioner (*i.e.* over age 65 if a man, 60 if a woman) is given the option of a visit at home or an interview at the local office.[23] The claim must, of course, be verified and the claimant must supply any information required in connection with it.[24] Where there is less than full documentation, payment may be withheld until a home visit is made, although for the interim period a provisional payment may be made, the balance being made up subsequently. The *Handbook* states specifically that "there is no question of benefit being refused simply because a claimant does not have an address" although it is not unknown for this to happen and in such circumstances benefit is more likely to be in kind (*e.g.* accommodation vouchers) than in cash.[25]

A beneficiary is required to keep the local office informed of any relevant change of circumstances[26] and if benefit is paid by reason of an omission or misrepresentation on the part of the claimant, even if unintentional, it will be recoverable. There appears to be no time limit on the right of recovery. Overpaid benefit may be recovered from the estate if the beneficiary dies in the meantime.[27] Any dispute as to repayment goes to a Supplementary Benefit Appeal Tribunal.[28] A criminal prosecution may result from a deliberate misrepresentation[29] but "dishonesty in a true sense" is required for conviction. If the claimant believes the omission or misrepresentation to be immaterial, even if he knows it to be false, he may avoid conviction.[30]

Only if there are exceptional circumstances explaining the delay may a retrospective claim be entertained, *e.g.* where the local office has misled the claimant as to his entitlement on first inquiry.[31] Any right to benefit is extinguished a year after entitlement unless good cause can be shown for the delay.[32]

Under section 14 (3) of the 1976 Act, benefit may be paid to a third party if this is necessary to safeguard the interests of the claimant and his family. The power is exercisable in respect of both supplementary pensions and allowances and whether or not the claimant consents. Alternatively, the claimant may request that payment be made to someone else. The most controversial use of this power concerns the payment of rent directly to a landlord. This was done 51,000 times in 1975, roughly double the number of times the year before.[33] The Commission are reluctant to make such an order without the consent of the claimant and will do so only if he persistently defaults in payment of his rent.

The Act creates a power to pay to a third party. It does not, in terms, impose a duty. This is appreciated by the Parliamentary Commissioner in one case[34] where the Commission was held not to be at fault for declining to pay rent direct to a landlady in spite of her repeated requests (apparently justified by the subsequent default of the tenants) that they should do so. In an earlier case,[35] the Parliamentary Commissioner had referred to "a duty to ensure that this rent allowance was paid to the local authority landlord" but there is no statutory obligation to protect the interests of a landlord as such. The most that he can hope for is to benefit incidentally to the Commission's furthering the interests of tenants. It is possible to end up furthering nobody's interests. In a third Parliamentary Commissioner case[36] the Commission arranged to pay rent to a landlord quarterly in arrears but, not knowing this, the landlord took proceedings to secure the eviction of the tenants. If good administration cannot avoid such a consequence, a more comforting remedy than the exhortations of the Parliamentary Commissioner ought to be available.

Difficulty may arise if a landlord subsequently chooses to sue a tenant for non-payment of rent which has been paid direct by the Commission. It is hard to see how the Commission can be regarded as the tenant's agent where the tenant has expressly refused to consent to such an arrangement. The tenant seems clearly to be in breach although the landlord's damages are nominal.

The Commission are reluctant to make an order even at the request of the tenant unless "there are serious rent arrears or ... the claimant is incapable of managing his own affairs."[37] "On the one hand it can be argued that claimants have the right to be as free as any other member of the community to manage their finances and accept responsibility for their actions even if these lead to eviction. The danger of paying rent direct is that the claimant and his family will cease to see rent as a personal responsibility and will regard it as an automatic right which requires no action from them ... on the other hand it cannot be in the claimant's interests to build up large and avoidable debts, nor can it be right to take advantage of ... local authorities who wish to avoid evicting tenants.... The Commission have a responsibility to see that this public money (rent allowance) is spent for the purpose for which it is awarded and to prevent the situation arising in which it may have to make a lump sum payment to a tenant to save him from being evicted."[38]

The Finer Committee recommended an extended use of these powers and their exercise "as a matter of course" where a request is made by the tenant backed by a suitable organisation.[39] As a result, the Commission has relaxed its stance and will make an order where the claimant persistently defaults in payment.[40]

Payment of Benefit In Kind

The Act[41] authorises the payment of benefit in kind where, due to exceptional circumstances, this form of payment best meets the claimant's needs. It is not a power which is resorted to frequently.[42] In view of the overriding obligation imposed on the Commission to promote the welfare of beneficiaries, it is clear that the Commission's function is not confined solely to income provision. Special welfare officers are appointed whose task it is to ensure that beneficiaries receive such support from other welfare agencies as is appropriate in their case, as well as their cash benefit entitlement.[43] In a similar vein, the Commission has assumed responsibility for advising claimants as to whether they would be in a more favourable position claiming housing benefits instead of supplementary benefits, but deny that they are under any statutory obligation to do so.[44] There is certainly the general, overriding, obligation above-referred to to promote the welfare of beneficiaries and there is, in addition, the responsibility which arises from creating an expectation that advice will be given if it is appropriate, leading to a claimant's inferring from silence that more favourable benefits are not obtainable.

The Commission will not normally pay national insurance contributions even where a claimant is close to qualifying for benefit, although an exception may be made in the case of a female claimant who gives up work in order to care for aged and infirm parents, provided she claims supplementary benefit and the parents are unable to supplement the daughter's income themselves.[45] The Act empowers the Commission to reimburse to a claimant any travelling expenses incurred in claiming benefit.[46] The Commission may make grants to voluntary organisations doing work similar to that performed at reception or re-establishment centres.[47] Guidelines for eligibility are published in Appendix 7 to the Supplementary Benefits Commission Annual Report, 1975.

Under section 1 of the Children and Young Persons Act 1963, local authorities are empowered to make cash payments in

exceptional circumstances to avoid the need to commit a child
into care. Considerable concern has been expressed that payments under the Act are being made in lieu of exceptional needs
payments under the 1976 Act.[48]

As under the family incomes supplement scheme, a supplementary beneficiary is eligible for a number of other income-
related benefits—free milk and vitamins for young children and
expectant mothers, free school meals, free prescriptions, fares
for travel to hospital,[49] remission of optical and dental charges
and legal advice under section 1 of the Legal Aid Act 1974.[50]

Review

If a claimant is dissatisfied by the decision and makes a written
complaint, or if circumstances have changed, a number of opportunities for revision of the original decision open up. They fall
into two main categories; administrative review and judicial
review.[51]

Administrative review

The Commission enjoys wide powers of review of its own
previous decisions. Decisions are, of course, made on the basis
of the circumstances assumed to be prevailing at the time of
claim. If those circumstances change, a decision can be reviewed.
Equally, if the original decision involved a mistake of law, the
Commission has power to review it. Where the decision is based
upon a mistake of fact (including ignorance of a material fact)
the Commission can review it. In this latter case, the Commission may not only review its own decision but also that of
an appeal tribunal.[52]

The Commission may receive as many as six or seven million
claims in a year. The vast majority of these are disposed of in
the first instance by relatively junior officials. It is quite possible
for such junior officials to make erroneous determinations either
because they lack the time and expertise to deal with sophisticated claims, or because they are not empowered to depart from
the established policy even in an unusual case. It is therefore
the Commission's policy for a more senior official or officials
to review a determination appealed against and, in an appropriate case, to vary it before appeal. If, as a result of the

variation, a prospective appellant gets what he wants, he will obviously not proceed with an appeal.

The importance of this procedure is well brought out in a recent survey[53] covering the year down to October 31, 1969. Of 26,000 original determinations re-examined, either by review or by appeal, 9,000 never reached a Supplementary Benefit Appeal Ttribunal hearing, about 6,000 of them being varied, as a result of review, in the appellant's favour, the remaining 3,000 being dropped without alteration. Thus, only 17,000 eventually went to hearing of which 3,300 succeeded. In all, however, it will be seen that the review process resulted in the variation in the appellant's favour of about 9,300 of the original 26,000 cases (*i.e.* 36 per cent., as opposed to 19 per cent. successes in appeals actually heard).

4. ENTITLEMENT TO BENEFIT

(a) *The Basic Conditions*

The supplementary benefit scheme, embodied in the 1976 Act, performs the same function as did the old poor law—the relief of destitution. Benefit is paid, in terms as of right, to any person over the age of 16 "whose resources are insufficient to meet his requirements" and who satisfies any other conditions stipulated in the Act.[54] There are four basic conditions which must be satisfied in all cases. Even, however, if these basic conditions are satisfied, the Commission may have power to impose further ones or even, exceptionally, not to make available resources to meet requirements at all. It is in this sense and in this sense only that a claimant who satisfies the basic conditions can be said to be "entitled" to benefit. The basic conditions are:

1. The claimant must be present in Great Britain (under the Northern Ireland scheme, five years' residence was formerly required[55]).

2. He must be over the age of 16 years.

3. His resources must be insufficient to meet his requirements according to the statutory criteria.

4. He must be independent, *i.e.* as a dependant, his requirements and resources must not fall to be aggregated with and treated as those of another person.[56]

These conditions require elaboration.

(i) Presence

It is sufficient merely to be "in Great Britain." Nationality, domicile and residence are equally irrelevant. The purpose of the different requirement in Northern Ireland was ostensibly to prevent the crossing of the land frontier by persons resident in the Republic of Ireland for purposes of claiming benefit. Since no limitation at all is imposed in the case of those crossing the Irish Sea, five years' residence seemed a somewhat excessive requirement in the Northern Ireland case.

(ii) Age

A child of the age of 16 years or less will normally either be dependent upon another person or liable to the operation of the child care legislation.[57]

(iii) Need

In the normal case, requirements and resources are calculated in accordance with the provisions of Parts II and III respectively of Schedule 1 to the 1976 Act. These provisions are considered in greater detail below in connection with calculation of benefit.

(iv) Independence

Cohabitation

For purposes of entitlement to benefit, the family is treated as a unit and benefit is paid to the head of the household, normally a husband. For this purpose, the family means not merely the family *de jure* but also families *de facto*. Schedule 1, paragraph 3, of the 1976 Act provides:

"(1) Where—

(*a*) a husband and wife are members of the same household, their requirements and resources shall be aggregated and treated as the husband's;

(*b*) two persons are cohabiting as husband and wife, their requirements and resources shall unless there are exceptional circumstances be aggregated and treated as the man's.

(2) Where a person has to provide for the requirements of

another person who is a member of the same household, not being a person falling within section (1) above:

(a) the requirements of that other person may, and if he has not attained the age of 16 shall, be aggregated with, and treated as, those of the first mentioned person; and

(b) where their requirements are so aggregated, their resources shall be similarly aggregated."

The result of the rules is that if a man is in full-time employment not only he but also an unemployed wife or mistress with whom he is living will be disentitled to benefit.

The policy behind the requirement of aggregation of resources and requirements is the perfectly sensible one of ensuring that public funds are not used to augment the resources of a person who is already adequately provided for, whatever the source of that provision. This is why the wife's resources and requirements are aggregated with the husband's. The "cohabitation rule" is an attempt to assimilate the positions of wife and mistress. "It cannot be right to treat unmarried women who have the support of a partner as if they had no such support, and better than if they were married."[58] There may be an argument for treating married women as beneficiaries in their own right rather than relegating them to an inferior status so far as claiming is concerned, but any proposal to do away with the aggregation rule in the present economic climate is clearly ruled out unless it is of a fundamental character. And to retain the aggregation rule for married women whilst abolishing it for unmarried "wives" is regarded as discriminating unfairly against the former, even if it were economically viable.[59]

The non-discrimination argument has force, but it would be more compelling if it were not the case that in other areas of social security law, unmarried women are discriminated against. Certain benefits, particularly widow's benefits, become available on the death of a lawful husband but not on the death of a lifelong sole cohabitant. Even more relevant for present purposes, increases of benefits are available in respect of a wife, but not a mistress. The husband is under an obligation to maintain his wife and family; not so in the case of a mistress. This is the case not merely under the common law but also under the statutory provisions contained in the 1976 Act itself. As a last resort, a wife can sue for maintenance from a husband receiving benefit on her behalf. A mistress cannot.[60]

The main criticism of the rule is that it makes an assumption which in some cases is wholly unwarranted, namely that financial support is in fact forthcoming from the man. Where it is not, genuine financial hardship can arise from a refusal of benefit. It is true that aggregation need not be resorted to if there are "exceptional circumstances" and it is the Commission's policy to abate need in at least some such cases on these grounds. Circumstances may be regarded as "exceptional" where there are children of another union in a family the income of which is insufficient to support all its members at the appropriate level. If this is so, the Commission is prepared to make discretionary payments[61] based upon the children's requirements in order temporarily to tide the family over. Allowance is usually paid for a four-week period but this may be extended if necessary. The Commission have, however, rejected proposals to put such payments on an automatic or permanent basis.[62] A lump sum payment may be made to meet essential requirements[63] and section 4 of the 1976 Act confers a general power upon the Commission to pay benefit in urgent cases, *e.g.* where the man refuses to support his mistress, but it is rarely exercised in cohabitation cases.[64] The fear is not that the powers are inadequate, however, but rather that they are exercised with excessive concern to prevent fraud and too little willingness to risk improper payment in the cause of adequate provision.

The main source of difficulty is the concept of "living together as husband and wife." It is a concept which is relevant in other areas of social security law, affecting entitlement to widow's benefits, the special child benefit premium for single parents, and family incomes supplement. Moreover it causes similar problems under the Matrimonial Proceedings (Magistrates' Courts) Act 1960 and the Matrimonial Causes Act 1963) where questions of desertion and separation are in issue. Much doctrine has developed under this legislation and it is surprising that more use has not been made of it by determining authorities under the social security schemes.

The difficulties are attributable to the fact that the incidents which attach to a man and wife relationship are many and varied and 'none of them necessary in law. The law does not disown marital status if the parties live apart, are financially independent, refrain from sexual relations and adopt different names. Such a marriage might well be regarded as abnormal, but it does not follow that a "normal" marriage need have any one or more of these specific incidents. An elderly couple might well share the same house and name but abstain from sex and each be financially independent; for professional reasons, a wife might retain her own name and be obliged to live apart from her husband, but have sexual relations and be financially dependent on him.

The invariable problem in cohabitation cases is that where one or more of these incidents is present in a relationship between a man and woman who are not married and it has to be decided whether they are "cohabiting as man and wife." If the policy of the law were borne in mind, some at least of the difficulty would disappear.

This policy is not, however, the sole governing consideration. The prevailing mores relating to sanctity of marriage seem to influence the law here. There is certainly a reluctance to focus primarily upon the question of actual dependency and to attach perhaps too much importance to the existence of sexual relations which, strictly speaking, are relevant only as offering weak evidence of the likelihood of dependency. This, however, is not the purport of the existing law.

Cohabitation in law

The objective of the law is "to disqualify a 'woman' who (is) really in the position of a married woman and obtaining support as such." This statement of Lord Anderson in *Paterson* v. *Ritchie*[65] provides judicial endorsement of the avowed policy of the law. The actual rules applied, however, depart from it.

There are two problems in approaching the question whether or not parties are cohabiting in any given case, a fact confused here as elsewhere in the law by characterising the question as "one of fact."[66] The first problem is the evidentiary one—exactly what is the relationship between the parties? Does he support her? Do they reside together? Do they have sexual relations? Does she call herself "Mrs. X"? This is an evidentiary problem of the same nature as "Did the accused pull the trigger?" and it will not always be easy to solve. Certain types of evidence (such as to the financial arrangements between the parties) may be hard to obtain from any source other than the parties themselves, and from them it may be highly coloured by self-interest and therefore unreliable. But these are the normal difficulties encountered in seeking to establish facts.

The second problem is the legal one—what is the legal significance of the facts found? Do they constitute cohabitation in law? This second question is the area of doubt solely because of the indeterminateness of the criterion of cohabitation.

Where cohabitation is admitted, the need for proof does not arise. This is unlikely to occur before a tribunal, but may do so, as in *R(P) 6/52* where it was admitted incidentally to a claim that it had ceased. In deciding whether cohabitation exists, it is legitimate to have regard to the relationship of the parties at an earlier period.[67]

Where cohabitation is denied, it must be proved by the Commission's officer. What is required is proof of the mere fact of conscious cohabitation. In *R(I) 29/60*, the parties had gone through a ceremony of marriage and the woman thought she was married. The marriage was, in fact, bigamous. Her contention that she had not consented to cohabitation was rejected —the fact was enough. This may seem harsh at first blush, but it is in line with policy. She had been supported by the man for the relevant period; had she actually been married, their resources would undoubtedly have been aggregated. Where there has been a ceremony of marriage, the burden is on the claimant to prove non-cohabitation.[68]

Where it is to be proved, evidence as to sexual relations, one party holding himself out as the spouse of the other, shared financial arrangements and common residence will be relevant; it is not, however, inconsistent with cohabitation that one or possibly even more of these should, in any given case, be absent.

There is no clear definition of cohabitation. There is some judicial indication as to its meaning and the Commission have laid down guidelines for the determination of particular cases. They have, however, declined to give statutory force to any definition on the grounds that it would be too difficult to draft a provision encompassing every situation which might arise.[69] A less interested view of what is needed is that of the Fisher

Committee that "greater precision is necessary so that claimants will know exactly how the cohabitation test will be operated in practice. It is difficult to see how this can be done without amending the statute in the direction of greater precision. The alternative of publishing non-statutory guidance as to how the statute will be interpreted would be less satisfactory since the adjudicating authorities would not be bound by the guidance given and might disagree with it."[70] The Fisher Committee, the promised High Court appeal in supplementary benefit cases and common sense all argue for consistency in the determination of claims involving alleged cohabitation whether in relation to supplementary or other social security benefits. The consideration which follows draws upon all available social security sources in which the evidence above referred to (as to common residence, sexual relations, holding out, financial arrangements etc.) looms large.

COMMON RESIDENCE

The couple must be members of the same household, *i.e.* normally and regularly live in the same house or flat.[71] In *R(G) 11/55* the evidence was that the man and woman loved each other and wished to marry but were unable to do so because of the refusal of the man's wife to divorce him. The only evidence as to cohabitation was common residence. The parties had shared a four-roomed house and had moved together to another one. The man was ostensibly a lodger and there was no proof of sexual relations or as to any other financial arrangement. The Commissioner found it impossible in these circumstances to resist the conclusion that they were living together as man and wife. Mere common residence is not, however, conclusive, as is witnessed by *R(G) 14/59*, considered below. Many different types of relationship may involve a sharing of accommodation: "There is the relationship of a man and his housekeeper in which sometimes the relationship is strictly that of employer and employee and sometimes is a euphemistic description of a man and his mistress; or the relationship may be one of companionship. A man and woman might be living together in the same household each under their own names, each earning their own living and each contributing to the general expenses."[72] Not all are cohabitation. In particular, the Commission attaches great importance to the continuity and stability of the arrangement,[73] although they have declined to lay down any rigid time limit beyond which benefit must be withheld. The time contemplated is clearly a matter of weeks, not of months. During this period, benefit may continue to be paid in circumstances where the arrangement is clearly intended to be temporary.[74]

SEXUAL RELATIONS

Evidence of stable sexual relations is not conclusive but goes a long way towards establishing cohabitation.[75] "The fact that the couple have such a relationship ... obviously does not of itself imply that they must be regarded as living as husband and wife. ... What has to be decided is whether the relationship *as a whole* of a couple living together in the same household has the character of that of husband and wife."[76] In *R(G) 2/64* the claimant and the father of the youngest child had been living in a caravan and sharing a double bed. He intended to marry her if his wife divorced him. This was held to constitute overwhelming evidence of cohabitation notwithstanding that there was evidence of separate financial arrangements. Clear evidence of the absence of any sexual relations is equally weighty in the other direction. "Since a sexual relationship is a normal and important aspect of marriage ... it would seldom, if ever, be reasonable to hold that a claimant was living with a man as his wife if there was no reason to suppose that they had ever had such a relationship.[77] Presumably the case of an elderly couple setting up home together on a basis of close companionship but without sexual relations would be one of the rare cases.

There is a presumption of sexual relations from the surrounding circumstances and proof of actual sexual intercourse is not required. This results from the nature of the system of administration. "An insurance officer is not in a position to decide such questions" and "neither the local authority nor the Commissioner, who have no authority to compel the attendance of witnesses, have the necessary facilities for deciding such questions."[78] The danger is that if the presumption is too readily made, and if too great an importance is attached to the presumed sexual relations, the award of benefit begins to look less like abatement of need and more like a reward for sexual conformity.

HOLDING OUT

Evidence that the woman takes the man's name, holding herself out to be his wife, is relevant. It will normally be some indication that the substantial relationship is of a "husband and wife" type. "There is cogent evidence that a man and a woman are cohabiting together as man and wife when they are not only using the same accommodation but the woman has assumed the surname of the man, as in the present case. Whatever may be the reason, whether to avoid gossip or to acquire the benefit of accommodation in the event of death, in such circumstances the inference is unavoidable, in the absence of compelling evidence to the contrary, that the woman wishes to pass herself off as the wife of the man with whom she is living."[80] It is not, however, essential that there should be "holding out." In *CP 97/49 (KL)* a local tribunal which had held that a woman was not cohabiting because she was "not pretending to be his wife" was overruled by the Commissioner.

FINANCIAL ARRANGEMENTS[81]

Evidence that the household fund is made available by the man to the woman is, in policy terms, exactly in point and is frequently adduced. But its absence "cannot be taken as positive evidence that the relationship is not comparable to that of husband and wife."[82] Perhaps it should be, if the evidentiary difficulties could be surmounted, but this is not easy for "household and financial arrangements are personal matters not easy to ascertain."[83] This apart, the Commission fears that any other rule would offer an incentive for abuse by the parties. A distinction may be drawn, however, between "the commercially determined basis of a lodger's payments" and a husband's practice of paying what he can reasonably afford.[84] Presumably it would be significant if the payments were irregular and varied in size.

CHILDREN[85]

The role played by the man within the household may be significant as, for example, where he cares for the children, helps with domestic chores and engages in leisure activities with the woman and children.[86] Where there are children of the union there is a strong presumption that the couple are living together as man and wife.

Where the facts are all clearly known, it should be possible to assess their legal significance. Some legal problems involve an evaluation, for example as to whether conduct was reasonable or fair, but that has never been suggested to be the situation so far as cohabitation is concerned. Nevertheless, the lawyer cannot give an accurate forecast because the law itself has not become sufficiently clear and settled. X, a widower, takes a housekeeper. The financial arrangements throughout are that he provides her with a weekly sum to cover the cost of keeping house for both and five pounds besides. After a while he habitually has sexual relations with her. Later this ceases. Later still, she "retires" though continues to live in his house and be kept by him, he employing another housekeeper. The above authorities do not enable us to say with anything near certainty, at any point in this history, whether or not they are cohabiting. We can do better than this.

CESSATION OF COHABITATION

When cohabitation ceases, so does the liability to aggregation of resources for benefit purposes. Whereas the onus of proving cohabitation is on the Commission, once it has been established or admitted it is up to the claimant to establish that it has ceased and "very cogent evidence is necessary to prove that this relationship has ended if they continue to live in the same house."[87] It is not unknown, however, for this onus to be discharged. In *R(G) 14/59*, the man left in June 1957 but returned in September 1957 to the woman's house, occupying the upper part and shopping and cooking for himself, sharing the kitchen. They were joint owners and shared payment of mortgage interest and other outgoings. The woman alleged that she had allowed him to return purely for economic reasons and, the nature of the relationship being completely different, it was held that cohabitation had ceased.

Similarly, since aggregation need only be effected during the continuance of cohabitation, benefit may be payable during breaks in it. A distinction is to be drawn, however, between an actual break in cohabitation and a mere interruption of common residence for some other purpose. In *R(G)* *11/59*, there had been a separation as a result of a quarrel which was later made up. For a time, however, the relationship had been suspended and so, therefore, had disentitlement by reason of cohabitation. However, "the mere absence of a husband from his wife for purposes of business or holiday would not be any ground for holding that they were no longer living together, which is what cohabiting means, but where there are no marital obligations, and the absence is not caused by reasons of business or holiday, but is attributable to a dispute or quarrel between the parties, even though it is subsequently made up after the lapse of quite a short time, I do not think that the claimant and the man concerned can be said to be cohabiting."

WITHDRAWAL OF BENEFIT ON GROUNDS OF COHABITATION

There has been considerable controversy in the past about the method of withdrawing benefit on grounds of alleged cohabitation. The Press has made a great deal of fuss about "Ministry spies" and unsavoury methods of inquiry. There is a genuine problem here—that of finding a way of reconciling respect for privacy with the prevention of improper or fraudulent claims and whilst there should obviously be proper direction and control of the activities of investigating officers so as to minimise offence, investigation is inherent in the nature of the present scheme. Some of its more offensive manifestations are obviated, though at a cost, by the presumption of sexual intercourse above referred to.

The decision to investigate suspected fraud is taken at regional level. Investigations, which may involve keeping watch on the house or making inquiries of neighbours, are carried out by a team of special investigators and the decision is made by the local office on the basis of their evidence. If the decision is to withdraw benefit, the woman must be given a written statement of the reasons.[88] These procedures should be resorted to only where there is no reasonable alternative.[89] It is estimated that some 8,000 claimants annually have benefit reduced or withheld as a result of decisions on cohabitation, 4,000 of them after investigation. 400 prosecutions resulted.[90]

The Fisher Committee criticised the lack of co-ordination between the supplementary benefit and national insurance authorities in investigating cases of suspected cohabitation as a result of which, either as a matter of fact or of law, it was possible for a woman to be found to be cohabiting for the purpose of one benefit but not so far as another was concerned.[91] Brooke has asked whether it is "just that benefit can be withdrawn when the allegation (of cohabitation) is made rather than after a hearing of the evidence"[92]; and although more than a mere allegation is required, something other than mere abstract justice is involved. Removing an order book on the basis of a simple decision by the Commission looks very like depriving the subject of his rights contrary to the principles of natural justice, an argument which has yet to be addressed to an adjudicating authority but which has a compelling appearance. The practice must, however, be viewed in context. It must be remembered that in the nature of administration of the scheme, rights are conferred in the first place "without a hearing." Benefit is awarded upon the "allegation" of an officer that a claimant is entitled to it. The procedure does not take the form of our standard justice; the officer is at once "prosecution" and judge. And the practice of withdrawing benefit on a mere "allegation" is not confined to cohabitation cases. Whenever any of the conditions of entitlement cease to be fulfilled, benefit can be and is stopped without a hearing. If the allegation turns out to be unsubstantiated on appeal, full benefit is restored and payable retrospectively. It has been suggested that benefit should continue to be paid until the appeal but this has been rejected because of the opportunities it gives for abuse.[93] The Finer Committee recommended, however, that benefit should be paid pending appeal in a case where the claimant disputes the facts alleged. Both the Fisher and Finer Committees proposed that greater use should be made by the Commission of its power to award urgent needs payments pending appeal. The Commission, however, are reluctant to do so too regularly, again for fear of abuse, and conclude that although "local officers must be responsive to evidence of genuine need, claimants should (not) be given any encouragement to suppose that emergency payments will be made indiscriminately."[94]

It has been suggested that in cases of withdrawal of benefit on grounds of cohabitation there should be an appeal on a point of law to the National Insurance Commissioner,[95] or, alternatively, that exclusive power to order the withdrawal of benefit on grounds of cohabitation should be vested in the local tribunal. In view of current developments concerning supplementary benefit appeals there is little point in commenting in detail on these proposals. It may be considered, in passing, however, that benefit can be withdrawn on grounds other than cohabitation and that to single out cohabitation cases for a special appeals procedure is apt to create more anomalies than it removes. On the second proposal above, one's confidence in its ability to effect improvement must vary directly in proportion to one's confidence in the capacity of supplementary benefit appeal tribunals to make good decisions.

Aggregation of children's resources and requirements

The resources and requirements of dependent children are also aggregated with those of their parents under para. 3 (2) of the First Schedule to the 1976 Act. Aggregation is mandatory in the case of children under 16 and customary in the case of older children still at school although it may be waived where there are "exceptional circumstances."[96] Circumstances may well be treated as exceptional where, for example, the child is handicapped and unlikely to find work, or where he is the head of a family himself.[97]

It should be noted that Schedule 1 applies only where "a person *has to* provide for the requirements of another." Ambiguity centres around the italicised words. They might mean that aggregation is required when there is an obligation to provide, (regardless of whether provision is in fact made or not); or that it is required where provision has, as a matter of fact, to be made because the other person has no other means of support. In *K.* v. *JMP Ltd.*[98] it was held that a person (a mother) did not "have to" provide for her children where in fact they had sufficient means of their own to meet the necessaries of life which, by virtue of an award of damages under the Fatal Accidents Act, they had.[99]

If these four basic conditions—presence, age, need and independence,—are fulfilled, a claimant is prima facie entitled to benefit of some kind. This prima facie entitlement may, however, be defeated. The wording of section 4 (above) is consistent with allowing benefit to be paid to people in low-paid employment but it is the accepted objective of the scheme that benefit should only be awarded when all else has failed. If a claimant is in work, or capable of work, or provided for otherwise, or capable of becoming trained for work, all else, it is assumed, has not failed.

(b) *Grounds of Disentitlement*

(i) **Persons in employment**

The arguments for withholding entitlement from persons in or with the opportunity for low-paid employment are not compelling. Once the state has determined what it considers to be the minimum acceptable subsistence level of living, and decided to ensure that people reach it, it seems strange to pay full benefit to those who cannot earn at all, yet withhold part benefit from those who earn what little they can. The alleged justifications are that not to do so would add greatly to the cost of the scheme and would interfere with the free market in fixing wage-levels, in effect subsidising employers. That neither of these principles is sacrosanct is evidenced by the institution of the family incomes supplement scheme. The bar nevertheless remains in section 6 of the 1976 Act: "... for any period during which a person is engaged in remunerative full-time work he shall not be entitled to supplementary benefit."

The section empowers the Secretary of State to make provision by regulations for continuing benefit after the claimant has engaged in full-time work. Similarly, benefit in such circumstances may be paid by the Commission in the exercise of its overriding discretion in urgent cases under section 4 though in this case repayment may be required if the Commission is satisfied that recovery would be equitable. The exclusion under section 6 does not operate in the case of self-employed persons whose earning power in relation to others in his field is diminished by reason of disability. "Full-time work" is not defined.

(ii) The employable unemployed

A number of controls are designed to operate so as to ensure that unemployed persons support themselves and their dependants by securing work where possible rather than by relying on supplementary benefits. Amongst these are:

1. The Commission's power to require persons under pensionable age to register for employment as a condition of receipt of benefit.[1] Invocation of this power is the rule rather than the exception. Where the power is exercised but the claimant does not register, no benefit is payable; the Commission may not even exercise its discretion to make an emergency payment under section 4.

2. The Commission has power to refer to an appeal tribunal the cases of claimants or beneficiaries who refuse or neglect to maintain themselves or their dependants. On such a reference, the tribunal may direct that the Commission make payment of benefit conditional upon attendance on an approved course of instruction or training, or upon residence in a re-establishment centre.[2] Exercise of this latter power may bear a close resemblance to a sentence of imprisonment in some cases.[3] It does not exclude payment of benefit in exercise of the emergency payment discretion under section 4.

3. Disentitlement of a claimant, though not of his dependants, may result from involvement in a trade dispute. Section 8 of the 1976 Act is couched in terms almost identical with those of section 19 of the Social Security Act 1975 in relation to unemployment benefit[4] and the grounds of disqualification are in this case appealable to a national insurance tribunal.[5] Where a claimant who has been refused benefit by reason of the trades dispute disqualification re-enters employment, he may be paid benefit notwithstanding the work bar under section 6 above for not more than the first 15 days after his return to work but in this case any benefit paid may be recoverable from him,[6] and certain sums received by him may rank as resources for the purposes of calculating entitlement.[7]

The Commission's overriding discretion in cases of emergency is available here.

4. In addition to the above controls which operate so as to deny benefit, control of voluntary unemployment may also be effected by restricting the term for which benefit is awarded with a view to pressing the claimant to seek work urgently. Until 1974, the Commission followed a practice of granting allowances of limited duration to claimants capable of work in areas where work was considered to be available. This practice worked most severely in the case of single, able-bodied men under the age of 45 who were subjected to a "four-week" rule. The Fisher Committee favoured the retention of the modified "four-week" rule[8] but its effect and legality remained in doubt and the Commission itself eventually replaced the former practice of interviewing claimants in order to see if a continuation of benefit was justifiable with a new practice of interviewing for exhortatory purposes but with the threat of withdrawing benefit in exceptional cases. It is not known to what extent substantial change results.

(iii) Schoolchildren etc.

Persons attending school "or receiving full-time instruction of a kind given in schools" are not entitled to benefit though the Commission has a discretion to award benefit to one who would otherwise be entitled, where there are exceptional circumstances (s. 4). According to the *Handbook*,[9] "the Commission may accept a claim from a young person still receiving secondary education ... *e.g.* where he is so handicapped as to be unlikely to be able to work or is a 'head of household'."

Some doubt arises where the claimant is pursuing a course of full-time instruction after school but before entering work. The criterion offered by section 7 (*i.e.* whether the instruction is "of a kind given in schools") is vague and is exactly the sort of question which would be much more easy to answer were doctrine surrounding it developed and published. There is, of course, none. It is, however, worthwhile pointing out that a claimant has a right to benefit unless he falls within section 7 and that it is not relevant that the Commission has a discretion under that section which it would be prepared to exercise benevolently in an appropriate case.

(iv) Overriding discretion in cases of urgency

We have considered disentitlement under sections 6 to 10 inclusive. Notwithstanding disentitlement, the Commission has a discretion to award benefit in an urgent case where the disentitlement falls under sections 6–8 or 10, though, of course, in all cases the basis conditions must be fulfilled. If this discretion is exercised in favour of a person in work, the Commission may stipulate for repayment of a whole or part as it thinks appropriate.

(c) *Benefit*

(i) Benefit as of right and discretionary benefit

In the normal case of a claimant present in Great Britain or Northern Ireland, of age and in need, and not disentitled under any of the disentitling provisions, benefit in an amount such that his resources are adequate to meet his requirements will normally be paid as of right in the form of a weekly sum continuing so long as he remains entitled. As we have seen, there is a discretion to pay benefit in an urgent case, notwithstanding disentitlement. There is also discretion, under section 3 to make a lump sum payment in cases of exceptional need; and under paragraph 4 of Schedule 1, the statutory entitlement may be varied, upwards only in the case of persons of pensionable age, but either upwards or downwards in all other cases where there are exceptional circumstances.[10]

Payments in case of exceptional need under section 3 form an important part of the functions of the Commission. It is under this head that *ad hoc* grants for clothing and furniture may be made in appropriate circumstances. In considering claims for such grants the Commission has regard to standard lists of reasonable stocks of such items.[11] The second important area of discretionary benefits is that under paragraph 4, above, under which additions to benefit may be paid in respect of matters such as special diets and the cost of domestic assistance in appropriate cases. In the case of discretionary benefits, the Commission's officer will normally have regard, in the first instance, to departmental instructions (usually contained in the "A Code") as to how the discretion should be exercised. It should be noted, however, that if the circumstances of the individual case are not considered, the discretion is not properly exercised and an application to the Divisional Court for correction of the decision may succeed.[12]

(ii) Types of benefit

As above indicated, the normal benefit is in the form of a weekly sum. A lump sum may be paid under section 3. Under section 11, benefit in kind as opposed to cash may be paid "where it appears to the Commission that, by reason of exceptional circumstances, the requirements of any person can best be met by the provision of goods or services instead of the whole or part of any payment." Benefit payable to a person over pensionable age is called a "supplementary pension"; otherwise it is called a "supplementary allowance."[13]

(iii) Calculations of benefit

Subject to exceptions, "the amount of any benefit to which a person is entitled shall be the amount by which his resources fall short of his requirements."[14] Requirements and resources fall to be calculated in accordance with Parts II and III respectively of Schedule 1 of the 1976 Act.

(a) *Requirements*

The basic scale requirements (there are separate and more generous scales for blind persons) are designed to cover normal needs "including food, fuel and light, the normal repair and replacement of clothing, household sundries (but not major items of bedding and furnishing) and provision for amenities such as newspapers, entertainments and television licences."[15] The rates are, however, fixed, although actual needs may differ according to personal characteristics and locality. It will be noted that there is no mention of rent in the above list. The statutory requirements include, in addition to the scale rates, the net rent payable by a householder (or such part of it as is reasonable) or, in the case of non-householders, a weekly sum of £1·20, presumably for lodging. Where there are joint tenants each is, strictly speaking, a householder but, in such circumstances, the Commission has preferred to treat each joint tenant as entitled to the non-householder's allowance being prepared, if necessary, to "top up" to the level of the actual reasonable rent by the exercise of the exceptional circumstances discretion. Whilst recognising that legally each tenant is a "householder," the Court of Appeal has applauded the Commission's approach as being "the better way of administering the Act" and declined to issue certiorari accordingly.[16]

This separate treatment of the rent question derives from the Beveridge Report and recognises that rent forms an important part of small household budgets and may vary considerably from one case to another.

The basic scale (the "A" scale in the latest legislation) is not meant to cover long-term needs, such as the major items (bedding, furnishings etc.) excluded above. Augmented scales (the "B" and "C" scales) are therefore applicable where such long-term needs may be presumed, *i.e.* in the case of pensioners and other beneficiaries of two years' standing (provided not required to register for work), and in the case of persons over 80 respectively.[17] Where a beneficiary qualifies for an augmented scale rate and also an exceptional circumstances addition under paragraph 4, he receives only so much of the latter as exceeds 50p per week (scale "B") or 75p per week (scale "C") unless the addition is in respect of certain specified matters such as extra heating.[18]

In certain cases, the Commission may depart from the list of statutory requirements. This arises where a claimant required to register for work under section 5 is disqualified for receiving unemployment benefit by virtue of section 20 (1) of the Social Security Act 1975 or would be so disqualified if he claimed.[19] In this case, his personal requirements are taken to be 60 per cent. only of the scale rate to which he would otherwise be entitled.

(b) *Resources*

In so far as possible, a claimant should meet his requirements out of his own resources, both capital and income. Certain sources of capital and income may, however, be disregarded, *e.g.* the capital value of the house in which he resides,[20] death grant, maternity grant[21] and capital resources up to £1,249 together with any income derived therefrom.[22] In addition, the first few pounds of net weekly earnings may be disregarded, The limits here are £2 in the case of claimants required to register for work, £6 for parents of one-parent families and £4 in other cases.[23] There is a further disregard of £4 in the case of income other than earnings and certain other social security benefits.[24]

CAPITAL

Capital resources which do not fall to be disregarded are to be converted into notional weekly income for the purposes of calculating entitlement.[25] The Commission is expected to use common-sense criteria for the characterisation of capital rather than the technical doctrines which operate in some areas of law though an application for certiorari might succeed if the Commission's or a tribunal's determination were clearly improper.[26] All aggregable capital must be aggregated; since the only express disregards do not extend beyond the capital value of the claimant's interest in his dwelling-house, this theoretically includes all his other property—furniture, the tools of his trade, car, clothes etc. In practice, however, it is almost unknown for these items to be taken into account.

When the total value of the available capital is ascertained, it is translated into weekly income at the rate of 25p per week for each complete £50 above the £1,200 disregard, equivalent to 26 per cent. per annum. The object is not to find an equivalent of the income which the capital might reasonably yield but rather a crude equivalent of the annuity which it might be expected to purchase; the claimant is expected to live out of capital to some extent. On the present scale rates, the entitlement of married pensioners paying a modest rent would disappear with total capital resources in excess of £7,000.

INCOME

All income, including child benefit and national insurance benefits other than those specifically excepted, must be brought

into account subject to the disregards. The Act provides that
when a person who has been involved in a trade dispute returns
to work, any advance of wages made or offered during the first
15 days after the return is to count as net weekly earnings for
the week during which it is received.[27]

It used to be the case that in calculating resources during
a strike, the claimant's income tax refunds and strike pay would
be disregarded up to the level of his personal requirements
negating disqualification to this extent. The 1976 Act[28] now
provides for these sums to be treated as income, while section
9 of the 1976 Act empowers the Commission to require repayment of benefits paid in certain cases out of earnings on resumption of work.

The Act also contemplates attempts to establish entitlement
by a deliberate abandonment of resources. Such resources may
be counted in calculating entitlement.[29] The *Handbook* instances
only the case of transferring money or property to others. The
mechanism might well, however, be available much more extensively. Whether it would extend to a deliberate spendthrift
policy is not clear; the Commission has in fact a measure of
discretion whether to include it or not. It is interesting to note
that in the student grant cases discussed below no attempt was
made by the Commission to use this power.

NOTIONAL RESOURCES

Entitlement depends upon the resources available to a
claimant. The Act clearly contemplates that the resources shall
be actually available. Express provision is made where the Commission is allowed to take into account resources which are not
actually available, as in the case above, where they were available but have been deliberately abandoned. It has now become
clear that in administering benefit, the Commission has at times
presumed, without evidence, that resources were available and
has seemed to make determinations of benefit dependent upon
"notional" resources. In *R. v. Preston Supplementary Benefit Appeal
Tribunal, ex pe. Moore*[30] the Commission "credited" the claimant
with the amount of a notional vacation allowance of £1·90
per week included in his student grant which, however, he had
spent. In *R. v. West London Supplementary Benefit Appeal Tribunal,*

ex p. Clarke[31] the Commission had treated a mother-in-law as
being in receipt of weekly maintenance in an amount which
rendered her entitlement to benefit nil on the basis of an undertaking by her son-in-law to maintain her. And in *R.* v. *Barnsley
Supplementary Benefit Appeal Tribunal, ex p. Atkinson*[32] another
student claimant was presumed to have received the annual
parental contribution assumed by the local authority in paying
him the minimum student grant of £50 per annum.

It must be abundantly plain that the Commission is no more
warranted in resorting to the concept of "notional" resources
than is the prosecution in a murder trial allowed to establish
its case by reference to the "notional" death of a victim actually
in robust good health. In the *Moore* case, it might have been
justifiable to treat the £1·90 per week vacation allowance as
being a resource deliberately abandoned. In the *Clarke* and *Atkinson* cases, however, it was surely simply a matter of evidence
as to whether the resources were available or not. In these cases,
there was not even any legal entitlement to maintenance from
the source (son-in-law, parents) in question, as there is in the
case of the thousands of deserted wives who, rightly, are treated
as being without resources. The conclusion that the Commission
was, in these and, no doubt, other cases, abusing its power so
as to achieve justice according to subjective notions seems
irresistible. In *Moore*'s case, they succeeded—at least to the extent
that the courts declined to intervene even if there had been
an error in law. In the *Clarke* and, ultimately, the *Atkinson* case,
they failed.

It is not argued here that no account should be taken of
resources which a claimant actually receives even though he
has no enforceable right to them. Such resources should clearly
be taken into account, must as much as a win on the Pools.
What is argued is that the Commission should base its determination on the evidence as to whether actual resources are in fact
available rather than presuming, as a matter of policy and convenience and perhaps in the face of the facts, that they are.

SPREADING

As in other areas of social security law, the problem of attributing to particular weeks for benefit purposes a larger sum paid

in respect of an indeterminate period may arise. The courts have again, here, accorded a wide measure of latitude to the Commission as to the manner in which it seeks to spread the larger sum over a period of weeks. There are, however, limits. In *R.* v. *West London Supplementary Benefit Appeal Tribunal, ex p. Taylor*[33] the Commission, endorsed by the local tribunal, had sought to attribute a large sum paid by way of arrears of maintenance to that number of weeks which would minimise the Commission's liability, rather than to a larger number. They might well have treated it as capital and translated it into income as indicated above. Once having chosen to treat it as income, however, it was to be attributed on the basis on which it had been received (*i.e.* as the accrual of a large number of weekly sums) and not, arbitrarily, in the manner which best suited the Commission.

ENTITLEMENT

The actual sum of entitlement is arrived at by deducting the resources available from the statutory requirements which they are available to meet and paying the balance as benefit. The sum thus arrived at used to be subject to the notorious wage-stop whereby the total amount of benefit receivable was not allowed to exceed what the claimant would normally have earned in his usual occupation but this has now been abolished.[34] The sum remains, however, liable to alteration in the exercise by the Commission of the exceptional circumstances discretion now contained in paragraph 4 of Schedule 1 to the 1976 Act.

Paragraph 4 authorises the Commission to adjust the sum arrived at upwards in the case of pensioners or either upwards or downwards in the case of other beneficiaries, as may be appropriate to take account of those circumstances. There has been a marked tendency to view this discretion as being in the widest terms.[35] In its terms, it might have been thought not to be available if the circumstances taken into account were not exceptional as, for example, affecting a very large class of claimants. What seems clear is that the existence of exceptional circumstances (whatever that might mean) does not allow the Commission to do anything at all, but merely to adjust "as may be appropriate to take account of those circumstances."

5. SUPPLEMENTARY BENEFITS AND FAMILY BREAKDOWN

The 1976 Act imposes a statutory duty on the husband and wife to maintain each other and their children, legitimate or otherwise,[36] during the subsistence of their marriage. The duty between husband and wife ceases on divorce but remains with regard to any children. The obligation to maintain is, unlike the common law's,[37] fully reciprocal. Section 17 (1) provides:

"For the purposes of this Act—

(a) a man shall be liable to maintain his wife and his children; and

(b) a woman shall be liable to maintain her husband and her children."

The Act contains a number of devices which seek to ensure that a relative liable to maintain under section 17 (1) does not thrust his obligation onto the taxpayer and provides for the reimbursement by a husband of any sums paid to his dependants by the Commission. For the purposes of the Act, however, an obligation to maintain exists where and only where it is stated to do so by section 17 (1). It does not extend to, for example, a parent, step-parent, or parent-in-law.[38]

Under section 18, the Commission may itself take proceedings in a magistrates' court for an order against a relative liable to maintain. There is a similar provision under section 19 (2) in respect of affiliation orders. Difficulty arises in determining how far the obligation under section 17 (1) extends. The section is couched in unqualified terms and prima facie appears to render a husband liable to maintain an adulterous wife; it might be thought to follow that the Commission could recover from a husband in such a case sums paid to the wife, under section 18.

Adultery is an absolute bar to the provision of financial relief under section 27 of the Matrimonial Causes Act[39] and under the Matrimonial Proceedings (Magistrates' Courts) Act 1960. On the other hand, financial provision in divorce proceedings is unaffected by matrimonial misconduct unless it is "gross and obvious."[40]

It has been held that section 17 (1) is not unqualified as, prima facie, it might appear to be, though significantly different reasons have been offered for this conclusion. The view taken in *National Assistance Board* v. *Parkes*[41] was that the existence of a matrimonial offence (though not a mere separation[42]) was one of the circumstances to which magistrates were obliged, by section 18, to have regard and that accordingly it was proper to refuse an order in such a case. In *National Assistance Board* v. *Wilkinson*[43] however, Lord Goddard C.J. preferred simply to read section 17 as not creating an absolute obligation but as importing the common law rules at least to the extent of excusing maintenance in the case of a matrimonial offence.

This difference is significant because of section 25 of the Act which renders persistent refusal or neglect to maintain a criminal offence. This section makes no mention of "having regard to all the circumstances of the case" and it has been suggested[44] therefore that no account could be taken of a "matrimonial offence" as a defence to a charge under section 25. It is believed, however, that this conclusion is not inevitable. Section 25 only extends to a failure to maintain "any person whom for the purposes of this Act he is liable to maintain" which must be taken as referring back to section 17 therefore raising the question of the extent of the obligation to maintain under that section, and calling for an examination of the court's reasoning in *Wilkinson's* case.[45] The view expressed by Lord Goddard C.J. in that case was couched in the following terms:

"It is perfectly possible to give an intelligent meaning to section 42 (1) [now section 17 of the 1976 Act], while bearing in mind to the full the prefatory words, without construing it in such a manner as would make a husband liable, for the first time in the history of the law, to maintain a wife who was either living in adultery or refusing to live in the home which he had provided and where he was willing to receive her, and indeed would equally compel a wife to maintain a husband from whom she had been obliged to depart by reason of his brutality, or who might himself be living in open adultery with another woman. It is impossible to suppose that Parliament intended this section to have any such effect. In my opinion, it was inserted for the purpose of limiting the class of persons who were liable to maintain a family. The obligation of children

to maintain their parents has disappeared, the obligation by
grandparents or to grandparents has disappeared. From the
passing of the Act husband and wife have to support each other
and have to support their children, but it is not necessary to
hold that this section takes away from either spouse the defences
which have always been open to them against a claim, whether
arising out of the common law or the poor law statutes, and,
in my opinion, a husband is no more liable since the Act of
1948 to support an adulterous or deserting wife than he was
before."

Devlin J. took the same view.

There are certainly difficulties involved in simply applying
the common law rules. What, for instance, is the position of
an adulterous husband under section 17 (1)? In *Parkes'* case,
Romer L.J. disapproved the statement of Lord Goddard quoted
above, but he did not, in doing so, contemplate what the effect
would be so far as section 25 is concerned and the interpretation of section 18 which he prefers is no more compelling that
that offered by Lord Goddard. Nevertheless, the interpretation
offered in *Parkes'* case is generally accepted as authoritative.
In *Gray* v. *Gray*[46] in 1976, it was stated that the duty to maintain "was a duty created by the section for the purposes of
the 1948 Act [predecessor of the 1976 Act] and in particular
for the purposes of the recovery of expenses by the board. It
did not purport to confirm, amend or abolish the duty to maintain at common law, or under the various Acts relating to
matrimonial proceedings.... Thus as a matter of strict law,
adultery or continuing desertion which prevented a duty to
maintain arising in matrimonial proceedings did not excuse the
husband from the duties imposed by section [17] on him. It was,
however, 'a strong circumstance' affording an answer in law
to the claim."

A problem likely to be of increasing importance is the status
of parties to polygamous unions under section 17. It has been
held[47] that the wife in a polygamous marriage is liable to maintain the husband and can be made the subject of a section
18 order. By parity of reasoning, a husband in such a union
would seem to be liable to maintain all his wives.[48] Whether
one wife who had maintained the husband could secure contribution from others who had not must remain doubtful. The

words of section 17 are not apt to require one wife to maintain another.

Section 19 allows the Commission to stand in the shoes of a mother for purposes of obtaining an affiliation order. The Act and decisions make it clear, however, that the Commission is in a more favourable position than the wife. Thus, although the mother must act within 12 months, this does not bar the Commission from acting at any time up to three years after the last payment.[49] Equally, a subsequent marriage debars the mother, but not the Commission.[50] Even if the mother has tried and failed to get an affiliation order, the Commission may challenge the facts as found in securing its own order.[51] The only bar to the Commission's seeking an order is if an affiliation order is "in force." This has been held not to be the case where there is merely an adjudication of paternity but no order for payment. The "order" referred to is the payment order.[52]

These provisions have a peculiar and perhaps unanticipated effect by virtue of section 19 (6) which allows an order to be varied, on the application of the Commission, so as to substitute the mother for the Commission. This may happen even if the wife has lost her right to an affiliation order by lapse of time or marriage. If this happens, the mother may in effect obtain what Casey aptly calls "an affiliation order by the back door."[53]

Obviously, difficulties will arise as to the *quantum* of maintenance payable to a separated wife in receipt of supplementary benefits. Few men, particularly those whose circumstances are such as to require them to be subjected to magistrates' court proceedings, are in a position to support two families and "it is the almost inescapable consequence of the principles on which the supplementary benefits scheme is founded that whenever there is not enough money for the husband to support two women, it is the one with whom he is not living who has to resort to the Supplementary Benefits Commission."[54] If, however, he is able to support two families there is no good reason why the cost should be thrown onto public funds. The Commission has a dual function in these circumstances: first, to assist the wife, and secondly to seek reimbursement from the husband. Where the wife has not applied for an order, the policy of the Commission is to try and reach an informal arrangement with the husband whereby he will pay whatever is reasonable in view of his means. For this purpose, his own requirements are treated as being the supplementary benefit scale rates plus an allowance for rent and a quarter of his earnings. Anything above this can be regarded as available for the wife.

If the relative liable to maintain is in a position to fulfil his obligations but refuses to do so, then either the Commission or the wife may take proceedings against him. Formerly, the latter was encouraged to take proceedings herself. The Finer committee disapproved this practice on the ground that it put undue pressure on the wife at a time when she was most vulnerable and it has now ceased. "The question of proceedings against the husband is now discussed with the wife and it is made clear to her that the decision whether or not to take her own proceedings is entirely a matter for her and, whatever her decision may be, the Commission will ensure that she continues to receive the full supplementary benefits to which she is entitled."[55]

If the wife does not wish to go to the trouble of taking proceedings—and she will almost invariably have nothing to gain by so doing since the only effect of obtaining an order will be to reduce her supplementary benefit entitlement *pro tantó*—the Commission may take proceedings under section 18. An award made under section 18 is limited to whatever is appropriate and in many cases may be considerably less than the amount paid by way of benefit.

The next question which arises is whether the assessment of maintenance in the courts is affected by the fact that the claimant is in receipt of supplementary benefits. "The first rule is that the liable relative is not permitted to shift his responsibility to the Supplementary Benefits Commission. He is not permitted to argue that since the payment of maintenance will benefit the Commission rather than his wife, in the sense that it will reduce the burden on the Commission without increasing her income, this relieves him of liability ... but secondly, the maintenance order should not be pitched at a level which would reduce the liable relative to below subsistence level ... If there is sufficient to go round, the courts aim at producing equality at supplementary benefit levels."[56]

In a recent case[57] the question arose whether as a matter of principle the courts should fix a sum bringing the husband below supplementary benefit levels under the Attachment of

Earnings Act 1971. It was held that although there was nothing to prohibit the making of such an order, nevertheless in most cases it would be unreasonable to do so since supplementary benefits are not usually payable to help a man discharge his obligations under a court order.

The Finer Committee severely criticised the lack of co-ordination generally of the activities of the Commission, magistrates' courts and the divorce courts and drew attention to the fact that subsistence level in the latter in fixing maintenance orders is taken to be the supplementary benefit scales whilst a higher disregard is permitted by the Commission in making informal arrangements. In a slightly different but analogous context in *Williams* v. *Williams*[58] Finer J. remarked: "There is something radically unsatisfactory in the state of the law, by which I mean not only the matrimonial law but also the law of social security which allows two authorities—the courts and the Supplementary Benefit Commission—when dealing with precisely the same people in the identical human predicament, to make different determinations each acting in ignorance of what the other is doing and applying rules which only tangentially meet each other." In the latest case[59] the Family Division has adopted supplementary benefit guidelines on an appeal from a variation of a maintenance order.

Once an order has been made, the wife is able to relieve herself of responsibility for its enforcement by assigning it to the Commission, provided she is in receipt of supplementary benefit on a regular basis at a higher rate than the amount of the order. "The effect is that the wife receives her full entitlement regularly whether the maintenance order is paid in full, intermittently, or not at all. She is relieved of the anxiety of regular payments and the harassment and indignity of commuting between different officials and different procedures."[60] The Finer Committee concluded that "within the confines in which it operates which are determined by the overlap of entitlement as to maintenance and supplementary benefits the diversion procedure represents a victory of realism over bureaucracy."[61]

The Committee recommended the abolition of the dual system of magistrates and divorce courts and its replacement by a unified family court. Independently of this, they made a number of proposals designed to relieve the wife of the anxieties involved in court proceedings. Their first was to throw responsibility for the assessment and enforcement of maintenance wholly on the Commission by means of a new administrative order which was to be legally enforceable.[62] The order would not exceed supplementary benefit rates and there would be a right of appeal from it. It would only be at the appellate stage that disputed allegations of adultery would be relevant. They further recommended the introduction of a new one-parent social security benefit because the above reforms were inherently unsatisfactory in assisting one-parent families; even if maintenance payments were to be more strictly enforced, the single parent would still be forced to rely on supplementary benefits because of the low level of the order. As yet, none of these recommendations has found favour with the government.

Criminal proceedings may be taken against a liable relative for persistent refusal or neglect to maintain.[63] In 1975, such proceedings were taken in 624 cases resulting in 591 convictions. The futility of imprisonment in such circumstances is self-evident and the Finer Committee recommended its abolition.[64]

The object of the above provisions is to spare public funds burdens which others should and can carry. This seems to be a desirable policy[65] but is not pursued as consistently as it might be in other branches of the law where it is relevant. In *Re E.* (*decd.*)[66] an application was made for an order that reasonable provision be made out of E.'s estate for his dependants under the Inheritance (Family Provision) Act 1938 which imposed restrictions on a testator's right to will the estate away from needly dependants. He can do so provided adequate provision is otherwise available and in *Re E.* (*decd.*) the applicant was a wife receiving national assistance. It was held that the availability of national assistance "was a . . . reason for regarding the deceased as not having failed to make reasonable provision." "Where a deceased's estate is so small, and the means of the claimant so exiguous, that the only effect of making provision for the claimant would be *pro tanto* to relieve the national assistance fund, it would not be unreasonable for the deceased to make no provision for the claimant; but the fact that people who are very badly off can obtain national assistance does not justify a deceased in making no provision for a claimant out of a large estate."

In *Re E.* (*decd.*), reliance was placed on *Re Watkins* (*decd.*)[67] where Roxburgh J. decided similarly in the case of a widow hospitalised under the national health service. The situations are not, however, analogous. The national health service is a universal scheme, not means-tested, and would have been available to the widow whether she benefited from her husband's estate or not. Public funds were not therefore being devoted to financing the husband's posthumous beneficence. The opposite is the case where supplementary benefits are concerned. To the extent that dependants are supported out of the estate, they have resources which are taken into account in assessing entitlement to benefit.

The decision in *Re E.* (*decd.*), which may well have influenced the administration of many thousands of small estates, means that public funds are being resorted to to support those disinherited, perhaps in favour of persons not in need, by a testator who, in his life, was liable to maintain them. It is strange to suggest that lawyers should advise clients whose estates are so small as to yield an income lower than supplementary benefit levels that they would do no harm by willing it away from dependants if the latter would thereby qualify for benefit.

6. CONCLUSION

A critique of the supplementary benefits scheme ought fairly to begin by viewing it in its historical and functional context. Its foundations were laid at a time when certain values prevailed in society and when certain assumptions about social progress seemed warranted. When the Beveridge Report was compiled the English noncomformist virtues of industry, providence and thrift seemed to be more influential in social planning than they would be today. And the planners looked forward to a post-War era in which the whole social services would be mustered in the cause of social progress; full employment would result from education and economic planning, a national health service would take care of the sick and disabled.

In this context, it made sense to look mainly to contributory schemes for social security and to expect that the numbers needing social assistance would decline and remain few. Events have gone a long way to vitiating this concept of social security and have radically altered the role of social assistance.

The total cost of social security (defined here as embracing child benefit, national insurance, industrial injuries and supplementary benefit) is now of the order of £10,000 million per annum and rising. Less than half of this is derived from contributions payable under the insurance schemes by employers and employees (including graduated contributions). The largest single contributor is the Exchequer. Social security benefits deriving from the contributory schemes are now usually insufficient by themselves to provide a subsistence income. We have departed very far from the idea of self-support by statutory providence and thrift.

It might have been more purposeful to nurture the virtue of industry if the opportunities for exercising it had been enhanced. But 30 years after the Second World War, unemployment has reached its highest level since before the War. Education and economic planning have not worked the miracles hoped from them; the resources made available to the health services have not been sufficient to relieve the private purse of all the cost of sickness and disablement.

It is in this context that the supplementary benefits scheme falls to be criticised, and it should be made clear immediately that whilst there are serious defects, they are defects inherent in the scheme in the context in which it now finds itself, and not defects in its administration. No human institution is perfect; it is possible to argue that some junior Commission officers could be more sympathetic in their relations with claimants; the appeal tribunals may at times work inefficiently and, apparently, mysteriously as a result of the extreme informality of their proceedings. The overall picture remains that of a difficult and thankless job being done as well as is reasonably to be expected in the circumstances.

The cardinal point is that it is a difficult job. The supplementary benefits scheme is now expected to do a job that it was never designed to and is, in many respects, not well-fitted to do. In spite of the facts of industrial life and the now widespread recognition that unemployed persons are much more likely to be the victims of imperfectly planned and evolved social development rather than of vicious indolence, the rules of the scheme (and, therefore, its administration) still give its face a deterrent aspect. There is an immense apparatus of overlapping safeguards against voluntary unemployment; there are hardly any devices for ensuring that the truly needy are actually sought out and helped.

Many of the consequent vices will be removed if and when the new system of tax credits is instituted. But not all will fade. Much of the old law will find a place in the new scheme, and if we are not careful much that reflects discredited and inapt ideals may be imported with it.

Chapter 13

ADJUDICATION

INTRODUCTION

THE notion of a right to appeal against a refusal to give seems incongruous; and for a long time, social security was viewed as being a species of charity. It is otherwise when the payment of benefit by the administration becomes seen as a matter of right for the beneficiary; refusal of benefit may be denial of a right. In contributory schemes it is easy to establish the psychology of entitlement on a proprietory or, at least, pseudo-proprietory basis—the beneficiary has performed his part of the bargain by paying contributions into the fund; the fund must now play its part by paying him benefit. Less securely and more gradually, the idea of entitlement may also be founded on social responsibility—the casualties of a given method of social organisation designed to benefit most are the persons called upon to bear the burdens of that method of organisation and are entitled to the benefits prescribed as part of the package.

Where benefit is a right, it is hard to see how justice can be regarded as being seen to be done if the power to make decisions as to the granting of the benefit are vested exclusively in the administration. Whatever may be the actual position, the appearance is that of a party judging in his own cause—a lack of impartiality. This, however, is not the only consideration. Cost effectiveness comes into it. The first level of administration must reflect the need to keep the costs of administration within reasonable bounds and the resources available. It cannot be the highest quality of administration; that must be reserved for the more difficult cases and those resulting in dissatisfaction. Such a higher tier of administration is perfectly possible intra-departmentally and, indeed, does exist. The two birds of impartial decision-making and higher-quality administration can, however, be killed with one stone—an independent appeal structure.

The case against using the courts has been restated innumerable times; they tend to be costly, dilatory and geared to a purely adversarial process. In relation to social security, the void has been filled by tribunals. The full range of tribunals presently involved in the determination of social security claims and questions may be illustrated as follows:

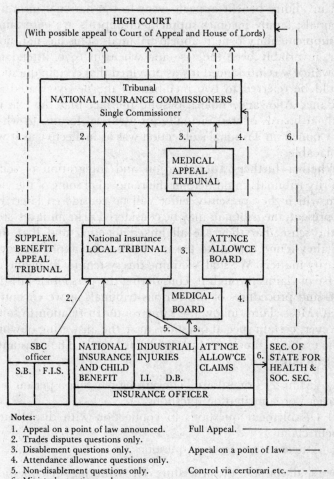

Notes:

1. Appeal on a point of law announced.
2. Trades disputes questions only.
3. Disablement questions only.
4. Attendance allowance questions only.
5. Non-disablement questions only.
6. Minister's questions only.

Full Appeal. ——————

Appeal on a point of law — — —

Control via certiorari etc. —— - —— -

This present structure bears witness to the partial success of the Franks Committee's exhortation to avoid proliferation of

tribunals and, where possible, to rationalise the jurisdictions
of existing ones. Family allowances (now replaced by child
benefit) claims were originally appealed to their own Umpire;
in 1959, however, his jurisdiction was vested in the national
insurance tribunals. As new benefits have been introduced,
jurisdiction to entertain appeals concerning them has usually
been vested in the existing tribunals. Child's special allowance
and invalidity benefit appeals went to the national insurance
tribunals; family incomes supplement appeals are entertained
by supplementary benefit appeal tribunals. This has not, however, invariably been the case and when, in 1970, attendance
allowance was introduced it was provided that certain questions
should be referred to two members of the newly-created Attendance Allowance Board, despite the fact that the existing
medical boards offered virtually an identical forum, to which
the Council on Tribunal's objection was as ineffective as it was
implacable.

Whether further rationalisation and integration of social
security tribunals could help in the removal of some of the vices
from which they presently suffer will be considered later. For
the present, the tribunals may be considered as forming a system
in the sense that they are all linked together and that they
and they alone constitute the mechanism for appeal in social
security matters. We shall examine this system by following the
course of claims through it, considering the personnel, jurisdictions and procedures of the various tribunals as we encounter
them. Most claims follow the same route. In relation to some,
however, certain special questions arise the answering of which
is the exclusive function of particular tribunals. These instances
are as follows:

1. "Minister's questions," concerning whether a person is an
"earner" or contribution questions, etc.;
2. Disablement questions in connection with disablement
benefit claims;
3. Attendance allowance questions.

We shall consider the procedures for answering such questions
as they arise.

DETERMINATION OF CLAIMS IN GENERAL

Supplementary benefit and family income supplement claims follow their own route, dealt with later. Under the Social Security Act 1975, claims are submitted in the first instance to an insurance officer[1] who is a civil servant.[2] He must dispose of it, so far as practicable, within 14 days,[3] by deciding it in favour of the claimant or adversely to the claimant, or by referring it to a local tribunal,[4] in which latter case he must notify the claimant in writing.[5] If he decides in favour of the claimant, that is an end of the matter—he can not himself appeal against his own decisions.[6] If, however, he decides adversely to the claimant, the claimant has a right of appeal to a local tribunal,[7] unless it is certified that the sole reason for the adverse decision is the adverse determination of one of the special questions referred to above, in which case the leave of the chairman of the local tribunal is required.[8] The time for appealing is 21 days from the date of the adverse decision.[9]

Local Tribunals

A local tribunal consists of three members, although with the consent of the claimant, an appeal may be heard by fewer.[10] The chairman is appointed by the Secretary of State[11] from a panel of persons appointed by the Lord Chancellor or, in Scotland, the Lord President.[12] There are no formal qualifications for appointment as chairman of a local tribunal but the practice has been pursued of seeking to secure the appointment of legally-qualified persons, and the vast majority of appointments in Great Britain are of such persons.

Of the other two members (often referred to as the "wingmen") one is drawn from a panel composed of persons representing employers and persons representing earners other than employed earners and the other is drawn from a panel of persons representing employed earners.[13] Although the main concern of local tribunals is with appeals from insurance officers under the Social Security Act, they also exercise jurisdiction in appeals from the reduction by the Supplementary Benefit Commission of claims for benefit on grounds of the trade dispute disqualification, this latter unusual course being designed to ensure uniformity of decision-making in trade dispute cases.[14]

Appeal lies from the decision of a local tribunal to a Commissioner. An insurance officer, the claimant or, in industrial injuries cases, a person adversely affected may appeal.[15] So, also, may a trade union or similar body where the claimant (or person in respect of whose death benefit is claimed) was a member at all relevant times.[16]

Notice of appeal must be given within three months of the decision of the local tribunal, though a Commissioner may extend the time for special reasons. The notice, in writing and stating grounds of appeal on the prescribed form, must be given to the claimant, if by an insurance officer, and otherwise to the local office.[17]

Commissioners

The Commissioners (a Chief National Insurance Commissioner and so many others as are thought fit, presently nine) are appointed by Her Majesty from among barristers or advocates of not less than 10 years' standing.[18] When it is remembered that a barrister with no experience of social security matters may be appointed but a solicitor with a long and successful record as chairman of a local tribunal may not, this has the appearance of a blatant restrictive practice endorsed by Parliament.

A Commissioner normally sits alone but in cases of exceptional importance or difficulty, a tribunal of three Commissioners may entertain the appeal.[19] A Commissioner may have the assistance of an expert assessor where questions of fact of special difficulty are involved.[20] Medical assessors are the most obvious type. A different procedure is for a Commissioner to refer a question to a medical practitioner for examination and report.[21]

Commissioners also entertain appeals on a question of law from the Attendance Allowance Board and from Medical Appeal Tribunals.[22] There is no appeal from the decision of a Commissioner, though he is subject to the supervisory jurisdiction of the High Court, as is any other inferior tribunal, and all decisions, whether of an insurance officer, a local tribunal or of a Commissioner, are subject to review by an insurance officer (and, on reference by him, by a local tribunal) on certain grounds. The grounds are that the decision under review must have been given in ignorance of, or based on a mistake as to, some material fact (as to which there must be fresh evidence if it is a Commissioner's decision under review); or that there has been a relevant change of circumstances since the original decision was given.[23]

Appeals heard by a local tribunal or a Commissioner are by way of re-hearing—evidence may be asked for anew if necessary. The local tribunal or Commissioner are not confined to entertaining only the questions determined by the insurance officer.[24]

Insurance officers work out of local offices of the Department of Health and Social Security. Local tribunals are found in most areas. The Commissioners sit in London, Edinburgh and Cardiff (and the Northern Ireland Commissioner in Belfast). There are no costs of appeal and reasonable expenses incurred in connection with the appeal by claimants and witnesses may be refunded. Legal aid is not available (although its introduction has been recognised as desirable, at all events in some types of case and it may soon be extended). Advice is, however, available under the £25 ("Green form") scheme under the Legal Advice and Assistance Act 1972, and a claimant may be represented by a solicitor or counsel (not uncommon in trade union cases) or by a friend. It has not been considered necessary or desirable to provide for the administration of the oath or the issue of subpoenas to witness. The best evidence ought to be tendered, but the tribunals do not operate the strict rules of evidence (such as the "hearsay" rule), preferring, rather, to attach such weight (which may, in the case of "hearsay" evidence be slight) as the evidence in question may warrant.

Notions of precedent, similar to those which operate in relation to court decisions at common law, exist within the tribunal structure. Distinctions are drawn between the *ratio decidendi* of decisions (*i.e.* the rule or principle of law, explicit or implicit, underlying and necessary to the decision in the case) and *obiter dicta* (*i.e.* propositions of law uttered in a case but incidental to the point and not necessary for its decision). So far as the former is concerned, the notion of precedent is that a decision of a higher tribunal "binds" lower tribunals. So, a decision of a tribunal of Commissioners is considered to bind a single Commissioner in a subsequent case[25] and a decision of a single Commissioner is considered to bind local tribunals[26] and, even more, insurance officers.[27] A tribunal on the same level is not regarded as bound by previous decisions on the level. So, a tribunal of Commissioners in a subsequent case is not, strictly, "bound" by prior decisions of such tribunals, at all events where the prior tribunal did not intend to state a principle of general application, but the usual tendency will be to follow the precedent unless there are compelling reasons for departing from it.[28] Similarly, the prior decisions of single Commissioners do not bind a single Commissioner in a subsequent case though, again, the tendency is to follow and it is a tendency which may prevail notwithstanding the hardship caused to a claimant.[29]

Although not binding, decisions of tribunals under former schemes (*i.e.* prior to the establishment of the modern tribunals in the post-War legislation)[30] are treated as being persuasive but must be treated with caution in view of the possibility of intervening legislative change. Decisions of Great Britain tribunals may be cited in Northern Ireland tribunals and Northern Ireland decisions are now sometimes cited in Great Britain cases. They are treated, again, as persuasive and, in view of the virtual identity of the two schemes, can be relied upon more readily as relevant. Decisions of other tribunals, *e.g.* Industrial Tribunals, on similar points, *e.g.* unfair dismissal cases in relation to misconduct cases[31] are rarely to be trusted, the similarity of the points often being more apparent than real.

In those areas where the superior courts have been provided with the opportunity to consider questions of social security law, their decisions are supposed to attract the highest respect of all. They are most frequently cited in industrial injuries cases where a half-century of workmen's compensation litigation yielded a handsome harvest.

These "statutory authorities"—insurance officers, local tribunals and Commissioners—who alone may determine claims, are the spine of the system of adjudication. In certain specific cases, however, other entities play an important and sometimes crucial part. These are cases where one of the "special questions" referred to above arises.

Minister's questions

The statutory authorities may not determine certain questions arising in connection with claims. Only the Secretary of State can do so. These include questions whether the contribution conditions for a particular benefit are satisfied in the particular case but also a number of others.[32] Obviously, whenever a claim is made for a benefit in respect of which there is a contribution condition it must be ascertained that that condition is fulfilled before benefit can be awarded. Normally, the point will be verified in an informal manner. If, however, the point is contested or controversial, it may be determined more formally and the Secretary of State may appoint a person to hold an inquiry into the matter.[33] He may, if he thinks fit, refer a question of law to the High Court or Court of Session[34] and a person aggrieved by his decision may appeal to the High Court or Court of Session on a question of law.[35] Costs may be ordered against the Secretary of State even if successful.[36]

Attendance allowance questions[37]

A question whether or not a claimant satisfies the attendance conditions set out in section 35 (1) of the 1975 Act must be determined by the Attendance Allowance Board.[38] A person aggrieved by the first decision of the Attendance Allowance Board must first of all seek review by the Board before appealing and,[39] even if he is then still aggrieved, may appeal on a question of law only, and with the leave of a Commissioner only, to a Commissioner.[40] The Board may delegate any of its functions in an individual case to one or more medical practitioners; the general practice is to delegate to two.

Disablement questions

In relation to a claim for disablement benefit it must be decided, *inter alia*, whether the accident has resulted in a loss of faculty and at what degree the extent of disablement resulting from a loss of faculty is to be assessed and in respect of what period.[41] These questions fall to be answered in the first instance by a medical board and must be referred by an insurance officer to a board.[42] Medical boards are appointed by the Secretary of State and consist of two or more medical practitioners of whom one acts as chairman.[43] With the consent of the claimant, the questions may be referred to a single medical practitioner. In practice, both disablement and attendance allowance questions are determined in the first instance by two doctors, occasionally one.

A medical board may consider a single case on a number of occasions; it may not be possible to make final assessment on the first reference and a provisional assessment, subject to reassessment later, may be made. Even a final assessment may be reviewed if either it was founded on non-disclosure or misrepresentation by the claimant or if there has been an unforeseen aggravation of the results of the injury.[44]

A claimant who is dissatisfied with the decision of a medical board may be able to appeal to a medical appeal tribunal. His right of appeal only exists where a final assessment has been made or where two years have elapsed since he was first provisionally assessed.[45] Although, however, he has no right of appeal in these circumstances, the Secretary of State may at any time instruct an insurance officer to refer a case to a medical appeal tribunal and a dissatisfied claimant may request such a reference.[46]

A medical appeal tribunal consists of a chairman and two medical practitioners.[47] The chairman is usually legally-qualified. Appeal lies from the decision of a medical appeal tribunal to the Commissioner on a point of law at the instance of the claimant, his trade union or a similar association or the Secretary of State. The leave either of the medical appeal tribunal or of a Commissioner is required.[48] A medical appeal tribunal may at any time refer a question of law to a Commissioner.[49]

The Secretary of State, the Attendance Allowance Board and the medical authorities have exclusive jurisdiction to entertain and determine these special questions. One implication of this is that any attempt to answer them by the statutory authorities (insurance officer, local tribunal and Commissioner) is a nullity and should it appear at any time in proceedings before the statutory authorities that such questions arise, they must be referred to the appropriate authorities for answer.

This has caused particular difficulty in the case of the disablement questions. Entitlement to disablement benefit via the accident route[50] turns upon there being (1) personal injury, (2) caused by accident, (3) resulting in loss of faculty, (4) assessable at the appropriate degree. The structure of the legislation requires that (1) and (2) be determined by the statutory authorities and that (3) and (4) be determined by the medical authorities. This becomes problematical, however, where the statutory authorities and the medical authorities are disposed to take different views on the question of causation of the loss of faculty, as well they may be. It may seem, to an insurance officer, to be the case that a particular injury has resulted from accident, and he may so find. On further examination, however, a medical board may be disposed to take the view that the appropriate degree at which to assess such loss of faculty *as results from the accident* is nil, it being attributable to some other cause, *e.g.* a pre-existing condition. But an assessment of nil per cent. has the appearance of a denial that there was a cognisable injury caused by accident.

This division of jurisdiction as between the statutory and medical authorities has been considered by the House of Lords on a number of occasions. The first of these was in the *Dowling* case[51] in which, on appeal, a Commissioner had decided that the injury was caused by accident and that injury benefit was accordingly payable. On a subsequent claim for disablement benefit, a medical appeal tribunal decided that there was no loss of faculty resulting from the accident, since the relevant injury was neither caused nor aggravated by the accident. The legislation then in force[52] provided that the Commissioner's decision that the accident caused the injury was "final and conclusive" and the House of Lords took the view that this meant final and conclusive not only so far as the injury benefit claim was concerned but also so far as the disablement benefit claim went. Accordingly, the medical appeal tribunal was wrong in seeking to make a determination inconsistent with that decision.

In the *Jones* and *Hudson* cases[53] the position was similar except that on this occasion, because two separate injuries were claimed to result from the accident, it was possible to uphold the medical authorities' finding that the disabling injury was not due to the accident consistently with the statutory authorities' award of injury benefit (the latter being referable to the other, non-disabling, injury). The House of Lords nevertheless took the view that the medical authorities were wrong and certiorari was issued.

In none of these cases was the decision of the House of Lords unanimous and in none, furthermore, was the compulsion of the argument wholly with the majorities. An attempt to clarify and settle the position was made in 1972 and the result of that attempt now appears in the 1975 Act.[54] Decision of any claim or question in accordance with the Act or regulations is final; but no finding of fact or other determination embodied in or necessary to a decision is conclusive for the purposes of any further decision. This seems to mean that in the type of situation encountered in the above decisions, the decision of neither the statutory authorities nor the medical authorities on any matter which it is for them to decide in accordance with the Act or regulations is conclusive for the purposes of the other. Accordingly, notwithstanding that the statutory authorities have decided that an accident has resulted in personal injury it remains open for the medical authorities to decide that the same accident has not resulted in a loss of faculty. If this is the intent of section 117, then certainty is fostered but at the cost of anomaly—the result may be that the severance of a hand is found to result from the accident but that the loss of its use is not.

One other jurisdiction incidental to industrial injuries claims may be mentioned. In some cases, an industrial accident may occur which does not immediately result in incapacity leading to injury benefit or loss of faculty leading to disablement benefit though it may clearly do so later. Whether a claim for either of these benefits is made or not, there is something to be said for providing for the determination at this stage of such questions as it is possible to answer, in particular whether an accident arose out of and in the course of the employment, whether that employment was in employed earner's employment, and whether the circumstances are such as to avoid disqualification by reason of being outside Great Britain. On some of these matters, evidence later may be more difficult to obtain and less reliable when obtained; and such fruits as may be harvested from the administrative effort so far put in may as well be gathered. The legislation therefore provides that in such circumstances, a declaration may be made by the statutory authorities to the effect that an accident was an industrial accident, *i.e.* if the above questions are answerable in the affirmative.[55] Such a declaration is final, subject to review on the grounds applicable to reviews generally,[56] and a subsequent claim would turn upon the answers to the other, as yet unanswered, questions.

The Role of the High Court

In some of the instances above dealt with, appeal lies to the High Court on a question of law. Even without this, however, the High Court's supervisory jurisdiction over all inferior courts and tribunals is available. Appeal is the creature of statute; the supervisory jurisdiction, exercisable via orders in the nature of prerogative writs, derives from the prerogative.

Grounds of appeal on a question of law are not confined to the narrow question of the particular point of substantive law raised by the proceedings in the inferior tribunal. The proper procedures must also be observed and even findings of fact are controllable to the extent that as a matter of law they must be reasonably supportable by the evidence.[57] The High Court is, unfortunately, not always entirely clear as to whether the point under consideration is one of law, in which case the appeal will succeed if the court takes a different view, or fact, in which case the fact that the court might have found differently is not, by itself, enough.

In the case of social security tribunals, the almost invariable way in which it is sought to invoke the supervisory jurisdiction of the High Court is by applying for an order of certiorari. This is an order whereby, in effect, the court orders the tribunal to "put right" its decision and, obviously, such an order will not be issued unless the court takes the view that the tribunal decision challenged is wrong for some reason. Such a reason might consist in the fact that the tribunal had no power to make the decision which it purported to make (*ultra vires*); or that its decision was arrived at in a manner contrary to the "principles of natural justice"; or that there is an error of law on the face of the record; or, possibly, on the ground that the decision is wholly unreasonable. The "principles of natural justice" do not allow an appeal to moral principles; confusingly, they refer to the requirement that proper procedures, calculated to conduce towards fairness, are adopted in the process of making the decision. So it would be contrary to the principles of natural justice for a tribunal to listen only to the case of one party, or for a member of it to have a significant interest in the proceedings. "Error of law on the face of the record" means that on the basis of what is actually stated on the forms or necessarily implicit in it, the decision which the tribunal arrived at can only be explained on the basis of a wrongful understanding of the relevant legal principles.

Certiorari is a discretionary remedy. This means that even if one of the above grounds is clearly established, the court may nevertheless decline to issue the order. Lord Denning M.R. in the Court of Appeal has, indeed, stated that in applications for certiorari in supplementary benefit cases, the courts should exercise their discretion against the issue of certiorari even in cases of error of law unless either manifest injustice to a claimant would be thereby condoned, or unless the case was one of a type which might well affect a large number of claimants in a significant way.[58]

CHILD BENEFIT ADJUDICATION

Child benefit claims are processed in the same way as national insurance claims in relation to which the special questions do not arise. All questions are determined by the statutory authorities: insurance officers, local tribunals and National Insurance Commissioners.[59] A separate tribunal structure closely resembling the national insurance structure was contemplated for the now superseded child interim benefit.[60]

THE WORK-LOAD OF NATIONAL INSURANCE TRIBUNALS

The number of appeals handled by national insurance local tribunals and the Commissioners during 1975, together with the number of successes by appellants, is indicated overleaf:

It will be seen that overall, the average success rate before local tribunals is about 20 per cent. and, before a Commissioner,

Benefit, allowance, etc.	Local tribunals		Commissioners	
	Appeals*	Successes	Appeals	Successes
Unemployment	16,872	3,106	898	225
Sickness	5,321	805	225	52
Industrial Injuries	3,677	1,344	429	135
Invalidity	2,536	493	163	41
Retirement	748	131	101	27
Family	657	62	30	3
Maternity	370	59	21	3
Widow's	212	40	16	3
Attendance	74	11	26	8
Death Grant	45	6	2	0
Guardian's	21	1	3	0
Totals	30,533	6,058	1,914	497

Source: *Social Security Statistics, 1975*
(* appeals not including references.)

about 25 per cent. The most significant deviations arise in connection with industrial injuries claims before local tribunals and, although the numbers are small, attendance allowance appeals before a Commissioner. The success rate is lowest in sickness benefit and maternity benefit cases before local tribunals. It is worth observing that although there is a steady success rate of the order of 25 per cent. before Commissioners, appeals to them from local tribunals are pursued in only approximately 2 per cent. of cases,[61] including appeals by insurance officers and others.

It was the view of the Franks Committee that national insurance tribunals functioned well. "The impression which we have gained of the working of the system of adjudication for national insurance and industrial injuries claims is most favourable. The system is generally considered to have operated smoothly for many years, and we are satisfied that no structural changes are called for."[61] More recent and more scientific research has tended to confirm this view.[62] Such research, however, is necessarily subject to the inherent limitations of social science research method and ought not to induce complacency. Accurate measurement of such dissatisfaction as there may be amongst potential customers of the tribunals will not necessarily be obtained by inquiry of those who chose to resort to them in the first place; the vast majority choose not to appeal. And some facets of the work of tribunals is not readily measurable at all, such as the efficiency of their procedure or the quality of their decisions. There may be inequality of arms as between an expert insurance officer and an unrepresented claimant and this will not readily be compensated for by the undoubted fair-mindedness of most insurance officers (who frequently present arguments for claimants) and tribunal members. The frequency with which wingmen serve may be thought to be insufficient to maximise their usefulness; part-time chairmen may tend to be spare-time chairmen and a sufficient mastery of social security law so as to enable a chairman properly to discharge the inquisitorial role on all occasions may not readily be acquired in the spare moments of a busy professional man. Some argue that clerks, whose *cursus honorum* leads back into mainstream DHSS work, will necessarily have mixed loyalties.

One error in particular seems particularly commonplace and that is that questions of law arise relatively uncommonly in cases before tribunals. That is an error which probably derives more from an inability to recognise its features than from an unwillingness to observe the scene.

Supplementary Benefit Appeals Tribunals (SBATs)

SBATs entertain appeals in supplementary benefit cases (except those concerning the trades disputes disqualification which go to national insurance local tribunals) and family incomes supplement cases. The Supplementary Benefits Act 1976 (formerly the Ministry of Social Security Act 1966) continues the practice formerly prevailing of providing for appeals to SBATs whose determinations remain "conclusive for all purposes"[63] although the government's intention of providing for appeals to the courts has been announced.

The SBATs entertain appeals against determination of the Supplementary Benefits Commission and also against refusals by the Commission to review such determinations, on any of a number of grounds whose scope is such that the tribunals' jurisdiction is potentially very wide. On an appeal, a tribunal may confirm the original determination, or substitute therefore any other determination which the Commission itself could have made.[64] An award may thus be confirmed, increased or reduced. The number of appeals has increased enormously in recent years (from 9,565 in 1965 to 32,759 in 1975) largely as the result of a marked increase in the interest of voluntary groups in this area. The same period has witnessed no enduring significant increase in the work of the national insurance tribunals. The over all success rate before SBATs remains fairly constant around the 20 per cent. mark,[65] although there are apparently variations as between particular tribunals.

In addition to entertaining appeals on the initiative of a disappointed claimant, SBATs also have jurisdiction to entertain references from the Commission in cases where it appears to the Commission that there is a refusal or neglect to maintain himself by a person claiming or in receipt of benefit.[66] There is a further jurisdiction under section 26 (2) on a reference by the Secretary of State on the question of whether benefit is recoverable by him on grounds of misrepresentation etc.

Each tribunal consists of a chairman and two other members, all appointed by the Secretary of State, and has jurisdiction in respect of a particular geographical area assigned by him. The chairman is not required to be legally qualified and hitherto no policy has been pursued of trying to secure the appointment of legally-qualified chairmen. This, however, is expected to follow in the wake of the establishment of appeals from the decisions of SBATs. There are at present 120 SBATs in Great Britain. Their procedure is governed by regulations[67] under which they are required to give written reasons for their decisions. The manner in which this obligation is discharged has failed to satisfy the Council on Tribunals but its blandishments on the point appear so far to have been resisted. The vice is, however, unlikely to survive the institution of an appeals system.

Appeals to an SBAT must be made in writing. Normally, they should be made within 21 days of the relevant decision (*i.e.* the original determination or refusal to review) but the tribunal has discretion to extend the period and appeals have been entertained even after a year.[68] The appeal is by way of re-hearing and there are no formal pleadings, but any issue which the claimant wishes to have settled should be expressly stated. Regulations require the tribunal to hold a hearing "as soon as may be" and provision is made for an accelerated hearing in appropriate cases. This is facilitated by providing for appeals to be heard by a tribunal of two with the consent of the claimant.

Tribunal hearings must be held in private. The tribunal staff and parties, together with representatives, must obviously be present, and there is provision for persons bona fide engaged in research to be admitted with the consent of the claimant and chairman. The Franks Committee accepted the need for privacy on the ground that it will often be necessary to discuss the private affairs of claimants with the result that fear of publicity might inhibit resort to the tribunals. This is no doubt an entirely proper policy and it is thus a matter for regret that it is abandoned when, as sometimes happens, supplementary benefit cases reach inferior and superior courts. But one remains in any case at a loss as to why the public should be excluded willy-nilly even if the claimant would wish them to attend, a choice which could be opened without fear by the simple addition of a tick-box to the appeal form. As long as this opportunity is denied to claimants there may remain a suspicion, however unworthy, that some other, unarticulated, interest may be served by privacy.

Legal aid is not available before SBATs and therefore legal representation is rare, though again advice and assistance is available under the Legal Advice and Assistance Act 1972 (the "£25" or "Green form" scheme). Few solicitors, however, have any great expertise in supplementary benefit matters and much representation is handled by voluntary associations such as the Child Poverty Action Group. As is the case of national insurance tribunals, the notion has long prevailed that questions of law rarely arise before SBATs. The recent spate of applications for certiorari to the High Court[69] may indicate that some enlightenment on this point has already dawned and may prompt more.

SBATs do not take evidence on oath and cannot compel the attendance of witnesses. They must reach their decisions as soon as possible (though they may adjourn before doing so) and normally notify a claimant of the result of his appeal by post within a day or two.

Applications to the High Court

Although there is as yet no right of appeal from the decisions of SBATs the supervisory jurisdiction of the High Court over inferior tribunals is available. Until 1973, no application was reported, but since that date a number of cases have been the subject of application. The experience has been encouraging and then discouraging by turns. The first decision, in *R.* v. *Birmingham Appeal Tribunal, ex p. Simper*[70] reminded us that the grounds for review were by no means narrow. It was there held that the statutory scheme conferred a discretion which must therefore be exercised in each individual case and certiorari would lie to quash a determination made by reference only to a hard-and-fast departmental rule that the determination should be made in a particular way. The tribunal's decision was accordingly quashed. The triumph was short-lived—the particular decision was negatived by regulations shortly thereafter, but the principle remained and still holds good. The dicta of Lord Denning M.R. in *Moore*'s case, referred to above,[71] added discouragement. His reasons for the non-exercise of discretion to issue certiorari (and therefore to restrict the scope for control by the High Court) undoubtedly contain a truth. It was, no doubt, the intention of Parliament that the SBATs should handle appeals and that their decisions, indeed, should be final. But "final" in this context has not been regarded as excluding the supervisory jurisdiction of the High Court and it may certainly be doubted if it was the intention of Parliament that SBATs should be free from supervision even when wrong in law in making their decisions.

The grounds for withholding certiorari stated by Lord Denning have not, in the event, proved too restrictive. In subsequent cases[72] the Court has on a number of occasions seen fit to intervene.

The Future of SBATs

It will rightly be inferred from the above that it is relatively easy, at least in a technical if not always in a psychological sense, to take an appeal before an SBAT and that procedure before such a body is extremely informal. A price is paid for this informality. The Council on Tribunals has drawn attention to the amount of time spent by SBATs in explaining to claimants under a misunderstanding as to their rights (particularly under the family incomes supplement scheme), why they do not qualify for benefit. It may be some consolation to realise that ignorance of the law is by no means confined to social security and that the same phenomenon would undoubtedly occur more frequently before ordinary courts were they as readily accessible to claimants as are tribunals and were professional advice as hard to come by as it is in the field of social security. If there is some truth in the complaint that members of the public are ill-informed about their rights to social security benefits, it is still the case that a greater effort at information is made in this field than in most other branches of the law.

A price is, however, paid for informality and it is arguably more costly. Acknowledging to the full the need to put appellants at their ease and the possibility that many claimants may not easily acquire a complete understanding of what is going on, the fact nevertheless remains that informality can easily slide into lack of clarity about the actual issues and can impede their satisfactory determination. Without going very far along the road towards written, formal, pleadings, there is a case to be made out for increased efficiency on the part of some tribunals in isolating and explaining the relevant issues to the parties. Clarity is consistent with simplicity; it does not involve verbosity and delay, but it does require an articulate chairman with some analytical skill and not all chairmen possess these qualities. An argument for entitlement has on more than one occasion been received as a prayer for the benevolent exercise of a discretion.

In recent years, SBATs have come under increasing criticism. It is by no means always well-informed and some of it seems to express little but a dislike of the policy underlying the supplementary benefit scheme which is, after all, the result of endorsement by Parliament and hardly the fault of the tribunals. Other criticism is, however, more substantial.[73] Cases are not always as well presented as they could be; claimants go unrepresented when they want and need representation; the role of clerks is not always satisfactory; wingmen acquire insufficient experience; chairmen are again spare-time and lack knowledge and some relevant skills; procedures are weak; the policy of the Commission may be mistaken for law or at least "quasi-law"; evidence is insufficiently scrutinised and improperly weighed; reasons are inadequately stated; there is an over all lack of supervision and control and insufficient sanction for the ensuring of high-quality decision-making.

Various sovereign remedies have been proposed but, bearing in mind that national insurance adjudication is not entirely free from vice, the chief ills of both systems point overwhelmingly in the direction of a reform of the whole of social security adjudication in a way which creates opportunities for the development of a corps of skilled personnel. Claimants need advice and representation of high quality; tribunals need the services of clerks whose career structure will inspire loyalty towards the tribunal service. Adjudication is too important a function to be left to the spare-time of busy men however well-intentioned. And at a higher level of decision-making, selection should be made from amongst those who have acquired experience in the service.[74] What is needed is an integrated system of tribunals for all social security appeals, supervised by the Commissioners, within which there exists a single career structure within which full-time personnel can graduate from adviser and clerk to Chief Commissioner in the tribunal service. This is not just an option for reform; it is the only way in which a sustained assault can be mounted upon all the serious vices of the system.

INTRODUCTION

1 Wickwar, *Social Services*, pp. 9–10.
2 *Ibid*. p. 11.
3 T. H. Marshall, "The Role of the Social Services" in *The Future of the Social Services*, ed. Robson and Crick, pp. 11–22.
4 It is interesting to note that the only significant opposition to the Workmen's Compensation Bill in 1896 came from Members of Parliament voicing trade union and friendly society interests.
5 *Social Insurance and Allied Services*, Cmd. 6404 (hereinafter, Report).
6 *Social Insurance*, Cmd. 6550, 6551.
7 See *post*, pp. 302–306.
8 See *post*, pp. 385–439.
9 *Post*, p. 447.
10 1975 Act, s. 99(2)(c).
11 *Ibid*. s. 100(1).
12 *Ibid*. s. 101(2)(c) and (3).
13 *Ibid*. s. 104.
14 *Ibid*. s. 97(2).
15 *Ibid*. s. 97(3).

CHAPTER 1

FINANCE AND FUNDING

1 Report, para. 9.
2 Although it may be noted that it does not seem to attach to non-contributory family allowances.
3 Cmd. 6550, para. 6.
4 H.C.Deb., Vol. 781, col. 762. Contributions are now much more earnings-related, though the existence of an upper earnings limit and of flat-rate Class II contributions still lends them a regressive bias.
5 These figures describe the situation which prevailed five to six years ago.
6 Abel-Smith, *Socialism and Affluence*, p. 23.
7 See Department of Health and Social Security Annual Report 1975, p. 75. On finance generally, see 1975 Act, ss. 1–11 (contributions) and 133–137 (the Fund etc.). It should be noted that the Fund (now amalgamated with the Industrial Injuries Fund) meets only the cost of contributory benefits. Most non-contributory benefits, even under the 1975 Act (*i.e.* attendance allowance, non-contributory invalidity pension, invalid care allowance, Category C and D retirement pension and corresponding benefits and age addition), are met out of general exchequer (s. 135). Anomalously guardian's allowance (which is a non-contributory benefit (s. 38) is not included in this list.
8 Policy is largely dictated by the legislation, see 1975 Act, s. 133.
9 See *post*, pp. 20–21.
10 The "big spenders" on the non-contributory side (supplementary

benefits and family benefits) fall outside the scheme of the 1975 Act altogether and are funded from the Consolidated Fund. On pensions funding, see pp. 258–271, *post*.

11 See *post*, pp. 258–307.

12 s. 1(2).

13 *Ibid*. s. 2(1).

14 See Contributions Regulations, especially regs. 7–19, 72–117 and Sched. 1; Categorisation of Earners Regulations.

15 See 1975 Act, Sched. 20, *s.n.* "contract of service."

16 See *e.g. Vandyk* v. *Minister of Pensions and National Insurance* [1955] 1 Q.B. 29; *Benjamin* v. *Minister of Pensions and National Insurance* [1960] 2 Q.B. 519, *A.E.U.* v. *Minister of Pensions* [1963] 1 W.L.R. 441, *Ready Mixed Concrete Ltd.* v. *Minister of Pensions* [1968] 2 Q.B. 497, *Whittaker* v. *Minister of Pensions* [1967] 1 Q.B. 156, *Stagecraft Ltd.* v. *Minister of National Insurance*, 1952 S.C. 288, *Market Investigations* v. *Minister of Social Security* [1969] 2 Q.B. 173, *Global Plant Hire Ltd.* v. *Secretary of State for Health and Social Security* [1972] 1 Q.B. 139, *Argent* v. *Minister of Social Security* [1968] 1 W.L.R. 1749, *Rennison* v. *Minister of Social Security* [1970] 10 K.I.R. 65, *Maurice Graham Ltd.* v. *Brunswick* (1974) K.I.R. 188, *C.S.43/48(KL)*, *40/48(UB)*, *C.P.7/49(KL)*, *C.S.133/49(KL)*, *C.S. 509/50(KL)*, *R(S)17/52*, *R(P)7/54*, *R(S)27/54*, *R(P)2/56*, *R(S)8/56*, *R(U)8/60*, *R(S)1/62*, *R(G)1/64*, *R(P)1/65*, *R(P)4/67*, *R(P)1/69. R(U)6/70*.

17 The literature on this subject is immense. See, in addition to the cases mentioned in the note above, *Gould* v. *Minister of National Insurance* [1951] 1 K.B. 731, *Ready Mixed Concrete* v. *Cox* (1971) 10 K.I.R. 273; see, in connection with the *Argent* case above, Second Report of the Parliamentary Commissioner for Administration, session 1971–72, Annual Report for 1971, Case No. C. 139/S, p. 109; Selected Decisions of the Minister on Questions of Classification and Insurability, *passim*. (Insurability, a largely otiose concept, disappears from the latest legislation.)

18 See *Market Investigations Ltd.* v. *Minister of Social Security* [1969] 2 Q.B. 173.

19 See P.C.A. Case No. C.139/S, n. 17 above. But see now the S.S. (Categorisation of Earners) Amendment Regs. 1977 and H.C. Paper No. 418 (1976–77).

20 s. 4.

21 Contribution Regulations, reg. 40.

22 *The Gee-Whiz* [1951] 1 All E.R. 876.

23 Contribution Regulations, reg. 19.

24 *Ibid*. reg. 16. See Social Security (M.P.) Act 1977, s. 18, and S.S. (Contributions) (Employment Protection) Regs. S.I. 1977 No. 622.

25 *Ibid*. reg. 17.

26 1975 Act, s. 146(1).

27 *Ibid*. s. 148(1)(a).

28 *Ibid*. s. 93(1).

29 *Ibid*. s. 7. Regulations may exempt low earners.

30 *Ibid*. s. 9.

31 *Ibid*. s. 2(1)(a).

32 *Ibid*. Sched. 20, *s.n.* "employment."

33 Contribution Regulations, regs. 20–23, 50–52.

34 1975 Act, s. 2(2)(*b*).

35 Categorisation of Earners Regulations, Sched. I, Pt II.

36 1975 Act, s. 8.

37 Contribution Regulations, reg. 24(3).

38 *Ibid.* reg. 25.

39 See *e.g.* Case No. C.225/V, Fifth Report of the Parliamentary Commissioner for Administration, 1975–76, p. 116; Case No. C.406/V, *ibid.*, p. 122; Case No. C.372/J, *ibid.* Fourth Report, 1974–75.

40 See Credits Regulations.

41 *Ibid.* reg. 3.

42 *Ibid.* regs. 4 and 5.

43 *Ibid.* reg. 9. In the case of unemployment, the contributor must be available for work.

44 1975 Act, ss. 146(1), 147.

45 *Ibid.* s. 147(1).

46 *Ibid.* s. 149(2).

47 *Ibid.* s. 150; *Shilvock* v. *Booth* [1956] 1 W.L.R. 135, *Morgan* v. *Quality Tools & Engineering (Stourbridge) Ltd.* [1972] 1 W.L.R. 196.

48 *Ibid.* s. 152(4). He and other agents of the company may also be prosecuted in certain circumstances, *ibid.* s. 147(7).

49 *Department of Health and Social Security* v. *Wayte* [1972] 1 W.L.R. 19.

50 1975 Act, s. 147(3), (4).

51 *Post*, pp. 443, 447.

52 *Post*, p. 447.

CHAPTER 2

BENEFIT

Chapter 2, pp. 24–34

1 Report, para. 27.

2 *Ibid.* (italics supplied).

3 1975 Act, ss. 124–126. See, however, *The* Metzger *v.* D.H.S.S. *The Times*, March 26, 1977.

4 This is the long-term trend. Due to factors such as the non-taxability of social security benefits and the non-raising of the tax base for earnings in a time of high inflation, the short-term trend is for social security benefits to compare slightly more favourably with low earnings in net terms than previously.

5 Report, especially paras. 193–232.

6 Contributions Regulations, reg. 34.

7 Unemployment, Sickness and Invalidity Benefit Regulations, reg. 14; Maternity Benefit Regulations, reg. 8; Widow's Benefit and Retirement Pensions Regulations, reg. 5.

8 Hospital In-Patients Regulations, regs. 3–7, 9–13.

9 *Ibid.*

10 *Ibid.* reg. 15.

11 *R(P)2/62* and see *post*, p. 288.

12 See *e.g.* *65/49(SB)* and *R(S)9/52*.

13 *R(S)2/52, R(S)2/54.*

14 *R(S)2/52, R(S)13/52, R(S)2/54.*

15 *C.S.591/49.* Note that the decision here may turn upon the particular contract and is not necessarily applicable to contracts of employment generally.

16 *R(S)4/53.*

17 *R(S)8/51.*

18 *R(P)1/67.*

19 *R(S)28/52.*

20 *R(S)2/52.*

21 *R(S)1/54.*

22 *R(S)12/56.*

23 See *post*, pp. 218–221.

24 See *e.g. R(S)26/64, R(S)15/55, R(S)6/58.* As to what constitutes "residence" in prescribed accommodation, see *R(P)17/55.*

25 Hospital In-Patient Regulations, reg. 21.

26 See Overlapping Benefits Regulations 1975.

27 *Ibid.* reg. 3(4).

28 *Ibid.* reg. 3(2).

29 *Ibid.* reg. 8.

30 *R(S)9/58*; see also *C.S.11/49(KL).*

31 See *e.g.* Overlapping Benefits Regulations, reg. 5 and Sched. See also *C.G.186/50(KL), R(S)13/55.*

32 Overlapping Benefit Regulations, *ibid.*; *C.S.166/49(KL).*

33 Overlapping Benefit Regulations, *ibid.*; *R(G)7/54.*

34 Overlapping Benefit Regulations, reg. 2, *s.n.* "training allowance"; and see *R(U)38/56.*

35 *Post*, pp. 248–252.

36 *Post*, pp. 253–257.

37 *Post*, pp. 361–385.

38 See *post*, pp. 398–439.

39 1975 Act ss. 41–43, especially 41(1), as amended by the Child Benefit Act 1975, s. 21, Sched. 4, para. 13.

40 *Post*, pp. 361–385.

41 *Post*, pp. 33–34.

42 *Post*, pp. 40–41.

43 1975 Act, s. 42(2); see also s. 42(3).

44 *Post*, pp. 366–368.

45 *Post*, pp. 36–37.

46 *Post*, pp. 361–385.

47 1975 Act, s. 43(1); General Benefit Regulations, regs. 7–10.

48 *Post*, pp. 34–35.

49 1975 Act, s. 41(6); see *post*, pp. 35–36.

50 Overlapping Benefits Regs., reg. 12 as substituted by the S.S. (Child Benefit Consequential) Regs. 1977, reg. 10.

51 *Post*, pp. 34–35.

52 1975 Act, ss. 44(1)(*a*), 45(2)(*a*), 47(1).

53. *Ibid.* ss. 44(1)(*a*)(ii), 45(2)(*b*), 47(1)(*a*).

54 *Ibid.* ss. 44(3)(*a*), 47(1)(*a*).

55 *Ibid.* s. 44(1)(*b*).

56 Maternity Benefit Regulations, reg. 9(1)(*a*). *Sed quaere* could she receive earnings from employment yet not do any work? Possibly yes, see *R(S)2/55* and *R(S)8/58*.

57 1975 Act, s. 45, and see *post*, pp. 290–298.

58 See *post*, p. 298.

59 See *R(S)23/51*, *R(S)12/55*.

60 See *R(P)7/51*, *R(U)30/52*, *R(S)11/56*, *R1/60(UB)*, *R(S)3/61*.

61 *R(S)2/55*, *R(S)8/58*.

62 *Cf. R(S)27/54* and *R(S)6/56*.

63 *R(P)1/70*.

64 *C.S.11/48(KL)*, *C.G.3/49(KL)*.

65 *R(S)9/61*.

66 See *e.g. R(U)1/68*.

67 *C.G.203/49(KL)*.

68 *C.G.53/50(KL)*.

69 *38/49(P)*.

70 *R(G)1/51*.

71 *R(G)2/70*.

72 *R(P)1/51*, *R(G)1/55*, *R(G)7/56*, *R(G)8/56*, *R(G)1/71*.

73 *R(S)4/59*.

74 *R(G)1/68*.

75 *R(G)10/53*.

76 *R(G)2/63*.

77 See *R(G)3/72*, not following *R(G)1/53*.

78 See Matrimonial Causes Act 1973, s. 16.

79 *R(G)2/71*.

80 On the position prior to the enactment of the Family Allowances and National Insurance Act 1956, s. 3, see *R(G)6/51*, *C.G.116/51*, *R(G)18/52*, *R(G)11/53*, *R(G)3/55*, *R(G)7/55* and Webb, (1956) 19 M.L.R. 687–690. See also *R(G)2/56*.

81 *i.e* "when neither party to it has any spouse additional to the other . . . ," Polygamous Marriage Regulations, reg. 2.

82 *Ibid.* reg. 3.

83 Social Security (Dependency) Regulations 1977, reg. 9(1) and Sched. 1.

84 *Ibid*; Adoption Act 1976, s. 39.

85 *C.S.7/48(KL)*.

86 National Insurance Act 1965, s. 43(9); 1975 Act, Sched. 20, *s.n.* "relative."

87 See *C.S.33/48(KL)*.

88 *Post*, pp. 34–35.

89 *Post*, pp. 40–41.

90 1975 Act, ss. 44(3)(*b*), 47(1)(*b*).

91 Social Security (Dependency) Regulations 1977, reg. 9(2)(*a*) and (*b*).

92 *Ibid.* reg. 9(2)(*a*), *post*, pp. 35–36.

93 *Ibid.* reg. 9(2)(*d*)(ii).

94 Inaccurate because in common parlance no child is required.

95 1975 Act, ss. 44(3)(*c*), 46(2).

96 General Benefit Regulations, regs. 3 and 4.
97 See *422/48(SB)*.
98 See *C.U.257/50(KL)*.
99 See *C.S.55/49(KL)*.

Chapter 2, pp. 34–46

1 *R(S)17/54.*
2 *C.S.726/49(KL).*
3 *Ibid.*
4 *R(S)20/54.*
5 *C.U.201/50(KL).*
6 See *post*, pp. 48–50.
7 *R(P)15/56.*
8 *Ibid.*
9 *R(S)14/52.*
10 S.S. Benefit (Persons Residing Together) Regs. 1977.
11 *R(P)7/53, R(U)14/59.*
12 *C.S.185/50(KL), C.S.541/50(KL).*
13 *R(U)6/54; cf. C.S.31/48* (unrep.).
14 See *C.S.3/48(K).*
15 *R(S)10/55.*
16 *C.S.541/50(KL).*
17 *R(S)10/55.*
18 *R(S)15/51.*
19 See above and n. 10 above.
20 See *e.g. C.S.3/48(K), C.S.6/48(K), C.S.70/49(K), 134/50(SB), R(S)15/51, R(S)22/52, R(S)26/52, R(S)31/52.*
21 See n. 10 above; *R(S)8/60.*
22 1975 Act, Sched. 20, *s.n.* "incapable of self-support."
23 *C.S.185/50(KL); C.S.41/49(KL).*
24 *C.S.343/49(KL).*
25 *C.S.288/50(KL).*
26 *Ibid.*
27 *R(S)2/56.*
28 Social Security Benefit (Dependency) Regulations 1977, regs. 3, 5, 11.
29 *R(U)25/59.*
30 Social Security Benefit (Dependency) Regulations 1977, reg. 5.
31 *R(U)11/71.*
32 *R(U)11/62.*
33 *R(U)15/64.*
34 Social Security Benefit (Dependency) Regulations 1977, reg. 5(4).
35 *R(U)2/65.*
36 Social Security Benefit (Dependency) Regulations 1977, reg. 3(1).
37 *R(S)3/74.*
38 *Post*, pp. 355–385.
39 *R(U)37/52.*
40 *C.U.80/48(KL).*
41 *Post*, pp. 368–369.

42 *C.S.638/49(KL)*.

43 *R(S)7/58*.

44 *C.U.303/50(KL)*.

45 *R(S)22/52*.

46 On supplementary benefits, see now S.S. (Dependency) Regs. 1977, reg. 4.

47 See *e.g. C.U.80/48(KL)*.

48 *R(S)6/52*.

49 *R(U)3/66*.

50 Social Security Benefit (Dependency) Regulations 1977, reg. 11.

51 *C.U.303/50(KL)*, where maintenance had been paid only from the date of a court order but was held to suffice. *Cf R(U)3/66*.

52 Social Security Benefit (Dependency) Regulations 1977, reg. 2.

53 *C.S.58/49(KL)*.

54 *R(U)5/54*.

55 *R(S)26/52*.

56 *R(S)1/59*.

57 *C.S.58/49(KL)*.

58 *Ibid.*; see also *134/50(SB)*, *C.S.801/49(KL)*.

59 *R(S)1/51*, *R(S)7/58*, *R2/61(SB)* and *cf. C.S.801/49(KL)*.

60 Social Security Benefit (Dependency) Regulations 1977, reg. 2(2).

61 *C.S.547/49(KL)*.

62 *Post*, pp. 258–30.

63 National Insurance Act 1966, s. 2; 1975 Act, s. 14(7).

64 1975 Act, s. 22(4).

65 *Ibid.* s. 24(3).

66 *Ante*, pp. 16–20.

67 *Post*, pp. 302–306.

68 1975 Act, s. 14(7) and see *post*, pp. 131–133.

69 *Ibid.* s. 22(4).

70 *Ibid.* s. 24(3).

71 *i.e.* the tax year last ending before the beginning of the current benefit year, *ibid.* Sched. 6, para. 1(2).

72 *Ibid.* Sched. 6.

73 See below.

74 Claims and Payments Regulations, reg. 20.

75 *C.W.G.6/50(KL)*.

76 1975 Act, s. 82(1).

77 See *R(U)7/64*, *R2/69(FA)*.

78 1975 Act, s. 119(2).

79 The editor, *Digest of Commissioners' Decisions*, Vol. 1, p. 465 (he is a former legal adviser in the Ministry of Pensions and National Insurance).

80 *R(G)9/62*.

81 *e.g. R(G)5/51*; see also *R(P)18/52*.

82 See decisions summarised in *R(G)2/54*.

83 See *e.g. C.S.4/50(KL)*, *R(S)34/52*.

84 *R(P)13/53*.

85 *5/56(P)*.

86 *R(G)7/51*.

87 Case No. C.269/J, 3rd Report of the P.C.A., 1974–75, p. 119.
88 *Post*, pp. 393–439.
89 1975 Act, s. 146(3).
90 [1971] 1 W.L.R. 141.
91 1975 Act, s. 144.
92 See *ibid.* ss. 144(2)–(5) and 145.
93 *Ibid.* s. 145(1).
94 *Ibid.* s. 145(3).
95 *Smith* v. *Hawkins* [1972] 1 W.L.R. 141.
96 1975 Act, s. 145(3)(4).
97 (1972) I.L.J. 177.
98 1975 Act, s. 147.

CHAPTER 3

GENERAL DISQUALIFICATIONS

1 See *e.g.* in relation to unemployment benefit, *post*, pp. 145–203.
2 1975 Act, s. 82(1); Claims and Payments Regulations 1900, regs. 3–9, 13.
3 See Sheridan "Late National Insurance Claims: Cause for Delay" (1956) 19 *M.L.R.* 341.
4 1975 Act, s. 82(2).
5 1975 Act s. 82(3).
6 Italics supplied.
7 *C.U.28/49(KL)*, but see *post*, pp. 52–54.
8 *C.U.54/48(KL)*.
9 *R(S)1/66*.
10 *C.S.U.14/48(KL)*.
11 *Ibid.*
12 *C.P.93/49(KL)*, *R(S)23/52*, *R(S)8/59*.
13 Persons Abroad Regulations 1975.
14 *Ibid.* reg. 4(1).
15 *Ibid.* reg. 9(3).
16 *Ibid.* reg. 9(4) and (5). See below.
17 *Ibid.* reg. 9(6).
18 *Ibid.* reg. 7(2).
19 *Ibid.* reg. 7(1).
20 *Ibid.* reg. 4(2).
21 *Ibid.* reg. 10.
22 Attendance Allowance Regulations, reg. 2.
23 *Ibid.* reg. 2(2)(*b*) and see reg. 2(2)(*c*).
24 Persons Abroad Regulations, reg. 9(4) and (5), (6 months and 3 months absence respectively).
25 *Ibid.* reg. 8.
26 *Ibid.* reg. 5.
27 *Levene* v. *Commissioners of Inland Revenue* [1928] A.C. 217, *per* Viscount

Cave L.C. at p. 225, cited with approval in *R(G)2/51, R3/60(FA), R(F)1/62*
and see *C.G.165/50*.

28 *Levene*'s case, above.
29 See *R(P)1/72*.
30 *C.G.202/49(KL), C.G.204/49(KL), C.G.206/49(KL)*.
31 *R(G)5/52*.
32 *R(P)1/72*.
33 *R(G)1/54, C.G.32/49(KL)*.
34 *C.G.32/49(KL), 55/50(MB)*.
35 *R(P)4/54*.
36 *R(F)1/62*.
37 Persons Abroad Regulations, reg. 13.
38 *Ibid.* reg. 3.
39 *Ibid.* reg. 2.
40 *Ibid.* reg. 2(1)(*a*)–(*c*).
41 *Ibid.* reg. 9(1).
42 *Ibid.* regs. 2(2) and 9(2).
43 *R4/62(SB)*.
44 *R(S)5/59*.
45 *R(S)9/55*.
46 *9/59(SB)*; see also *C.S.317/49(KL), R(S)1/57, R(S)1/75*.
47 *R(S)3/54*.
48 *C.S.S.71/49(KL), R(S)6/61*.
49 *R(S)16/51, R(S)35/52*.
50 *R(G)13/59*.
51 *R. v. National Insurance Commissioner, ex. p. McMenemey* (1966), (Div. Ct.)
(published as an appendix to *R(S)2/69*). See also *R4/62(SB), R(S)1/69*.
52 *C.S.474/50(KL)*.
53 *C.S.S.71/49(KL), R(S)10/52*.
54 *R(S)5/61, R(S)4/74*. The latter also decides that "treatment" has a
similar meaning for the purposes of the EEC arrangements, *post*, pp. 52–54.
55 *R(S)2/59*.
56 *R(S)1/65*.
57 *R(S)6/61*.
58 *C.S.77/49(KL)*.
59 *R(S)9/59, R(S)1/75*.
60 *R(G)3/54*.
61 *R(G)5/53*.
62 See *e.g. R(S)10/53, R(S)6/54, R(S)8/54*, Mariners' Benefit Regulations,
reg. 4.
63 National Insurance Act (N.I.) 1966, s. 18(7) (now repealed).
64 See *ante*, pp. 48–50.
65 See *R5/62(UB)* and authorities there cited.
66 See now 1975 Act, s. 143, S.S. and C.B. (Reciprocal Arrangements)
Order 1977.
67 See *e.g.* Regulation No. 1408/71 as amended. For a statement of the
similarities and dissimilarities between the European schemes, see Van Langendonck, "Social Security Legislation in the EEC," (1973) I.L.J. 17.

68 See *e.g.* *R(A)4/75*.

69 See Cases Nos. C.72/V, and C.100/V, First Report of the Parliamentary Commissioner for Administration, 1975–6, pp. 134, 137, and Annual Report for 1975, para. 20.

70 There remain considerable opportunities for enterprise via the Irish Sea ferries.

71 See Calvert, (1970) 5 *Irish Jurist (N.S.)* 70.

72 [1955] 1 Q.B. 139.

73 *R(S)20/53, R(S)21/53, R(S)22/54, R(P)10/54, R(S)3/55, R(S)4/55*. For this reason, administrative detention has been held not to disqualify in Northern Ireland, *R. (O'Neill)* v. *National Insurance Commissioner* [1974] N.I.

74 *C.S.16/48(KL), R(S)11/52*.

75 General Benefit Regulations, regs. 11, 12 and 15.

76 *Ibid.* reg. 11(2).

77 *Ibid.* reg. 11(3).

78 *Ibid.* reg. 11(4).

79 *R(S)1/71*.

CHAPTER 4

UNEMPLOYMENT BENEFIT

Chapter 4, pp. 57–76

1 See, generally, Field, "Unemployment: The Facts," *Poverty* pamphlet No. 20; *Poverty* special issue, No. 32, Autumn 1975 on "Unemployment"; Ogus, "Unemployment Benefit for Workers on Short-time" (1975) 4 I.L.J. 12.

2 For provisions specially relating to unemployment benefit, see regs. 12 and 14 and Scheds. 1, 2, para. 1, and 3.

3 Claims and Payments Regulations, Sched. 1.

4 *Ibid.* Sched. 2, para. 1. Claims must be made in person at an unemployment benefit office, *ibid.* reg. 4.

5 *R(U)6/75*.

6 Claims and Payment Regulations, reg. 7.

7 Certain benefits (generally, those following immediately and automatically upon another benefit) are payable without claim, *ibid.* reg. 3. Unemployment benefit is not one of these.

8 *R3/61(UB)*.

9 Claims and Payments Regulations, reg. 7(1). He must also, "if reasonably so required ... attend at such office or place as the Secretary of State may direct." *Ibid.*

10 *R14/59(UB)*.

11 *R24/60(UB)*.

12 *R(U)14/59*; *post*, pp. 76–88.

13 *Post*, pp. 145–203.

14 1975 Act, s. 13(6)(d).

15 *Ibid.* Sched. 3, para. 1.

16 *Ibid.* s. 13(3).

17 *Ibid.* s. 14(2)(*b*).

18 *Ibid.* s. 14(2)(*c*).

19 *Ibid.* s. 12(2).

20 *Ibid.* s. 14(8).

21 1975 Act, s. 18. For "period of interruption of employment" see *post*, pp. 131–132.

22 Unemployment, Sickness and Invalidity Benefit Regulations, reg. 11.

23 *i.e.* over 16 hours per week, 1975 Act, s. 18, S.S. (Miscellaneous Provisions) Act 1977, s. 17(1).

24 See 1975 Act, Sched. 4.

25 See Claims and Payments Regulations, reg. 14.

26 *Ante*, p. 58.

27 *Per* Commissioner Shewan in *R(U)1/76*.

28 See, for example, Unemployment, Sickness and Invalidity Benefit Regulations, reg. 5 (the "nightworkers" regulation, *post*, pp. 118–121).

29 *R(U)4/71*.

30 *Decision 13129/34*.

31 *R1/68(UB)*.

32 *R(U)6/68*. See, also, *C.U.28/48* (school bus attendant paid a "retaining fee" of half-wages during school holiday), *R(U)8/54* (ship's musician receiving half-pay between voyages which he was contractually bound to make).

33 *R(U)28/52* (this decision must now be read subject to ss. 17(3) and 167 of the 1975 Act.

34 *R(U)33/56*.

35 *R(U)5/75*. This case was decided under the pre-1975 law under which the crucial question was whether the claimant was "gainfully occupied" and it was well-settled that he was "gainfully occupied" if he worked in the hope or expectation of remuneration or profit even if that hope or expectation was not, at the end of the day, fulfilled. The 1975 Act uses, instead, the concept of "gainful employment" and it remains to be decided what the exact scope of this latter phrase is and whether the change in wording is significant.

36 *Post*, pp. 65–70.

37 *R(U)11/73*. This was a "three-day week" case. The rearranged schedules enabled the claimant to earn his normal basic five-day rate on three days; he was nevertheless entitled to benefit, not being either earning or on call on the days off.

38 *91/51(UB)*.

39 "Employment" includes any trade, business, profession, office or vocation, 1975 Act, Sched. 20, *s.n.* "employment." It will be unusual for a self-employed person to satisfy the contribution conditions for unemployment benefit, but it is perfectly possible, as where he was, until recently, employed by another.

40 See *R28/60(UB)*, following Case No. 6978 of 1924.

41 See cases mentioned *ante*, p. 62.

42 See *R1/68(UB)* in which the payment was held, in the event, not to be gratuitous, and *R(U)11/64*.

43 *R(U)6/68*.

44 *C.W.U.42|50(KL).*
45 *C.U.236|50(KL), 43|50(UB).*
46 *18|59(UB).*
47 See above. See also Employment Protection Act 1975, s. 113.
48 *R(U)30|56*; see *C.U.137|49(KL).*
49 *R(U)40|56.*
50 *R(U)21|56.*
51 *Decision No. 1|33* (unrep.), an unsatisfactory statement of the rule as now operated.
52 *Decision No. 215|47.*
53 *C.U.137|49(KL), R(U)23|55.*
54 *C.S.U.49|50(KL).*
55 *R(U)27|51.*
56 *R(U)23|55.*
57 *R(U)13|51, R(U)25|55.*
58 See also *R(U)30|56, R(U)5|58, R(U)16|58.*
59 *R(U)7|60*; see also *R(U)21|56.*
60 *R(U)13|51, R(U)21|56, R(U)17|58, R(U)1|59.*
61 *R(U)2|58.*
62 *Ante,* p. 62.
63 *R(U)1|76.*
64 As before *R(U)21|56*, see *R(U)13|51, R(U)25|55.*
65 *R(U)10|73. Cf. R(U)11|73.*
66 *R(U)1|75.*
67 ss. 22–28.
68 *Decision No. 4903.*
69 The 1975 Act does not define "employed" and "employment" for this purpose other than to say that the latter term includes "any trade, business, profession, office or vocation." (1975 Act, Sched. 20). The reasoning in *R(U)4|59* holds good, but now it stands on common law and the common meaning of "employment" rather than on an express statutory basis.
70 See *R(U)2|67.*
71 See *post,* pp. 108–118.
72 See the quite extraordinary provision contained in s. 1 of the National Insurance etc. Act 1969, since repealed. See now 1975 Act, s. 17(3).
73 *i.e.* a "normal idle day," the phrase used in regulations.
74 *i.e.* either a day of unemployment or a day of incapacity, 1975 Act, s. 17(1)(c).
75 1975 Act, s. 17(1)(b).
76 Unemployment, Sickness and Invalidity Benefit Regulations, reg. 16.
77 *R1|61(UB).*
78 *Decision 16930 of 1931.*
79 *R(U)16|59, R(U)17|59, R(U)18|59, R(U)13|60, R1|61(UB).*
80 *Post,* pp. 105–108.
81 *Post,* pp. 88–94.
82 *Post,* pp. 95–104.
83 This seems to be the effect of reg. 16 of the Unemployment, Sickness and Invalidity Benefit Regulations providing that for the purposes of the

normal idle day rule, employment is to be treated as if it had been terminated if "it has been treated as having been terminated for the purpose of section 17(1)(*b*) as substituted by section 17(3)(*a*)." What is meant by "has been treated" is not clear. Presumably a claimant's employment will not be treated as having been terminated until the question of his entitlement to earnings-related supplement has arisen and been answered, and even then the position is doubtful. Section 17(1)(*b*) as substituted by section 17(3)(*a*) does not provide for employment to be treated as being terminated; it offers an alternative to termination as a condition of entitlement to supplement.

84 *R(U)16/59*.
85 *R1/61(UB)*.
86 *R(S)30/57, R(I)17/59, R(U)18/59*.
87 See *post*, pp. 151–154.
88 See *R(U)20/57, R(U)21/57, R(U)16/59*.
89 *R(U)16/59*; see *post*, pp. 151–154.
90 Unemployment, Sickness and Invalidity Benefit Regulations, reg. 16(2).
91 *Ibid*. reg. 16(6). For other exceptions, see paras. (3)–(5).
92 *Ibid*. reg. 16(3)(*a*).
93 *R(U)16/59, R(U)13/60, R1/61(UB)*.
94 *R(U)16/59, R(U)17/59*.
95 *R1/61(UB)*.
96 *R(U)13/59*.
97 *R1/61(UB)*.
98 *R(U)18/59*.
99 *R1/61(UB)*.

Chapter 4, pp. 76–97

1 See post, pp. 78–79.
2 Unemployment, Sickness and Invalidity Benefit Regulations, reg. 7(1)(*e*).
3 *Ibid*. This relates to determining "normality" (below) and is relevant to the same function in relation to the normal idle day rule, *ibid*. reg. 16(3)(*d*) and (5).
4 *Ibid*. reg. 7(2). An identical provision operates in relation to the normal idle day rule, see *ibid*. reg. 16(6).
5 *R(U)13/62*.
6 See *U.D.4149/38* explained in *R(U)33/53*.
7 *R(U)14/60*.
8 In considering "normality" in its reference to the normal idle day rule (above pp. 72–76), the relevant provision is Unemployment, Sickness and Invalidity Benefit Regulations, reg. 16(6).
9 *R(U)28/58*.
10 *R(U)9/54, R(U)13/55, R(U)5/57, R(U)19/58, R(U)9/62*.
11 *C.U.518/49(KL), R(U)36/51, R(U)2/52, R(U)13/55, R(U)9/56, R(U)16/58, R(U)22/58, R(U)28/58, R(U)13/60*.
12 *C.U.518/49(KL), R(U)36/51, R(U)2/52, R(U)9/56, R(U)16/58, R(U)22/58, R(U)13/60*.
13 *R(U)13/55*.
14 *R(U)19/58*.
15 See now *R(U)1/72*.

16 *R(U)17/60*; and see *R(U)2/73*.

17 *R(U)17/60*.

18 *R(U)14/60*.

19 *R(U)2/52*. See also *R(U)36/51* and *C.U.151/49(KL)*.

20 *R(U)29/56*.

21 See now *R(U)3/74* where an employee who had previously worked a six-day week was immediately re-engaged by his old employers on a three-day week basis after attaining retirement age. He was actually paid benefit for nearly a year but the Commissioner eventually expressed the view that the new normality should have been recognised long before.

22 *R(U)15/60*.

23 See now *R(U)3/74*.

24 *Cf. R(U)15/61*.

25 In applying the normal idle day rule, see, however, Unemployment, Sickness and Invalidity Benefit Regulations, reg. 16(3)(4).

26 *Cf. R(U)1/72*, where one of two contracts occupying the claimant for three days a week had finally expired and the "normality" thus became reduced to two days.

27 *R(U)10/62*.

28 *C.U.518/49(KL)*.

29 *R(U)5/57*.

30 *C.U.518/49(KL)*.

31 The original "year period test" as established in *C.U.518/49(KL)* was endorsed in *R(U)9/56*, *R(U)33/57*, *R(U)16/58*, *R(U)19/58*, *R(U)22/58* and *R(U)28/58*. The adapted, non-pattern version of it was applied in *R(U)13/60*, *R(U)14/60* and *R(U)17/60*.

32 *R(U)14/60*, *R(U)21/60*.

33 *R(U)14/60*.

34 *R(U)22/58*, where regard was had to the whole year, notwithstanding a marked change in the employment, in applying the original test.

35 *R(U)17/60*, *R(U)21/60*.

36 *C.U.518/49(KL)*.

37 "Group" presumably means a number of employers not necessarily associated in any way otherwise than by employing the same employee.

38 See *R(U)33/57*, *R(U)28/58*, *R(U)13/60*, *R(U)17/60*, *R(U)21/60*.

39 *R(U)13/60*.

40 *R(U)2/73*.

41 See *R(U)33/57*, *R(U)28/58*, *R(U)17/60*, *R(U)21/60*.

42 *R(U)33/57*.

43 *R(U)17/60*.

44 *Fitzgerald* v. *Hall, Russell & Co.* [1970] A.C. 984.

45 *R(U)13/62*.

46 *Ibid.*

47 *R(U)33/53*.

48 *R(U)5/57*.

49 *R(U)15/59*.

50 In *R1/65(UB)*.

51 *R(U)2/68*.

52 See *e.g. 172/50(UB), R(U)12/53, R(U)13/54, R(U)32/58.*

53 *R(U)9/57.*

54 Continuity of payment was never required in the case of termination of fixed term contracts, see *R(U)9/57.*

55 *R(U)4/54.*

56 *R(U)9/73.*

57 See below. There is apparently no objection to agreeing less notice than that contractually required, see dicta in *R(U)6/73.*

58 *R(U)5/73,* and see *R(U)6/73*—"if a payment ... is wholly referable to past services, it is not a payment in lieu of, etc., for the purposes of regulation 7(1)(*d*)."

59 See below.

60 *R(U)7/73, R(U)8/73.*

61 *Ibid.*

62 See above.

63 *R(U)7/73, R(U)8/73.*

64 *R(U)29/55, R(U)4/56, R(U)10/58.*

65 *R(U)29/52.*

66 *R(U)7/73.*

67 *R(U)17/52, R(U)4/56, R(U)10/58.*

68 *R(U)4/56.*

69 *R(U)5/74.*

70 *R(U)2/68, R(U)3/68.* But see now Employment Protection (Recoupment of Unemployment and Sickness Benefit) Regulations 1977.

71 See *e.g. R(U)5/53, R(U)37/53, R(U)9/57, R(U)10/58, R(U)5/60, C.U.27/61* (unrep.) *R(U)8/63, R(U)10/64.*

72 *R(U)10/58, R(U)5/74.* A reasonable period may exceed that stipulated in the Contracts of Employment Act 1972.

73 See also *R(U)6/73, R(U)7/73, R(U)9/73.*

74 See *per* Chief Commissioner Micklethwait in *R(U)7/73.*

75 *R(U)3/68.*

76 See also *C.U.27/61* (unrep.), *R(U)2/68, R(U)3/68.*

77 *R(U)37/53, R(U)10/58, R(U)10/64.*

78 *C.U.286/50(KL), R(U)37/53, R(U)5/60.*

79 See *R(U)8/70.*

80 *R(U)7/73, R(U)8/73.*

81 *Per* Chief Commissioner Micklethwait in *R(U)7/73.*

82 See the majority decision, *ibid.*

83 *R(U)3/68.*

84 See below.

85 *R(U)21/53, R(U)4/71.*

86 See *1/53(UB).*

87 *C.U.21/48.*

88 *3/54(UB).*

89 *15/59(UB).*

90 *C.U.62/48(KL), R(U)38/52.*

91 Now, as amended, Unemployment, Sickness and Invalidity Benefit Regulations, reg. 7(1)(*d*), *Ante*, pp. 88–94.

92 See *e.g. 30/48(UB)*, *C.U.401/49(KL)*.

93 See in particular *R(U)45/52*, *30/48(UB)*, *C.U.72/48(KL)*, *213/49(UB)*, *C.U.401/49(KL)*, *C.U.532/49(KL)*, *R(U)40/52*.

94 *Ante*, p. 89.

95 *C.U.21/48(KL)*, *C.U.62/48(KL)*.

96 *Ante*, pp. 88–92.

97 *e.g. C.U.401/49(KL)*, *R4/60(UB)*.

98 *R(U)7/68*, see *ante*, pp. 73–75.

99 *Post*, pp. 108–118.

Chapter 4, pp. 97–119

1 See *C.W.U.7/48(KL)*, *C.W.U.88/48(KL)*, *R(U)27/57*, *R11/62(UB)*, *R3/63(UB)*, *R(U)8/64*, *R(U)1/66*, *R(U)2/66*. Dicta of the Deputy Commissioner in *R(U)4/66*, para. 8, are incorrect where the employment has been terminated.

2 Unemployment, Sickness and Invalidity Benefit Regulations, reg. 7(1)(*i*)(i).

3 *Ibid.* reg. 7(1)(*i*)(i).

4 *Ibid.* reg. 7(1)(*i*)(ii).

5 *R(U)8/68*.

6 See also *R(U)7/54*, where the contract ran from August to June each year, *R(U)18/64*, where the claimant was employed on a daily basis, and *R10/62(UB)*, in all of which the claim failed.

7 *R11/62(UB)*, *R3/63(UB)*.

8 *R(U)1/66*, *R(U)2/66*.

9 See *C.W.U.7/48(KL)*, *R(U)8/64*.

10 Referred to in *R(U)7/56*.

11 *102/51(UB)*.

12 See also *R(U)18/54*.

13 In *Decision No. 53/48* (revised)(unrep.).

14 *C.W.U.7/48(KL)*; see also *R3/63(UB)*.

15 Equivalent to "recognised."

16 Equivalent to "customary."

17 *Decision No. 18284/32*.

18 *7/54(UB)*.

19 *Decision No. 4796/37*, *R(S)3/53*.

20 [1972] 1 Ch. 305 (C.A.).

21 *Decision No. 4616/37*.

22 *Decision No. 18284/32*, *R(U)11/53*.

23 See also *C.S.U.29/49(KL)*.

24 See also *R(U)27/58*, *R(U)24/59* even though, in this latter case, the reason for the regular closure was shortage of orders following upon the Whitsun holiday.

25 *15/59(UB)*.

26 *R(U)4/67*.

27 See Ogus, (1975) 4 I.L.J. 13.

28 1975 Act, ss. 14(8), 16(3).

29 *Ibid.* s. 17(1)(*e*).

30 Unemployment, Sickness and Invalidity Benefit Regulations, reg. 4.

31 *Ante*, pp. 72–76; see *R(U)15/60*.

32 *Post*, pp. 133–143.

33 *Ante*, pp. 62–65.

34 See *post*, p. 108.

35 National Insurance Act 1966, s. 3(1)(*a*).

36 1975 Act, s. 17(3).

37 National Insurance etc. Act 1969, ss. 1(2), (3).

38 1975 Act, s. 167(1)(*b*).

39 *Ante*, pp. 69–70.

40 1975 Act, s. 17(3)(*a*).

41 *Ibid.*

42 Unemployment, Sickness and Invalidity Benefit Regulations, reg. 6(2).

43 *Ibid.* reg. 6(3).

44 *Post*, pp. 121–131; *ibid.* reg. 7(1)(*h*).

45 *Ibid.* reg. 6(1).

46 *Ibid.* reg. 7(1)(*h*).

47 See *ante*, pp. 73–75.

48 *R(U)2/75.*

49 Miss Herbison, Secretary of State for Health and Social Security, H.C.Deb., Vol. 724, col. 42.

50 1975 Act, s. 17(1)(*a*)(i).

51 *C.U.235/49(KL).*

52 *R(U)44/57.*

53 *R(U)20/51, R(U)12/52.*

54 See *e.g. R(U)20/60, 120/52(UB), R(U)18/55, R(U)12/52, R(U)36/52.*

55 See also *R(U)33/58.*

56 *R(U)31/51, R(U)1/52, R(U)23/52, R(U)4/53, R(U)15/58.*

57 *Decision No. 938/29.*

58 See *C.W.U.47/49(KL), 142/50(UB), C.U.162/50(KL).*

59 Form U.I. 672H.

60 *Decision No. 7550/35.*

61 *R(U)1/55.*

62 *R1/60(UB), R5/60(UB).*

63 *C.U.427/50(KL), R(U)2/57.*

64 *Decision No. 7550/35.*

65 *R(U)3/65.*

66 *26/49(UB).*

67 See, *re* aliens, *R(U)13/57.*

68 *R(U)11/51, R(U)1/53.*

69 *R(U)1/76.*

70 *R(U)34/53.*

71 *R(U)12/55, R(U)11/56, R(U)24/58, R(U)8/59.*

72 *R(U)1/69.*

73 *R(U)36/52.*

74 See, in addition to decisions considered below, *C.U.10/49(KL), C.U.235/49(KL), R(U)25/51.*

75 See *R(U)18/55.*

76 *R(U)12/52*; see also *R(U)15/51*, *C.U.109/48(KL)*, *R(U)36/52*, *R2/62(UB)*.

77 *R(U)17/57, R(U)6/72*.

78 *R2/62(UB)*.

79 *108/51(UB), R(U)20/60*.

80 *R3/60(UB)*.

81 *108/51(UB)*. Reg. 8 of the Married Women and Widows Special Provisions Benefit Regulations allows "such consideration of the responsibilities arising from her marriage as is reasonable" in the case of a married woman to be taken account of in determining questions of *disqualification* under s. 20 of the 1975 Act. Presumably she would still be liable to disentitlement by reason of unavailability. Regulation 8 is not, of course, available to married men, see *R(U)6/59*.

82 Unemployment, Sickness and Invalidity Benefit Regulations, reg. 7(1)(*a*).

83 *R(U)15/58*.

84 *R(U)4/57*.

85 See *ante*, pp. 84–86.

86 *R(U)6/72*.

87 *R(U)3/59*. It may be doubted whether, in view of *R(U)15/58* above, and bearing in mind the refusal to work for the whole day claimed, the applicability of the regulation need have been considered at all. See also *R(U)6/59*.

88 See also *R2/62(UB)*.

89 *R(U)3/59*.

90 Of the old regulations, in identical terms with the modern regulation 7(1)(*b*)(iii).

91 For examples of consideration of what is "reasonable," see *R(U)31/58, R(U)20/60, R(U)6/72*.

92 *Post*, pp. 177–203.

93 See Case No. C.369/J, Fourth Report of the Parliamentary Commissioner for Administration for 1974–75, p. 93.

94 1975 Act, s. 17(1)(*a*)(i).

95 *Post*, pp. 207–209.

96 See also Unemployment, Sickness and Invalidity Benefit Regulations, reg. 7(1)(*j*) and (*k*).

97 *Ante*, pp. 62–65.

98 Unemployment, Sickness and Invalidity Benefit Regulations, reg. 5.

99 *Ibid*. reg. 5(2).

Chapter 4, pp. 119–141

1 See *R(S)18/53* in which a claimant was held disentitled to sickness benefit notwithstanding that he had been certified as incapacitated in respect of a day on which he started a shift at 11 p.m., and *R(U)33/53* and *R(U)37/56* in which claimants the bulk of whose shifts did not fall on the Saturday were nevertheless held disentitled in respect of the Saturday.

2 *R(U)20/52, R(U)15/60*.

3 *R(U)20/52*.

4 See also *R(U)10/56*.

5 Unemployment, Sickness and Invalidity Benefit Regulations, reg. 7(1)(*h*).
6 See Unemployment and Sickness Benefit Regulations 1967, reg. 7(1)(*i*).
7 1975 Act, Sched. 20, *s.n.* "employment."
8 *Ibid.* s. 2.
9 *Ibid.*
10 *R(U)11/57.*
11 *C.P.7/49(KL), R(P)7/54.*
12 *R(G)1/64, 82/50(UB), R(U)11/57.*
13 *Decision No. 588/28.* See also *Decisions Nos. 269/36* and *285/49(UB).*
14 *Decision No. 11363/33* (rep.); *C.U.235/50(KL).*
15 *Benjamin* v. *Minister of Pensions and National Insurance* [1960] 2 Q.B. 519
at pp. 530–531; *R(U)1/67.*
16 *Cf. C.U.235/50(KL)* and *C.U.30/49(KL)* and see *285/49(UB).*
17 See also *R(U)16/64.*
18 *R(P)7/51.*
19 *R(U)6/61, R(U)3/72, R(U)1/73.*
20 *211/49(UB), R(U)22/64, R(U)3/72.*
21 *C.U.235/50(KL).*
22 *C.U.13/66,* referred to in *R(U)1/67.*
23 *R(U)4/74.*
24 Unemployment, Sickness and Invalidity Benefit Regulations, reg.
7(1)(*a*), see *ante,* pp. 108–118.
25 *Ante,* pp. 108–118.
26 See *R(U)24/58, R(U)8/59.*
27 *R(U)12/55, R(U)12/57, R(U)12/59, R(U)24/59, R(U)2/67.*
28 Such as *R(U)12/57* and *R(U)12/59.*
29 See *R(U)15/56, R(U)16/56, R(U)12/57, R(U)26/58.*
30 See *post,* pp. 190–191.
31 See National Insurance Act 1965, s. 1(2)(3), *C.S.P.1/48(KL),*
C.U.12/48(KL), C.S.P.28/49(KL) and *C.U.277/49(KL).*
32 1975 Act, s. 2(2) and Contribution Regulations.
33 1975 Act, s. 14.
34 *Ibid.*
35 *Ibid.* s. 14(3).
36 *17/59(UB).*
37 *R(S)1/56,* Unemployment, Sickness and Invalidity Benefit Regulations,
reg. 11(1).
38 *Post,* pp. 191–192.
37 Claims and Payments Regulations, reg. 13(1)(*b*).
38 Unemployment, Sickness and Invalidity Benefit Regulations, reg.
7(1)(*b*).
39 *Ibid.* reg. 11. See *R(U)5/75.*
40 *R(U)5/75.*
41 See *e.g.* Members of the Forces Regulations, Mariners' Benefits Regulations, Airmen's Regulations.
42 *R(U)8/64.*
43 Unemployment, Sickness and Invalidity Benefit Regulations, reg. 19.
44 *Ibid.* reg. 19(2).

45 *R(U)19/57.*

46 *R(U)4/55.*

47 *R(U)3/51, R23/60(UB).*

48 *R(U)3/52, R(U)5/53, R(U)7/59.*

49 *R(U)4/61.*

50 *R(U)5/64.*

51 *24/49(UB)*; see also *R(U)21/52, 8/53(UB).*

52 *C.U.168/49(KL).*

53 *R(U)11/55. Re* "normal employment" see also reg. 19(2).

54 *R(U)3/51.*

55 *R14/60(UB).*

56 *R(U)36/56, R23/60(UB)*; and see reg. 19(2): "in construing the expression 'normal employment', regard shall be paid to factors inherent in the nature of conditions of the occupation or occupations in which that person is engaged, and not to factors abnormal to that occupation or occupations notwithstanding that those factors persist for a prolonged period." The decisions, however, do not treat factors peculiar to the worker as being "abnormal to the employment."

57 *8/54(UB).*

58 *R(U)20/53.*

59 *R(U)3/51.*

60 *R(U)14/53.*

61 *R(U)6/64.*

62 *R(U)4/75.*

63 Rejection of the statutory definition previously was not arbitrary. "Year" is defined for the purposes of the regulation and the three-year rule is a creature of the Commissioners, not part of the regulation.

64 Reg. 19(2); *R(U)6/60.*

65 Reg. 19(2).

66 See also *3/53(UB).*

67 *R(U)9/71.*

68 *R(U)19/54.*

69 *R(U)8/71,*

70 *R(U)19/60.*

71 *R(U)6/55,* where a likely change was in prospect.

72 Reg. 19(2).

73 *R2/68(UB).*

74 *218/49(UB).*

75 Reg. 19(2).

76 *R(U)27/53.*

77 *R(U)9/51.*

78 *R(U)5/64.*

79 *R(U)7/59.* This decision also breaks another apparently circular argument—Whether one is a seasonal worker depends upon the characteristics of one's on- and off-season; whether one has an on- and off-season depends upon whether one is a seasonal worker! In fact, whether one is a seasonal worker depends upon the characteristics of those parts of the year when one mainly works and not which, if they justify the conclusion that one is a

seasonal worker, may be properly characterised as the on- and off-seasons respectively.

80 *R(U)5/53, R(U)29/51.*
81 *R(U)29/51.*
82 *Post,* pp. 141–142.
83 Reg. 19(3).
84 *R(U)17/53.*
85 *R(U)13/56.*
86 *R(U)10/59.*
87 *R(U)25/55.*
88 *R(U)4/55.*
89 *R(U)7/52.*
90 *R(U)19/60.*
91 *R(U)5/64.*
92 *R(U)3/51.*
93 *R(U)16/51, R(U)9/55, R(U)10/55, R(U)21/55, 11/59(UB).*
94 *R(U)16/51.*
95 *R(U)9/55.*
96 *R(U)29/51.*
97 *R(U)10/55.*
98 *R(U)21/55.*
99 *R(U)29/51, R(U)21/55.*

Chapter 4, pp. 141–144

1 *R(U)9/55.*
2 *R(U)3/51.*
3 *R(U)5/55, R(U)6/60.*
4 *R(U)6/60.*
5 *R(U)5/64.*
6 *R(U)3/51* above.
7 *R(U)10/55.*
8 *R(U)5/55.*
9 *Ibid.*
10 *R(U)3/51.*
11 *R(U)10/55.*
12 Ogus, "Unemployment Benefit for Workers on Short-time," (1975) 4 I.L.J. 12.

CHAPTER 5

DISQUALIFICATION FOR UNEMPLOYMENT BENEFIT

Chapter 5, pp. 145–166

1 *Ante,* pp. 48–54.
2 *Ante,* pp. 54–56.
3 Claims and Payments Regulations, reg. 13.
4 *R(U)5/71.*
5 *R(U)2/54.* See however *R19/60(UB).*
6 *R(U)2/71.*

7 See Case No. C.206/V, 3rd Report of the Parliamentary Commissioner for Administration 1975–76.

8 Cmnd. 3623, paras. 953–968.

9 *R4/63(UB)*. There is a case for treating lockouts differently from strikes (although it is not always easy to determine which a particular stoppage is). Strikers are, by definition, parties to the dispute; lockouts can be and usually are undiscriminating as between parties and others.

10 *R(U)19/55.*

11 *R(U)21/59.*

12 1975 Act, s. 19(1).

13 *Ibid.*

14 s. 111.

15 Approving the test laid down in *Decision No. 2575.*

16 *19/59(UB).*

17 *Ibid.*

18 *130/52(UB).*

19 See *R(U)1/74.*

20 *e.g. Decision No. 7197/32.*

21 *Decision No. 1767/26, R(U)30/55, R(U)29/59.*

22 *Decisions Nos. 1953/25 and 7197/32, R(U)19/56.*

23 *R(U)6/71.*

24 *R(U)30/55.*

25 *R(U)8/58*; see also *R(U)10/57, R(U)26/57, R(U)29/57, R(U)30/57, R(U)31/57.*

26 *R(U)29/57.*

27 *R(U)3/58.*

28 *R(U)20/57.*

29 *R(U)21/57*; see also *R(U)30/57.*

30 *R(U)26/57*; see also *R(U)8/58.*

31 *R(U)8/58.*

32 *R(U)6/71.*

33 *C.U.54/52* (unrep.), *Decision No. 3508/29, R(U)11/52.*

34 *R(U)12/61, R(U)32/55.*

35 *R(U)3/69.*

36 See also *R(U)19/53.*

37 *R(U)17/52* as explained in *R(U)1/65.*

38 1975 Act, s. 19(2)(*b*).

39 *R(U)21/59.*

40 *Ibid.*

41 *R(U)36/58*, concerning the distinction drawn for purposes of the Industrial Disputes Order 1951, a distinction which might well have been thought apt for unemployment benefit purposes.

42 *R(U)3/69.*

43 *Decision No. 306/29, Decision No. 80/48* (unrep.), referred to in *R20/60(UB).*

44 Donovan Report (above), paras. 993–994.

45 *R20/60(UB).* The implications prompt doubts as to the rule's validity.

46 *R(U)2/53, R(U)3/69.*

47 *R(U)1/74.*

48 *R(U)6/51.*

49 Several opportunities to clarify this point in the legislation have been declined. It matters because not every disagreement is a dispute (*ante*, p. 155).

50 *Post*, pp. 157–158.

51 *R(U)1/74.*

52 *R(U)12/60.*

53 *Decisions Nos. 2031/36* and *1400/32* (unrep.).

54 *Ante*, p. 155.

55 *R(U)17/52*, following *Decisions Nos. 2461/28, 458/20* and *415/27.*

56 *Decisions Nos. 9959/29* and *3127/35.*

57 *115/51(UB), C.W.U.18/49(KL).*

58 *R(U)36/53, R(U)12/60, R(U)27/56.*

59 *Decision No. 2461/28.*

60 *R(U)12/60.*

61 1975 Act, s. 19(2)(*a*).

62 *R(U)1/70.*

63 *Ibid.*

64 *Ibid.*

65 *Ibid.*

66 *R(U)26/57, R(U)30/57, R(U)4/58, R(U)8/71.*

67 *R(U)1/70.*

68 This was almost certainly an erroneous finding of fact. Trim manufacture is "commonly carried on as a separate business." Ford's could find only one *who was big enough to take on their work.*

69 *R(U)24/57.*

70 *R(U)23/64.*

71 Report, paras. 970–972.

72 *R(U)17/52, ante*, pp. 153–154.

73 *Ibid.*

74 See also *8/59(UB).*

75 *R(U)17/56.*

76 *Decision No. 4850/26.*

77 *R(U)19/51.*

78 *Ibid.*

79 *R(U)7/58.*

80 *Ibid.*

81 *R(U)39/56.*

82 *Ibid.*

83 *R(U)6/74.*

84 *111/49(UB), R(U)3/55.*

85 *Ante*, p. 159.

86 *R(U)28/57.*

87 As from the coming into force of s. 111 of the Employment Protection Act 1975, the "financing" and "grade or class" provisions will disappear. It is expected that that provision will be brought into force during 1977.

88 *R(U)3/56, R(U)4/58.*

89 *R(U)5/66.*

90 *R3/68(UB)*.

91 *R(U)5/66*.

92 *R(U)3/69*.

93 *R(U)14/64*, dissenting from *R(U)22/57*.

94 *Punton* v. *Ministry of Pensions and National Insurance* (No. 2) [1963] I W.L.R. 1176, *per* Phillimore J.

95 *Decisions Nos. 1677/25, 1764/25, 1765/25*. This again raises the question whether the illegality would taint the "dispute."

96 *Decision No. 1022/38*, approved in *R(U)3/69*.

97 *R(U)3/69, R(U)1/74*.

98 Report, para. 982.

99 *Ibid.* para. 984.

Chapter 5, pp. 167–189

1 See *R(U)15/55* and cases referred to below.

2 *R(U)12/71*.

3 *R15/60(UB)*.

4 *R(U)8/71*. This decision suggests that a part of the subscriptions must reach central funds out of which strike payments are made. It might be more accurate to say that a proprietory interest in central funds must result from membership of the branch.

5 *R(U)12/71*.

6 *Decision No. 84/36*.

7 *R(U)2/70* and pre-War decisions there cited.

8 *R(U)2/70*.

9 *Ibid.*

10 [1956] A.C. 104.

11 Report, paras. 983–991.

12 See *R(U)14/71* where some hourly workers struck about a claim for all hourly workers.

13 *R(U)14/64*.

14 *R(U)3/69*.

15 *R(U)4/65*.

16 *R(U)3/69*.

17 *R(U)3/69, 245/49(UB)*.

18 *R(U)18/58*.

19 *R(U)1/60*.

20 *245/49(UB)*; see also *R(U)25/56*.

21 *R(U)3/56, R(U)14/64*.

22 *R(U)13/71, R(U)14/71*.

23 *Cf. R(U)25/56, R(U)3/56* and *R(U)1/60* with *C.U.16/59* (referred to in *R(U)1/60* and *R(U)30/59*) and *cf. R(U)13/71* and *R(U)14/71*.

24 Report, para. 992.

25 *Ibid.*

26 *R(U)13/71*.

27 *R(U)14/71*.

28 *R(U)22/55*.

29 *R3/62(UB)*.

30 *R(U)32/53*.

31 *R(U)22|57.*
32 *R(U)8|52.*
33 See also *R(U)34|55* and *R(U)25|53.*
34 See also the decision in *R(U)23|56.*
35 Report, para. 973.
36 *Ibid.* para. 980.
37 See *R(U)1|70.*
38 *R(U)5|59.*
39 *C.U.14|65, R(U)4|72.*
40 *C.U.190|50(KL).*
41 s. 20(1).
42 See below.
43 On these "escape" provisions, see *R(U)5|71.*
44 *R(U)2|60.*
45 *Ibid.*
46 *R(U)7|61, R7|62(UB).*
47 1975 Act, s. 20(1)(*a*).
48 *R(U)10|71.*
49 *R(U)24|55.*
50 *R(U)14|57.*
51 *R(U)20|50.*
52 *R(U)7|57, R1|64(UB), R2|61(UB).*
53 Example cited in *R(U)7|57; R2|61(UB).*
54 *R(U)10|53.*
55 *R(U)13|57.*
56 *R(U)7|57,* italics supplied.
57 *R6|62(UB).*
58 See *C.U.381|51* (unrep.).
59 *R(U)26|56.*
60 *R(U)10|54.*
61 *R(U)12|56.*
62 *R(U)27|52.*
63 *R(U)41|53.*
64 *R(U)34|52.*
65 *R(U)24|55, R(U)2|74.*
66 See *R(U)23|58, R(U)22|52, 4|48(UB).*
67 *R(U)11|59.*
68 *42|51(UB), R(U)35|58.*
69 *R(U)35|58.*
70 *R9|60(UB).*
71 *R17|60(UB).*
72 *R(U)14|56.*
73 *R17|60(UB).*
74 *R(U)17|64,* and see *124|51(UB), R(U)10|52, R(U)13|53.*
75 *R6|62(UB).*
76 See also *R1|64(UB).*
77 *R(U)10|54.*
78 See also *R(U)24|55.*

79 See Lewis, "Unemployment Insurance" (1976) 5 I.L.J. 119.

80 *R(U)2/74.*

81 *R(U)9/59.*

82 *R(U)2/54.*

83 *R(U)9/59.*

84 *R9/62(UB).*

85 *R(U)7/74,* (refusal to work overtime not contractually required and to take alternative work not requiring overtime in lieu).

86 *Ante,* pp. 180–181.

87 *C.U.164/50* (unrep.), quoted in *R(U)20/64;* see also *R(U)14/55, R(U)23/59.*

88 *Ibid.*

89 *R(U)14/52.*

90 See also *post,* pp. 198–201.

91 *R(U)22/52,* and see *R(U)4/73.*

92 *R2/67(UB).*

93 *R(U)18/57* and see *R(U)33/51* where employees issued an ultimatum.

94 See *e.g. R3/65(UB), 181/49(UB).*

95 *C.U.96/48(KL).*

96 See also *C.U.248/49(KL), R(U)15/53, R(U)38/53, C.U.46/59* (unrep.), and *C.U.1/64* (unrep.).

97 *R(U)38/53.*

98 *R(U)4/51.*

99 *4/54(UB).*

Chapter 5, pp. 189–203

1 *C.U.542/49(KL).*

2 *312/49(UB).*

3 *R(U)32/59.*

4 *R(U)31/59.*

5 See also *R(U)14/52, R(U)19/52.*

6 *R(U)14/55.*

7 *R(U)25/51, R(U)4/70.*

8 *Post,* pp. 288–290.

9 *R(U)4/73* (existing employment precarious and part-time); claimant already in receipt of social security benefits).

10 *29/48(UB).*

11 *226/49(UB).*

12 *R(U)3/73.*

13 See also *R(U)4/73.*

14 1975 Act, s. 20(5)(a).

15 See *R(U)5/71.*

16 *Ibid.*

17 *Ibid.*

18 *R(U)28/55.*

19 1975 Act, s. 20(5)(b).

20 *R8/62(UB).*

21 *Ibid.*

22 *2/57(UB).*

23 *Ibid.*

24 *R(U)20|55.*

25 *R25|60(UB).*

26 *R(U)26|52.*

27 *e.g. R(U)36|51, R16|60(UB).*

28 See *e.g. R(U)25|52, R(U)32|56.*

29 See *e.g. 13|48(UB), 12|52(UB), R26|60(UB), R29|60(UB), R2|63(UB).*

30 *R(U)26|52.*

31 *R(U)32|52.*

32 *R(U)14|54.*

33 *R(U)5|68.*

34 *R(U)3|63.*

35 *R(U)10|61, R(U)15|62.*

36 *R(U)36|52*; but note that he may render himself unavailable, *ante*, pp. 108–118.

37 *R(U)40|53.*

38 *R(U)32|52.*

39 See *e.g. 1|59(UB), 4|59(UB).*

40 *R(U)34|58.*

41 1975 Act, s. 20(4)(c).

42 *Ibid.*

43 *Ibid.* s. 20(4), concluding words; see *R(U)10|61*; *R(U)15|62.*

44 *R(U)14|54.*

45 *R(U)25|52.*

46 See *e.g. R6|60(UB), R26|60(UB), R29|60(UB).*

47 *Jones* v. *Chillington Tool Co. Ltd.* (1948) 41 B.W.C.C. 12.

48 *13|48(UB).*

49 *12|52(UB).*

50 *R2|63(UB).*

51 *R(U)23|51.*

52 See also *112|49(UB).*

53 *Ante*, pp. 188–190.

54 *1|48(UB).*

55 *R(U)18|51.*

56 See *e.g. 21|48(UB), C.U.365|49(KL), C.U.542|49(KL), R(U)14|52, R(U)19|52, R(U)6|53.*

57 Married Women and Widows Special Provisions Benefit Regulations reg. 8.

58 *R(U)20|60.*

59 See *e.g. C.U.248|49(KL), R(U)18|52, 3|55(UB).*

60 *Ante*, pp. 146–177.

61 See *R(U)35|52.*

62 *211|59(UB)* (unrep.).

63 *R18|60(UB), R21|60(UB)*; on change of work, see *e.g. C.U.3|48(KL), R(U)41|52, 6|53(UB), 5|54(UB), R(U)34|56, R27|60(UB), R44|62(UB).*

64 See *e.g. R(U)13|52, R10|60(UB), R22|60(UB)*, and cases discussed above.

65 *R10|60(UB), R22|60(UB).*

66 *R(U)17/54.*

67 *R(U)8/74.* Decisions before this case tend to be coloured by the view taken in *R(U)17/54* and must be read with caution.

68 *C.U.190/50(KL), R(U)5/54.*

69 *C.U.190/50(KL).*

70 *R(U)5/54.*

71 See *e.g. C.S.3/48(KL), R(U)18/51, R(U)13/52, R(U)4/70.*

72 *R(U)27/59.*

73 *R9/62(UB).*

74 *C.U.190/50(KL).*

75 *R(U)13/53.*

76 *R(U)1/71.*

77 *Decision No. 98/28,* approved in *106/51(UB).*

78 *R(U)2/72.*

79 *R(U)11/59.*

80 *R(U)11/59, 4/48(UB), 105/50(UB).*

81 *R(U)35/53, C.U.155/50(KL).*

82 See *162/50(UB).*

83 *Ante,* pp. 89, 96–97.

84 *C.U.155/50(KL), 162/50(KL).*

85 *C.U.19/48.*

86 *R(U)24/56.*

87 *R(U)1/57.*

Chapter 6

BENEFITS RELATING TO SICKNESS

Chapter 6, pp. 204–222

1 The anomaly is now heightened by earnings-related supplement which attaches to sickness benefit but not to industrial injury benefit and as a result of which the former may be higher or lower than the latter quite capriciously.

2 See *ante,* pp. 26–27 (hospital in-patients).

3 1975 Act, s. 36.

4 1975 Act, s. 37.

5 *Ibid.* s. 37A. These benefits have now been introduced. See App. I.

6 Claims and Payments Regulations, Sched. 1.

7 See *C.S.33/49* allowing them and *C.S.174/49(KL)* disallowing them.

8 Medical Evidence Regulations, reg. 3; Claims and Payments Regulations, reg. 11.

9 *R(S)1/55.*

10 1975 Act, s. 14(1).

11 For reduced entitlement to benefit, see *ibid.* s. 33 and *R(S)27/52.*

12 1975 Act, ss. 13 and 14(2) and Sched. 3, Pt. I, para. 1.

13 *Ibid.*

14 See G. de N. Clark, "Industrial Law and the Labour-only Sub-contract," (1967) 30 M.L.R. 6.

15 Italics supplied.

16 1975 Act, s. 15.

17 There is statutory elaboration of the meaning of the phrase for other purposes, see Unemployment, Sickness and Invalidity Benefit Regulations, regs. 8 (invalidity allowance) and 17 (earnings-related supplement) but not for the present purpose (entitlement to invalidity pension). The decisions discussed in the text relate to an analogous problem no longer relevant for sickness benefit purposes.

18 See also *R(S)14/53.*

19 1975 Act, s. 14(1).

20 See *ante*, pp. 131–132.

21 Meaning "work which the person can reasonably be expected to do," 1975 Act, s. 17(1)(*a*). It might be reasonable to expect a person to work even though he suffers from a very serious illness provided it is not at all disabling; and see *R(S)1/75.*

22 *C.S.363/49(KL).*

23 *R(S)7/52, C.S.363/49(KL), R(S)18/53.*

24 *C.S.37/53* (unrep.).

25 Unemployment, Sickness and Invalidity Benefit Regulations, reg. 5; *ante*, pp. 118–120.

26 *C.S.363/49(KL).*

27 Unemployment, Sickness and Invalidity Benefit Regulations, reg. 3(2).

28 1975 Act, s. 17(1).

29 *R(S)4/56.*

30 *R(S)2/53.*

31 *Ibid.* and see *post*, pp. 218–221.

32 National Insurance Act 1965, s. 19(7); National Insurance Act 1966, s. 3(3).

33 *C.S.221/49(KL), R2/62(SB).*

34 Meaning "work which the person can reasonably be expected to do," 1975 Act, s. 17(1)(*a*).

35 *R(S)9/59.*

36 *Ante*, p. 113.

37 *Post*, p. 214.

38 *C.S.69/50(KL)*; see also *C.W.I.20/49(KL).*

39 *R4/61(SB).*

40 *R1/62(SB).*

41 *R(S)20/52, R(S)13/52, R(S)9/59, R(S)7/60.*

42 *R(S)7/60.*

43 *Ibid.*

44. *C.S.561/50(KL), R(S)24/51, R(S)20/52.*

45 *R(S)20/52.*

46 *R3/62(SB).*

47 See Categorisation of Earners Regulations, reg. 2 and Sched. 1, Pt. III; *C.W.S.2/48(KL).*

48 *R(S)8/55.*

49 *R(S)10/61, R8/52(SB), R(S)37/52, R(S)24/52, C.S.499/50(KL).*

50 *R(S)37/52.*

51 *R(S)10/61.*

52 *R8/52(SB). R(S)2/74* offers a good recent illustration.

53 See *R1/69(SB).*

54 *11/58(SB).*

55 *R(S)33/52.*

56 See the examples provided in *R(S)2/61.*

57 *R(S)5/51, R(S)34/52, R5/57(SB), R5/61(SB).*

58 *R(S)11/51*, applied in *R3/60(SB).*

59 Unemployment and Sickness Benefit Regulations 1967 (S.I. 1967 No. 330), reg. 3; *ibid.* (Northern Ireland), 1961, reg. 3.

60 *R6/62(SB).*

61 The Medical Evidence Regulations, reg. 3, require a claimant to furnish evidence by a formal certificate or by "such other means as may be sufficient in the circumstances of any particular case". See Case No. 123/J., Third Report of the Parliamentary Commissioner for Administration, 1974–5, p. 105.

62 *Ibid.*

63 See *ibid.* Sched. 1, rr. 10 and 11. See H.C. Paper No. 349 for 1975–6.

64 *Ibid.* regs., Sched. 1, r. 3.

65 Third Report of the Parliamentary Commissioner for Administration, 1974, Case No. 346/T.

66 *R(S)7/53.*

67 *R(S)15/54.*

68 See *R(S)1/58.*

69 Although the statutory authorities are legally-empowered to accept "other means" of proof, see n. 61 above.

70 See *ante*, pp. 208–209 and *R(S)8/55, R(S)1/53, R(I)13/55, R(S)16/54* and *R(S)1/58.*

71 *R(S)1/58, C.I.40/49* (unrep.).

72 *R(S)1/58*, and *cf. R(S)6/59.*

73 *R(S)12/59.*

74 *R(S)16/54.*

75 See *e.g. R4/59(SB), R(S)1/67.*

76 See *R(S)17/51, R(S)29/52, R(S)1/53, R(S)10/54, 30/58(SB), R(S)4/60* and *3/61(SB).*

77 *R(S)17/51.*

78 See Medical Evidence Regulations, Sched. 1, rr. 10 and 11.

79 *R(S)9/63.*

80 *R(S)24/51*; see however *R(S)1/56, ante*, p. 207, on disentitlement.

81 See *ante*, pp. 50–52, for disqualification on grounds of absence abroad in its special relation to sickness benefit.

82 Unemployment, Sickness and Invalidity Regulations, reg. 12.

83 *R(S)2/53.*

84 *R34/58(SB)*; *cf.* unreported Decisions *C.S.439/50* and *C.S.4/55.*

85 By analogy with the decision in *R(S)3/57*, considered below.

86 See *ante*, p. 121.

87 *C.W.S.25/50(KL)*.

88 *R(S)5/52*.

89 *4/53(SB)*.

90 *C.W.S.25/50(KL)*.

91 See *R(S)21/52, C.W.S.25/50(KL)* and *cf. R(S)9/51* and *R(S)6/55*.

92 *R(S)10/60*.

93 *R(S)9/51*.

94 *165/50(SB)*.

95 *R(S)4/61*.

96 *Post*, pp. 290–298.

97 Increases for dependants are also at a higher rate, 1975 Act, Sched. 4, Pt. IV, 1975 Act, s. 16.

98 1975 Act, s. 16 (as amended from 1979 by the S.S. (Pensions) Act.

99 *Ante*, pp. 218–221.

100 For the post-1979 position, see S.S. (Pensions) Act 1975, ss. 14–16.

Chapter 6, pp. 223–229

1 See *post*, pp. 253–257.

2 1975 Act, s. 135(2)(*a*).

3 See Attendance Allowance Regulations, reg. 2.

4 1975 Act, s. 35(1)(*a*), (*b*). Normally, "person" when used in a statute, includes artificial persons (corporations etc.) as well as natural persons. In the context of the attendance allowance legislation, however, a contrary intentions appears, see *R(A)3/75*.

5 See the decisions summarised in *R(A)4/74*.

6 See Northern Ireland appeal Decision No. *1/72(AA)*.

7 Unreported Decision No. *C.A.9/72*.

8 Northern Ireland appeal Decision No. *1/72(AA)*.

9 *R(A)3/74*.

10 [1974] 1 W.L.R. 1290.

11 *R(A)3/74*, in which helping the disabled person to bath or eat his food, cooking for him, or dressing a wound, are cited as examples.

12 *R(A)1/73*. More recent decisions suggest a perhaps stronger requirement, see *e.g. R(A)1/75*.

13 *R(A)1/73*.

14 Northern Ireland appeal Decision No. *12/72(AA)*; *R(A)4/74*.

15 *R(A)1/73, R(A)1/75*.

16 *R(A)2/74*, which also holds that indirect attendance qualifies as attendance for the purposes of allowance.

17 *R(A)1/73*.

18 As to informal claims, see P.C.A. Decision C.347/V, (First Report, P.C.A., 1975–76, p. 149.

19 1975 Act, ss. 103(1)(*a*), 105(3); and see *R(A)4/75*.

20 1975 Act, s. 105, Sched. 11.

21 Annual Report for 1969–70, para. 47.

22 See *R(A)1/72* and Carson, (1972) 122 *New Law Journal*, 973–974.

23 1975 Act, s. 35(4).

24 *Ibid.* s. 35(2).

25 *Ibid.*

26 1975 Act, s. 119(2) and see *ante*, pp. 44–45.

27 Attendance Allowance Regulations, regs. 8 and 9.

28 *Ibid*. regs. 10–14.

29 *Ibid*. reg. 9(2).

30 *R(A)1/72*. See also *R* v. *National Insurance Commissioner, ex p. Secretary of State for Social Services* [1974] 1 W.L.R. 1290; *R(A)1/75*.

31 Attendance Allowance Regulations, regs. 3–5, 7.

32 *Ibid*. regs. 6 and 7.

33 *Ibid*. regs. 4 and 7(1)(*b*).

34 *R(A)2/73, R(A)3/73*.

35 *R(A)1/74*.

36 *R(A)3/74*.

CHAPTER 7

WIDOW'S BENEFITS

1 Report, paras. 346–347.

2 *Ibid*. para. 153.

3 Under the existing scheme, widows of pensionable age may qualify for retirement pension (see *post*, pp. 258–307) and may be disqualified for widow's benefit, see 1975 Act, s. 24(1)(*a*).

4 Report, para. 156.

5 Cmd. 6550, para. 122. Entitlement has since been extended, see *post*, pp. 235–236.

6 See *ante*, pp. 31–33.

7 Cohabitation merely suspends the right to benefit which is restorable when cohabitation ceases. Promiscuity may be the most prudent course and cohabitation preferable to marriage. See 1975 Act, ss. 24(2), 25(3) and 26(3). On "cohabitation," see *post*, pp. 408–419.

8 *R(G)18/52*.

9 1975 Act, s. 162 and Polygamous Marriages Regulations, reg. 2. The corollary is that a *de facto* polygamous marriage does not disqualify until there is a sole surviving husband, when it does disqualify. In the unlikely event of a wife losing one husband and marrying two more, she would lose the benefit in respect of the first upon losing one of the two later ones. The moral seems to be always to keep an adequate supply.

10 *R(G)10/53*, see also *R(G)1/53*.

11 *R(G)3/72*.

12 Not surprisingly, the position where the marriage was actually annulled after title to widow's benefits had accrued in virtue of it was never considered.

13 Nullity of Marriage Act 1971, s. 5, now repealed by the Matrimonial Causes Act 1973 but replaced by s. 16 of the 1973 Act.

14 *R(G)2/73*.

15 *Ibid*. The decisions here discussed relate to the position under the law of England and Wales. S. 16 of the Matrimonial Causes Act 1973 does not extend to Scotland and Northern Ireland.

16 *R(G)1/62*; see also *R(G)4/57* (review of original decision in light of new circumstances).

17 *R(G)1/62*, concerning the Presumption of Life Limitation (Scotland) Act 1891.

18 See *post*, pp. 235–236.

19 For a detailed treatment of "cohabitation," the effects of which are best-known in relation to supplementary benefits, see *post*, pp. 408–419. See now S.S. (Miscellaneous Provns.) Act 1977, s. 22(2).

20 Child's special allowance, payable in respect of children on the death of a father divorced from the mother and maintaining the children prior to his death (*post*, pp. 253–257), is similarly affected by remarriage and co-habitation.

21 There will, of course, be cases where title to benefit would accrue by the death of an estranged husband. Cohabitation may even have preceded the death. There is a case for making special provision in such cases as part of a general reorientation of the scheme towards actual dependency.

22 1975 Act, s. 24(2).

23 *Ibid.* For contribution conditions see Sched. 3, Pt. I, para. 4.

24 *Ibid.* s. 25. For contribution conditions see Sched. 3, Pt. I, para. 5.

25 *Post*, pp. 355–392 and see C.B. (Dependency) Regs. 1977, reg. 4.

26 *R(G)3/61*.

27 *R(G)9/53*.

28 See *ante*, pp. 34–55; *R(G)1/57*.

29 1975 Act, Sched. 3, Pt. I, para. 5.

30 *Ibid.* s. 26(1)(*a*).

31 *Ibid.* s. 26(1)(*b*).

32 *R(G)2/55* and see *R(G)3/62*.

33 I guess this to be the law. The present governing provision is reg. 16 of the Widow's Benefit and Retirement Pensions Regulations which provides: "Where before January 7, 1957 a widow ceased to be entitled to a widow's *pension* under the National Insurance Act 1965 and when she so ceased she was incapable of self-support by reason of infirmity...." Reg. 1 (4) allows us to substitute "1946" for "1965" but one is still left with problems if the italicised word is correct. Entitlement to widow's pension can cease (1) by the death of the pensioner; (2) by attaining age 65 (neither of which events can be referred to in reg. 16, the first *ex hypothesi* and the second because the regulation only confers title to benefit for any period during which she is under 65; (3) by cohabitation and (4) by remarriage. If regulation 16 is intended to apply to (3) and (4) then one of two anomalous results follows. Her entitlement to benefit is "as if she was over the age of 50 when her husband died." If this means that her entitlement is fixed as it was at the death of her husband, the purport of the regulation seems to be that she can receive pension even though she is cohabiting or has remarried. If, however, as seems the correct view, her entitlement is subject to suspension or disqualification as provided by the Act, the regulation is self-defeating. The explanation seems to be that precursors of the present regulation have been erroneously paraphrased and adapted. The National Insurance Act 1965, Sched. 11, para. 4(1) provided "Section 18(3) of the Act of 1946 (by virtue

of which a widow who would otherwise have *ceased to be entitled to widow's benefit* at a time when incapable of self-support by reason of infirmity may be granted a widow's pension), ... shall be specially saved; and where a widow *entitled to a widow's pension* by virtue of the said section 18(3) *ceases to be so entitled.*" The third italicised phrase seems to refer back to the first, whereas it seems to have been assumed, in drafting regulation 16, that it refers back to the second.

34 1975 Act, s. 26(2).

35 *R(G)8/53.*

36 Widow's Benefit and Retirement Pensions Regulations, reg. 16(20); *R(G)8/53.*

37 *C.G.4/48, R(G)12/53.*

38 *R(G)22/52.*

39 *R(G)16/52.*

40 *R(G)3/56.*

41 *R(G)4/51.*

42 *R(G)16/52.*

43 *C.G.30/49(KL).*

44 *C.G.3/48*; "A person is 'incapable of self-support' if (but only if) he is incapable of supporting himself by reason of physical or mental infirmity and is likely to remain so for a prolonged period.

45 See *R(G)2/57, R(G)3/57, R(G)2/58.*

46 Widowers may be entitled to death benefit under the industrial injuries scheme, *post*, pp. 347–348. From 1979, invalidity and retirement pension may be paid to a widower on the basis of his spouse's contribution record, S.S. (Pensions) Act 1975, ss. 8, 16.

CHAPTER 8

MINOR BENEFITS

Chapter 8, pp. 237–250

1 See George, *Social Security*, pp. 128–134.

2 H.C.Deb., Col. 835 (December 19, 1975).

3 D.H.S.S. Annual Report for 1975, p. 17.

4 Formerly ss. 16–18 of the Social Security Act 1973. For Northern Ireland, see the Social Security (N.I.) Act 1975, especially ss. 21–23, and regulations made thereunder.

5 1975 Act, ss. 21(1) and (5).

6 Maternity Benefit Regulations, reg. 3.

7 1975 Act, s. 21(1)(a) and Sched. 3.

8 *Ibid.* s. 13(1).

9 *Ibid.* Sched. 3, Pt. I, para. 2.

10 *Ibid.* para. 4(a).

11 *Ibid.*

12 Maternity Benefit Regulations, reg. 3(b).

13 1975 Act, Sched. 3, Pt. I, para. 2(2)(*b*).

14 *Ibid.* paras. 2(3) and (4)(*b*); in relation to satisfying contribution conditions, see also the Short-term Benefits (Transitional) Regulations.

15 1975 Act, s. 21(1)(*b*).

16 On concubinage, see *C.G.3/49(KL)*; on polygamous marriages, see *ante*, pp. 32–33.

17 1975 Act, s. 162 and Family Allowances Act 1965, s. 12, as substituted by the Social Security (Consequential Provisions) Act 1975. See Child Benefit (General) Regulations 1976 due to come into force in August 1978.

18 *R(G)2/68.*

19 *R(G)2/68, R(G)1/52.*

20 1975 Act, s. 21(2).

21 *R(G)1/65, R(G)1/67.*

22 1975 Act, s. 22(1)(*a*) and (8); Maternity Benefit Regulations, reg. 6(1)(*a*).

23 1975 Act, s. 22(1)(*a*), (6); Maternity Benefit Regulations, reg. 4(2).

24 See also Maternity Allowance (Transitional) Regulations and Transitional (Amendments) Regulations; Married Women and Widows (Amendment and Transitional) Regulations, reg. 3(1).

25 1975 Act, s. 13(1).

26 Maternity Benefit Regulations, reg. 8(1). See also Employment Protection Act 1975, ss. 35–51.

27 Note Maternity Benefit Regulations, reg. 12: substantive entitlement is enough; she need not have claimed or received benefit.

28 1975 Act, s. 22(4).

29 *Ibid.* s. 22(8)(*a*); Maternity Benefit Regulations, reg. 6(1)(*a*).

30 Maternity Benefit Regulations, reg. 6(2)(i).

31 *Ibid.* reg. 6(2)(ii).

32 *Ibid.* reg. 6(3).

33 1975 Act, s. 22(2).

34 *e.g. C.G.266/49(KL).*

35 *R(G)8/55, R(G)2/61.*

36 *R(G)8/55.*

37 Maternity Benefit Regulations, reg. 5(1).

38 *Ibid.* reg. 5(2), (3).

39 1975 Act, s. 21(9); Maternity Benefit Regulations, reg. 9(3).

40 *R1/64(MB).*

41 1975 Act, s. 23(1)(*a*); see *R(G)4/56* as to the method of calculation of the 28 week period. See also *R(G)12/59.*

42 *R1/62(MB).*

43 *C.S.G.3/49(KL).*

44 1975 Act, s. 22(3), Maternity Benefit Regulations, reg. 10. The significance of this is in its enabling contributions to be credited during the maternity allowance period.

45 Claims and Payments Regulations, reg. 9(1).

46 *Ibid.* reg. 10(1).

47 *R(S)1/74.*

48 Medical Evidence Regulations, reg. 2(3).

49 *Ibid.* Sched. 2.

50 As to which, see *C.W.G.1/49(KL)*.

51 Report of the Committee on One-Parent Families, para. 290.

52 *Ibid.* para. 291.

53 George, *Social Security, supra*.

54 The Finer Committee (Report, above, para. 293) put the additional cost at about £1m. p.a. Mr. R. C. Brown, however, in a reply to a written question, put the figure at slightly under £2m., H.C.Deb., col. 337 (May 24, 1974).

55 An amendment put down in the House of Lords during the passing of the Social Security Bill 1973 to the effect that maternity grant should be non-contributory was defeated.

56 *R(G)2/55*.

57 Robson (1947) 10 M.L.R., at 177.

58 See also Beveridge Report, paras. 157–160.

59 Robson, *loc. cit.* above. The distinction of the need as being "self-inflicted" is not quite as clear-cut as might seem. It may be argued that the cultural milieu dictates the need in much the same way as it dictates the margin of other needs beyond the biological and functional.

60 1975 Act, s. 32.

61 1975 Act, s. 32(1); see also Death Grant Regulations.

62 1975 Act, s. 32(2), (3) and (4); Death Grant Regulations, regs. 2 and 3, and C.B. (Consequential) Regs., reg. 19.

63 *R(G)3/51*.

64 *R1/68 (DG)*.

65 *C.G.213/50* (unrep.).

66 Claims and Payments Regulations, reg. 7(4).

67 1975 Act, s. 32(5).

68 Persons Abroad Regulations, reg. 7.

69 Death Grant Regulations, reg. 5.

70 Claims and Payments Regulations, reg. 27(2).

71 *Ibid.* reg. 27(4).

72 *R(G)21/52*.

73 Claims and Payments Regulations, reg. 27(4).

74 *C.G.65/50(KL)*, *C.G.145/50(KL)* affirmed in *R(G)2/52*.

75 But see Death Grant Regulations, reg. 2(2).

76 Claims and Payments Regulations, reg. 27(1).

77 *C.G.145/50(KL)*.

78 *Ante*, pp. 233–234.

79 Claims and Payments Regulations, reg. 27(2).

80 *C.G.66/50(KL)*.

81 *R(G) 13/52*, overruling on this point *R(G)8/52*, *C.G.65/50(KL)*.

82 1975 Act, Sched. 4, Pt. II.

83 Cmd. 6550, para. 60.

84 s. 38(1).

85 The original section 38(1) referred to "family allowances." "Child benefit" was substituted by the Child Benefit Act 1975, Sched. 4, para. 12(a).

86 See Guardian's Allowance Regulations.

87 1975 Act, s. 38(3).

88 See 1965 Act, s. 29.

89 See *C.G.53/50(KL), R(G)8/62, C.G.244/49(KL)*.

90 Guardian's Allowance Regulations, reg. 6(1) as substituted by S.S. (C.B. Consequential) Regs., reg. 9(1).

91 *Ibid.* reg. 6(3).

92 *Ibid.* reg. 7.

93 *Post*, pp. 355–385.

94 *R(G)4/52*, decided in the context of the Family Allowance Acts.

95 *R(G)12/55*, following *R(G)8/51*.

96 Guardian's Allowance Regulations, regs. 3, 6(3).

97 [1955] 2 Q.B. 479.

98 1975 Act, s. 38(2)(*b*).

99 See also, *R(G)4/59*.

Chapter 8, pp. 251–257

1 1975 Act, s. 38(2)(*c*), (first instituted as reg. 5A by S.I. 1962 No. 1270).

2 *Ibid.* and s. 38(4) (*b*); Guardian's Allowance Regulations, regs. 5(1) and (9).

3 Guardian's Allowance Regulations 1973, reg. 6(6) and see *R(G)1/74*.

4 See particularly *R(G)13/56*.

5 Guardian's Allowance Regulations, reg. 3. See *R(G)15/52*, holding that paternity was "admitted" and "prima facie established" by the entry on the birth certificate of the person in question as "father" and informant.

6 *Ibid.* reg. 3(2).

7 1975 Act, s. 38(6).

8 Child Benefit Act 1975, Sched. 4, para. 12, amending 1975 Act, s. 38(5) and S.S. (C.B. Consequential) Regs., reg. 9(2).

9 *Ibid.* s. 24(5).

10 As amended by Child Benefit Act 1975, Sched. 4, para. 10.

11 As amended by Child Benefit Act 1975, Sched. 4, para. 15.

12 Child's Special Allowance Regulations, reg. 3.

13 *R(G)3/69*.

14 1975 Act, Sched. 3, para. 6.

15 Still fixed at 25p by the Child's Special Allowance Regulations, reg. 2.

16 *C.G.11/58, R(G)5/59, R(G)6/59, R(G)15/59, R(G)3/60*.

17 *R(G)5/59*.

18 *R(G)3/59*.

19 *R(G)6/59*.

20 *Social Security Statistics 1975*, pp. 78, 218–220. No other benefit comes near the five-fold increase in outgo on child's special allowance during the last decade.

CHAPTER 9

RETIREMENT PENSIONS

Chapter 9, pp. 258–281

1 *Social Security Statistics 1975*, pp. 88, 89, 157. A further 94 thousand persons of pensionable age relied exclusively upon supplementary pension.

2 Supplementary Benefit Commission Annual Report 1975, Cmnd. 6615.

3 Lister, *The Reform of Social Security*, C.P.A.G., 1975.

4 Social Security Benefits Uprating Order 1976 (S.I. 1976 No. 1029).

5 The decreasing number of pensioners on Supplementary Benefits (28 per cent. in 1968–72, 22·7 per cent. in 1975) probably reflects the increasing number having graduated pensions, occupational pensions, rent and rate rebates etc. It is certainly not due to any marked increase in the level of retirement pension rates by comparison with supplementary benefit rates.

6 "Better Pensions," Cmnd. 5713, iii, 6.

7 *Strategy for Pensions*, Cmnd. 4755 (1971), p. 4. See also H.C.Deb., Vol. 885, col. 186–187.

8 Social Security Pensions Act 1975.

9 Report, para. 403 and Appendix A.

10 Cmd. 6550, para. 82. For a more detailed consideration of policy, see Townsend, *Socialism and Affluence*, pp. 60–62; Marshall, *Social Policy*, Chap. 8, Titmuss, *Commitment to Welfare*, pp. 174–184, 200–204; Atkinson, *Poverty in Britain and the Reform of Social Security*, pp. 44–77, 96–97, 105–130; Walley, in *The Future of the Social Services* (ed. Crick & Robson), pp. 147–179; Priest, *Three Banks Review*, June 1970.

11 National Insurance Act 1959.

12 Cmnd. 5713, p. 2.

13 Claims and Payments Regulations, reg. 13(1), Sched. 1, para. 5, Sched. 2, para. 4(1).

14 *Ibid*. reg. 13; Social Security Act 1975, s. 82(2).

15 Annual Report of the Parliamentary Commissioner for Administration, First Report, 1970, Case No. C.540/L, p. 108.

16 Claims and Payments Regulations, Sched. 2, para. 4(4).

17 1975 Act, ss. 28, 29.

18 *Ibid*. s. 27(1).

19 1976, Cmnd. 659, 7, 17.

20 The *Annual Abstract of Statistics, 1973*, estimated that a woman of 60 could, on average, expect to live to 80 whilst a man at 60 could expect to live to 75. In 1975, retirement pensions were distributed by age and sex as follows:

Age	Men	Women
	%	%
60–64	—	10·4
65–69	13·3	16·9
70–74	10·8	15·6
75–79	5·9	11·7
80 plus	4·5	11·7
Total	34·6	66·4

(Source: *Social Security Statistics 1975*, p. 90)

21 The DHSS Research Division estimated that in 1971, of a total of 620,000 one-parent families, some 100,000 were motherless, although it must be added that at least half of these were households incorporating another adult; Report of the Committee on One-Parent Families (Finer), Cmnd. 5629, Vol. 2, p. 79.

22 Shenfield, *Social Policies for Old Age.*

23 Report of the Committee on Equal Status for Men and Women in Occupational Pension Schemes, 1976, p. 735.

24 H.C.Deb., Vol. 888, (March 10, 1975).

25 *Ibid.* Vol. 905, col. 546 (February 16, 1976).

26 *Ibid.* Vol. 899, col. 102 (November 4, 1975).

27 Cmnd. 659.

28 Family Law Reform Act 1969, s. 9.

29 *C.P.11/49(KL), R(P)3/65, R(P)1/75.* On review on grounds of fresh evidence, see *R(P)3/73.*

30 *C.P.48/49(KL), C.P.1/50(KL), R1/59(P), R4/61(P).*

31 Claims and Payments Regulations, reg. 15(2).

32 *Ibid.* reg. 15(9), *C.S.P.15/49, R(P)2/73;* see Report of the Parliamentary Commissioner for Administration, 3rd Report, 1974–75, Case No. C.207/J, p. 113.

33 Widow's Benefit, Retirement Pension and Other Benefits (Transitional) Regulations 1974 (S.I. 1974 No. 1757), reg. 6(1).

34 1975 Act, ss. 28(1)(*b*), 29(6), Sched. 3, para. 5(2).

35 *Ibid.* Sched. 3, para. 5(3).

36 *Ibid.* s. 27(2).

37 *Ibid.* Sched. 3, para. 5(4). Amendment of the contribution conditions by the Social Security Pensions Act 1975 is due to come into effect in 1978.

38 Social Security Pensions Act 1975, s. 19(4). Note also the modification of this condition by the Widow's Benefit, Retirement Pensions and Other Benefits (Transitional) Regulations 1974 (S.I. 1974 No. 1757), reg. 11(1) and (2).

39 Married Women and Widow's Special Provisions Regulations, reg. 4(1), (3).

40 Widow's Benefit, Retirement Pension and Other Benefits (Transitional) Regulations 1974 (S.I. 1974 No. 1757), reg. 6(2).

41 *Ibid.* reg. 7(2).

42 1975 Act, s. 28(3), Sched. 7. The Social Security Pensions Act 1975, s. 20 extends this cover to a spouse whose marriage has terminated, as from April 6, 1979. See also s. 9.

43 Married Women and Widow's Special Provisions Regulations, reg. 4(1), (3).

44 Widow's Benefit and Retirement Pension Regulations, reg. 5(1); Married Women and Widows Special Provisions Regulations, reg. 9(1).

45 Widow's Benefit and Retirement Pensions Regulations 1972 (S.I. 1972 No. 606), reg. 7(1) and Sched. 1 (see 1975 Act, s. 115).

46 Report of the Parliamentary Commissioner for Administration, First Report for 1975–6, Case No. C.128/V, p. 140

47 *C.P.96/50(KL).*

48 *C.S.P.21/50.*

49 1975 Act, s. 28(1)(*a*).

50 *C.P.70/50(KL).*

51 1975 Act, s. 27(3)(*a*).

52 *Ibid.* s. 27(5).

53 *Ibid.* s. 27(3).

54 See *ante*, pp. 16–17.

55 *C.P.21/49(KL)*.

56 1975 Act, Sched. 20, *s.n.* "employment."

57 *C.P.30/49(KL)*, *C.P.7/49(KL)*.

58 *C.P.129/50(KL)*.

59 *Quaere* is there any other kind? See Partnership Act 1890, s. 1.

60 *R(P)19/56*. *Cf. R(P)9/56*.

61 *Benjamin* v. *Minister of Pensions* [1960] 2 Q.B. 519, 530, *per* Salmon J., approved and applied in *R(P)1/65*, where a member of the court of a Livery Company who had undertaken to serve and did serve for motives of family pride and loyalty before he even knew that fees were payable was nevertheless held to be "gainfully occupied."

62 *Ante*, pp. 16–17.

63 *Ante*, pp. 28–42.

64 *R(P)4/67*.

65 *R(P)1/69*.

66 *R(P)17/52*.

67 *19/49(P)*.

68 *141/49(P)*, citing *U.P.68/47*.

69 *Ibid.*; see also *R(P)3/54* holding an intention to quit for a fortnight to involve a "misunderstanding of the nature of retirement". Retirement for a fortnight is, of course, possible, provided that resumption of employment is not intended and planned beforehand. The need produced by cessation of employment exists in both cases; it does not depend on the intention of the particular claimant. Again, one must question the relevance of the retirement condition.

70 *R(P)3/54, 114/49(P)*.

71 *R(P)8/52*.

72 *C.P.49/49(KL)*.

73 *R(P)10/53*.

74 *R(P)8/52*.

75 *C.P.49/49(KL)*.

76 *R(P)8/52*. *Cf. 2/60(P)* and *R(P)8/51*.

77 *R(P)1/52, R(P)1/53*.

78 *Ibid.*

79 *206/48(P), R(P)15/52, 15/59(P), R(P)4/61*.

80 para. 17.

81 See *R1/60(P)*, where the Northern Ireland Commissioner avoids the heresy; and *R(P)1/54* manifesting the simpler approach. There, the only grounds put forward concerned hours and pay; no reference was made to condition (iii).

82 *R(P)16/55*.

83 *R(P)11/55*; see also *R(P)15/55*.

84 *R(P)16/56, R(P)5/51, R(P)7/52*.

85 *R(P)6/55*.

86 *R(P)2/53*; see also *R(P)3/53, R(P)12/53, R(P)10/55, R(P)13/55, R(P)6/54, R(P)6/55, R(P)1/54*.

87 *C.P.33/49(KL)*, quoting *U.P.4/47*.

88 *U.P.4/47.*

89 *C.P.33/49(KL).*

90 *e.g. R(P)5/52, R(P)1/54, R(P)8/55, R(P)6/55, R(P)11/55, R(P)16/55, R(P)2/61, R(P)4/61.*

91 *C.W.P.1/59.*

92 *C.P.7/49(KL).*

93 *R(P)16/56.*

94 *R(P)9/54, R(P)15/55, 58/49(P).*

95 *R(P)2/53.*

96 *R(P)15/55.*

97 *R(P)8/54.*

98 *C.P.176/49(KL).*

99 *R(P)10/55.*

Chapter 9, pp. 282–297

1 See also *R(P)16/55.*

2 See, in addition to the decisions discussed above, *R(P)5/51, R(P)9/52, R(P)6/53, R(P)9/53, R(P)9/54, R(P)6/55, R(P)13/55, R(P)6/56, R(P)2/61,* and *R(P)3/61.* The earlier decisions are comprehensively rehearsed in *R(P)11/56.* For Northern Ireland, see *R3/60(P).*

3 Relaxation of Earnings Regulations 1975.

4 Annual Report of the Parliamentary Commissioner for Administration, 4th Report for 1974–75, Case No. C.368/J, p. 195.

5 1975 Act, s. 27(4); Claims and Payments Regulations, Sched. 2, para. 4(2) (3).

6 Claims and Payments Regulations, Sched. 2, para. 4(3).

7 *R(P)4/52, R(P)17/56* and *2/56(P).*

8 *R(P)5/55.*

9 Claims and Payments Regulations, Sched. 2, paras. 4(1) and (2).

10 *R(P)8/51, R(P)13/53.*

11 *R(P)13/53, R(P)11/53.*

12 *R(P)8/51.*

13 Claims and Payments Regulations, Sched. 2, para. 4(2).

14 *R(P)14/55.*

15 1975 Act, s. 28; Widow's Benefit, Retirement Pensions and Other Benefits (Transitional) Regulations, regs. 6 and 7.

16 Social Security Benefits Upratings Order 1976 (S.I. 1976 No. 1029); 1975 Act, s. 29(7)(i).

17 1975 Act, s. 29(7)(ii).

18 *Ibid.* s. 29(2)(b), (3)(b), (4)(b).

19 *Ibid.* s. 29(5).

20 1975 Act, s. 29(1).

21 *Ibid.* s. 29(2)(3)(5).

22 *Ibid.* s. 29(4).

23 *Ibid.* s. 29(2)(3).

24 Married Women and Widow's Special Provision Regulations 1974 (S.I. 1974 No. 2010), reg. 4(2).

25 1975 Act, s. 27(6).

26 Social Security Pensions Act 1975, s. 25(1) (2).

27 *Ibid.* ss. 9 and 10.

28 *Ibid.* s. 8.

29 1975 Act, s. 30(3).

30 Widow's Benefit and Retirement Pension Regulations, reg. 2(2)(*c*).

31 *Ibid.* reg. 2; 1975 Act, s. 30(4).

32 *Ibid.* reg. 2.

33 *R(P)6/60.*

34 Reference is made to the dicta of Cozens-Hardy M.R. in *Shanly* v. *Ward* (1913) 29 T.L.R. 714, 715 (C.A.).

35 Widow's Benefit and Retirement Pension Regulations, reg. 2(3).

36 *Ibid.*

37 *Ibid.* reg. 2(4)(*b*).

38 *Ibid.* reg. 2(3).

39 *Ibid.* reg. 2(4)(*b*); *R(P)1/61.*

40 *Ibid.* reg. 2(1) 3.

41 *Ibid.* reg. 2(2)(*a*).

42 See Social Security (Miscellaneous and Transitional Provisions) Regulations 1975, reg. 3.

43 Persons Abroad Regulations, reg. 6.

44 1975 Act, s. 6. No Class I or II contributions will be payble by any person over pensionable age after April 1978—Social Security Pensions Act 1975, s. 6. A deficient contribution record will presumably be remediable by payment of Class III contributions.

45 National Insurance Act 1965, s. 31; Social Security Act 1973, s. 24(4).

46 Widow's Benefits, Retirement Pensions and Other Benefits (Transitional) Regulations 1974 (S.I. 1974 No. 1757), reg. 12(1).

47 *Ibid.* reg. 12(2).

48 National Insurance (Contributions) Regulations 1969 (S.I. 1969 No. 1696), reg. 28, saved by Contribution Regulations, Sched. 7.

49 Parliamentary Commissioner for Administration, Fifth Report, 1975–76, Case No. C.3/K, p. 151.

50 1975 Act, s. 28(4).

51 Widow's Benefit and Retirement Pensions Regulations 1974 (S.I. 1974 No. 2059), reg. 4(1).

52 1975 Act, s. 29(10) as modified by the (Pensions Act) 1975 and S.S. (M.P.) Act 1977.

53 See *R(P)3/67.*

54 1975 Act, s. 29(12); see also Widow's Benefit, Retirement Pension and Other Benefits (Transitional) Regulations 1974, reg. 12.

55 *Ibid.* reg. 14(1).

56 *C.P.125/49.* See also *R(P)5/53.*

57 *R(U)33/53* followed in *R(G)10/59.*

58 *R(G)10/59.*

59 Claims and Payments Regulations, reg. 15(6).

60 1975 Act, s. 3 and Sched. 20.

61 Computation of Earnings Regulations.

62 See *1/57(P)*, *2/57(P)* and *R(G)9/55*, *R(G)14/56* on widow's pension.

63 General Benefit Regulations 1948, reg. 4(1)(*a*).

64 *R(G)14|56.*

65 *R(G)14|56.*

66 *C.P.7|49(KL).*

67 See also *R5|61(P)* and authorities there cited.

68 *R(G)9|55.*

69 *R(P)7|61, R(P)1|70.*

70 *R(G)9|55.*

71 Computation of Earnings Regulations, reg. 1(2).

72 *R(P)5|53.*

73 *R(P)7|61.*

74 Computation of Earnings Regulations, reg. 2(3).

75 *C.P.3|48(KL).*

76 *C.G.178|50(KL).*

77 *R(G)7|59.* Christmas bonuses up to £10 are deductible—Computation of Earnings Regulations, reg. 3(1)(*b*) and (2) and see below.

78 *C.P.43|49.*

79 *R(P)2|51.*

80 *R(P)2|51.*

81 Computation of Earnings Regulations, reg. 3(1)(*a*).

82 *Ibid.* reg. 3(1)(*b*).

83 *Ibid.* reg. 4.

84 See *ibid.* reg. 2(2).

85 *R(G)7|52, R(G)12|52, C.G.114|49(KL).*

86 *R(G)7|52.*

87 *R(G)12|52.*

88 *C.G.114|49(KL).*

89 *R(P)4|56, R(P)1|64.*

90 *R(G)7|53.*

91 *R(G)9|51.*

92 See *R(G)7|62.*

93 *Ibid.*

94 *R(P)3|56* (PAYE tax deductible, other income tax not so).

95 *Ibid.*

96 *R(G)6|54.*

97 *R(G)9|54.*

98 *R(G)5|57.*

99 *R(P)1|66.*

Chapter 9, pp. 298–307

1 Computation of Earnings Regulations, regs. 5 and 6.

2 *Ibid.*; for self-employed persons, see *R(P)1|73.*

3 *Ibid.* reg. 7.

4 *R(G)20|52.*

5 *4|59(P).*

6 Beveridge Report, para. 17.

7 National Insurance Act 1965, s. 36(2).

8 Social Security Pensions Act 1975, s. 25, taking effect from April 6, 1978.

9 Graduated Benefit Rights Regulations.

10 Social Security Pensions Act 1975, s. 24.

11 *Ibid.* s. 6.

12 Rates of Category B retirement pension (for a widow), Widowed Mother's allowance, widow's pension and Invalidity pension are calculated in the same way.

13 Social Security Pensions Act 1975, s. 19(3)(4).

14 See, esp. Lister, *op. cit.* p. 40; George, *op. cit.* p. 34. *Cf.* Fogarty, *op. cit.* p. 45.

15 National Insurance (Non-participation—Transitional Provisions) Regulations, S.I. 1974 No. 2057.

16 See also S.I.s 1960 No. 1103; 1961 No. 1378; 1963 Nos. 1265, 1988, 676; 1959 No. 1860; 1960 No. 1210.

17 Social Security Pensions Act 1975, s. 27(6).

18 *Ibid.* s. 32(4). The parts of the Act relating to the issue, cancellation, and modification of certificates are already in force but do not take effect until 1978. See also the Social Security Occupational Pension Schemes (Certification of Employments) Regulations, S.I. 1975 No. 1927.

19 Social Security Pensions Act 1975, s. 32(3)(b). See also, Occupational Pensions Schemes (Contracting Out) Regulations, S.I. 1975 No. 2102.

20 Social Security Pensions Act 1975, s. 29, S.S. (M.P.) Act 1977, s. 3(3).

21 *Ibid.* ss. 34(1), 35(4)(b).

22 *Ibid.* s. 36(6).

23 *Ibid.* s. 37(1).

24 *Ibid.* s. 39(3).

25 *Ibid.* ss. 40 and 41; Social Security (M.P.) Act, 1977, s. 22(9).

26 Social Security Act 1973, Sched. 16.

27 Social Security Pensions Act 1975, ss. 38, 43(3); Social Security Act 1973, s. 9(1); Occupational Pension Schemes (Preservation of Benefit) Regulations, S.I. 1973 Nos. 1469 and 1784; 1974 No. 1324; 1976 No. 140.

28 Social Security Pensions Act 1975, ss. 42 and 43.

29 *Ibid.* s. 44.

30 *Ibid.* s. 35(5).

31 *Ibid.* s. 45.

32 Contracted-Out Employments (Notification of Premium Payment and Miscellaneous Provisions) Regulations 1976 (S.I. 1976 No. 143), reg. 4(2)(a).

33 *Ibid.* reg. 4(3).

34 Social Security Pensions Act 1975, s. 31(4).

35 *Ibid.* s. 43(3).

36 Contracted-out Employments (Notification of Premium Payments and Miscellaneous Provisions) Regulations, S.I. 1976 No. 143, reg. 4(1).

37 Social Security Pensions Act 1975, s. 53.

38 Occupational Pensions Schemes (Equal Access to Membership) Regulations 1976 (S.I. 1976 No. 142), reg. 4.

39 Social Security Pensions Act 1975, s. 53(4).

40 Equal Pay Act 1970, s. 6A, as modified by the Sex Discrimination Act 1975, Sched. 1.

41 Social Security Act 1973, s. 86(1); Social Security Pensions Act 1975, s. 60(4).

42 See s. 27(1).

43 Widow's Benefit and Retirement Pensions Regulations, reg. 6.

44 *Ibid.* regs. 8–11.

45 National Insurance Act 1971, s. 5(1).

46 1975 Act, s. 39(3).

47 1975 Act, s. 39(2).

48 *Ibid.* s. 125.

49 National Insurance Act 1971, s. 5(1).

50 1975 Act, s. 40(1).

51 Claims and Payments Regulations, reg. 17(1). See also S.I. 1975 No. 2079.

52 Persons Abroad Regulations, reg. 5(1)(3). On the meaning of "residence" in this context, see *R(P)2/67.*

CHAPTER 10

INDUSTRIAL INJURIES BENEFIT

Chapter 10, pp. 308–325

1 Workmen's Compensation Act 1897, s. 1.

2 *Noble* v. *Southern Railway Co.* [1940] A.C. 583, 600.

3 In a vast number of cases the decision appears almost a matter of caprice. *Cf.* the inferences of fact drawn in cases of unexplained death in cases such as *Bender* v. *Owners of Steamship Zent* [1909] 2 K.B. 41 (C.A.) and *Owners of Ship Swansea Vale* v. *Rice* [1912] A.C. 238 (H.L.).

4 See Beveridge Report, paras. 77–80. To the Beverage list should be added the defect revealed in the Northern Ireland scheme in the case of accidents occurring outside the jurisdiction to workers resident in and working for employers established in it; see *Cash* v. *Rainey* [1941] N.I. 52; *Macklin* v. *Concrete Piling Ltd.* (1941) 75 I.L.T.R. 6.

5 Report, para. 79.

6 *Ibid.*

7 "Danger money," of course figures in collective bargaining in hazardous industries and to that extent the Beveridge justification involves paying twice although, as Beveridge pointed out, the "danger money" will not necessarily be put aside to meet the contingency. Nevertheless special provision could be made for hazardous industries—see the Colliery Workers' Supplementary Scheme, *post*, p. 352.

8 Atiyah first stated a compelling case for reform in *Accidents, Compensation and the Law.*

9 Cmnd. 6551.

10 The 1973 Act consolidated in the 1975 Act.

11 On the transition to the new scheme, see *Mobberley and Perry Ltd.* v. *Holloway* [1952] A.C. 133; *Hales* v. *Bolton Leathers Ltd.* [1951] A.C. 531; *Harris* v. *Rotol Ltd.* [1950] 2 K.B. 573.

12 See now Industrial Injuries and Diseases (Old Cases) Act 1975 (The "Old Cases Act 1975").

13 See Old Cases Act 1975, s. 7(3) and Industrial Injuries Benefit Regulations 1975 (S.I. 1975 No. 559) (referred to in this chapter as "the Regulations"), reg. 12.

14 1975 Act, s. 50(1).

15 *Ibid.* s. 76(1).

16 *Ibid.* s. 50(2).

17 See *post*, pp. 343–348.

18 DHSS Annual Report 1975, p. 75.

19 Claims and Payments Regulations, reg. 13 and Sched. 1.

20. *Ibid.* reg. 13(2).

21 See *post*, p. 340.

22 Claims and Payments Regulations, reg. 13 and Sched. 1. A pension in lieu of a gratuity (*post*, p. 340) is treated as a pension.

23 *Ibid.*

24 1975 Act, s. 107(1).

25 *Ibid.* s. 107(2).

26 *Ibid.* s. 107(3).

27 *Ibid.* s. 107(4)(5).

28 1975 Act, s. 93(1)(*d*).

29 *Ibid.* s. 94.

30 *Post*, p. 346.

31 *Post*, p. 347.

32 1975 Act, s. 95(1)(*b*).

33 *Ibid.* s. 95(1)(*c*). There is no appeal against the decision upon these latter questions though a review may be sought (s. 96) and applications for prerogative orders are not excluded.

34 1975 Act, s. 98(2)(*b*).

35 *Ibid.* s. 108(1).

36 *Ibid.* s. 108(2).

37 *Ibid.* s. 109(2).

38 *Ibid.* s. 109(3).

39 For adjudication, see pp. 440–459 *post*.

40 See *ante*, pp. 16–19.

41 1975 Act s. 51.

42 Employed Earners Employments for Industrial Injuries Purposes Regulations, regs. 2, 3 and Sched. 1. For the consequential categorisation of "employers" see *ibid.* Sched. 3.

43 Categorisation of Earners Regulations, reg. 2, Sched. 1, Pt. I.

44 1975 Act, s. 156.

45 *R(I)7/56.*

46 See *Re Haines* [1945] 1 All E.R. 349.

47 *R(I)7/56.*

48 *Coulter* v. *Coltness Iron Co. Ltd.*, 31 B.W.C.C., Supp. 111; *Graham* v. *Christie*, 10 B.W.C.C. 486; *Marriott* v. *Maltby Main Colliery Co. Ltd.* 13 B.W.C.C.; *C.W.I.12/49, C.I.256/49, C.I.172/50; R(I)49/52; cf. R(I)22/59.*

49 Lord Macnaghten in *Fenton* v. *Thorley & Co.* [1903] A.C. 443, 89 L.T. 314 at p. 316.

50 *Stewart* v. *Wilson & Clyde Coal Co. Ltd.* (1902) 5 F. (Ct. Sess.) 120.

51 *Hensey* v. *White* [1900] 1 Q.B. 481 (C.A.).

52 [1903] A.C. 443.

53 It is derived from a pre-1897 insurance case, echoing dicta of Lord Halsbury L.C. in *Hamilton, Fraser & Co.* v. *Pandorf* 12 App.Cas. 518. See also the dicta of Lord Lindley in *Fenton*'s case: "... an accident means any unintended and unexpected occurrence which produces hurt or loss. But it is often used to denote any unintended and unexpected loss or hurt apart from its cause and if the cause is not known the loss or hurt itself would certainly be called an accident." See also, *Oates* v. *Earl Fitzwilliam Collieries* [1939] 2 All E.R. 498 (C.A.); esp. *per* Clauson L.J.

54 Lord Macnaghten's thinking appears in this dictum: "It does seem to me extraordinary that anybody should suppose that when the advantage of insurance against accident at their employer's expense was being conferred on workmen, Parliament could have intended to exclude from the benefit of the Act some injuries ordinarily described as *accidents* which beyond all others merit favourable consideration ..." (italics supplied).

55 [1905] A.C. 230. See also *Innes* v. *Kynach* [1919] A.C. 765; *Burrell (Charles) & Sons Ltd.* v. *Selvage* (1921) 126 L.T. 49; *Fitzsimmons* v. *Ford Motor Co. Ltd.* [1946] 1 All E.R. 429 (C.A.); *Hughes* v. *Lancaster Steam Coal Collieries Ltd.* (1947) 177 L.T. 313; *Pyrah* v. *Doncaster Corporation* [1949] 1 All E.R. 883 (C.A.); *Reg. (Curry)* v. *National Insurance Commissioner* [1974] N.I. 102.

56 (1905) 93 L.T. 357.

57 (1905) 93 L.T. 360.

58 The term "process" is used in the head-note of *Steel* v. *Cammell, Laird* (n. 56 above) but not in the body of the report itself. Whether the credit (or discredit) for coining its use in this context belongs to a most diligent editor or to Collins M.R. remains a mystery.

59 12 B.W.C.C. 78; *sub.nom. Innes (or Grant)* v. *Kynoch* [1919] A.C. 765.

60 (1921) 126 L.T. 49. See also *Hughes* v. *Lancaster Steam Coal Collieries* (1947) 177 L.T. 313; *Fitzsimmons* v. *Ford Motor Co. Ltd.* [1946] 1 All E.R. 429 (C.A.); *Williams* v. *Guest, Keen & Nettlefolds Ltd.* [1926] 1 K.B. 497.

61 [1949] 1 All E.R. 883 (C.A.).

62 [1948] W.N. 246.

63 It was not required, in the early "series" cases that each specific instance be "ascertainable." On the contrary, it was inferred from the nature of the injury that they must have occurred, and that is all.

64 The other leading judgment, that of Lord Simonds, follows a similar course.

65 *R(I)77/51.*

66 *R(I)42/51.*

67 *R(I)4/62*; see also *C.I.123/49(KL)*, *R(I)18/54*, *R(I)43/61*, *R6/63(II)*.

68 *R(I)19/56*; see also *C.I.257/49(KL)*, *R(I)7/66*.

69 *C.I.83/50(KL)*, *C.I.244/50(KL)*, *R(I)25/52* (emphasising continuity rather than duration); *C.I.125/50(KL)*.

70 *R(I)31/52.*

71 *R(I)54/53.*

72 *R(I)49/52.*

73 *Post*, pp. 349–351. Even if prescribable, prescription by no means neces-

sarily follows and, even if it does, may well be a very lengthy process. Many claims may fail in the meantime. See *e.g. C.I.325/50(KL), R(I)25/52, R(I)11/74* (reported, after application to the divisional court as *R.* v. *Industrial Injuries Commissioner, ex p. William Storr*, as an appendix to *R(I)11/74.*)

74 See, since the *Dorothea* case, *C.I.27/49(KL)*. A bold attempt at a brief analysis of the post-*Dorothea* position (but not, alas, a successful one) is to be found in the judgment of Denning L.J. (as he then was) in *Pyrah* v. *Doncaster Corporation* [1949] 1 All E.R. 883, 890.

75 The distinction in some of the earlier cases seems sometimes to be between requiring strict discharge of the onus and readily inferring accidental cause. The point recurs in post-1948 decisions. See *C.I.244/50(KL)*. See now *R(I)7/73*.

76 *C.S.I.2/48(KL)*.

77 [1940] 3 All E.R. 157.

78 See *e.g. R(I)9/51, R(I)67/52, R(I)27/54*.

79 See 1975 Act, ss. 50(3) (*post*, p. 331) and 55 (*post*, p. 337).

80 *e.g.* in relation to the significance of "obligations" and "matters reasonably incidental," below.

81 *i.e.* broadly speaking, "in the course of his employment," see below.

82 *i.e.* arise "out of" it.

83 *R(I)10/52*, (italics supplied).

84 [1924] A.C. 59, overruling *Cremins* v. *Guest, Keen & Nettlefolds Ltd.* [1908] 1 K.B. 469.

85 See *Newton* v. *Guest, Keen & Nettlefolds Ltd.* (1926) 19 B.W.C.C., 119; *R(I)9/51*; *Vandyk* v. *Fender* [1970] 2 Q.B. 292. See however, *post*, pp. 335–336.

86 *C.S.I.2/48(KL)*.

87 *Clark* v. *Stephen, Sutton & Co.* (1937) 30 B.W.C.C. 340; *R(I)20/57, R(I)23/55*; *Northumbrian Shipping Co.* v. *McCullum* (1932) 25 B.W.C.C. 284.

88 *Weaver* v. *Tredegar Iron & Coal Co. Ltd.* [1940] 3 All E.R. 157 (H.L.).

89 *Hill* v. *Butterley & Co.* [1948] 1 All E.R. 233 (C.A.).

90 *R.* v. *National Insurance Commissioner, ex p. Fieldhouse* (Appendix to *R(I)9/74*); *R(I)12/74*.

91 *Bell* v. *London & North Eastern Ry. Co.* [1938] A.C. 126 (H.L.).

92 *Dunn* v. *Lockwood* [1947] 1 All E.R. 446 (C.A.); dubiously, because it places a man who has been allowed to arrive late in an advantageous position by comparison with those who have not sought such a concession.

93 *R.* v. *Industrial Injuries Commissioner, ex p. Amalgamated Engineering Union* [1966] 1 All E.R. 97 (C.A.) (the "A.E.U. case," also frequently referred to as "*Culverwell's* case").

94 See *Armstrong, Whitworth & Co.* v. *Redford* [1920] A.C. 757 (H.L.); *Harris* v. *Associated Portland Cement Manufacturers* [1939] A.C. 71 (H.L.); *R(I)52/52, R(I)11/54, R(I)1/59, R(I)14/61*.

95 See *per* Lord Macmillan in *Northumbrian Shipping Co. Ltd.* v. *McCullum* (1932) 25 B.W.C.C. 284, at pp. 292–302; see also *per* May J., in *Ex p. Michael* (n. 3 below): "it is quite clear on many authorities which need not be specifically cited that a *particular act of a servant* or a *particular accident* in which he becomes involved will in law be considered to arise out of and in the course of his employment if *that act* is done *or* if *the accident* is

sustained in circumstances which make *it* reasonably incidental to that servant's employment" (italics supplied).

96 Otherwise one could have an "employment" without a "course."

97 See the compound example given by Lord Atkin in *Harris* v. *Associated Portland Cement Manufacturers Ltd.* [1939] A.C. 71 (H.L.)

98 See *per* Lord Denning L.J. in *R.* v. *Industrial Injuries Commissioner, ex p. A.E.U.*, n. 93 above: "Was what Mr. Culverwell did ... reasonably incidental to his employment? Was he *merely* overstaying his break negligently or even dishonestly? Or was he doing something *entirely* different, using this extended break for purposes of his own for an indefinite time quite unconnected with his employment?" (italics supplied). One might, quite unobjectionably, answer both questions both negatively and affirmatively. "Overstaying a break" and "doing something different from the employment" are by no means necessarily mutually exclusive alternative characterizations of Culverwell's position. It is not nonsense to say of him that he was doing both. The substantial question must be as to the degree to which what he is doing has become remote from what he was employed to do.

99 Printed as an appendix to *R(I)16/75*.

Chapter 10, pp. 325–340

  1 See the *A.E.U.* case (n. 93 above); *R(I)16/62, R(I)2/63, R(I)3/63*.

  2 *Cf. R(I)3/62* and *R(I)11/54*.

  3 It is, on the contrary, not clear that there is a point of law here at all. Speaking of the analogous position with respect to arbitrators under the old scheme Lord Loreburn said, in *John Stewart & Son (1912) Ltd.* v. *Longhurst* [1917] A.C. 249, "... in every case the question for the arbitrator is whether the facts come within the words of the Act ... most of the decisions are instances of the application of those words. They do not qualify the Act itself and there is always a danger of arguing from analogy from the facts of one case to the facts of another, or of treating the opinions of judges which are true in regard to the case before then as though they were putting a glass on the statute ..." See *Michael*'s case below.

  4 [1976] 1 All E.R. 566. (Div. Ct.).

  5 A cop-out?

  6 See also *per* May J., at p. 569.

  7 *Ibid. per* May J., p. 568. See, now, [1977] 2 All E.R. 420.

  8 *Upton* v. *Great Central Railway Co.* (1923) 16 B.W.C.C. 269, *per* Viscount Haldane, at p. 272; see also *Weaver* v. *Tredegar Iron Co.* [1940] 3 All E.R. 157, *per* Lord Wright; *R(I)16/61*.

  9 *Per* Viscount Haldane, n. 7 above.

 10 *R(I)16/61*.

 11 *Ibid.*

 12 *Karemaker* v. *S.S. Corsican (Owners)* (1911) 4 B.W.C.C. 295 (doubted in *Craig* v. *Dover Navigation Co. Ltd.* (1939) 32 B.W.C.C. 300); *R.* v. *National Insurance Commissioner, ex p. Richardson* [1958] 1 W.L.R. 851, and see s. 50(3), *post*, pp. 330–332; *Brooker* v. *Thomas Borthwick & Sons (Australasia) Ltd.* [1933] A.C. 669, 676, *per* Lord Atkin; *R(I)41/51*; *cf. R(I)3/72, R(I)4/61*.

 13 See *post*, pp. 337–338.

 14 See *e.g. R(I)3/72*.

15 *Per* Viscount Maugham in *Craig* v. *Dover Navigation Co. Ltd.* (1939) 32 B.W.C.C. 300, 303. See also *per* Lord Atkin *ibid.* at pp. 305–306; *Dennis* v. *A. J. White & Co.* [1917] A.C. 479 (H.L.); *R(I)41/51*.

16 See *per* Russell L.J. in *Lawrence* v. *George Matthews (1924) Ltd.* [1929] 1 K.B. 1, 19; *per* Viscount Haldane in *Upton* v. *Great Central Ry. Co.* (1923) 16 B.W.C.C. 169, 272.

17 *R(I)4/61*.

18 *R(I)1/76*.

19 *Ibid.* see also *Oates* v. *Earl Fitzwilliam's Collieries* [1939] 2 All E.R. 498.

20 *C.I.5/49(KL)*.

21 See *Clover, Clayton & Co. Ltd.* v. *Hughes* [1910] A.C. 242, p. 247, *per* Lord Loreburn.

22 The same reasoning would apply to a peculiar susceptibility to mental injury.

23 *R(I)73/51*; *C.I.5/49*.

24 The treatment in the authorities of pre-existing conditions and intervening new causes frequently fails to distinguish between the questions whether the injury was caused by accident and whether the accident arose out of the employment. Both types of question arise; (most cases concern the situation where the "injury is the accident" (*ante*, pp. 317–321)) and are considered together here for convenience.

25 All these expressions are used; see *R(I)38/51*, *R(I)12/58*, *R(I)15/61*.

26 *Ibid.*

27 *R(I)38/51*; *R(I)12/58*.

28 *R(I)12/58*; *R(I)15/61*; *cf.*, however, *Brown* v. *Kent* (1913) 6 B.W.C.C. 745 (C.A.) where compensation was awarded "even though the industrial accident was not an *effective* cause."

29 *Cf. e.g. R(I)3/56* (Second accident merely aggravating first) and *C.I.114/49* (similar injury caused by later non-industrial accident after complete recovery from prior injury). See also *C.I.5/49* and *cf. C.I.384/50*, *R(I)33/53*, *R(I)27/58*.

30 See *e.g. R(I)16/55*. See also *R(I)30/60* where the accident was caused by inflammable materials at the place of work being ignited by the workman's cigarette and the claim disposed of by reference to the fact that the accident was "caused" by the workman's smoking.

31 *Bender* v. *Owners of Steamship Zent* [1919] 2 K.B. 41 (C.A.).

32 *Ibid.*

33 See *e.g. C.I.3/49(KL)*.

34 See *e.g. Owners of Ship Swansea Vale* v. *Rice* [1912] A.C. 238 (H.L.).

35 National Insurance (Industrial Injuries) Act 1946, s. 7(4).

36 Italics supplied.

37 *C.I.3/49(KL)*.

39 *R.* v. *National Insurance (Industrial Injuries) Commissioner, ex p. Richardson* [1958] 1 W.L.R. 851.

40 "Evidence fit to be left to the jury" was Devlin J.'s expression, *ibid.* p. 691.

41 It could be said, consistently with many of the cases cited above, that

the exigencies of his employment took him to the spot where he was exposed to the risk.

42 *Quaere* would evidence that on previous occasions the youths had attacked indiscriminately be admissible as evidence that they were attacking indiscriminately on the occasion in question?

43 See s. 55 below.

44 *R(I)1/64.*

45 More specifically it might fail to arise "out of or in the course of" or merely "out of" the employment depending on the circumstances. *Quaere* whether the basic common law and industrial injuries law tests are the same. *Cf. Kay* v. *I.T.W. Ltd.* [1968] 1 Q.B. 140 and *R.* v. *d'Albuquerque, ex p. Bresnahan* [1966] 1 Lloyd's Rep. 69, and see *R(I)1/70* and the observations of Lord Parker L.C.J. in *R.* v. *Deputy National Insurance Commissioner, ex p. Jaine,* unreported but discussed in *R(I)1/70.*

46 1975 Act, s. 52, formerly National Insurance (Industrial Injuries) Act 1946, s. 8). The provision originated in the Workmen's Compensation Act 1923, s. 7.

47 *C.I.182/49(KL).*

48 *C.I.220/49(KL), R(I)96/53; Howells* v. *Great Western Ry. Co.* (1928) 21 B.W.C.C. 18; *Goring* v. *Southern Ry. Co.* (1938) 31 B.W.C.C. 68.

49 *C.I.11/49(KL).*

50 Coal Mines (Explosives) Order 1956 (S.I. No. 1767), Sched., para. 32(5). See *R(I)12/61* which contains a detailed discussion of all the prior authorities. *Quaere* would express authorisation of the illegal act satisfy the condition? See *R(I)7/57.*

51 *e.g.* general health and safety prohibitions.

52 n. 45 above.

53 *e.g. R(I)17/61; R(I)1/58.*

54 The original provision (Workmen's Compensation Act 1923, s. 7; Workmen's Compensation Act 1925, s. 1(2)) did not contain condition 1. It seems to have been assumed that it was not necessary. Judicial decisions narrowed the operation of the provision by requiring the effective content of what is now condition 1—see *Matthews* v. *Victoria Spinning Co. Ltd.* (1936) 29 B.W.C.C. 242 (H.L.).

55 To regard either as completely contained within the other is to treat one as being otiose.

56 See *Kerr or M'Aulay* v. *James Dunlop & Co. Ltd.* [1926] A.C. 377.

57 See the discussion in *Davies* v. *Gwauncaegurwen Colliery Co.* (1924) 17 B.W.C.C. 181 (C.A.), *per* Pollock M.R., at pp. 187–188, *per* Warrington L.J., at pp. 191–192: "These words [*i.e.* condition 2] clearly indicate an intention to prevent the section applying to acts which are merely incidental to the employment...."

58 *e.g. C.I.220/49(KL), R(I)6/55, R(I)25/55, R(I)8/59.*

59 *Ante,* pp. 323–326.

60 1975 Act, s. 53(1).

61 *Ibid.* s. 53(1)(*a*); *R(I)40/55.*

62 *Ibid.* s. 53(2).

63 *Ibid.* s. 53(1)(*b*).

64 *R(I)48/54; R(I)67/52; R(I)79/51.*

65 *R(I)9/51; C.I.49/49*

66 *R(I)40/55.*

67 *R(I)8/62.*

68 *R(I)48/54*

69 See *R(I)5/60.*

70 *Cf. C.I.101/49(KL)* (farm worker injured travelling to work in transport provided in pursuance of arrangements made with County Agricultural Executive Committee without reference to the employer) and *R(I)49/53* (worker injured travelling from work in transport provided in pursuance of arrangements made with main contractor with concurrence and participation of employer).

71 *R(I)67/51.*

72 See *R(I)49/53, R(I)15/57, R(I)3/59.*

73 *R(I)15/57.*

74 *R(I)49/53.*

75 *R(I)15/57.*

76 *R(I)3/59.*

77 See *R(I)15/57.*

78 *R(I)46/60, R(I)11/51.* It may be regarded as within the course of employment of a quite different type to cope with minor incidental emergencies—*C.I. 280/49(KL).*

79 This would not include the highway—*R(I)52/54*—unless the highway "about" premises etc. See *R(I)6/63.*

80 *Cf.* s. 52 above where the Act must be done "for the purposes of *and in connection with* the employer's trade or business." What, if any, is the effect of the added italicised words has baffled the courts. One is not, however, it appears, about the employer's business if one is merely on one's way to work —*C.I.35/50(KL).*

81 Lesser emergencies are not covered—*C.I.280/49(KL).*

82 This will not occur all that commonly. It will usually be enough that the employer is exposed to a risk, which otherwise he would have avoided, by the exigencies of his employment, see *ante,* pp. 326–327.

83 *Ante,* pp. 330–332; see Family Allowances and National Insurance Act 1961, s. 2. See also *R(I)5/59, R(I)16/61* and cases considered therein.

84 Not necessarily a fellow-employee.

85 1975 Act, s. 55(1)(*b*).

86 *Ibid.* s. 55(1)(*c*).

87 *Ibid.* s. 56.

88 *Ibid.* see s. 57(4). A day does not rank as a "day of incapacity" for injury benefit purposes if no claim is made or if the claimant is disqualified— Industrial Injury Benefit Regulations, reg. 4.

89 *Ibid.* s. 56(2).

90 *i.e.* the first 3 days; *cf.* unemployment benefit, *ante.*

91 1975 Act, Sched. 4.

92 For qualification for and calculation of earnings-related supplement, see *ante,* p. 131.

93 See *Social Security Statistics 1975,* pp. 100–140, 223, 236.

94 1975 Act, s. 57(1). Disablement benefit is also payable for disabilities resulting from prescribed diseases, *ibid.* s. 77. In this section, references to "accident" include references to "diseases" unless the context otherwise indicates.

95 *Ibid.* s. 57(2).

96 *Ibid.* s. 57(4).

97 *Ibid.* s. 57(5). An existing disablement pensioner who becomes entitled to a later gratuity may elect to have a higher pension in respect of the total disablement—Industrial Injuries Benefit Regulations, reg. 34; *R(I)42/55.*

98 *Ibid.* s. 57(6).

99 *Ibid.* s. 57(5); Industrial Injuries Benefit Regulations, reg. 6 and Sched. 2.

Chapter 10, pp. 340–353

1 *Post*, pp. 447–451.

2 "This is a logical and not necessarily a time sequence; in some cases some of the items in it may be simultaneous or even indistinguishable"; *R(I)7/63.* It may be noted that if the links between these various elements are truly causal there is necessarily a time-sequence, however short. One concludes that the links are not always truly causal. The only necessary true causal connection is that between the force which brings about the disablement and the disablement which results. A claimant whose arm is severed by a machine finds himself thereby injured, without a faculty, and disabled thereby. These three things are not identical but they are all qualities of the condition which results and all are necessary if he is to obtain disablement benefit.

3 1975 Act, Sched. 8, para. 1(*a*).

4 *Ibid.* para. 1(*c*).

5 *Ibid.* para. 4.

6 *Ibid.*

7 *Ibid.* para. 5.

8 *Ibid.* s. 57(1).

9 See Industrial Injuries Benefit Regulations, Sched. 2.

10 1975 Act, Sched. 8, para. 5.

11 Industrial Injuries Benefit Regulations, Sched. 1.

12 See below.

13 Industrial Injuries Benefit Regulations, reg. 2(6). This formulation of the regulation obviates the difficulties encountered in *R. v. Industrial Injuries Commissioner, ex p. Cable* [1968] 1 All E.R. 9 and *R. v. Medical Appeal Tribunal, ex p. Burpitt* [1957] 2 Q.B. 584 in applying the old "paired organs" rule.

14 Industrial Injuries Benefit Regulations, reg. 2(2).

15 *R(I)8/74.*

16 Industrial Injuries Benefit Regulations, reg. 2(4), degrees taken from the tariff, *ibid.* Sched. 1.

17 *Ibid.* reg. 2(5).

18 *Ante*, p. 342.

19 Industrial Injuries Benefit Regulations, reg. 34(1).

20 See *ibid.* reg. 34(2), (3).

21 1975 Act, s. 58(1). It may not attach to a gratuity—*R(I)48/59.* On "incapable of work," see *C.I.44/49(KL), C.I.99/49(KL), R(I)58/52, R(I)43/54.*

22 *Ibid.* s. 58(3). The amount currently prescribed is £364 p.a.—Industrial Injuries Benefit Regulations, reg. 8.

23 *Ibid.* s. 14(5)(*b*).

24 *Ibid.* Sched. 4.

25 *Social Security Statistics 1975*, p. 135.

26 1975 Act, s. 59.

27 *Ibid.* Sched. 4; and see *ante*, pp. 222–223.

28 *Social Security Statistics 1975*, p. 135.

29 1975 Act, s. 60(5). See also Industrial Injuries Regulations, regs. 9 and 10.

30 *Ibid.* s. 60(1); (subsidiary occupations are to be ignored and equivalent jobs must be in an employed earner's capacity: *ibid.* s. 60(2)). This is not a "disablement question" so as to be within the exclusive competence of the medical authorities. The statutory authorities are bound by the findings of the medical authorities on the disablement questions for pensions purposes (see *post*, pp. 447–451) but may take note of changes in the degree of disablement for purposes of special hardship allowance—*R.* v. *Industrial Commissioner, ex p. Ward* [1965] 2 W.L.R. 19.

31 *Ibid.* s. 60(6) and Sched. 4.

32 [1971] 1 All E.R. 740 (C.A.).

33 *Ibid. per* Buckley L.J.

34 *Ibid. per* Denning M.R. who, in relation to part-time work, approves *R(I)6/68* and *R(I)7/68* and disapproves *R(I)10/66*. See also *R(I)10/65*.

35 *R.* v. *Industrial Injuries Commissioner, ex p. Humphreys* [1966] 2 Q.B. 1.

36 See *R(I)14/62*. On the allowance generally and on "regular occupation" and prospects, see *R(I)6/75*.

37 1975 Act, s. 61.

38 Industrial Injuries Benefits Regulations, reg. 13; see below.

39 *Ibid.* reg. 11.

40 *Ibid.* reg. 12.

41 1975 Act, s. 62(1).

42 See Industrial Injuries Benefit Regulations, reg. 7 and Sched. 3.

43 *Ibid.* reg. 14. See also reg. 13.

44 *Social Security Statistics 1975*, p. 135.

45 1975 Act, s. 63.

46 *Social Security Statistics 1975*, p. 135.

47 See below.

48 1975 Act, s. 64(1); and see Industrial Injuries Benefit Regulations, regs. 24–32.

49 *Ibid.* s. 64(1)(*b*).

50 *Ibid.* ss. 64, 65 as amended by the Child Benefit Act 1975, Sched. 4, paras. 21, 22; Industrial Injuries Benefit Regulations, reg. 24.

51 1975 Act, s. 66(1)(*a*)(*b*).

52 1975 Act, s. 66(1)(*c*); Industrial Injuries Benefit Regulations, reg. 25, Sched. 4.

53 1975 Act, s. 66(1)(*d*) as amended by Child Benefit Act 1975, Sched. 4, para. 23; Industrial Injuries Benefit Regulations, reg. 26.

54 *Ante*, pp. 28–42.

55 1975 Act, s. 50(1)(2)(*c*).

56 *Ibid.* s. 76.

57 *Ibid.* ss. 67–75; See Industrial Injuries Benefit Regulations, regs. 15–23, Scheds. 6, 7.

58 1975 Act, Sched. 9; Industrial Injuries Benefit Regulations, Sched 7.

59 1975 Act, s. 67.

60 *Ante*, pp. 235–236.

61 1975 Act, s. 68(1)(2), as amended by Child Benefit Act 1975, Sched. 4, para. 24.

62 *Ibid.* s. 69.

63 *Ibid.Ibid.* s. 69(2).

64 *Ibid.* s. 70, as amended by Child Benefit Act 1975, Sched. 4, para. 25.

65 *Ante*, pp. 234–235.

66 1975 Act, s. 71; Industrial Injuries Benefit Regulations, Sched. 5.

67 1975 Act, s. 72; Industrial Injuries Benefit Regulations, Scheds. 4, 5.

68 *Ibid.* s. 73.

69 *Social Security Statistics 1975*, p. 109.

70 *Ibid.* pp. 110–111.

71 *Ibid.* p. 112.

72 *Ibid.* p. 116. The total number of spells had declined markedly in recent years.

73 *Ibid.* p. 133.

74 *Ibid.* pp. 133, 134.

75 1975 Act, s. 76(2).

76 *Ibid.* s. 77(3). See Prescribed Diseases Regulations, reg. 4.

77 *Ibid.* s. 141 and Sched. 16.

78 Prescribed Diseases Regulations, reg. 3.

79 *Ibid.* Sched. 1, para. 19.

80 *Ibid.* Sched. 1, para. 37(*b*).

81 *Ibid.* reg. 4.

82 *Ibid.* Sched. 1, para. 38.

83 1975 Act, s. 78; Prescribed Diseases Regulations, regs. 36, 36A.

84 *Ibid.*

85 Prescribed Diseases Regulations, regs. 40–47.

86 For recent examples, see *R(I)5/76, R(I)8/76.*

87 1975 Act, s. 82(5), *ante*, pp. 47–56.

88 Industrial Injuries (Airmen's Benefit) Regulations, regs. 2–4.

89 Industrial Injuries (Mariners' Benefit) Regulations, regs. 2–5.

90 Industrial Injuries Benefit Regulations, regs. 36, 37.

91 *Ibid.* reg. 40.

92 *Ibid.* reg. 41.

93 *Ibid.* reg. 42.

94 1975 Act, s. 158. Sched. 19.

95 *Ibid.* Sched. 19, para. 1.

96 S.I. 1970 No. 376.

CHAPTER 11

FAMILY PROVISION

Chapter 11, pp. 354–382

1 See *ante* and *post*.

2 Income and Corporation Taxes Act 1970, ss. 10 and 11.

3 *Poverty and Equality in Britain*, p. 98.

4 Beveridge Report, para. 411.

5 *Ibid*. para. 413.

6 *Ibid*. para. 410.

7 Cmd. 6550.

8 Cmnd. 5116 (1972).

9 *The Tax Credit Scheme and Redistribution of Income*, Institute of Fiscal Studies (1973).

10 *New Society*, June 17, 1976.

11 Child Benefit Act, s. 5 and see A. and M. Wynn in *Poverty*, pamphlet No. 33 (1975–6).

12 Child Benefit Act, s. 1(2).

13 *Ibid*. s. 5(5).

14 H.C.Deb., Vol. 892, col. 440.

15 Child Benefit Act, s. 24(3).

16 *Ibid*. s. 16(1); Child Benefit (General) Regulations 1976 (S.I. 1976 No. 965) reg. 16(1).

17 Child Benefit Act, s. 24(1).

18 Annual Report of the Parliamentary Commissioner for Administration, 4th Report for 1972–73, Case No. C.333/9, p. 102.

19 *R(F)4/60, R(F)7/64, R(S)2/68, R(S)3/70*.

20 *R(F)7/64*.

21 See also *R2/68(FA)*.

22 See *R2/68(FA)*.

23 For the old law, see also *R3/66(FA)* in which title lapsed in the case of a child moving to a school in Canada because the predominant cause of his removal from the school was not transfer to the new school but assisting the family in preparing for the move.

24 Child Benefit Act, s. 2(3).

25 Child Benefit (General) Regulations 1976, reg. 20.

26 Child Benefit Act, Sched. 1, para. 2(1).

27 Child Benefit (General) Regulations, reg. 8.

28 Family Law Reform Act 1969, s. 9.

29 Child Benefit Act, s. 3(1).

30 Child Benefit Act 1975, s. 30(1).

31 Under the family allowances scheme, priority was given to persons linked by "issue" rather than by "maintenance," although to qualify as "issue" the child had to be "living with" or "provided for by" the parent.

32 See also *R(G)4/62*.

33 Child Benefit Act, Sched. 2, para. 4(1).

34 Child Benefit Act, s. 2(2); Child Benefit (General) Regulations, reg. 4.
35 Child Benefit Act, s. 3(3) and (4).
36 *Ibid.* s. 3(3)(*c*); Child Benefit (General) Regulations, regs. 3 and 4.
37 Child Benefit Act, s. 3(2).
38 [1955] 1 W.L.R. 899.
39 See also *R(G)1/57.*
40 Child Benefit Act, s. 3(1)(*b*).
41 See *ibid.* s. 24(1).

42 The statement in Halsbury's *Laws of England* (3rd. ed.), Vol. 27, pp. 885–886, (note r) that "money paid by a husband under a court order or separation deed amounts to payment by the wife," relying upon the analogy in tax law in *Stevens* v. *Tirard* [1940]1 K.B. 204, and *Spencer* v. *Robson* (1946) 27 T.C. 198 would seem to need qualification in the light of the above.

43 Although the *principles* here illustrated hold good under the new scheme, if such *facts* arose under the new scheme, the persons with whom the children were living would be entitled against others.

44 [1962] 1 W.L.R. 1296.
45 Now s. 3(1)(*b*).
46 See *R(F)1/73.*
47 See *C.F.6/62.*

48 It may be that the decision was reached having regard to the potential unfairness of the old priority rules. Since these no longer apply, it may be that there is less justification for treating contributions in kind differently.

49 Child Benefit and Social Security (Fixing and Adjustment of Rates) Regulations 1976 (S.I. 1976 No. 1267).
50 *Cf. R(F)2/63.*
51 See also, *R(F)3/73.*

52 See also *R(F)3/73.* The generally accepted view of conflicts of law, as expressed in *Re Valentine's Settlement* [1965] Ch. 831 is that the child's domicile is not relevant because of his dependent status and that the adoptive parent's domicile must govern. Lord Denning suggests that the child's residence (as opposed to its domicile) should be considered but this view was not shared wholeheartedly by Dankwerts L. J. There seems to be a considerable measure of disagreement amongst academic writers as to the requirements needed to be satisfied. See *Morris and Dicey on Conflicts*, p. 478 and *Cheshire on Private International Law*, (9th ed.), p. 473.

53 Child Benefit (General) Regulations, reg. 21.
54 Child Benefit (Residence and Persons Abroad) Regulations, reg. 2.
55 *Post*, pp. 393–439.
56 *Ante*, pp. 230–236.
57 Child Benefit Act, s. 24(5).
58 Child Benefit (General) Regulations, reg. 17(1).
59 *Ibid.* reg. 17(2).
60 Child Benefit and Social Security (Fixing and Adjustment of Rates) Regulations, *ante*, n. 49, reg. 2(3).
61 Child Benefit Act, Sched. 2, para. 1.
62 Child Benefit (General) Regulations, reg. 13(1).
63 *Ibid.* reg. 2.

64 *R(F)1/74*; R. v. *Hoxton Local Tribunal, ex p. Sinnot* [1976] *The Times*, March 12.

65 Council Regulation No. 1408/71.

66 See Child Benefit (General) Regulations, reg. 16(2).

67 Children and Young Persons Act 1933, s. 53, Criminal Procedure (Scotland) Act 1975, ss. 198, 206, 403 and 406.

68 Child Benefit (General) Regulations, reg. 16(3).

69 *Ibid.* reg. 16(4).

70 See *ibid.* reg. 16(5). The child must be in care under powers in the legislation there listed. See, on the effect of rescission of a parental rights resolution, *R(F)3/62*.

71 *Ibid.* reg. 16(6).

72 *Ibid.* regs. 9(11), 15(1) and (2); Child Benefit Act, Sched. 1.

73 This was a matter of considerable difficulty and controversy under the family allowances scheme, see *Fraser* v. *Minister of National Insurance* 1947 S.C. 594, and decisions listed in the first edition of this book at pp. 256–259.

74 *Ante*, pp. 70–72. See *R(U)3/67*, *R(U)2/67* and *R(F)2/73*.

75 Child Benefit (General) Regulations, reg. 8(2).

76 *Cf.* Family Allowances (Qualification) Regulations, reg. 17.

77 See *R(F)4/63* and *R1/68(FA)*.

78 Child Benefit (General) Regulations, reg. 20.

79 Common parlance was, in any case, too narrow a criterion for family allowances—trainee employee is much better. Allowances were never confined to children parties to deeds or contracts of apprenticeship.

80 Under the family allowances scheme, an earnings rule of £2 per week net applied in categorising apprentices as such. Earnings for this purpose meant "the return which a person receives for the work or services which he has rendered"; *R(F)2/73*. In that case, a learner was paid a grant for a training course exceeding the statutory maximum. It was held that the grant was not earnings but similar to that paid to a university student, to cover living expenses. The earnings rule was originally a creature of the statutory authorities but is now largely incorporated in the Family Allowances (Qualification) Regulations 1969 which allows certain deductions etc, see *R(G)2/65*. Problems of spreading arise, see *R(F)4/63*. Provision is made for interruptions on account of holidays, sickness etc.

81 Child Benefit Act, Sched. 2.

82 For the old law, see Family Allowances Act 1965, s. 4.

83 Child Benefit (Claims and Payments) Regulations, reg. 13(2).

84 *Ibid.* reg. 13.

85 *Ibid.* reg. 10.

86 Child Benefit Act, s. 12.

87 For an illustration of a typical fact situation, see *R.* v *Curr* [1968] 2 Q.B. 944.

88 [1952] N.I. 172.

89 *Ibid. per* Sheil J.

90 Child Benefit Act, s. 11(2), Child Benefit (Claims and Payments) Regulations, reg. 14.

91 *Cf.* Family Allowances (Claims and Payments) Regulations 1970 (S.I. 1972 No. 1524), reg. 9.

92 Child Benefit Act, s. 6(1).

93 For the old law, see Family Allowances Act 1965, s. 6(3) and *R(F)1/66.*

94 Social Security Act 1975, ss. 82(3) and 119.

95 Child Benefit (Determination of Claims and Questions) Regulations, regs. 17–22.

96 Social Security Act 1975, s. 119(2).

97 [1968] 2 Q.B. 944.

98 Child Benefit Act, s. 11(6).

99 *Ibid.* s. 11(8).

Chapter 11, pp. 382–392

1 Family Allowances Act 1965, s. 20; Family Allowances (Qualification) Regulations 1969, reg. 2.

2 Child Benefit Act, s. 13(3); Child Benefit (Residence and Persons Abroad) Regulations.

3 Child Benefit (Residence and Persons Abroad) Regulations, reg. 4(2) as amended.

4 *Cf. Fox* v. *Stirk etc.* [1970] 2 Q.B. 463.

5 Child Benefit (Residence and Persons Abroad) Regulations, reg. 2(2)(iii).

6 *Ibid.* reg. 4(3).

7 *Ibid.* reg. 5.

8 S.I. 1975 No. 1504.

9 See S.I. 1976 No. 1003.

10 See, now, the S.S. and C.B. (Reciprocal Arrangements) Order, S.I. 1977 No. 425.

11 See *ante*, pp. 52–54; Council Regulation 1408/71, art. 73.

12 *R(F)1/76*; Council Regulation 1408/71, art. 76, Council Regulation 574/72, art. 10 (now Council Regulation 878/73).

13 Child Benefit (Claims and Payments) Regulations, reg. 13(2). It is believed that art. 80(3) of Council Regulation 574/72 dealt only with the question of payment, not with that of entitlement.

14 The decision on this point was taken some years after the event. It should be noted that absence now ceases to be temporary after a fixed period of six months subject to certain limited exceptions. See above.

15 See Tony Lynes, *Penguin Guide to Supplementary Benefits*; Legal Action Group, *Guide to Supplementary Benefits 1976.*

16 See, in particular, Lister, "Take-up of Means-Tested Benefits," *C.P.A.G.* pamphlet No. 18, 1974; *Poverty*, pamphlet No. 34 (1976).

17 "The finances presume we shall have 85 per cent. take-up level. I will do my best to do that and better," Sir Keith Joseph, on the second reading of the Family Incomes Supplement Bill, H.C.Deb., Vol. 806, col. 227.

18 Over £1,830,000 has been spent on advertising Family Incomes Supplement since 1970, some £172,000 of this in 1976—H.C.Deb., col. 1055 December 6, 1976). See Supplementary Benefits Commission Annual Report, 1976, p. 85.

19 Sir Keith Joseph, H.C.Deb., Vol. 806, col. 1124.

20 Family Incomes Supplement Act, s. 1(1)(*a*).

21 Family Incomes Supplement Act, ss. 1 and 3(1) as substituted by the Child Benefit Act, Sched. 4(4).

22 *Ibid.* s. 1.

23 Family Incomes Supplement (General) Regulations.

24 Family Incomes Supplement (General) Regulations, reg. 5.

25 H.C.Deb., Vol. 806, col. 1135.

26 Family Incomes Supplement Act, s. 1(1)(*c*).

27 Family Incomes Supplement (General) Regulations, reg. 9.

28 *Cf.* the additional supplement payable to one-parent families under the Child Benefit Act, *ante*, pp. 373–374.

29 Boarding-out of Children Regulations 1955, Boarding-out of Children (Scotland) Regulations 1959. *Cf.* Child Benefit Act, s. 17(1)(*b*). Much has been made of the need to rationalise the various concessionary schemes for families. Less has been made of the need to harmonise their language. Thus, where the Social Security Act 1975 refers to "gainful employment" and, occasionally, "occupation," the Supplementary Benefit and Family Incomes schemes speak of "remunerative work." Where the Child Benefit Act refers to "full-time education at a recognised educational establishment" the supplementary benefit and family incomes supplement schemes still use "full-time instruction in a school." Generally, these are essentially differences in wording, not meaning.

30 Family Incomes Supplement (General) Regulations, reg. 7.

31 *Ibid.* reg. 3, substituted by Child Benefit Act, Sched. 4(4). Prior to April 1977, the additional amount paid for second and subsequent children was £4.50. It has been reduced to take into account child benefit which is treated as disregarded income. At the time of writing, no regulations to this effect have been published—see H.C.Deb, col. 789, January 7, 1977.

32 Family Incomes Supplement Act, s. 4(1).

33 *Ibid.* Family Incomes Supplement (General) Regulations.

34 *Ibid.* regs. 2(1) and (2).

35 *Ibid.* reg. 2(5).

36 *Ibid.* reg. 5 as substituted by reg. 2(3) of S.I. 1972 No. 1282 and amended by S.I. 1975 No. 1360. From April 1977, child benefit is disregarded in computing weekly income (see above). Family allowances were formerly taken into account in full.

37 *Ibid.* reg. 8.

38 Family Incomes Supplement (Northern Ireland) Act 1971. *Quaere* the effect of Council Regulation 1408/71 on the scheme?

39 See *post*, p. 402.

40 Family Incomes Supplement Act, s. 7(1).

41 See *post*, pp. 454–459.

42 Supplementary Benefit Commission Report 1975, p. 86, reports a failure rate of 95 per cent. It has varied between 93 per cent. and 98 per cent. since the supplement was instituted. See *Social Security Statistics, 1975*, p. 150.

43 Family Incomes Supplement (General) Regulations, reg. 11(1) and (2).

44 Family Incomes Supplement Act, s. 5(2), Family Incomes Supplement

(Claims and Payments) Regulations, reg. 2(6) as substituted by S.I. 1972 No. 1232.

45 *Ibid.* reg. 4(2).

46 Family Incomes Supplement Act, s. 6(2) as substituted by Pensions and Family Incomes Supplement Payments Act 1972, s. 3.

47 Family Incomes Supplement (Claims and Payments) Regulations, reg. 3(1).

48 *Ibid.* reg. 5(1) and (2).

49 Family Incomes Supplement (General) Regulations, reg. 4(1) and (2).

50 Family Incomes Supplement Acts, s. 8(3), Family Incomes Supplement (General) Regulations, reg. 10.

51 Supplementary Benefit Commission Annual Report 1975, s. 12(4).

52 *Social Security Statistics 1975*, p. 147.

53 s. 81, and see Regulations for Scholarships and Other Benefits 1945 (S.I. 1945 No. 666) as amended.

54 Report of the Working Party on Educational Maintenance Allowances 1957. See also 3rd Report of the Expenditure Committee on Education Maintenance Allowances, 1974, H.C. 306; 6th Special Report of the Expenditure Committee on Education Maintenance Allowances, DHSS. 1976, H.C. 428.

55 3rd Report, above, p. 75.

56 Report of the Working Party, above, 1957.

57 6th Special Report, above.

58 H.C.Deb., December 6, 1976, col. 26. See reports above cited and *Poverty*, pamplet No. 33, 75–76; Reddin and others, *Social Services for All* (Fabian Society); Milson, *Poverty*, pamphlet No. 9, p. 15.

59 Report of the Committee on One-Patient Families, Cmnd. 5629, para. 2(6), p. 7. George, *Poverty*, pamphlet No. 31, 1975, p. 6.

60 Report of the Committee on One-Patient Families, above, para. 2(6), p. 7.

61 *Ibid.*

62 *Ibid.*, Vol. 1., para. 5(36), p. 261.

63 *Post*, p. 426.

64 Finer Report, para. 106. Further recommendations are mentioned in Chap. 13, *post*.

65 H.C.Deb., Vols. 987–988, col. 53.

66 *Ante*, pp. 373–374.

67 See *Poverty*, pamphlet No. 31, 1975.

CHAPTER 12

SUPPLEMENTARY BENEFITS

Chapter 12, pp. 393–420

1 Riesenfeld and Maxwell, *Social Legislation*, p. 683.

2 For its history in Ireland, see Casey, "Social Assistance in Northern Ireland," (1968) 19 N.I.L.Q. 278.

3 "The truth is that the burden of maintaining public assistance in some of the poorer authorities was crushing local government almost out of existence." J. Griffiths, on the second reading of the National Assistance Bill, H.C.Deb., Vol. 518, col. 1710 (1947).

4 Wickwar, *The Social Services*, p. 31.

5 *Supplementary Benefits handbook* (hereinafter the *Handbook*), Supplementary Benefits Commission (hereinafter "the Commission"), HMSO, p. 1.

6 Beveridge Report, para. 369.

7 *Ibid.* paras. 369–371.

8 Supplementary Benefits Commission Annual Report 1975.

9 See S. A. de Smith, *Judicial Review of Administrative Action*, (3rd ed.), pp. 265–267.

10 *Handbook*, p. 3.

11 Supplementary Benefits Commission Annual Report 1975, Cmnd. 6615, p. 13.

12 Annual Report of the Council on Tribunals for 1971, p. 23.

13 Garner, *Administrative Law*, (2nd ed.), p. 181.

14 *Scott* v. *Scott* [1913] A.C. 417.

15 *e.g.* recovery of expenses etc.

16 Lynes, *The Fifth Social Service*, Fabian Society, pp. 123–124.

17 1976 Act, s. 27.

18 *Ibid.* s. 27(1). See also Supplementary Benefits Commission Annual Report 1975, pp. 2–4.

19 1976 Act, Sched. 3, para. 5.

20 *Ibid.* s. 27(3).

21 House of Commons Disqualification Act 1975, s. 1(2)(*f*); Northern Ireland Assembly Disqualification Act 1975, s. (1)(*f*).

22 See Supplementary Benefits (Claims and Payments) Regulations.

23 *Handbook*, p. 213.

24 Supplementary Benefits (Claims and Payments) Regulations, reg. 10.

25 Lynes, *op. cit.* pp. 31–35. See Fisher Report on Abuse of Social Security Benefits, p. 106.

26 Supplementary Benefits (Claims and Payments) Regulations, reg. 10.

27 *Secretary of State for Health and Social Security* v. *Solly* [1974] 3 All E.R. 922.

28 See the Legal Action Group *Lawyer's Guide to Supplementary Benefits*, 1976, p. 58.

29 1976 Act, s. 21.

30 *Moore* v. *Branton*, (1974) 118 S.J. 405.

31 See *Handbook*, p. 77, Lynes, *op. cit.* p. 37.

32 Supplementary Benefits (Claims and Payments) Regulations, reg. 9 as amended.

33 Supplementary Benefits Commission Annual Report 1975, table 17, p. 58.

34 Fifth Report of the Parliamentary Commissioner for Administration, Session 1975–6, Case No. C.455/V, p. 125.

35 *Ibid.* Case No. C.9/V, p. 98.

36 *Ibid.* Case No. C.458/V, p. 127.

37 *Ibid.* Case No. C.540/V, p. 135.

38 Supplementary Benefits Commission Annual Report 1975, p. 58.

39 Report on One-Parent Families, p. 396. 6.106(1).

40 See also Lynes, *op. cit.* pp. 58–59; *Handbook*, p. 62.

41 1976 Act, s. 11(1).

42 *Handbook*, p. 233.

43 First Report of the Parliamentary Commissioner for Administration, Session 1974–75, Case No. C.76/J, pp. 85, 87.

44 Fifth Report of the Parliamentary Commissioner for Administration, Session 1975–6, Case No. C.540/V, p. 135.

45 *Ibid.* Fourth Report, Session 1974–5, Case No. C.450/J, p. 107.

46 1976 Act, s. 14(4).

47 *Ibid.* Sched. 5, para. 4.

48 See Lister and Emmett, "Under the Safety Net," *Poverty*, pamphlet No. 25, 1976.

49 See *ante*, n. 44.

50 On the problem of take-up, see *Poverty*, pamphlet No. 34, Summer 1976.

51 For judicial review, see *post*, pp. 454–459.

52 Supplementary Benefit (General) Regulations, reg. 5.

53 See Coleman, "Supplementary Benefits and the Administrative Review of Administrative Action" *Poverty*, pamphlet No. 7, 1971.

54 1976 Act, s. 1.

55 *Cf.* unemployment benefit, *ante*, p. 52.

56 1976 Act, 1(2) and Sched. 1, para. 3(1).

57 1976 Act, s. 34(1). See Family Law Reform Act 1969, s. 9.

58 Finer Report on One-Parent Families, p. 340, 5.269. See also the Supplementary Benefits Commission Reports on *Cohabitation* in 1971 and *Living Together as Husband and Wife* in 1976 and its Annual Report for 1976, p. 319.

59 *Living Together as Husband and Wife*, p. 15 (SBC. HMSO).

60 See *K.* v. *JMP Ltd.* [1976] Q.B. 85. The confusion on the character of supplementary benefits is well-illustrated in this case, Cairns L.J. describing the award of the Commission as being a matter of "discretion" whilst Graham, J. speaks of "entitlement."

61 How far this is a matter of discretion is debatable. Once the Commission finds that there are "exceptional circumstances" the obligation to aggregate falls and "entitlement" should follow, subject to abatement or augmentation in exercise of the general "exceptional circumstances" discretion, *post*, pp. 422–423.

62 *Living Together as Husband and Wife*, p. 67. The Finer Committee recommended that the period be extended to three months.

63 *Ibid.* p. 66.

64 *Ibid.* p. 69.

65 1934 *S.C.(J)42.*

66 See *R(G)5/68.*

67 *R(G)3/71.*

68 *R(G)1/53.*

69 Yet the Commission manage to decide every situation which does arise.

The Commission either has a very primitive notion of the form and function of legislation (*i.e.* it cannot conceive that its criteria can be expressed in statutory form) or, more probably, it has not adequately articulated, even to itself, the criteria which are in fact applied in cohabitation cases.

70 Report of the Committee on Abuse of Social Security Benefits, para. 330.
71 *Living Together as Husband and Wife*, para. 55.
72 *R(G)5/68.*
73 *Living Together as Husband and Wife*, para. 55(2).
74 *Ibid.* para. 55(2).
75 See *R(G)3/71.*
76 *Living Together as Husband and Wife*, para. 55(4).
77 *Ibid.*
78 *R(G)5/68.*
79 *Living Together as Husband and Wife*, para. 55(6).
80 *R(G)5/68.*
81 *Living Together as Husband and Wife*, para. 55(3).
82 See *R(G)2/64.*
83 *R(G)5/68.*
84 *R(G)3/71.*
85 *Living Together as Husband and Wife*, para. 55(5).
86 *R(G)3/71.*
87 *R(P)6/52*, where it was alleged that the parties had become merely landlady and lodger.
88 *Living Together as Husband and Wife*, para. 82.
89 *Ibid.* para. 95.
90 *Ibid.* para. 94.
91 Report of the Committee on Abuse of Social Security Benefits, para. 332.
92 "Civic Rights and Social Services," in *The Future of the Social Services* (ed. Crick and Robson), pp. 36–37.
93 Report of the Committee on Abuse of Social Security Benefits, para. 343.
94 *Living Together as Husband and Wife*, para. 69.
95 n. 93 above, para. 341.
96 See 1976 Act, s. 7(1).
97 *Handbook*, p. 6.
98 [1976] Q.B. 85.
99 See Legal Action Group, *Lawyer's Guide to Supplementary Benefits*, p. 63.

Chapter 12, pp. 421–439

1 1976 Act, s. 5.
2 *Ibid.* s. 10.
3 See Lewis, *Public Law* (1973), 277.
4 See *ante*, pp. 146–177.
5 See *post*, pp. 440 *et seq.*
6 1976 Act, s. 9, Sched. 2, Pt. II.
7 *Ibid.*
8 Report of the Committee on Abuse of Social Security Benefits, para. 270.

9 Para. 6.

10 See cases discussed *post*, pp. 427–428.

11 See, for example, form B/O.40 on clothing stocks, and see *Handbook*, paras. 77–90 and Lynes, *op. cit.* pp. 86–107.

12 *R.* v. *Birmingham Appeal Tribunal, ex p. Simper* (1973) 117 S.J. 304.

13 1976 Act, s. 1.

14 *Ibid.*, Sched. 1, para. 1(1).

15 *Handbook*, para. 43.

16 *R.* v. *Sheffield Supplementary Benefits Appeal Tribunal, ex p. Shine* [1975] 1 W.L.R. 624.

17 1976 Act, Sched. 1, para. 6(1).

18 *Ibid.* para. 6(2), (3). This was originally a matter of discretion but was not, as the *Simper* case illustrated (*ante*, p. 424), treated as such by the Commission. The present, mandatory, reduction restores, with legislative authority, the practice condemned by the court in that case. In the result, one who needs a special diet must be presumed not to need a new pillow-case.

19 *Ibid.* para. 9. It is surely anomalous that appeals against the trades disputes disqualification should go to a national insurance local tribunal (1976 Act, s. 15(2)) but that determinations under para. 9 should depend upon "the opinion" of the Commission or a Supplementary Benefit Appeal Tribunal.

20 *Ibid.* para. 17.

21 *Ibid.* para. 18.

22 *Ibid.* paras. 19 and 20. Para. 19 exempts the first £1,200 and income derived therefrom. Para. 20 *post*, effectively exempts the next £49.

23 *Ibid.* para. 22.

24 *Ibid.* para. 23. See also paras. 24–26.

25 *Ibid.* para. 20.

26 *R.* v. *West London Supplementary Benefit Appeal Tribunal, ex p. Taylor* [1975] 1 W.L.R. 1048.

27 1976 Act, Sched. 1, para. 22(3).

28 Sched. 1, para. 26.

29 *Ibid.* para. 28.

30 [1975] 1 W.L.R. 624.

31 [1975] 1 W.L.R. 1396.

32 [1976] 1 W.L.R. 1047. The claimant succeeded on appeal to the Court of Appeal. See, now, S.S. (Miscellaneous Provisions) Act 1977.

33 [1975] 1 W.L.R. 1048.

34 Child Benefit Act 1975, s. 19.

35 See *per* Lord Widgery L.C.J. in the *Atkinson* case, n. 29 above.

36 s. 17(1).

37 Subject to some statutory modification, the common law obligation is confined to the husband's obligation to maintain the wife, see Matrimonial Causes Act 1965, s. 27(1) and Matrimonial Proceedings (Magistrates' Courts) Act 1960. The Law Commission (Working Paper No. 53, Report No. 77) recommends putting liability in all these cases on a purely reciprocal footing.

38 *R.* v. *West London Supplementary Benefit Appeal Tribunal, ex p. Clarke* [1975] 1 W.L.R. 1396.

39 *Gray* v. *Gray* [1976] Fam. 324.

40 *Wachtel* v. *Wachtel* [1973] Fam. 72.

41 [1955] 2 Q.B. 506.

42 See *Parkes'* case itself, *Stopher* v. *National Assistance Board* [1955] 1 Q.B. 486, *National Assistance Board* v. *Prisk* [1954] 1 W.L.R. 443.

43 [1952] 2 Q.B. 648.

44 See Casey, "The Supplementary Benefits Act: Lawyer's Law Aspects" (1968) 19 N.I.L.Q. 1, 8.

45 See n. 43, above.

46 See n. 39 above.

47 *Din* v. *National Assistance Board* [1967] 2 Q.B. 213.

48 The singular includes the plural, Interpretation Act 1889, s.1.

49 *National Assistance Board* v. *Mitchell* [1956] 1 Q.B. 53.

50 *National Assistance Board* v. *Tugby* [1957] 1 Q.B. 506.

51 *Clapham* v. *National Assistance Board* [1961] 2 Q.B. 77.

52 *Oldfield* v. *National Assistance Board* [1960] 1 Q.B. 635.

53 *Loc. cit.* p. 19; *Payne* v. *Critchley* [1962] 2 Q.B. 83.

54 Report of the Committee on One-Parent Families, 4.182.

55 Supplementary Benefits Commission Annual Report 1975, p. 112.

56 Report of the Committee on One-Parent Families, 4.205; *Ashley* v. *Ashley* [1968] P. 582.

57 *Billington* v. *Billington* [1974] Fam. 24.

58 [1974] Fam. 55.

59 *Smethurst* v. *Smethurst* [1977] *The Times*, March 30.

60 Report of the Committee on One-Parent Families, 4.208.

61 *Ibid.* 4.209.

62 *Ibid.* p. 153.

63 1976 Act, s. 25.

64 Report of the Committee on One-Parent Families, 4.212.

65 See Casey, *loc. cit.* pp. 20–23.

66 [1966] 1 W.L.R. 709.

67 [1949] W.N. 125.

Chapter 13

ADJUDICATION

1 1975 Act, s. 98.

2 *Ibid.* s. 97.

3 *Ibid.* s. 99.

4 *Ibid.* s. 99(2).

5 *Ibid.* s. 99(3).

6 But a person adversely affected by the decision may have a right of appeal in some industrial injuries cases, *Ibid.* s. 100(7).

7 *Ibid.* s. 100(1).

8 *Ibid.* s. 100(3).

9 *Ibid.* s. 100(4). The time may be extended by the chairman of the local

tribunal for good cause. See Determination of Claims and Questions Regulations, regs. 9 and 10.

10 *i.e.* in the absence of one of the "wingmen," *ibid.* reg. 11.

11 1975 Act, s. 97(2), Sched. 10.

12 Tribunal and Inquiries Act 1971, s. 7.

13 1975 Act, s. 97(2)(*a*) and (*b*).

14 Supplementary Benefits Act 1976 (formerly the Ministry of Social security Act 1966 and referred to in this chapter as "the 1976 Act"), s. 18(2). Further appeal lies to the Commissioner, see *R(U)3/71.*

15 1975 Act, s. 101; Determination of Claims and Questions Regulations, reg. 13.

16 *Ibid.* s. 101(2)(*c*), (3) and (4).

17 *Ibid.* s. 101(5).

18 *Ibid.* s. 97(3), Sched. 10.

19 1975 Act, s. 116.

20 1975 Act, s. 101(6).

21 *Ibid.* s. 101(7).

22 See below.

23 1975 Act, s. 104.

24 *Ibid.* s. 102. Adjournment may be necessary to satisfy the requirement of fairness.

25 *R(U)15/62.*

26 *R(G)3/62.*

27 *Ibid.*

28 *R(U)18/64.*

29 See *e.g. R(U)8/63.* Failure to observe these "rules" of precedent does not nullify a decision. They are precepts sometimes lacking any effective sanctioning mechanism. There is no appeal, for example, from a decision of single Commissioner to a tribunal of Commissioners where the former has declined to follow a prior decision of the latter.

30 See *R(U)4/51.*

31 See *ante,* p. 185.

32 See 1975 Act, ss. 93, 95, S.S. (Miscellaneous Provisions) Act 1977, s. 22(5).

33 *Ibid.* s. 93(3).

34 *Ibid.* s. 94(1).

35 *Ibid.* s. 94(3).

36 *Ibid.* s. 94(8). See also Determination of Claims and Questions Regulations, regs. 6–8.

37 See *ante,* pp. 223–226.

38 1975 Act, s. 103(1)(*a*).

39 *Ibid.* s. 106(2), Attendance Allowance Regulations, regs. 8–14.

40 *Ibid.*

41 See *ante,* pp. 340–343.

42 1975 Act, ss. 103(1)(*b*), 108; Determination of Claims and Questions Regulations, regs. 16–19.

43 1975 Act, Sched. 12, para. 1.

44 *Ibid.* s. 110.

45 *Ibid.* s. 109(2).

46 *Ibid.*

47 *Ibid.* Sched. 12, para. 2; Determination of Claims and Questions Regulations, reg. 20.

48 1975 Act, s. 112(1)–(3).

49 *Ibid.* s. 112(4). See Determination of Claims and Questions Regulations, regs. 21–30.

50 *Ante*, pp. 316 *et seq.*

51 *Minister of Social Security* v. *Amalgamated Engineering Union* [1967] 1 A.C. 725.

52 National Insurance (Industrial Injuries) Act 1946, ss. 36(3) and 49(4).

53 *Jones* v. *Secretary of State for Social Services, Hudson* v. *Same* [1972] A.C. 944.

54 s. 117.

55 1975 Act, s. 107.

56 See *ibid.* ss. 107(6), 117(3).

57 See in relation to appeals on a point of law to the Commissioner from decision of the Attendance Allowance Board, *R(A)1/72.*

58 *R.* v. *Preston SBAT, ex p. Moore*; *R.* v. *Sheffield SBAT, ex p. Shine* [1975] 1 W.L.R. 624.

59 Child Benefit Act 1975, s. 7.

60 *Ibid.* s. 16(7) and (8); Child Interim Benefit (Determination of Questions) Regulations 1975 (S.I. 1975 No. 1925), regs. 5–12.

61 Report, para. 171.

62 See Bell, Collison, Turner and Webber, "National Insurance Local Tribunals: A Research Study" (1973) *Journal of Social Policy*, Vol. 3, Pt. 4; (1974), *ibid.* Vol. 4, Pt. 1.

63 ss. 18, 28.

64 *Ibid.* s. 18.

65 *Social Security Statistics 1975*, p. 155.

66 1966 Act, s. 12.

67 Supplementary Benefit (Appeal Tribunal) Rules 1971.

68 See *Poverty*, pamphlet No. 9, p. 4.

69 See below.

70 (1973) 117 S.J. 304.

71 *Ante*, p. 452.

72 See *ante*, pp. 393–438.

73 Annual Report for 1971–2, p. 23.

74 See particularly *Justice, Discretion and Poverty*, ed. Adler and Bradley. See also Bell, *Research Study on Supplementary Benefit Appeal Tribunals, Review of Main Findings*; *Conclusions*; *Recommendations*, (DHSS); Lister, *Social Security: the Case for Reform.*

75 See *Justice, Discretion and Poverty*, ed. Adler and Bradley.

FURTHER READING

WELFARE Law is now the subject of a vast amount of literature. Two publications are of particular value in this field. These are *Poverty* (by the Child Poverty Action Group) and *LAG Bulletin* (by the Legal Action Group). Reference should also be made to *New Society* and to the *Industrial Law Journal* and similar journals. For a fuller bibliography see *Welfare Rights: A Bibliography on Law and the Poor 1970–75* by M. Partington, J. Hull and S. Knight; and *Bibliography of British and Irish Labour Law* (1975) by Hepple, Neeson and O'Higgins.

GENERAL

B. Abel Smith and P. Townsend, *The Poor and The Poorest* (1965) Occasional Papers on Social Administration No. 17.

B. Abel Smith and Others, *Socialism and Influence* (Fabian Society 1967).

P. S. Atiyah, *Accidents, Compensation and the Law* (2nd ed., 1976).

A. B. Atkinson, *The Economics of Inequality* (1975).

A. B. Atkinson, *Poverty in Britain and the Reform of Social Security* (1969).

Z. Bankowski and G. Mungham, *Images of Law* (1976).

A. H. Boulton, *The Law and Practice of Social Security* (1976).

R. G. S. Brown, *The Management of Welfare* (1975).

D. Bull, *Action Welfare Rights* (Fabian Society 1970).

D. Bull (ed.), *Family Poverty* (1972).

K. Coates and R. Silburn, *Poverty: The Forgotten Englishman* (1973).

F. Field (ed.), *Low Pay* (1975).

F. Field (ed.) *Is Low Pay Inevitable?* (1976).

F. Field, "What is Poverty?" [1975] *New Society* 688.

V. George and P. Wilding, *Ideology and Social Welfare* (1976).

V. George, *Social Security: Beveridge and After* (1968).

V. George, *Social Security and Society* (1973).

J. C. Kincaid, *Poverty and Equality. A Study of Social Security and Taxation* (1975 revised).

R. Lister, *Social Security. The Case for Reform* (C.P.A.G. 1974).

D. C. Marsh, *The Future of the Welfare State* (1964).

D. C. Marsh, *The Welfare State* (1970).

T. H. Marshall, *Social Policy in the Twentieth Century* (4th ed., 1975).

W. Robson and P. Crick, *The Future of the Social Services* (1970).

W. Robson, *Welfare State and Welfare Society. Illusion and Reality* (1976).

L. Scarman, *English Law, the New Dimension* (Hamlyn Lectures) 1974.

J. F. Sleeman, *The Welfare State; It's Aims, Benefits and Costs* (1973).

Smith and Hoath, *Law and the Underprivileged* (1975).

H. Street, *Justice in the Welfare State* (1968 Hamlyn Lectures 2nd ed., 1975).

R. M. Titmuss, *Commitment to Welfare* (1976).

R. M. Titmuss, *Essays on "The Welfare State"* (2nd ed., 1963).

R. M. Titmuss, *Income Distribution and Social Change. A Study in Criticism* (1962).

R. M. Titmuss, *Social Policy, An Introduction* (1976).

P. Townsend (ed.), *The Concept of Poverty* (1970).

P. Townsend, *Sociology and Social Policy* (1975).

P. Townsend and Others, *Social Service For All* (Fabian Tract 1968).

Sir J. Walley, *Social Security: Another British Failure?* (1972).

M. Young (ed.), *Poverty Reports 1974–77.*

AN HISTORICAL OUTLINE

Beveridge, Social Insurance and Allied Services (Cmnd. 6404 (1942).

L. N. Brown and G. C. F. Forster, "Poor Relief to National Insurance. A Historical Outline" (1957) 121 J.P. 529.

M. Bruce, *The Coming of the Welfare State* (4th ed., 1968).

M. Bruce (ed.), *The Rise of the Welfare State. English Social Policy. 1601–1971* (1973).

H. Catchpole, "Workmen's Compensation under the Beveridge Plan" (1944) 6 N.I.L.Q. 31.

S. E. and E. O. A. Checkland (ed.), *The Poor Law of 1834* (1974).

J. Clarke, "Social Insecurity" (1945) 16 P.Q. 30.

D. Fraser, *The Evolution of the British Welfare State* (1973).

D. Frazer (ed.), *The New Poor Law in the Nineteenth Century* (1976).

B. Gilbert, *The Evolution of National Insurance in Great Britain* (1966).

B. Gilbert, *British Social Policy 1914–1939* (1970).

Gregory (Chairman) Report of the Royal Commission on Unemployment Insurance Cmd. 4185 (1900).

D. G. Hanes, *The First British Compensation Scheme 1897* (1968).

E. P. Hennock, "The Poor Law Era" [1968] *New Society* 306.

E. P. Hennock, "Social Security: A System Emerges" [1968] *New Society* 336.

H. Hilton, "The State and The Unemployed: Report of the Royal Commission" (1933) 4 P.Q. 16.

B. Keith-Luce, "A Local Act for Social Insurance in the Eighteenth Century" 11 C.L.J. 191.

T. Lynes, "Unemployment Assistance Tribunals in the 1930's" *Justice, Discretion and Poverty* (1975) 5.

"Mass Observation: Social Security and Parliament" (1943) 14 P.Q. 245.

J. Moss, "From the Poor Law to Social Security, Health and Welfare" (1973) 137 L.G.R. 12.

G. W. Oxley, *Poor Relief in England and Wales 1601–1834* (1974).

W. Robson, "The Beveridge Report—An Evaluation" (1943) 14 P.Q. 150.

White Paper, Social Insurance, Cmnd. 6550 and 6551 (1942).

B. Wootton, "Record of the Labour Government and the Social Services" (1949) 20 P.Q. 101.

H. and W. Wickwas, *The Social Services: An Historical Survey* (1949).

THE NATIONAL INSURANCE SCHEME

The C.P.A.G. have published several extremely useful guides to rights in this area: P. Moore, *Unemployed Workers and Strikers Guide to Social Security* (1974); P. Moore, *Students Rights* (1975) and Richard Drabble, *Contributory Benefits* (1977).

Further reading

P. S. Atiyah, "Common Law Damages and Social Security" (1969) 50 L.G. 17.

P. S. Atiyah, "Damages or Social Security?" (1970) 60 L.G. 23.

J. Bradshaw and S. Baldwin, "Attendance Allowance" [1974] *New Society* 292.

H. G. Calvert, "Social Security Law and the Three-Day Week" (1974) 27 C.L.P 146.

H. G. Calvert, "Parity in Social Security in Northern Ireland" (1970) 5 Irish J. 70.

D. Carson, "The Attendance Allowance" (1975) 26 N.I.L.Q. 291.

J. P. Casey, "Unemployment Benefits and Damages—The Need for a New Approach" (1969) 14 Juridical Review 206.

J. P. Casey, "Damages and Social Security—Recent Developments" (1972) Juridical Review 22.

J. Coussins, *Maternity Rights for Working Women* (N.C.C.L. 1976).

J. Coussins (ed.), "Come Back Pecksniff" (1973) 123 N.L.J. 309.

Disablement Income Group, *Realising a National Disablement Income— A Policy Statement* (D.I.G. 1974).

Donovan (Chairman), Report of the Royal Commission on Trade Unions and Employees' Associations 1965–68, Cmnd. 3623 (1967).

F. Field, "Unemployment: The Facts" (1975) *G.P.A.G.* Pamphlet No. 20.

F. Field, "The New Corporate Interest" (1976) *C.P.A.G.* Pamphlet No. 23.

Fisher (Chairman), Report of the Committee on Abuse of Social Security Benefits, Cmnd. 5228 (1973).

J. Gennard and R. Lasko, "Supplementary Benefits and Strikers" (1974) B.J.L.R. p. 1.

J. A. G. Griffith, "The Place of Parliament in the Legislative Process" (1951) 14 M.L.R. 279 at 433.

J. A. G. Griffith, "Delegated Legislation—Some Developments" (1949) 12 M.L.R. 297 at 311.

D. Harris, "Accident Compensation and New Zealand" (1974) 37 M.L.R. 361.

T. Hartley, "Polygamy and Social Policy" (1969) 32 M.L.R. 155 at 165.

R. A. Hasson and J. Mesher, "No Fault—Private or Social Insurance" (1975) 41 N.L.J. 168.

R. Hill and R. G. Brewer, "Voidable Marriages—Some Wider Implications" (1975) 119 S.J. 144.

M. Hill, "Policies for the Unemployed. Help or Coercion?" (1974) *G.P.A.G.* Pamphlet No. 15.

R. Howell, *Why Work? A Challenge to the Chancellor* (Conservative Political Centre 1976).

The Law Commission, Working Party No. 21, "Polygamous Marriages" p. 61.

The Law Commission, Report No. 42 on Polygamous Marriages, 125.

R. Lasco, "The Payment of Supplementary Benefit for Strikers' Dependants—Misconception and Misrepresentation" (1975) 38 M.L.R. 31.

P. Lawrie, *On the Dole—Your Guide to Unemployment Benefit and Other Things You Need to Know* (1976).

D. Lewis, "Unemployment Insurance" (1976) 5 I.L.J. 119.

I. Lustergarten and M. Elliott, "Benefit Uprating: a Problem in Administrative Law" (1976) 126 N.L.J. 756.

T. Lynes, "Taxing Strikers' Savings" [1971] *New Society* 354.

J. Mesher, "Earnings Related Benefits" (1974) 3 I.L.J. 118.

A. Morris, *Needs Before Means* (1974).

H. Monro, "The Golden Handshake" (1973) 129 N.L.J. 411.

D. Neligan, "Some Aspects of Social Security Law" (1969) 113 S.J. 883.

National Insurance Advisory Committee, Report on the Time Limit of Claiming Benefit, Cmnd. 8483.

A. I. Ogus, "Unemployment Benefit for Workers on Short-Time" (1975) 4 I.L.J. 13.

J. Reid, "Equal Pay and Opportunity: The Implications for Social Security" (1974) 3 I.L.J. 174.

J. Reid, "Strikes and State Benefit" (1973) 2 I.L.J. 111.

J. Reid, "Recent Unemployment Benefit Cases" (1975) 4 I.L.J. 51.

L. A. Sheridan, "Late National Insurance Claims: Cause for Delay" (1956) 19 M.L.R. 341.

Society for Conservative Lawyers, *Financing Strikes* (C.P.C. 1974).

E. D. A. Topliss, *Provision for the Disabled* (1975) Chap. 5.

P. R. Webb, "Polygamy Problems under the National Insurance Acts 1946–1956" (1956) 19 M.L.R. 687.

D. Williams, "State-Financed Benefits for Personal Injury Cases" (1974) 37 M.L.R. 281.

PENSIONS

N. A. Barr, "Labour's Pension Plan—A Lost Opportunity?" (1975) B.T.R. 107, 155.

N. Bosanquet, "New Deal for the Elderly" 1975 *Fabian Society* 435.

K. Burton, "Better Pensions—But Not for Present Pensioners" [1975] *Accountant* 724.

P. Burgess, *Selected or Neglected?—Welfare Rights and the Elderly* (Age Concern 1974).

R. H. Crossman, *The Politics of Pensions* (1972).

D. Gilling Smith, "Occupational Pensions and the Social Security Act 1973" (1973) 2 I.L.J. 197.

P. Hewitt and P. Lewis, *Your Rights* (Age Concern 2nd ed., 1975).

K. D. Johnson, "Divorced Wife's Pension Rights" (1968) 14 N.L.J. 689.

J. Mesher, "The Social Security Pensions Act 1975" (1976) 39 M.L.R. 321.

M. McKelvey, "National Pensions" (1970) B.T.R. 310.

H. Munro, "Retirement Pensions After Divorce" (1971) 121 N.L.J. 159.

Occupational Pensions Board, Equal Status for Men and Women in Occupational Pension Schemes, Cmnd. 6599.

Occupational Pensions Board, The Role of Members in Running of Schemes, Cmnd. 6514.

J. Reid, "Social Security Pensions Act 1975" (1976) 5 I.L.J. 54.

R. M. Titmuss, "Pension Schemes and Population Changes" (1955) 26 P.Q. 152.

The Times, "Pensions Special Report" April 27, 1977.

White Paper, *Better Pensions*, Cmnd. 5713 (1974).

White Paper, Strategy for Pensions, Cmnd. 4755 (1974).

INDUSTRIAL INJURIES

P. S. Atiyah, *Accidents, Compensation and the Law*, Chap. 15.

R. L. Denyer, "Special Hardship Allowance" 122 N.L.J. 543.

B. Douglas-Mann and Others, *Accidents at Work, Compensation for All* (Society of Labour Lawyers 1974).

F.H.C. "National Insurance Medical Tribunals" 1969 113 S.J. 137.

Hepple and O'Higgins, *Employment Law* (2nd ed., 1976).

Industrial Law Society, "Compensation for Industrial Injuries" (1975) 4 I.L.J. 195.

Jarrett (Chairman), Report of the Committee on the Assessment of Disablement, Cmnd. 9827.

R. Micklethwait, *The National Insurance Commissioners* (1976 Hamlyn Lectures).

R. Micklethwait, (1969) 37 Medico-Legal Journal 172.

D. Payne, "Compensation for Industrial Injuries" (1957) 10 C.L.P. 85.

A. I. Ogus, "Recent Decisions on Unemployment Benefit" (1976) 5 I.L.J. 188.

J. Reid, "Disablement Benefit" (1972) 1 I.L.J. 109.

J. Reid, "Recent Decisions on Disablement Benefit" (1975) 4 I.L.J. 122.

J. Reid, "Industrial Injuries and the Tea Break" (1966) 29 M.L.R. 389.

R. Rideat, *Principles of Labour Law* (2nd ed., 1976) Chap. 16.

Robson (Chairman), Report of the Committee on Health and Safety, Cmnd. 5034.

N. D. Vandyk, "Appeals from the Medical Appeals Tribunals" (1962) 106 S.J. 1020.

C. A. Webb, *Industrial Injuries—A New Approach* (Fabian Society 1974).

FAMILY PROVISION

A. B. Atkinson, "Tax Credits Examined" [1972] *New Society* 145.

A. B. Atkinson, "The Tax Credit Scheme and Redistribution of Income" (1973) I.F.S. No. 9.

D. Barber (ed.), *Single Parent Families* (1975).

J. Bradshaw and I Wakeman, "The Poverty Trap Updated" (1972) 43 P.Q. 459.

E. Bull (ed.), *Family Poverty* (1972).

J. M. Eekelaar, "Public Law and Private Rights: The Finer Proposals" (1976) P.L. 64.

F. Field and P. Townsend, "A Social Contract for Families" (1975) C.P.A.G. Pamphlet No. 19.

F. Field and D. Piachaud, "The Poverty Trap" [1971] *New Statesman* 772.

Finer (Chairman), Report of the Committee on One Parent Families, Cmnd. 5629 (1974).

"Killing a Commitment: The Cabinet v. The Children" [1975] *New Society* 630.

I. Knight and J. Nixon, *Two Parent Families in Receipt of F.I.S. 1972* (HMSO 1975).

R. Lister, *Take-Up of Means Tested Benefits* (C.P.A.G. 1974).

T. Lynes, "Credit Progress" [1973] *New Society* 16.

I. Muller Fembeck and A. I. Ogus, "Social Welfare and the One Parent Family in Germany and Britain" (1976) 25 I.C.L.Q. 382.

M. Meacher, *Rate Rebates—A Study of the Effectiveness of Means Tests* (1972 C.P.A.G. Research Set 1).

National Consumer Council, "Means Tested Benefits" A Discussion Paper 1976.

National Council for One Parent Families, *The Finer Report Recommendations and Responses* (1976).

D. Piachaud, "Poverty and Taxation" 1971 P.Q. 31.

A. R. Prest, "Proposals for a Tax Credit System" 1973 B.T.R. 6.

P. Payne, "Aid for a Pupil" [1973] *New Society* 397.

J. Reid, "In the GMA World" (1975) 38 M.L.R. 52.

J. Reid, "Proposals for a Tax Credit System" (1973) 2 I.L.J. 52.

Report of the Expenditure Committee on Educational Maintenance Allowances (1974; H.C. 306).

Select Committee on Tax Credits (1972–73; H.C. 341).

J. Scegg, "Tax Credits—the New System" (1972) N.L.J. 907.

Weaver (Chairman), Report of the Committee on Educational Maintenance Allowances 1957.

M. Wynn, *Family Policy* (1972).

ADJUDICATION

M. Adler and A. Bradley, *Justice, Discretion and Poverty* (1975), (J.D.P.).

K. Bell and Others, *Research Study on Supplementary Benefit Appeal Tribunals. Review of Main Findings: Conclusions: Recommendations* (HMSO 1975).

K. Bell, "N.I.L.T.s A Research Study" British Journal of Social Policy 3 p. 289 and 4.1.

A. Bradley, "Reform of Supplementary Benefit Appeal Tribunals—the Key Issues" (1976) 27 N.I.L.Q. 96.

J. A. Farmer, *Tribunals and Government* (Chap. 4).

Franks (Chairman), Report of the Committee on Administrative Tribunals and Inquiries, Cmnd. 218 (1957).

J. Fulbrook, *The Appellant and his Case* (Poverty Research, Series 5).

J. Fulbrook and Others, "Tribunals—A Social Court" (1974) Fabian Tract No. 427.

N. Lewis, "Supplementary Benefit Appeal Tribunals" (1973) P.L. 257.

R. Lister, *Justice for the Claimant* (Poverty Research, Series 4).

M. Herman, *Administrative Justice and Supplementary Benefits* (1972).

H. Hodge, "Judicial Withdrawal" (1975) 125 N.L.J. 595.

R. Micklethwait, *The National Insurance Commissioners* (Hamlyn Lectures 1976).

M. Partington, "Some Thoughts on a Test Case Strategy" (1974) 124 N.L.J. 236.

A. Safford, "The Creation of Case Law under the National Insurance and National Insurance (Industrial Injuries) Acts" (1954) 17 M.L.R. 197.

C. Smith, "Judicial Attitudes to Social Security" (1975) 2 British Journal of Law and Society 217.

S. A. DeSmith, "Half a Yard Onwards" (1963) 26 M.L.R. 297.

S. A. DeSmith, "Half an Inch Onwards" (1964) 27 M.L.R. 458.

"Supplementary Benefit Appeals" (1974) 125 N.L.J. 1009.

N. D. Vandyk, "The Minister of National Insurance as a Judicial Authority" (1953) P.A. 331.

T. Wadling and A. Rattenbery, *Tribunals and the Law* (Student Praxis 4).

R. E. Wraith and P. G. Hutchesson, *Administrative Tribunals* (1973).

SUPPLEMENTARY BENEFITS

More attention has been focused on this area of social security law than any other. The S.B.C. itself publishes a useful if uncritical guide to the Law. The most comprehensive treatment is given by Tony Lynes in his *Penguin Guide to Supplementary Benefits* (1974). Reference should also be made to L.A.G.'s *A Lawyer's Guide to Supplementary Benefits* (1976), and to Ruth Lister's *Supplementary Benefit Rights* (1974) and *National Welfare Benefits Handbook 1976*.

A. B. Atkinson, "Poverty in the Test of Policy" [1975] *New Society* March 13.

A. Bissett-Johnson and D. W. Pollard, "Maintenance, Divorce and Social Security" (1975) 13 M.L.R. 449R.

L. N. Brown, "National Assistance and the Liability to Maintain One's Family" (1955) 18 M.L.R. 110.

L. N. Brown, "Separation Agreements and National Assistance" (1956) 19 M.L.R. 623.

Bryant and J. Bradshaw, "Welfare Rights and Special Action" (1971) *Poverty Report*.

D. Bull (ed.), *Dear David Donnison. A five part open letter to the new chairman of the Supplementary Benefits Commission* (1976).

J. P. Casey, "The Supplementary Benefits Act: Lawyer's Law Aspects" (1968) 19 N.I.L.Q. 1.

J. P. Casey, "Social Assistance in Northern Ireland" (1968) 19 N.I.L.Q. 278.

"Cohabitation. How to do Injustice" (1972) 122 N.L.J. 506.

R. J. Coleman, "Supplementary Benefits and the Administrative Review of Administrative Action" *Poverty* Pamphlet No. 7.

F. Field, "Poverty: The Facts" (1975) *Poverty* Pamphlet No. 21.

M. Hill, "The Exercise of Discretion in the National Assistance Board" 1969 P.A. 75.

M. Johnson and M. Rowland, "Fuel Debts and the Poor" (1976) *Poverty* Pamphlet No. 24.

B. Jordan, *Freedom and the Welfare State* (1976).

R. Lister and T. Emmet, "Under the Safety Net" (1976) *Poverty* Pamphlet No. 25.

R. Lister, *As Man and Wife. A Study of the Cohabitation Rule* (Poverty Research, Series 2 1973).

T. Lynes, "Welfare Rights" Fabian Tract 395.

A. Milner, "Maintenance and National Assistance" (1961) 111 L.J. 55.

R. Page, *The Benefits Racket* (1972).

C. Smith, "Discretion or Rule of Thumb?" (1973) 123 N.L.J. 267.

C. Smith, "Discretion or Legislation?" (1974) 124 N.L.J. 219.

C. Smith, "The Abolition of the Four Week Rule" (1974) 3 N.L.J. 249.

P. Snow, "Child of the Family: Liability to Maintain and Supplementary Benefits" (1974) 5 Family Law 72, 112.

O. Stevenson, *Claimant or Client? A Social Worker's View of the Supplementary Benefits Commission* (1973).

O. Stone, "The Public Nature of Domestic Responsibilities" (1957) 20 M.L.R. 509.

R. M. Titmuss, "Welfare Rights Law and Discretion" (1971) 42 P.Q. 113.

J. Tunnard, "No Father No Home" (1976) *Poverty* Pamphlet No. 28.

Supplementary Benefit Administrative Papers:
  Living Together As Husband and Wife (1975).
  Training of Staff (1973).
  Cohabitation (1971).
  Exceptional Needs Payments (1973).

K. Watson, "Affiliation Orders via the National Assistance Board" (1962) 112 L.J. 366.

EUROPE AND THE FUTURE

D. Callund, *Employee Benefits in Europe—An International Survey of State and Private Schemes in 16 Countries* (1975).

H. G. Calvert, "Appeals Structures of the Future" J.D.P. Ch. 14.

A. Cambell, *Common Market Law* (vol. 3, 529).

Central Office of Information (Reference Div.) *Britain in the European Community Social Policy* (1976).

A. Christopher and Others, "Policy for Poverty etc." 1970 1 E.A.

Disablement Income Group, *Social Security and Disability—a study of the financial provisions for disabled persons in seven Western European countries* (D.I.G. 1971).

Finer Report, Income Maintenance for One Parent Families in Other Countries, Cmnd. 5629 (1974) App. 3.

A. M. Helstädt, *Unemployment Benefits and Related Payments in Seven Major Countries* (O.E.C.D. 1975).

J. van Langendonck, *Prelude to Harmony as a Community Theme Health Care Insurance in the Six and Britain.*

J. van Langendonck, "Social Security Legislation in the EEC" (1973) 2 L.L.J. 17.

R. Lawson and B. Reed, "Social Security in the European Communities" P.E.P. 1975.

P. R. Kairn Caudle, *Comparative Social Policy and Social Security: A Ten Country Study* (C.P.C. 1973).

V. O'Donovan, "The Co-ordination of Social Security Benefits with the EEC" 1976 126 N.L.J. 913, 1017.

M. Shonfield, *Modern Capitalism* (1969).

"Social Security Arrangements for People Moving within the EEC" 123 N.L.J. 417.

R. Titmuss, "Social Security and the Six" [1971] *New Society* 927.

T. Wilson (ed.), *Pensions Inflation and Growth* (1974).

APPENDIX I

INVALID CARE ALLOWANCE
(See 1975 Act, s. 37; Social Security (Invalid Care Allowance) Regulations, 1977)

ATTENDANCE allowance is designed to meet some of the needs of the disabled person; invalid care allowance to meet those of his attendant. Title to allowance is restricted to prescribed relatives who are engaged in caring for a severely disabled person. The latter phrase is exhaustively defined in regulations to mean a recipient of either an attendance allowance, war disablement pension or certain industrial injury benefits where constant attendance is required.

A beneficiary may not be under 16 nor in receipt of full-time education. Invalid care allowance is regarded as a substitute for earnings which would have been earned by the attendant had he not had to remain at home to look after his charge. Married women, if they are residing with or maintained by their husbands, are excluded on the grounds that they would probably have remained at home in any event. The exclusion also operates in the case of a woman who lives with a man as his wife. Further conditions must be satisfied before entitlement is established. The beneficiary must be "regularly and substantially engaged in caring for" a disabled person, *i.e.* for at least 35 hours per week. If less than 35 hours are worked, in a week, the condition is regarded nonetheless as satisfied provided the reduction in hours is a temporary measure, and normal hours would have been worked for 22 weeks and have been worked for 14 weeks out of the 26 weeks preceding that week, had the beneficiary or his charge not been admitted to hospital as an inpatient for the purposes of treatment. Gainful employment is, of course, regarded as inconsistent with the proper performance of the duties of a state-subsidised attendant and therefore operates as a bar to entitlement. For this purpose, gainful employment means employment from which earnings of at least £6 are derived (Computation of Earnings Regs. 1977). There are further conditions relating to residence and presence in Great Britain.

The allowance is not generally available to a person over pensionable age, but provision has been made to continue payment where entitlement was established prior to that age; in the case of persons over retirement age, this is so even where the person ceases to meet the basic requirements of entitlement. As with other benefits, family responsibilities are recognised and an increase of benefit is payable in respect of dependants.

NON-CONTRIBUTORY INVALIDITY PENSION
(See 1975 Act, s. 36; Social Security (Non-contributory
Invalidity Pensions) Regulations 1977)

"It is palpably wrong to deny altogether basic benefit as of right to people who because of severe disablement have not been able to establish themselves as contributors in the insurance scheme. At the same time, it would be inconsistent with the maintenance of the contributory basis of that scheme and inequitable in comparison with the treatment of those already over pension age ... to pay non-contributory invalidity pension at the full contributory rates to people under pension age." (Social Security Provision for Chronically Sick and Disabled People 1974 H.C. 276 p. 55). Hence the introduction of a new non-contributory invalidity pension, paid as of right, from general taxation, and at a rate substantially lower than its contributory counterpart designed to meet some of the needs of sick and disabled people, ineligible for membership of the insurance scheme, and hitherto dependent on means-tested supplementary benefits (for service benefits see Chronically Sick and Disabled Persons Act 1970).

The pension is paid to a person who is incapacitated for work for at least 196 consecutive days and who satisfies the age, residence and presence conditions, *i.e.* over 16 and not engaged in full-time education, as prescribed. Incapacity for work has the same meaning as for sickness and invalidity benefit purposes. Persons over pensionable age are generally ineligible for benefit, but the statutory requirements have been relaxed in the case of those entitled to pensions immediately prior to attaining pension-able age.

Pensions will be available to housewives if they are incapable of performing normal household duties, a welcome development and one benefiting a group which have probably suffered more than any other through the inconsistencies and anomolies of our patchwork accident compensation cover. Grounds of disqualification are the same as for sickness and invalidity benefit. At present the pension is £9·20 plus increases for dependants.

MOBILITY ALLOWANCE
((See 1975 Act, s. 37A; Mobility Allowance (Vehicle Scheme Beneficiaries) Regulation 1977

Severely disabled people between the ages of five and 65 (60 for a woman) may be eligible for a £5 per week cash allowance paid specifically for the purposes of facilitating locomotion. Section 37A of the 1975 Act as amended provides that "... a person who satisfied prescribed conditions as to residence or presence in Great Britain shall be entitled to a mobility allowance for any period throughout which he is suffering from physical disablement such that he is either unable to walk or virtually unable to do so." A person satisfies the physical requirements "if his physical condition as a whole is such that, without having regard to circumstances peculiar to that person as to place of residence or as to place of, or nature of employment—

(a) he is unable or virtually unable to walk; or

(b) the exertion required to work would constitute a danger to life or would be likely to lead to a serious deterioration in his health." Entitlement is conditional on two further factors: his physical condition must be likely to persist for 12 months from the date of claim, during most of which he must be in a position to benefit from enhanced facilities for locomotion. Mobility Allowance "... is an allowance for locomoter disability and not a general expenses allowance for severely disabled people ... The sole criterion will be locomotive disability or inability to walk. (Alf Morris H.C.Debs., Vol. 893, Col. 471). Thus a person in a permanent coma would clearly not qualify.

Disqualification may ensue for a refusal to submit for medical examination if required. Medical questions subject to certain exceptions are referred to a medical practitioner, then to a medical board, with further appeal to a medical appeal tribunal. The usual provisions for leap frogging and review are contained in the regulations.

INDEX